# MASTERING

# EXCEL 97
## FOURTH EDITION

# MASTERING

# EXCEL 97

## *Fourth Edition*

## *Thomas Chester and*
## *Richard H. Alden*

SYBEX

**San Francisco • Paris • Düsseldorf • Soest**

Associate Publisher: Amy Romanoff
Acquisitions Manager: Kristine Plachy
Associate Developmental Editor: Neil Edde
Editor: Michelle Nance
Project Editor: Linda Good
Technical Editor: Betsy Walker
Book Design Director: Catalin Dulfu
Book Designers: Catalin Dulfu, Patrick Dintino
Template Designer: Tony Jonick
Electronic Publishing Specialist: Tony Jonick
Production Coordinator: Nathan Johanson
Indexer: Ted Laux
Cover Designer: Design Site
Cover Photo Direction: Ingalls & Associates
Cover Photographer: Mark Johann

Screen reproductions produced with Collage Plus

Collage Plus is a trademark of Inner Media Inc.

SYBEX is a registered trademark of SYBEX Inc.
Mastering is a trademark of SYBEX Inc.

Library of Congress Card Number: 96-70738
ISBN: 0-7821-1921-2

Manufactured in the United States of America

10 9 8 7 6 5 4

# Acknowledgments

We would like to thank the many people who have contributed to this book.

First, many thanks to the dedicated people at Sybex who made this book possible: Richard Mills, Neil Edde, Linda Good, Michelle Nance, Betsy Walker, Molly Sharp, Nathan Johanson, Tony Jonick, and Patrick Dintino. Thanks also to Douglas Hergert who put together the Master's Reference section at the end of this book.

Thanks to our many friends and associates at Microsoft who have been supportive over the years, especially Corey Salka and Eric Wells (not to mention the many outstanding individuals who designed and developed Excel).

There are many talented Excel practitioners with whom we've had the pleasure of exchanging ideas over the years: our colleagues Tim Tow and Robert Affleck deserve special recognition. Thanks also to Will Tompkins, Mike Sessions, Bob Umlas, Chris Kinsman, and Reed Jacobson. Thanks for sharing your knowledge.

Over the years, our clients have asked us to deliver world-class software. This constant challenge helps keep us on our toes. Special thanks go to Dick Paris and Carl Spaulding—you've taught us a lot, and we've had fun along the way.

Last but not least, thank you to Karen, Kaitlin, Miles, and Susan.

# Contents at a Glance

# TABLE OF CONTENTS

## PART II • BASIC SKILLS

## PART III • TAPPING EXCEL'S POWER

# PART IV • GRAPHICS AND CHARTS

## PART V • WORKING EFFECTIVELY WITH DATABASES

# PART VI • PIVOT TABLES

# Introduction

Spreadsheets started out as electronic versions of hard copy accounting worksheets with one major purpose: simple row-and-column arithmetic. These programs have evolved dramatically over the past decade, and now comprise one of the most widely used categories of software products. Excel has long been the leading graphical spreadsheet. With the Windows 95 interface, Excel 97 (also referred to as Excel 8) is even more versatile—it has more user interface features in common with other Microsoft Office 97 applications, easier file access and management, longer file names, improved online help, and many other new features.

## New in Excel 8

You'll find detailed information throughout this book (and especially in Chapter 1) about all of Excel's exciting new features, but here are a few of the highlights you can look forward to:

- Larger worksheets (up to 65,536 rows!) and higher cell character limits
- Natural language formulas, which alleviate the need to understand the intricacies of naming
- Shared workbooks, allowing multiple users to edit the same workbook at the same time
- New chart types and shapes, including Bar Of Pie and Pie Of Pie
- Enhanced drawing and graphics capabilities
- A Query Wizard for use with Microsoft Query
- Data validation, which allows you to set data entry rules
- Internet features, including a Web toolbar and the ability to create hyperlinks and to save files using a Save As HTML option

# How Excel Is Used in the Workplace

Excel is used for a wide variety of applications. Here are some of the most common.

## Basic Spreadsheet Applications

Even though Excel is a multifaceted tool, a considerable percentage of users still employ it as an electronic replacement for the hard copy accountant's worksheet. In this capacity, you can use Excel to help automate financial statements, business forecasting, transaction registers, inventory control, accounts receivable, accounts payable—the list of potential applications is endless.

## Financial Modeling

You can create financial models that let you play "what if." By changing one or more variables, the model recalculates, and a new set of results can be presented in tabular and/or graphical format. You can perform multilevel data consolidation or rollups automatically. For example, cost centers can roll up into departments, which roll up into divisions, which roll up into company summaries.

## Scientific and Engineering

While spreadsheets are usually thought of as tools for business, Excel provides many statistical, analytical, and scientific functions. It is used in many scientific and engineering environments to analyze numerical data and present findings.

## Presentation Graphics

Excel is a powerful, flexible graphical presentation tool. Worksheets can include charts and graphs, and can be formatted for high-impact presentations.

## Database Management

Excel is a highly adept data management tool. For many database requirements, users find that Excel's interface allows them to get up to speed very quickly in comparison to "real" database management programs. It is very easy to enter, edit, sort, and filter databases in Excel.

## Database Front End

Excel database manipulation is simple, yet spreadsheets inherently lack certain features found in actual database management programs. By using Excel as a database front end, you can realize the best of both worlds. Excel is able to access data stored in a wide variety of database formats, and is an ideal tool to analyze and manipulate data and to create high-impact reports and graphical presentations.

## Custom Applications

Excel is a powerful application development tool. Many of the world's largest corporations have utilized Excel to create serious, large-scale custom applications. It uses *Visual Basic, Applications Edition* (VBA), the programming language used throughout Microsoft Office applications.

# A Mastering Excel Road Map

The book is divided into eight parts, followed by Appendices and a Master's Reference.

## Part One: Getting Started

This part of the book is important for beginners, but even veterans can learn about some important new features.

- Chapter 1 explains the elements of the Excel workspace, including features such as tabbed dialog boxes and submenus.
- In Chapter 2, you'll learn about the workbook concept and get an introduction to such basic skills as saving your work.
- Chapter 3 is essential for novices. It explains how to enter and edit information, how to navigate the worksheet, and how to copy and move information.

## Part Two: Basic Skills

Part Two is where you learn many of the most important basic skills.

- In Chapter 4, learn how to enter formulas and functions. You also get a clear explanation of a topic that sometimes confuses new users—cell references.
- Chapter 5 covers the many different ways you can format cells.
- Learn about the nuances of printing in Chapter 6.
- Chapter 7 provides a number of productivity tips. You will probably learn some

important skills, regardless of how much Excel experience you already have.

## Part Three: Tapping Excel's Power

This section of the book provides important insights on how to get the most out of Excel.

- Using names is vitally important, and Chapter 8 provides a thorough discussion of this topic.
- Chapter 9 provides a comprehensive discussion of the handful of worksheet functions considered essential for serious Excel users.
- Don't skip Chapter 10! Templates are an important topic, and this chapter explains not only how to use them, but why.
- Chapter 11 explains how to audit, protect, and document workbooks and worksheets.

## Part Four: Graphics and Charts

You might have a lot of fun in this part of the book.

- Chapter 12 shows you how to place graphics on worksheets, and how to format them.
- Learn all of the important charting skills in Chapters 13, 14, 15, and 16.

## Part Five: Working Effectively with Databases

This part of the book is vitally important, even if the problems you are trying to solve do not appear to be database problems.

- Chapters 17 and 18 show you how to work with internal databases (or *lists*)—data that resides on a worksheet.
- Excel is a powerful tool for accessing external databases, and Chapter 19 explains how to do it.

## Part Six: Pivot Tables

Arguably, pivot tables are the most important feature in Excel, and they are covered in depth in Chapters 20, 21, and 22.

## Part Seven: Customizing Excel

Excel is easy to customize, so don't be put off if you are not a programmer.

- In Chapter 23, learn how to place controls, such as list boxes and option buttons, on worksheets. (It's easy!) You'll also learn how to create custom dialog boxes.
- Chapter 24 provides an introduction to macros, and shows you how to use the macro recorder effectively.
- Create a powerful, graphical, custom application, start to finish, in Chapter 25.

## Part Eight: Solving Real-World Problems

This part of the book covers many special skills to help you solve real-world problems.

- Consolidation, a vital topic, is covered in Chapter 26.
- Chapter 27 shows how to use three important what-if features: Goal Seek, Solver, and Scenario Manager.
- Learn how to work with add-ins—including the Report Manager, the Lookup Wizard, the Conditional Sum Wizard, and the Analysis ToolPak—in Chapter 28.
- In Chapter 29, learn how to share workbooks among users and how to link workbooks locally or via the Internet. You also learn how to import and export data and how to make the transition from Lotus 1-2-3.

## Appendices

In the three appendices, you'll find supplemental information that will help you master Excel.

- Appendix A provides you with a comprehensive list of built-in worksheet functions and Analysis ToolPak functions.
- Appendix B lists numerous keyboard shortcuts that can help you speed up your work.
- Appendix C documents the symbols you can use as part of a numeric formatting code.

## Master's Reference

Finally, the Master's Reference is an alphabetical quick-reference guide to using the most important Excel features. As you work, you can turn directly to this guide when you need a reminder of how to perform a specific task.

## Conventions Used in This Book

Features that are new to Excel 8 are indicated by the icon shown at left.

- The plus sign is used to indicate when one key is held down while another key is pressed. For example, Shift+Tab means to hold down the Shift key while pressing the Tab key.
- Menu commands are expressed using the following convention: File ➤ Print.

- Toolbar shortcuts are indicated with an icon in the left margin, as pictured here.
- At the beginning of each chapter is a "Featuring" list, which provides a quick overview of the most important topics covered in the chapter.

In addition, look for these three elements to give you extra help along the way:

> **NOTE**
>
> Notes provide you with information that is important for particular commands or features, but that does not appear in the associated discussion.

> **TIP**
>
> Tips provide you with information that will make the current task easier. Tips include shortcuts and alternative ways to perform a task.

> **WARNING**
>
> Read all Warnings so you can avert a possible disaster. The Warnings will help you avoid losing important data and save you the time that must be spent replacing lost data.

# PART

# I

## Getting Started

## LEARN TO:

- *Start Excel*

- *Use menu commands*

- *Create workbooks*

- *Insert worksheets*

- *Enter data*

- *Move and copy cells*

- *Adjust column width*

- *Search and replace cell contents*

# Chapter

# 1

## The Excel Environment

## FEATURING

# The Excel Environment

**M**ake no mistake about it, Excel 8, also referred to as Excel 97, represents a major upgrade to the world's leading spreadsheet program. For several years now, Microsoft has made major enhancements to Excel and other Microsoft Office programs with every other release. Excel 4 to 5 was a major upgrade. Excel 5 to 7 (Excel 95) was a minor one. (There never was a version 6, incidentally.) And now, the move to Excel 8 (Excel 97) is another major upgrade, with a wealth of new features and plenty of revamped old ones.

**NOTE**

Don't miss the "What's New in Excel 8" section at the end of this chapter.

Everyone will appreciate everyday usability features such as color-coded ranges, which simplify entering and changing formulas. Excel's charting capabilities have been improved across the board. Pivot tables have been massively enhanced. Shared workbooks are an important new addition. And, as you might expect, there are plenty of new Internet-related features. You'll find an overview of these and many other new features at the end of this chapter. You'll also get an overview of the Excel working environment, where we'll introduce the basic tools you'll need to get started working with Excel.

# Getting Started

As with any program, the first Excel skills you'll need to learn are the most basic: how to start and exit the program itself.

## Starting Excel

You may have purchased Excel by itself, or as a part of Microsoft Office. In either case, we assume you have run the setup program, and installed Excel on your computer. (Otherwise, follow the setup instructions that come with Excel.) The setup program installs all of the required files to your hard disk.

Starting Excel is no different than starting most any other Windows program. Here are the three most common methods:

- Click on the Start button on the Windows 95 Task bar, choose Programs, then click on the Microsoft Excel menu item.
- From Windows Explorer, double-click on any Excel file. Excel will start *and* the file will be opened.
- Double-click the Excel shortcut icon on your Windows 95 desktop (if one is present).

As you can see, starting Excel is no different that starting most Windows applications. To learn more about Windows 95, a good source is the book *The ABCs of Windows 95* by Sharon Crawford.

**NOTE** Because you can easily customize Excel, the screen you see when you first start up the program will probably not look exactly like the screen you might see on your coworkers' machines. Excel's default appearance is based on settings that were chosen when the program was installed and on various settings that are available from within Excel.

## Exiting Excel

There are several ways to exit Excel, all of which will be familiar if you have used other Windows programs:

- Click on the × button in the upper-right corner of the Excel workspace.
- Choose File ➢ Exit.

- Click on the Excel icon in the upper-left corner of the Excel window to display the Control Menu, then choose Close. (Or, double-click on the Excel icon.)
- Press Alt+F4.

When you exit, you are prompted to save any unsaved work before Excel does the final shutdown.

# Interacting with Excel

Perhaps the biggest advantage of the Windows interface is the commonality found from program to program. If you have used other Windows programs, finding your away around Excel won't be very difficult. Better yet, if you are familiar with another Microsoft Office program, such as Word or PowerPoint, the Excel interface will be strikingly familiar. This is because programs belonging to the Microsoft Office suite have become more and more alike over the years. Learning a new program no longer necessitates starting from ground zero.

This section covers the rudiments of the Excel workspace. However, even if you are a veteran Excel user, this section covers several new features that will likely be of interest.

## Navigating the Windows Interface

Excel 8 runs under Microsoft Windows 95 and adheres to Windows interface standards. If you have used other Windows programs, you will see many familiar controls, such as the application controls, window controls, menu bar, and scroll bars (see Figure 1.1). These controls work the same way in other Windows programs.

**NOTE**

If you are new to Microsoft Windows, a good starting point is the "guided tour." Click on the Windows Start button and choose the Help command. A Help Topics - Windows Help dialog box appears. Click on the Contents tab at the top of the dialog box, then choose Tour: Ten Minutes To Using Windows.

## Using the Command System

As we said earlier, choosing commands in Excel is pretty much the same as with other Microsoft Office programs. There are a menu system, various shortcut menus, an array of toolbars, and countless keyboard shortcuts for those who are less mouse-inclined. When you add it all up, there are several ways to execute most Excel commands.

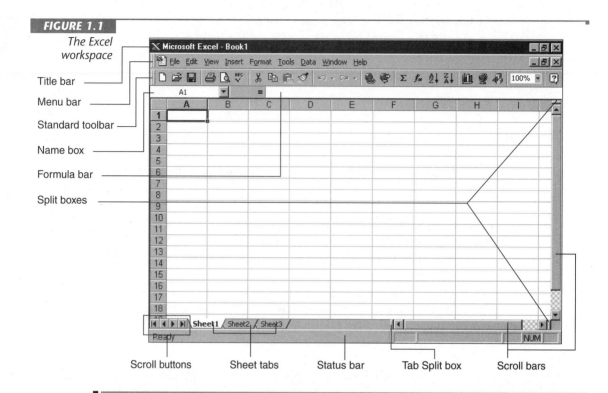

**FIGURE 1.1**

*The Excel workspace*

Title bar

Menu bar

Standard toolbar

Name box

Formula bar

Split boxes

Scroll buttons     Sheet tabs     Status bar     Tab Split box     Scroll bars

## Observe the Status Bar

The status bar (see Figure 1.1) displays a variety of status messages and other information that can be very useful—especially if you are new to Excel. For example, the status bar usually displays the message "Ready," which means that the workspace is ready for new activity.

When Excel is carrying out certain activities, such as saving a workbook, a status indicator is shown on the status bar. If Excel is performing a lengthy operation, such as opening a file with many links, you might think Excel has locked up.

Look at the status bar before forcing a shutdown. You will see a message such as "Link" followed by a timeline that measures the progress of the operation.

Sometimes the status bar displays instructions on what to do next. For example, when you cut or copy cells, the status bar instructs you to "Select destination and press Enter or choose Paste." On the right side of the status bar are boxes that display the on/off status of several keyboard modes, like Caps Lock, Number Lock, and Overwrite mode.

**NOTE**
We assume that readers of this book already know how to choose a command from a menu and how to click on a button.

## Discovering Submenus

An important feature of the Excel interface is the *submenu*, sometimes referred to as a *cascading menu*. The submenu displays more choices that cascade to the side when you select a menu command. Menu commands that display submenus are indicated by the triangle symbol:

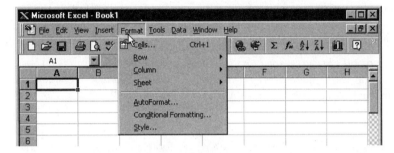

For example, the Format ➤ Row command, when selected, displays a submenu with several options to choose from:

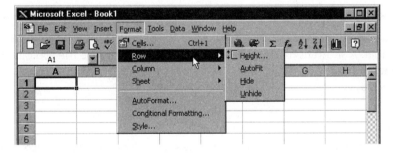

## Toolbars—Quick Access to Commands

Toolbars provide shortcuts for the most common Excel commands. There are many different toolbars, each of which contains several individual commands. The *Standard toolbar* is displayed by default. Many of the toolbars automatically appear when applicable. For example, the PivotTable toolbar automatically appears when the active worksheet contains a pivot table. (See Chapter 20 to learn about pivot tables.)

## What Is a Command Bar?

When discussing menus, there is some confusing terminology to reckon with. Prior to Excel 8, there were *menu bars* and *toolbars,* and they were different animals entirely. In Excel 8, the user interface still includes the familiar menus and toolbars. However, in actuality, menu bars and toolbars have merged into the same type of object: *command bars.*

A command bar can contain textual commands (as with "menu bars"), and/or icons/controls (as with "toolbars"). The default worksheet menu bar is simply a command bar containing textual commands. The default toolbar is a command bar containing icons/controls. Both are command bars.

You can customize the built-in command bars or create new ones using the Tools ➤ Customize command. This topic is covered in Chapter 7.

Excel's online documentation and this book use the terms *menu bar, toolbar,* and *command bar* interchangeably.

To show or hide toolbars, choose View ➤ Toolbars. The dialog box shown in Figure 1.2 appears. Select the toolbars you want to view, and deselect the ones you want to hide. This dialog box also lets you customize toolbars; this topic is discussed in Chapter 7.

**TIP**

A quick way to show or hide toolbars is to right-click on the menu bar or on any toolbar. A shortcut menu appears, where you can choose the toolbar you want to show or hide.

## Displaying Pop-Up Tool Explanations

The function of a tool is often hard to determine by looking at the icon. Fortunately, there is an easy way to discover the function of a given toolbar button. Point to the button with your mouse, but don't click on it—let the mouse pointer hover for a moment over the button. A description of the tool should appear in the form of a yellow pop-up note.

Getting Started

**FIGURE 1.2**

*The Toolbars tab of the Customize dialog box. The Worksheet menu bar and Standard toolbar are checked by default.*

If the pop-up note fails to appear, try this: choose Tools ➤ Customize and select the Options tab. Make sure Show ScreenTips On Toolbars is selected.

By default, toolbar buttons are relatively small, and, depending on your monitor, it may be difficult to clearly discern them. Here's how to make them larger: choose Tools ➤ Customize ➤ Options, then select the Large Icons setting.

## Moving Toolbars

By default, toolbars are docked underneath the menu bar. To move a toolbar, place the mouse pointer on the bar anywhere around or between the tool buttons, and drag the bar to a different location. If the toolbar is dragged to the top, bottom, left, or right edge of the Excel workspace, it is docked on that edge of the window. If it is dragged anywhere else, it "floats" (see Figure 1.3). You can resize floating toolbars by dragging their borders.

You can drag toolbars outside of the Excel workspace entirely. This is particularly useful if you are customizing workbooks intended for use by others (and you have a large monitor!). Here's why: as the developer, you can place toolbars being used solely for development purposes outside of the Excel workspace. The workspace is then more accurately emulating the target desktops where the workbook will be used.

**FIGURE 1.3**

*An example of a
floating toolbar*

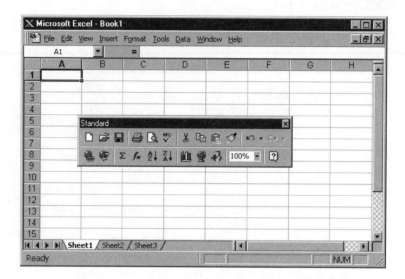

## Getting More Options: Drop-Down Palettes

Some tools have an arrow button next to them. An example is the Borders tool shown at left, found on the Formatting toolbar. You can click on the arrow to display a drop-down palette of choices:

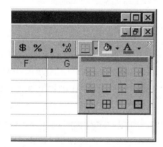

Suppose you are using the Borders palette frequently. You can tear it away from the toolbar by following these steps:

**1.** Click on the drop-down arrow to display the palette.

**2.** Carefully click on the bar along the top of the palette, hold the mouse button down, and drag the palette away from the toolbar.

**3.** Release the mouse button to drop the palette.

To hide a floating palette, click on the small × icon in the upper-right corner of the palette.

## Introducing the Standard Tools

Table 1.1 describes the functions of the tools on the Standard toolbar. You can customize toolbars and tools to suit your tastes and needs—see Chapter 7 to learn how.

**NOTE**

Most of the tools on the standard toolbar are there for good reason: these are commands that are used frequently. However, tools for creating maps and surfing the Web may be doing little more than consuming valuable screen real estate. Chapter 7 explains how to customize toolbars so that they contain *your* most often used commands.

**TABLE 1.1:** FUNCTIONS OF THE STANDARD TOOLBAR TOOLS

| Tool | Command Equivalent | Function |
|------|--------------------|----------|
| | File ➢ New | Opens a new workbook |
| | File ➢ Open | Opens an existing workbook |
| | File ➢ Save | Saves an active workbook |
| | File ➢ Print | Prints an active workbook |
| | File ➢ Print Preview | Previews what printed pages will look like |
| | Tools ➢ Spelling | Checks spelling |
| | Edit ➢ Cut | Moves selected cells |
| | Edit ➢ Copy | Copies selected cells |

**TABLE 1.1:** FUNCTIONS OF THE STANDARD TOOLBAR TOOLS (CONTINUED)

| Tool | Command Equivalent | Function |
|------|--------------------|----------|
| | Edit ➤ Paste | Pastes cut or copied cells |
| | N/A | Format painter (see Chapter 5) |
| | N/A | Undoes last actions, sequentially |
| | N/A | Redoes undone actions |
| | Insert ➤ Hyperlink | Inserts a hyperlink to another document at a remote location (see Chapter 29) |
| | View ➤ Toolbars ➤ Web | Displays or hides the Web toolbar (see Chapter 29) |
| $\Sigma$ | Insert ➤ Function ➤ Sum | AutoSum—enters the SUM function in selected cells (see Chapter 4) |
| $f_x$ | Insert ➤ Function | Displays the Paste Function dialog box |
| | Data ➤ Sort | Sorts selected cells in ascending order |
| | Data ➤ Sort | Sorts selected cells in descending order |
| | Insert ➤ Chart | Starts the ChartWizard (see Chapter 13) |
| | Insert ➤ Map | Places a map on worksheet |

**TABLE 1.1**: FUNCTIONS OF THE STANDARD TOOLBAR TOOLS (CONTINUED)

| Tool | Command Equivalent | Function |
|------|---------------------|----------|
|  | View ➢ Toolbars ➢ Drawing | Displays the Drawing toolbar |
| 100% ▼ | View ➢ Zoom | Reduces/enlarges worksheet magnification |
| ? | N/A | Starts Office Assistant |

## Working with Shortcut Menus

One of the most convenient ways to choose commands is to use context-sensitive menus, also known as *shortcut menus*. A shortcut menu is a menu that you display by pointing at a certain object, then clicking the right mouse button. The shortcut menu will contain frequently used commands that pertain to the object you clicked on.

Perhaps the most useful shortcut menu is the one displayed when you right-click on a cell. Commands like Cut, Copy, Paste, and Format are available. To get rid of a shortcut menu, press Esc or click elsewhere on the worksheet.

Another useful shortcut menu is one that appears when you right-click on a toolbar. This menu allows you to quickly hide or unhide the toolbar.

Here's a rarely used shortcut menu that is invaluable when your workbook contains many worksheets: right-click on the sheet tab scroll buttons in the lower-left corner of the window (refer back to Figure 1.1). The shortcut menu lists the worksheets—click on the worksheet you wish to activate.

## Speeding Things Up with Keyboard Shortcuts

Many menu commands have keyboard shortcuts, which appear to the right of the command. For example, Ctrl+C is the shortcut for the Edit ➢ Copy command, and Ctrl+G is the shortcut for Edit ➢ Go To, as you can see in the Edit menu. You can learn most of these shortcuts just by observing the menu commands as you use them.

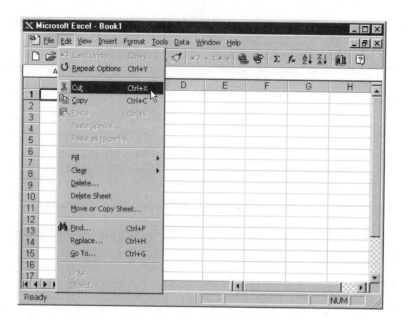

 **NOTE**
Appendix B contains a complete list of keyboard shortcuts.

## Commands with Checks

Some menu commands, such as View ➤ Status Bar, sometimes have a check mark next to the command:

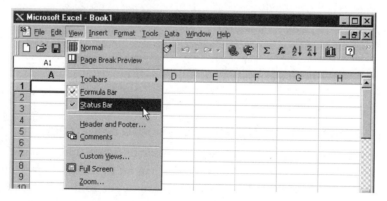

These commands are toggles—the check mark is an indicator specifying whether the setting is on or off. Choosing the command switches the toggle.

## Dimmed Menu Commands

A dimmed menu command is a command that, for one reason or another, is unavailable for use. For example, the Window ➤ Unhide command in the following menu is available only when there is a hidden window; otherwise it is dimmed:

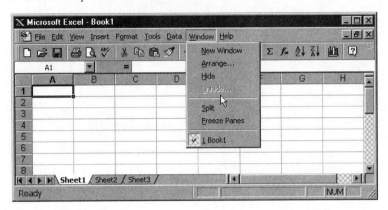

## Which Commands Stop for Input?

Menu commands that display dialog boxes have an ellipsis (...) after the command. For example, the View ➤ Header And Footer... command in the View menu displays a dialog box (Page Setup), whereas the View ➤ Formula Bar command takes immediate action.

There are exceptions to this interface convention. Some commands are immediate in certain situations and display a dialog box in others. For example, when you are saving a file that has never been saved, the File ➤ Save command displays a dialog box. Otherwise the command acts immediately. Such commands do not include an ellipsis.

# Tabbed Dialog Boxes

Another important Excel feature is the *tabbed dialog box*. Tabbed dialog boxes group related settings, and minimize screen clutter in the process. A good example is the dialog box displayed by the Format ➤ Cells command shown in Figure 1.4.

**FIGURE 1.4**

*A tabbed dialog box is like a stack of manila file folders. The Format Cells dialog box is shown here. You'll learn more about cell formatting in Chapter 5.*

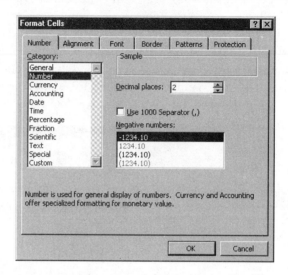

All the cell formatting commands are grouped together in the Format Cells dialog box. Click on the tabs on top of the dialog box to activate them.

**TIP**

Tabbed dialog boxes remember which tab was last used—when you redisplay the dialog box, the last tab used is the active tab.

## Understanding Workbooks

An Excel document is called a *workbook*. Workbooks are containers for one or more *worksheets* (and other types of sheets, as you will later discover). Here are some things to keep in mind:

- Think of a workbook as a binder.
- Think of every worksheet as a page in the binder.

Upon starting up Excel, the first thing you'll see is a workbook named *Book1* similar to that shown in Figure 1.1. Book1 is a new, unsaved workbook that is displayed by default.

**TIP**

You can change the number of worksheets that are, by default, in new workbooks. Choose Tools ➢ Options ➢ General, then change the Sheets In New Workbook setting.

## Opening Files Created in Earlier Versions of Excel

Excel 8 is capable of reading and writing files created by earlier versions of Excel. Opening an old Excel file involves no special procedure—use the File ➤ Open command.

When you save the file, Excel asks if you want to convert to the new format. If you answer no, the file stays in the older format, though any formulas and formats you may have used that are new to Excel 8 will not be saved (see Figure 1.5). If users within your organization are still using an older version of Excel, you can still transfer files back and forth. Just remember *not* to update the file to the new Excel 8 format. See Chapter 2 to learn about workbooks and worksheets.

---

**FIGURE 1.5**

*When you save a file created in an earlier version of Excel, you will be asked if you want to save it in the previous version or update it to the new Excel format.*

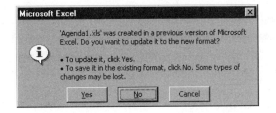

## Managing Worksheets within Workbooks

Worksheets are the pages within a workbook. A worksheet consists of a grid of *cells*, very similar to an accounting worksheet. Cells, which are oriented in rows and columns, are used to store numbers, text, and formulas. Worksheets are not limited to numbers and text—they can also contain graphical objects, such as charts, arrows, and pictures.

By default, a workbook includes three worksheets, named *Sheet1*, *Sheet2*, and *Sheet3*, though there is no limit to the number of worksheets other than available memory. Typically, you would store related worksheets in a single workbook to keep them together. For example, you might keep regional sales projections in one workbook, with information for each region stored on individual worksheets. Another worksheet within the same workbook might be used to consolidate the regions.

At the bottom of the workbook are tabs, which are used to activate the worksheets within that workbook. Activating a worksheet is the equivalent of opening a book to that page. See Chapter 2 for more information on worksheets.

# Working with Cells

Each worksheet is made up of a tabular grid of *cells*. There are 65,536 rows of cells, numbered 1 through (you guessed it) 65,536 along the left margin of the worksheet. There are 256 columns along the top margin of the worksheet. Usually these columns are labeled alphabetically (A through IV), using a single-digit and then a double-digit alphabetization scheme.

**TIP**

You can also label columns with numbers by changing the cell reference style, as you'll learn in Chapter 4.

This means that every worksheet contains over 16 million cells. You can enter text, numbers, and formulas into cells. Keep in mind that there are practical limitations to consider: if you were to place data in every cell, you would probably encounter memory problems.

## Cell References—Finding Your Way around the Worksheet

Cells are referred to using the column label followed by the row number. For example, the cell coordinate A2 would refer to column 1, row 2. In spreadsheet terminology, a cell's row and column coordinates are called the *cell reference*. See Chapter 4 to learn more about cell references.

## The Active Cell

When you select a cell by either clicking on it or moving to it using the keyboard, it becomes the *active cell*. The *Name box*, on the left of the formula bar (shown earlier in Figure 1.1), displays the reference of the active cell.

# Creating High-Impact Presentations: Charts and Graphics

Excel worksheets are not limited to numbers and text. You can place charts and other graphical objects on worksheets, allowing you to create high-impact graphical presentations. Here are a few points to keep in mind when working with charts and graphical objects:

- There are several ways to create charts, but the *ChartWizard* is the quickest and easiest. The ChartWizard, accessed by clicking on the ChartWizard tool shown at left, gives you a variety of basic chart types to work with, as shown in Figure 1.6. The ChartWizard tool is on the Standard toolbar.

**FIGURE 1.6**

*Some of the chart types available through the ChartWizard*

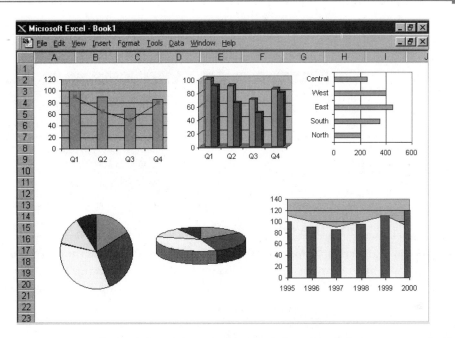

- Charts are usually linked to data stored on worksheets, and change automatically when the data on the worksheet changes. See Chapter 13 for more detail on creating charts.
- Excel has a powerful drawing program that is used in common with other Microsoft Office 97 applications. The drawing tools allow you to draw various objects on worksheets (covered in Chapter 12).
- You can paste graphics from other programs onto a worksheet. See Chapters 12 and 29 to learn how to incorporate graphics from other programs.
- You can apply many formatting options, such as fonts, borders, and colors, directly to cells. See Chapter 5 to learn how to format cells.

# Using Online Help

Excel's online help system is extensive. In addition to allowing you to search a traditional index of help topics, it also offers features such as the Office Assistant, an animated help figure providing context-sensitive help. There are a number of ways to access Excel's various help features.

## The Help Menu

The most obvious place to access online help is the Help menu. The Help menu provides several entry points into the online help system.

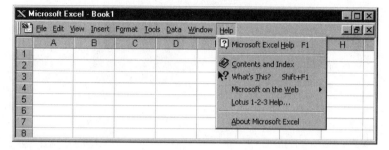

## Using the Office Assistant

The Help ➢ Microsoft Excel Help command displays the *Office Assistant*, an animated help figure that provides a shortcut to context-sensitive help topics and productivity tips. As its name implies, the Office Assistant is available throughout Microsoft Office.

Once the Assistant is visible, you can click on it any time to get help or ask it a question. When the Assistant displays a light bulb, click on it, then click on the Tips button. A tip will appear, explaining a quicker way to perform a certain action. You can also type a free-form question, and the Assistant will provide a list of help topics that may answer your question.

The Assistant is configurable. Click on it, then click on the Options button to display the Office Assistant dialog box shown here:

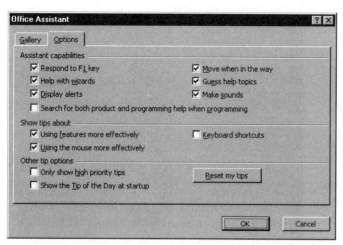

This dialog box determines which topics the Assistant will provide help for. To change the animated character, click on the Gallery tab, where you can scroll through the gallery of characters, and choose one that suits you.

## Searching the Help Index

Choosing Help ➤ Contents And Index displays a tabbed Help Topics dialog box. This is probably the most useful way to access online help.

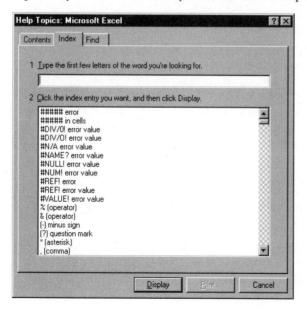

- The Contents tab displays a table of contents for the online help system.
- The Index tab displays an index of all the topics available for online help.
- The Find tab lets you search for help on a certain topic.

## Getting Context-Sensitive Help with the Help Tool

The Help ➢ What's This? command transforms your mouse pointer into a Help pointer—a normal mouse pointer with a large question mark next to it. With this pointer, you can click on any object, or choose any menu command, and context-sensitive help will appear (if available). To cancel the Help pointer, press Esc.

## Other Help Features

The Help ➢ Microsoft On The Web command launches your Web browser program and jumps you to the chosen Web site. See Chapter 29 for more information on how to use Excel's Internet-related features.

The Help ➢ Lotus 1-2-3 command provides help for new Excel users who are converting from Lotus 1-2-3.

### Searching for a Topic in Help

What if you want to check the spelling in a worksheet, but you can't quite remember how to do it? There are a couple ways to get online help about a specific subject. You can choose Help ➢ Contents And Index, choose the Contents tab, and sort through layers of overview information until you locate the pertinent help topic. But the quickest way to get help on a specific topic is by searching. To search for help, choose Help ➢ Contents And Index and click on the Find tab. The first time you click on the Find tab, you must build an index—a wizard walks you through this simple process.

Begin typing the topic. As you type, Excel moves through the list of help topics, getting closer to the topic you want with each letter you type. In this case, you only have to type **spel** to get to the list of spell check topics. Click on a topic (for instance, Spelling Checking), and then click on the Display button. Specific help topics will be listed in the lower half of the Find dialog box. Double-click on a topic that looks useful, or select the topic and click on Display.

When a dialog box is displayed, you can get help for any of its elements. Click on the question mark button in the upper-right corner of the dialog box, and then click on the item in question. A pop-up window appears with an explanation.

# What's New in Excel 8?

Here is an overview of the major enhancements you'll find in Excel 8, with pointers to the chapters where each feature is discussed in detail.

## Basic Features

Look for these new basic features and enhancements in Excel:

**Larger Worksheets:** The number of rows in a worksheet has been increased from 16,384 to 65,536. For a segment of the Excel community, this is one of the most important enhancements, bar none.

**Cell Limit Expanded:** Cells are no longer limited to 255 characters. A cell can now contain up to 32,000 characters.

**Natural Language Formulas:** In the past, Excel users had to learn the intricacies of naming to derive the benefits now provided by natural language formulas, discussed in Chapter 4.

**Multilevel Undo:** Like its Microsoft Word sibling, Excel now supports more than one level of Undo actions. You can use the Edit ➤ Undo command to undo your last 16 actions. See Chapter 7 to read more about the Undo command.

**Color-Coded Ranges:** When you are entering formulas that refer to one or more ranges, the formula and the ranges are color-coded in a way that makes editing complex formulas much easier. This feature is discussed in Chapter 4. In addition, color-coded ranges are used in conjunction with charting, which is discussed in Chapter 13.

**Page Break Preview:** This new feature vastly simplifies setting and changing page breaks. See Chapter 6 to learn how.

**Insert Function Command:** This feature, covered in Chapter 4, has been overhauled, simplifying the entry of functions.

**Shared Workbooks:** For many organizations, this is one of the most important new features in Excel 8. The Tools ➤ Share Workbook command allows more than one person to edit the same workbook at once. Read more about shared workbooks in Chapter 29.

# Formatting Features

There are several new cell formatting options you will find on the Format ➤ Cells dialog box, discussed in Chapter 5. These include merged cells, rotated text, indented cells, and more:

**Merged Cells:** Two or more cells can be merged together into one large cell using the Format ➤ Cells ➤ Alignment command. If this feature seems superfluous, refer to the discussions in Chapters 5 and 10 to see the usefulness of merged cells.

**Rotated Text:** The alignment tab of the Format ➤ Cells dialog box allows you to rotate the text.

**Conditional Formatting:** Check out the Format ➤ Conditional Formatting command. It allows cells to be formatted conditionally, using cell values and worksheet functions to determine the formatting. (This is one of the features most requested by advanced Excel users.)

# Charting and Graphics Features

The charting engine in Excel 8 is the beneficiary of a major overhaul. Here are but several of the multitude of new features:

**New Chart Types:** Several chart types and formatting options have been added. There are new pie-of-a-pie, bar-of-a-pie, and bubble chart types. There are new shapes: pyramids, cones, and cylinders. Charting is covered in Chapters 13 through 16.

**More Data Points:** Here's an important enhancement if you chart large volumes of data: a data series in a 2-D chart has a limit of 32,000 points, up from 4,000 in Excel 7.

**Chart Tips:** When a chart is active and you point to an object within the chart, a pop-up tip appears containing the name of the object. Given the number of objects that exist within a chart, and how close they are to one another, this small feature will be welcomed heartily by charting aficionados.

**Time-Scale Axes:** If you are charting data where an axis is based on dates, a time-scale axis is automatically used (see Chapter 16).

**Drawing:** Excel's drawing and graphics capabilities have been dramatically enhanced. The new drawing toolbar, common to all Microsoft Office programs, contains countless shapes and options. It is discussed in Chapter 12.

**New Graphics Filters:** Support for GIF and JPEG formats allow you to export charts for use on the World Wide Web.

## Data Analysis Features

Several new and revamped data analysis features await you in the new version of Excel:

**Pivot Tables:** This vital analytical tool has been dramatically enhanced. Of particular note is the addition of calculated fields and calculated items, in addition to the long list of other improvements. Pivot tables are covered in Chapters 20 through 22.

**Microsoft Query:** This program (included with Excel) has been simplified with a Query Wizard, which walks the novice through the process of defining a database query (see Chapter 19).

**AutoFilter:** This database feature, covered in Chapter 17, now allows you to view the top 10 items in a field.

**Background Queries:** Database queries can be performed in the background, allowing you to continue using Excel while the query is being processed. This is discussed in Chapter 19. Pivot tables based on external data also support background queries (see Chapter 22).

**Data Validation:** Here is another exciting new feature for advanced users. Data validation allows you to set cell data entry rules. For example, you can define a cell to accept only values between 1 and 10. Read about this feature in Chapter 10.

**GETPIVOTDATA:** This new worksheet function allows you to reference data contained in a pivot table. You can learn about it in Chapter 22.

## Excel and the Internet

A host of new Internet-related features have been added to Excel 8. These topics are all discussed in Chapter 29.

**Hyperlinks:** Even if you are not an Internet user, don't overlook this feature—it is incredibly useful within the confines of Excel. Also read about the HYPERLINKS worksheet function.

**The Web Toolbar:** This toolbar, available throughout Microsoft Office, allows you to navigate Office documents the same way you navigate the World Wide Web.

**Saving HTML Format:** Learn how to save tables and charts in HTML format for use on a Web page.

In this chapter, you've gotten acquainted with the overall look and feel of the Excel environment, and you've read about what's new in Excel 8. In the next chapter, you'll learn how to create, save, and manipulate basic Excel documents, and how to modify the Excel workspace to better suit your tastes.

# Chapter

## 2

### Managing Workbooks, Worksheets, and Windows

## FEATURING

# Managing Workbooks, Worksheets, and Windows

**T**his chapter covers the essential skills needed for managing workbooks, worksheets, and windows. Some of the skills you learn in this chapter are applicable to other Microsoft Office programs. For example, as you learn to create, open, and save workbooks, you will be using techniques that are virtually identical in Word and PowerPoint.

## Using Workbooks

All Excel documents are workbooks, and can contain the following:

- Worksheets (covered in this chapter)
- Chart sheets (covered in Part Four)
- Macro sheets, modules, and dialog box sheets (covered in Part Seven)

When you start Excel, a workbook named Book1 is automatically displayed. Book1 is a new, unsaved workbook that is ready for input. (However, if the first thing you do is open an existing workbook, Book1 is closed automatically—there's no need to close it on your own.)

## Creating New Workbooks

There are several ways to create a new workbook. When Excel is already running, you can open a workbook by choosing File ➢ New, or by clicking on the New Workbook button on the Standard toolbar. Each workbook you create during an Excel session is automatically named using a sequential number; i.e., Book1, Book2, and so on. The first time a workbook is saved, you can assign it a name of your choosing.

You can also create a new workbook by putting an icon on your Windows 95 desktop. Simply right-click on your desktop to display a context-sensitive menu, and choose New ➢ Microsoft Excel Worksheet. This will create an icon on your desktop that automatically starts Excel and opens a new workbook called Book1.

## Opening Existing Workbooks

To open a workbook that has been previously saved to disk, choose File ➢ Open or click on the Open Workbook button on the Standard toolbar. The Open dialog box will appear (see Figure 2.1). If you have used other Microsoft Office applications, such as Word, this dialog box should look familiar. You can select the file from the list of files, or type in a file name. You can also type a full path to a file that is not located in the current folder (for example, C:\BUDGET\EAST).

**FIGURE 2.1**

*The Open dialog box*

| Open | | | ? X |
|---|---|---|---|
| Look in: | Business File | | |

Budget96
Budget97
Budget98
Expenses
Income
Regional Sales
Sales96
Sales97
Sales98

Open
Cancel
Advanced...
☐ Read Only

Find files that match these criteria:

| File name: | | Text or property: | | Find Now |
|---|---|---|---|---|
| Files of type: | Microsoft Excel Files | Last modified: | any time | New Search |

9 file(s) found.

The Open dialog box has eight important buttons in its upper-right section. The functions of these buttons are described below:

 **Up One Level:** Moves up one level in the folder (directory) hierarchy.

 **Search the Web:** Starts your Web browser.

 **Look In Favorites:** Displays files that are saved in your *Favorites* folder which stores shortcuts to files you use frequently.

 **Add To Favorites:** Highlight a file, then click on this button to add the file to your Favorites folder.

 **List:** Displays the list of files without showing detailed information, as shown previously in Figure 2.1.

 **Details:** Displays file name, size, type, and date last modified, as shown here:

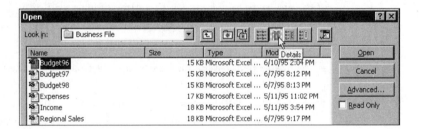

 **Properties:** Displays specified properties of highlighted file as shown here

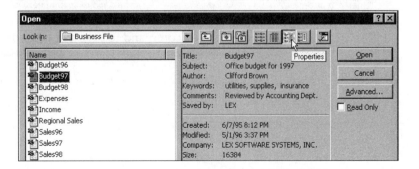

**NOTE**

The next two buttons perform file management functions that are explained in more detail in Chapter 11, "Auditing and Protecting Your Work."

 **Preview:** Displays a preview of the selected file in the Open dialog box.

 **Commands And Settings:** When you click on this button, a menu of file options appears.

## Finding Workbooks

You can also use the Open dialog box to search for files. Click on the Find Now button in the Open dialog box to search for a workbook based on file name, location, file type, text or property, or time last modified. For more information on file searches, see Chapter 11, "Auditing and Protecting Your Work."

## Opening Files Read-Only

Check the Read Only setting in the Open dialog box if you want to open the file *without* the ability to save changes. Opening a file as read-only does not prevent you from making changes—it prevents you from *saving* the changes to a file with the same name. The read-only option serves several useful purposes:

- You can open a workbook as read-only to avoid accidentally changing a file that you don't want to change.
- A read-only workbook may be shared by more than one user on a network; if you open a file as read-only, another user can still open it, change it, and save it under a different name.
- If another user on the network has a file open with write permission (in other words, not read-only), you will still be allowed to open it as read-only.

**TIP**

What if you make changes to a read-only workbook, and want to save the changes? Choose the File ➢ Save As command to save it under a different file name.

Excel 8 now has the ability to share workbooks; if a workbook is shared, more than one user can open it and make changes at the same time. See Chapter 29 to learn about shared workbooks.

## When Another User on the Network Has Your File Open

What if someone else on the network is using a file you need, and you require read/write access to the file as soon as possible? You can try to open it every few minutes (which is aggravating), or you can have Excel notify you as soon as the file becomes available.

When you attempt to open a file that is in use by someone else on the network, the File Reservation dialog box appears. Click on the Notify button to ask Excel to alert you when the file is available for read/write access. The file will initially be opened as read-only, and as soon as the file becomes available for read/write access, a dialog box will appear to notify you. When you click on the Read-Write button, the file is automatically closed and then reopened. Remember not to make any changes to the file until you have read/write access.

## Accessing Different Types of Files

The Files Of Type list in the Open dialog box determines which files are displayed. You can open files created in Lotus 1-2-3, dBase, and QuattroPro, and you can open text files. See Chapter 29 for more information on the types of files Excel is capable of working with.

## Opening More Than One File at a Time

The list box in the Open dialog box is a multi-select list box. Using the mouse, you can select more than one file by holding down the Ctrl or Shift keys while selecting from the list:

- To select noncontiguous files, hold down the Ctrl key while clicking on each file name.
- To select a contiguous range of files, click on the first file, then hold down Shift and click on the last file. All files in between will be selected.

## Opening Recently Used Files

By default, Excel keeps track of the last four files used and displays them in a numbered list at the bottom of the File menu.

Simply choose the file name from the File menu to open it. You can change the number of recently used files displayed on the File menu by choosing Tools ➤ Options. In the Settings area on the General tab of this dialog box, uncheck the Recently Used File List check box to remove them all, or change the Entries value to change the number of files displayed.

## Working with More Than One Workbook

As implied above, Excel supports what is known as the *multiple document interface*, or MDI. MDI allows you to have more than one workbook open at a time. Each time you create a new file or open an existing file, another workbook is added to the workspace. The Window menu will list all open workbooks at the bottom, with a checkmark next to the *active* workbook, as shown below left.

The active workbook is the workbook that you are working in. To activate a different open workbook, select it from the Window menu or simply click on it. Later in this chapter, you will learn how to arrange your workspace so that you can view more than one window at a time.

## Managing Your Workbooks with Microsoft Office

If you are using Excel as part of the Microsoft Office software package, you can create new workbooks and open existing ones from either the Start menu or the Microsoft Office Shortcut bar.

Getting Started

## Managing Workbooks from the Start Menu

To create a workbook from the Windows 95 Start menu, click on the Start button to display the Start menu, and then click on New Office Document. This command accesses the New dialog box (see Figure 2.2), a tabbed dialog box that allows you to create a variety of new documents from any of the Office applications.

FIGURE 2.2

The Office New
dialog box

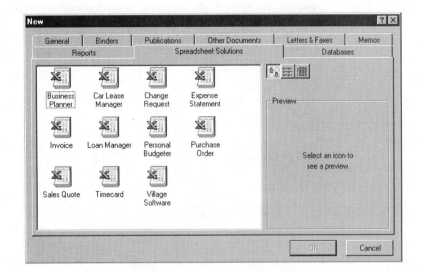

- To create a new Excel workbook, either click on Blank Workbook from the General tab, or click on the Spreadsheet Solutions tab and select an Excel workbook template (see Chapter 10, "Using Templates," for more information on workbook templates).
- To open an existing workbook, click on the Start button, and then click on Open Office Document. The Open dialog box will appear (see Figure 2.1), allowing you to browse through your folder hierarchy and select files.

## Managing Workbooks from the Microsoft Office Shortcut Bar

To create a new workbook from the Shortcut bar, click on the Start A New Document icon on the Office Shortcut bar.

To open an existing workbook, click on the Open A Document icon.

## Saving Your Work

Once you've made changes to a workbook, choose File ➤ Save to save it to disk. You can also click on the Save button on the Standard toolbar. The first time you save a workbook, Excel displays the Save As dialog box (Figure 2.3) so you can give the file a name.

*The Save As dialog box*

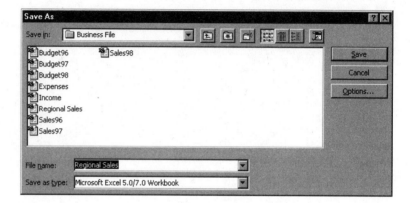

Subsequent File ➤ Save commands automatically use the current file name to save the file.

**NOTE**
File names in Excel aren't subject to the DOS file name limitation of eight characters followed by a three-character extension, nor are you required to add the default .XLS suffix. However, you can still use and display file extensions by starting Windows Explorer, choosing View ➤ Options, and unchecking the Hide MS-DOS File Extensions check box.

You can use the File ➤ Save As command to save an existing file under a different name. The command's dialog box is identical to the one displayed the first time you saved a file (see Figure 2.3 above). This feature is useful when you want to save different versions of a document on which you are working.

### Creating Different Types of Files

The Save As Type drop-down list in the Save As dialog box lets you save the file in one of many different file formats. For example, you can save a file in Excel 5/7 format, so that other users who have yet to upgrade to Excel 97 can use it. See Chapter 29 to learn how to work with different types of files in Excel.

## Options for Saving Files ·

To access a variety of save options, click on the Options button in the Save As dialog box. The Save Options dialog box appears:

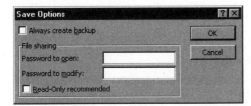

The File Sharing options in this dialog box provide protection for the workbook. File protection is covered further in Chapter 11, "Auditing and Protecting Your Work." Check the Always Create Backup setting to make Excel automatically create a backup of the file each time it is saved. See Chapter 7, "Enhancing Your Productivity," to learn more about this setting.

## Closing a Workbook

Choose File ➤ Close to close the active workbook. If there are unsaved changes, you will be asked if you want to save them.

**TIP**

To close all open workbooks with one command, hold down the Shift key, then click on the File menu. The Close command will be changed to Close All, and you can select this command to close all workbooks.

# Managing Worksheets

A workbook can contain one worksheet or hundreds of worksheets, depending on your computer's memory. Typically, worksheets within a workbook are related to one another. For example, you may create one worksheet for each department in your company, or one sheet for each month.

## Activating Worksheets

To activate a worksheet using the mouse, click on the worksheet tab at the bottom of the workbook.

To activate a worksheet using the keyboard, do either of the following:

- Press Ctrl+Page Down to activate the next worksheet.
- Press Ctrl+Page Up to activate the previous worksheet.

The active worksheet is indicated by the highlighted tab.

## Scrolling the Tabs

Several worksheet tabs may be visible at a given time. Use the tab scrolling buttons pictured in Table 2.1 to scroll the sheet tabs. These four buttons control which tabs are displayed, but they do not change the active worksheet.

**TABLE 2.1:** TAB SCROLLING BUTTONS

| Click on this button | To display |
| --- | --- |
| ⏮ | First tab in workbook |
| ◀ | Previous tab (left) |
| ▶ | Next tab (right) |
| ⏭ | Last tab in workbook |

You can control the number of visible sheet tabs in the workbook by moving the Tab Split box to the left or right. Move the mouse pointer over the Tab Split box until it changes to parallel lines with arrows pointing in opposite directions (see the graphic below). Then click and drag to the left or right. To view more sheet tabs, drag to the right; to view fewer tabs, drag to the left.

## Inserting and Deleting Worksheets

To insert a worksheet into the active workbook, choose Insert ➤ Worksheet. Or, right-click on a tab, then choose Insert from the shortcut menu that appears.

To delete a worksheet from a workbook, activate the sheet, then choose Edit ➤ Delete Sheet. Excel will display a dialog box confirming the deletion. Or, right-click on the sheet tab, then choose Delete from the context-sensitive menu.

# Copying and Moving Worksheets

Worksheets can be moved or copied within a single workbook or to a different workbook.

## Moving and Copying Worksheets within the Same Workbook

To move a worksheet within the same workbook, first activate the worksheet, then use either of the following methods:

- Click on the worksheet tab, then drag and drop it to a new location along the row of worksheet tabs.
- Choose Edit ➤ Move Or Copy Sheet. The Move Or Copy dialog box appears (see Figure 2.4). Select the insertion point from the Before Sheet drop-down list and click on OK.

FIGURE 2.4

**FIGURE 2.4**

The Move Or Copy dialog box, where you can move sheets within workbooks

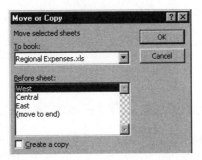

To copy a worksheet within the same workbook, follow the procedure for moving a worksheet described above, making these modifications:

- With the mouse, select the tab, then hold down the Ctrl key while you drag and drop the tab.
- With the menu command, check the Create A Copy check box on the Move Or Copy dialog box. A copy of the worksheet is inserted.

## Moving or Copying to a Different Workbook— The Easy Way

The simplest way to move or copy a sheet to a different workbook is to drag and drop the worksheet tab. Both workbooks must be open and visible. (The discussion on windows later in this chapter will explain how to make more than one workbook visible at the same time.) To move a sheet, drag and drop the tab to the row of tabs on the destination workbook. To copy, select the tab, then hold down Ctrl while you drag and drop.

## Moving or Copying to a Different Workbook— The Hard(er) Way

If you do not want to rearrange workbooks to make them both visible, or if you want to move/copy to a *new* workbook, use the following procedure:

1. Choose Edit ➤ Move Or Copy Sheet. The Move Or Copy dialog box appears, as shown previously in Figure 2.4.
2. Specify the destination workbook in the To Book drop-down list. All open workbooks will appear in this list, as will a *(New Book)* choice.
3. Specify in the Before Sheet list where the sheet will be placed in the destination workbook.
4. Check the Create A Copy setting to copy the sheet, or uncheck it to move the sheet.
5. Click on OK.

# Manipulating Multiple Worksheets

The procedures described above for copying, moving, and deleting a sheet can be performed on multiple sheets at the same time. This is accomplished by selecting more than one sheet before performing the desired operation. Selecting multiple tabs involves a procedure that is similar to selecting multiple items in a multi-select list box:

- To select and deselect noncontiguous tabs, hold down the Ctrl key while clicking on them.
- To select adjacent tabs, hold down the Shift key while clicking on them.

To cancel multiple tab selection, either click on a tab that is not selected, or right-click on a tab and choose Ungroup Sheets from the shortcut menu that appears.

Once you have selected the worksheets that you want to move or copy, simply hold down the Ctrl key while you drag and drop them to their new location.

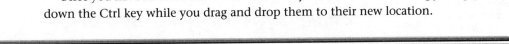

You can edit and format multiple worksheets simultaneously by selecting more than one tab. You'll learn about this technique in Chapter 7, "Enhancing Your Productivity."

## Using Meaningful Worksheet Names

You are not required to use Excel's default worksheet names. Worksheet tabs become a very useful interface for navigating a workbook when sheets have names like *Sales Analysis* and *Forecast* instead of *Sheet1* and *Sheet2*. To rename a worksheet, do one of the following:

- Choose Format ➤ Sheet ➤ Rename.
- Right-click on a sheet tab, then choose Rename from the shortcut menu.
- Double-click on the sheet tab.

Each of these procedures will cause the sheet name on the tab to be highlighted. Simply type the new name, then press ↵.

## Controlling the Default Number of Worksheets in New Workbooks

By default, there are three worksheets in a new workbook. To change the number of worksheets shown by default in a new workbook, choose Tools ➤ Options and select the General tab in the Options dialog box that appears (see Figure 2.5).

Change the Sheets In New Workbook setting according to your preference. Although there is no limit to the number of sheets that can be added other than that imposed by available memory, oddly, the default Sheets In New Workbook setting has a maximum limit of 255.

## Working with Windows in Excel

It comes as a surprise to many users to learn that *windows* and *workbooks* are not synonymous. One workbook can be displayed in more than one window. One of the greatest benefits of this feature is the ability to view two or more worksheets in the workbook simultaneously. For example, if you keep statistics about your company's sales trends organized in worksheets by month, you can compare the information

**FIGURE 2.5**

The General tab
in the Options
dialog box

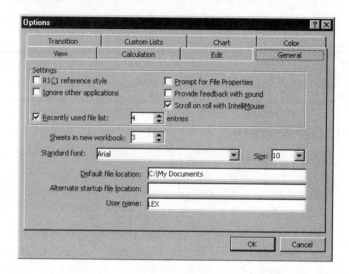

about several months of sales by opening multiple windows. Or, you might want to view numerical data on one sheet, and simultaneously view a chart that resides on a different sheet.

**NOTE**

If you are just learning about workbooks and worksheets, there is no compelling reason to tackle the windows topic right away—you may want to get comfortable with workbooks and revisit this section later.

## Displaying a Workbook in More Than One Window

Assume that you have an active workbook called Book1. If you want to display Book1 in separate windows, choose Window ➤ New Window to create a second window. There will now be two open windows: Book1:1 and Book1:2. These are windows into the same workbook. Entries made in one window will reflect in the other, and vice versa.

### Arranging Windows

There are several ways to quickly arrange multiple windows so that you can see them. To understand all the options, try this short exercise:

**1.** Create three or more windows by choosing Window ➤ New Window a few times.

**2.** Choose Window ➤ Arrange. The Arrange Windows dialog box appears:

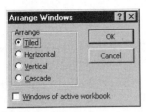

**3.** Now choose one of the Arrange options from the dialog box:

| | |
|---|---|
| **Tiled** | Each window is made fully visible, and Excel decides how best to arrange them based upon the number of open windows. |
| **Horizontal** | Each window is made fully visible and arranged horizontally. |
| **Vertical** | Each window is made fully visible and arranged vertically. |
| **Cascade** | Windows are overlapped, with the title of each window visible. |

**Arranging the Active Workbook Only** - If you have more than one workbook open, and you have created multiple windows for each workbook, you can use the Windows Of Active Workbook check box to limit the arranging of windows to the active workbook only:

- If checked, only the windows of the active workbook are arranged.
- If unchecked, all windows of all open workbooks are arranged.

## Moving between Windows

There are various ways to move from one window to another in Excel:

- The bottom of the Window menu lists all open windows—choose the one you want to activate.
- If the windows are arranged so that more than one is visible, click on the window you want to activate.
- Press Ctrl+F6 to activate the next window, or Ctrl+Shift+F6 to activate the previous window.

PART

I

Getting Started

# Closing Displayed Windows

When manipulating the display of multiple windows of a workbook, use the Control menu. For example, when you want to close a window, the File ➤ Close command won't necessarily be the right choice all of the time—if the workbook is displayed in multiple windows, *all* of the windows will be closed. To close only one window, you must use the Close command on the Control menu for that specific window. Open the active window's Control menu by clicking on the control box on the left side of the window's title bar, as shown in Figure 2.6.

**FIGURE 2.6**

*Click on the active window's control box to display its Control menu.*

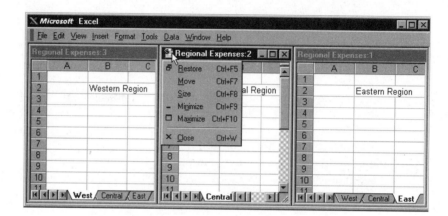

To close the window, click on the control box, then choose Close from the menu. Or just double-click on the window control box. (The commands on the window Control menu are Microsoft Windows conventions, and not specific to Excel.)

## Hiding Windows

To avoid cluttering your workspace, you may want to temporarily hide a window instead of completely closing it. Choose Window ➤ Hide to hide the active window, and choose Window ➤ Unhide to unhide a window.

**NOTE**

Remember, workbooks and windows are not necessarily synonymous—one workbook can be displayed in multiple windows. If a workbook is displayed in only one window, then the window and workbook are virtually synonymous—closing the window closes the workbook.

# Controlling the Display

There are many different settings that control how elements on your screen are displayed, and these settings apply at different levels—workspace, workbook, worksheet, or window. For example, one workspace setting controls whether the status bar is visible or not. You may want more viewable screen area by default, so that Excel always starts with the status bar hidden. Or, in a given worksheet, you may want to hide the row and column headings. In this section, you will learn to change the most common settings.

## Controlling the Workspace Display

Workspace level settings are global to the entire Excel workspace, and are not specific to any workbook or worksheet.

### Hiding the Formula Bar and Status Bar

There is one primary reason for hiding the formula and status bars: gaining additional screen real estate. If you want to hide these bars, do the following:

- Select View ➤ Formula Bar to hide or display the formula bar.
- Select View ➤ Status Bar to hide or display the status bar.

These settings are persistent—Excel "remembers" them from session to session, so if you hide the formula bar and exit Excel, the formula bar will still be hidden the next time you run Excel.

### Displaying the Full Screen

The View ➤ Full Screen command maximizes the Excel workspace by hiding the toolbars, title bar, status bar, menu bar, and scroll bars and displaying the work area across the full screen. A full-screen display yields extra screen real estate, and is often used for overhead presentations. Excel remembers this setting from session to session.

You can also use the Full Screen toolbar to switch back and forth from normal to full-screen view: just select View ➤ Toolbars ➤ Full Screen.

## Controlling the Workbook or Window Display

Workbook settings are saved with the workbook. If you change any of these settings and then save the workbook, close the workbook, and later reopen it, the setting remains in effect. Access these settings by choosing Tools ➤ Options, then choosing the View tab (see Figure 2.7).

**FIGURE 2.7**

*The View tab
in the Options
dialog box*

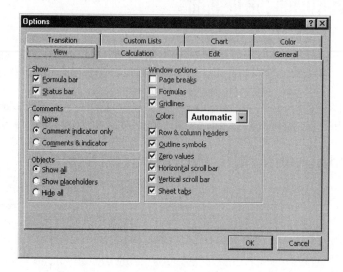

Let's take a look at several of the more commonly used settings in this tab:

**Horizontal Scroll Bar/Vertical Scroll Bar** - Horizontal and/or vertical scroll bars can be displayed or hidden by checking or unchecking the appropriate check box in the Window Options area of the View tab.

**Sheet Tabs** - This option controls the display of the worksheet tabs at the bottom of the workbook. You may want to hide the tabs if you are distributing a workbook with multiple sheets but only one sheet is intended to be viewed. In this case, you would uncheck the Sheet Tabs check box in the Window Options area of the View tab.

## Controlling the Worksheet Display

Worksheet settings are applied only to the active worksheet, and are saved only for that worksheet. Worksheet settings, like the settings for controlling the display of workbooks and workbook windows, are accessed by choosing Tools ≻ Options, then choosing the View tab (see Figure 2.7 again). These are the worksheet options:

**Row & Column Headings** - If this setting is checked, row and column headings are displayed; otherwise they are hidden.

**Gridlines** - If this setting is checked, gridlines are displayed on the worksheet. If unchecked, gridline display is turned off for both the screen worksheet and the printed worksheet.

Getting Started

Gridlines are not the same as cell borders—gridlines are an all-or-nothing proposition, whereas cell borders can be applied selectively. Cell borders, covered in Chapter 5, are far more effective when gridlines are turned off. Use the Gridlines setting in the dialog box shown previously in Figure 2.7.

**Gridlines Color** - You can select a different gridline color from the drop-down Color list shown previously in Figure 2.7. Try experimenting with a light gray color to create less obtrusive gridlines.

**Page Breaks** - If this setting is checked, automatic page breaks are displayed as broken lines along the gridlines where page breaks occur. If unchecked, page breaks will not be displayed until the page is printed. (Page break lines only show on the screen— they do not appear on the hard copy printout.)

**Zero Values** - If this setting is checked, cells containing zero values display zero; otherwise they display as blank. Remember, this setting applies to the entire worksheet. Chapter 5 shows some formatting techniques to suppress zeros selectively.

## Splitting Window Panes

Windows can be split into *panes*, resulting in either two or four separate scrollable regions on the window. One common reason for splitting panes is to create row and/ or column headings that do not scroll out of view. Another reason is to simply view two different regions of the sheet at the same time.

To split windows into panes, first select the cell(s) to represent the split point:

- Select an entire column to split panes vertically.
- Select an entire row to split panes horizontally.
- Select a single cell to split panes immediately above and to the left of the cell.

Then choose Window ➤ Split to automatically split the window. Figure 2.8 shows a window with both vertical and horizontal splits. The four regions are *separately scrollable;* i.e., you can scroll around them just as if they were separate windows.

**Freezing Split Panes** - If the purpose of the split panes is to freeze row and/or column titles in place, choose Window ➤ Freeze Panes to lock the split in place. The following changes will occur:

- The split bar or bars turn into solid lines.
- The pane above a horizontal split can no longer be scrolled.
- The pane to the left of a vertical split can no longer be scrolled.

**FIGURE 2.8**

*Split windows. This split was created by selecting cell F9, then choosing the Window ➢ Split command.*

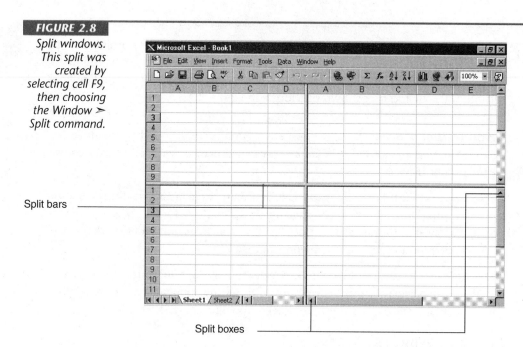

Split bars

Split boxes

Try the following steps to practice splitting and freezing panes:

**1.** Enter text into a blank worksheet as shown here:

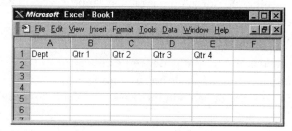

**2.** Select cell B2.

**3.** Choose Window ➢ Split. You should now have four panes, similar to those shown in Figure 2.8, each of which is separately scrollable.

**4.** Choose Window ➢ Freeze Panes. Row 1 and column A are now frozen in place. When you scroll the worksheet, the headings stay in view.

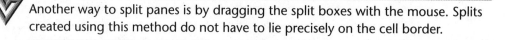

**TIP**

Another way to split panes is by dragging the split boxes with the mouse. Splits created using this method do not have to lie precisely on the cell border.

**Removing Splits** - You can do either of the following to rejoin split windows:

- Choose Window ➤ Remove Split to remove both horizontal and vertical splits.
- If the window is unfrozen, double-click on a split bar to join the panes, or drag the split boxes all the way to the top or left with the mouse. If the window is frozen, choose Window ➤ Unfreeze Panes first.

## Zooming In and Out

To reduce or increase the magnification of the window display, select a magnification level from the pull-down list on the Standard toolbar. You can also choose View➤ Zoom to display the Zoom dialog box, shown below. Zooming out is one of the handiest ways to step back and get the big picture of your worksheet model. Zooming in is a great way to avoid eye fatigue while working on a particular section of the sheet.

**TIP**

If you are using a new Microsoft mouse with a central wheel button, you can use the wheel to zoom in and out of the window display.

You can choose one of several preset zoom settings in the dialog box shown below, or you can specify your own magnification setting using the Custom option. If you choose the Fit Selection option, the selected range is zoomed to fill the window up to a maximum of 400%.

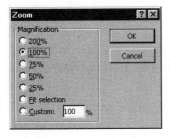

Getting Started

**NOTE**

Splitting panes, freezing panes, and zooming do not affect the printed document.

You now have the basic information for starting and using Excel, and for managing and customizing the Excel workspace and its component workbooks, worksheets, and windows. In the next chapter, you will be introduced to the skills you'll need to work with cells, the basic element of Excel worksheets.

# Chapter

# 3

Working inside
Worksheets

# Working inside Worksheets

**T**his chapter covers the basics of working inside a worksheet. While the previous chapters have discussed the Excel interface, commands, and workbook and worksheet organization, it is inside the worksheet where the real work takes place. Worksheets are composed of individual cells, and cells can contain numbers, text, formulas, etc. Cells also provide data fields for charts, lists, and tables. Working within the worksheet is learning the art of cell manipulation, how to present and synthesize data, and interrelate cells to provide different perspectives.

## All About Cells

The basic element of an Excel worksheet is the cell. Cells possess these basic properties:

- They can contain text or numbers.
- They can contain formulas, which are used to perform calculations.
- They can be formatted using a wide variety of formatting options, such as font, borders, color, and alignment of data within the cell.

Cells are identified by their position in the worksheet grid, with letters used to designate the column, and numbers used to designate the row. For example, cell B4 is located at the intersection of the second column and fourth row. A cell address, such as B4, is called a cell *reference*.

**NOTE**

You can label columns with numbers by changing the cell reference style to R1C1 (Choose Tools ➢ Options, and select the General tab to change reference style). You'll learn more about reference styles in Chapter 4.

## The Active Cell

One cell is always the *active cell*. The reference of the active cell is displayed in the *Name box*, on the left part of the formula bar (see Figure 3.1). One easy way to activate a cell is by clicking on it with the mouse. Then, whatever you type is entered into the active cell.

**NOTE**

There are times when there is *not* an active cell, such as when a graphical object is selected.

## Selecting Multiple Cells

There will be times when you need to copy, move, or otherwise manipulate a group of cells. For such cases, Excel allows you to select a *range* of cells. The easiest way to select a range is to click on a cell, hold down the left mouse button, drag the mouse pointer across several cells, then release the mouse button. From the keyboard, a range of cells can be selected by holding down the Shift key and pressing one of the arrow keys. The selected cells are referred to as the *selection*. Even when a range of cells is selected, one cell is still the active cell.

**FIGURE 3.1**

*The Worksheet grid—the cell reference for active cell is shown in the Name box.*

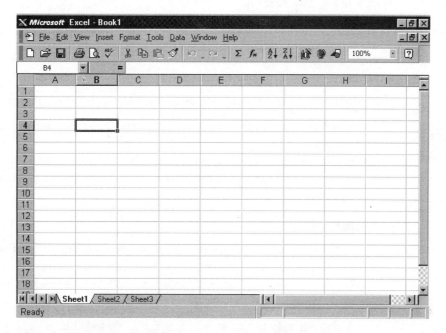

In the selection shown here,

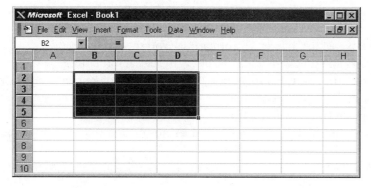

- Cell B2 is the active cell.
- The selected range is referred to as B2:D5—the colon is shorthand for the word *through*.

# Types of Cell Data

There are four distinct types of data that can reside in a cell: text, numbers, logical values, and error values. Let's take a look at each type.

## Text

Text in a cell can include any combination of letters, numbers, and keyboard symbols:

- A cell can now contain up to 32,000 characters (previous versions of Excel were limited to 255).
- If column width prevents a text string from fitting visually in a cell, the display extends over neighboring cells. However, if the neighboring cells are occupied, the display is truncated.

## Numbers

Performing numeric calculations is the most common thing that is done with spreadsheet programs, and over the course of the next several chapters, you will learn many ways to perform calculations, and to format numbers on the worksheet. Here are some important things to understand about the way Excel treats numbers:

- A number may be displayed using commas, scientific notation, or one of many built-in numeric formats. Do not confuse a number's *display format* with the *underlying value*. The *display format* is what you see in the cell, and the *underlying value* is the calculated value (which you can see in the formula bar). (Numeric formatting is covered in Chapter 5, "Formatting Worksheets.")
- Dates and times are numbers, but with special formatting.
- Excel tries very hard to guess the "meaning" of numeric input, and format it accordingly. If you try to enter **1–9** as a text string, Excel will interpret this as a date and display it as **9-Jan**.
- When an unformatted number does not fit in a cell, it is displayed in scientific notation.
- When a formatted number does not fit in a cell, number signs (####) are displayed.

## Logical Values

You can enter the logical values TRUE and FALSE into cells. Logical values are often used in writing conditional formulas. Also, there are many formulas that can return logical values.

### Error

Formulas, covered in Chapter 4, "Using Formulas and Functions," can result in errors. An error value is a distinct type of data. For example, if a formula attempts to divide a number by zero, the result is the #DIV/0! error value.

# Entering, Editing, and Clearing Cells

Here are the common procedures for entering data into a cell, editing data in a cell, and clearing the contents of a cell.

## Entering Data into a Cell

To enter data into a cell, simply do the following:

1. Select the cell by clicking on it.
2. Type numbers, text, or a combination of both.
3. Press ↵ (or click on the green check mark that appeared in the formula bar as you were typing).

Notice that when you select the cell, the data contained in the cell is displayed on the formula bar. This will become more important later on when you start working with formulas. The formula bar displays the formula contained in the active cell, whereas the resulting value is displayed in the cell.

### Entering Numbers

1. A numeric entry can include one or more digits and the special characters shown in Table 3.1. The underlying numbers that Excel supports can be as large as $9.99999999999999^{307}$ (roughly, 1 followed by 14 zeros, raised to the 307th power) and as small as $-9.99999999999999^{307}$.

**TIP**

You can enter numbers with fixed decimal points by choosing Tools ➢ Options, then choosing the Edit tab. Check the Fixed Decimal check box, and select a number of decimal places. Accountants often prefer to work with two fixed decimals, because the decimal point does not have to be typed. If you are entering a long list of dollar values, you can type just the numbers (Excel inserts the decimal point automatically).

**TABLE 3.1: ALLOWABLE CHARACTERS FOR NUMERIC ENTRIES**

| Character | Function |
| --- | --- |
| 0 through 9 | Any combination of numerals |
| + | Indicates exponents when used in conjunction with E |
| - | Indicates negative number |
| ( ) | Indicates negative number |
| , (comma) | Thousands marker |
| / | Fraction indicator (when fraction is preceded by a space) or date separator |
| $ | Currency indicator |
| % | Percentage indicator |
| . (period) | Decimal indicator |
| E | Exponent indicator |
| e | Exponent indicator |
| : | Time separator |
| (single space) | Separators for compound fractions (e.g. 4 1/2); and date time entries (e.g. 1/2/94 5:00[*]) |

[*] (Note: various alphabetic characters may also be interpreted as parts of a date or time entry, e.g., 4-Jan or 5:00 AM).

## Entering Numbers as Text

An inventory product code may consist of only numeric characters, yet you may not want Excel to treat such data as numeric. As in the above example, if you enter **1–9** intended as a product code, Excel displays **9-Jan**. To force an entry to be text, use an apostrophe as the first character. The apostrophe will not be displayed in the cell, nor will it print out. It will be displayed when you edit the cell, however. When you use an apostrophe to force a number to become text, the cell can no longer have number formats applied to it, nor can the number be used in calculations.

Getting Started

## Entering Dates and Times

When you enter a number that Excel interprets as a date or time, the cell display will automatically be formatted as such.

> **TIP**
>
> By default, text is left-aligned within the cell, and numbers are right-aligned. This provides a quick visual cue as to whether Excel interpreted your entry as text or numeric.

# Editing a Cell

Don't worry if you discover a mistake that you made when entering data into a cell. There are two places where you can do your editing: in the formula bar or in the cell itself.

**Formula Bar**: Select the cell, then click in the formula bar. The insertion point is placed into the formula bar.

**In-Cell**: Double-click on the cell, or select the cell and press F2 (see Figure 3.2). The insertion point is placed at the end of the cell contents.

**FIGURE 3.2**

*Double-clicking on cell C6 here lets you perform in-cell editing.*

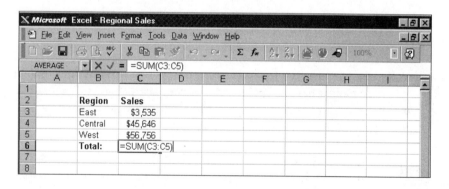

You can turn on or off the in-cell editing feature. Choose Tools ➢ Options, select the Edit tab, then check or uncheck the Edit Directly In Cell check box. There are several advantages to turning off in-cell editing:

- Double-clicking on a cell with a comment allows you to edit the comment (see Chapter 11 to learn about cell comments).
- Double-clicking on a cell that refers to other cells takes you to the other cells.

Whether you are editing in-cell or in the formula bar, use basic text-editing techniques to change the contents of a cell:

- Double-click on a word to select it. Use the mouse to position the insertion point or to select text.
- Highlighted text is replaced by whatever you type.
- Press Home to go to the beginning, or End to go to the end.
- Use the left and right arrow keys to move left and right.
- While editing cell references in formulas, F2 toggles the function of the left and right arrow keys. The arrow keys can be used to edit a cell reference by allowing you to navigate the sheet to select a new reference, rather than only being used to navigate within the formula.

Press ↵ or click on the enter box on the formula bar to finish editing.

## Undoing Cell Entries and Edits

If you change your mind about an entry or edit while you are making it, you can undo it before moving on to the next entry:

- If you haven't yet pressed ↵ while entering or editing, you can cancel your changes by pressing Esc or clicking on the Cancel button (the Cancel button is only visible while you are editing a cell—it is the small button in the formula bar which has an × in it).
- If you've already pressed ↵, you can choose Edit ➤ Undo, or click on the Undo button.

Excel allows you to reverse your actions sequentially. The Undo button on the Standard toolbar has a drop-down list of your last 12 actions. As you "back up" and undo your actions, Excel keeps replenishing the list with the previous actions you performed since you opened the workbook.

**NOTE**
See Chapter 7 for information on the Undo and Redo commands.

## Clearing a Cell

Clearing a cell is like erasing a mistake, unlike deleting a cell with Edit ➤ Delete, which causes cells below and/or to the right to shift position. The quickest way to clear cells is to select the cell or cells, then press the Delete key. This clears the contents, but leaves formatting and cell notes intact. Edit ➤ Delete deletes the cell.

**TIP**

For more on clearing vs. deleting, see the sidebar on this topic later in the chapter.

Choose Edit ➤ Clear if you want greater control over what you are clearing, and choose one of the following commands from the Edit ➤ Clear submenu:

**All:** Clears everything (contents, formats, and notes) from the selected cell(s).

**Formats:** Clears formats.

**Contents:** Clears just contents. This is the same as pressing the Delete key.

**Comments:** Clears just cell comments (see Chapter 11).

**TIP**

If you want to replace a cell's contents with a different entry, there is no need to clear the cell first. Select the cell and begin typing the new entry; the old entry will be replaced.

# Navigating Worksheets Using the Mouse

You can use some special mouse techniques, such as jumping to specific cells, for more efficient movement across the worksheet. This allows you to avoid wasting time scrolling around. We'll take a look at some of these techniques in the following sections.

## Jumping to the Beginning or the End of the Block

When you are working with a block of data, you often need to move to the beginning or end of that block to add to or edit the data. A quick way to jump to the end of a block of filled or blank cells is by double-clicking on the *cell border* of the selected cell in the direction you want to move. For example, to move to the bottom of a column of data, double-click on the bottom border of the selected cell. To move to the end of a row of data, double-click on the right cell border. The selected cell will be the last (or first) cell in the row or column.

## Moving Directly to Specific Cells

You can also move to a specific cell or range of cells anywhere in the worksheet. The fastest way to go directly to specific cells is to use the Name box in the formula bar. You can jump to a specific cell using either of these methods:

- Click on the Name box and type a cell reference, then press ↵.
- If the cell or range is named, click on the name from the Name box drop-down list (see Chapter 8 to learn about cell names). Click on the drop-down arrow on the left side of the formula bar to open the Name box drop-down list.

## Moving to a Cell with Go To

You can also use the Go To command to move to a specified cell or range of cells, especially if you want to go back to a previous cell and can't remember where it was:

**1.** Choose Edit ➤ Go To (or press F5). The Go To dialog box appears (see Figure 3.3).

**FIGURE 3.3**

*The Go To
dialog box*

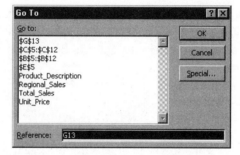

**2.** Select a cell or range from the list of names, or type a cell reference into the Reference box. It is not necessary to type in dollar signs.

**3.** Click on OK.

Excel remembers the last four cell locations you selected using the methods described above and lists them at the top of the Go To list in the Go To dialog box. Any named cells in the workbook will be listed below the last four locations.

# Navigating Worksheets Using the Keyboard

Most of the time, you'll use your mouse to move around in Excel, but sometimes using the keyboard to move between cells is more efficient (and easier on the wrist). Table 3.2 explains the keystrokes you can use to navigate worksheets.

> **TIP**
>
> Make sure that Scroll Lock and Num Lock are off. With the Scroll Lock on, the arrow keys scroll the worksheet instead of moving to the selected cell, and some keyboards don't have separate arrow keys.

**Getting Started**

**TABLE 3.2:** MOVING AROUND A WORKSHEET USING KEYSTROKES

| This Keystroke | Moves |
|---|---|
| Arrow keys (→←↑↓) | Right, left, up, and down (one cell at a time) |
| Ctrl+arrow keys | To the edge of the current data region (region the cell is currently in) |
| Page Up, Page Down | Up or down one window |
| Home | To the beginning of row |
| Ctrl+Home | To cell A1 |
| Ctrl+End | To lower-right corner of worksheet |
| End, Arrow key | By one block of data, within current row or column |
| End, ↵ | To the last cell in current row |
| End (with Scroll Lock on) | To the lower-right corner of window |
| Home (with Scroll Lock on) | To the upper-left corner of window |

## Moving within a Range of Cells

If you are working with a specific block of cells, you might want to move around just within that block. You can select a range of cells (see the section below for more on selecting cells), and then use the keystrokes in Table 3.3 to navigate the selected range.

> **TIP**
>
>
> If you scroll to a distant area of the worksheet using the mouse and scrollbars, and you haven't selected a new cell, you can return to the active cell quickly by pressing Ctrl+Backspace.

**TABLE 3.3:** KEYSTROKES FOR MOVING WITHIN A SELECTION

| Press | To Move |
|---|---|
| ↵ | Down one cell |
| Shift+↵ | Up one cell |
| Tab | Right one cell |
| Shift+Tab | Left one cell |

# Selecting Cells

When you want to work with a range of cells (for example, to change their format, delete their contents, or perform a calculation on them), you must first select the range. You can use either the mouse, the keyboard, or a combination of two to select ranges of cells.

## Selecting a Range with the Mouse

There are several ways to select cells using the mouse, as explained in the following sections.

**Dragging a Range** - Here's how to select a range of cells by dragging:

1. Click on a cell at a corner of the range, but don't release the mouse button.
2. Drag the mouse to select the range.
3. Once the desired range is selected, release the mouse button.

**NOTE**

While selecting a range of cells, the Name box displays the dimensions of the selected range. If the selection is four rows by two columns, 4R x 2C will appear. These dimensions only display *while you are selecting*—as soon as you release the mouse button, the dimensions are replaced with the active cell reference.

**Selecting a Large Range without Dragging** - Selecting a very large range by dragging the mouse can be cumbersome. Here's another way to do it:

1. Click on a cell in one corner of the range.
2. Hold down Shift and click on the cell in the opposite corner of the range.

The entire range is automatically selected.

**Other Ways to Select with the Mouse** - Table 3.4 illustrates the variety of ways cells can be selected using the mouse (along with the keyboard in some cases).

**TABLE 3.4:** SELECTING CELLS WITH THE MOUSE

| Do This | To Select |
| --- | --- |
| Click on row number at left side of worksheet | One row |
| Click and drag up or down through row numbers | Multiple rows |
| Hold down Ctrl while selecting row numbers | Noncontiguous rows |
| Same as rows, but click on column letters | Columns |
| Click on Select All button on upper-left corner of worksheet (see Figure 3.1) | Entire worksheet |
| Hold down Ctrl while selecting | Multiple ranges |
| Select cell within data region, click on Select Current Region tool, a custom editing tool. See Chapter 7 for information on custom tools. | Current data region |

## Selecting Cells Using the Keyboard

If you prefer to keep your hands on your keyboard, you can also select ranges of cells using keystrokes only. Table 3.5 defines the keystrokes to use for making a wide variety of cell selections.

**TABLE 3.5:** KEYSTROKES FOR SELECTING GROUPS OF CELLS

| This Keystroke | Selects |
| --- | --- |
| Ctrl+Spacebar | Entire column |
| Shift+Spacebar | Entire row |
| Ctrl+Shift+Spacebar | Entire worksheet |
| End, Shift+Arrow keys | Extends selection to end of data block |
| End, Shift+Home | Extends selection to lower-right corner of worksheet |

**TABLE 3.5:** KEYSTROKES FOR SELECTING GROUPS OF CELLS (CONTINUED)

| This Keystroke | Selects |
| --- | --- |
| End, Shift+↵ | Extends selection to last cell in current row of data block. |
| Ctrl+Shift+* (asterisk) | Current data region |
| F8, Arrow keys | Same as holding down Shift while using arrow keys, except that F8 is a toggle. You can release the F8 key and then just use the arrow keys. (Press F8 or Esc again to turn it off.) |

### MASTERING THE OPPORTUNITIES

#### Keyboard Shortcuts for Selecting Regions

Quite often you will need to select an entire region of adjacent cells to do something, such as copy the table, chart a pivot table, apply an outline border, or format a range of cells. New users typically use the mouse to select the region by dragging, which is usually efficient. But what if the region is larger than the window? The fastest way to select an entire region of adjacent cells is to press Ctrl+Shift+*.

There are two other ways to select the current region: if you don't want to remember keystrokes, place the Select Current Region tool on a toolbar, and click on the tool to select the current region (see Chapter 7 to learn how to customize toolbars); otherwise, bring up the Go To dialog box from the Edit menu (by pressing F5), click on the Special button, and then select the Current Region option.

## Moving and Copying Cells

There are many times when it is easier to copy the contents of a cell or range of cells than to key the data in again. For example, a cell may contain a complex formula. You can copy cells using drag and drop or menu commands.

# Moving and Copying Cells Using Drag and Drop

The easiest way to moving cells it to use the mouse to drag and drop them. Here's how to move a cell using drag and drop:

1. Select the cells you want to move (the range must be contiguous).
2. Point to an outside border of the selected range using the mouse. The mouse pointer will turn into an arrow.

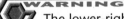

3. Click on the selection, drag the cells to a new location, then release the mouse button.

The cells will now be positioned in the new location.

**WARNING**

The lower-right corner of the selected cells has a special marker called the *fill handle*. When you point at the fill handle, the mouse pointer becomes cross-hairs. When dragging and dropping, be sure not to accidentally use the fill handle. (See Chapter 7 for information about the fill handle and AutoFills.)

Copying via drag and drop is the same as moving, except you hold down the Ctrl key while you drag. The cursor arrow displays a plus (+) to show that you are copying rather than moving.

**NOTE**

The drag-and-drop feature can be turned on or off by choosing Tools ➢ Options, selecting the Edit tab, and checking or clearing the Allow Cell Drag And Drop setting.

## Using the Drag and Drop Shortcut Menu

If you hold down the right mouse button while dragging and dropping cells, the following shortcut menu will be displayed when the cells are dropped:

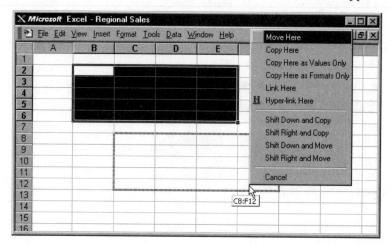

The commands on this shortcut menu are described in Table 3.6.

**NOTE**

See Chapter 4 for more information on links and Chapter 29 for more on hyperlinks.

**TABLE 3.6:** DRAG AND DROP SHORTCUT MENU COMMANDS

| Command | Function |
| --- | --- |
| Move Here | Moves cut cells to destination |
| Copy Here | Copies cells to destination cells |
| Copy Here As Values Only | Copies values only |
| Copy Here As Formats Only | Copies formats only |
| Link Here | Links destination to copied cells |
| Create Hyperlink Here | Hyperlinks destination to copied cells |
| Shift Down And Copy | Inserts copied cells, shifts existing cells down |

| TABLE 3.6: DRAG AND DROP SHORTCUT MENU COMMANDS (CONTINUED) | |
|---|---|
| **Command** | **Function** |
| Shift Right And Copy | Inserts copied cells, shifts existing cells right |
| Shift Down And Move | Inserts cut cells, shifts existing cells down |
| Shift Right And Move | Inserts cut cells, shifts existing cells right |

## Copying and Moving Using Menu Commands

Drag and drop is very efficient when you are copying or moving cells short distances. Menu commands (and toolbar shortcuts) may prove more effective when the target cells are a long distance from the source cells.

### Moving Cells Using Menu Commands

Here's how to move cells using menu commands:

**1.** Select the cell(s) to be moved.
**2.** Choose Edit ➤ Cut, or click on the Cut button on the Standard toolbar.
**3.** Select the upper-left cell of the region where the cells are to be pasted.
**4.** Choose Edit ➤ Paste, or click on the Paste button on the Standard toolbar.
 The cells are moved to the new location.

### Copying Cells Using Menu Commands

Copying cells using menu commands is very similar to moving cells:

**1.** Select the cell(s) to be copied.
**2.** Choose Edit ➤ Copy, or click on the Copy button on the Standard toolbar.
**3.** Select the upper-left cell of the region where the cells are to be pasted.
**4.** Choose Edit ➤ Paste, or click on the Paste button.
 The cells are copied to the new location.

## Inserting and Deleting Cells

Once you have created a worksheet, you may discover that you need to insert or delete cells to accommodate your changing information. Excel makes it easy to insert or delete cells, rows, and columns, as you'll learn in the following sections.

The number of rows and columns in a worksheet is fixed—inserting does not actually create new cells, but rather shifts cells. An insertion will not cause data that is located at the end of the worksheet to "fall off the edge." For example, if there is data in cell IV2 (the second row of the *last* column) and you insert a column, Excel displays a warning and will not allow the insertion to occur.

**NOTE**
Inserted cells will assume the formatting of the region into which they are inserted.

## Inserting Cells

To insert cells, select the cell(s) where you want to perform the insertion. This can be one cell, a range of cells, entire rows, or entire columns. If you select two rows, Excel will insert two rows, and so on. You can insert cells using the following method:

1. Right-click on the selection to display the shortcut menu, and choose Insert.
2. From the Insert menu, do one of the following:

   • Choose the Rows command to insert entire rows.
   • Choose the Columns command to insert entire columns.
   • Choose the Cells command to insert a range of cells. The Insert dialog box is displayed, asking how the insertion should occur.

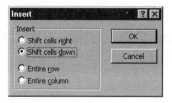

## Inserting Cells Cut or Copied from Another Location

Cells that have been moved or copied can be inserted into existing data using either menu commands or drag and drop.

### Inserting Using Menu Commands

To insert cut or copied cells using menu commands, follow these steps:

1. Select the cells, then cut or copy them.
2. Select the cell where you want the insertion to occur.

**3.** Choose either Copied Cells or Cut Cells from the Insert menu, depending on which operation you performed in step 1.

**4.** The Insert Paste dialog box (pictured below) will appear, letting you specify how to insert the cells.

## Inserting Using Drag and Drop

To insert cut or copied cells using drag and drop, use the same procedures you used to move or copy cells with drag and drop (covered earlier in this chapter), but hold down the Shift key while dragging cut cells, and Shift+Ctrl when dragging copied cells. A gray insertion marker appears. The keystroke combinations get confusing when copying.

The precise steps for a copy-insert are as follows:

**1.** Select the cells to be moved or copied.

**2.** Point to the edge of the range until the mouse pointer becomes an arrow. Click and hold down Shift while dragging the cells to their new location. You'll see a gray insertion bar between rows and columns instead of a range outline.

**3.** Hold down Ctrl+Shift when dragging copied cells to their insertion location.

# Deleting Cells

When you delete one or more cells, the cells beneath or to the right shift position. (*Clearing* cells, on the other hand, does not cause other cells to shift position.)

To delete a cell or cells, follow these steps:

**1.** Select the cells that you want to delete. This can be one cell, a range of cells, entire rows, or entire columns.

**2.** Choose Edit ➣ Delete:

- If you select an entire row or column, the row or column is deleted immediately.
- If you select a single cell or a group of cells, the Delete dialog box (shown below) is displayed, giving you the opportunity to specify what to delete.

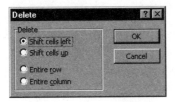

**MASTERING TROUBLESHOOTING**

### Deleting Cells vs. Clearing Cells

New users are often confused by the difference between *clearing* cells and *deleting* cells. Clearing a cell means emptying a cell of its contents (or formatting or notes). Clearing a cell does not affect the worksheet structure. Deleting a cell removes the cell from the worksheet, like pulling a single brick out of a brick wall; yet unlike a brick wall, the worksheet is not left with a hole in it. Cells below or to the right of the deleted cell shift to fill in the hole. Confusion is compounded by the fact that the Delete key does not delete cells—it *clears* cells by deleting the cells' contents.

- If you want to delete selected cells from the worksheet, choose Edit ➢ Delete.

- If you want to clear a cell of its contents, choose Edit ➢ Clear, or press the Delete key.

Don't make the mistake of typing a space in a cell to erase the cell's contents—Excel considers the space a character, even though you can't see it; therefore, the cell is not blank. This can create problems with worksheet functions and database commands, and is difficult to uncover.

## Controlling Row Height and Column Width

When you have a cell containing a large amount of data, you may want to increase the column width or row height to make the data easier to read. There may also be times when you want to reduce column width and row height. As with many Excel features, you can change row height and column width using either menu commands or the mouse.

### Setting Column Width

To size columns using menu commands, select any cell(s) in the column you want to resize. Then choose Format ➢ Column. The following submenu appears:

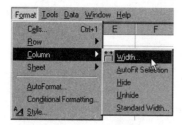

Table 3.7 explains the commands available on the Format ➤ Column submenu.

**TABLE 3.7:** COMMANDS ON THE FORMAT ➤ COLUMN MENU

| Command | Function |
|---|---|
| Width | Displays dialog box prompting for column width |
| AutoFit Selection | Sizes column(s) according to the widest entry within selected range |
| Hide | Hides selected column(s) from view |
| Unhide | Unhides hidden columns |
| Standard Width | Sets column to default column width |

To use the mouse to change the column width, follow these steps:

**1.** Point to the line between column letters. The mouse pointer becomes a two-way arrow.

**2.** Click and drag to resize the column. (While dragging, the new width is displayed as a pop-up note.)

**TIP**

You can size several columns at once with the mouse. Select the columns you want to size (hold down Ctrl to select noncontiguous columns), and drag the border of any *one* of the selected columns.

## Resizing for the Best Fit

You can use the mouse to quickly perform the same function as the Format ➤ Column ➤ AutoFit Selection command. Double-click on the right border between column headings. The column will be sized according to the widest value within the entire column.

Similarly, you can use the mouse in place of the Format ➤ Row ➤ AutoFit command. Double-click on the lower border between the row headings. The row will be sized according to the tallest value within the entire row.

**TIP**

If you see ##### in a cell, it means the column is too narrow to display the number. Use the double-click technique described above to instantly size the column so all values will fit.

## Adjusting Row Height

Row height works just like column width, except that rows will automatically increase in height to account for changing font size or wrapped text. Select a row or a cell in the row, and choose the appropriate Format ➤ Row commands to specify height or to hide/unhide rows. Row AutoFit is based on the largest font or wrapped text in the row.

**TIP**

You can unhide a hidden row or column using the mouse. To unhide a column, place the mouse pointer just to the right of the column header where the column is hidden, so that the pointer becomes a split double arrow (rather than the solid double arrow you usually see between column headers). Drag the split double arrow to the right to unhide the column. To unhide a row, place the mouse pointer just below the row header where the row is hidden (so that it becomes a split double arrow), then drag the split double arrow downward.

# Searching and Replacing

Use the Edit ➤ Find and Edit ➤ Replace commands to search the worksheet for user-specified values, and, optionally, to replace them with a different value. For example, suppose you have a worksheet that keeps track of payroll information, and employee Jane Smith changes her name to Jane Jones. Excel can search for every occurrence of *Jane Smith* and replace it with *Jane Jones*.

## Finding a Value

To find a value on an active worksheet, follow these steps:

**1.** Choose Edit ➤ Find. The Find dialog box appears (see Figure 3.4).
**2.** Type the characters you want to find in the Find What box.
**3.** Click on Find Next to find the next cell containing the search value.

**FIGURE 3.4**

*The Find dialog box*

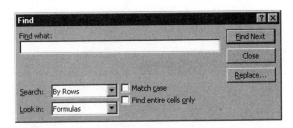

If you need to narrow the search parameters, continue with the following steps:

**4.** Use the Look In list box to specify where to search:

> **Value:** searches cell values
>
> **Formula:** searches formulas
>
> **Comments:** searches cell comments

**5.** Specify the row or column search sequence using the Search list.

**6.** Checking Match Case will limit the search to text strings that match the Find What entry in upper- and lowercase (for instance, if you search for *Bill*, the search will ignore *bill*).

**7.** Checking Find Entire Cells Only will limit the search to exact matches. For example, if you are searching for *Rob*, the search will find *Robert* and *Robin*, but if you check Find Entire Cells Only, only *Rob* will be found.

## Replacing a Value

The Replace option works like Find, but allows you to replace the found value with another value. Try the following exercise:

**1.** Enter the following data into a blank worksheet:

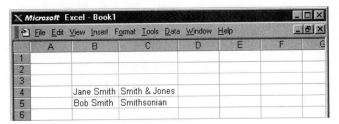

**2.** Choose Edit ➢ Replace. The Replace dialog box appears (see Figure 3.5).

**3.** Type **Smith** in the Find What box.

**FIGURE 3.5**

*The Replace
dialog box*

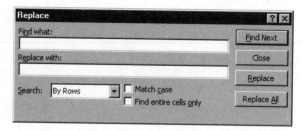

4. Type **Jones** in Replace With.
5. Click on Replace All to replace all instances of *Smith* with *Jones*.

## Specifying the Search Range

You can search an entire worksheet, a range of cells, or multiple worksheets within a workbook. Before choosing the edit or replace command, do one of the following:

- Select only one cell to search the entire sheet.
- Select a range of cells to search the range only.
- Select multiple sheets to search multiple sheets (see Chapter 2).

## Using Wildcards

The question mark (?) and asterisk (*) can be used in your search text as wildcard characters.

- The asterisk represents one or more characters—a search for *A*Z* will find *ABZ* and *ABCZ*.
- A question mark represents only one character—a search for A?Z will find *ABZ* and *ACZ*, but not *ABCZ*.

**TIP**

If you want to search for a question mark or asterisk, precede these characters with a tilde (~). For example, to search for the string *QUIT?* and not find *QUITO*, enter *QUIT~?* as the search string.

In Part One you have learned how to manipulate the overall structure and appearance of Excel's basic components, workbooks, worksheets, and cells. As you proceed to Part Two, you'll add some skills needed to apply formulas and functions to your Excel documents, learn formatting and printing, and gain some valuable techniques to increase your productivity.

# PART — II

## Basic Skills

## LEARN TO:

- *Use formulas and functions*

- *Apply cell references*

- *Format worksheets*

- *Print Excel data*

- *Create file links*

- *Use AutoFills*

- *Create custom command bars*

- *Master Excel productivity skills*

# Chapter

# 4

## Using Formulas and Functions

# Chapter 4

# Using Formulas and Functions

A spreadsheet is only as good as the operations you can perform on it. Excel offers its users a wealth of options for charting and calculating the data in worksheets. In this chapter, we'll cover some of the most important topics for new Excel users. You'll learn to use cell references, external references, and file links, and you'll discover how to use functions to write formulas. You will also learn how to apply complex conditions to formulas and how to perform simultaneous calculations on multiple worksheets.

## Performing Calculations with Formulas

In Chapter 3 you learned about entering text and numbers into cells. In this chapter, you will learn how to perform calculations using *formulas*. Formulas provide the real power when doing analysis and *modeling*—creating functioning spreadsheet systems—in Excel. You can perform a wide variety of numeric calculations, including addition, subtraction, multiplication, and division. You can also manipulate text and look up values in tables. By using formulas, entering a number into a single cell can cause a ripple effect throughout a complex model.

A formula is essentially a sequence of values and operators that begins with an equal sign (=) and produces a new value. Excel comes with several hundred built-in formulas, called *functions*, which are designed to perform many different kinds of calculations. The SUM function provides a simple demonstration of how formulas work, and is easily entered using the AutoSum tool on the Standard toolbar.

Formulas in Excel share some basic properties:

- All formulas begin with an equal sign.
- After a formula is entered, the *resulting value* is displayed in the cell.
- When a cell containing a formula is selected, the underlying formula is displayed in the formula bar.

## Using the AutoSum Tool

The SUM function is probably the most often used function, and the AutoSum tool makes it very easy to enter SUM functions onto your worksheet. Try the following exercise to see how it's done:

**1.** Enter the following data into a blank worksheet:

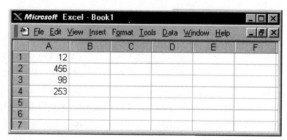

**2.** Select cell A5.

**3.** Click on the AutoSum tool on the Standard toolbar.

**4.** Press ↵ (or click on the Enter box in the formula bar).

Excel determines which cells you want to sum by examining the adjacent cells—the formula in cell A5 sums cells A1:A4 (the answer is 819). It is important to verify the range that Excel guesses at—unintended blank cells will cause sum ranges to be truncated. Also, keep in mind that whenever Excel is unsure if you want to sum a column or a row, AutoSum defaults to column.

The AutoSum tool is not limited to a single cell. Suppose there are numbers in cells A1:C3. If you select A4:C4, then click on AutoSum, sum formulas will be entered for all three columns.

**TIP**

You can enter sum totals across the bottom of an entire table of numbers with one click. First, select the entire table range by choosing a cell in the range and pressing Ctrl+Shift+*. Then click on the AutoSum tool.

## Entering a Formula Manually

To enter a formula into a cell, simply select the cell in which you want the formula located and begin typing. The first character must be an equal sign, as you will see in this brief example:

**1.** Select cell A1 on a blank worksheet.
**2.** Enter **=1+2,** then press ↵. The resulting value, 3, appears in the cell.

This simple formula uses only constant values (1 and 2); you might as well enter the number 3 into the cell instead of a formula. Soon, you will see the real power of formulas by learning how to refer to other cells, and not just constant values.

## Editing Formulas

The procedure for editing formulas is the same as for editing numbers and text, which was covered in Chapter 3. You can edit in either the formula bar or in the cell. When you double-click on a cell containing a formula, the formula is displayed in the cell, but something else also happens. Excel highlights the source cells for the formula with colored borders; these are color-coded ranges. You can edit or move the source cells in the formula by dragging the range borders, and you can expand or contract the source cells for the formula by using the fill handles. In some ways, color-coded ranges act a lot like selected cells, but they manipulate elements of a formula. Chapter 13 further discusses color-coded ranges in conjunction with charting.

**TIP**

Do you want to see all of the formulas in a worksheet at once, instead of viewing them one by one in the formula bar? Press Ctrl+` (Ctrl plus the grave apostrophe, usually found to the left of the exclamation point) to switch back and forth from displaying formulas to displaying values on the worksheet. This is useful if you want to know which cells contain values and which contain formulas, or if you want to document the formulas used in the worksheet.

## Formatting Formulas with Line Breaks for Readability

Long formulas are often difficult to decipher. Suppose you have a long formula that just can't be shortened—how can you make it easier to read? You can insert line breaks into the formula. Here's a long formula:

=(A1+A2)*5-(A3+A4)/12-A5+2

The same formula with line breaks might look like this:

=(A1+A2)*5

-(A3+A4)/12

-A5+2

To enter a line break, press Alt+↵.

## Arithmetic Operators in Formulas

You can perform all the standard operations on data in an Excel worksheet. Table 4.1 lists the arithmetic operators Excel supports in formulas.

**TABLE 4.1:** ARITHMETIC OPERATORS SUPPORTED IN FORMULAS

| Symbol | Function |
| --- | --- |
| + | Addition |
| - | Subtraction |
| * | Multiplication |
| / | Division |
| ^ | Exponentiation |
| % | Percent when placed after a number |

Below are examples of formulas using arithmetic operators:

| | |
| --- | --- |
| =1+1 | Add 1 plus 1 |
| =10-5 | Subtract 5 from 10 |
| =4/2 | Divide 4 by 2 |
| =2*2+10 | Multiply 2 times 2, then add 10 |
| =3^2 | Square 3 |
| =435.67*10% | Returns 10% of 435.67 |

# Order of Calculation

It is very common for formulas to include more than one operator. Excel performs calculations in a specific order, and you'll need to be aware of this as you enter and edit formulas. Table 4.2 explains the order in which operators are evaluated:

**TABLE 4.2:** ORDER OF EVALUATING OPERATORS

| Order | Operator | Function |
|-------|----------|----------|
| 1 | - | Negation |
| 2 | % | Percent |
| 3 | ^ | Exponentiation |
| 4 | * and / | Multiplication and division |
| 5 | + and - | Addition and subtraction |
| 6 | & | Joining text (covered below) |
| 7 | =<>, <=, >=, <> | Comparison |

Following the order of precedence shown in the table, you can see that the multiplication operator is evaluated before the addition operator; therefore, the formula

    =1+2*5

yields 11 (1 plus the result of 2 times 5), not 15 (the sum of 1 plus 2, which equals 3, times 5).

When there is more than one operator with the same priority level, the operators evaluate from left to right. For example, since multiplication and division are at the same priority level, the formula

    =10/5*2

yields 4 (10 divided by 5, times 2), not 1 (10 divided by the product of 5 times 2).

## Changing the Evaluation Order

Parentheses can be used to group expressions within a formula. An expression within parentheses evaluates *before* all arithmetic operators.

    =1+2*3        Yields 7
    =(1+2)*3      Yields 9

## Joining Text

The ampersand character (&) joins text—a process referred to as *concatenation*. For instance, if you join the text string *ABC* with *XYZ*, the result is *ABCXYZ*. Consider a worksheet used as an invoice form: suppose the invoice total of $500 is in cell D10, and on the bottom of the invoice, you want to show "Your balance due is $500." On the bottom of the worksheet, you can enter a formula that concatenates a text constant with the value of cell D10:

```
="Your balance due is $"&D10
```

evaluates to

```
Your balance due is $500.
```

The same result could be obtained using the CONCATENATE function, though most users prefer the & operator since it requires fewer keystrokes. (Worksheet functions are covered later in this chapter.)

## When Formulas Return Errors

When there is a problem with a formula, an error value is returned. One of the most common errors occurs when attempting to divide by zero. Enter the formula **=1/0** into a cell and the error #DIV/0! is returned. Table 4.3 explains the different errors that can result from an erroneous formula.

**TABLE 4.3**: ERROR VALUES

| Error Value | Cause |
| --- | --- |
| #DIV/0! | Divided by zero |
| #N/A! | Different meanings depending on circumstance (usually means no value available or inappropriate argument was used) |
| #NAME? | Reference to an invalid name |
| #NULL! | Reference to intersection of two areas that do not intersect (e.g., if named areas January and Profits do not intersect, =January Profits returns #NULL!) |
| #NUM! | Incorrect use of a number (unacceptable numeric argument, such as SQRT(-1), or formula returns a number too large or too small to be represented in Excel) |
| #REF! | Invalid cell reference |
| #VALUE! | Usually caused by incorrect argument(s) or operand(s) |

**MASTERING TROUBLESHOOTING**

PART

**II**

Basic Skills

## What Is a Circular Reference (and What Can You Do about It?)

Suppose you have entered the formula =B1+C1 into cell A1. You press ↵ and are surprised by an alert that warns you against making circular references in formulas. A *circular reference* is a reference that refers to itself, either directly or indirectly. It is a formula that depends on its own value. After clicking on OK on the alert, the Circular Reference toolbar appears; you should also take a look at the status bar. It says "Circular: A1," for example, which means that A1 is the cell that contains the circular reference; i.e., one of the cells in the formula also contains a formula dependent on a value in A1. See Chapter 11 for a description of the Circular Reference toolbar.

Usually circular references happen by mistake, and you can fix the problem by editing the formula. But occasionally, circular references are a valid approach to solving a problem, and Excel can resolve them if you set calculation to use *Iterations*, or repeated calculations. To turn on Iterations, choose Tools ➤ Options. Select the

Calculation tab, and place a check in the Iteration check box. By default, Excel allows a maximum of 100 iterations. This means that Excel recalculates the formulas 100 times, each time getting a little closer to the correct value. This process is called *convergence*. Excel keeps track of how much the value changes with each iteration, and when the amount of change is reduced to the Maximum Change (or the maximum number of iterations is reached), Excel stops converging.

You can change the Maximum Iterations and Maximum Change values in the Tools ➤ Options ➤ Calculation dialog box. You can make the calculation faster by setting fewer iterations and a larger maximum change value, or you can reach a more accurate solution by setting more iterations and a smaller maximum change value. You may want to set Calculation to Manual when you set Iteration—otherwise Excel will recalculate the circular references each time you make a cell entry. Iteration and convergence are also the means by which Solver and Goal Seek solve problems. You can learn more about Solver and Goal Seek (and iteration and convergence) in Chapter 27.

## Freezing Values

There are times when you will want to "freeze" a range of cells by replacing formulas with values. For instance, you might print a report that is distributed to other people in your organization. Later, it may be important that you see exactly what was contained on the original report—formulas make it all too easy to change the report.

Follow this procedure to freeze a range of cells:

**1.** Select the cell(s) you want to freeze.
**2.** Choose Edit ➤ Copy.
**3.** Choose Edit ➤ Paste Special.
**4.** Select the Values option from the Paste Special dialog box, then click on OK.

All formulas in the range are replaced with constant values.

# Understanding Cell References

A *cell reference* is the cell's address, and it can be either the absolute location of a specific cell on a specific worksheet (e.g., Sheet1!$B$2), or simply the location of a cell relative to a specific cell. Most of the sample formulas presented so far in this chapter contain text and numeric *constants*. But a formula with only constants has limited uses. To get the most out of functions, you can use cell references to incorporate *variables* into formulas, by using cell references you can vary the output of formulas depending on the value you place in the referenced cells, as demonstrated in the following examples:

| | |
|---|---|
| =A1*2 | Multiplies the value in cell A1 by 2 |
| =A1*B1 | Multiplies the value in cell A1 by the value in cell B1 |
| ="ABC"&A1 | Concatenates (joins) the characters ABC and the value in cell A1 |
| =A1&B1 | Concatenates the value in cell A1 and the value in cell B1 |

Try this simple exercise on a blank worksheet to see how cell references work:

**1.** Enter the number **2** in cell A1.
**2.** Enter the number **4** in cell A2.
**3.** Enter the formula **=A1+A2** in cell A3 (the value returned is 6).
**4.** Change the value in A1 to **8**, and watch the value in A3 change automatically to 12.

You've just seen one of the basic features of a spreadsheet program—automatic recalculation of formulas as cell values change. Once your needs progress beyond the most simplistic calculations, it becomes vital that you fully understand every nuance of cell references.

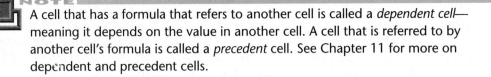

**NOTE** A cell that has a formula that refers to another cell is called a *dependent cell*—meaning it depends on the value in another cell. A cell that is referred to by another cell's formula is called a *precedent* cell. See Chapter 11 for more on dependent and precedent cells.

## Excel Reference Styles

Excel supports two styles of cell references:

**A1 Style:** This is the Excel default. Columns are labeled with letters A through IV, allowing for the maximum 256 columns. Rows are labeled by number, 1 through 65536.

**R1C1 Style:** Rows and columns are both referred to by number. For example, R3C2 in this system is the same as B3 in the other system.

For better or for worse, A1-style references are the de facto standard for almost all spreadsheet products, including Excel. There is no compelling reason to work with both reference styles, and the inclusion of both styles in the Excel manuals only serves to further complicate an already complex subject. This book focuses exclusively on the A1 style. Once you understand A1, it is easy to go back and understand R1C1.

## Distinguishing between Types of Cell References

You have just read about the two reference styles—A1 and R1C1. Regardless of which style you use, there are also three *types* of cell reference. A cell reference can be *relative*, *absolute*, or *mixed*. To illustrate the differences between these types, we will use a street address analogy to show how the different types would refer to the same house:

**Absolute Reference:** An absolute reference refers to a specific cell or cells. In this analogy, a specific home address, such as 123 Elm Street.

**Relative Reference:** A relative reference refers to cell(s) relative to a given position, such as "go one street down and two houses over."

**Mixed Reference:** In a mixed reference, one of the coordinates is absolute, but the other is relative. "Turn right on Elm Street. Ms. Jones lives three houses down."

**NOTE** Excel supports three-dimensional cell references, which are used in conjunction with functions. Three-dimensional references are used to refer to multiple worksheets.

### Understanding Absolute References

A dollar sign in front of the cell coordinate denotes an *absolute* reference:

**$A$1** is an absolute reference to cell A1.

**$B$2** is an absolute reference to cell B2.

PART

II

Basic Skills

An absolute reference does not change when copied to another cell. The following exercise will demonstrate this:

1. Enter **=$A$1** into cell B1.
2. Copy and paste cell B1 to B2.

The formula in cell B2 is unchanged; it still reads =$A$1.

## Understanding Relative References

In the A1 style, a relative reference is denoted simply by the column letter followed by the row number, as in B13 or C34. Use relative references to refer to cells *relative to the cell containing the formula*. The formula =A1, when entered into cell B1, actually means "the contents of this cell are equal to the contents of the cell that is now one to the left" (A1 being one to the left of B1). Since the formula uses a relative reference, the reference automatically adjusts when the cell is copied to another location.

Try this example:

1. Enter **=A1** into cell B1. This gives B1 the same content as A1, its neighbor directly to the left.
2. Copy and paste cell B1 to B2.

The formula in cell B2 automatically changes; Excel has adjusted it to read =A2, giving B2 the same content once again as its neighbor directly to the left (in this case A2).

**NOTE**
Unlike copy/paste, if you *cut* and paste a cell with relative references, the references will not change.

## Absolute vs. Relative References

When should you use absolute references and when relative references? Here is an example to illustrate the difference between the two. Enter the constants shown in Figure 4.1 into a blank worksheet:

**Doing It the Wrong Way** - Here's one way to enter the values, but not the best way:

1. Enter the formula **=$B$5*$C$5** (absolute references) into cell D5.
2. Copy the formula in D5 to cells D6 and D7.

Since absolute references were used, cells D6 and D7 mistakenly extend (multiply) the figures on row 5—not what we intended.

**Doing It the Right Way** - Here is a much better way to enter the data:

**FIGURE 4.1**

*Column D is intended to extend (multiply) the numbers in columns B and C.*

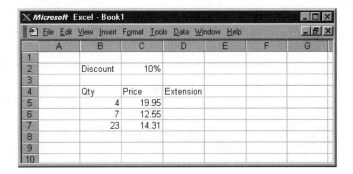

1. Enter the formula **=B5\*C5** (relative references) into cell D5.
2. Copy the formula in D5 to cells D6 and D7. Better yet, use the fill handle to drag the formula.

   Since D5 contains relative references, Excel automatically adjusts the references when copied, and the extensions are now correct.

   Now we will add an absolute reference to the equation. Assume that the discount in cell C2 applies to each row:

1. Enter the formula **=(B5\*C5)-((B5\*C5)\*$C$2)** into cell D5. In English, this formula says "The contents of this cell equals Extension minus Discount." Notice that cell C2 is being referred to absolutely.
2. Copy this formula into cells D6 and D7. Excel will adjust the relative references, but leave the absolute reference alone.

**NOTE**

The formula in step 1 above has extra parentheses that were added to enhance the readability of the formula. They do not affect the order of calculation.

## Understanding Mixed References

You have now used absolute references (with a dollar sign in front of the coordinate), and relative references (with no dollar sign). A *mixed reference* has one absolute coordinate and one relative coordinate. A$1 and $A1 are both examples of mixed references. The coordinate with a dollar sign is absolute, and the coordinate without a dollar sign is relative. For instance, $A1 refers to an absolute column (A) and a relative row (1).

PART

II

Basic Skills

**TIP** Instead of constantly typing and deleting dollar signs to switch reference type, simply place the cursor anywhere within the cell reference, then press the F4 key to toggle between the different reference types available.

To gain a clearer understanding of mixed references, enter the following constants into a blank worksheet:

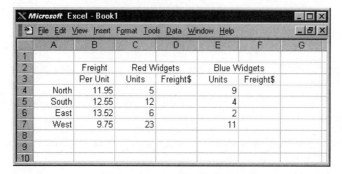

In this scenario, the freight cost calculations for both red widgets and blue widgets are based on the Freight Per Unit in column B. Formulas are required in columns D and F to calculate freight. The following sections offer two ways to solve the problem.

**Doing It the Inefficient Way** - Here's one not-very-efficient way to solve the problem:

1. Enter the formula **=B4*C4** in cell D4, and copy it to cells D5 through D7.
2. Enter the formula **=B4*E4** in cell F4, and copy it to cells F5 through F7. (If the formula in D4 is copied to column F, it would be incorrect because of the use of purely relative references.)

While the resulting values are correct, there is a quicker way. By using a mixed reference, you can enter the *same* formula in columns D and F. This may seem like a trivial saving of time and energy, but this is a simple example after all. Anytime you can get away with using the same formula, you'll save yourself a lot of time and hassle when you initially enter the formula and when you go back later to change it.

**Doing It the Efficient Way** - Here is a much better way to enter the formula:

1. Enter the formula **=$B4*C4** in cell D4. $B4 is a *mixed* reference—the first coordinate is absolute and the second coordinate is relative.
2. Copy D4 to cells F4 through F7.

Check out the formulas in columns D and F after you have copied them. Excel has adjusted the relative portion, but left the absolute portion alone.

**TIP**

The use of names can greatly simplify references. Names also add clarity: a formula that reads =Sales–Cost makes a lot more sense than =$B$25–$B$47. See Chapter 8 for more on naming.

## Referring to Multiple Cells

In all of the examples so far, references have been made to *single* cells. A cell reference can also refer to a *range* of cells. In the cell reference A1:A3, the starting cell is A1, the colon means *through*, and A3 is the ending cell. (References to ranges of cells will take on greater significance as you learn more about worksheet functions later in this chapter.)

Here is a simple illustration of how references to ranges work:

**1.** Press F5 (the shortcut for Edit ➤ Go To).

**2.** Enter **A1:A3** as the reference, then click on OK.

The range of cells A1 through A3 will be selected.

## Marking Cell References by Pointing and Clicking

Fortunately, it is not necessary to actually type cell references when entering or editing formulas. You can enter references into formulas by pointing to individual cells or cell ranges, then clicking. Try this exercise:

**1.** Enter numbers into cells A1 and A2 on a blank worksheet.

**2.** Select cell A3. Type an equal sign to start a formula.

**3.** Click on cell A1. Notice in the formula bar that the cell reference A1 has been added to the formula.

**4.** Type a plus sign.

**5.** Click on cell A2 to add it to the formula.

**6.** Press ↵ to complete the formula, which adds cells A1 and A2.

## Referring to Other Worksheets within the Same Workbook

In all of the examples so far, references have been made to cells located on the same worksheet. You can also refer to cells that are located on different worksheets. We'll return to the street address analogy to illustrate this point. The address you're now interested in is located in another city (let's say Chicago), so instead of saying *123 Elm Street*, you must say *123 Elm Street, Chicago*. The same is true with references to other

PART

II

Basic Skills

worksheets—the worksheet becomes part of the cell reference, as you will see in the next exercise. Try these steps in a new workbook:

1. On Sheet1, enter **10** into cell A1.
2. Activate Sheet2 by clicking on its tab.
3. Enter an equal sign into cell B1 to begin a formula.
4. Activate Sheet1 by clicking on its tab (notice that the formula is still being built).
5. Click on cell A1 to add it to the formula.
6. Press ↵ to complete the formula.
7. The formula in cell B1 (on Sheet2) will read =Sheet1!A1 and the number 10 will appear in the cell.

Notice that the cell reference is preceded by the sheet name and an exclamation point. (The exclamation point separates the sheet name from the cell reference.) Don't be confused by references to other worksheets—they are essentially the same as references to the same sheet. All of the same rules apply.

If a worksheet name has a space in it, references to the sheet from other sheets must enclose the sheet name in single quotes, as in

```
='Sales Forecast'!B3
```

However, if a space is added to a sheet name *after* references have been made to the sheet, Excel automatically places single quotes in dependent cells for you.

## Why Refer to Other Sheets?

Referring to cells on other worksheets is a very common practice. A workbook might contain departmental forecasts, with one worksheet for each of four departments. A fifth sheet might be used to summarize the departments, and this summary sheet might refer to cells on each of the four departmental sheets.

# External References: Pointing to a Worksheet in Another Workbook

A reference to another workbook is called an *external reference*. In our street address analogy, the address is not only located in another city, but in another state. And of course, the state must become part of the address. Try this exercise:

1. Create two new workbooks, Book1 and Book2. Arrange them horizontally using the Window ➤ Arrange command.
2. On Sheet1 of Book1, enter **Hello** into cell A1.
3. On Sheet 1 of Book2, enter an equal sign into cell B1 to begin a formula.
4. Activate Book1 by clicking anywhere on the workbook.

**5.** Click on cell A1 (on Sheet1, Book1) to add it to the formula.

**6.** Press ⏎ to complete the formula.

**7.** The formula in cell B1 (Sheet1, Book2) will now read as follows:

```
=[Book1]Sheet1!$A$1
```

and Hello will appear in the cell.

The reference begins with the book name, enclosed in square brackets. (Notice that the reference defaults to absolute.)

## What Happens to References As Cells Are Moved?

Various things can happen to cell references when cells are moved, depending on how and where they're moved:

**Same Sheet:** When you move a cell to a different location on the same worksheet, cells that refer to that cell (dependent cells) are automatically updated to point to the new cell reference, regardless of the method you use to move the cell. This is true even if the dependent cell is located in a dependent workbook—but only if the dependent workbook is open when the cell is moved.

**Different Sheet:** When you cut and paste a cell to a different worksheet (in the same workbook or a different workbook), dependent cells are left with #REF! (a reference error).

**Dependent Cell:** When you move a dependent cell, it will still point to the same cell(s) it originally pointed to, regardless of the method you use to move the cell. This holds true even if the dependent cell is moved to a different worksheet or workbook.

PART

**II**

Basic Skills

# Linking Files Using External References

When an external reference is entered, something special happens—a file *link* is automatically created. A file link always involves two workbooks: the *dependent* workbook and the *source* workbook:

**Dependent workbook:** The dependent workbook contains the external reference and is thus dependent on the other workbook.

**Source workbook:** The source workbook contains the source cell(s) and is referred to by the external reference.

The dependent workbook is *linked* to the source workbook. The source workbook is not linked—it has no idea that one or more dependent workbooks may be linked to it.

## R1C1 Reference Style

Although the A1 reference style is the style you will most likely use, and is the style used throughout this book, you may want to know a bit more about the R1C1 style.

You have already learned the A1 style refers to cell addresses by column letter and row number, and you can see the column letters and row numbers on your worksheets. R1C1 style refers to cell addresses by row and column numbers, and you can see numbered rows and columns on your worksheets if you choose the Reference Style as R1C1 in the Tools ➤ Options dialog box, General tab. If you change the reference style in the Tools ➤ Options dialog box, all the A1-style references in your workbook will change to R1C1 references.

As with A1 style, R1C1 style has both relative and absolute reference types. The absolute cell address R2C2 is equivalent to $B$2—it refers to a specific row/column intersection. Relative cell addresses are defined by their relationship to the cell containing the formula, rather than by worksheet coordinates. For example, the relative cell address R[-2]C[3] means "the cell 2 rows up and 3 columns to the right." Positive row and column numbers indicate rows down and columns right. Negative row and column numbers indicate rows up and columns left. No number indicates "this row" or "this column."

# Advantages of Using Links

Linked workbooks are used quite commonly, even in relatively simple models. Linked workbooks provide several key advantages compared to using multiple worksheets in one workbook:

- Different users can concurrently edit workbooks: the manager of the western region can be editing WEST while the manager of the eastern region is editing EAST.
- You don't have to open an entire model at once, making opening, recalculating, and saving workbooks faster. Also, a large model stored in one workbook may not "fit" in memory.
- Multilevel roll-ups (e.g., rolling up, or consolidating, data from several corporate levels into a single summary) can be achieved using multilevel linked workbooks (covered in Chapter 26).

Although a particular link always refers to a single workbook, a workbook can be linked many times, in many ways:

- One workbook can be linked to many different source workbooks.
- One source workbook can have many dependent workbooks.
- One workbook can be both a dependent workbook and a source workbook. That is, workbook A can be linked to workbook B and workbook B can be linked to workbook C.
- Two workbooks can be linked to each other, in which case each is dependent on the other.

## Recognizing Link Paths

Excel tracks the full path of the source book, and when the source book is closed, the full path appears in the external reference. For example, an external reference to a source workbook named SALES, located in a folder named FILES on the C drive, would appear as follows:

When the source workbook is open:

```
=[SALES.XLS]Sheet1!$A$1
```

When the source workbook is closed:

```
='C:\FILES\[SALES.XLS]Sheet1'!$A$1
```

## Changing a Link

One way to change a link is by editing the formula containing the external reference. But what if a dependent workbook contains dozens of external references? Choose Edit ➢ Links to display the Links dialog box pictured in Figure 4.2.

---

**FIGURE 4.2**

*The Links dialog box lists all source workbooks for the active workbook.*

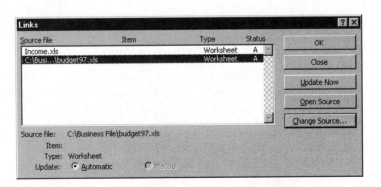

Select the source file you want to change, then click on the Change Source button to display the Change Links dialog box (Figure 4.3).

**FIGURE 4.3**

*The Change Links dialog box*

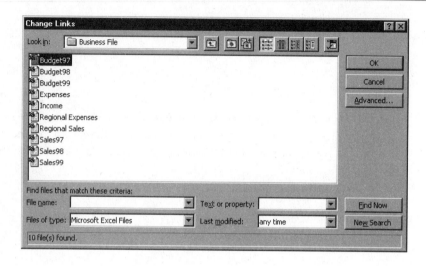

The Change Links dialog box looks and behaves very similarly to the Open dialog box. You can navigate the file system to find the workbook you want to link to. Once you have selected a new source file to link to, all affected external references are automatically changed in one fell swoop. Assume you have changed the source file EAST to WEST. Every external reference in the dependent workbook is automatically changed to WEST.

## Opening a Dependent Workbook

Excel behaves differently depending on whether the source workbook is opened or closed at the time the dependent book is opened.

- If the source workbook is already open, the dependent workbook recalculates automatically (unless you are in manual calculation mode).
- If the source workbook is not open, Excel will display the following dialog box. Click on Yes to update the external references.

**TIP** When such formulas that refer to closed workbooks recalculate, current values are retrieved from the closed workbook file without the workbook being opened. However, some functions, such as OFFSET and VLOOKUP, do not work when the source workbook is closed—these functions are too complex. (These functions are covered in Chapter 9.)

## Avoiding Large Workbook Files When Using External Links

Behind the scenes, dependent workbooks invisibly save values contained in source workbooks (external values). For example, if workbook A refers to A1:A999 in workbook B, all 999 values are saved inside workbook A. There is one problematic manifestation of this feature: sometimes a seemingly small workbook consumes an inexplicably large amount of disk space. To set a workbook so that it does *not* save external values, choose Tools ➢ Options, select the Calculation tab (Figure 2.4), and then uncheck the Save External Link Values setting. However, if you uncheck this setting, the source workbook must be recalculated when it is opened, otherwise the dependent cells will contain errors.

**WARNING** Linking to a workbook that has *never* been saved is not a good idea; if you close the source workbook without saving it, the dependent workbook is linked to a workbook that does not exist. In general, it is good practice to save source workbooks before saving dependent books.

## Hyperlinks

There are two types of hyperlinks in Excel. The first type of hyperlink works just like hyperlinks in HTML documents on the Internet (Web pages); when clicked on, they allow you to jump from place to place. The second type of hyperlink in Excel is the HYPERLINK function. Hyperlinks and the HYPERLINK function will be discussed in Chapter 29.

## Using Worksheet Functions

Picture a worksheet with numbers in cells A1 through A9, and imagine that these numbers need to be summed. You could enter the following formula to sum them:

```
=A1+A2+A3+A4+A5+A6+A7+A8+A9
```

**FIGURE 4.4**

*The Calculation tab in the Options dialog box*

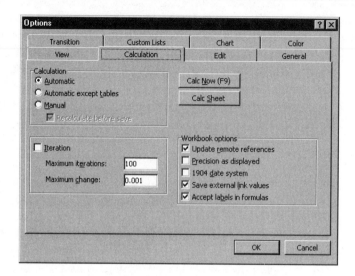

## MASTERING TROUBLESHOOTING

### Avoiding the Update Links Alert

When you open a workbook that contains external or remote references, an alert will be displayed which says, "This document contains links. Re-establish links?" This alert causes a great deal of confusion for novice users. Clicking on Yes will update all the links in the newly opened workbook. Clicking on No means formulas that contain external or remote references will not recalculate with current data.

There is a way to prevent the question from being asked, so that links are always updated automatically: Choose Tools ➢ Options, click on the Edit tab, and clear the Ask To Update Automatic Links check box. This is a global setting, and cannot be applied to individual workbooks. Another way to avoid the alert is by opening the source workbook before opening the dependent workbook.

This method is tiresome when summing nine cells, and becomes downright impossible if thousands of cells need to be summed. The same result could be achieved using the SUM function:

```
=SUM(A1:A9)
```

The SUM function is one of several hundred built-in functions. These functions provide the real power when it comes to the manipulation of text and numbers in Excel. A function can be used by itself, as with the SUM function above, or within a complex formula (referred to as *nesting*).

Most functions need to be provided with one or more pieces of data to act upon, referred to as *arguments*. The arguments are enclosed in parentheses following the function name, as in =SUM(A1:A9) above. If there are multiple arguments, they are separated by commas. A function is *not* preceded by an equal sign unless the function is at the start of the formula.

## MASTERING TROUBLESHOOTING

### Matching Parentheses Inside Formulas

When you are first learning to write formulas (and even when you get to be an expert), getting all the parentheses matched up correctly can be quite a chore, particularly in long formulas. Sometimes Excel figures out what you want and does it for you. For example, in simple formulas, like a SUM or an INDEX function with no nested functions, the closing parenthesis can be omitted. When you press ↵, Excel adds the closing parentheses automatically. In more complex formulas, Excel will

not close the parentheses for you. Instead, an alert will be displayed which says "Parentheses do not match," and the offending portion of the formula will be highlighted. When you enter a closing parenthesis, the matching opening parenthesis will be highlighted briefly.

Even more helpful is this trick for finding all the matching pairs of parentheses in a formula: use the arrow keys to scroll through the formula character by character. Each time you cross a parenthesis, both parentheses in the pair will be highlighted briefly.

# Using Functions in Formulas

The following exercise demonstrates the application of several critical skills:

- Assigning arguments to functions
- Using *nested* functions, where one function serves as an argument for another function
- The use of the IF function, used to calculate a value conditionally

**NOTE**

The functions used in this exercise do not have special significance—they are intended to illustrate general syntax only.

In this exercise, you will use the AVERAGE function to calculate average test score, the LEFT and SEARCH functions to determine the student's last name, and the IF function to calculate the grade:

**1.** Enter the following constants onto a blank worksheet.

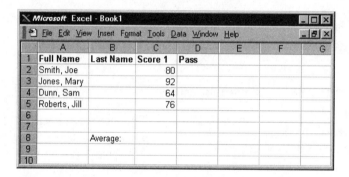

**2.** Enter the following formula into cell C8 to calculate the average score:

`=AVERAGE(C2:C5)`

This averages the values in cells C2 through C5. The range C2:C5 is the argument for the AVERAGE function. (Remember, ranges don't have to be typed—they can be entered using the point and click method.)

**TIP**

You can enter functions in lowercase. If entered correctly, they automatically convert to uppercase.

**3.** Enter the following formula into cell B2 to determine the student's last name, based on the information in column A:

`=LEFT(A2,SEARCH(",",A2)-1)`

This is an example of a formula containing *nested* functions. To fully understand this formula, it would be valuable to read about the LEFT and SEARCH functions in Chapter 9. But you can still get the general idea by understanding these two key points:

- The LEFT function takes two arguments—it is used to find text that resides at the leftmost side of a text "string," and in this instance, it searches for last names.
- The SEARCH function (minus one) serves as the LEFT function's second argument—it finds the location of specified characters within a text string; in this example it finds the position of a comma inside of A2 (since comma is the separator between first and last names).

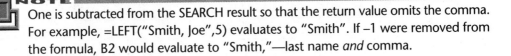

**NOTE**
One is subtracted from the SEARCH result so that the return value omits the comma. For example, =LEFT("Smith, Joe",5) evaluates to "Smith". If –1 were removed from the formula, B2 would evaluate to "Smith,"—last name *and* comma.

4. Copy the formula in cell B2 to cells B3 through B5.
5. The following formula, entered into cell D2, will display No if the student failed, or Yes if the student passed:

```
=IF(C2<65,"No","Yes")
```

This is an example of the all important IF function, which breaks down into five pieces:

| | |
|---|---|
| **IF** | Function keyword |
| **C2<65** | Condition |
| **"No"** | Value if condition is true |
| **,** | ELSE clause (implied with a comma) |
| **"Yes"** | Value if condition is false |

In plain English, the formula reads: "If the score is less than 65 then *No*, otherwise *Yes*."

6. Copy the formula to cells D3 through D5. If the formulas were entered correctly, the worksheet will appear as shown in the graphic on the next page.

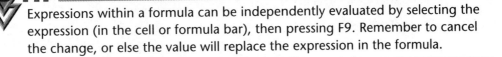

**TIP**
Expressions within a formula can be independently evaluated by selecting the expression (in the cell or formula bar), then pressing F9. Remember to cancel the change, or else the value will replace the expression in the formula.

PART

**II**

Basic Skills

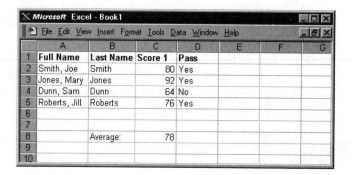

# Checking Complex Conditions—AND and OR Functions

In the previous exercise, the IF function was used to apply conditional logic in a formula. The AND and OR functions allow more complex conditions to be tested.

## AND Checks Whether More Than One Condition Is True

The AND function has the following syntax:

```
=AND(logical1,logical2,...)
```

There can be up to 30 expressions as arguments to the AND function, and *all* must evaluate true for the AND function to evaluate true.

The general syntax of AND used with IF is as follows:

```
=IF(AND(Expression1, Expression2),Value if TRUE,Value if FALSE)
```

On the following worksheet, it is OK to leave cells B1 and B3 blank. But, you enter a first name in B1, you must enter a last name into B3.

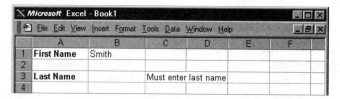

The following formula, entered into cell C3, will remind the user to enter a last name if a first name has been entered:

```
=IF(AND(ISTEXT(B1),ISBLANK(B3)),"Must enter last name","")
```

In plain English, the formula reads "If there is text in B1 *and* B3 is blank, display a reminder or else display nothing." (The empty quotes represent null text.)

### OR Checks Whether One Condition Is True

Unlike the AND function, which requires that *all* expressions be true, the OR function only requires that *one* expression be true in order for the function to evaluate true. The syntax of the OR function is identical to that of the IF function.

## Creating Formulas with Insert Function

Excel includes over 300 built-in functions, and no one—not even the most advanced user—is familiar with each and every one. The Insert ➤ Function command (also known as the Paste Function tool) is a great way to explore, learn about, and build functions. It automates and goof-proofs the creation of formulas that use functions by guiding you through the arguments and syntax required by each function.

Users of earlier versions of Excel may be familiar with the Formula Wizard, a stepped series of dialog boxes that helped you create formulas. In Excel 97, however, there is no Formula Wizard. Formulas are even easier to create, though, because once you choose a formula from the Paste Function dialog box and click on OK, Excel displays a dialog box specific to that function; you just fill in the blanks for the arguments.

In the following exercise, you'll use Insert Function to create a formula that uses the Text function to return the first four characters of a text string:

1. Open a blank worksheet and enter **Smithers** into cell A1.
2. Select cell B1 and choose Insert ➤ Function (or click on the Paste Function tool). You'll see the Paste Function dialog box.

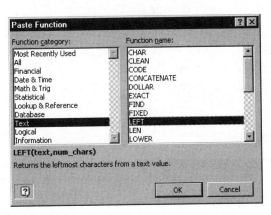

PART

II

Basic Skills

**3.** From the Function Category list, select Text to create a Text function.

**4.** From the Function Name list, select LEFT to tell Excel to count characters from the left side of the string of text.

**5.** Click on OK. The LEFT dialog box appears.

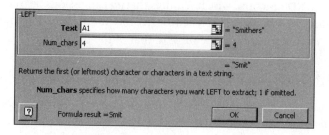

**6.** Click on cell A1 to place its reference in the first argument of the LEFT function. The value in the cell appears next to the Text argument.

**7.** Type **4** in the Num_chars argument to tell Excel how many characters to return.

**8.** Click on OK. Cell B1 returns the value *Smit*, the four leftmost characters from the text value in cell A1.

## Calculations Using 3-D References

Use 3-D cell references to reference cells in multiple, adjacent worksheets within a workbook. An example where this would be useful is if you had four sets of budget data on four separate sheets of a workbook, one worksheet for each region, let's say. You can use a 3-D reference to write a formula that refers to the same cell on each worksheet. The following exercise demonstrates how to use a 3-D cell reference and the SUM function to sum cells spanning workbooks:

**1.** Create a new workbook.

**2.** Enter a number into cell A1 on Sheet1, Sheet2, and Sheet3.

**3.** Activate Sheet1. In cell B2, type **=SUM(**

**4.** Select Sheet1 through Sheet3 as a group (select Sheet1, hold down Shift, and select Sheet3).

**5.** Select cell A1.

**6.** Type **)** and press ↵.

This formula sums cell A1 on sheets 1 through 3, and places the result in cell B2 on Sheet1. You can also type the reference into the formula as follows:

```
=SUM(Sheet1:Sheet4!A1)
```

# Natural Language Referencing

*Natural Language References* are simply cell references based on row and column labels. When you create a table of data, you can use the labels you create at the top of columns or either side of rows of data, and refer to them in formulas. In previous versions of Excel you would have to create specific names (see Chapter 8) for cell ranges first, but with natural language referencing, the names are created automatically. Let's take a look at ways you might use this feature.

**TIP**

Be careful when trying to use a label that is also a cell reference when writing formulas. For example, if you have used Q1 as a column label and you are trying to write the formula =Q1 East, referencing the intersection of column Q1 with the row East, Excel will look at cell Q1, and not the column labeled Q1.

## Referencing a Row-and-Column Intersection

Suppose you have a budget with columns labeled by month (January, February, etc.) and rows labeled by category (Supplies, Utilities, etc.). What if you want to refer to March Utilities, or October Supplies? There is a special way to reference a cell that lies at the intersection point of a given row and column (for instance, March and Utilities): use a space character. The *space character* implies an intersection. For example, the formula =C:C 2:2 is a roundabout way of referring to cell C2, and breaks down as follows:

| | |
|---|---|
| C:C | Reference to column C |
| Space | Intersection operator |
| 2:2 | Reference to row 2 |

While an intersection reference does not require the use of names or labels, its power is realized when used in conjunction with them. In the following exercise, you will refer to cells that are at the intersection point of two cell ranges.

**1.** Enter the following values onto a new worksheet:

| Book1 | A | B | C | D | E |
|---|---|---|---|---|---|
| 1 | | | | | |
| 2 | | | East | West | |
| 3 | | Gadgets | 3897 | 4123 | |
| 4 | | Gizmos | 9000 | 2721 | |
| 5 | | Widgets | 8521 | 9699 | |
| 6 | | | | | |
| 7 | | | | | |

PART

II

Basic Skills

**2.** The five labels represent the following cell ranges:

| Name | Refers to |
| --- | --- |
| Gadgets | C3:D3 |
| Gizmos | C4:D4 |
| Widgets | C5:D5 |
| East | C3:C5 |
| West | D3:D5 |

**3.** The following formulas can be used to refer to the intersection point of these ranges:

| Formula | Refers to |
| --- | --- |
| =East Gadgets | C3 (3897) |
| =West Widgets | D5 (9699) |
| =Gizmos East | C4 (9000) |

Once you create labels, you can use them in formulas just like cell addresses, as in the following:

| Formula | Refers to |
| --- | --- |
| =SUM(Gadgets) | Sum of cells C3:D3 |
| =West Widgets/2 | Cell D5 divided by 2 |
| =AVERAGE(Gizmos) | Average of cells C4:D4 |

## Implied Intersections

Labels can act like relative cell references. For example, using the worksheet from the above exercise, enter the formula **=East+West** into cells E3, E4, and E5. Even though East and West are ranges, the formulas calculate correctly based on the values on the same row. This is due to an *implied intersection*. Now enter the formula **=East+West** into cell E6. The number 0 will display because no values exist in the adjoining cells in row 6.

While writing natural language formulas, if you have more than one label with the same name, Excel may select the first label it finds, usually the upper-leftmost, or it may ask you to specify which label you want to use with the following dialog box:

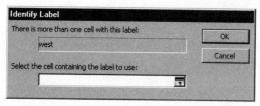

Sometimes it is not convenient for labels to be allowed in cell formulas. To disable this feature, first select Tools ➤ Options, then the Calculation tab, and uncheck the Accept Labels In Formulas setting (shown earlier in Figure 4.4).

# Controlling Worksheet Calculation

By default, Excel calculates worksheet formulas when changes to cell values so require. The calculation options are possibly the most important features of a spreadsheet program, and it is important to understand how to control them. To set the calculation options, choose the Tools ➤ Options command, then select the Calculation tab (see Figure 4.4 again).

## Calculation Modes

Calculation mode is a setting that is global to the workspace—it is not a workbook setting. The three Calculation modes available are described here:

**Automatic:** Automatic is the default calculation mode. Calculation automatically occurs if a cell value is changed and there are formulas referring to the changed cell. While calculation is taking place, a message is displayed on the status bar indicating what percentage of the calculation is complete.

**Automatic Except Tables:** This option is a special mode that recalculates everything except data tables. (Data tables are fairly obscure, and are mentioned briefly in Chapter 27.)

**TIP**

You can continue to work while Excel is calculating, though the calculation process pauses until you stop working.

**Manual:** Use the Manual calculation mode to speed up response time. When working with a large model, it will make your life easier if you keep this option checked until after you've entered all the data, at which time you switch back to automatic calculation mode. The word *Calculate* will appear on the status bar as a reminder that recalculation is required. Press the Calc Now (F9) button in the dialog box to perform a one-time calculation, yet remain in manual calculation mode. Click on the Calc Sheet button to calculate just the active worksheet rather than the entire workspace.

PART

**II**

Basic Skills

## The Precision As Displayed Setting

The value that appears in a cell is not necessarily the same as the actual value stored in the cell. Excel stores numbers with 15-digit accuracy, yet a cell may be formatted to display dollars and cents. (The formula bar always displays the actual underlying value.) Variation between formatted numbers and underlying values can cause incorrect results, which vexes accountants to no end. To recalculate based on the formatted values, again choose Tools ➤ Options, select the Calculation tab, and then check the Precision As Displayed setting.

**WARNING**
This is a workbook setting that is saved with the workbook, unlike the automatic and manual calculation settings.

# Putting Formulas and Functions to Work

Now you'll put what you've learned in this chapter into action. This section demonstrates how you can use formulas and functions to create two simple but useful worksheets: a loan calculator and a loan amortization table.

## Creating a Loan Calculator

Suppose you are taking out a car loan, and want to analyze the various loan options that are available. This exercise will show you how to create a simple, reusable loan calculator to determine what the monthly payments will be, based on the loan amount, interest rate, and term.

Enter the following information onto a blank worksheet:

| Cell | Entry |
|------|-------|
| B2 | **Loan Calculator** |
| B5 | **Interest Rate** |
| C5 | **Term (months)** |
| D5 | **Loan Amount** |
| G5 | **Monthly Payment** |
| G6 | **=PMT(B6/12,C6,-D6)** |
| B6 | **10.0%** (be sure to type the % sign) |

| Cell | Entry |
|------|-------|
| C6 | **24** |
| D6 | **2000** |

After appropriate cell formatting, your worksheet should look something like the one shown here:

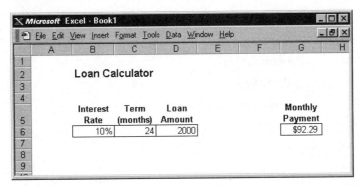

You can play "what if?" by changing the interest rate, the number of monthly payments, and the loan amount.

## Creating a Loan Amortization Schedule

The loan calculator tells you what the monthly payment is. Suppose you want to know how much interest is being paid in a given year. This exercise will add a loan amortization schedule to the loan calculator.

These are the basic calculations used in the table:

**Beginning balance (except for initial):** The ending balance from previous period

**Interest (compounded monthly):** The annual interest rate divided by 12, multiplied by the beginning balance for the period

**Principal:** The payment less interest

**Ending balance:** The beginning balance less principal

Now create the schedule:

**1.** On the same worksheet as the loan calculator, make the following entries:

| Cell | Entry |
|------|-------|
| B10 | **Amortization Schedule** |
| B17 | **Period** |
| C17 | **Beginning Balance** |
| D17 | **Payment** |
| E17 | **Interest** |
| F17 | **Principal** |
| G17 | **Ending Balance** |
| B18 | **May-97** |
| C18 | **=$D$6** |
| D18 | **=$G$6** |
| E18 | **=$B$6*C18/12** |
| F18 | **=D18-E18** |
| G18 | **=C18-F18** |
| B19 | **Jun-97** |
| C19 | **=G18** |
| D19 | **=$G$6** (copy from D18) |
| E19 | **=$B$6*C19/12** (copy from E18) |
| F19 | **=D19-E19** (copy from F18) |
| G19 | **=C19-F19** (copy from G18) |
| C14 | **Totals:** |
| D13 | **Payments** |
| E13 | **Interest** |
| F13 | **Principal** |
| D14 | **=SUM(D18:D378)** |
| E14 | **=SUM(E18:E378)** |
| F14 | **=SUM(F18:F378)** |

After you repeat the above steps for filling columns B through G for succeeding months, your worksheet should look similar to the one shown below:

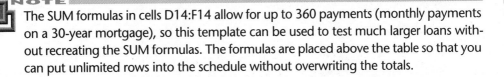

**NOTE**

The SUM formulas in cells D14:F14 allow for up to 360 payments (monthly payments on a 30-year mortgage), so this template can be used to test much larger loans without recreating the SUM formulas. The formulas are placed above the table so that you can put unlimited rows into the schedule without overwriting the totals.

2. Select cells B19:G41. Choose Edit ➤ Fill ➤ Series, select the AutoFill option, then click on OK. (See Chapter 7 to learn more about AutoFill.)
3. Select cells C18:G41, then choose Format ➤ Cells and select the Number tab. Select the Custom Category and the format code: #,##0.00.
4. Click on OK. (See the next chapter to learn more about cell formatting.)

**NOTE**

Excel performs these calculations with 15-digit precision, and will display the full precision unless you format the cells otherwise. Changing the format doesn't change the actual underlying cell value.

## Expanding a SUM Formula to Include Inserted Rows

Suppose you have values in cells A1:A10, and the formula =SUM(A1:A10) in cell A11. You want to add another value to the bottom of the list, so you insert a new row at row 11 (directly above the SUM function) and enter the new value in cell A11. But the new value is not included in the summed range. How can you insert a new value at the end of a list, and have the summed range expand automatically to include the new value? There are a couple of tricks to accomplish this.

First, you can leave a blank row at the bottom of the range (in this case, row 11), and include the blank row in the sum formula. The formula in this instance would be =SUM(A1:A11). Then insert a row above the blank row (row 11) whenever you want to add a value to the list, and the summed range will automatically adjust to include the new row.

As an alternative, you can use this formula to sum a range which always includes the cell above the formula:

```
=SUM(first_cell:INDEX
(column:column,ROW()-1))
```

The argument `first_cell` refers to the first cell in the summed range (in this example, cell A1). The argument `column:column` refers to the column being summed (in this example, $A:$A). In this case, the formula in cell A11 would be =SUM($A$1:INDEX($A:$A,ROW()-1)). See Chapter 9 to learn more about the INDEX and ROW functions.

The worksheets created at the end of this chapter were formatted with borders and special fonts for illustrative purposes. In the next chapter, you'll learn how to format your own worksheets for optimum presentation and clarity.

# Chapter

## 5

## Formatting Worksheets

## FEATURING

# Formatting Worksheets

Some people believe that the substance of a document is all that counts. Even if you are in this camp, keep in mind that much of the world would disagree. As a user of a graphically rich spreadsheet program, consider how important a report's appearance can be. Fairly simple formatting practices can yield numerous benefits:

- You can highlight important information with formatting.
- You can use simple formatting procedures to greatly enhance overall readability of reports.
- You can use styles to easily create a consistent look—and consistency enhances professionalism.
- You can use conditional formatting to highlight information when conditions or values change.

This chapter will cover many formatting options, including text, background, and borders, all of which are easy to apply: you just select the cell(s) you want to format, then choose the desired formatting command.

In addition, Excel 8 includes a number of new formatting features, including conditional formatting, merged cells, and angular text alignment, which we'll discuss in this chapter.

# Working with Fonts

One of the most basic ways you can enhance the appearance and usefulness of your worksheet is to use font formatting. In Excel, the font format property encompasses several aspects of the character:

- Typeface, such as Times New Roman, Arial, and Courier
- Size measured in points
- Boldface and/or italic
- Color
- Underline
- Special effects—strikethrough, superscript, and subscript

For ideas about how to create an attractive worksheet, see the sidebar "A Few Design Tips" later in this chapter.

Excel has made things easier for almost every conceivable business environment with three often-requested font formatting features:

- Accountants will appreciate the support of underlining that adheres to rigid accounting standards.
- Scientists and engineers will appreciate the option of superscript and subscript as global font options.
- Everyone will appreciate that fonts can be applied to individual characters within a cell.

## Applying Font Formats

Applying special font formatting is a simple procedure. As with all cell-level formatting commands, the first step is to select the range you wish to format. Choose Format➢Cells to display the Format Cells dialog box, then click on the Font tab to display the dialog box pictured in Figure 5.1. Select the font properties you want to apply and click on OK. We'll take a look at the options below.

**Font:** The list of fonts that are available to choose from are not part of Excel. Rather, these fonts either came with Windows, or were installed later.

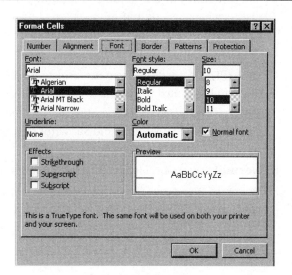

**FIGURE 5.1**

*The Font tab in the Format Cells dialog box*

PART

II

Basic Skills

**TIP**

You can right-click on the selected cell(s) to display a shortcut menu with the Format ➢ Cells command.

- TrueType fonts are indicated by a TT symbol next to the typeface. TrueType is a scalable font technology built into Microsoft Windows.
- Fonts available for the currently selected printer are indicated by a printer symbol next to the typeface.

**Font Style:** Allows you to boldface and/or italicize the font.

**Size:** Font size is measured in points. There are 72 points per inch (measured from the top of the *b* upstroke to the bottom of the *p* downstroke), so a 12-point font is 1/6th of an inch from top to bottom when printed. When you enlarge a font, the row height is automatically enlarged so that the characters display properly.

**Underline:** While the several varieties of underlines described below may seem excessive to some, accountants and financial analysts must often adhere to strict formatting standards when preparing financial reports.

- Single and Double underlines apply to all characters.

- Single Accounting and Double Accounting underlines apply to the entire cell if text, or characters only if number. Accounting underline styles, when applied to a dollar format, underline only the digits, not the dollar sign (unlike normal underline styles, which underline the dollar sign as well).

  **Color:** The Color drop-down list displays a palette containing the many colors that can be applied to the contents of a cell.

  **Effects:** The Strikethrough setting causes a line to be placed through the characters. The Superscript and Subscript settings are typically used for scientific data.

  **Normal Font:** Checking Normal Font resets font selections to default settings.

  **Preview Window:** The Preview window shows what the formatted characters will look like once you click on OK.

## Changing the Default Workbook Font

To change the default workbook font, choose Tools ➢ Options, then select the General tab. The Standard Font and Size settings determine the default font. This setting is applied every time you create a new workbook. (Excel must be restarted before changes in this setting take effect.)

## Tools for Setting Fonts

Table 5.1 displays the various font tools available in Excel. Note that the tools marked with * do not appear on a built-in toolbar—see Chapter 7 to learn how to display them by customizing toolbars.

**TABLE 5.1:** FONT FORMATTING TOOLS

| Tool | Function |
| --- | --- |
| Arial | Font (typeface) |
| 10 | Size (in points) |
| **B** | Bold |

| **TABLE 5.1:** FONT FORMATTING TOOLS (CONTINUED) | |
| --- | --- |
| **Tool** | **Function** |
| *I* | Italic |
| U | Single Underline |
| D | Double Underline * |
| ABC | Strikethrough * |
| A | Increase Font Size * |
| A | Decrease Font Size * |
| A | Font Color Palette |
| | Fill Color Palette |

# Adding Cell Borders

Cell borders add clarity and organization to a worksheet, and when used judiciously are one of the most useful formatting options. To add borders to selected cells, choose Format ➤ Cells, then select the Border tab to display the dialog box shown in Figure 5.2.

## Understanding the Border Options

The following options are available from the Border tab in the Format Cells dialog box:

**Style:** Controls the line style of selected borders, including varied line weight, solid or broken, and single or double.

**Color:** Controls the color of selected borders.

FIGURE 5.2

The Border tab
in the Format
Cells dialog box

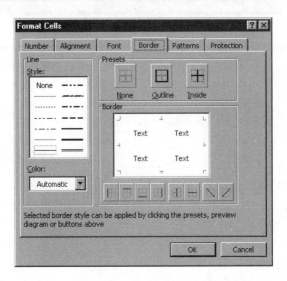

**Border:** Provides a preview of cell borders and controls which borders are applied to selected cells. The buttons below and to the left of the preview window are used to apply or remove selected borders. You can also use the mouse to click on a border in the preview window to add or remove it. The preview also displays the Style and Color selected for each border.

**Presets:** Use the Outline button to place a border around selected cells, and the None button to remove it (see Figure 5.2, above). When more than one cell is selected, an additional Preset option is available that allows borders to be placed between cells.

Sometimes when you remove a border, the border doesn't disappear from the cell. This happens because there are two borders applied to the gridline—for instance, the left border of the selected cell and the right border of the adjacent cell to the left—and you must remove both.

## Gridlines vs. Borders

Cell gridlines are not the same as cell borders. Gridlines are global to the worksheet, and they diminish the impact of borders. To remove gridlines, choose Tools ➤ Options, select the View tab, and uncheck the Gridlines option.

**TIP**

Light gray borders and/or thin borders can be less visually obtrusive and provide a more professional look. The appearance of these effects will vary depending on monitor or printer resolution.

# Tools for Applying Borders

The Border tool displays a palette of various border styles. Table 5.2 describes each tool on the Border tool palette.

**TABLE 5.2:** BORDER FORMATTING TOOLS

| Tool | Function |
|------|----------|
|  | No border (removes existing borders) |
|  | Bottom |
|  | Left |
|  | Right |
|  | Bottom double |
|  | Bottom heavy |

PART

**II**

Basic Skills

**TABLE 5.2:** BORDER FORMATTING TOOLS (CONTINUED)

| Tool | Function |
|------|----------|
| | Top and bottom |
| | Top and double bottom |
| | Top and heavy bottom |
| | Outline (each cell in selection) |
| | Outline (around selection) |
| | Heavy outline (around selection) |

# Applying Patterns and Colors

Patterns and colors can improve the appearance of a worksheet or emphasize specific information. For example, if you were creating a spreadsheet to track sales, you could use a patterned background to indicate all sales above a certain amount, calling attention to these high figures. Or, you can enhance the readability of large tables by shading every other row in a light color or gray, as shown here:

| | A | B | C | D | E | F | G | H |
|---|---|---|---|---|---|---|---|---|
| 1 | | | | | | | | |
| 2 | 840 | 581 | 438 | 300 | 111 | 457 | 568 | 585 |
| 3 | 400 | 316 | 883 | 75 | 855 | 498 | 692 | 957 |
| 4 | 376 | 777 | 448 | 745 | 220 | 909 | 162 | 209 |
| 5 | 935 | 862 | 126 | 983 | 980 | 733 | 137 | 204 |
| 6 | 40 | 990 | 522 | 735 | 487 | 30 | 889 | 658 |
| 7 | 321 | 294 | 654 | 635 | 271 | 738 | 938 | 257 |
| 8 | 528 | 67 | 310 | 487 | 758 | 89 | 654 | 187 |
| 9 | 954 | 797 | 144 | 608 | 388 | 968 | 893 | 344 |
| 10 | 360 | 472 | 750 | 210 | 672 | 131 | 288 | 602 |

To apply patterns and colors to selected cells, choose Format ➤ Cells, then select the Patterns tab.

> **TIP**
>
> You can mute bright colors by mixing them with a white pattern, or by applying the bright color as a pattern over a white background.

## Tools for Applying Colors

The Fill Color and Font Color tools are on the Formatting toolbar. When clicked on, they display a tear-off palette of colors that you can use to format the text and background colors of selected cells.

# Aligning Items within Cells

*Alignment* refers to the positioning of characters within the cell. By default, text is left-aligned and numbers are right-aligned. To change the alignment within a cell, choose Format ➤ Cells, then select the Alignment tab to display the dialog box shown in Figure 5.3. The horizontal and vertical alignment of text in selected cells is controlled by two list boxes.

**FIGURE 5.3**

*The Alignment tab in the Format Cells dialog box*

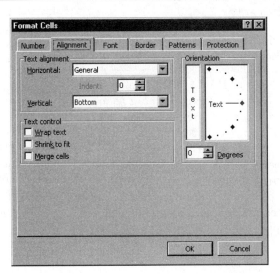

Basic Skills

## Controlling Horizontal Alignment

The following options are available for aligning the text horizontally using the Horizontal list box:

**General:** Aligns text to the left, numbers to the right.

**Left (Indent):** Aligns cell contents to the left.

**Center:** Centers characters within the cell.

**Right:** Aligns cell contents to the right.

**Fill:** Fills selected cells evenly with a single character.

**Justify:** Aligns wrapped text right and left (text is automatically wrapped). Results are visible only with multiple lines.

**Center Across Selection:** Centers text across multiple columns.

The Indent control changes the left alignment of text in the selected cells, similar to tab stops.

**MASTERING THE OPPORTUNITIES**

### Filling a Cell with a Single Character

Suppose you are creating a form in which you want some cells to be filled in with a specific character, perhaps ———— or ####### or $$$$$$. The Fill option on the Format ➢ Cells dialog box's Alignment tab will fill a selected cell or cells with a single character for you. You can also fill cells with a repeating string of characters, such as *abc* (the cell will fill with *abcabcabc*). You might think it simple to fill the cell by typing the character until the cell is filled, but what happens when you change the width of that column? If you have typed, for instance, nine characters, there will be nine characters in the cell, no matter what the width of the column is. But if you fill the cell using the Fill option, the cell will be filled with the character regardless of the column width.

You can also use the Fill option to fill several cells (or an entire row) with a single character, and the line of characters will look unbroken. If you typed characters to fill each cell, you would see discrete groups of characters, with spaces left for gridlines between cells.

## Centering across Selections

The *Center Across Selection* option is very useful for titles, as it centers the text across the selected cells regardless of varying column widths. For example, suppose you want to center the title *1998 Quarterly Review* over columns A through F (in row 2), as shown here:

| | A | B | C | D | E | F | G | H |
|---|---|---|---|---|---|---|---|---|
| 1 | | | | | | | | |
| 2 | | | 1998 Quarterly Review | | | | | |
| 3 | | | | | | | | |
| 4 | | | | | | | | |
| 5 | | | | | | | | |

**1.** Enter text in cell A2.
**2.** Select cells A2:F2.
**3.** Choose Format(Cells and select the Alignment tab.
**4.** Choose Center Across Selection from the Horizontal list box, and click on OK.

## Centering and Merging

The old Center Across Columns button on the formatting toolbar is now called the *Merge And Center* button. This is because of a new function added to the tool, the ability to merge cells. The tool not only horizontally centers cell contents across the selected cells, but also merges the selected cells.

Merged cells act as one big cell, and do not affect the formatting of surrounding cells. They are particularly useful for labeling ranges of cells. To separate cells, first select them, and then select Format ➢ Cells, click on the Alignment tab, and deselect the Merge Cells option. Chapter 10 discusses merged cells in more detail.

# Controlling Vertical Alignment

The Vertical list box controls alignment between the top and bottom of the cell. These are the options:

**Top:** Positions contents at the top of the cell

**Center:** Centers contents vertically within the cell

**Bottom:** Positions contents on the bottom of the cell

**Justify:** Justifies lines vertically, from top to bottom of the cell, and automatically wraps text

### Reapplying the Center Across Cells Format

Suppose you have centered a worksheet title across six cells using the Center Across Cells format. Now you want to re-center the title across just five cells. The common mistake most users make is to select the five cells, then apply the Center Across Cells format. But this won't work, because when you apply the Center Across Cells format to a range, the format is applied to each cell in the range individually. The sixth cell will retain the center-across format until you specifically remove it.

The easiest way to change the centering is to select the sixth cell and remove the center-across format (click on the Center Across Cells tool to toggle the format off). To add a cell to the center-across range, apply the Center Across Cells format to the next cell on the right side of the range. To remove a cell from the center-across range, remove the Center Across Cells format from the last cell on the right side of the range.

To demonstrate the effect of vertical alignment, try this exercise:

1. Enter some text in cell B2.
2. Increase the height of row 2, say to 50 or so.
3. Change the vertical alignment in cell B2 to Top.

Notice that the vertical alignment in a cell is not apparent unless the row height is increased.

## Changing Text Appearance with Text Control

The Text Control section of the Alignment tab changes several aspects of the way text appears in a cell or group of cells, and on the worksheet. These are the text control options:

**Wrap Text:** The Wrap Text option breaks a long line of text into multiple lines to fit within the cell. Excel breaks the lines to fit column width, but you can insert specific line breaks with a "soft" return, Alt+↵. Row height automatically increases to fit multiple lines of text.

| | A | B | C | D | E | F | G | H |
|---|---|---|---|---|---|---|---|---|
| 1 | | | | | | | | |
| 2 | | | | | | | | |
| 3 | | You can wrap text to change the row height, or... | | | | | | |
| 4 | | | | | | | | |
| 5 | | | | | | | | |
| 6 | | Shrink to fit | | | | | | |
| 7 | | | | | | | | |

**Shrink To Fit:** The Shrink To Fit option changes the font size instead of the row height, shrinking the text to fit in the cell. This is a handy feature when text is just a little too big for the selected cell, as shown above, but if you try to shrink too much text without changing the cell size, the text can be too small to read without zooming.

**Merged Cells:** The Merged Cells option is an extremely useful new feature. It allows you to merge several cells together to act as one, without changing row heights and column widths. By merging cells, you can place addresses, labels, or explanatory text on worksheets, and maintain the formatting integrity of accompanying data. This is especially useful when you are creating documents such as invoice templates. In the image shown below, cells B3:D6 have been merged to create space for the company address, but the widths of the adjoining columns of data are intact.

| | A | B | C | D | E | F | G |
|---|---|---|---|---|---|---|---|
| 1 | | | | Invoice | | | |
| 2 | | | | | | | |
| 3 | | Penumbrous Projections, Inc. | | | | | |
| 4 | | 3373 Groundhog Highway | | | | | |
| 5 | | Suite 1922 | | | | | |
| 6 | | Punxsutawney, PA | | | | | |
| 7 | | | | | | | |
| 8 | | Item No. | Quantity | Cost | Extension | | |
| 9 | | 302-041 | 144 | 0.83 | 119.52 | | |
| 10 | | 156-070 | 80 | 1.75 | 140.00 | | |
| 11 | | 440-003 | 12 | 2.25 | 27.00 | | |
| 12 | | 237-011 | 12 | 16.75 | 201.00 | | |
| 13 | | 997-001 | 24 | 74.34 | 1784.16 | | |
| 14 | | 886-010 | 60 | 3.75 | 225.00 | | |

PART

II

Basic Skills

> **NOTE**
> We'll discuss more about creating templates using merged cells and other formatting techniques in Chapter 10.

## Orienting Text within a Cell

The Orientation settings on the Alignment tab control how the text is oriented within the cell. The settings on the dialog box display what the text will look like.

You can control the angle of text within cells plus or minus 90 degrees from horizontal by either clicking on and dragging the Text Orientation indicator or by scrolling the Degrees spinner. In the image below, the years shown in cells B2:G2 have been rotated to 90 degrees above horizontal, and the names shown in cells B5:G5 have been rotated 55 degrees.

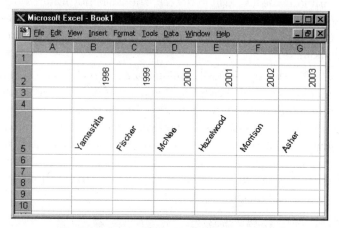

> **NOTE**
> Row height automatically adjusts when the cell is oriented vertically, sideways, or at an angle. For instance, if you format a cell for vertical orientation, the row height will increase to fit the entire entry into the cell.

## Working with Alignment Tools

Table 5.3 lists and describes some of Excel's alignment tools. Note that the tools marked with * do not appear on a built-in toolbar. Many other formatting tools are available for adding to existing toolbars or creating custom ones; see Chapter 7 to learn how to display them by customizing toolbars.

**TABLE 5.3:** ALIGNMENT TOOLS

| Tool | Function |
| --- | --- |
|  | Left-align |
|  | Center-align |
|  | Right-align |
|  | Justify * |
|  | Merge and Center |
|  | Vertical orientation * |
|  | Angle Text Upward |
|  | Angle Text Downward |
|  | Sideways (read bottom-to-top) * |
|  | Sideways (read top-to-bottom) * |

PART

II

Basic Skills

# Formatting Numbers

Number formats control how numbers, including dates and times, are displayed. Excel allows you to display numbers in a vast array of number, time, fraction, currency, accounting, and scientific formats, as well as a General or default format.

## Using Number Formats

There are a wide variety of built-in number formats available, and they are grouped by categories, each relating to a particular field or topic such as Accounting, Time, Scientific, and Currency, to name a few. To apply a number formatting to a cell or group of cells on your worksheet, do the following:

1. Choose Format ➤ Cells to call up the Format Cells dialog box, then select the Number tab (see Figure 5.4).
2. Select a format Category (to narrow the search for a formatting type).
3. Select a Format Type. (The Sample area displays the selected format applied to the active cell.)
4. Click on OK.

**TIP**

When you enter a formula that refers to other cells, the cell inherits the number formatting of the first referenced cell in the formula (unless a specific format has already been applied to the cell containing the formula).

## Understanding Format Symbols

Excel's number formats are controlled by the use of format symbols. You can combine format symbols to specify the appearance, length, and alignment of numbers, and even to add a text description to a number.

**NOTE**

Excel's number, date, and time format symbols are listed in Appendix C.

### Date and Time Formatting Symbols

When a date or time is entered in a cell, it is recognized and displayed in a default date or time format. Sometimes it is necessary to display a different format. Appendix C shows the variety of other formats available for dates and times. Keep in mind that a date cannot be used in calculations if entered as text.

Basic Skills

FIGURE 5.4

The Number tab
in the Format
Cells dialog box

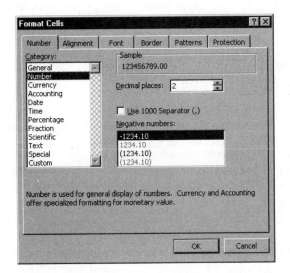

FIGURE 5.4

The Number tab
in the Format
Cells dialog box

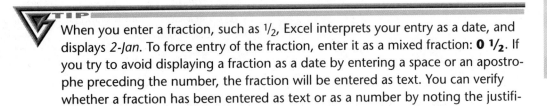

**TIP**

When you enter a fraction, such as ½, Excel interprets your entry as a date, and displays *2-Jan*. To force entry of the fraction, enter it as a mixed fraction: **0 ½**. If you try to avoid displaying a fraction as a date by entering a space or an apostrophe preceding the number, the fraction will be entered as text. You can verify whether a fraction has been entered as text or as a number by noting the justification. By default Excel left-justifies text and right-justifies numbers.

# Using Custom Number Formats

You are not limited to the built-in number formats. Using the format symbols in Appendix C, you can construct your own custom number formats.

## Creating a Custom Number Format

In this section, you will learn how to create a simple custom number format. Suppose that you have a worksheet with very large numbers, and to make the data more readable, you want to display numbers in thousands, without changing the actual cell values. A custom number format can do the job:

**1.** Select cell A1 and enter **1234567**.

**MASTERING THE OPPORTUNITIES**

## Custom Number Formatting for Elapsed Time

Suppose you keep track of your daily work hours by recording start times and stop times. Every morning and evening you type Ctrl+Shift+: (colon) to enter the current time on your time worksheet—then you subtract the start time from the stop time to calculate the elapsed work time, and format the result as hours. You get 8 or 9 (or 10 or 12) hours worked daily—no problem.

Now you want to total up your work hours for the week—you sum the daily elapsed times and get 16 hours, even though you expected an answer of 40!

This happened because Excel's standard time formatting allows for a maximum of 24 hours (and 60 minutes, and 60 seconds). Don't despair, it's easy to fix the formatting to display the full elapsed time in hours (or minutes, or seconds).

Special formatting is required to display an elapsed time value that is more than 24 hours, or 60 minutes, or 60 seconds. Enclose the time code in brackets to remove the limitation. For example, the custom format code [h]:mm will display a 40-hour work week as 40 hours (and a fractional hour as minutes). The custom code [mm] will display your 40-hour week as 960 minutes, and [ss] will display it as 57600 seconds.

**2.** Choose Format ➤ Cells, then select the Number tab.

**3.** Select the Custom Category and enter **#,###,** in the Type box (be sure to type both commas).

**4.** Click on OK. The number will display as 1,235.

## Applying Custom Number Formats

Once you define a custom number format, it is stored in the workbook and can be applied just like built-in formats. Custom formats will display in the Number tab of the Format Cells dialog box (see Figure 5.4, above) at the end of the Custom category.

## Deleting Custom Number Formats

Custom number formats are stored in the workbook in which they were defined. To delete them, activate the workbook, then follow these steps:

**1.** Choose Format ➤ Cells, then select the Number tab.

**2.** Select the Custom category.

**3.** Select the custom format you want to delete, then click on the Delete button.

PART

**II**

Basic Skills

## Three Ways to Hide Zeros on a Worksheet

Suppose you have assembled a worksheet which contains a lot of zeros. A worksheet with a profusion of zeros may be hard to read because there is too much information on it. How can you hide the zeros so that the worksheet will be easier to read? There are three ways, and the method you choose will depend on the circumstances in which you want to hide zeros.

- If you want to hide zeros throughout the worksheet, choose Tools ➢ Options, select the View tab, and clear the Zero Values check box. The zeros can be displayed again by checking the check box.

- If you only want to hide the zeros in specific cells, you can format the cells

to hide zeros by adding a semicolon at the end of the format code. Choose Format ➢ Cells and select the Number tab, then customize the format code in the Code text box. Here are some sample "hide zero" format codes:

#,##0_);(#,##0);

#,##0.00_);(#,##0.00);

$#,##0_);($#,##0);

- If you want to hide zeros that are the result of a formula, you can use an IF function. For example, say you have a formula that reads =A1-B1, and if the result is zero you don't want it to be displayed. You can nest the formula in an IF function to hide a zero result like this: IF(A1-B1=0,"",A1-B1). This formula reads "if A1-B1 is zero, then display null text, otherwise display A1-B1."

## Conditional Formatting

Using the custom number formatting methods described above, you can format a cell to display, for example, negative numbers in red. However, font color alone may not represent or highlight data the way you want. Now, with conditional formatting, you can format numbers, text, cell background, and borders to all display differently, based on cell values. Conditional formatting can be dependent on the values within the selected cells, or based on values in other cells. Conditional formatting is also *dynamic*; formats change as values change. With conditional formatting, you can create "stoplight" charts that display favorable data in green, negative data in red, and precautionary conditions in yellow. For example, actual sales for a given period may exceed, fall below, or barely meet projected sales for that period. A stoplight chart can dramatically display sales performance, and warn of changes.

Here's how to apply conditional formatting:

1. Select cells to be formatted.
2. Choose Format ➢ Conditional Formatting to display the Conditional Formatting dialog box.

**FIGURE 5.5**

*The Conditional Formatting dialog box*

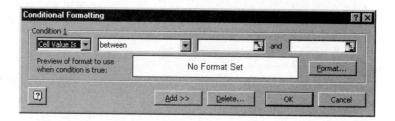

In the following exercise, conditional formatting is used to create a simple stoplight chart based on the values in the selected cells.

1. Enter the following data onto a worksheet.

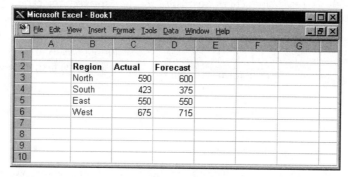

2. Select cell C3.
3. Choose Format ➢ Conditional Formatting.
4. In the Conditional Formatting dialog box under Condition 1, select Cell Value Is from the first list box and Equal To from the second list box, then enter **=D3** (use

relative references) for the forecast value in the right-most text box, and click on the Format button.

> **TIP**
>
> You can expand the middle range using the Between function and entering upper and lower limits.

**5.** Select the Patterns Tab on the Format Cells dialog box, select yellow from the palette, and click on OK.

**6.** Click on the Add button on the Conditional Formatting dialog box.

**7.** Change the criterion in the second list box of Condition 1 to Greater Than, again enter **=D3**, format the cell pattern to green, and click on Add.

**8.** Add the third criterion to the formatting scheme, Less Than, again enter **=D3**, format the cell pattern to red, and click on OK.

**9.** Copy cell C3, select cells C4 through C6, and choose Edit ➢ Paste Special. Select Paste Formats, and click on OK.

The formats in cells C3:C6 will now change automatically as you change the values in the cells. Chapter 10 covers conditional formatting in greater detail, including how to conditionally format cells based on the contents of other cells.

> **NOTE**
>
> By using the relative reference D3, you are essentially telling Excel: "Format the selected cell (C3) based on the value in the cell to the right." That way, when you copy and paste the format to cells C4:C6, they will base their formats on their corresponding values in column D, not cell D3. If you point-and-click your cell references, Excel will use absolute references.

**PART**

**II**

Basic Skills

# Using the Format Painter

A powerful feature in Excel is the Format Painter tool, available on the Standard toolbar. Format Painter copies and pastes formats by "painting" them onto cells. This can be an enormous time-saver: if you want to repeat formats on different cells, you don't have to go through all the steps of recreating the format; you can just use the Format Painter tool.

Here's how to use Format Painter:

**1.** Select a cell containing formatting you want to copy.

**2.** Click on the Format Painter tool.

**3.** Click and drag through cells where you want to apply the formatting.

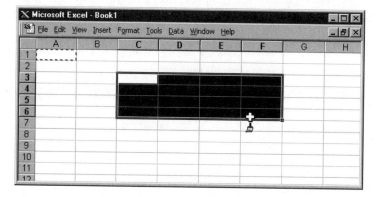

You can paint formatting repeatedly without clicking on the tool each time by double-clicking on the Format Painter tool. The Format Painter cursor remains active until you click on the Format Painter tool again.

You can clear formats fast using Format Painter. Select an unformatted cell, click on Format Painter, then select (paint) the cells to be cleared.

# Taking Advantage of AutoFormats

An AutoFormat is a built-in table format that you can quickly apply to a range of cells. AutoFormats include formatting for numbers, alignment, font, border, pattern, color, row height, and column width.

## Applying an AutoFormat

Follow these steps to apply an AutoFormat to a range of cells:

**1.** Select a range of data (either an entire contiguous range or a single cell within a range of data).

**2.** Choose Format ➤ AutoFormat. The AutoFormat dialog box appears (see Figure 5.6).

**FIGURE 5.6**

*The AutoFormat dialog box*

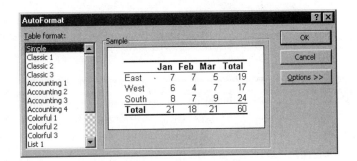

**3.** Select an AutoFormat from the Table Format list.

**4.** Click on OK.

## Selectively Applying an AutoFormat

An AutoFormat includes six attributes—Number, Font, Alignment, Border, Patterns, and Width/Height—but when you apply an AutoFormat you can elect to include only selected attributes. When the AutoFormat is then applied, it won't erase previously applied formatting. For example, suppose you want to apply an AutoFormat without changing the current row and column sizing on the worksheet:

**1.** Select a range of data and choose Format ➤ AutoFormat.

**2.** Select an AutoFormat from the Table Formats list, then click on the Options button. The AutoFormat dialog box expands to include the new Formats To Apply area (see graphic on next page).

**3.** Under Formats To Apply, uncheck the Width/Height option.

**4.** Click on OK. The AutoFormat will be applied without altering any column width or row height attributes.

PART

II

Basic Skills

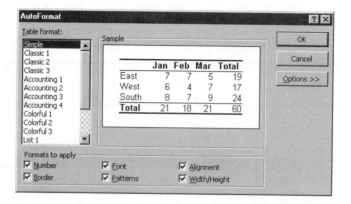

> **TIP**
> Format Painter will paint an AutoFormat from one table to another (but without row/column sizing). Select the entire range that has an AutoFormat applied to it, click on Format Painter, then select (paint) the entire range to be formatted.

# Working with Styles

Picture a worksheet that has dozens of subheadings, each formatted in 12-point, bold-faced Times New Roman, with a bottom border. It can be time-consuming to apply these formats to dozens of subheadings, and more time-consuming if you decide to change all the subheadings to font size 14. But you can define a *style*, which is a named combination of formats, then rapidly apply the style to cells. If you change the style, all cells using the style change automatically.

Styles are vitally important when it comes to simplifying sheet formatting. The small amount of time it will take you to learn about styles will save you a lot of time and hassle in the long run. Here are some of the benefits of styles:

- They save time when you are initially formatting worksheets.
- They simplify changing formats later.
- They establish formatting standards.

## Creating Styles by Example

When you create a style by example, you first format a cell, then define a style that uses the formatting of the cell. (This is the fastest way to create a new style.)

**1.** Format a cell using the desired formatting commands, and leave that cell selected.

## Making Cells Look Three-Dimensional

By using cell borders creatively, you can create 3-D effects that add a professional touch to worksheets that are viewed on the screen. (Depending on your printer, the effect will work for printed documents as well.) Notice that some of Excel's built-in table AutoFormats use a 3-D effect. Here, you see how to create the same effect selectively. The technique involves the creative use of cell borders. The following procedure shows how to make one cell appear raised, or embossed:

1. Format a range of cells (at least a 3 × 3 range) as dark gray. (On the color palette of the Patterns tab, use the gray on the second row, last column.)
2. Select a cell inside the gray range, choose Format ➤ Cells, and click on the Border tab.

3. Apply a light gray border to the left and top borders
4. Apply a black border to the right and bottom borders.

The cell will now appear to be raised. To make the cell look sunken, reverse the borders: make the left and top borders black, and make the right and bottom borders light gray. You do not have to use a dark gray background to achieve this effect. The cell borders simply have to be one shade lighter, and one shade darker, than the background color.

At first glance, the practical benefits of this technique may seem limited, but in fact there is an important benefit to be realized—the 3-D effect lets you highlight cells without using color. Users who are new to a graphical environment often go overboard with the use of color, instead of using color judiciously.

Basic Skills

2. Choose Format ➤ Style. The Style dialog box is displayed (see Figure 5.7).
3. Type a name for the new style into the Style Name text box.
4. Click on OK.

The new style will contain all the formatting characteristics of the selected cell.

TIP

You can create a new style by typing the name directly into the Style drop-down list rather than using the Style dialog box. To use the Style drop-down list, add it to a toolbar (see Chapter 7 to learn how).

**FIGURE 5.7**

*The Style
dialog box*

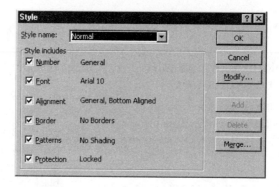

## Creating Styles Explicitly

Previously, you learned how to create by example. You can also define a style explicitly by using the options available in the Style dialog box.

1. Choose Format ➢ Style.
2. Type a name for the new style in the Style Name text box.
3. Click on Modify. The Format Cells dialog box is displayed.
4. Select the formatting options you want from the dialog box tabs, then click on OK.
5. The Style dialog box is displayed again:

   • To apply the new style, click on OK.
   • To define the style without applying it, click on Add, then click on Close.

The Style dialog box displays a list of the six attributes a style can include (see the Style Includes area in Figure 5.7), and the settings for each attribute in the selected style. You can uncheck any attributes that you don't want to include. For example, you can create a style that doesn't include border or patterns attributes, so that the style, when applied, won't alter existing borders or patterns.

**NOTE**
Row height and column width are not part of the style definition.

## Changing a Style Definition

The steps involved in changing the style are very similar to creating a style:

1. Choose Format ➢ Style.

2. Select or type the name of the style you want to change:

- If you *select* the name, the existing style formats serve as the starting point for changes.
- If you *type* the name, the formatting of the active cell serves as the starting point for changes.

3. Click on Modify and change the formats using the Format Cells dialog box tabs.
4. Click on OK. The Style dialog box is displayed again.
5. Click on OK to apply the new style, or click on Add to keep the Style dialog box open (to create or redefine more styles).

# Applying a Style

You have learned how to create styles. Here is the procedure for *applying* a style to one or more cells:

1. Select the cell(s) to which you want to apply the style.
2. Apply the style in one of two ways:

- Choose Format ➢ Style, select a style from the Style Name list, then click on OK.
- Select a style from the Style text box, a formatting tool available for custom toolbars (see Chapter 7 to learn how to customize toolbars).

**TIP**

Use styles in conjunction with templates to create standardized worksheet formats. See Chapter 10 to learn about templates.

## Deleting a Style

Styles are stored inside the workbook in which they were created. Here's how to delete a style:

1. Activate the workbook containing the style.
2. Choose Format ➢ Style.
3. Select the style to delete from the Style Name list.
4. Click on Delete, then click on OK.

Any cells still defined with the deleted style will revert to normal style.

**NOTE**

You can't delete the Normal style, but you can change its properties.

PART

II

Basic Skills

## Merging Styles into Different Workbooks

Assume that you have created some styles in a workbook, and want to merge them into a different workbook without having to redefine them. The procedure for merging styles is as follows:

1. Open the *source* workbook containing the style(s) to be copied from, and the *target* workbook the style(s) are to be merged into.
2. Activate the target workbook.
3. Choose Format ➤ Style to open the Style dialog box.
4. Click on Merge. The Merge Styles dialog box appears:

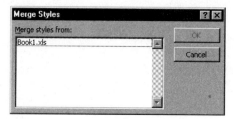

5. Select the source workbook from the Merge Styles From list.
6. Click on OK to copy the styles into the target workbook—all styles in the source workbook will be merged into the target workbook.
7. Click on OK to close the Style dialog box.

**NOTE**

If both workbooks have a style with the same name, Excel will prompt "Merge styles that have same names?". If you choose Yes, the incoming style (from the source workbook) will replace the style in the target workbook.

## Copying Formats and Styles to a Different Workbook

When you copy a cell from one workbook to another, the formatting moves with the cell. This is most beneficial with custom number formats and styles, since it can be time-consuming to recreate the definitions.

To copy a custom number format or style to another workbook, select a cell containing the format or style and copy it to the new workbook. Custom number formats and styles will be added to the lists in the new workbook.

## Changing Built-In Styles

There are a handful of built-in styles that come with Excel. The Normal style is one of these built-in styles—Normal is the default style for all cells in a new workbook, and is the style to which cells revert when you clear formatting. But what if the Normal style doesn't provide what you want? For example, you may want your worksheets to be created in the font Times New Roman 12 instead of Arial 10.

You can change the definition of Normal style in the active workbook the same way that you change any style definition. Choose Format ➤ Style, select Normal from the list of Style Names, then click on the Modify button. Make the changes in

the Format Cells dialog box, then click on OK to close it. Click on OK again to close the Style dialog box.

Now you've changed the Normal style in one workbook. Suppose you want to use the new Normal style in all workbooks? You can redefine Normal style in every new workbook you create, but that's inefficient. You can change the Normal style for all new workbooks by redefining Normal in a global workbook template. Name the template **Workbook**, and save the template in the Excel Startup Folder (see Chapter 10 to learn more about templates). All new workbooks will be created from this template, and will have the Normal style that you defined.

# Formatting Worksheet Backgrounds

Why settle for a drab-looking worksheet? Excel's Format ➤ Sheet ➤ Background command lets you select a variety of graphic and picture file formats from the Sheet Background dialog box. To make your worksheets more attractive, you can select a clip art background motif as shown below, put your corporate logo on a "cover" worksheet of your workbook, or add a JPEG image of your family dog.

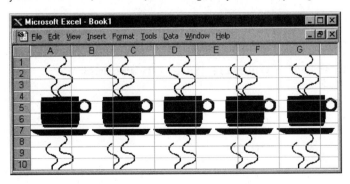

To clear the worksheet background, choose Format ➤ Sheet ➤ Delete Background.

## A Few Design Tips

Here are some simple tips for designing aesthetically pleasing and easy-to-use worksheets:

- **Keep it simple!** Too many fonts and colors can be overwhelming. Limit a given worksheet to one or two type-faces, with variations in size and style (boldface, italic).

- **Use scaleable fonts,** such as True-Type, to keep your figures sharp and clear on the screen.

- **Use color meaningfully,** to high-light information or focus the reader's attention. Use muted colors, like gray, for backgrounds.

- **Turn off gridlines,** and use borders for clarity.

- **Incorporate plenty of white space**—a lot of condensed data can be difficult to digest.

- **Incorporate graphic features** (charts, logos, etc.) to make the worksheet more visually appealing. See Chapter 12 to learn more about graphic objects.

# A Formatting Exercise

As an exercise, let's create the sample worksheet shown in Figure 5.8 and then take the steps to format it differently. (Don't worry about having to enter all the numbers as shown here; in these steps you'll learn how to use a function that will fill in the number cells with random data.)

**1.** Open a new worksheet and enter the following:

| Cell | Entry |
|------|-------|
| B2 | **Northwest Athletic Wear** |
| B3 | **Quarterly Sales - By Product** |
| B6 | **Shoes** |
| C7 | **Qtr 1** |
| D7 | **Qtr 2()** |

**FIGURE 5.8**

*A typical hard-to-read worksheet*

```
            Northwest Athletic Wear
          Quarterly Sales - By Product


    Shoes   Qtr 1   Qtr 2   Qtr 3   Qtr 4
          --------------------------------
   Running    616     963     539     119
    Tennis     21     539     647     140
Basketball    807     663     487     958
          =======  =======  =======  =======
  subtotal   1444    2165    1673    1217

   Shirts   Qtr 1   Qtr 2   Qtr 3   Qtr 4
          --------------------------------
       Tee    106     321     853     728
      Polo    608     515     205     570
     Sweat    447     228     507     449
          =======  =======  =======  =======
  subtotal   1161    1064    1565    1747
          =======  =======  =======  =======
     Total   2605    3229    3238    2964
```

| Cell | Entry |
|------|-------|
| E7 | **Qtr 3** |
| F7 | **Qtr 4** |
| B8 | **Running** |
| B9 | **Tennis** |
| B10 | **Basketball** |
| B11 | **subtotal** |
| C11 | **=SUBTOTAL(9,C8:C10)** |
| D11:F11 | (copy formula from C11) |

**2.** Apply the following formatting:

| Cell | Formatting |
|------|------------|
| B2 | Boldface, italic, 16 points |
| B3 | Boldface, italic, 12 points |
| B2:B3 | Center across worksheet (select B2:F3; choose Format ➤ Cells, Alignment tab, Center Across Selection setting) |

| Cell | Formatting |
|------|-----------|
| B6 | Boldface, italic, 11 points |
| B8:B11 | Right-align |
| B11:F11 | Boldface |
| C7:F7 | Boldface, center-align |
| C8:F10 | Thin, gray borders to left, right, top, and bottom |
| C11:F11 | Gray double borders to top; built-in Custom number format **#,##0** |
| C8:F10 | Custom number format **[Red][<300]#,##0;[Blue][>600]#,##0;#,##0** |

**3.** Turn the gridlines off.

**4.** Create a style for the title cells:

- Select cell B6.
- Choose Format ➢ Style, type **Title** in the Style Name text box, then click on OK.

**NOTE**

If you change the properties of a style, all the cells using that style will change. This may seem a minor efficiency with only a few titles, but picture a worksheet with hundreds of titles. If the titles have been formatted using a style, a single change to the style will automatically change the formatting of all of the titles.

**5.** Create a second section by copying the first:

- Select cells B6:F11.
- Copy and paste to cell B13.

**6.** Change these values in the second section:

- Enter **Shirts** in cell B13.
- Enter **Tee**, **Polo**, and **Sweat** in cells B15:B17.

**7.** Enter the following function to enter random data:

- Select cells C8:F10 and C15:F17 (hold down Ctrl to select both ranges).
- Type **=INT(RAND()*1000)** and press Ctrl+↵.

**8.** Freeze the random values:

- Select C8:F10, choose Edit ➤ Copy, choose Edit ➤ Paste Special, select Values, and click on OK.
- Repeat this freeze procedure for cells C15:F17.

**9.** Create a Grand Total row:

- Enter **Total** (right-aligned and boldfaced) in cell B19.
- Enter the formula **=SUBTOTAL(9,C8:C10,C15:C17)** in cell C19, then copy the formula to cells D19:F19 (see Chapter 9 to learn more about the SUBTOTAL function).

**10.** Apply a gray double border to the tops of the Grand Total cells.

**11.** Give the totals some visual separation from the data:

- Select rows 11, 18, and 19.
- Choose Format ➤ Row ➤ Height, and enter a row height of **19**.

When completed, the exercise worksheet should look like Figure 5.9.

PART

**II**

Basic Skills

---

**FIGURE 5.9**

*The worksheet from Figure 5.8, newly formatted*

### Northwest Athletic Wear
#### Quarterly Sales - By Product

**Shoes**

|            | Qtr 1 | Qtr 2 | Qtr 3 | Qtr 4 |
|------------|-------|-------|-------|-------|
| Running    | 616   | 963   | 539   | 119   |
| Tennis     | 21    | 539   | 647   | 140   |
| Basketball | 807   | 663   | 487   | 958   |
| subtotal   | 1444  | 2165  | 1673  | 1217  |

**Shirts**

|          | Qtr 1 | Qtr 2 | Qtr 3 | Qtr 4 |
|----------|-------|-------|-------|-------|
| Tee      | 106   | 321   | 853   | 728   |
| Polo     | 608   | 515   | 205   | 570   |
| Sweat    | 447   | 228   | 507   | 449   |
| subtotal | 1161  | 1064  | 1565  | 1747  |
| Total    | 2605  | 3229  | 3238  | 2964  |

We hope you enjoy the formatting techniques you've read about in this chapter. In the next chapter, you will learn everything you ever wanted to know about printing!

# Chapter

# 6

## Printing Worksheets

# Printing Worksheets

**D**espite trends toward the paperless office, hard copies of business reports and printed worksheets will likely be office fixtures for the foreseeable future. Fortunately, Excel offers all sorts of options for setting up worksheets to print out your data. You can set margins and fonts; include headers, footers, and titles; and print multiple copies of the entire worksheet or just certain pages. Before you waste any paper (and printer time), you can preview your worksheets to see just how they'll look when you print them.

## Setting Up Worksheets for Printing

Before you actually print your worksheets, you'll need to set up the pages you want to print. The File ➢ Page Setup command displays a tabbed dialog box that provides access to most print-related settings. The four tabs are as follows: Page, Margins, Header/Footer, and Sheet.

## Determining the Look of Printed Pages

You'll find the options for controlling the basic layout of the printed pages on the Page tab in the Page Setup dialog box, shown in Figure 6.1.

**FIGURE 6.1**

*The Page tab in the Page Setup dialog box*

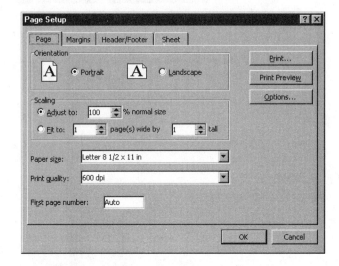

The options available on the Page tab are described here:

**Orientation:** Select portrait (tall) or landscape (wide).

**Scaling—Adjust To:** Allows you to enlarge or reduce the printed worksheet without changing the size of the onscreen display. You can reduce the printed worksheet to as low as 10% to fit more of the worksheet on a page, or enlarge up to 400% to enhance detail.

**Scaling—Fit To:** Fits a worksheet onto a specific number of pages, based on how many pages wide and how many pages tall you want the printed worksheet to be. The relative dimensions of the worksheet will be preserved.

**NOTE**

If you choose the Fit To option, Excel will ignore any page breaks you have set, and fit the entire worksheet or print area to the specified number of pages.

**Paper Size:** Select paper size from drop-down list.

**Print Quality:** Select resolution (dpi) from list.

**First Page Number:** Begins numbering at specified page number.

> **NOTE**
> On each of the four Page Setup dialog box tabs, there is an Options button—this button displays the Setup dialog box for the selected printer. Any changes you make in the Page Setup dialog boxes that affect the printer setup (such as changing paper size) will automatically be made in the Printer Setup dialog box.

## Adjusting Margins

You can set the margins and determine the position of headers, footers, and print areas from the Margins tab in the Page Setup dialog box, shown in Figure 6.2.

**FIGURE 6.2**

*The Margins tab in the Page Setup dialog box*

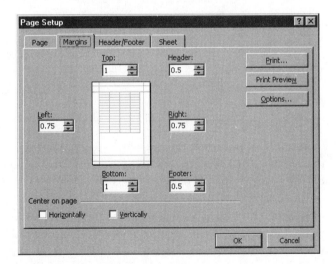

The Preview area on the dialog box provides a visual illustration of how the margins are set. (Select a margin, and the corresponding line on the dialog box Preview picture will be highlighted.) Other options on the Margins tab include the following:

**Top, Bottom, Left, Right:** Sets margins (inches from edge).

**From Edge:** Sets header/footer placement (inches from edge)—should be less than top/bottom margins.

PART

**II**

Basic Skills

**Center On Page:** Check to center the print area vertically or horizontally between margins.

# Creating Page Headers and Footers

You enter and format headers and page footers on the Header/Footer tab, shown in Figure 6.3.

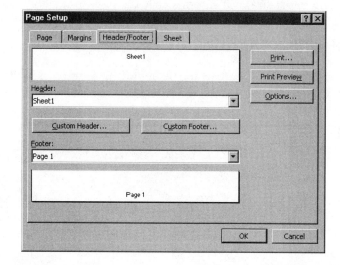

Headers are printed at the top of every page, and footers are printed at the bottom of every page. Headers are commonly used for company names and report titles (the default header is the file name); footers are commonly used for page numbers and printout dates/times.

Headers and footers are not actually a part of the worksheet—they are part of the printed page—and are allotted separate space on the printed page. How much space the header and footer are allotted is controlled on the Margins dialog box tab (the header occupies the space between the Header margin and Top margin; the footer, that between the Bottom and Footer margins).

Headers and footers work exactly alike—you can choose a built-in header/footer, or define a custom one.

## Using Built-in Headers/Footers

Select from a variety of built-in headers and footers using the respective drop-down lists on the Header/Footer tab. The lists include several commonly-used header/footer formats, such as the page number, worksheet name, user name, date, and combinations of these.

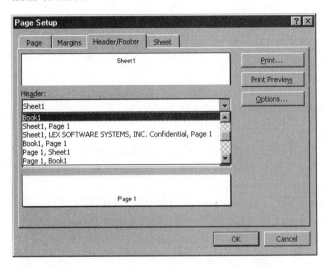

## Creating Custom Headers/Footers

Click on the Custom Header or Custom Footer buttons to customize headers/footers. A dialog box appears with three text boxes—Left Section, Center Section, and Right Section. These text boxes allow you to justify the text of your headers and footers to the left, center, or right of the page.

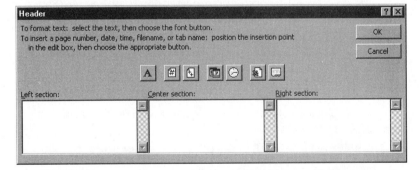

Click on the section where you want to place a header/footer entry. Type text into any of these three sections. (Press ↵ for a new line.) The buttons in the center of the dialog box above are used to format the text, and to insert special values into the header/footer. They are as follows:

- Font format (Select text, click on button, select formatting options.)

- Page number
- Number of pages
- Current date
- Current time
- Workbook name
- Worksheet name

A common custom footer is (page #) of (# pages) (e.g., **1 of 12**), which is created by combining header/footer codes and text. Follow these steps to create this custom footer:

1. Choose File ➤ Page Setup, then select the Header/Footer tab.
2. Click on the Custom Footer button (see Figure 6.3), then click in the center section on the Footer dialog box.
3. Click on the Page Number button, type **of**, then click on the Number Of Pages button.
4. Click on OK to close the Footer dialog box.

The preceding steps will insert the code *&[Page] of &[Pages]* into the center section of the Footer dialog box, and a preview of the footer will be displayed on the Header/Footer dialog tab. The code will also be added to the drop-down list of footers for the workbook.

**NOTE**

The ampersand (&) is a code symbol for headers and footers, and doesn't print. So what if you want to print an ampersand in your header (*Brown & Brown*, for instance)? Type two ampersands—enter **Brown && Brown** as the custom header.

## Modifying Sheet Options

You can specify a print area, print titles, and several other print options on the Sheet tab, shown in Figure 6.4.

The following list describes the options found on the Sheet tab:

**Print Area:** Select area of worksheet you want to print (either select or type area reference).

**Print Titles:** Select or type rows/columns to print on every page.

**Gridlines:** Turns gridlines on/off (only affects printed pages).

**Black And White:** Prints all pages in black and white (no shades of gray for colors).

Basic Skills

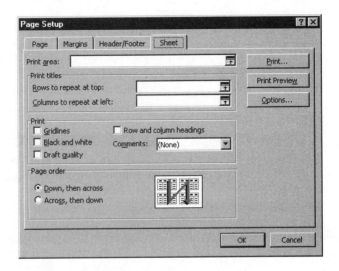

**FIGURE 6.4**

*The Sheet Tab in the Page Setup dialog box*

**Comments:** Allows printing cell comments either in place or at end of sheet (See Chapter 11).

**Draft Quality:** Gridlines will not print, nor will most graphics and many types of cell formatting, reducing printing time.

**Row And Column Headings:** Includes row and column headings on printed page.

**Page Order:** Select page order for multiple-page worksheets (see Figure 6.4, above, for an illustration of printing order).

**TIP**

Turning off the workspace gridlines (choose Tools ➢ Options, then select the View tab) will automatically turn off the printed gridlines (on the Sheet tab in the Page Setup dialog box), and vice-versa. But you can print gridlines without displaying them in the workspace if you *first* turn off the Gridlines setting on the View tab, *then* check the Gridlines check box on the Sheet tab.

## Setting a Print Area

If you want to print only specified areas of a worksheet, you can set a Print Area from the Page Setup dialog box. To set a Print Area, click in the Print Area edit box of the Sheet tab, then select a range of cells using the mouse (or type in a cell range reference).

The collapse dialog button in the Print Area edit box will minimize the dialog box while you make your selection.

Alternatively, you can set a Print Area quickly using one of the following methods:

- Select the range to print and then choose File ➢ Print Area ➢ Set Print Area.
- Select the range to print and then click on the Set Print Area tool on a customized toolbar. This tool is not available on a built-in toolbar. See Chapter 7 to learn how to add the Set Print Area tool to a customized toolbar.

**TIP**

You don't have to define a print area in order to print a certain range of cells. Select the cells to print, choose File ➢ Print, and choose Selection from the Print What options.

## Setting Multiple Print Areas on the Same Worksheet

Suppose you have a worksheet with several tables, and you want to print each table sequentially on its own page. You can set lots of page breaks all over the worksheet, but what if the tables are different sizes and don't fit neatly between page breaks? Also, the pages you create with page breaks will print in the order defined on the Sheet tab in the Page Setup dialog box (either across then down, or down then across—see Figure 6.4). What if you want to print the tables in a specific order, rather than in the order designated on the Sheet tab? In Excel you can set multiple print areas on a worksheet, and you can determine the order in which they print.

To set multiple print areas and specify the order in which they are printed, do the following:

1. Choose File ➢ Page Setup, and select the Sheet tab. (Don't use the Print Area tool, as it can only set one print area on a worksheet.)
2. Click in the Print Area edit box, then select the first area by dragging on the worksheet; hold down Ctrl to select the next range.

In the Print Area edit box, you will see the selected ranges separated by commas; you can manually specify subsequent print areas by typing a comma after the first print areas, then selecting (or typing) the next area. You can set as many print areas as you want, in whatever order you want, by separating the print area references with commas. The area you set first will print on page one, the second area will print on page two, and so on.

## Setting Print Titles

When printing a multiple-page document, you may want certain rows or columns to appear on each page. For example, suppose you have a worksheet of scientific air-quality data, with a year's worth of daily readings from 150 sites. The worksheet is 365 rows (dates) long by 150 columns (sites) wide, and requires several pages to print. Each data point must be identified by date (down the left column) and by site (along the top row). A page containing, for example, data for Sites 99–105 in June must have appropriate dates and sites along the left and top of the page, as shown here.

| Site# | 99 | 100 | 101 | 102 | 103 | 104 | 105 |
|---|---|---|---|---|---|---|---|
| 6/1/97 | 564 | 252 | 879 | 469 | 349 | 821 | 773 |
| 6/2/97 | 828 | 163 | 681 | 912 | 426 | 231 | 827 |
| 6/3/97 | 589 | 933 | 656 | 993 | 988 | 605 | 505 |
| 6/4/97 | 960 | 709 | 659 | 196 | 820 | 777 | 53 |
| 6/5/97 | 56 | 23 | 243 | 791 | 354 | 602 | 377 |
| 6/6/97 | 913 | 398 | 980 | 333 | 512 | 352 | 584 |
| 6/7/97 | 425 | 153 | 675 | 509 | 559 | 947 | 172 |
| 6/8/97 | 983 | 244 | 110 | 505 | 175 | 56 | 995 |
| 6/9/97 | 555 | 96 | 26 | 199 | 371 | 809 | 669 |
| 6/10/97 | 425 | 256 | 811 | 296 | 894 | 984 | 925 |
| 6/11/97 | 19 | 943 | 636 | 311 | 9 | 107 | 787 |
| 6/12/97 | 691 | 993 | 871 | 115 | 363 | 837 | 135 |
| 6/13/97 | 19 | 760 | 914 | 862 | 148 | 613 | 893 |
| 6/14/97 | 115 | 331 | 611 | 922 | 229 | 659 | 554 |
| 6/15/97 | 925 | 310 | 972 | 104 | 22 | 767 | 141 |
| 6/16/97 | 180 | 435 | 198 | 520 | 41 | 225 | 627 |
| 6/17/97 | 49 | 440 | 452 | 540 | 354 | 614 | 408 |
| 6/18/97 | 430 | 921 | 471 | 722 | 754 | 820 | 46 |

The page shown is just one page out of 144 pages (the worksheet is 12 pages tall by 12 pages wide). In this case, setting the Date column (column A) and the Site row (row 1) as print titles makes it possible to print any range of cells in the worksheet without having to paste in the identifying dates and sites; the appropriate date and site titles are printed automatically with whatever portion of the worksheet is printed.

**NOTE**

Print titles are not the same as page headers, though they can be used for similar purposes. Also, a page can be set up for both print titles and page headers.

Here's how to set print titles:

**1.** Choose File ➤ Page Setup, then select the Sheet tab.

**2.** Click on the Collapse Dialog Box button in the Rows To Repeat At Top edit box.

**3.** On the worksheet, select the rows that you want for your print titles, or type the cell reference. Click again on the Collapse Dialog Box button to set the row selection.

PART

II

Basic Skills

**4.** Click on the Collapse Dialog Box button in the Columns To Repeat At Left edit box.

**5.** On the worksheet, select the print title columns, or type the cell reference. Click again on the Collapse Dialog Box button to set the column selection.

**6.** Click on OK.

## Deleting a Print Area or Print Titles

If you have defined a print area and want to print the entire worksheet, you must first delete the print area.

To delete the print area, choose File ➢ Print Area ➢ Clear Print Area, or choose File ➢ Page Setup, then select the Sheet tab and clear the Print Area edit box. To delete print titles, you must manually clear any references in the Rows To Repeat At Top and/or Columns To Repeat At Left edit boxes in the Page Setup dialog box.

When you set the print area or print titles, range names are automatically defined on the worksheet. Setting the print area causes the name *Print_Area* to be defined. Setting print titles causes the name *Print_Titles* to be defined. If you want to see either of these ranges, select them from the drop-down list in the Name box. Because they are named ranges, they can be deleted using the Insert ➢ Name ➢ Define command. (See Chapter 8 to learn more about names.)

**NOTE** Named ranges are also automatically deleted when you clear the ranges.

# Previewing Your Worksheet before Printing

Choose File ➢ Print Preview, or click on the Print Preview button on the Standard toolbar, to see what the printed pages will look like before you actually print them. There are also several settings that you can control while in print preview mode. Figure 6.5 shows the Print Preview workspace.

## Zooming In on the Previewed Worksheet

When you are in print preview, the mouse pointer becomes a magnifying glass. Click on the part of the worksheet that you wish to zoom in on. The sheet will be magnified, and the pointer will change to an arrow. Click on the worksheet again to zoom back out. (Alternatively, you can use the Zoom button on the top of the window to zoom in and out of the worksheet.)

**FIGURE 6.5**

*The Print Preview workspace*

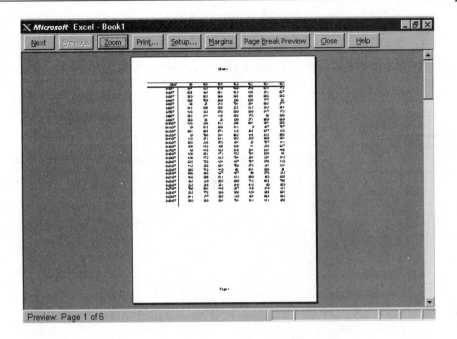

## Print Preview Buttons

The following list explains the buttons displayed along the top of the workspace in print preview mode (see Figure 6.5):

**Next:** Displays the next page (dimmed when there is no next page).

**Previous:** Displays the previous page (dimmed when there is no previous page).

**Zoom:** Toggles between magnified and full page display.

**Print:** Displays the Print dialog box.

**Setup:** Displays the Page Setup dialog box.

**Margins:** Toggles on/off lines depicting page margins, header/footer margins, and column width.

**Page Break Preview:** Displays a view mode of your worksheet that shows your page breaks, and allows you to adjust them. Click on the Print Preview button to return to that mode, or select View ➤ Normal to exit either preview.

**Close:** Closes the Preview window and returns to the worksheet.

PART

II

Basic Skills

The Margins button, which toggles the display of margin and column lines, is a particularly useful feature. When margin and column lines are in view, you can drag them with the mouse to a new position. To reposition a guide line, place the mouse pointer on a margin line, a column gridline, or a handle at the edge of the page, and drag the line with the two-headed arrow (Figure 6.6). Margin settings (in inches) or column widths (in column width units) are displayed on the status bar while you drag margin/column lines. Sometimes it's easier to drag the lines if you zoom in first.

**FIGURE 6.6**

*Dragging a column gridline*

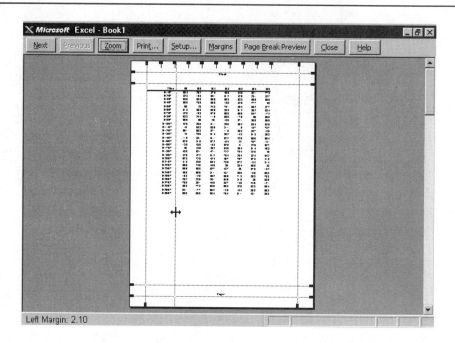

The inner horizontal margins are text margins (i.e., they define the worksheet); the outer horizontal margins are header/footer margins. The extra handles along the top of the page correspond to column lines.

## Setting Page Breaks

When you print, Excel automatically creates page breaks where needed. If automatic page breaks cause a page break to occur in an undesirable place on the worksheet, however, you can insert manual page breaks.

## Setting Excel to Display Page Breaks Automatically

By default, automatic page breaks are not indicated on the worksheet until the sheet is printed (or print previewed) for the first time. To display page breaks, choose Tools ➢ Options, select the View tab, and then check the Page Breaks option. Page breaks are indicated by broken lines which run along the gridlines.

## Customizing Page Breaks

Suppose you are working with a multiple-page worksheet that includes a table of numbers, and an automatic page break is occurring in the middle of the table (causing the table to print on pages two and three). If the table isn't too long, you can fit it on a single page by placing a manual page break just before it begins. You can do this using Page Break Preview. Page Break Preview shows you a zoomed-out view of your worksheet with page breaks shown as boldface lines. Using the mouse, you can move the page breaks by clicking and dragging, as shown in Figure 6.7.

**FIGURE 6.7**

*Dragging a page break in Page Break Preview*

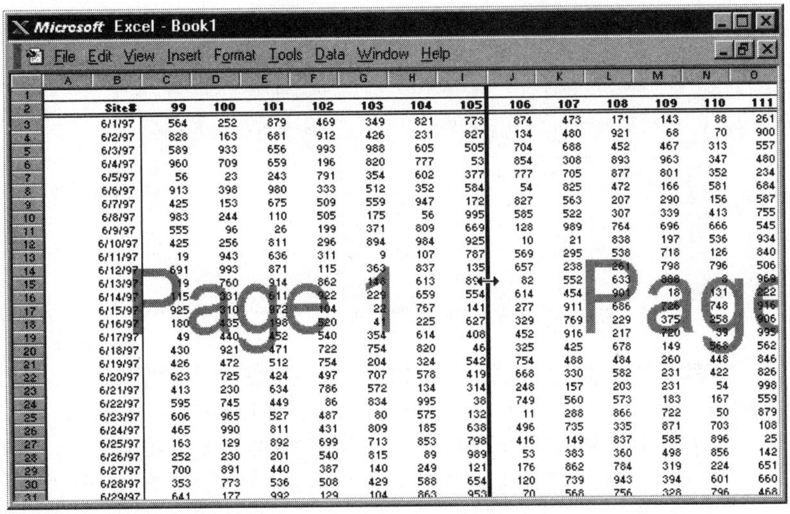

Although Page Break Preview is a view option, and thus an important formatting tool, it is also valuable when printing or setting print areas. You can access it in one of the following ways:

- Choose View ➢ Page Break Preview.

- Click on the Page Break Preview button in the Print Preview dialog box (see Figure 6.6, earlier in the chapter).

You can also insert page breaks directly from the worksheet or in Page Break Preview mode by selecting row and column headers. There are three types of page breaks—vertical, horizontal, and a combination of the two:

| To Insert This: | Do This: |
| --- | --- |
| Vertical page break | Select the column to the right of the desired break, and choose Insert ➤ Page Break. |
| Horizontal page break | Select the row below the desired break, and choose Insert ➤ Page Break. |
| Vertical and horizontal page break | Select a single cell, choose Insert ➤ Page Break. (Breaks insert along top and left side of cell.) |

Manual page breaks are indicated by heavier broken lines than automatic page breaks when displayed on the worksheet, as shown below. Automatic page breaks automatically adjust when manual page breaks are inserted.

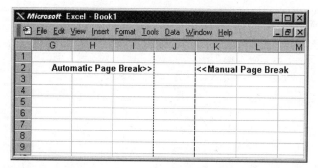

**NOTE** If you attempt to print a worksheet and find your page breaks are ignored, you probably have the Scaling—Fit To option selected. Choose File ➤ Page Setup, select the Page tab, and change the Scaling option to Adjust To.

## Removing a Manual Page Break

To remove a manual page break, select a cell to the right of a vertical break or immediately below a horizontal break, and choose Insert ➤ Remove Page Break. (If the Insert menu doesn't list the Remove Page Break command, there is no manual page break at the selected cell.)

# Worksheet Printing Options

The File ➤ Print command displays a dialog box that offers options for printing selected cells, specific sheets or pages, or an entire workbook (see Figure 6.8). The Print dialog box is common to Microsoft Office applications, so if you're already printing Microsoft Word documents, for example, Excel provides the same features.

**FIGURE 6.8**

*The Print dialog box*

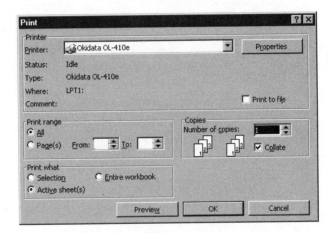

The Print button on the Standard toolbar will print the selection immediately without displaying a dialog box. The default Print dialog box settings will be used (i.e., selected sheet, one copy, all).

The options available in the Print dialog box are described briefly here:

**Printer:** Displays selected printer from a drop-down list, printer status, type, and the port that your computer is using to print.

**Print To File check box:** Allows you to create a disk file for the selected printer.

**Page Range—All:** Prints all pages in worksheet.

**Page Range—From/To:** Prints specified pages.

**Selection:** Prints selected cells.

**Active Sheet(s):** Prints only selected worksheet.

**Entire Workbook:** Prints open workbook.

**Number Of Copies:** Prints specified number of copies of selected pages.

**Collate check box:** Allows you to collate multiple copies.

**Preview button:** Switches from the Print dialog box to the print preview mode, allowing you to get a final view of your document before you print it.

**Properties button:** Displays a tabbed dialog box that controls the following printing options:

> **Paper:** Selects printer paper and envelope size, orientation of printing, and paper source.

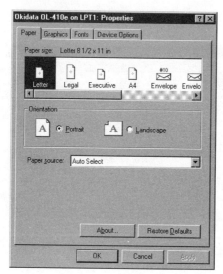

**Graphics:** Allows you to control resolution, dithering, and intensity of printed graphics.

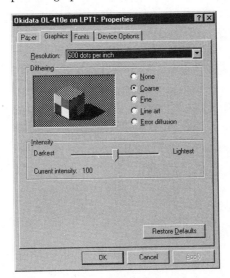

**Fonts:** Allows you to download TrueType fonts to selected printer as bitmap soft fonts, or print them as graphics.

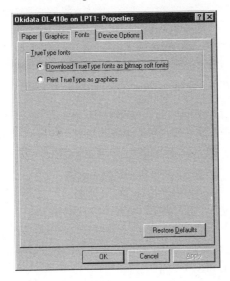

Basic Skills

**Device Options:** Controls print density and allows you to adjust printer memory tracking; i.e., you can try to "force" a complex document to print, even though the selected printer may not have enough memory.

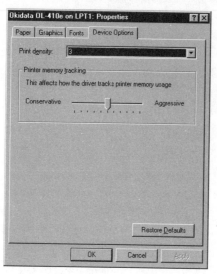

**NOTE**

To print a color worksheet in black and white (no shades of gray), choose File ➤ Page Setup, then select the Sheet tab and check the Black And White check box.

## Selecting a Printer

If you work in an office environment, your computer may be connected to more than one printer. If so, you can switch between printers and choose the one that is free to speed up your print jobs. Try out the steps below to learn how to select which printer to use.

**1.** Choose File ➤ Print.

**2.** Select the desired printer from the Printer drop-down list.

**3.** Click on OK.

The Print dialog box displays the print queue status, the printer port being used, and whether the printer is busy or idle.

## Printing Sections of a Worksheet

Often, you won't want to print an entire worksheet. For example, you might have a year's worth of data accumulating in a given worksheet, and want to print just one month's worth, or perhaps you want to print it all but in small chunks.

To print just a section of a worksheet, select the range of cells to print and choose File ➢ Print. Under Print What, choose Selection to print the selected cells. Excel ignores any Print Area that has been set and prints the selected range.

To print several worksheets with one command, select all the sheets you want to print and choose File ➢ Print, then choose the Selected Sheet(s) option under Print What (the worksheets must be within the same workbook). See Chapter 3 to learn how to select multiple sheets.

## Printing a Few Pages

By default, Excel prints all the pages in the workbook. However, you may want to print selected pages of a workbook. Follow these steps to print selected pages from a multiple-page printout. For example if you wanted to print only pages two and three of a workbook, you would do the following:

1. Choose File ➢ Print.
2. Under Page Range, select Page(s).
3. Type **2** in the From box, and type **3** in the To box.

> **NOTE**
> If you want to print a single page, type the page number in *both* the From and To boxes. If, for instance, you want to print just page 3, and you enter **3** in the From box but not in the To box, Excel will print everything from page 3 on.

## Printing Formulas

By default, a worksheet is printed as displayed onscreen. Although the workspace normally displays formatted values instead of the underlying formulas, you can print the underlying formulas instead (to document the internal logic of the worksheet, or for audit or inspection). Here's how to print formulas:

1. Display the formulas by choosing Tools ➢ Options, then selecting the View tab and checking the Formulas check box (or press Ctrl+`).

**2.** Print the worksheet.

| | A | B | C | D |
|---|---|---|---|---|
| 1 | Full Name | Last Name | Score 1 | Pass |
| 2 | Smith, Joe | =LEFT(A2,SEARCH(",",A2)-1) | 80 | =IF(C2<65,"No","Yes") |
| 3 | Jones, Mary | =LEFT(A3,SEARCH(",",A3)-1) | 92 | =IF(C3<65,"No","Yes") |
| 4 | Dunn, Sam | =LEFT(A4,SEARCH(",",A4)-1) | 64 | =IF(C4<65,"No","Yes") |
| 5 | Roberts, Jill | =LEFT(A5,SEARCH(",",A5)-1) | 76 | =IF(C5<65,"No","Yes") |
| 6 | | | | |
| 7 | | | | |
| 8 | | Average: | =AVERAGE(C2:C5) | |
| 9 | | | | |

Microsoft Excel - Book1

**TIP**

Make the formula printout more useful by printing row and column headings. Choose File ➤ Page Setup, then select the Sheet tab and check the Row And Column Headings option.

## Printing Ranges from Different Worksheets on the Same Page

Suppose you have four worksheets, each containing a small table that you want to print. Rather than printing four separate pages, each with a small table, you can trick Excel into printing all the tables on a single page. The trick is to place pictures of all four tables onto one worksheet:

**1.** Select the first table, then choose Edit ➤ Copy.

**2.** Activate the worksheet where you want to paste the tables and select a cell where you want to paste the picture. Hold down Shift and choose Edit ➤ Paste Picture Link. This pastes the copied cells as an object on the worksheet.

**3.** Repeat steps 1 and 2 for each table.

**4.** You can use the worksheet grid to align the pictures with each other—hold down Alt while dragging to snap each picture into a cell grid position.

**5.** Choose File ➤ Print Preview to check the layout of the worksheet before you print.

By default, the pictures are linked to the source cells. When you select a linked picture, the source cell reference is displayed on the formula bar. You can edit the source reference on the formula bar, or clear the reference entirely. When the reference is cleared, the picture becomes static. See Chapter 12 to learn more about linked pictures.

## MASTERING TROUBLESHOOTING

### Handling Common Printing Problems

Some common problems that occur during printing include improperly placed page breaks, printing in the wrong font, etc. Most of these problems can be fixed by using the File ➤ Page Setup and File ➤ Print dialog boxes. Sometimes your worksheets won't print at all. If your worksheets won't print, here are a few important details to check:

- There should be plenty of hard drive space (at least 5–6MB) available while in Windows. Windows creates temporary print files, and the space must exist on your hard disk.

- The printer should have at least 1MB of memory, and preferably 2MB or more for printouts that include a lot of graphics.

- Many print problems can be attributed to the printer driver. Make sure you have the most current driver for your printer. Sometimes, reinstalling a print driver can correct problems cause by a corrupted driver file.

This chapter has demonstrated Excel's versatility in printing. Excel's many printing options and features allow you to emphasize important data and trends and to produce impressive documents in a broad variety of printing formats.

The previous chapters have presented an introduction to the Excel workspace and to the basic techniques of spreadsheet manipulation, but before we go on to more advanced topics, the next chapter will show you a collection of useful skills that can enable you to master Excel more quickly.

# Chapter 7

## Enhancing Your Productivity

# Enhancing Your Productivity

T his chapter covers a wide variety of skills, techniques, and shortcuts that will enhance your overall productivity and allow you to get the most out of Excel. Hey, we confess—this grab-bag contains all kinds of miscellany that didn't quite find a proper home elsewhere in the book. Nonetheless, as the title of this chapter indicates, there are some truly useful skills to be learned here!

## Worksheet Skills

The following sections cover a number of skills that will help you to effectively enter and edit formulas and fix mistakes.

### Undoing Mistakes

Many things you do in Excel can be undone if you use the Edit ➢ Undo command. In fact, Excel 8 has expanded this feature, and now supports 16 levels of undo. This means, with several notable exceptions, you can undo your last 16 actions. You can undo typing, editing, inserting, deleting, and many other tasks where errors often occur. You need not undo several actions sequentially (i.e., by repeatedly clicking on the Undo button); Excel 8 has a drop-down list on both the Undo and Redo buttons that allows you to select multiple (consecutive) actions and undo them all with one click of the mouse

However, some things cannot be undone, either because of their inherent nature or because of memory restrictions. For example, you cannot undo a File ➢ Save command or File ➢ Close command, and you cannot undo deleting or inserting a worksheet, deleting a name, or setting a page break.

**NOTE** If you do not notice a serious mistake until it is too late to be undone, a measure of last resort is to close the file without saving it, and then reopen it.

## Repeating the Last Command Using Edit ➢ Repeat

You can use the Edit ➢ Repeat command to quickly repeat the last command that you issued. For example, you might format a cell, a process that takes several keystrokes. You could then repeat the procedure on other cells using Edit ➢ Repeat.

## Transposing Rows and Columns

Suppose you have data oriented in rows, and you want to reorient it in columns. Consider the worksheet shown here:

| | A | B | C | D | E | F | G | H | I |
|---|---|---|---|---|---|---|---|---|---|
| 1 | | | | | | | | | |
| 2 | | Q1 | Q2 | Q3 | Q4 | | | | |
| 3 | | 374 | 750 | 410 | 409 | | | | |
| 4 | | | | | | | | | |

After entering the constants onto a blank worksheet, follow these steps to transpose the data:

1. Select cells B2:E3.
2. Choose Edit ➢ Copy.
3. Select cell B5.

**4.** Choose Edit ➤ Paste Special. The Paste Special dialog box appears.

**5.** Place a check in the Transpose setting and click on OK. The data is transposed from rows into columns.

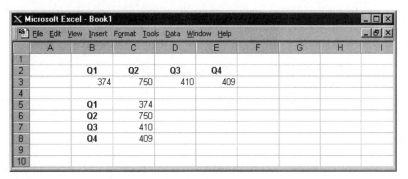

# Pasting Copied Cells Using ↵

Copied cells can be pasted by pressing ↵ rather than using a Paste command. Here's how:

**1.** Copy the desired cell(s).

**2.** Select the cell where you want to paste.

**3.** Press ↵.

You can also use ↵ to fill a range:

**1.** Copy a cell.

**2.** Select the range to fill.

**3.** Press ↵.

PART

II

Basic Skills

## Evaluating Expressions within a Formula

Often a formula refers to cells that are out of view. When entering, editing, or debugging this kind of formula, you can spend a lot of time scrolling the sheet to check the value of the cell(s) being referred to.

Instead of wasting your time this way, you can highlight the cell reference within the formula bar (or in the cell), and press F9. The cell reference is replaced with the cell value. This technique is not limited to cell references; you can highlight any expression, such as **(A1*B1)/C1**, and when you press F9, the entire expression is replaced with the calculated value.

After evaluating an expression, remember to cancel the changes (by pressing Esc). Otherwise, if you press ↵, the expression is replaced with the calculated value.

## Entering the Same Formula into Multiple Cells

When you are creating and formatting new worksheets, you often need to apply an equivalent formula to many different cells. The following procedure allows you to enter the same formula (or constant) into multiple cells:

1. Select the cells (selections can be noncontiguous).
2. Type the entry.
3. Press Ctrl+↵ instead of ↵.

## Displaying More Than One Line in a Cell

Suppose there are several words in a cell, and you want to display them on more than one line. There are two ways to tackle this problem. The first is by using formatting. Choose Format ➢ Cells ➢ Alignment and place a check in the Word Wrap selection. However, the Word Wrap feature does not give you control over where the line breaks will occur.

Here's another method: you can insert hard breaks by pressing Alt+↵ at the point where you want the line to break.

## Quickly Creating a Table of Numbers

When you design a new worksheet model, be it simple or complicated, you'll need to test the model periodically as you build it. Sometimes you don't have actual data available, and you use random test data instead. Test data can also be faster to enter than real data, which can save you a lot of time in the testing process. Here is a technique to help you quickly place a range of random numbers onto a worksheet:

1. Select a range of cells.
2. Enter the formula **=RAND( )**, then press Ctrl+↵. This places the random number function into the range of cells.

To keep the RAND functions from recalculating and returning new random values every time the worksheet recalculates, do the following:

1. Select the range of cells, then choose Edit ➤ Copy to copy them.
2. Choose Edit ➤ Paste Special, select Values, and click on OK.

This procedure copies the cell values and replaces the formula in each cell with its corresponding value.

The numbers generated by the RAND function are fractions. Here are two variations:

| | |
|---|---|
| =RAND( )*1000 | Creates random numbers between 1 and 1000 |
| =INT(RAND( )*1000) | Creates *whole* random numbers between 1 and 1000 |

## Entering Numbers with Automatic Decimal Places

Accountants typically prefer to enter numbers with two automatic decimal places. Excel can be configured for this type of data entry:

1. Choose Tools ➤ Options, then select the Edit tab (see Figure 7.1). Place a check in the Fixed Decimal box.
2. Enter the desired number of decimal places.
   See Chapter 5 for more information on custom number formatting.

## Moving the Active Cell Automatically After Pressing ↵

By default, the active cell selection moves down one cell after you press ↵. In some situations (entering a column of numbers, for instance) this behavior is very useful. At other times, however, it may be more convenient to have the active cell move up, to the right, to the left, or not at all after pressing ↵. Here's how to change this option:

1. Choose Tools ➤ Options, then select the Edit tab (shown in Figure 7.1).
2. Place a check in the Move Selection After Enter box, then select the desired direction from the Direction drop-down list.

PART

II

Basic Skills

*FIGURE 7.1*

*The Edit tab in the Options dialog box*

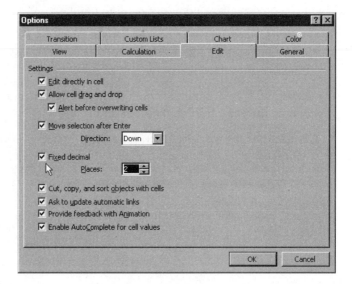

## Editing Multiple Worksheets Simultaneously

Workbooks often contain many similar worksheets. You can save a lot of time by editing and formatting these sheets simultaneously. When you edit multiple worksheets, the basic layout of each sheet should be identical; if you change a value in cell B5 for example, the value in cell B5 will be changed on all the selected worksheets. Select the group of worksheets that you want to edit. All input, editing, and formatting are applied to each sheet in the group.

One way to select multiple sheets is to hold down the Ctrl key while clicking on the worksheet tabs. See Chapter 2 for other ways to select groups of worksheets.

# Entering Numbers and Dates

Excel provides numerous formats for numbers and dates, and also allows you to create custom ones. Sometimes however, Excel will infer a format to apply. For example, if you enter the part number 9-2 into a cell (or the fraction 9/2), Excel will infer that you want to enter the date September 2nd, apply a date instead of a number format, and 2-Sep (or another preset date format) will appear in the cell. To override this tendency, simply enter a preceding space before the number. Here are some other cell formatting shortcuts:

**Entering a Number as Text** - Sometimes a number should be entered as text (for example, the zip code 07384, which will lose its leading zero if entered as a number). To enter a number as text, type an apostrophe first, such as: **'07384**.

**Formatting Numbers to Retain Leading Zeros** - At times you may want to enter numbers with leading zeros. Let's suppose you wanted to inventory all the parts stored in a given warehouse, and all parts were assigned a five-digit number (for example, inventory part number 00284). The solution is the custom number format **00000**, which retains leading zeros in a five-digit number. To apply a custom number format to selected cells, choose Format ➢ Cells and select the Number tab and the Custom Category. Type the format in the Type text box.

**Entering the Current Date and Current Time** - The following keystrokes will place the current date or time into a cell, or into the middle of a formula:

| | |
|---|---|
| Ctrl+; | (Ctrl+semicolon) Enters the current date |
| Ctrl+: | (Ctrl+colon) Enters the current time |

# Working with Workbooks, Worksheets, and Windows

The following sections will help you work more effectively with workbooks, worksheets, and windows.

## Activating a Worksheet: A Shortcut

When a workbook contains many worksheets, using the tab scrolling buttons, located in the lower-left corner of the Excel workspace, can be cumbersome. It might take several clicks to find the worksheet you are looking for. Here's a handy shortcut: right-click anywhere on the tab scrolling *buttons* (not the tabs)—a list of worksheets pops up, allowing you to select a sheet to activate.

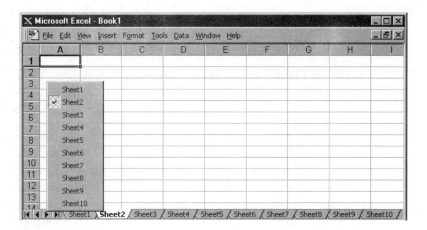

## Saving the Workspace

Perhaps there are several workbooks you use regularly, and the process of opening each of them and arranging them on the screen is time-consuming. When you choose File ➢ Save Workspace, Excel "remembers" the names of all open workbooks and how the windows are arranged. This information is saved in a workspace file with an .XLW extension. Later, when you open the workspace file using the File ➢ Open command, the individual workbooks are opened and arranged automatically.

**WARNING**

Workbooks are not physically stored inside the workspace file—only the workbook names and the way the windows are arranged are saved. Thus, saving a work-space file does not eliminate the need to save the workbooks (Excel will prompt you to save each workbook before closing the workspace).

## Creating Automatic File Backups

You can choose a setting that automatically creates a copy of your file prior to saving it. Choose File ➢ Save As, click on the Options button, then place a check in the Always Create Backup box.

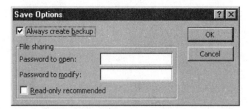

**WARNING**

Automatic backups are saved with an .XLK extension. If you have a workbook named FINANCE.XLS and a template named FINANCE.XLT in the same directory, and both files are set to create backups, Excel will not save both backups as Backup Of FINANCE.XLK. Excel will only create a backup of the first file saved.

This setting provides an extra safety net. For example, say you make mistakes editing a file named REPORT98, and the mistakes cannot be undone using Edit ➢ Undo. If the file is set to create backups, you can revert to an older copy of the file using one of these two methods:

- If the mistake was made *after* the file was last saved, choose File ➢ Open REPORT98. You will be prompted with the following message:

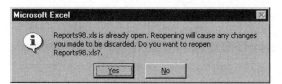

Click on Yes. All changes made since the file was last saved will be lost.
- If the mistake occurred *before* the file was last saved, close the file without saving it. Choose File ➢ Open Backup Of REPORT98.XLK. Since it is unwise to resume work on a file with an .XLK extension, immediately save the file under a different name.

**WARNING**

Automatic backups in no way take the place of "real" disk backups (backup copies on floppy disk or tape), which you should perform diligently.

# Speeding Up Data Entry with AutoFill

The AutoFill feature, explained in this section, is an important feature that can save you countless hours of data entry by expanding a series of numbers, days of the week, quarters, etc. from a given cell to adjacent ones. For example, you can enter a day of the week in a selected cell, and then use the Fill Handle to fill in the rest of the days of the week in adjacent cells.

PART

**II**

Basic Skills

## Using the Fill Handle

The Fill Handle provides a shortcut for automatically filling a range of cells with a series of values. The fill handle is the small black square located on the lower-right corner of the selected cell(s).

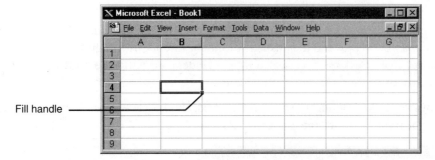

Fill handle

**NOTE**

If the fill handle does not appear on a worksheet, choose Tools ➢ Options, select the Edit tab, and make sure the Drag And Drop setting is checked.

Follow these steps to fill month names in a range of cells:

1. Enter **Jan** into cell A1.
2. Point to the fill handle with the mouse—the mouse pointer will become crosshairs.
3. Click and drag through cell L1, then release the mouse button. **Jan** through **Dec** will be filled into cells A1 through L1.

**TIP**

As you drag the fill handle, a pop-up note will appear showing you the cell entry for the last element in the range; therefore, if you want to enter the months in one year starting with January and ending with December, just drag the fill handle until the pop-up note says December—no need to count the cells.

## Establishing an AutoFill Trend

In the previous exercise, each AutoFill was based on a single starting value. If two or more values are selected as the starting range for an AutoFill, Excel tries to determine a trend and AutoFills accordingly.

## More Simple AutoFills

Some of the other types of data that can be filled are shown below:

If you want to see how the AutoFill feature works with this data, enter the values in the first column on a blank worksheet, select the cells, and then click and drag the fill handle to the right.

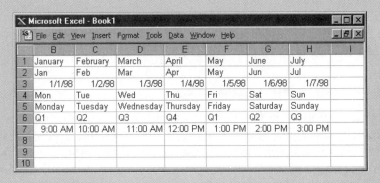

| | B | C | D | E | F | G | H | I |
|---|---|---|---|---|---|---|---|---|
| 1 | January | February | March | April | May | June | July | |
| 2 | Jan | Feb | Mar | Apr | May | Jun | Jul | |
| 3 | 1/1/98 | 1/2/98 | 1/3/98 | 1/4/98 | 1/5/98 | 1/6/98 | 1/7/98 | |
| 4 | Mon | Tue | Wed | Thu | Fri | Sat | Sun | |
| 5 | Monday | Tuesday | Wednesday | Thursday | Friday | Saturday | Sunday | |
| 6 | Q1 | Q2 | Q3 | Q4 | Q1 | Q2 | Q3 | |
| 7 | 9:00 AM | 10:00 AM | 11:00 AM | 12:00 PM | 1:00 PM | 2:00 PM | 3:00 PM | |
| 8 | | | | | | | | |
| 9 | | | | | | | | |
| 10 | | | | | | | | |

**1.** Enter the following values:

| | A | B | C | D | E | F | G | H |
|---|---|---|---|---|---|---|---|---|
| 1 | 2 | 4 | | | | | | |
| 2 | Jan | Apr | | | | | | |
| 3 | Mon | Wed | | | | | | |
| 4 | 1995 | 2000 | | | | | | |
| 5 | 1:00 | 1:15 | | | | | | |
| 6 | | | | | | | | |
| 7 | | | | | | | | |
| 8 | | | | | | | | |

**2.** Select cells A1 through B5.

**3.** Select the fill handle, and drag through cell H5. The result will be as shown:

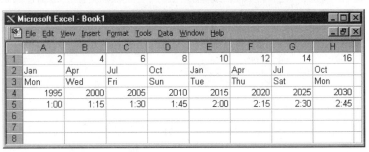

| | A | B | C | D | E | F | G | H |
|---|---|---|---|---|---|---|---|---|
| 1 | 2 | 4 | 6 | 8 | 10 | 12 | 14 | 16 |
| 2 | Jan | Apr | Jul | Oct | Jan | Apr | Jul | Oct |
| 3 | Mon | Wed | Fri | Sun | Tue | Thu | Sat | Mon |
| 4 | 1995 | 2000 | 2005 | 2010 | 2015 | 2020 | 2025 | 2030 |
| 5 | 1:00 | 1:15 | 1:30 | 1:45 | 2:00 | 2:15 | 2:30 | 2:45 |
| 6 | | | | | | | | |
| 7 | | | | | | | | |
| 8 | | | | | | | | |

Each series has been expanded according to the trend established in the first two columns.

# AutoFill Based on Adjacent Cells

You can AutoFill a range of cells adjacent to a range of data by double-clicking on the fill handle:

1. Type numbers into cells B1 through B4.
2. Enter **Q1** into cell A1.
3. Double-click on the fill handle on cell A1. Cells A1 through A4 will be filled with **Q1** through **Q4**.

# Using Custom AutoFills

The AutoFill feature lets you quickly fill a range of cells with months, dates, numbers, and certain text values. This section explains how to define custom lists that are recognized by AutoFill. For example, suppose your company operates in four regions (North, South, East, and West), and you are constantly typing the regions onto worksheets. A custom AutoFill will save you a lot of data-entry time.

## Defining Custom Lists

Follow these steps to define a custom list:

1. Enter the list into a (contiguous) range of cells, in a row or column.
2. Select the range of cells containing the list.
3. Choose Tools ➢ Options, then select the Custom Lists tab (see Figure 7.2).
4. Click on the Import button—the list will be displayed in the Custom List box. Click on OK.

**TIP**

You do not have to enter the list into cells first. The list can be typed into List Entries (pictured in Figure 7.2), though cells are generally easier to work with.

Custom lists are *not* stored in a specific workbook. Once a custom list is defined, it is available for use in all workbooks.

**FIGURE 7.2**

*Custom lists
can be filled
using AutoFills.*

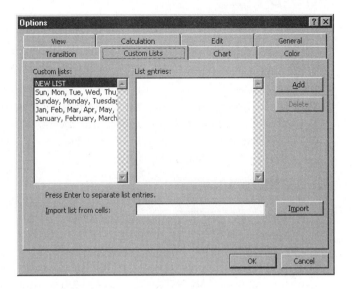

## Performing a Custom AutoFill

Performing an AutoFill with a custom list is no different from performing one with a
built-in list. Follow these steps:

**1.** Enter any one of the values from the list into a cell.

**2.** Grab the fill handle with the mouse, and drag it (in any direction).

For example, suppose you create a list consisting of the regions North, South,
East, and West. You can enter any of the four regions into a cell, and then perform
the AutoFill.

## Editing and Deleting the List

The Custom Lists dialog box, shown in Figure 7.3, can be used to edit or delete a custom list. Display the dialog box, select a list in the Custom Lists box, and then do one
of the following:

- To delete the list, click on the Delete button.
- To edit the list, edit the contents of the List Entries box.

**TIP**

You can also use custom lists to sort data in other than ascending or descending
order. See Chapter 17 to learn how.

PART

II

Basic Skills

## Using 3-D Fills

Use the Edit ➢ Fill ➢ Across Worksheets command to fill (copy) information across multiple sheets. Create a new workbook, and try this exercise:

1. On Sheet1, enter some information into B2:C3.
2. Select B2:C3.
3. With the Ctrl key held down, click on the sheet tabs to select the worksheets you want to fill—for this exercise, Sheet2 and Sheet4.
4. Release the Ctrl key, and then choose Edit ➢ Fill ➢ Across Worksheets—the following dialog box is displayed:

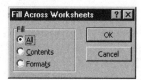

5. Select the information you want to fill—in this case All—and click on OK.

The information in Sheet1!B2:C3 is copied to the same range on Sheet2 and Sheet4.

**T I P**

To ungroup sheets, Shift+click the tab of the active worksheet.

# Customizing Command Bars

Prior to Excel 8, toolbars and menu bars were different animals entirely. Toolbars consisted of buttons and other icons. Menu bars, such as the default worksheet menu bar (containing the File, Edit, and other menus) consisted of text. Both objects served the same purpose—providing an interface for issuing commands. Now, they have converged into the same animal, often referred to as *command bars*. A command bar may contain buttons, text, and drop-down menus. This provides not only a more flexible interface, but also means you have less to learn—when learning to build command bars, one set of skills replaces what used to require two different skills. In the following discussion, the term a *command bar* is used to describe both menu bars and toolbars.

There are twenty-plus different command bars, in addition to the default Excel menu bar (which is a command bar in its own right). If they were all displayed, there would be very little screen real estate left for viewing worksheets. However, you can customize one or more command bars to contain the commands you use most often, and you can even build your own command bars.

# Adding Commands to a Built-In Command Bar

In order to customize a command bar, it must be visible. You can use the View ➤ Tool-bars command (or right-click on the Excel menu bar), which displays a list of command bars to choose from.

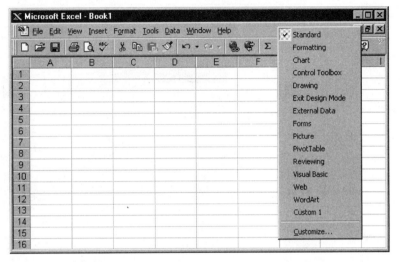

Another way to specify which command bar(s) to show is the Tools ➤ Customize ➤ Toolbars command, which displays the dialog box shown in Figure 7.3. Check those command bars you want to display, and uncheck the ones you wish to hide.

**FIGURE 7.3**

*The Tools ➤ Customize ➤ Toolbars command allows you to show and/or hide multiple command bars at a time.*

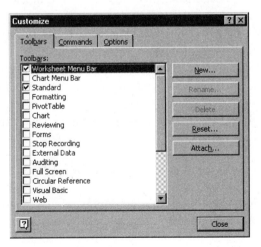

Suppose you want to add a command to the Standard command bar. Display the dialog box shown in Figure 7.3, and make sure that the Standard toolbar is checked (displayed). Next, click on the Commands tab on the top of the dialog box. This dialog box, shown in Figure 7.4, is where the fun occurs.

There are countless commands available. Many of them, such as File ➤ Save, will be familiar. Some of the commands are quite obscure. To see a description of a command, select it (by clicking on it once) and then click on the Description button. To add a command to a command bar, simply drag the command on top of an existing command bar, then drop it. To remove a command, display the Customize dialog box, and drag the button back onto the dialog box.

You can also customize your menu bar by selecting Tools ➤ Customize to display the dialog box, then either dragging a command directly to the menu bar, or by opening a menu and adding or removing commands by dragging them to and from the dialog box. In this mode, you can also tear whole menus off the menu bar and onto another command bar, or simply drop them on the workspace to hide them. To restore your menu bar, choose Tools ➤ Customize, select the Toolbars tab, check the Worksheet Menu Bar check box, and click on Reset.

## Creating a New Command Bar

You just learned how to add a command to a built-in command bar. To create a new custom command bar, click on the New button on the Customize/Toolbars dialog box shown earlier in Figure 7.3. After entering a name for the command bar (toolbar), a new empty command bar appears. Adding commands to it is no different than adding commands to a built-in command bar—simply drag and drop them from the Customize/ Commands dialog box shown earlier in Figure 7.4.

Three other buttons on the Customize/Toolbars dialog box (see Figure 7.3 again), pertain only to custom command bars. Each of these buttons requires that you first select a custom command bar (toolbar) in the Toolbars list:

**Rename:** Click on this button to rename the selected custom command bar. You will be prompted for a new name.

**Delete:** Click on this button to delete the selected custom command bar. You will be asked to confirm this action.

**Attach:** Use this feature to attach a custom command bar to a specific workbook. (The command bar then exists inside the Excel file.) Subsequently, when you distribute the workbook to other users, the custom command bar is displayed when the workbook is opened.

# Using Array Formulas

*Array formulas* are special formulas that operate on data arrays (matrices). They have been favored by Excel power users for years and are used to perform matrix arithmetic calculations. In the following discussion, you will learn how to enter array formulas and see a couple of examples where they might be applied.

You enter an array formula into a contiguous, rectangular range of cells, even if the range consists of just one cell. The following exercise uses a primitive example intended to show the mechanics of entering array formulas:

**1.** On a blank worksheet, select cells B2:C3.

**2.** Enter the following formula: **=1**.

**3.** Complete the formula by holding down Ctrl+Shift while pressing ↵.

The single array formula is entered into all four cells. On the formula bar, there are braces around the formula: *{=1}*, indicating that this formula has been *array-entered*. If you were to actually type the braces, you would enter a text constant, not an array formula.

Array formulas impose several restrictions:

• You cannot change an individual cell within an array formula. You must select the entire array, then change the formula.

• You cannot insert or delete cells within an array formula.

**TIP**

To select an entire array, select any cell within the array, choose Edit ➤ Go To, click on Special, choose the Current Array option, and click on OK. The keyboard shortcut is Ctrl+/.

- When you edit the formula, you must terminate the entry, using Ctrl+Shift+⏎, just as when the formula was first entered.
- An array formula is limited to approximately 1600 cells.

**NOTE**

Arrays can be expressed as constants. See Chapter 8 to learn about named constants.

## Putting Array Formulas to Work

Here are a few examples that illustrate the use of array formulas.

### Avoiding Interim Calculations

Consider the following worksheet:

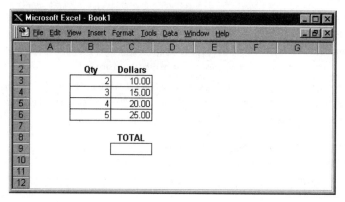

Suppose you want to know the total of Qty × Dollars. The traditional way to solve this problem is to add formulas to D3:D6 that multiply column B by column C, then add a formula that sums column D. The following array formula, entered into a single cell (C9), can perform the same calculation in one step:

```
{=SUM(B3:B6*C3:C6)}
```

Remember, the formula must be terminated with Ctrl+Shift+⏎—do not type the braces, Excel will insert them automatically as a visual indicator that this is an array formula.

## Performing Matrix Calculations

In the next example, an array formula entered into a range of cells performs a calculation on another range. On the following worksheet, suppose that in F5:G8 you want to display the word *High* where the population growth exceeds 3 percent.

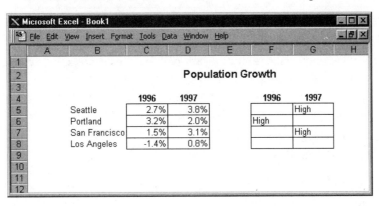

This exercise performs the calculation with one array formula. After entering the constants onto a blank worksheet, do the following:

**1.** Select F5:G8.

**2.** Type the following:

```
=IF(C5:D8>0.03,"High","")
```

**3.** Press Ctrl+Shift+↵.

The one formula calculates which cells in C5:D8 are greater than 3 percent.

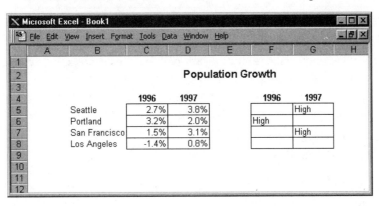

**TIP**

Using Ctrl+Shift+↵ to enter the formula will save you some time. It enters the formula into *all* the selected cells, otherwise you would have to copy the formula from the cell it was entered into the rest of the range.

## Using Array Functions

Matrix theory, or *linear algebra*, is used in a wide variety of applications in mathematics, science, business, and engineering. There are a number of worksheet functions that can be used to perform array calculations. The following exercise uses the MMULT function to perform matrix (array) multiplication.

On the following worksheet, suppose you want to find the product of matrix A (B2:C5) and matrix B (E2:G3) as shown below:

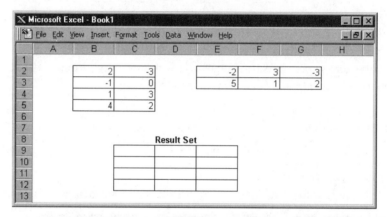

In order for the statement A × B = C to be true, the number of columns in A must equal the number of rows in B. The product of B × A is not defined because this is not the case. Unlike numbers, the multiplication of matrices is not always commutative.

The dimensions of resulting matrix C (Result Set) will be four rows by three columns in this case, reflecting the four rows of matrix A and the three columns of matrix B. After entering the constants onto a blank worksheet, do the following:

**1.** Select C9:E12.

**2.** Type the following:

    =MMULT(B2:C5,E2:G3)

**3.** Press Ctrl+Shift+↵.

The array formula calculates as follows:

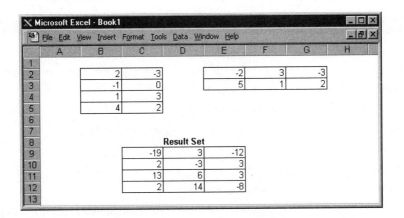

**NOTE**

Historically, a special syntax for array formulas has been used to conditionally sum a range of cells and to perform other types of summarization. By and large, these uses for array formulas have been obviated by pivot tables, which summarize, and by the worksheet functions SUMIF and COUNTIF (covered in Chapter 8), which perform conditional calculations.

Table 7.1 lists other worksheet functions that are applicable when performing array operations.

**TABLE 7.1:** FUNCTIONS USED IN ARRAY OPERATIONS

| Function | Comments |
| --- | --- |
| COLUMN | Returns array when argument is a range |
| COLUMNS | Argument must be array or range |
| GROWTH | Argument can be array or range—can return an array |
| HLOOKUP | Argument must be array or range |
| INDEX | Argument must be array or range—can return array |
| LINEST | Always returns array |
| LOGEST | Always returns array |
| LOOKUP | Argument must be array or range |
| MATCH | Argument must be array or range |
| MDETERM | Argument must be array |

PART

II

Basic Skills

**TABLE 7.1:** FUNCTIONS USED IN ARRAY OPERATIONS (CONTINUED)

| Function | Comments |
|---|---|
| MINVERSE | Always returns array |
| MMULT | Always returns array |
| ROW | Returns array when argument is a range |
| ROWS | Argument must be array or range |
| SUMPRODUCT | Argument can be array, range, or values |
| TRANSPOSE | Always returns array |
| TREND | Argument must be array or range—can return an array |
| VLOOKUP | Argument must be array or range |

Before we go on to Excel's drawing, charting, and database features, in the next few chapters we'll introduce you to more advanced Excel skills that will broaden your foundation in worksheet basics—skills like advanced naming techniques and worksheet functions, creating templates, and protecting your work.

# PART III

# Tapping Excel's Power

## LEARN TO:

- *Simplify formulas using names*

- *Define range names*

- *Use global and local names*

- *Use powerful worksheet functions*

- *Create and use workbook templates*

- *Validate data that is entered into cells*

- *Merge cells*

- *Protect and document your work*

- *Use the Auditing toolbar*

# Chapter

# 8

## The Power of Names

# The Power of Names

I n its simplest form, a name is a recognizable and memorable label for a cell or range of cells. For example, the name *Sales1998* is easier to recognize and remember than the cell reference B4:G18.

Using names is an important practice overlooked by many Excel users. If you are creating models of moderate complexity, or even simple models with linked workbooks, it is important that you learn basic naming techniques. In this chapter, you'll learn how to name cells, constants, and formulas, and how to use those names within formulas.

Natural language referencing, discussed in Chapter 4, has *partially* obviated the use of "real" names—but only partially. You may want to read about natural language referencing before proceeding with this chapter.

## Why Use Names?

There are a variety of important benefits to knowing how to use names. The use of names can add clarity, ensure reference integrity, improve functionality, and increase productivity.

## Clarity and Documentation

Later in this chapter, you will learn about important functionality provided by names. But, they are worthwhile just for the added clarity they provide. Spreadsheets are notorious for the "spaghetti code" syndrome (a tangled mess!), and names are an important tool for minimizing this problem:

- Names make formulas easier to understand and maintain. The formula =Sales-Cost makes a lot more sense than =C3-B3, especially six months later when you need to revise the worksheet.
- Organization-wide naming conventions let users of shared workbooks better understand formulas.

If you are developing models of even moderate complexity, names should be an integral part of your strategy.

## Integrity of External References

In a single workbook model, names provide clarity. But if you fail to use names, it's not the end of the world. When an insertion or deletion causes a value to move, formulas referring to the original cell will automatically adjust. (See Chapter 4 to learn about cell references.) But multiple-workbook models are an entirely different story: it is *vital* to use names, so that cross-workbook references will retain their integrity. Here's a real-world scenario to help illustrate why:

> Two workbooks, DETAIL and SUMMARY, are open. SUMMARY has an external reference pointing to cell A3 on DETAIL. You then close the dependent workbook, SUMMARY. Next, you add a new row at the top of DETAIL. The value in cell A3 is now in cell A4. When SUMMARY is reopened, the external reference incorrectly points to cell A3 instead of A4.

When a cell moves, its name moves with it. Had the external reference on SUMMARY been referring to cell DETAIL!A3 by name, there would be no adverse side-effect caused by the insertion.

## Improved Functionality

Names are more than cosmetic! The advanced naming techniques covered in this chapter provide important *functional* benefits:

- Named formulas serve to centralize logic (as explained later in this chapter), and can be used as powerful building blocks in complex formulas.

- Names can be used to create ranges that expand and contract depending on how many items are included (see the section "Using Named Formulas to Create Dynamic Named Ranges," later in this chapter).

## Increased General Productivity

Names can help to make you more productive by speeding up worksheet navigation, and by simplifying the entering of formulas:

- You can use the Name box drop-down at the left of the formula bar to rapidly go to a named range.
- Names reduce errors caused by typing incorrect cell references. But when a name is typed incorrectly in a formula, an error is displayed.
- Inserting names into formulas simplifies writing formulas.

# Valid and Invalid Names

There are several rules you must adhere to when defining names:

- A name can only contain the following characters: A–Z (upper- or lowercase allowed), 0–9, period, and underscore.
- The first character must be a letter or underscore.
- Names cannot be longer than 255 characters.
- A name cannot be the same as a cell reference, such as B3 or Y1998.

Here are some examples of valid and invalid names:

| Valid Names | Invalid Names (reason) |
|---|---|
| Last.Year.Sales | 97.Sales (starts with a number) |
| Profit_1997 | Gross Profit (contains a space) |
| UnitPrice | A1 (same as a cell reference) |
| Labor | R2C2 (same as a cell reference) |

## Names: Case-Retentive, but Not Case-Sensitive

Names are *not* case-sensitive. If you define the name SALES, then define the name Sales, the second name will replace the first. However, names *are* case-retentive. When a name is used in a formula, it will automatically revert to the same case used when the name was defined. If a name is defined as GrossProfit, and you enter the formula =grossprofit, the formula will automatically change to =GrossProfit when you press ↵.

**TIP**

There is a benefit to always using mixed case when entering names. Formulas are typically entered in all upper- or all lowercase. Since names revert to their original case, you get immediate visual feedback if you misspell a name—it will not revert to mixed case.

# Naming Cells

There are several ways to name cells: using the Name box, using the Define Name dialog box, and using the Create Names dialog box.

## Using the Name Box

The quickest and easiest way to name cells is with the Name box, found on the left part of the formula bar. To name a cell from the Name box, do the following:

**1.** Select the cell(s) you want to name.

**2.** Click in the Name box itself (not on the drop-down arrow):

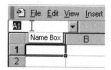

**3.** Type the name, then press ↵.

**WARNING**

The Name box won't let you accidentally overwrite a previously used cell name (the named cell will be selected), but it *will* let you overwrite a named constant or formula without warning.

## Using the Define Name Dialog Box

The Define Name dialog box lets you name cells as well as constants and formulas, which you'll learn more about later in the chapter. Here's how you name a range:

**1.** Select the cell(s) you want to name.

**2.** Choose Insert ➤ Name ➤ Define (or press Ctrl+F3) to display the Define Name dialog box shown in Figure 8.1.

**FIGURE 8.1**

*The Define Name dialog box is the only place where you can define any type of name— named ranges, named constants, named formulas, global names, and local names.*

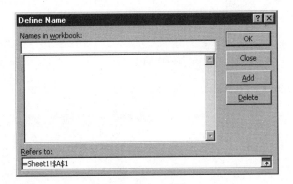

**3.** Type a valid name in the Names In Workbook text box.

> **TIP**
> Excel will suggest a name if the active cell or an adjacent cell contains text, and the text is not already used as a name.

**4.** The Refers To entry defaults to the current selection. (If you want to name a range other than the current selection, you can enter a new cell reference—this is a range edit which can be filled in by pointing and clicking on the worksheet, or by using the *Collapse Dialog Box* button found at the right end of the text box.)

**5.** Click on OK to finish (or click on Add to accept the name without closing the Define Name dialog box).

> **WARNING**
> The Define Name dialog box will let you overwrite previously used names without warning, though existing names are displayed in the Names In Workbook list and can be scanned to see if the name is in use.

## Using the Create Names Dialog Box

The Create Names dialog box is a source of considerable confusion for many users, because the difference between this dialog box and the Define Name dialog box is somewhat obscure. In terms of pure functionality, the Define Name dialog box lets you do a number of things which you simply can't do using the Create Name dialog box (which you will read about later in this chapter). However, the Create Name dialog box provides two key advantages over the Define Name dialog box:

PART

**III**

Tapping Excel's Power

- You are warned if you attempt to overwrite an existing name.
- You can name many cells with one command.

Choose Insert ➢ Name ➢ Create (or press Ctrl+Shift+F3) to display the Create Names dialog box pictured in Figure 8.2.

**FIGURE 8.2**

*The Create Names dialog box*

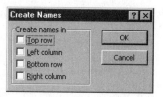

The Create Names dialog box lets you name cells based upon the contents of adjacent cells. For instance, suppose cell A1 contains *East,* and cell A2 contains *West.* Cells B1 and B2 can both be named, in one step, using the text in A1 and A2 as the names for cells B1 and B2. The following exercise illustrates the concept. Using one command, you'll create three names.

**1.** On a blank worksheet, enter the values pictured below.

|   | A | B | C | D |
|---|---|---|---|---|
| 1 | Name1 | | | |
| 2 | Name2 | | | |
| 3 | Name3 | | | |
| 4 | | | | |
| 5 | | | | |
| 6 | | | | |

**2.** Select cells A1 through B3, then choose Insert ➢ Name ➢ Create. The Left Column setting should be checked.

**3.** Click on OK.

Cells B1, B2, and B3 have *each* been named according to the text in cells A1 through A3. Cell B1 is named *Name1*, cell B2 is named *Name2*, and cell B3 is named *Name3*. Now, even if you clear the values in A1:A3, cells B1, B2, and B3 each retain their name. Use the Name box to test your newly created names—choose a name from the list, and the named range is selected.

If a name is already used, the following warning is displayed:

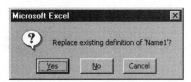

Click on Yes to replace the old name, click on No to leave the old name alone, or click on Cancel to cancel the entire operation.

## Naming Noncontiguous Cells

A named range does not have to be contiguous. You can name noncontiguous ranges using the Define Name dialog box or the Name box (you can't use the Create Names dialog box). It's simple: select two or more noncontiguous ranges (select a range, then hold down Ctrl while selecting another). Then use the Define Name dialog box or the Name box in the same manner as when you name a simple range.

If you are attempting to name a range consisting of many noncontiguous sections, the Refers To entry can become quite long. Be careful, because Refers To is limited to 255 characters.

## Deleting Names

Follow these steps to delete a name, regardless of the type of name (cell, constant, or formula):

1. Choose Insert ➢ Name ➢ Define to display the Define Name dialog box shown earlier in Figure 8.1.
2. Select the name you want to delete in the Names In Workbook list.
3. Click on the Delete button.

**WARNING**
Any cell referring to a deleted name will display the #NAME? error, since the name will no longer be valid.

**PART**

**III**

Tapping Excel's Power

# Referencing Named Cells

Very simply, a named cell or range of cells is an *absolute cell address*. The following formulas assume that cell $A$1 is named *Profit* and cells $B$1:$B$3 are named *Detail*.

| | |
|---|---|
| **=Profit** | Equal to cell A1 |
| **=Profit*2** | Multiply A1 by 2 |
| **=SUM(Detail)** | Sum cells B1:B3 |
| **=AVERAGE(Detail)** | Average cells B1:B3 |
| **=Profit+SUM(Detail)** | Add A1 to the sum of B1:B3 |

As in natural language formulas, referring to cells by name in formulas is just a matter of using the cell name in place of the cell address in your formulas.

## Pasting Names into Formulas

While entering or editing a formula, you can paste names into the formula rather than typing them. This is a helpful procedure if you forget the name, don't want to misspell it, or are too lazy to type the name. The following exercise illustrates how:

1. Name cell A1 **GrossProfit** and enter **100** into it.
2. Select cell B1. Type an equal sign to begin the formula.
3. Choose Insert ➢ Name ➢ Paste, pick **GrossProfit** from the Paste Name list, and click on OK. The name is inserted into the formula.
4. Type **\*2** (to multiply by 2), then press ↵. Cell B1 will equal 200.

**NOTE**

The Name box only lists named cells and named ranges. To paste in a name that refers to a formula or constant, use the Insert ➢ Name ➢ Paste command.

# Applying Names After the Fact

In the short run, it is easier to construct formulas by clicking on cells, but this places cell addresses in your formulas. Using names in formulas requires that the names be defined before they are used. Here is an example of how to work quick and dirty with cell references, and then quickly clean up later using the Apply Names dialog box:

1. On a blank worksheet, enter the formula **=A1** into cells A2, A3, and A4.

**2.** Name cell A1 **TestApply**.

**3.** Choose Insert ➤ Name ➤ Apply; the Apply Names dialog box (Figure 8.3) is displayed.

**FIGURE 8.3**

*The Apply
Names
dialog box*

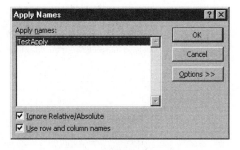

**4.** Make sure **TestApply** is selected in the Apply Names dialog box list. Click on OK.

**5.** Look at the formulas in cells A2, A3, and A4—they now refer to cell A1 by name.

Make certain that when you apply names to a formula, you select all names in the Apply Names dialog box that you want to appear in the formula.

The following sections describe the other settings on the Apply Names dialog box.

## The Ignore Relative/Absolute Check Box

The Ignore Relative/Absolute check box toggles between two useful settings:

- If checked (the default setting), it will replace the reference with a name, regardless of whether the reference is relative, absolute, or mixed.

- If unchecked, it will only replace absolute references with absolute names, relative references with relative names, and mixed references with mixed names.

## The Use Row And Column Names Check Box

The Use Row And Column Names option uses intersection names (covered above) if an actual cell name does not exist. For example, if an unnamed cell sits at the intersection of a column named *January* and a row named *Profits*, this setting allows Excel to apply the name *January Profits*.

PART

**III**

Tapping Excel's Power

## Advanced Options

Click on the Options button to expand the dialog box to include the options pictured in Figure 8.4. The following sections discuss these settings.

*Advanced Apply Names options appear at the bottom of the dialog box.*

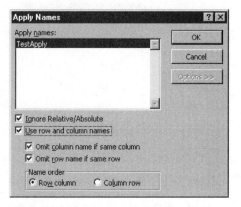

**Omit Column Name If Same Column** - This setting causes formulas that reside in the same column as a named range to omit that name from the adjusted formula. Here's an example: in the worksheet pictured here, the columns and rows are named ranges. Profit is equal to Revenue less Expenses.

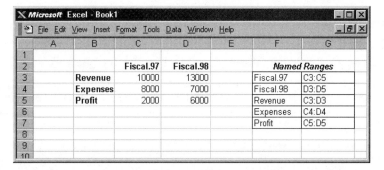

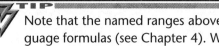

Note that the named ranges above are also labels that can be used in natural language formulas (see Chapter 4). When you create named ranges that already have labels, the Create Name dialog box will display (or suggest) the label as the name. Names must be defined for the Apply Names dialog box to be available.

Suppose you set up the profit formulas quickly, using point-and-click cell references (e.g., the formula in C5 is =C3-C4), and you want to replace the cell references with cell names. If you apply names with the Omit Column Name If Same Column setting checked (default), the formula in cell C5 will be =Revenue-Expenses. If you clear the setting and apply names, the formula in cell C5 will be =Fiscal.97 Revenue–Fiscal.97 Expenses.

**Omit Row Name If Same Row** - This is the same as the previous setting, but pertains to rows instead of columns. It causes formulas which reside in the same row as a named range to omit that name from the adjusted formula.

**Name Order** - The Name Order settings determine the name order for an intersection name: row-column or column-row.

# Naming Constants

So far, the names used in this chapter have all been named cells. You can also name *constants*. The name refers to a constant value, such as *25*, *10%*, or *East*, rather than a range. Probably the most common reason for naming a constant is to discourage users from inadvertently changing values.

Suppose, for instance, that a commission rate of 12% is to be used throughout a sheet. Knowing that the commission rate may change, you don't want to embed the 12% constant in formulas throughout the sheet. If the 12% is stored in a cell, the user is invited to change it. A named constant provides the flexibility of a named cell, with some added security.

## Defining a Named Constant

To name a constant, follow these steps:

1. Choose Insert ➢ Name ➢ Define. The Define Name dialog box appears.
2. Enter the name in the Names In Workbook text box.
3. In the Refers To text box, type in a constant value. The constant can be a number, text, logical (TRUE/FALSE), or even an array.

**4.** Click on OK to add the name and close the dialog box, or click on Add to add the name and keep the dialog box.

**TIP**

When you define a named constant, Excel automatically places an equal sign (and quotation marks surrounding text constants), in the Refers To text box. Remember, you do not have to type the equal sign or quotation marks—let Excel do it for you.

**MASTERING TROUBLESHOOTING**

### Fixing #NAME? Errors

When a formula has a nonexistent value in the Refers To text box, the #NAME? error message appears in the cell. If this happens, check that all of these things are true:

- Name(s) in the formula are typed correctly.

- Function name(s) in the formula are typed correctly.

- The name is not enclosed in quotes.

**NOTE**

The remainder of this chapter deals with advanced naming techniques. You may want to revisit this section after becoming comfortable with the topics covered earlier in the chapter. You will also need to understand external references (covered in Chapter 4).

## Names That Refer to Cells on Other Worksheets

A name can refer to cells on external workbooks. This technique is critically important when developing templates (see Chapter 10), and in worksheet development in general. Suppose that the names below are defined in Book1:

| Name | Refers to: | Comments |
|------|-----------|----------|
| Sales | =[STUDY.XLS]Sheet1!A1:A3 | Refer by cell address |
| Profit_1 | =[DEPT1.XLS]Sheet1!Profit | Refer by cell name |
| YTD.Table | =SUM([SALES.XLS]Sheet1!A1:A3) | Refer to range |

Formulas in Book1 can now use the names *Sales*, *Profit_1*, and *YTD.Table* as if the ranges were actually in Book1, without concern for the book name prefix. The following formulas are valid:

**=SUM(Sales)**

**=ROWS(Sales)**

**=INDEX(Sales)**

**=Profit_1*2**

## Applying Names to External References

To apply a name to an external reference, follow these steps:

1. Choose Insert ➢ Name ➢ Define.
2. Type in the name.
3. In the Refers To text box, type **=[BOOK1.XLS]Sheet1!*MyCell,*** where BOOK1 is the name of the external workbook and MyCell is the cell reference, or in this case the cell name.

## Saving External Link Values

Any time you create names referring to other workbooks, you should be aware of the Save External Link Values setting, which you access by choosing Tools ➢ Options and then clicking on the Calculation tab. Suppose you have a workbook (DEPENDENT) with formulas referring to ranges in another workbook (SOURCE). When this setting is checked for DEPENDENT, the referenced values in SOURCE are saved inside DEPENDENT, though these values are not visible. This allows the formulas in DEPENDENT to work without having to refresh the link. Consider the following scenario:

> The name YTD.Sales, created in Book1, refers to the external range SALES98.XLS!Database, which is 5000 rows by 20 columns. The Tools ➢ Options ➢ Calculation Save External Link Values setting is checked by default. This causes the values from SALES98.XLS!Database to be stored, invisibly, in Book1. When Book1 is saved, a huge workbook has been created because the external link values were saved.

Uncheck the Save External Link Values setting if the external values do not need to be saved with the sheet. This will often be the case.

PART

III

Tapping Excel's Power

## Naming External References

You already know how to name a range of cells, but you may not know that a name can refer to a range of cells in a different workbook. These named external references are important constructs if you are doing serious Excel modeling. A worksheet might have many references to a range in an external workbook. Such references are difficult to work with, as they include the name of the source workbook. And, if the source workbook is closed, they include the full path as part of the reference. By naming the external range, your formulas become easier to enter, edit, and read.

Naming an external range is not much different than a "normal" named range. Just include the workbook name in the Refers To text box in the Define Name dialog box. You can do this by typing the reference or by pointing and clicking on the external workbook. Suppose that you want to create a name in workbook REPORT.XLS that refers to a range in workbook STUDY.XLS, and that both workbooks are open. Activate REPORT.XLS, then choose Insert ➤ Name ➤ Define. Type a name, then place the cursor in the Refers To text box. Use the Window menu to activate book STUDY.XLS.

Select the range with the mouse, then click on OK.

Now, instead of entering a formula like this:

```
=SUM([STUDY.XLS!Sheet1]!$A$
1:$A$3
```

you can enter this:

```
=SUM(Sales)
```

# Centralizing Logic Using Named Formulas

By now you should be accustomed to naming cells and constants. If you observe the syntax of defined names using the Define Name dialog box, you will notice that references for *all* names begin with an equal sign in the Refers To text box. *All names are essentially named formulas*—some more complex than others. Almost any formula that can be entered into a cell can also be defined as a *named formula*.

One important way that named formulas are used is to centralize logic—one complex named formula can vastly simplify the formulas residing in multiple cells. Consider the following problem:

You've used a complex formula to calculate the rate of return for an investment, and this same formula is used in hundreds of cells on a sheet (the cells are not contiguous). What do you do if the formula needs to be changed? You can do a find/replace, but there are other similar formulas that you must be careful not to overwrite.

You can solve this problem by defining a single named formula, and then referring to this formula by name. Because the Refers To text box in the Define Name dialog box is awkward to work with, it is easier to name formulas by first entering the formula into a cell, and then copying it into the Define Name dialog box. The following exercise illustrates how to do this:

**1.** Enter the following constants onto a blank worksheet:

| | A | B | C | D | E | F |
|---|---|---|---|---|---|---|
| 1 | | | | | | |
| 2 | | Item | Qty | Price | Extension | |
| 3 | | Widgets | 7 | 22.95 | | |
| 4 | | Gadgets | 15 | 19.55 | | |
| 5 | | Gizmos | 11 | 8.98 | | |
| 6 | | | | | | |
| 7 | | | | | | |

*Microsoft Excel - Book1*
File Edit View Insert Format Tools Data Window Help

**2.** Enter the formula **=C3*D3** into cell E3.
**3.** Select the formula (on the formula bar, or using in-cell formula editing), then choose Edit ➢ Copy.
**4.** Press Esc (since you are not editing E3, but just copying its formula).
**5.** Choose Insert ➢ Name ➢ Define to display the Define Name dialog box.
**6.** Enter the name **Extension** (if Excel has not already entered it for you).
**7.** Clear the entry in the Refers To text box.
**8.** Choose Edit ➢ Paste to paste in the formula.
**9.** Click on OK.

At this point, the named formula Extension has been defined, but has not yet been used:

**10.** Select cells E3:E5.
**11.** Type **=Extension**, then press Ctrl+↵ to place the formula in all three cells.

Select cell E3, display the Define Name dialog box, and select the name Extension. It will refer to =Sheet1!C3*Sheet1!D3. Close the dialog box, select E4, and look at the definition of Extension again. It will refer to =Sheet1!C4*Sheet1!D4. The definition depends on the active cell because it contains relative references.

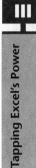

### The CellAbove Trick

Suppose there are numbers in cells A1:A10, and the formula =SUM(A1:A10) in cell A11. You need to add another value to the list which must be included in the SUM formula. If you insert a row in the middle of the column, the SUM range expands automatically. But more commonly you will need to add the new value to the bottom of the list—when you insert at row 11, the formula (now in row 12) must be edited to include row 11. One way around this problem is to create a named formula, using a *relative reference*, that refers to the cell one above. In the following example, cell A2 is the active cell:

1. Choose Insert ➤ Name ➤ Define and enter **CellAbove** as the cell name.
2. In the Refers To text box, enter =A1, then click on OK.
3. Now, you can enter the formula =CellAbove into any cell on the sheet (except row one) and it will refer to the cell one row up.

Back to the SUM problem. The formula will read =SUM(A1:CellAbove), which in lay terms means *sum cells A1 through the cell one cell above the formula*. You can insert rows immediately above the SUM formula, and the relative reference in the named formula causes the SUM to expand automatically.

# Creating Dynamic Named Ranges with Named Formulas

*Dynamic named ranges* are ranges that automatically change based upon certain conditions, such as a column that has a variable number of entries. There is no formal dynamic named range construct; they are simply named formulas that refer to a range of cells. Consider the following problem:

> A range of cells is named *Portfolio_Details*. Various complex formulas and charts refer to the named range Portfolio_Details for the purpose of analyzing the portfolio. The need to analyze two portfolios emerges. Using traditional methods, a second set of complex formulas and charts can be created that refer to the second portfolio range. Since the model requires modification to accommodate a second portfolio, a design that will easily accommodate a third and fourth portfolio is highly desirable.

You can solve the problem using a dynamic named range—with no change to the complex formulas that refer to Portfolio_Details. User input will determine which portfolio is being analyzed.

## Analysis Using a Dynamic Named Range

In the following exercise, you'll use a dynamic named range as a mechanism for analyzing one of two different portfolios:

**1.** Enter the following onto a blank worksheet:

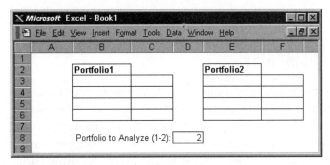

**2.** Name cells B2:C6 **Portfolio1**.

**3.** Name cell E2:F6 **Portfolio2**.

**4.** Name cell D8 **Choice**. (User input into this cell determines which portfolio is analyzed.)

**5.** Choose Insert ➢ Name ➢ Define.

**6.** Enter **Portfolio_Details** as the name.

**7.** Enter the following formula in the Refers To text box:

```
=CHOOSE(Choice,Portfolio1,Portfolio2)
```

**8.** Click on OK.

Now test the dynamic name:

**9.** Enter **1** into cell Choice.

**10.** Choose Edit ➢ Go To. Type the name **Portfolio_Details** in the Reference text box and click on OK. The range Portfolio1 will be selected.

**11.** Enter **2** into cell Choice, then repeat step 10.

Suppose that, in the future, a third portfolio is added. All you need to do is add the portfolio data, name it **Portfolio3**, then change the definition of Portfolio_Details to refer to

```
=CHOOSE(Choice,Portfolio1,Portfolio2,Portfolio3)
```

> **NOTE**
>
> Excel will not display dynamic named ranges in the Go To dialog box or in the Name box drop-down.

PART

**III**

Tapping Excel's Power

In the example above, formulas and charts that use the name Portfolio_Details as a cell reference are dynamic and dependent on user input in the cell named *Choice.* For example, if you wanted to sum a group of numbers in the right-hand column of Portfolio_Details you could use the INDEX function (See Chapter 9 ) to write the following formula:

```
=SUM(OFFSET(Portfolio_Details,1,1,4,1))
```

# Named Array Constants

For advanced users, array constants are useful, though awkward to create. An array constant is similar to a range of cells, but it does not reside in rows and columns and thus is not easily visible. One use of array constants is to store tables of data out of view from the user of the worksheet. As with other named constants, array constants are defined using the Insert ➤ Name ➤ Define command, which displays the Define Name dialog box pictured in Figure 8.1 (above).

An array constant stores multiple values which, like cells, are oriented in rows and columns. But since the array does not reside in the worksheet grid, the rows and columns are indicated by the use of two separators:

**Comma:** Denotes new column

**Semicolon:** Denotes new row

In the following examples, the boldfaced entries indicate what would be typed into the Refers To text box of the Define Name dialog box to create the arrays that follow:

| | |
|---|---|
| `={2;4;6;8}` | 4 rows, 1 column of numbers |
| `={"East",12,100;"West",15,135}` | 2 rows, 3 columns of text and numbers |
| `={"A",TRUE,99.99}` | 1 row, 3 columns—text, logical, and number |

Accessing the data in an array constant is similar to accessing data stored in cells. The INDEX function, discussed in Chapter 9, can be used to refer to an individual data element. The ROWS functions will return the number of rows in the array, and the COLUMNS function will return the number of columns.

**TIP**

Application developers often store information in array constants, but the process of building the arrays is controlled programmatically. This allows the use of the construct, without the tedium of defining the names. Also, since names that are defined programmatically can be hidden, another layer of security can be achieved.

# Applying Names at the Workbook or Worksheet Level

Names can be *global* to the workbook, or can be *local* to a specific worksheet. This is a distinction that is very important to understand in order to use names effectively.

## Global Naming

By default, all names are global to the workbook. This means that when cell B2, on Sheet1 in Book1, is named *Total*, the implications are as follows:

- The name *Total* can be referred to from any worksheet (in the same workbook) without having to specify the sheet name prefix—Sheet2 can contain the formula =Total.
- Regardless of which sheet is active, the name will appear in the Name box drop-down.
- If a sheet from a different workbook with the global name Total is moved or copied to Book1, the original name on Sheet1 takes precedence—the name defined on the just-copied sheet is changed to a local name.

## Local Naming

A local name is defined by including the sheet name as part of the name using the Define Name dialog box (see Figure 8.1, above), or the Name box. To create a local name Total on Sheet1, follow these steps:

1. Activate Sheet1.
2. Select cell(s) you want to name.
3. Enter the name **Sheet1!Total** in the Name box—the sheet name is included as part of the name. After the local name is defined, it will appear in the Name box without the prefix Sheet1!, and it will only appear in the Sheet1 Name box (it will not appear in the Name boxes of any other sheets).

**NOTE**

The Name box cannot be used to name constants or formulas, only cells, ranges, and objects. Also, the only names that will appear in the Name box are global cell and range names, and local cell and range names for the active worksheet.

The implications of the local name Total, defined on Sheet1, are as follows:

- Total can be referred to from any worksheet, but the sheet name prefix must be included (e.g., Sheet2 can contain the formula =Sheet1!Total).
- The formula =Total entered onto Sheet2 will return a #NAME? error.
- Total can be defined on other worksheets, and Sheet1!Total will *not* be overwritten (even if the new definition for Total is global).
- If Total is redefined on Sheet1 with the sheet name prefix omitted (as if it were a global name), it will still be a local name.

**NOTE**

The explanations of global and local names above use named cells to illustrate the concept. The same rules apply for all other worksheet names, including named formulas and named constants.

### A Shortcut for Defining Local Names

Since the Create Name dialog box does not have an option for creating local names, there is no obvious way to quickly create local names without going through the painstaking process of defining them one at a time using the Define Name dialog box.

Suppose you have a worksheet with monthly data for January, and you have used lots of names on the sheet. Now it's February, and you want to create another worksheet in the same workbook, using the same names that were used on the January sheet. (And in subsequent months, the process must be repeated.)

You would first need to make a copy of sheet January in the same workbook (hold down Ctrl while you drag and drop the January sheet tab to a new position). A new worksheet will be created – rename the sheet **February**. The new February worksheet will contain the same names as the January sheet, but they will be local to the February sheet.

## Naming Conventions

Once you start to use names, you're apt to use them a lot. A complex model might contain hundreds of names, and the list of names in the Define Name dialog box can become unwieldy. However, you can use special prefixes and/or suffixes to help document and manage the names. The naming conventions in the following examples are not intended to be used verbatim, but rather to provide ideas on how to create meaningful conventions that work for you.

## Conventions Based on Name Type

The naming conventions listed in Table 8.1 are based on the type of name created:

**TABLE 8.1:** CONVENTIONS BASED ON TYPE OF NAME

| Prefix | Meaning |
| --- | --- |
| NF | Named formula |
| AC | Array constant |
| ER | External reference |
| DB | Database table |
| CR | Calculated (dynamic) range |

## Conventions Specific to a Model

Naming conventions can also be specific to a worksheet model, as in the following examples:

- Several ranges on one sheet that are printed as separate reports—Use Report as a prefix, as in Report_Summary and Report_Detail.
- When a worksheet contains data for multiple regions, use Region as a prefix, as in Region_East and Region_West.
- For a worksheet used to track investments, use a prefix identifying type of investment, as in Stock.IBM, Stock.ATT, Bonds.Muni, Bonds.TB.

PART

III

Tapping Excel's Power

## Seeing All Names at Once

A complex workbook might contain hundreds of names. The Define Name dialog box only lets you view the definition for one name at a time. The Insert ➢ Name ➢ Paste command displays the following dialog box:

Click on the Paste List button to paste all of the definitions onto the active worksheet, starting at the active cell. All global names are pasted, as are all local names that are defined on the active worksheet. Local names defined on worksheets other than the active sheet are not pasted.

**WARNING**

Since the names are pasted starting at the active cell, you must be careful not to overwrite data on the worksheet. One way to avoid this pitfall is to add a new worksheet to the workbook, then paste the names into the new worksheet. Be aware, however, that the pasted list will contain all global names in the workbook, and local names only for the active worksheet.

In this chapter, you have seen how names can significantly increase your ability to use Excel to its fullest. You've learned that names can refer to individual cells, ranges of cells, formulas, or constants. You've also discovered how names can be used in formulas and how to create dynamic named ranges.

In the next chapter, you will learn some essential worksheet functions that, when used in conjunction with naming techniques, will further enhance your understanding of Excel's potential and your mastery of it.

# Chapter

# 9

# FEATURING

# Essential Worksheet Functions

There are hundreds of built-in Excel functions, and it is a given that most users will use the ones needed for basic worksheet arithmetic, such as SUM. (See Chapter 4 for more on basic worksheet functions.) But as you start to create more powerful models, the inherently dry nature of Excel's function reference falls short—it fails to point out which functions are *essential* for serious worksheet modeling and data analysis.

What makes a particular function essential? Even the most obscure functions are at times essential when required to solve a specific problem. But the functions covered in this chapter are important generic tools. A case in point is the OFFSET function—the thought of doing even simple modeling and analysis without OFFSET is inconceivable, yet few Excel users are even *aware* of it.

This chapter covers the following worksheet functions:

| | |
|---|---|
| Totals and Subtotals | SUMIF, SUBTOTAL |
| Lookup and Reference | VLOOKUP, MATCH, INDEX, OFFSET, INDIRECT, ROW, ROWS, COLUMN, COLUMNS |
| Counting | COUNT, COUNTA, COUNTBLANK, COUNTIF |

| Text | LEN, LEFT, RIGHT, MID, SEARCH, FIND |
|---|---|
| Date and Time | TODAY, NOW, DATE, DAY, HOUR, MINUTE, MONTH, WEEKDAY, YEAR |

# Calculating Totals and Subtotals

The SUMIF and SUBTOTAL functions are very important features in Excel, and serve to streamline two very common calculations: *conditional totals* and *nested subtotals*. Conditional summation is important to filter data that meets certain criteria, and nested subtotals can give intermediate values (not just sums) that can exist on the worksheet, yet be ignored in final calculation.

## Calculating Sums Conditionally with SUMIF

In some previous versions of Excel, there were two ways to conditionally calculate a sum of certain of the cells within a range (based on specified criteria):

- Array formulas—powerful but inordinately complex
- Criteria ranges combined with the DSUM function—again, powerful but tedious to construct

Array formulas and criteria ranges are still important functions, but SUMIF provides simple solutions for common conditional summing problems.

### SUMIF Syntax

The following options are used with SUMIF:

```
SUMIF(CheckRange,Criteria,SumRange)
```

**CheckRange:** A range of cells being compared against the *Criteria*

**Criteria:** An expression specifying which cells in *CheckRange* meet the evaluation criteria

**SumRange:** A range of cells being summed—only cells that correspond to qualifying CheckRange cells are summed

## SUMIF in Action

The formulas given below apply to the worksheet shown here:

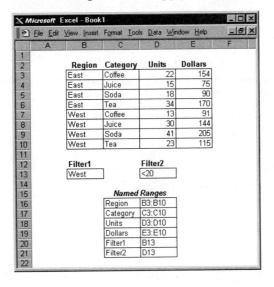

=SUMIF(C3:C10,"Soda",E3:E10)

Returns *295*—total dollars for category Soda.

=SUMIF(Category,"<>Tea",Dollars)

Returns *759*—total dollars for all categories except Tea.

=SUMIF(Region,Filter1,Units)

Returns *107*—total units for region West.

=SUMIF(Units,Filter2,Dollars)

Returns *256*—total dollars for every row where units are less than 20.

## Alternatives to SUMIF

Sometimes you don't want to just *add* values conditionally: you may want to count the *number of values* that meet specified criteria. Sometimes you just want to make a preliminary or side calculation that doesn't figure in to the final formula. Here are some alternatives to using the SUMIF function:

- Use the COUNTIF function, covered in this chapter, to count values conditionally.
- Use the SUBTOTAL function to place nested subtotals in a row or column.

PART

**III**

Tapping Excel's Power

# Working with the SUBTOTAL Function

The SUBTOTAL function is not merely a sum function, but one that can be used to calculate a variety of intermediate values within a given range of data, such as an average or maximum value:

- You can easily calculate subtotals using several calculation methods.
- You can nest multiple levels of subtotals in a column, and a grand subtotal will ignore nested subtotals.
- Rows that are hidden as a result of a data filter (see Chapter 17) are not included in the calculation.

## SUBTOTAL Syntax

The following options are used with SUBTOTAL:

```
SUBTOTAL(Type,Ref)
```

**Type:** A number from 1 to 11 that specifies type of calculation, as listed below:

| | | |
|---|---|---|
| **1** | AVERAGE | (arithmetic mean of values) |
| **2** | COUNT | (count numeric values) |
| **3** | COUNTA | (count non blanks) |
| **4** | MAX | (maximum value) |
| **5** | MIN | (minimum value) |
| **6** | PRODUCT | (multiply) |
| **7** | STDEV | (standard deviation based on a sample) |
| **8** | STDEVP | (standard deviation based on entire population) |
| **9** | SUM | (add values) |
| **10** | VAR | (variance based on a sample) |
| **11** | VARP | (variance based on entire population) |

**Ref:** The range being subtotaled

## SUBTOTAL in Action

The following exercise demonstrates the versatility of the SUBTOTAL function. You'll learn how user input can determine the type of calculation performed with SUBTOTAL.

**1.** Enter the following on a blank worksheet:

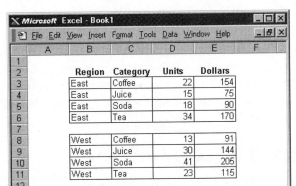

**2.** Enter the following formulas to calculate subtotals and a grand total:

| Cell | Formula |
| --- | --- |
| E7 | =SUBTOTAL(9,E3:E6) |
| E12 | =SUBTOTAL(9,E8:E11) |
| E13 | =SUBTOTAL(9,E3:E12) |

So far, SUBTOTAL is doing nothing that couldn't have been done with the simpler SUM function. The second part of this exercise makes the formulas dynamic and demonstrates the versatility of SUBTOTAL:

**1.** Name cell F16 **CalcType**.

**2.** In each of the three SUBTOTAL formulas, replace the Type argument **9** with a reference to cell **CalcType** (don't worry about the #VALUE! error, it will be taken care of in Step 3); for example:

```
=SUBTOTAL(CalcType,E3:E6)
```

**3.** Enter numbers from **1** to **11** in cell CalcType and watch the SUBTOTAL calculations change.

User input is now determining the type of calculation being performed by the SUBTOTAL functions.

The Data ➢ Subtotals command can quickly insert embedded subtotals, without the need to manually insert rows, and will create an outline in the process. See Chapter 17 to learn more about this command.

Tapping Excel's Power

PART III

# Lookup Functions

A worksheet is one great big table, which in turn often contains one or more tables of data. Accordingly, the ability to access data stored in tables is an essential skill, regardless of the type of analysis and modeling you are performing. Lookup functions such as INDEX, OFFSET, and VLOOKUP are some of the most important worksheet functions for serious users. These functions are especially useful when using Excel in conjunction with external databases.

## Searching with the VLOOKUP Function

The VLOOKUP function is used to search the leftmost column of a range (or array) for a specific value, then return a corresponding value from a different column in the table. Use VLOOKUP for the following:

- Traditional table lookups requiring exact matches—retrieving a customer address by using a customer code, or retrieving sales figures using a product number
- Searches for the closest value less than or equal to a search value, then retrieving a value from a corresponding column—for example, lookups into tax tables
- When the search is *not* case-sensitive

**NOTE**

The VLOOKUP function is generally used only when the values in the leftmost column of the range are unique, such as Social Security numbers or customer ID numbers.

### VLOOKUP Syntax

The following options are used with VLOOKUP:

```
VLOOKUP(LookupValue,LookupRef,ColumnNo,Nearest)
```

**LookupValue:** The value being searched for in the first column of LookupRef

**LookupRef:** A rectangular range or array

**ColumnNo:** The column number within the range containing the lookup value; must be a number greater than or equal to 1, and less than or equal to the number of columns in the table

**Nearest:** Specifies whether the search value must be an exact match to a value in the first column of LookupRef

- If Nearest is TRUE, the first column of LookupRef is searched for the closest value less than or equal to LookupValue in the first column of *LookupRef*. The values in the first column of LookupRef must be sorted in ascending order, otherwise VLOOKUP will not work properly.
- If Nearest is FALSE, the first column of LookupRef is searched for an exact match to LookupValue. Values in the first column of LookupRef do not have to be sorted.

## VLOOKUP Exact Lookups

The formulas given below apply to the worksheet shown here:

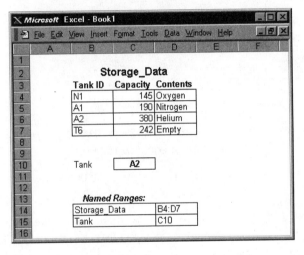

| =VLOOKUP("T6",B4:D7,2,FALSE) | Returns *242*—T6 is located in the fourth row, and 242 is found in the second column of range. |
| =VLOOKUP(Tank,Storage_Data,3,FALSE) | Returns *Helium*. |
| =VLOOKUP(Tank,Storage_Data,2,TRUE) | Mistakenly returns *#N/A* due to improper use of TRUE as the *Nearest* argument. |

PART

III

Tapping Excel's Power

## VLOOKUP Based on Closest Value

The formulas given below apply to the worksheet shown here:

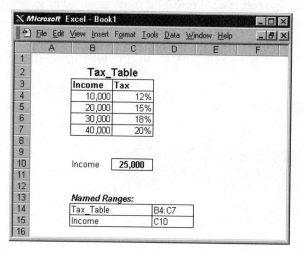

=VLOOKUP(15000,B4:C7,2,TRUE)

Returns *.12* (12%)—10,000 is the closest value less than or equal to 15,000.

=VLOOKUP(Income,Tax_Table,2,TRUE)

Returns *.15* (15%)—20,000 is the closest value less than or equal to 25,000.

=VLOOKUP(5000,Tax_Table,2,TRUE)

Returns *.#N/A*—there is no value equal to or less than 5000 in the first column of Tax_Table.

**NOTE** There are two functions closely related to VLOOKUP: HLOOKUP and LOOKUP. The HLOOKUP function is identical to VLOOKUP, except that it searches a row for a given value and returns a value from a corresponding row—once you understand VLOOKUP you will understand HLOOKUP. The LOOKUP function is not covered in this chapter because the sort requirements severely limit its usefulness (see Appendix A for a description of LOOKUP).

# Determining Position with the MATCH Function

Use MATCH when you have a known value, and you want to determine its position (first, second, third, etc.) in a one-dimensional list. Use MATCH for the following:

• Input verification, when an input value must exist within a list in order to be valid

- To determine the exact position of a value within a list where the list may or may not be sorted
- To determine where a given value falls within a sorted list (without the requirement for an exact match)

## MATCH Syntax

The following options are used with MATCH:

```
MATCH(LookupValue,LookupRef,Type)
```

**LookupValue:** The value being searched for

**LookupRef:** The range, or array constant, being searched; the range or array must be one-dimensional (a single row or column)

**Type:** The type of match being performed, as listed below:

| | |
|---|---|
| **0** | Search for an exact match—if match not found returns *#N/A* |
| **1** | Search for the largest value that is less than or equal to the LookupValue; LookupRef must be sorted in ascending order; if all values in Ref are greater than LookupValue, returns *#N/A* |
| **-1** | Search for the smallest value that is greater than or equal to LookupValue; LookupRef must be sorted in descending order; if all values in Ref are less than LookupValue, returns *#N/A* |

## MATCH Examples: Exact Matches

The formulas given below apply to the worksheet shown here:

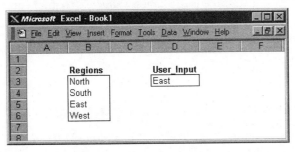

There are two named ranges in the graphic: Regions (B3:B6) and User_Input (D3).

| | |
|---|---|
| `=MATCH("South", B3:B6,0)` | Returns *2*, because *South* is the second value within the range B3:B6. |
| `=MATCH(User_Input, Regions,0)` | Returns *3*, because cell User_Input is the third value within the named range Regions. |

PART

III

Tapping Excel's Power

| | |
|---|---|
| `=MATCH("Central", Regions,0)` | Returns *#N/A*, because *Central* is not found in the named range Regions. |
| `=IF(ISNA(MATCH (User_Input,Region s,0)),"Invalid region!","")` | Returns text string intended as an error message if the entry in cell User_Input is not found in the range Regions, otherwise returns null text. |

## MATCH Examples: Match Closest Value

The formulas given below apply to the worksheet shown here:

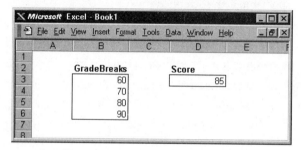

The following names have also been inserted into the workbook: GradeBreaks (B3:B6) and Score (D3).

| | |
|---|---|
| `=MATCH(92,B3:B6,1)` | Returns *4*, because the fourth value in the range is the largest value less than or equal to 92. |
| `=MATCH(Score, GradeBreaks,1)` | Returns *3*, because the third value in the range is the largest value less than or equal to 85. |
| `=MATCH(74, GradeBreaks,-1)` | Returns *#N/A*. Since GradeBreaks is sorted in *ascending* order, this is an improper use of match type -1. |

# Referring to Cells with the INDEX Function

The INDEX function is used to refer to a cell within a range of cells (or to an element within an array) when the position of the cell within the table is known. Use INDEX for the following situations:

- To refer to a cell within a range when the row and/or column is variable
- To perform lookups in conjunction with MATCH
- To refer into one-dimensional or two-dimensional ranges

## INDEX Syntax

The following options are used with INDEX:

    INDEX(LookupRange,Coordinate1,Coordinate2,AreaNum)

**LookupRange:** The range or array being referred to

**Coordinate1:** If LookupRange is one-dimensional, specifies row or column number within range; if LookupRange is two-dimensional, specifies row number

**Coordinate2:** Column number within LookupRange; use this argument only when LookupRange is two-dimensional

**AreaNum:** Specifies area number when LookupRange includes multiple noncontiguous areas

## INDEX Examples: One Dimensional Range

The formulas given below apply to the worksheet shown here:

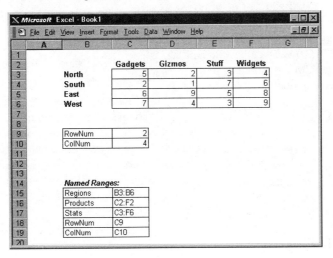

    =INDEX(B3:B6,1)

Returns *North*, the first element of range B3:B6.

    =INDEX(Products,RowNum)

Returns *Gizmos*, the second element of Products.

    =INDEX(Regions,5)

Returns *#REF!*—there are only 4 cells in Regions.

Tapping Excel's Power

PART III

## INDEX Examples: Two Dimensional Range

Using the same graphic as the previous example, these formulas refer to two-dimensional ranges; i.e., intersections of linear data.

`=INDEX(Stats,1,3)`

Returns *3*—the intersection of first row and third column of range Stats.

`=INDEX(Stats,RowNum,ColNum)`

Returns *6*—the intersection of second row and fourth column of range Stats.

## Using Functions That Refer to Closed Workbooks

In Chapter 8, you learned to write formulas that refer to closed workbooks. These formulas can include functions like SUM, INDEX, and SUBTOTAL. The following is an example of a SUM function that sums cells in a closed workbook:

`=SUM('C:\BUSINESS\[BUDGET.XLS]Sheet1'!$A$1:$A$5)`

Functions that refer to closed workbooks are exactly the same as functions that refer to open workbooks, except that the full path of each external reference is written out. You can type the full path into the formula,

but an easier way is to open the referenced workbook, enter the external references into your formulas by pointing and clicking, then close the referenced workbook. Excel will append the full path for each reference for you. You can also name the external reference and use the name rather than the full path in your function.

Most functions can refer to data in closed workbooks. This saves time and memory usage by not requiring additional workbooks to be opened. There are some functions which, because of their complexity, cannot refer to closed workbooks. These include OFFSET, COUNTIF, SUMIF, and INDIRECT.

## Referring to an Entire Row or Column

Referring to the graphic used in the previous examples, if zero is specified for either argument, the entire row or column is referred to:

`=SUM(INDEX(Stats,0,1))`

Returns *20*—the sum of the first column of Stats.

`=AVERAGE(INDEX(Stats,RowNum,0))`

Returns *4*—the average of the second row of Stats.

## INDEX Examples: Ranges Consisting of Multiple Areas

On the following worksheet, the noncontiguous range C4:F7,C12:F15 is named Calls.

| | A | B | C | D | E | F | G |
|---|---|---|---|---|---|---|---|
| 1 | | | | | | | |
| 2 | | | **Service Calls - 1997** | | | | |
| 3 | | | Q1 | Q2 | Q3 | Q4 | |
| 4 | | North | 961 | 24 | 273 | 211 | |
| 5 | | South | 127 | 25 | 106 | 493 | |
| 6 | | East | 328 | 544 | 34 | 573 | |
| 7 | | West | 778 | 174 | 977 | 687 | |
| 8 | | | | | | | |
| 9 | | | | | | | |
| 10 | | | **Service Calls - 1998** | | | | |
| 11 | | | Q1 | Q2 | Q3 | Q4 | |
| 12 | | North | 853 | 60 | 256 | 131 | |
| 13 | | South | 999 | 386 | 994 | 602 | |
| 14 | | East | 840 | 698 | 435 | 323 | |
| 15 | | West | 845 | 116 | 184 | 177 | |
| 16 | | | | | | | |
| 17 | | | | | | | |

`=INDEX(Calls,4,3,1)`    Returns *977*—the intersection of fourth row and third column within the first area of range Calls.

`=INDEX(Calls,4,3,2)`    Returns *184*—the intersection of fourth row and third column within the second area of range Calls.

**TIP**

When used together, MATCH and INDEX can be used to do lookups similar to lookups performed by the VLOOKUP and HLOOKUP functions. MATCH and INDEX require more effort (two functions instead of one) but with more flexibility.

# Reference Functions

The functions in this category, OFFSET, INDIRECT, ROW and COLUMN, are closely related to those in the Lookup category. They are used to refer to a cell or multiple cells based on position within the worksheet, not just individual values within a range of cells.

PART

III

Tapping Excel's Power

# The OFFSET Function

OFFSET is arguably the single most powerful general-purpose worksheet function. It allows you to refer to one or more cells that are *offset* from a given starting point by a specified number of rows and/or columns (for example, you can refer to a cell that is two rows below and three columns right of the starting point). Here are some important points to remember about OFFSET:

- It has similar uses to the INDEX function.
- Unlike INDEX, OFFSET is not limited to cells within a range.
- The range it refers to can be any height or width.

## OFFSET Syntax

The following options are used with OFFSET:

```
OFFSET(AnchorRange,RowOffset,ColOffset,Height,Width)
```

**AnchorRange:** The position on the worksheet being offset from

**RowOffset:** Vertical offset, measured in rows, from upper-left corner of AnchorRange:

- Positive number moves down
- Negative number moves up
- Zero performs no vertical offset

**ColOffset:** Horizontal offset, measured in columns, from upper-left corner of AnchorRange:

- Positive number moves right
- Negative number moves left
- Zero performs no horizontal offset

**Height:** The number of rows in the offset range; if omitted, defaults to same number of rows in AnchorRange

**Width:** The number of columns in the offset range; if omitted, defaults to same number of columns in AnchorRange

## OFFSET Examples: Referring to One Cell

The formulas given below apply to the worksheet shown here:

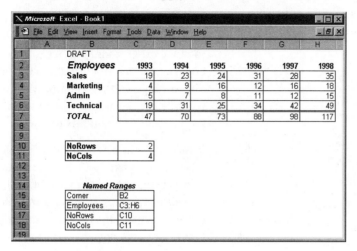

| =OFFSET(B2,1,3) | Returns *24*—one row down and three columns over from cell B2 (height and width default to 1—the same height and width of B2). |
| =OFFSET(Employees, 4,NoCols,1,1) | Returns *98*—four rows down and four columns over from upper-left corner of range Employees. |
| =OFFSET(Corner,-1,0) | Returns *Draft*—one row up, same column as cell Corner. |
| =OFFSET(Corner,NoRows,-3) | Returns *#REF!*—there is no column three to the left of cell (and two rows below) Corner. |

## OFFSET Examples: Referring to a Range of Cells

Using the same example, here are formulas for referring to a range of cells:

| | |
|---|---|
| `=AVERAGE(OFFSET (Employees,3,0,1,))` | Returns *33.33*—the average number of technical employees 1993 through 1998; refers to range offset from Employees three rows down and zero columns right, with dimensions one row high and six columns wide (defaults to six wide because last argument is omitted and Employees is six columns wide). |
| `=SUM(OFFSET (Employees,0,2,,1))` | Returns *73*—the total number of employees in 1995; refers to range offset from Employees by zero rows and two columns right, with dimensions four rows high and one column wide (defaults to four high because fourth argument is omitted and Employees is four rows high). |
| `=OFFSET (Employees,3,1)` | Returns *#VALUE!*—one cell cannot equal a range of cells; since last two arguments are omitted, offset range is four rows high and six wide. |

---

**TIP**

The OFFSET function actually returns a cell reference, but that reference is automatically converted to a value when the formula syntax so dictates. This is apparent when OFFSET is used as an argument to a function that expects a reference, such as the AVERAGE and SUM functions above. For a visual demonstration: select Edit ➢ Go To, then enter OFFSET(A1,1,2,3,4) as the reference—cells C2:F4 will be selected. You can perform a similar test with the INDEX function: go to the reference INDEX(A1:A9,3); cell A3 will be selected.

---

# The INDIRECT Function

The INDIRECT function is a powerful tool for advanced users. It allows a text string to be treated as a cell reference. You are better off if a problem can be solved *without* using INDIRECT because it is slower than other functions. But in special cases, INDIRECT can prove to be a unique, powerful function. Here are some important points to remember about INDIRECT:

- It is used in template development when trying to achieve extraordinary modularity (see Chapter 10).
- It should be used under the rare circumstances when a cell reference is only known in textual form.

## INDIRECT Syntax

The following option is used with INDIRECT:

```
INDIRECT(Text)
```

**Text:** Text that is equal to a cell reference

## INDIRECT in Action

The formulas given below apply to the worksheet shown here:

Microsoft Excel - Book1

| | A | B | C | D | E | F |
|---|---|---|---|---|---|---|
| 1 | | | | | | |
| 2 | | ABC | | | | |
| 3 | | | | | | |
| 4 | | B2 | | | | |
| 5 | | | | | | |
| 6 | | Sheet2!A1 | | | | |
| 7 | | | | | | |
| 8 | | | | | | |

`=INDIRECT("B2")`  Returns *ABC*—the contents of cell B2.

`=INDIRECT(B4)`  Returns *ABC*—since cell B4 contains *"B2"*, this returns the contents of cell B2.

`=INDIRECT("ABC")`  Returns *#REF!*—there is no cell reference ABC.

`=INDIRECT(B6)`  Returns the value in cell Sheet2!A1—INDIRECT can refer to cells on other worksheets on the same workbook, or other workbooks.

**PART III**

**Tapping Excel's Power**

**TIP**

In many cases, users solve problems with INDIRECT that could, and should, be solved with OFFSET and INDEX.

# Returning Row and Column Numbers

The ROW function returns the row number of a given reference. The COLUMN function returns a column number. Though seemingly obscure, these functions can play a key role in your modeling strategies. It is sometimes useful to refer to a cell by its position rather than its contents or address; for example, you may want to refer to cells in column C with the number 3 (the third column).

## ROW and COLUMN Syntax

The following option is used with ROW and COLUMN:

```
ROW(Reference)
COLUMN(Reference)
```

   **Reference:** The cell reference or name

## Using the ROW and COLUMN Functions

Here are some examples of how these functions work.

| | |
|---|---|
| =ROW(B3) | Returns *3*—the row number of cell B3. |
| =COLUMN(B3) | Returns *2*—the column number of cell B3. |
| =ROW(MyTable) | Returns the starting row number of a range named *MyTable*. |
| =ROW() | When Reference is omitted, row number of the cell containing the formula is returned. |
| =COLUMN() | When Reference is omitted, column number of the cell containing the formula is returned. |

# ROWS and COLUMNS

The ROWS function returns the number of rows in a given reference. The COLUMNS function returns the number of columns. Unlike the ROW and COLUMN functions, these functions count rows or columns, rather than return the row or column position.

## ROWS and COLUMNS Syntax

The following option is used with ROWS and COLUMNS:

```
ROWS(Reference)
COLUMNS(Reference)
```

   **Reference:** The cell reference or name

## Using the ROWS and COLUMNS Functions

Here are some examples:

| | |
|---|---|
| `=ROWS(B3:B4)` | Returns *2*—B3:B4 consists of 2 rows. |
| `=COLUMNS(B3)` | Returns *1*—B3 consists of 1 column. |
| `=ROWS(MyTable)` | Returns the number of rows in a range named *MyTable*. |

## Using ROWS with OFFSET to Keep a Range in Sync

Whenever a range of cells is named, a question arises about whether to include a header row as part of the named range. Some functions are easier to use one way and some the other. Both ranges can be named, but if a row is inserted immediately under the header row and the named range does not include the header row, the data area will not expand. The following exercise uses the OFFSET and ROWS functions, used in a named formula, to automatically keep a named data range in sync with the data-plus-header range:

**1.** Enter the following onto a blank sheet:

**2.** Name the range B2:C6 **Database**.

**3.** Use the Insert ➢ Name ➢ Define command to define the name Data to refer to the following:

```
=OFFSET(Database,1,0,ROWS(Database)-1)
```

This formula refers to the data area, less the header row.

**4.** Test the name by selecting Edit ➢ Go To and typing **Data** as the reference (it will not display in the list box). Cells B3:C6 should be selected.

**5.** Insert a row under the headings (at row 3). Go to Data again, and cells B3:C7 will be selected.

PART

III

Tapping Excel's Power

# Counting Functions

The various counting functions are important generic tools, and should be an integral part of your worksheet development strategy. They are used to count cells (within a given range) that meet certain criteria. These functions are often used as arguments in other functions, as you will see in later chapters.

## COUNT (and COUNTA, COUNTBLANK)

The COUNT function counts the numeric values found in a range of cells (or array). You can use COUNT for the following:

- To determine the number of entries in a column or row
- As an argument to functions such as INDEX and OFFSET

### COUNT Syntax

The following option is used with COUNT:

```
COUNT(Arg1, Arg2, etc.)
```

**Arg1:** There can be up to 30 arguments, each of which can be a constant or a range of cells.

### COUNT Examples

Here are some examples of the COUNT function.

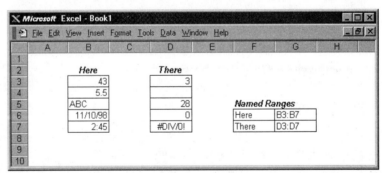

=COUNT(B3:B7)      Returns *4*—every value is numeric except for ABC.

=COUNT(There)      Returns *3*—every cell is numeric except for blank cell and cell with error.

=COUNT(Here,There)      Returns *7*—counts numeric values in both ranges.

## COUNTA and COUNTBLANK

Two related functions—COUNTA and COUNTBLANK—can also be useful at times:

- The COUNTA function is identical to COUNT, except it counts non-blanks (any cell with text, number, or error value).
- The COUNTBLANK function is identical to COUNT, except it counts blank cells (and it takes only a single range as an argument). Cells that are empty and cells containing space characters or null text ("") are both considered blank.

### Creating a Dynamic Named Range Using COUNTA with OFFSET

The following exercise uses the OFFSET and COUNTA functions in a named formula to create a dynamic named range that automatically expands based on the number of rows of data.

**1.** Enter the following values onto a blank sheet:

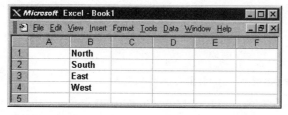

**2.** Use the Insert ➤ Name ➤ Define command to define the name Regions as follows:

```
=OFFSET($B$1,0,0,COUNTA($B:$B),1)
```

In lay terms, the named formula *Regions* is defined to start at $B$1, and the number of rows is based on the number of values found in cells in column B. (In other words, if there are five values anywhere within column B, Regions will contain five rows.)

**3.** Select Edit ➤ Go To and type **Regions** (the name will not appear in the list box)—if defined correctly, cells B1:B4 will be selected.

**4.** Enter a value in cell B5.

**5.** Select Edit ➤ Go To and type **Regions** again—cells B1:B5 will be selected, since the range has automatically expanded.

It is important to remember that the COUNTA function in the above formula counts only the number of nonblank cells in column B. Therefore, if there was a blank cell between North and South and you typed **Regions** in the Edit ➤ Go To dialog box, only cells B1:B4 would be selected (not cells B1:B5). Conversely, if column B had a column heading in cell B1, the COUNTA function would include it in the range of cells

Tapping Excel's Power

selected by the Regions formula. In this latter case, an alternative method of writing the formula would be

```
=OFFSET($B$2,0,0,COUNTA($B:$B)-1,1).
```

# The COUNTIF Function

The COUNTIF function was first introduced in Excel 5, and it partially obviated two other Excel constructs:

- Array formulas—powerful but rather complex
- Criteria ranges combined with the DCOUNT function—again, powerful but tedious to construct

Array formulas and criteria ranges are still applicable for counts requiring multiple criteria. But COUNTIF is a far simpler solution for counts based on a single criterion.

## COUNTIF Syntax

The following options are used with COUNTIF.

```
COUNTIF(Range,Criteria)
```

**Range:** The range of cells being counted

**Criteria:** An expression specifying which cells in *Range* are to be counted

## COUNTIF Examples

Here are some examples of the COUNTIF function.

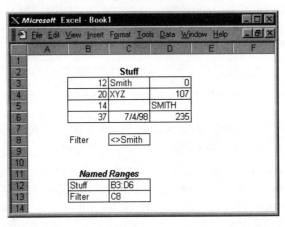

| | |
|---|---|
| `=COUNTIF(B3:B6,">30")` | Returns *1*—the number of cells greater than 30. |
| `=COUNTIF(Stuff,"Smith")` | Returns *2*—the number of cells equal to *Smith* (notice that COUNTIF is *not* case-sensitive). |
| `=COUNTIF(Stuff,Filter)` | Returns *10*—the number of cells not equal to *Smith*. |
| `=COUNTIF(Stuff,"<=20")` | Returns *4*—the number of cells less than or equal to *20* (notice that the blank cell and nonnumeric values were not counted). |

# Applying Text Functions

Excel has many powerful text-manipulation functions, most of which are very simple to learn and apply. Text functions when used in formulas are extremely useful, as they allow you to work with data based on names or text strings in your worksheet, and associate names or text with values or other data.

## Determining Length with the LEN Function

The LEN function determines the length of a text string (often used as an argument in other functions).

### LEN Syntax

The following option is used with LEN.

`LEN(Text)`

**Text:** Text string

### LEN Examples

Here are some examples of formulas using the LEN function, and the results they would produce:

| | |
|---|---|
| `=LEN("ABCDE")` | Returns *5*—there are five characters in the text string. |

PART

**III**

Tapping Excel's Power

| | |
|---|---|
| `=LEN(B2)` | Returns length of text string in cell B2. |
| `=IF(LEN(B2)>7,"Entry in B2 too long!","")` | Displays error message if text in cell B2 is longer than seven characters, or null text ("") if less than or equal to seven characters. |

## Returning LEFT and RIGHT Characters

The LEFT and RIGHT functions return the leftmost and rightmost characters of a text string.

### LEFT and RIGHT Syntax

The following options are used with LEFT and RIGHT.

```
LEFT(Text,Chars)
RIGHT(Text,Chars)
```

**Text:** Text string

**Chars:** Number of characters—defaults to 1 if omitted

### LEFT and RIGHT Examples

Here are some examples of formulas using the LEFT and RIGHT functions and the results they would produce:

| | |
|---|---|
| `=LEFT("ABCDE",3)` | Returns *ABC*—the left 3 characters of text string ABCDE. |
| `=LEFT("ABCDE")` | Returns *A*—when Chars argument omitted it defaults to 1. |
| `=RIGHT("ABC",5)` | Returns *ABC*—if Chars is larger than length of Text, entire text string is returned. |
| `=RIGHT(A1,2)` | Returns the two rightmost characters of text string contained in cell A1. |

## Returning Characters with the MID Function

The MID function returns characters from within a text string.

## MID Syntax

The following options are used with MID:

```
MID(Text,Start,Chars)
```

**Text:** Text string

**Start:** Starting character

**Chars:** Number of characters

## MID Examples

Here are some examples of formulas using the MID function and the results they produce:

| | |
|---|---|
| `=MID("ABCDE",2,3)` | Returns *BCD*—three characters beginning with the second character. |
| `=MID("ABCDE",1,2)` | Returns *AB*—two characters starting at the first character. |
| `=MID("ABCDE",4,99)` | Returns *DE*—if Chars extends beyond length of Text, entire text string beginning with Start is returned. |
| `=MID(A1,10,5)` | Returns 5 characters beginning at the tenth character of text string contained in cell. |

# Returning Positions of Nested Text Strings with SEARCH (and FIND)

The SEARCH and FIND functions return the position of one text string within another text string. Here are some important points to remember about SEARCH and FIND:

- SEARCH is not case-sensitive.
- SEARCH allows wildcard characters to be included in search text.
- FIND is case-sensitive.
- FIND does not allow wildcards.

## SEARCH and FIND Syntax

The following options are used with SEARCH and FIND:

```
SEARCH(find_text,within_text,start_num)
```

**find_text:** Text string being searched for—supports wildcards:

| | |
|---|---|
| * | Matches any sequence of characters |
| ? | Matches a single character |

**within_text:** Text string being searched for an occurrence of SearchText

**start_num:** Character number within SearchText to begin searching at; if omitted, defaults to 1

## Using the SEARCH Function

The following examples assume that cell A1 contains the text string Smith, Janet.

| | |
|---|---|
| `=SEARCH("C","ABCDE")` | Returns *3*—C is the third character of ABCDE. |
| `=SEARCH("Jan",A1)` | Returns *8*—*Jan* begins at the eighth character in cell A1. |
| `=SEARCH("T",A1,8)` | Returns *12*—the twelfth character is the first occurrence of T after the eighth character. |
| `=SEARCH("XYZ",A1)` | Returns *#VALUE!*—*XYZ* not found in cell A1. |
| `=SEARCH("J?N",A1)` | Returns *8*—question mark used as single-character wildcard. |
| `=SEARCH("J*T",A1)` | Returns *8*—asterisk used as multi-character wildcard. |
| `=LEFT(A1,SEARCH(",",A1)-1)` | Returns *Smith*—searches for comma and subtracts 1 in order to determine the last name. |

FIND works just like SEARCH except with the limitations mentioned previously.

# Working with Date and Time Functions

Working with dates and times is a common worksheet task, and Excel includes a rich set of date and time functions. First, it is important to understand how Excel works with date and time values:

- Date and time values are numbers, regardless of how the cells are formatted.
- Dates and times are stored as serial numbers—by default, Excel uses a 1900 date system in which serial numbers range from 1 to 65,380 corresponding to dates Jan 1, 1900 through Dec 31, 2078.
- In the serial number, digits to the right of the decimal point represent time of day (as a fraction of 24 hours); 12:00 PM is the equivalent of .5.
- The 1900 date system was employed for Lotus compatibility; a 1904 date system can be chosen (for Macintosh compatibility) using the Tools ➢ Options ➢ Calculation tab. This workbook option changes the starting date for date and time calculations from the 1900 to the 1904 date system.
- Excel automatically formats the serial number with a date or time format. To see the serial number, format the cell as General using the Number tab on the Format Cells dialog box.

In the next several sections, we'll take a look at some of the date and time functions and how you can put them to work for you.

## Returning the Serial Number of the Current Day with TODAY

The TODAY function returns the serial number of the current date. The TODAY function takes no arguments. It recalculates every time the worksheet recalculates.

### Using the TODAY Function

Here are some examples of formulas using the TODAY function and the results they would produce:

| | |
|---|---|
| `=TODAY()` | Returns *36068* on 9/30/98. |
| `=IF(DAY(TODAY())=15,"Check inventory today!","")` | Displays message on the fifteenth day of the month. |

PART

**III**

Tapping Excel's Power

**NOTE** If you enter the formula =TODAY( ) into an unformatted cell, Excel will automatically format the cell using the M/D/YY format. Do not confuse the formatted cell with the underlying value. This holds true for many of the date/time functions.

# Returning Current Date and Time Serial Numbers: the NOW Function

The NOW function returns the serial number of the current date and time (unlike TODAY, which returns only the date). The NOW function takes no arguments. It recalculates every time the worksheet recalculates.

## Using the NOW Function

Here's how the NOW function would work in a formula:

=NOW( )    Returns *36068.57639* on 9/30/98 at 1:50 PM (*36068* is the serial number for the date, and *.57639* is for the time).

**TIP** To freeze the date and time, use the Edit ➢ Copy and Edit ➢ Paste Special commands, then paste values.

# Returning the Serial Number of a Date

The DATE function returns serial number of a date.

## DATE Syntax

The following options are used with DATE:

DATE(Year,Month,Day)

**Year:** Number from 1900 to 2078 (1904–2078 if 1904 date system is selected)

**Month:** Number representing month of the year (can be greater than 12—see examples)

**Day:** Number representing day of the month (can be greater than number of days in month specified—see examples below)

### Using the DATE Function

Here are some examples of how the DATE function works in a formula:

`=DATE(98,9,15)`     Returns *36053*, the serial number for 9/15/98.

> **WARNING**
>
> Don't be fooled by the formatted date that displays after you enter this formula. When Excel detects an entry to be a date, it formats the cell as a date automatically. After entering the formula, change the format of the cell back to *Normal*, and 35688 will display.

`=DATE(97,14,15)`     Returns *35841*, the serial number for 2/15/98 (month 14 of 1997 translates to month 2 of 1998).

`=DATE(98,9,35)`     Returns *36073*, the serial number for 10/5/98 (day 35 of September translates to day 5 of October).

`=DATE(A1,A2,A3)`     Returns the serial number for the date defined by the year in A1, the month in A2, and the day in A3.

# Calculating the Day of the Month: The DAY Function

The DAY function calculates the day of the month (1–31) using dates entered as serial number or text.

### DAY Syntax

The following option is used with DAY:

`DAY(SerialNumber)`

   **SerialNumber:** The date as serial number or text

### Using the DAY Function

Here are some examples of formulas using the DAY function and the results they produce:

`=DAY(36053)`                                        Returns *15*—the day in 9/15/1998.

`=DAY("9/15/98")`                                    Returns *15*.

```
=DAY("15-Sep-98")
```
Returns *15*.

```
=DAY(A2)
```
Returns day of the date in cell A2.

```
=IF(OR(DAY(F2)=1,DAY(F2)=15),"Payday!","")
```
Displays message if date in F2 is first or fifteenth of month.

# Converting Serial Numbers to Hours

The HOUR function converts a serial number to an hour.

## HOUR Syntax

The following option is used with HOUR:

```
HOUR(SerialNumber)
```

**SerialNumber:** The time as serial number or text

## Using the HOUR Function

The examples below show formulas using the HOUR function and the results they produce:

```
=HOUR(0.75)
```
Returns *18*—0.75 times 24 hours equals 18 hours.

```
=HOUR("1:50 PM")
```
Returns *13*—the hour, using 24-hour clock, of the given time.

```
=HOUR(35688.75)
```
Returns *18*—the hour, using 24-hour clock, of 9/15/97, 6:00 PM.

```
=HOUR(NOW())
```
Returns hour of the current time.

```
=IF(HOUR(C9)>8,"Enter
reason for late
arrival","")
```
Displays message if time in C9 is later than 8:00 AM.

## Converting Serial Numbers to Minutes

The MINUTE function converts serial numbers into minutes, displayed as an integer from 1 to 59.

### MINUTE Syntax

The following option is used with MINUTE:

```
MINUTE(SerialNumber)
```

**SerialNumber:** The time as serial number or text

### Using the MINUTE Function

Here are some formulas using the MINUTE function and their results:

| | |
|---|---|
| `=MINUTE(0.3)` | Returns *12*—0.3 times 24 hours equals 7.2 hours, which equals 7 hours, 12 minutes. |
| `=MINUTE(36053.3)` | Returns *12*—the minutes of 9/15/98, 7:12 AM. |
| `=MINUTE("1:50:36 PM")` | Returns *50*—the minutes of the given time. |
| `=MINUTE(B3)` | Returns minutes of the time in cell B3. |

### Converting Time to Decimals

Suppose you calculate the payroll for your company, and one of your jobs is to translate timesheet times into decimal format to calculate hourly wages. An easy way to accomplish that is to use the formula =(*Time*-INT(*Time*))*24, where *Time* is the time in hours and minutes (e.g., 6:30) that you want to convert to a decimal (e.g., 6.5). As an example, enter time worked (using hour:minute format) into cell A1. In cell B1, enter the formula **=(A1-INT(A1))*24**. The result is shown in decimal format, and can be used to perform calculations.

PART

III

Tapping Excel's Power

## Converting Serial Numbers to Months

The MONTH function converts a serial number to a month.

### MONTH Syntax

The following option is used with MONTH:

```
MONTH(SerialNumber)
```

**SerialNumber:** The date as serial number or text

### Using the MONTH Function

Here are examples of formulas with the MONTH function and their results:

| | |
|---|---|
| `=MONTH("15-Sep")` | Returns *9*—the month number of the given date. |
| `=MONTH(35688)` | Returns *9*—the month number of the given date. |
| `=MONTH(B5)` | Returns month number of date in cell B5. |
| `=IF(MONTH(B5)=4,`<br>`"Tax Time!","")` | Displays message if date in B5 is in April. |

## Converting the Serial Number to the Day of the Week

The WEEKDAY function converts a serial number to the day of the week.

### WEEKDAY Syntax

The following options are used with WEEKDAY:

```
WEEKDAY(SerialNumber,ReturnType)
```

**SerialNumber:** The date as serial number or text

**ReturnType:** Number that determines type of return value:

| | |
|---|---|
| **1** | Returns 1 through 7 representing Sunday through Saturday. |
| **2** | Returns 1 through 7 representing Monday through Sunday. |
| **3** | Returns 0 through 6 representing Monday through Sunday. |

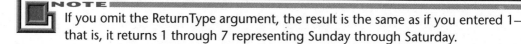

**NOTE** If you omit the ReturnType argument, the result is the same as if you entered 1—that is, it returns 1 through 7 representing Sunday through Saturday.

## Using the WEEKDAY Function

Here are formulas using the WEEKDAY function and the results they produce:

| | |
|---|---|
| `=WEEKDAY("9/15/98")` | Returns *3*—date is a Tuesday, ReturnType omitted. |
| `=WEEKDAY(35687)` | Returns *1*—date is a Sunday, ReturnType omitted. |
| `=WEEKDAY(35687,2)` | Returns *7*—date is a Sunday, ReturnType is 2. |
| `=IF(WEEKDAY(A1,2)>5,`<br>`"Entry must be`<br>`weekday!","")` | Displays error message if entry in A1 is not a weekday. |

# Converting the Serial Number to a Year

The YEAR function converts a serial number to a year.

## YEAR Syntax

The following option is used with YEAR:

`YEAR(SerialNumber)`

> **SerialNumber:** The date as serial number or text

## Using the YEAR Function

Here are some examples of the YEAR function at work in formulas:

| | |
|---|---|
| `=YEAR("9/15/98")` | Returns *1998*. |
| `=YEAR(36053)` | Returns *1998*. |
| `=IF(YEAR(A1)<>YEAR`<br>`(NOW()),"Entry must be`<br>`in current year.","")` | Displays error message if date in A1 is not in the current year. |

The functions covered in this chapter are some of the most useful when working in the Excel environment. These functions allow you to go beyond simple worksheet calculation, and write complex formulas that provide more specific information, for example, when using Excel to retrieve information from a database.

In the next chapter, "Using Templates," we'll use the functions we covered in this chapter in conjunction with named ranges (see Chapter 8) to create some powerful and useful worksheet models.

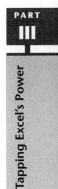

PART

III

Tapping Excel's Power

# Chapter

# 10

## Using Templates

# Using Templates

T emplates are patterns that can be used over and over again to produce similar objects. A carpenter might use a template as a reusable guide to produce the same item, such as a cabinet door, repeatedly. Templates simplify tasks, save time, and help you to avoid mistakes. You can use workbook templates to create reusable workbooks and worksheets, allowing you to work more effectively.

In addition to explaining how templates work, this chapter covers two nifty new features that are often used on templates, though their use is not restricted exclusively to templates: *data validation* and *merged cells*.

## What Is a Template?

This chapter will cover the subject of templates using two distinct definitions of the word. In this section, we'll explain both definitions so that you'll always know exactly what we mean.

## *Template*—The "Official" Excel Definition

In Excel terminology, a *template* is a special workbook (or sheet) that is used as a basis for creating new workbooks, or new sheets within a workbook. It's a lot simpler than it sounds: a template is just an ordinary workbook that has been identified as a template and saved into a special template folder.

The first part of this chapter is dedicated to explaining the simple task of creating and using such templates. You can create your own templates, or use one of Excel's built-in templates. When you select File ➤ New and select the Spreadsheet Solutions tab, Excel displays a variety of useful templates, among which are an Invoice form and a Purchase Order form. You can also select one of your own custom templates that you have previously saved in the Template folder.

## *Template*—The General Definition

Generally speaking, the word *template* implies a reusable form or model. Reusability is not limited to *official* Excel templates. Any workbook can be used as a template (though without the special characteristic of "official" templates described above). Gradually, this chapter will expand upon the topic of templates, and explain how to create powerful reusable worksheets that you can use as building blocks in worksheet development, whether or not the worksheets are part of an official Excel template.

# Working with Templates

In order to make Excel work the same as other Microsoft Office applications, Microsoft has made some minor changes to the way that templates are stored. There is now a TEMPLATE folder that is used by all Microsoft Office applications. Within the TEMPLATE folder are several subfolders that are used to create logical groupings of templates by category. (Under the Spreadsheet Solutions folder are several built-in templates, unless you chose not to install them when you installed Excel.)

**NOTE**

You are not limited to the pre-created template subfolders. You can create new ones in the same manner as you would create any new folder. Simply locate the TEMPLATE folder inside of Office, then create new subfolders within it.

## Opening New Files Based on Templates

Opening a template is different from opening a normal workbook in one respect: a copy of the template is placed into memory, rather than using the original file. Later, when you select File ➤ Save, the default file name is not the same as the original template, making it difficult to accidentally overwrite the original template. To clarify this point, assume that you have just opened a template named *REPORT*:

- The workbook in memory will be an unsaved file, similar to new workbooks created with the File ➤ New command (though it will be an exact copy of all the data, formulas, and formatting from the REPORT template).

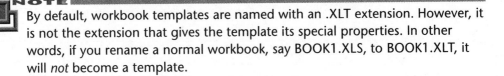

**NOTE**
By default, workbook templates are named with an .XLT extension. However, it is not the extension that gives the template its special properties. In other words, if you rename a normal workbook, say BOOK1.XLS, to BOOK1.XLT, it will *not* become a template.

- The unsaved workbook will be named REPORT1.
- If you open the template again (during the same Excel session) the workbook in memory will be named REPORT2. (There can be multiple copies of the same template open at the same time.)
- Saving REPORT1 is no different than saving any new workbook—by default, it is saved as a "normal" workbook.

**WARNING**
Never link other workbooks to a template. The link breaks when copies of the template are opened (since the name of the template is different when opened). However, you can link templates to other workbooks.

## Creating Your Own Templates

You can easily make any workbook into a template. To create a template from scratch, follow these steps:

1. Create a new workbook, or open an old one.
2. Enter constants, formulas, and formatting (anything goes—a template can include charts and macros).
3. Select File ➤ Save As to call up the Save As dialog box.

**4.** Select Template from the Save As Type drop-down list, as shown here:

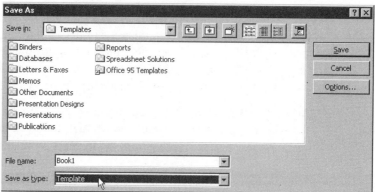

**NOTE**

Notice that when you select Template in the Save As Type list, Excel defaults to the TEMPLATES folder in the Save In drop-down list.

**5.** Enter a file name, then click on Save.

**MASTERING THE OPPORTUNITIES**

## Creating a Worksheet Template

You can create a template that governs the appearance of all newly created individual worksheets. These templates are called *autotemplates*. For example, suppose that any time you insert a new worksheet into an existing workbook using the Insert ➤ Worksheet command, you would like certain formatting to be in place, automatically. Here's how you could set this up:

**1.** Create a workbook consisting of one worksheet. Format the sheet as desired.

**2.** Save the file. Specify the file type as Template.

**3.** Name the file **SHEET** and save it in the XLSTART folder (within the MICROSOFT EXCEL folder) or the alternate startup folder.

## Using Workbook Templates

Once you have saved a workbook as a template, it appears as an Excel document icon whenever you select File ➤ New. For example, if you have saved a workbook as a template named INVOICE, the New dialog box would appear as follows:

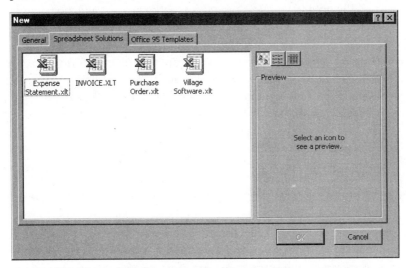

To create a new monthly invoice workbook from the INVOICE template, select the Invoice icon to highlight it, and click on OK. Excel will open a new workbook named Invoice1. Simply select File ➤ Save As to rename the new workbook.

## Making Changes to Existing Workbook Templates

In order to change an existing workbook template, open the file using the File ➤ Open command, just as you would open a "normal" workbook. When opened in this manner, the original template file is loaded into memory, rather than a copy. Simply make your changes, then save the file. Remember, changing a template file has no effect on files previously created using the template.

# Data Validation

Templates are often intended for use by many individuals within an organization, and are often used as input forms of one kind or another, such as invoices, expense statements, etc. In these situations, data validation is a key consideration. A date input needs to be a valid date. A numeric input might need to be restricted to a value between 1 and

99. Optimally, a product code would be selected from a list, rather than typed in. However, the very openness that makes spreadsheets so popular is a double-edged sword. Historically, it has been difficult to create worksheet models where data input is validated—no small amount of custom programming was required in order to implement rudimentary validation. A vital new feature in Excel 97 allows you to validate user input without the need to write custom macros—the Data ➢ Validation command.

There are two important points to understand before we get underway. First, though data validation is often used in templates, it is *not limited* to templates. That is, the Data ➢ Validation command can be used to implement validation in *any* workbook, be it an "official" template or not. Second, data validation is not limited to classical data entry applications, where user input is typically saved to disk. For example, say you have a chart that is intended to show data for one particular region, and the user gets to specify that region. You can use data validation to provide the user with a list from which to select the region. This is an example of data input that is not necessarily saved. Rather, the input is used to recalculate the worksheet, and in this case, the chart.

**TIP**

Another important device for restricting user input is *custom controls*, discussed in Chapter 23. You can place controls such as list boxes and check boxes on worksheets and link them to cells. You can find custom controls on the Forms toolbar.

## Validation Basics

Applying data validation rules to a cell, or a range of cells, is conceptually similar to cell formatting—the command acts upon the selected cell(s). First, select the cell(s) for which validation is to be applied. Then, select Data ➢ Validation. The tabbed dialog box shown in Figure 10.1 appears.

After you work with it briefly, you will probably find the Data Validation dialog box easy to use. However, this is one of those dialog boxes that changes (considerably) based on what you choose in the Allow list. The default for the Allow list is Any Value, as shown in Figure 10.1. As you might surmise, this allows any value to be entered into the cell. (Not much validation to be had there!) However, once you change the Allow setting to Whole Number, for example, things get more interesting. Take a look at Figure 10.2—this will be the starting point for our discussion of data validation.

## Validating Numbers, Dates, Times, and Text

Figure 10.2 shows the Data Validation dialog box with Whole Number chosen from the Allow list. In fact, the dialog box is virtually identical for Decimal, Date, and Time.

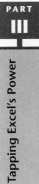

**FIGURE 10.1**

*The Data Validation dialog box lets you specify what data is allowed in a cell or range of cells.*

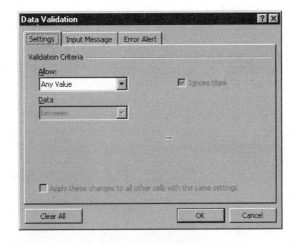

**FIGURE 10.2**

*The Allow list determines which other settings are provided in the Data Validation dialog box.*

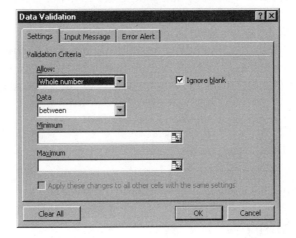

In each case, the Data drop-down list is enabled, allowing you to specify the next validation rule. The Data drop-down list provides the following choices:

| | |
|---|---|
| Between | Greater Than |
| Not Between | Less Than |
| Equal To | Greater Than Or Equal To |
| Not Equal To | Less Than Or Equal To |

Choosing Between or Not Between causes the dialog box to display two constraints: Minimum and Maximum. All other choices provide a singe constraint. Suppose you want to allow a whole number between 1 and 99 in a given cell. Try this simple exercise:

**1.** Select cell A1, then select Data ➢ Validation.

**2.** Now select Whole Number from the Allow list.

**3.** Select Between from the Data list.

**4.** Enter **1** as the Minimum and **99** as the Maximum. Click on OK.

Now, test your work: Try entering invalid data into cell A1—a number larger than 99, or text. The following error message appears:

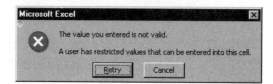

Click on Retry to undo your data entry, and you are put back into edit mode so that you can enter a different value. When you click on Cancel, the data entry is undone—you are *not* placed in edit mode.

This is a good time to explain the Ignore Blank setting, shown in Figure 10.2. Suppose you have a sales order form that has an input for the ship date—but the order has yet to ship. This is a situation where it might be OK to leave the cell blank. If the Ignore Blank setting is checked, Excel will allow the cell to be cleared, even if the Minimum and Maximum dates are specified.

## Validating Text

When Allow is set to Text Length, there is just one slight difference compared to numeric validation: the constraint(s) serve to limit the *length* of the text string.

# Validating with Lists

The List setting in the Allow list, shown in Figure 10.3, is used to validate a cell based on the contents of a list. For example, this feature could be used to force the user to enter a valid two-character state code.

In Figure 10.3, notice the In-Cell Dropdown setting. When this setting is checked and the dialog box is closed, a drop-down arrow automatically appears when the cell is selected. The drop-down list will contain the list specified in the Source text box. To see how this works, try the following exercise:

**1.** Enter the values **North**, **South**, **East**, and **West** into cells A1:A4.

**MASTERING THE OPPORTUNITIES**

## Using Variable Constraints

Here is a very powerful feature for advanced users: suppose you want to impose data validation on a cell where the constraints are variable. For example, you may have a cell that requires the user to enter a date. The most recent allowable input (End Date) is the current date; the oldest allowable input (Start Date) is 30 days ago. The Data Validation dialog box will accept *formulas* for these constraints. As with formulas entered into cells, the first character must be an equal sign. Here are entries for the Data

Validation dialog box that would apply the aforementioned validation logic:

| | |
|---|---|
| Allow: | Date |
| Data: | Between |
| Start Date: | =TODAY()-30 |
| End Date: | =TODAY() |

As you can see, the formulas may include Excel functions (in this case, the TODAY function). They can also reference cells. This technique is applicable for other types of inputs as well, not just dates.

**FIGURE 10.3**

*When Allow is set to List, the Source text box is used to specify the range that contains the list.*

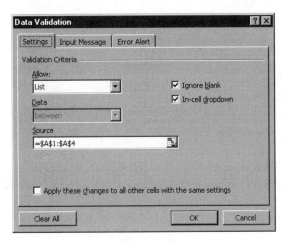

**2.** Select cell C2 and select Data ➤ Validation.
**3.** Select List from the Allow list.
**4.** With the cursor in the Source setting, select the range A1:A4.

PART III

Tapping Excel's Power

**5.** Be sure the In-Cell Dropdown setting is checked, then click on OK.

Now, select cell C2. A drop-down list will appear, as pictured below. Choose a region, and the value will be placed into C2.

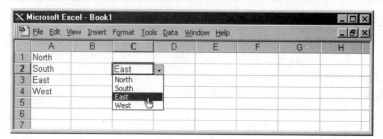

# Specifying an Input Prompt and Error Message

The second tab of the Data Validation dialog box, titled *Input Message*, lets you specify a title and a prompt to help the user understand what should be entered into the cell.

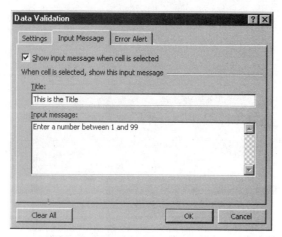

The third tab of the Data Validation dialog box—Error Alert—lets you enter an error message that is displayed if the user enters invalid data.

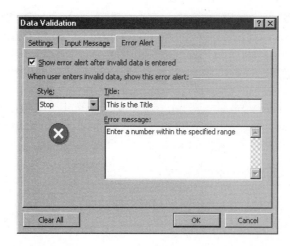

## Custom Validation

Advanced users will have a lot of fun with custom validation. When Allow is set to Custom, you can specify custom validation in the form of an Excel formula. The potential uses of this feature are limitless. Consider Figure 10.4: in this example, a dollar amount must be entered into cell B4 *only if* there is a number in cell B2. Conversely, if B2 is zero, B4 must also be zero.

**FIGURE 10.4**

*Custom validation allows cell B4 to be conditionally validated based on the contents of B2.*

Here's how it's done: with cell B4 selected, select Data ➤ Validation, and then select Custom from the Allow list. Then enter the following formula:

```
=IF(B2<>0,B4<>0)
```

Here's the layperson's translation: if Units is not zero, then dollars must be greater than zero. Please note, this is a simplistic example. These formulas become quite complex once you account for all possible input errors. For example, the above formula will not prevent a text entry into B4.

**TIP**

Advanced users, be aware that a formula used for custom validation can even include calls to custom VBA functions.

Now, let's take this concept a step further. In Figure 10.5, the same units/dollars problem is presented, but this time it pertains to an entire column of inputs. Dollar values must be entered into column C if the corresponding cell in column B (Units) is not zero. Here are the steps:

**1.** Select C2:C4, then select Data ➤ Validation.
**2.** Select Custom from the Allow list.
**3.** Enter this formula: =IF(B2<>0,C2>0).
**4.** Click on OK.

**FIGURE 10.5**

*The values in column C must be validated conditionally, based on the values in column B.*

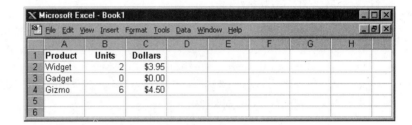

Now, the validation rules for column C are based on the corresponding cells in column B. The reason this works is because of the magic of relative references (covered in Chapter 4). Again, this is a simplistic example that would *not* prevent a text entry in column C.

## Maintaining Validation Settings

Depending on the layout of your worksheet, it's entirely possible that the same validation settings will be applied to numerous cells, perhaps even noncontiguous ones. This presents somewhat of a challenge when it comes time to change the validation settings, as it be difficult to tell which cells use which settings. There are three ways to overcome this problem, and to help with maintaining data validation in general.

• The first tab of the Data Validation dialog box has a setting Apply These Changes To All Other Cells With The Same Settings (shown previously in Figure 10.3).

When this option is checked, any changes that are made will be made to every cell with the same settings.

- The Go To Special dialog box contains new options to help find cells with data validation. To display this dialog box, select Edit ➤ Go To, then click on the Special button. The last set of option buttons provides the ability to select all cells with data validation, or just the cells with the same validation as the active cell.

- Suppose you want to copy data validation from one cell to another, but *not* copy anything else. The Paste Special dialog box has a setting that allows you to do this. To use this feature, select a cell with validation and select Edit ➤ Copy. Select the cell where you want to paste the validation settings, then select Edit ➤ Paste Special. Click on the Validation option, then click on OK.

# Data Validation Tips and Traps

Here is some more information about data validation to help you understand some of the limitations.

## Validation Settings are Affected by Copy/Paste

When you perform copy/paste operations, data validation behaves much as you would expect cell formatting to behave. Suppose that cell A1 has data validation. If you copy A1 to cell A2, then A2 will have the same data validation. Conversely, if you copy a cell with no validation, and paste it to A1, cell A1 will no longer have validation.

## Validation Does *Not* Detect Pasted Values

This is the most severe chink in the data validation armor. Suppose that cell A1 has data validation requiring a number from 1 to 9. Cell B1 contains the number 100. It would be logical to assume that data validation would detect the following:

1. Select cell B1, then select Edit ➤ Copy.
2. Select cell A1. Select Edit ➤ Paste Special, choose Values, and click on OK.

Data validation will *not* detect this illegal value that has been pasted in. Ultimately, this means that you must think of data validation as a useful tool for enhancing data integrity. But it is not a fortress—bulletproof data validation still requires custom programming.

PART

III

Tapping Excel's Power

# Merging Cells

There's an important new feature buried deep in the cell formatting dialog box that will be a major boon for template authoring—the ability to *merge cells*. Before explaining how to merge cells, we'll discuss the problem that merged cells solve. Suppose you have a template used as an invoicing form. Figure 10.6 shows just such a template, created in an earlier version of Excel. Notice that the column widths are sized for the body of the invoice, and the Bill-To area, in the header, is forced to use two columns as a result. Experienced spreadsheet developers will recognize this as a trivial example of a vexing, age-old problem: the endless battle with column widths in an attempt to satisfy all the sections of a form.

> **NOTE**
>
> Typically, with the type of form shown in Figure 10.6, gridlines would be removed and cell borders would be used to create bordered effects selectively. In this example, the gridlines were left in place to clearly indicate the column widths. Gridlines are turned on and off using the Tools ➢ Options ➢ View command, where you will find a Gridlines check box.

---

**FIGURE 10.6**

*In the past, creating high-quality forms meant battling the worksheet grid. Here, the column widths, set to accommodate the body of the form, fail to provide for the header section.*

| | A | B | C | D | E | F | G |
|---|---|---|---|---|---|---|---|
| 1 | | | | | | | |
| 2 | | Bill-To: | | | | | |
| 3 | | Company name | | | | | |
| 4 | | Address line 1 | | | | | |
| 5 | | Address line 2 | | | | | |
| 6 | | Address line 3 | | | | | |
| 7 | | | | | | | |
| 8 | | Product | | | | | |
| 9 | | Code | Description | | Qty | Price | Extension |
| 10 | | | | | | | |
| 11 | | | | | | | |
| 12 | | | | | | | |
| 13 | | | | | | | |
| 14 | | | | | | | |
| 15 | | | | | | | |
| 16 | | | | | TOTAL: | | |
| 17 | | | | | | | |

*Microsoft Excel - Book1*

File  Edit  View  Insert  Format  Tools  Data  Window  Help

Merged cells provides a partial solution to this problem. You can merge multiple cells to form one large virtual cell. Here's how it's done:

**1.** Select a range of cells, then select Format ➤ Cells. Click on the Alignment tab.

**2.** Check the Merge Cells setting, then click on OK.

To apply this technique to the template shown in Figure 10.7, you would merge B3 with C3, B4 with C4, etc. Then, the users of the form would not only be unable to enter data into cells C3:C6—they wouldn't even be able to select these cells!

In this chapter, you've learned the basics of Excel templates, and two important features that relate to templates (data validation and merging cells). There are many other skills that come into play when you are authoring templates. Pay particular attention to custom controls, discussed in Chapter 23. And don't miss the myriad of formatting features discussed in Chapter 5.

# Chapter

## 11

### Auditing and Protecting Your Work

Chapter

11

# Auditing and Protecting Your Work

Two of the biggest problems endemic to worksheet applications are maintaining security and enhancing flexibility. The most clever models are rendered useless if users are able to alter them easily. Similarly, complex models that are difficult to support or modify may eventually collapse under their own weight.

This chapter will provide you with some relatively simple security and troubleshooting skills that will allow you to keep users from accidentally altering worksheets and changing sensitive data. You'll also learn how to use the Auditing toolbar and how to organize and find information using file settings and search criteria.

## Implementing File-Level Security

There are several levels of protection that can be applied to a workbook. The topmost level of protection is set on the file level. If users can't access the file itself, they won't be able to change the information inside it. At the file level, you have several different protection options:

- You can require users to enter a password just to open the file.
- You can make the file read-only.

- You can require users to enter a password if they want to save changes to the file.
- You can have Excel create a backup copy of the file every time it is modified.

Let's take a closer look at each of these options.

## Applying Password Protection to a File

If you apply password protection to a file, a user must enter the file's password to open the file. To apply password-protection to an existing file, follow these steps:

**1.** Select File ➤ Save As to call up the Save As dialog box.

**2.** Click on Options. The Save Options dialog box appears.

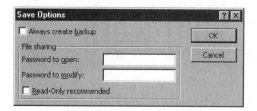

**3.** Enter the password you want used for the file in the Password To Open area of the Save Options dialog box and click on OK.

**4.** Re-enter your password in the Confirm Password dialog box and click on OK.

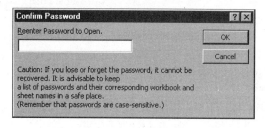

**5.** Click on the Save button in the Save As dialog box.

**6.** If the Replace Existing File dialog box appears, click on Yes to implement password protection.

The Password To Open entered in the Save Options dialog box is required to open or access the workbook. In general, this password is used on workbooks requiring the highest possible level of security. The password can be up to 15 characters, can include special characters, and is case-sensitive.

## Applying a Modification Password

The Password To Open option requires the user to enter a password just to open the file, but you can also set a password that the user must enter in order to save modifications to the file. Entering a password in the Password To Modify text box in the Save Options dialog box allows users to open the workbook in read-only mode. They can view and manipulate the workbook, but not save it without knowing the password. The modification password can be up to 15 characters long (including special characters) and is case-sensitive.

## Setting the Read-Only Recommended Option

The Read-Only Recommended setting is a handy solution for two situations:

- When a workbook is used by more than one person—users should generally open it read-only in case somebody else needs to change it.
- When a workbook requires only periodic maintenance—users are discouraged from accidentally changing a workbook that is not supposed to be changed on a day-to-day basis.

When you set the Read-Only Recommended option in the Save Options dialog box, Excel will display the following dialog box when the file is opened:

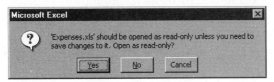

If you click on Yes and open the workbook as Read-Only, the text [Read Only] appears next to the file name on the title bar. If you click on No, the file is opened with full write privileges.

Read about shared workbooks, which allow multiple users to edit a file at the same time, in Chapter 29.

PART

**III**

Tapping Excel's Power

## Creating Backups When the File Is Saved

When checked, the Always Create Backup setting in the Save Options dialog box causes Excel to create a backup of the file every time it is saved. The backup file is saved as Backup Of *Filename* with a .XLK extension in the same folder as the original file. Open the backup file if one of these situations occurs:

- The original file becomes corrupted.
- You make mistakes, and do not realize it until *after* you have saved the file.

**WARNING**

Automatic backups are saved with a .XLK extension. If you have a workbook named FINANCE.XLS and a template named FINANCE.XLT in the same directory, and both files are set to create backups, Excel will not save both backups as Backup Of FINANCE.XLK. Excel will only create a backup of the first file saved.

# Opening a Password-Protected File

Each time you attempt to open a password-protected workbook, you will be prompted for the password.

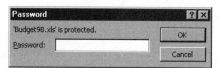

You will also be prompted for the password if a formula is entered into a different workbook that refers to cell(s) on the password-protected workbook (and the protected workbook is closed).

If you forget the password, there is virtually nothing you can do to recover the workbook—and you will not get assistance from Microsoft technical support.

## Opening Any File as Read-Only

Even when a modification password is not defined and Read-Only Recommended is not set, you can still open files in read-only mode. Click the Commands and Settings button in the File ➢ Open dialog box , and select the Open Read-Only menu command. The words *[Read-Only]* will appear next to the file name on the title bar.

## Removing Protection and Modification Passwords

Follow this procedure to remove a protection password or modification password from a document you have created:

**1.** Open the workbook. (You must enter the password to do this.)

**2.** Select File ➤ Save As, then click on the Options button.

**3.** Clear the password(s)—asterisks will appear when there is a password.

**4.** Click on OK to close the Save Options dialog box, then click on Save to save the file.

**5.** Answer Yes when the Replace Existing File dialog box is displayed.

# Protecting Data within the Workbook

The remainder of the security options serve to restrict what users can do *after* they've opened the workbook. Essentially, there are three levels of security:

- Workbook level
- Worksheet level
- Object level (cells and graphical objects)

Workbook is the highest level, followed by worksheet and then object. Let's take a look at each of these levels.

## Applying Workbook Protection

To apply protection to a workbook, select Tools ➤ Protection ➤ Protect Workbook to display the Protect Workbook dialog box, as shown in Figure 11.1.

*The Protect Workbook dialog box*

These are the options in the Protect Workbook dialog box:

**Structure:** If checked, prevents changes to worksheet structure; you are prevented from deleting, inserting, renaming, copying, moving, hiding, or unhiding sheets.

**Windows:** If checked, prevents changes to the workbook's window; the window control button becomes hidden and most windows functions (move, size, restore, minimize, maximize, new, close, split, and freeze panes) are disabled.

**Password (Optional):** Optional password up to 255 characters; it can include special characters and is case-sensitive.

Since a protected structure for workbooks prevents users from inserting new sheets, there are several unexpected side effects that you should be aware of. When a structure is protected you are unable to do the following:

- Add a new chart sheet with ChartWizard.
- Record a macro onto a new module or macro sheet.
- Use the Scenario Manager to create a new report (see Chapter 27 for more information on Scenario Manager).
- Display source data for a cell in a pivot table (see Chapters 20 through 22 for more information on pivot tables).

## Unprotecting a Workbook

To unprotect a workbook, open it and remove the password from the Save Options dialog box by using File ➤ Save As, then click on Save to save the file, and click on Yes to replace the protected file with the unprotected one.

# Applying Worksheet Protection

There may be times when you'll want to use worksheet protection to prevent users from changing the contents of an individual sheet. For example, you want users to be able to add data to this month's sales sheet, but not to the sheets for previous months. Select Tools ➤ Protection ➤ Protect Sheet to display the Protect Sheet dialog box, as shown in Figure 11.2.

These are the options available in the Protect Sheet dialog box:

**Contents:** Protects worksheet cells and chart items.

**Objects:** Protects graphic objects on worksheets (including charts).

*FIGURE 11.2*

*The Protect
Sheet dialog box*

**Scenarios:** Prevents changes to scenario definitions (see Chapter 27).

**Password (Optional):** Optional password up to 255 characters; it can include special characters and is case-sensitive.

## Unprotecting a Worksheet

To unprotect a worksheet, select Tools ➢ Protection ➢ Unprotect Sheet. You will be prompted for the password if one was specified when the worksheet was protected.

## Hiding Sheets and Cells

Another way to discourage users from changing cells is by hiding all or part of the sheet:

**Hiding an Entire Sheet:** Select Format ➢ Sheet ➢ Hide to hide a worksheet. To unhide a worksheet, select Format ➢ Sheet ➢ Unhide. Remember, you can't hide or unhide worksheets if the *workbook* structure is protected. So, to achieve the highest level of security, hide sheets first, then protect the workbook structure. (You will have to unprotect the workbook before you can unhide the sheets.)

**Hiding Rows:** Select the rows you want to hide, then select Format ➢ Row ➢ Hide.

**Hiding Columns:** Select the columns you want to hide, then select Format ➢ Column ➢ Hide.

You can make it difficult for a user to unhide hidden rows and columns by protecting the worksheet with the Tools ➢ Protection ➢ Protect Sheet command.

**TIP**

How do you unhide hidden rows or columns when you are unable to select them? To unhide a hidden row or column, select a contiguous range of cells that includes the hidden row or column, then select Format ➢ Row ➢ Unhide or Format ➢ Column ➢ Unhide. Alternatively, use the Name box to select a hidden cell, then unhide the row or column.

PART

**III**

Tapping Excel's Power

## Adding Cell Protection

Sometimes you may want to protect individual cells in a worksheet. Select Format ➤ Cells, then select the Protection tab (Figure 11.3).

*FIGURE 11.3*

*The Protection tab in the Format Cells dialog box*

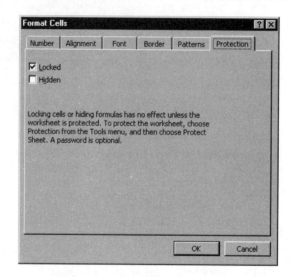

The following options are available from the Protection tab in the Format cells dialog box.

**Locked:** Cells can't be changed after sheet is protected.

**Hidden:** Hides formulas after sheet is protected.

Two simple facts can save you considerable confusion and frustration when working with cell protection:

- Cell protection does not take effect unless the worksheet is protected with Contents checked (think of sheet protection as a master breaker switch, and cell protection as a single outlet on the breaker).
- By default, each cell is individually set with Locked checked—you must individually unlock each cell that users will be allowed to change before you protect the worksheet.

**TIP**

You can navigate between unlocked cells on a protected worksheet using the Tab key.

## Protecting Graphical Objects

If graphical objects placed on a worksheet are not protected, users are able to move, resize, or even delete them. Here's how to protect a graphical object:

1. Select the object.
2. Select the Format ➤ Object command, then select the Protection tab.
3. Lock the object and/or object text.

**NOTE**

The Format command changes depending on the type of object you select. If you select a picture, the command will be Format ➤ Picture; if you select an AutoShape, the command will be Format ➤ AutoShape; and so forth. See Chapter 12 to learn how to work with graphic objects.

Object locking works like cell protection: by default, objects are set with Locked on (checked), and only need to be unlocked if you want specific objects unprotected on an otherwise protected sheet.

Keep these facts in mind when protecting objects:

- All objects have a protection setting called *Locked*; when checked, the object cannot be deleted, resized, moved, or formatted (if the worksheet is protected, that is; remember, there's a two-tier structure). If the object's format dialog box does not have a *Protection* tab, look under its *Properties* tab.
- Text boxes, buttons, and several controls have an additional setting called Lock Text; when checked, the text cannot be changed.

**TIP**

If you select the box in such a way that you have a flashing cursor inside the box, then when you select Format ➤ Text Box, you will only be able to format the text, not the box itself. Be sure to click toward the edge of the box when selecting it, this ensures the Format ➤ Text Box command will allow you to make the full range of format choices, including protection.

PART

**III**

Tapping Excel's Power

- Object protection does not take effect unless the worksheet is protected with Objects checked.

# Documenting Your Work

Spreadsheet applications have a notorious reputation for "spaghetti code" (formulas and macros which are disorganized and difficult to follow) and the blame falls directly on the shoulders of the people who build them. When spreadsheets were used solely for personal productivity, at least others weren't bearing the brunt of developers' bad habits. But spreadsheet programs have become popular tools used to create organizational solutions. Thorough documentation—cell notes that explain why a particular formula was used, where supporting information came from, and so on—is vitally important, particularly in complex models.

**TIP**

Though it may be a practice that defies human nature, you are a lot better off if you document as you work. The formulas and logic are fresh in your mind, and a tedious task is not left for the end.

There are three primary items used for documenting a worksheet model:

- Cell comments
- Text boxes and arrows
- Meaningful naming conventions (see Chapter 8)

# Enhancing Documentation with Cell Comments

Cell comments are an outstanding feature for documenting formulas, assumptions, and results. Cell comments are notes that are displayed when the cursor passes over a cell, or when the cell is selected. To add a cell comment to a worksheet, select a cell, then select Insert ➤ Comment to display a pop-up note box, as shown below.

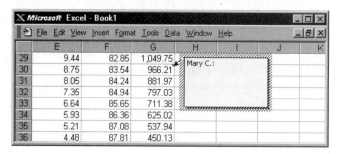

### Listing All the Names in a Worksheet

If you use names extensively, it doesn't take long before a workbook can contain hundreds of names. Whether you are documenting your work or troubleshooting a problem, having a complete list of the names in a worksheet is very helpful. To create a list of all the names in a worksheet:

1. Select a cell in an empty area of the worksheet, so that the pasted list will not overwrite other data. (The list will be pasted into two columns, beginning with the active cell.)
2. Select Insert ➢ Name ➢ Paste.
3. Click on the Paste List button on the Paste Name dialog box.

The pasted list will contain all the global names in the workbook, and local names only for the active worksheet. To compile a list including all the local names in the workbook, you must repeat this process for each worksheet in the book that contains local names. (See Chapter 8 to learn more about global and local names.)

To add a cell comment, type the comment in the comment box and select another cell. Selecting another cell finishes and closes the cell note, but leaves a small red marker in the upper-right corner of the noted cell. You can also insert a cell comment from the Reviewing or Auditing toolbars. Use View ➢ Toolbars ➢ Customize, and check the toolbar you want to display on the Toolbars tab of the dialog box.

## Viewing and Editing Comments

When a cell with a comment is selected, the Insert Comment command becomes an Edit Comment command. Cells with comments are indicated with a small red marker in the upper-right corner of the cell. Comment indicators and comments can be turned on and off individually using the Comments controls setting on the Tools ➢ Options ➢ View dialog box.

To view or edit a cell comment, select a cell with a comment marker, then use one of the following procedures:

- Double-click on the cell (if in-cell editing is turned off).
- Click on the Edit Comment tool on the Reviewing toolbar.
- Select Insert ➢ Edit Comment.
- Right-click on a cell with a comment to display a submenu that includes comment editing commands, select either Edit Comment, Delete Comment(s), or Show/Hide Comment.

**TIP**

You can use the Edit ➢ Find command to search cell comments for a given text string. You can find the Comments option in the Look In drop-down list of the Find dialog box.

## Reviewing Workbook Comments

One of the main reasons to include comments in a workbook is to allow review of your documents on a higher level, and to provide specific details that accompany bottom-line cell values. For example, your regional manager may want a monthly profit breakdown from each of several regions, but usually just looks at the total for each region. If the profits for a given region were less than expected because of the acquisition of a new building, for instance, a cell comment can instantly convey that information without digging for it.

When reviewing workbooks it is often desirable to simply look at all the comments before taking into account any data, or making any changes. If a workbook is modified or reviewed by others, they may want to address only specific areas, quickly make changes or add new comments, and move on.

To review all the comments in a workbook, use View ➢ Comments, this will display them and also the Reviewing toolbar shown below.

The buttons on the Reviewing toolbar provide an easy way to create, edit, add, or delete comments, and a few other useful document review tools. The Reviewing toolbar commands perform the following tasks:

 **New Comment:** Creates a new comment in the selected cell; if the cell already has a comment, this becomes the Edit Comment command.

 **Previous Comment:** Displays the previous comment in the workbook.

 **Next Comment:** Displays the next comment in the workbook.

 **Show/Hide Comment:** Shows or hides the comment in the selected cell.

**Show/Hide All Comments**: Shows or hides all comments in the workbook.

 **Delete Comment:** Deletes comments from the selected cell.

 **Create Microsoft Outlook Task:** Creates a Microsoft Outlook Task. Microsoft Outlook is an information management program that is part of the Microsoft Office 97 group.

 **Update File:** Updates changes made by other users.

 **Send to Mail Recipient:** Sends the file as an attachment to a mail message.

## Printing Comments

When you print a worksheet using the normal procedures, cell comments are not included in the printout. Follow these steps to print cell comments:

1. Select File ➢ Page Setup, then select the Sheet tab.
2. Check the Row And Column Headings setting to print the cell references before each note.
3. Check the Comments list box and select whether to print cell comments either *As displayed on sheet*, or at the end of the worksheet, then click on OK before printing.

 **NOTE**
When you want to print comments as displayed on the worksheet, they must actually be that: displayed. To display comments, use either View ➢ Comments, or right-click on the cell with the comment, and use the Show/Hide Comment command on the shortcut menu.

## Clearing Comments for Memory Efficiency

Sometimes cell comments are intended for the user of a worksheet to learn more about certain formulas or assumptions. Other times, comments are used by the developer, and are *not* intended for users. In the latter case, you may want to clear the comments (for memory efficiency) before deploying the workbook:

1. Save a copy of the workbook *with* comments for future reference.

PART

III

Tapping Excel's Power

**2.** Select all cells on the sheet (use the Select All button, located at the upper-left intersection of the row and column headings).

**3.** Select Edit ➢ Clear ➢ Comments.

Sometimes you'll want notes to stand out boldly. Text boxes, combined with other on-sheet graphical objects, can add important information to a report, with style. See Chapter 12 to learn more about text boxes and other graphical objects.

# Auditing Worksheets

One of the most tedious tasks in working with spreadsheets is troubleshooting complex spreadsheets. Tracing all the interrelated cells and formulas can be a time-consuming task. Excel has some powerful auditing features designed to simplify the process. For example, you can trace the source of data found in linked cells by tracing dependent or precedent cells.

## Understanding Dependent and Precedent Cells

When you begin to work with linked worksheets and workbooks, the ability to identify dependent and precedent cells is indispensable. Assume that cell B1 has the formula =A1.

- B1 is the *dependent* cell; it depends on A1.
- A1 is the *precedent* cell; it precedes B1.

On complex worksheets, there can be many levels of dependency, which makes it difficult to trace the flow of dependencies. The auditing commands provide a graphical representation of cell relationships (see Figure 11.4).

You can find auditing tools on both the Auditing and Circular Reference toolbars.

 **Precedent Tracer**     Select a dependent cell, then select Tools ➢ Auditing ➢ Trace Precedents; arrows are displayed pointing from precedent to dependent cells.

 **Dependent Tracer**     Select a source cell, then select Tools ➢ Auditing ➢ Trace Dependents; arrows are displayed pointing from precedent to dependent cells.

*Tracer arrows provide a graph-ical representa-tion of cell relationships.*

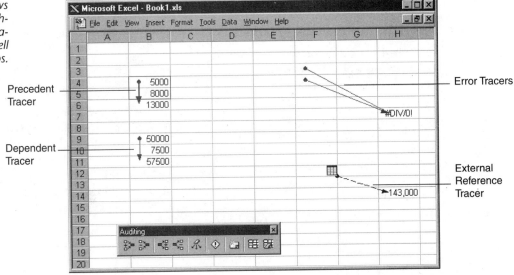

Precedent Tracer

Dependent Tracer

Error Tracers

External Reference Tracer

**Error Tracers**   Select a cell containing an error value, then select Tools ➢ Auditing ➢ Trace Error. Arrows are drawn from the error value in the active cell to the cells that might have caused the error.

**Removing Arrows**   Select Tools ➢ Auditing ➢ Remove All Arrows; all arrows on the worksheet are removed.

There are three types of tracer arrows:

- **Formula** tracers are solid blue arrows (solid black on black-and-white monitors).
- **Error** tracers are solid blue arrows from precedent formulas and precedent values.
- **External reference** tracers are dashed black lines.

PART III

Tapping Excel's Power

**TIP**

You can quickly locate cells containing links to other worksheets, workbooks, and applications by searching for an exclamation point (!). Select Edit ➢ Find, and type **!** in the Find What text box. Select Look In Formulas, and clear the Find Entire Cells Only check box.

## Troubleshooting a Link

When you move or copy a worksheet from one workbook to another, you may create unintended links in the new workbook. You may not notice the links until you open the new workbook and see the alert message "This document contains links. Re-establish links?" Sometimes links can be difficult to trace and eliminate. Here are some steps you can follow to find the cause of a link:

- Select Edit ➢ Links. The Links dialog box lists all workbooks that the active workbook is linked to, and lets you change the links.

- Names can point to ranges on other workbooks, which in turn create links that are hard to find. Select Insert ➢ Name ➢ Paste, then click on Paste List. It is easy to see external references in the list.

- Display the formulas on each worksheet by pressing Ctrl+` (grave accent), then scan the formulas for external references. Press Ctrl+` again to display values on the worksheet.

- If you create a chart in your workbook from data in another workbook, a link is created. These links are hard to isolate because you must examine each chart individually. Select the chart and click on the ChartWizard tool. The ChartWizard Step 1 dialog box will be displayed—click on Next to go to Step 2 and display source data and check for external references in the Data Range edit box. If the chart plots data from more than one worksheet, click on the Series tab and scroll through each chart series and look at their respective Name and Values edit boxes.

There are several ways to eliminate links once you've found them:

- If the links are caused by references in formulas, you can replace the formulas with values. Select the cells containing linked formulas, select Edit ➢ Copy, then select Edit ➢ Paste Special and check Values.

- If the links are in formulas and you want to keep the formulas, replace the external references with references in the current workbook. Use the Edit ➢ Replace command to speed up the process of replacing references.

- If the links are in names, either redefine or delete the names.

- If the link is in a chart, redefine the data source(s) for the chart.

## Selecting Special Cells

As you troubleshoot spreadsheets, you will often need to locate particular types of cells on the worksheet, such as cells containing formulas or constants. To select special cells, do the following:

1. Select Edit ➤ Go To. The Go To dialog box appears.
2. Click on the Special button to display the Go To Special dialog box, shown in Figure 11.5.

*FIGURE 11.5*

*The Go To Special dialog box*

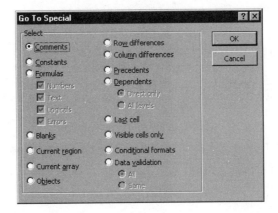

3. Make selections based on the following options available in the Go To Special dialog box:

   **Comments:** Selects all cells containing comments.

   **Constants:** Selects all cells containing constant values.

   **Formulas:** Selects all cells containing formulas; you can select cells containing formulas that return numbers, text, logical values (TRUE and FALSE), and error values.

   **Blanks:** Selects all blank cells.

   **Current Region:** Selects a rectangular range of data (the active cell must be within the data before choosing the command).

   **Current Array:** Selects the entire array that the active cell resides in (if it is part of an array).

   **Objects:** Selects all graphical objects (including chart objects).

PART

III

Tapping Excel's Power

**Row Differences:** Selects cells in the selected row which have contents that are different from the active cell.

**Column Differences:** Same as row differences, but in columns.

**Precedents:** Selects cells referred to by the formula in the active cell.

**Dependents:** Selects cells with either direct references only, or both direct and indirect references to the active cell.

**Last Cell:** Selects the last cell in the worksheet (or macro sheet) containing data or formatting.

**Visible Cells Only:** Selects only visible cells on the worksheet (so changes will not affect hidden rows or columns).

**Conditional Formats:** Selects cells to which conditional formatting has been applied (see Chapter 5).

**Data Validation:** Selects cells with Data Validation (See Chapter 10).

Once you've selected the desired cells, use the Tab key to cycle through them. If a range of cells is selected prior to choosing Edit ➤ Go To, only cells within the selected range will be searched.

Here are some shortcut keys for selecting special cells.

| This Keystroke | Selects |
| --- | --- |
| Ctrl +[ | Direct precedents |
| Ctrl+Shift+{ | All precedents |
| Ctrl+] | Direct dependents |
| Ctrl+Shift+} | All dependents |
| Ctrl+Shift+* | Current region |
| Ctrl+/ | Entire array |
| Ctrl+End | Last cell in worksheet |

TIP

Use the Edit ➤ Find command, covered in Chapter 3, to search for specific values or formulas. You can search cell values, formulas, or cell comments.

# Searching for Files

Searching for files and categorizing files using *summary information* are important skills to help you organize your work.

## Searching Based on the File Name

Suppose you have saved budget data for each year in workbooks with file names beginning with *BUDGET*, such as *BUDGET97* and *BUDGET98*. You now want to view the files, but don't remember what directory you saved them in. This procedure will locate the files for you:

**1.** Select File ➢ Open. The Open dialog box appears.
**2.** Enter these search parameters in the Open dialog box:

- In File Name text box, enter the file name, with optional wildcards—for example, enter **budget*** to search for every file beginning with *BUDGET* (see Table 11.1 for a list of supported wildcard characters).

**TABLE 11.1:** SUPPORTED WILDCARD CHARACTERS

| Character | Meaning |
|-----------|---------|
| ? (question mark) | Match single character |
| * (asterisk) | Match any number of characters |
| "" (double quotes) | Enclosed character is not wildcard (use to search for ?, *, &, etc.) |
| , (comma) | Indicates OR (search for information matching at least one item in list) |
| & (ampersand) | Indicated AND (search for information matching all items in list) |
| (space) | Same as &—indicates AND (search for information matching all items in list) |
| ~ (tilde) | Indicates NOT (exclude matching information from search) |

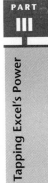

- In Look In, select a folder or drive—use the drop-down list to specify the drive, then type a folder name in the File Name text box, if desired.
- To search all subfolders of the Look In drop-down list, click on the Commands And Settings button and select Search Subfolders from the drop-down menu (see Figure 11.6).

**FIGURE 11.6**

*The Open dialog box*

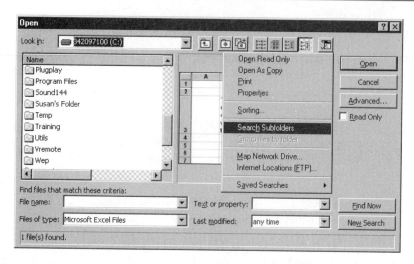

**3.** Click on the Find Now button. The Open dialog box is displayed again, with the results of the search displayed in the Name window.

To view file details, paths, or properties, click on either the List, Details, or Properties button in the Open dialog box (see Figure 11.7). (See Chapter 2 for more on the Open dialog box.) To display a preview of the file, click on the Preview button. This lets you quickly inspect the file before taking the time to actually open it (see Figure 11.8).

**FIGURE 11.7**

*The files are listed on the left, and properties for the selected file are displayed on the right.*

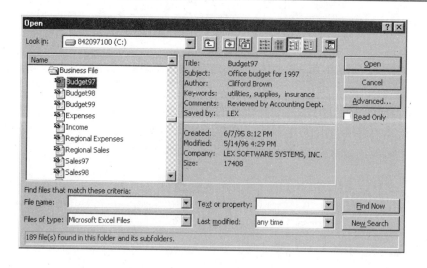

*FIGURE 11.8*

*The upper-left corner of the top sheet is displayed in the preview.*

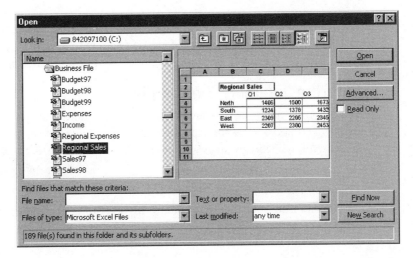

When you have completed the initial search, you can either click on the Open button to open the file, or click on the New Search button to conduct a new search.

## Commands and Settings Options

If you clicked on the Commands And Settings button in the Open dialog box in step 2 of the exercise above, you may have noticed that additional options were available from the drop-down menu (see Figure 11.6). These additional choices are described here:

**Open Read Only:** Opens selected workbook(s) read-only.

**Open As Copy:** Opens a copy of the document.

**Print:** Prints selected file

**Properties:** Displays a tabbed dialog box of general file properties.

**Sorting:** Displays Options dialog box for choosing how to sort listed files.

**Search Subfolders:** Searches through all subfolders of drive or folder specified in Look In.

**Group Files By Folder:** Displays folder hierarchy (path) for each file found in search.

**Map Network Drive:** Allows you to connect to a network drive.

**Add/Modify FTP Locations:** Allows you to connect to a File Transfer Protocol site (see Chapter 29).

**Saved Searches:** Displays list of previous searches by name specified in Advanced Find dialog box (see Figure 11.9).

PART

III

Tapping Excel's Power

## Performing an Advanced Search

There are several ways to search for files based on criteria other than the file name. For instance, your budget files may not always begin with *BUDGET*. Before you can understand advanced searches, you need to understand how to enter file properties.

### Entering Summary Information

You can enter file properties such as a title, subject, author, keywords, and comments for each workbook. This information can help you locate workbooks, and is particularly useful in a workgroup environment. Here's how to enter file properties:

**1.** Open the workbook.

**2.** Select File ➤ Properties.

**3.** Enter a title, subject, author name, any keywords that might be useful in a future search, and comments.

**4.** Click on OK.

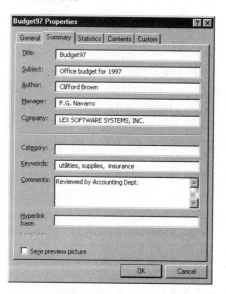

To display the Properties dialog box every time a new worksheet is saved (or when the File ➤ Save As command is used), select Tools ➤ Options, select the General tab, and check the Prompt For Workbook Properties setting.

## Searching Using Keywords

In the following exercise, you'll search for files where the word *BUDGET* was entered as a keyword in properties.

**1.** Select File ➤ Open. The results of the last search are displayed.

**2.** Click on the New Search button (to clear all previous search parameters).

**3.** Enter a Location in the Look In text box (including a path to narrow the search).

**4.** Click on the Advanced button. The Advanced Find dialog box appears (see Figure 11.9).

FIGURE 11.9

*The Advanced
Find dialog box*

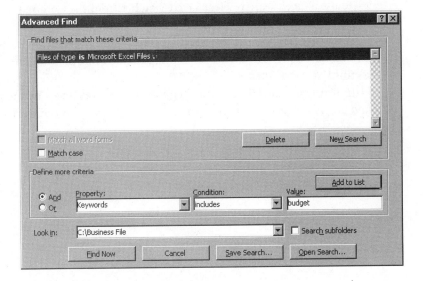

**5.** Select Keywords from the Property drop-down list.

- Select Includes from the Condition drop-down list.
- Enter **budget** in the Value box.
- Select the Add To List button.

**6.** Click on the Find Now button in the Advanced Find dialog box to begin the search.

## Saving the Search

Suppose this is a search that you want to perform regularly. Once a set of search criteria has been specified, you can name it and save it for future use. You can then perform the same search again at a later date without having to reenter the search parameters.

PART

**III**

Tapping Excel's Power

Follow these steps to name and save a search:

**1.** Specify the search criteria.

**2.** In the Advanced Find dialog box, click on Save Search.

**3.** Type a name for the search in the Search Name text box, and click on OK.

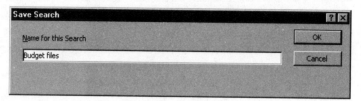

To use a saved search, select Saved Searches from the Command and Settings drop-down menu in the File Open dialog box.

Part Three has been an introduction into creating versatile worksheet models, using names, functions, and templates. It also provided information on auditing and protecting Excel documents.

In Part Four you will learn how enhance your worksheets by incorporating charts and graphic objects in the presentation and interpretation of worksheet data.

# PART IV

# Graphics and Charts

## LEARN TO:

- *Use the new Drawing toolbar*

- *Work with graphic objects placed on worksheets*

- *Create a chart with the ChartWizard*

- *Use the Chart toolbar*

- *Work with embedded charts and chart sheets*

- *Create a custom AutoFormat*

- *Dynamically chart different data sets*

- *Work with 3-D charts, picture charts, and other special chart types*

# Chapter

# 12

## Working with Graphic Objects

# Chapter 12

# Working with Graphic Objects

**T**raditionally, spreadsheet programs have been used for number crunching. But Excel is a powerful graphics package in its own right. You can enhance worksheets with company logos, text boxes, pictures, pointers, and shapes of all colors, sizes, and styles. In fact, the new package is so versatile it is practically a stand-alone application.

The new Excel drawing features are used in other Office programs. Once you've mastered the Excel drawing toolbar, you can apply the knowledge to Word and PowerPoint. One of the outstanding features of the new drawing package is its ability to quickly create *flowcharts,* an extremely valuable tool used in decision making and visualizing process flow.

Excel also includes WordArt, a special-effects text tool that replaces the WordArt program used by Microsoft Works, Publisher 95, and other Office applications.

**NOTE**

See Chapter 29 to learn how to import and export graphics to and from other applications.

# Drawing Graphic Objects

Suppose you have a worksheet with information that needs explanation or emphasis. In the worksheet shown below, we've used a simple text box, circle, and arrow to explain a figure on the worksheet. These objects were drawn on the sheet using tools found on the drawing command bar.

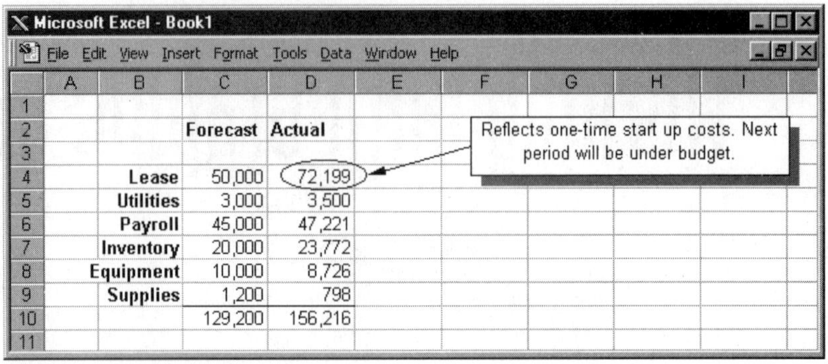


To add a graphic object to a worksheet, do the following:

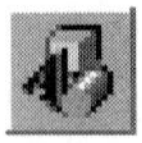

1. Choose View ➢ Toolbars, or click on the Drawing tool on the Standard toolbar to call up the Drawing command bar, shown here:

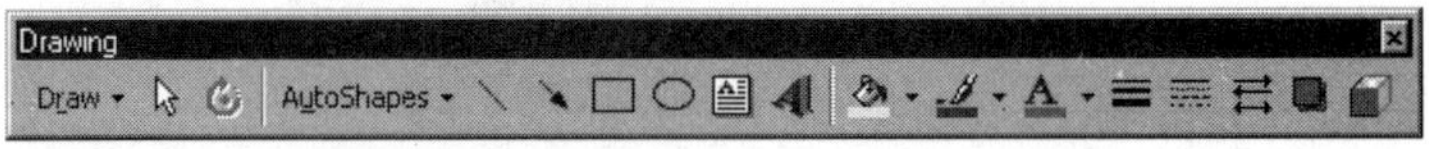


2. Select the tool for the object you want to draw, a rectangle for example (Table 12.1 explains the tools available). The mouse pointer becomes crosshairs.

**TABLE 12.1: DRAWING TOOLS**

| Tool | Function |
|---|---|
| 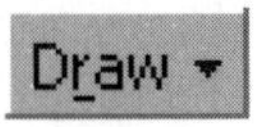 | Displays a drop-down menu of general drawing commands, and alignment and orientation tools |
|  | Selects multiple objects |
|  | Allows free rotation of selected object |

**TABLE 12.1:** DRAWING TOOLS (CONTINUED)

| Tool | Function |
| --- | --- |
| AutoShapes ▾ | Displays a drop-down palette of drawing shapes |
| | Draws straight lines |
| | Draws arrows |
| | Draws a filled rectangle |
| | Draws a filled oval |
| | Draws a text box |
| | Creates WordArt text |
| | Formats the fill color |
| | Formats the line color |
| | Formats the font style |
| | Formats the line style |
| | Formats the dash style |
| | Creates arrow effects |

| **TABLE 12.1:** DRAWING TOOLS (CONTINUED) | |
| --- | --- |
| **Tool** | **Function** |
| 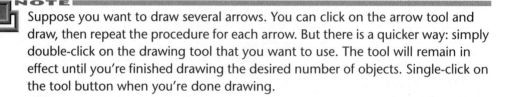 | Creates shadow effects |
| | Creates 3-D effects |

**3.** Click on the worksheet, and drag the mouse to form the desired object.

**4.** Release the mouse button when you're finished drawing.

**NOTE**

Suppose you want to draw several arrows. You can click on the arrow tool and draw, then repeat the procedure for each arrow. But there is a quicker way: simply double-click on the drawing tool that you want to use. The tool will remain in effect until you're finished drawing the desired number of objects. Single-click on the tool button when you're done drawing.

## Filled vs. Unfilled Objects

As implied in Table 12.1, there are *filled* and *unfilled* objects.

A *filled* object is colored or has a pattern—it obscures the underlying cells, as shown in Figure 12.1. (Some of the tools on the Drawing command bar create filled objects that are colored white—this can be hard to distinguish from an unfilled object if worksheet gridlines are turned off.)

**NOTE**

You will learn how to change the fill of an object in the formatting section later in this chapter.

An *unfilled* object is an outline with no fill—you can see the cells behind the object.

**FIGURE 12.1**

*The unfilled rectangle on the right leaves gridlines showing, whereas the filled rectangle on the left obscures the gridlines behind it.*

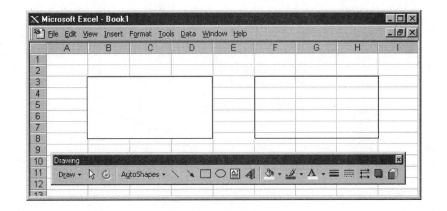

# Manipulating Objects

In this section you will learn how to select, group, move, resize, copy, and delete graphic objects.

## Selecting Objects

Before manipulating an object in any way, you must first select it. The procedure differs slightly depending on whether the object is *filled* or *unfilled*:

- To select a filled object , simply click anywhere on the object.
- To select an unfilled object, you must click on the object's border.

When you select an object, the name of the selected object appears in the Name box on the left of the formula bar.

**TIP**

It is impossible to select a cell behind a filled object by clicking on the cell, because you will select the object instead. To select a cell behind a filled object, you can use the Name box or the Edit ➢ Go To command, or use the arrow keys to navigate to the cell behind a filled object.

A selected object has small markers along the border—these are called *handles*. You'll learn more about object handles in the "Resizing an Object" section.

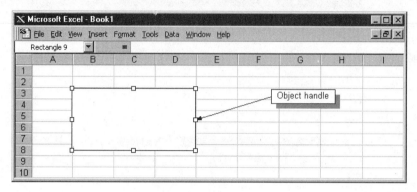

## Selecting Multiple Objects

You can have more than one object selected at the same time, allowing you to manipulate all of the selected objects at once. Suppose you want to move several objects, but retain their relative positions. You can select all of the objects and move them together, instead of moving them one by one. The following methods are available for selecting multiple objects:

- Hold down Shift while selecting objects with the mouse. This technique is probably the quickest if you need to select just two or three objects.
- Click on the Drawing Selection tool, then draw a rectangle around the objects that you want to select. When finished using the Drawing Selection tool, click on it again to turn it off. This tool is most useful when the objects you want to select are positioned close together.

# Moving an Object

To move an object, select it with the mouse, then drag it across the worksheet. An outline of the object is displayed until you release the mouse button.

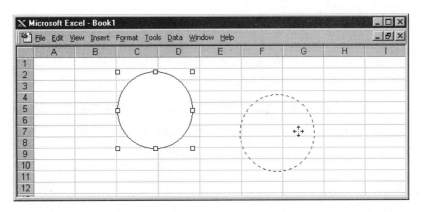

You can rotate or invert objects using the Draw ➤ Rotate Or Flip command on the Drawing command bar. The Rotate Left and Rotate Right commands rotate the selected object in 90° increments, while the Flip Horizontal and Flip Vertical commands invert the objects as though across a mirror plane.

When the Free Rotate command is selected, either directly from the Drawing command bar or from the Draw ➤ Rotate Or Flip menu, the selected object will have four green handles. Place the cursor on one of the handles and rotate the object by holding down the left mouse button while moving the mouse. In this way, you can spin the object as if it were nailed to the worksheet.

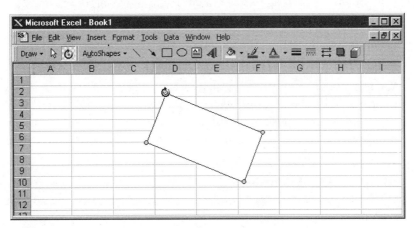

# Resizing an Object

To resize an object, select it, then drag one of its handles. An outline of the new size is displayed until the mouse button is released. When you click and hold on a handle, the cursor changes to a double-headed arrow, showing the direction(s) that you may resize.

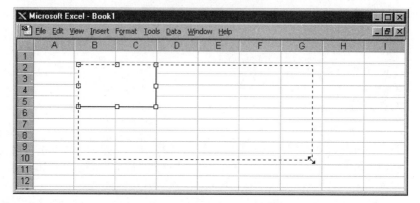

To retain the precise proportions when resizing an object, hold down the Shift key while dragging one of the corner handles.

**TIP**

Hold down the Shift key while drawing with the Oval tool to draw a circle, or with the Rectangle tool to draw a square.

## Aligning and Distributing Objects

You will often need to perfectly align several objects or make sure objects are the exact same size. When you try this freehand, no matter how careful you are, it is nearly impossible to align or size the objects perfectly. When you look at a worksheet with imperfectly aligned objects, you may not be consciously aware of the imperfections, but the brain detects them anyway.

**Using the Snap Command** - If you hold down Alt while moving or resizing an object, the object is snapped to the worksheet grid along its top and left margin—even if gridlines are not displayed.

If you select the object and then choose Draw ➤ Snap ➤ To Grid, when you move the object, it snaps to the grid. To disable this option, select the object and repeat the Draw ➤ Snap ➤ To Grid command.

You can also snap an object to another object to its left or above it by selecting the object and choosing Draw ➤ Snap ➤ To Shape. Then click on and drag the selected object to the object you want to connect it to. Repeat the command to undo it.

**Using the Nudge Command** - One of the handiest tools is the Draw ➤ Nudge command. Using the Nudge command, you can make small, precise movements to selected objects (this is especially useful for moving pointer arrows). You can nudge objects up, down, to the left, or to the right.

**Alignment vs. Distribution** - *Alignment* is the process of spatially arranging two or more objects to a common reference point; for example, to the worksheet grid. *Distribution* is juxtaposing three or more objects with respect to each other (see Figure 12.2).

To align two or more objects to the worksheet grid, select them (while holding down Shift) by clicking on them, or by using the Select Objects tool on the Drawing command bar. Choose the Draw ➤ Align Or Distribute command, then select either Align Left, Center, Right, Top, Middle, or Bottom.

You can also *distribute* three or more objects; that is, make the space between them equal. To do this, choose Draw ➤ Align Or Distribute ➤ Distribute Horizontally, or Draw ➤ Align Or Distribute ➤ Distribute Vertically. Use a combination of alignment and distribution commands to create a variety of effects. In the figure below, the three objects have been aligned *middle*, and distributed *horizontally*.

**FIGURE 12.2**

*The objects have been aligned along their middle and distributed horizontally.*

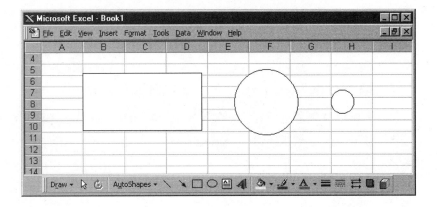

## Copying Objects

There are two ways to copy objects: by dragging and dropping, and by using menu commands.

### Copying Objects Using Drag and Drop

The most efficient way to copy an object to a nearby location is to drag it and drop it. Here's how:

**1.** Select the object.

**2.** Hold down the Ctrl key.

**3.** Drag and drop the object—a copy of the object is created.

## Copying Objects Using Menu Commands

To copy (or cut) an object using menu commands:

**1.** Select the object.

**2.** Choose Edit ➤ Copy or Edit ➤ Cut.

**3.** Select a cell where you want to paste the object.

**4.** Choose Edit ➤ Paste.

Alternatively, you can use the Cut, Copy, and Paste commands on the object shortcut menu.

# Grouping and Ungrouping Objects

While selecting multiple objects is a useful method for manipulating objects, there may be times when you'll want to *group* objects together. It's often a lot easier to move a group of objects rather than several smaller ones, and sometimes you create objects that are composed of several other objects (an AutoShape with a text box on it, for example) that need to be kept together when you move, copy, or resize them. When you group objects, a new object is created.

Try the following exercise to practice grouping objects:

**1.** Draw a text box and an arrow.

**2.** Select the text box and arrow, then choose Draw ➤ Group.

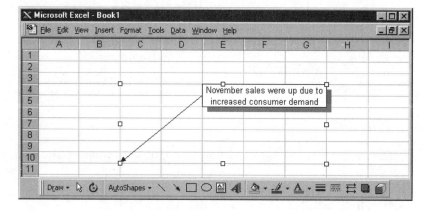

PART

**IV**

Graphics and Charts

Notice that the two objects are now a single object, and (if you display the formula bar) have a new name; e.g., Group 3. (Since Excel names objects using a sequential numeric suffix, the name of the new object depends on the number of objects that have already been created on the worksheet.)

To ungroup objects, select the group object, then choose Draw ➤ Ungroup. If you have ungrouped some objects and want to regroup them, you can select one of the members of the former group and use the Draw ➤ Regroup command to restore the group.

## Deleting Objects

Here's how to delete an object:

**1.** Select the object.
**2.** Press Delete (or choose Edit ➤ Clear ➤ All).

## Using the Object Shortcut Menu

When you click on an object with the right mouse button, the object is selected and a shortcut menu is displayed, as shown in Figure 12.3. Shortcut menus often have commands specific to the type of object selected. For example, if a text box is selected, then the Format command will read *Format Text Box* (as opposed to *Format Object*).

**FIGURE 12.3**

*Click on an object with the right mouse button to display the object shortcut menu.*

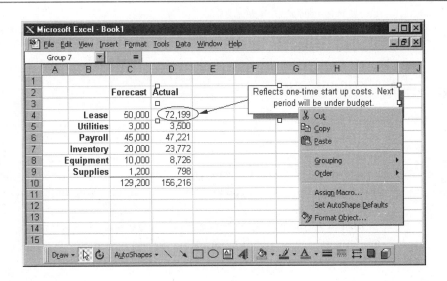

The shortcut menu can save you several keystrokes when working with objects. In addition to functions that have already been covered, such as Cut, Copy, and Paste, the following options are available from the object shortcut menu:

**Add Text:** Adds text to the selected object

**Grouping:** Groups, ungroups, or regroups objects

**Order:** Moves the selected object in front of or behind any stacked objects in its vicinity

**Assign Macro:** Assigns a macro to the selected object (the macro then runs when you click on the object)

**Set AutoShape Defaults:** Applies formatting of selected object to succeeding objects that you draw

**Format:** Displays the formatting dialog box for the selected AutoShape, text box, or other object (see the section on "Formatting Objects" later in the chapter)

## Renaming Objects

Each object is named automatically when it is drawn—the name is displayed in the Name box when the object is selected. Excel names the objects using a prefix consisting of the object type, and a suffix that is a sequential number. For instance, when you draw a text box on a new workbook, it is named *TextBox 1*. If you then draw a rectangle, it is named *Rectangle 2*.

To rename an object, simply select it, overwrite the name in the Name box with something more meaningful, and press ↵.

## Formatting Objects

There are several different format settings that you can apply to objects, such as font style or size, colors, and patterns, though the options available vary for different objects. Therefore, it is usually advisable to format objects before grouping them. As you group objects, you decrease your formatting options. For example, you can add text to a rectangle, but if you group it with an arrow, you can't format the text without ungrouping.

In spite of the fact that some objects have unique formatting properties, all objects are formatted by displaying the Format (*Object type*) dialog box pictured in Figure 12.4.

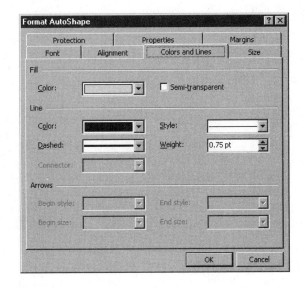

*The contents of the Format (Object type) dialog box vary depending on the type of object.*

There are three ways to display this dialog box:

- Double-click on the object.
- Choose Format Object (or Text Box or AutoShape) from the object shortcut menu.
- Select the object, then choose Format ➤ Object.

## Adding Visual Impact with Colors and Fills

There are three tools on the Drawing command bar that control the colors of selected objects: Fill Color, Line Color, and Font Color. All three tools have a drop-down palette of colors to choose from. The Fill Color and Line Color tools can also apply additional standard colors, fill effects, patterns, and custom colors. All of these options are also provided through the Format Object dialog box.

To change the color of an object, right-click on it and choose the Format command. In the Fill or Line areas of the dialog box, click on the arrow to open the Color drop-down menu and select a color from the palette, or choose More Colors to display the Colors dialog box. The Standard tab of the Colors dialog box allows you to select additional built-in colors, and the Custom tab allows you to create custom colors. Click on OK to set your new colors.

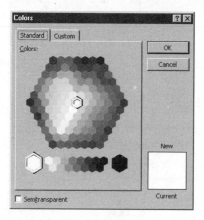 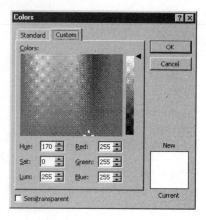

## Applying Patterns

The Format (Object type) dialog box also allows you to apply patterns to object fills and borders; just select the object and execute the formatting command. From the Color drop-down menus in the Fill and Line areas, choose Fill Effects (for fills), or Patterned Lines (for borders). To apply a pattern, click on the Pattern tab and choose Foreground and Background colors, click on a pattern, and click on OK twice.

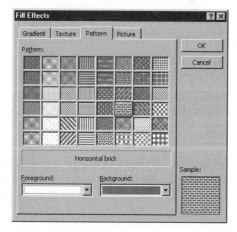

## Creating Fill Effects

In addition to colors and patterns, there are many types of fill effects for objects: gradient fills, textures, and pictures. The following tabs on the Fill Effects dialog box control these formatting properties:

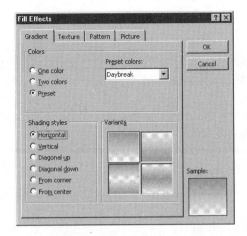

**Gradient:** Applies a gradual transition between two colors, or a gradual fading or darkening effect to a single color

**Texture:** Applies built-in textures from a palette or custom textures

**Picture:** Inserts a picture file or clip art as the object fill, such as WMF, GIF, or BMP files

The following exercise will show you how to format a text box using some formatting techniques:

**1.** Display the Drawing command bar and use the Text Box tool to draw a text box.
**2.** Enter some text into the text box (press Esc when you are done). The object will still be selected.

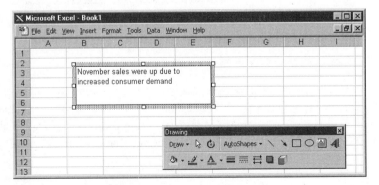

**3.** Choose Format ➢ Text Box, then select the Colors And Lines tab.

**4.** In the Fill area, click on the arrow to display the Color drop-down menu, and select a yellow fill.

**TIP**

To tone down the bright yellow, use a pattern. Display the Fill Color drop-down menu and choose Fill Effects, click on the Patterns tab and choose a yellow background and a white foreground, then select a pattern. Click on OK, and then move on to your next formatting task.

**5.** Click on the Font tab and select Bold for the style.
**6.** Select the Alignment tab, and align text to the center both horizontally and vertically.
**7.** Click on OK.
**8.** Click on the Shadow tool, and select shadow style 6 (hold the cursor over the shadow palette to get a pop-up label for each type).

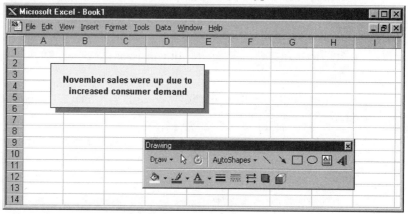

## Shadows and Shapes

As illustrated in the previous exercise, you can apply shadows to graphic objects using the Shadow tool. The Shadow tool displays a palette of 20 different shadow effects. The Shadow Settings button on the Shadow palette allows you to toggle shadows on and off, to change the colors of shadows, and to nudge shadows up, down, left, and right.

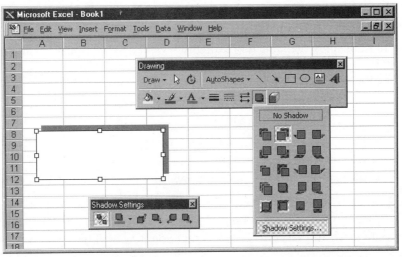

 You can make two-dimensional objects three-dimensional using the 3-D tool. Select the object, click on the tool, and Excel provides a palette of various 3-D shape styles. The 3-D Settings button on the palette displays a 3-D Settings toolbar that lets you toggle 3-D effects on and off, tilt them up and down or left to right, and adjust depth and perspective. The Lighting tool changes the illumination effects of the various surfaces of the 3-D object, while the Surface tool adjusts the texture of the respective surfaces. A drop-down color palette gives the full range of color options for the object.

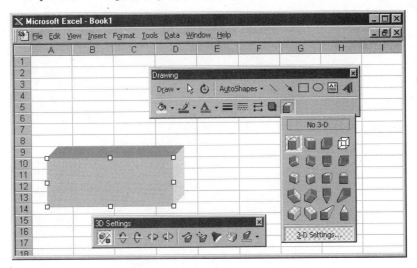

## Quickly Formatting Several Objects with the Format Painter Tool

You can apply the same formatting to several objects using the Format Painter tool (on the Standard toolbar). In the preceding exercise, seven steps were required to format the text box. Suppose you want to format several text boxes the same way—the Format Painter will let you do it quickly.

**1.** Select an object that is already formatted the way you want.
**2.** Double-click on the Format Painter tool.
**3.** Click on each object you want format.
**4.** Click on the Format Painter (or press Esc) to turn it off.

An alternative to the Format Painter is the Draw ➢ Set AutoShape Defaults command on the Drawing command bar; just select a formatted object, execute the command, and successive objects that you draw will have the same formatting.

# Understanding Object Properties

The Format (*Object type*) dialog box has a tab called Properties (see Figure 12.5). This tab is identical for all types of objects. The Properties tab controls object size and position relative to the underlying cells, and also whether the object prints out.

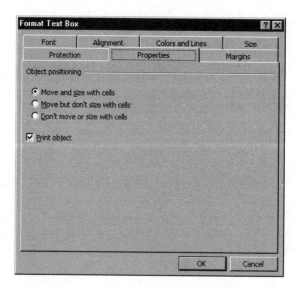

**MASTERING THE OPPORTUNITIES**

## Create Your Own Color Palette

Excel's color palette offers 56 built-in colors to choose from, but you are not limited to those 56 colors. You can choose from dozens of additional standard colors, or change any color in the palette to a custom color that you create using the Colors dialog box. It is especially useful to change the Chart Fills and Chart Lines colors because these are the default colors Excel uses when you create a chart. You can customize the colors in a specific order from left to right, and Excel will use the custom colors in the order in which you created them. For example, if you customize the Chart Fills colors as a succession of greens, then create a column chart, the chart series will be colored a succession of greens. Changing any of Excel's built-in colors is fairly simple:

1. Open the workbook in which you want to use custom colors.
2. Choose Tools ➢ Options, then select the Color tab.
3. Select the color you want to change, then click on Modify.

4. Select a new color from the Standard tab of the Colors dialog box, or create a new color using the Custom tab (this is the only tricky part—getting the color you want takes a bit of experimentation).
5. Click on OK to close the Colors dialog box, then click on OK to close the Options dialog box.

Your custom color palette will be saved with the workbook in which you created it. If you want to copy the custom palette into another workbook, follow these steps:

1. Open the workbook containing the custom color palette and the workbook you want to copy the palette into.
2. Activate the workbook you want to copy the palette into.
3. Choose Tools ➢ Options, then select the Color tab.
4. In the Copy Colors From text box, select the name of the workbook containing the custom color palette.

To restore the default color palette, click on the Reset button on the Color tab.

## Controlling Object Size and Placement Relative to Underlying Cells

Suppose you draw a text box, enter some text, then manually size the text box:

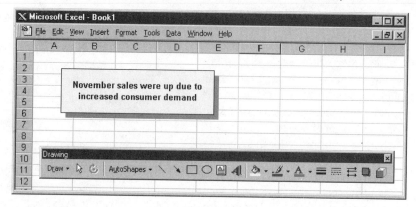

If you change the row height or column width of the underlying cells, the text box resizes accordingly:

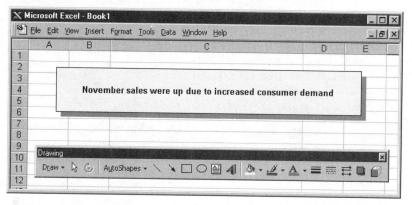

The Object Positioning options in the Properties tab control this behavior:

**Move And Size With Cells:** An object will move if rows/columns are inserted or deleted. The object size will change as the row height or column width of underlying cells changes.

**Move But Don't Size With Cells:** An object will move with the underlying cells, but will not resize.

**Don't Move Or Size With Cells:** An object will not move with the underlying cells, and will not resize.

Graphics and Charts

## Do You Want the Object to Print?

By default, all objects (except buttons) are included on the printout when the worksheet is printed. But some objects may be intended to display on the screen and not print. For example, a text box may instruct the user on how to enter data; this text box would be inappropriate on the printout. The *Print Object* setting determines whether an object will print or not. Just click on the Properties tab on the Format dialog box, and check (or uncheck) the Print Object setting.

### Cutting, Copying, and Sorting Objects with Cells

You have seen how the size and position of an object relative to the underlying cells are controlled by the Format ➤ Object ➤ Properties dialog box tab. You can also copy, cut, sort, and delete objects with their underlying cells. This behavior is controlled by an option on the Edit tab in the Tools ➤ Options dialog box. When the Cut, Copy, And Sort Objects With Cells option is selected, objects on a worksheet are virtually attached to the underlying cells. If you move or copy the cells under an object, the object is also moved or copied. If you delete a cell using the Edit ➤ Delete command, objects attached to the cell will also be deleted. If an object fits entirely within a single cell, the object will sort with the cell.

## Protecting Objects

Like cells, objects are protected (locked) by default. To unlock an object, select the object, then choose Format ➤ Object. Select the Protection tab, then clear the Locked check box. The Protection settings do not take effect unless the worksheet is protected. See Chapter 11 to learn about worksheet protection.

# Types of Objects

So far in this chapter, you have read about objects in general. This section will describe the unique properties of the various object types.

## AutoShapes

Excel includes a drawing tool called AutoShapes. AutoShapes are pre-existing "templates" for commonly drawn shapes, like lines, polygons, and arrows, as well as freeform lines and two-dimensional shapes. The following drawing tools are available from the AutoShapes menu:

**Lines:** Allows you to draw straight or curved lines, arrows, freeform lines, and shapes

**Connectors:** Draws straight, curved, or orthogonal lines and arrows that connect objects

**Basic Shapes:** Provides a palette of basic two-dimensional shapes, plus arcs and brackets

**Block Arrows:** Draws two-dimensional arrows

**Flowchart:** Creates standard two-dimensional flowchart symbols

**Stars and Banners:** Makes two-dimensional star and banner shapes

**Callouts:** Displays a palette of shapes for text insertion, dialogue, thought clouds, and line callouts

To draw an AutoShape, use the AutoShapes menu on the Drawing command bar, select a shape from one of the submenus, hold down the left mouse button, and drag the mouse to draw the shape. Figure 12.6 illustrates just a few of the basic AutoShapes. For most 2-D shapes, the tool stops drawing when you release the button, and the object is selected. When drawing lines, however, releasing the left button only changes direction of the line; you must double-click on it to exit the drawing mode and select the object. You can also add text to most AutoShapes: simply right-click on the object and select the Add Text or Edit Text command.

**NOTE**

The Edit Text command is not available for some shapes, such as freeform polygons. This does not mean that these shapes cannot contain text; you can always place a text box on top of the shape.

When certain AutoShapes are selected, such as block arrows and arcs, small, yellow handles appear in addition to the resizing handles. The yellow handles are used to change the object by clicking and dragging. They can change the relative proportions of an object, such as a block arrow, or extend the curve of an arc, depending on the type of object selected.

FIGURE 12.6

*Some basic
AutoShapes*

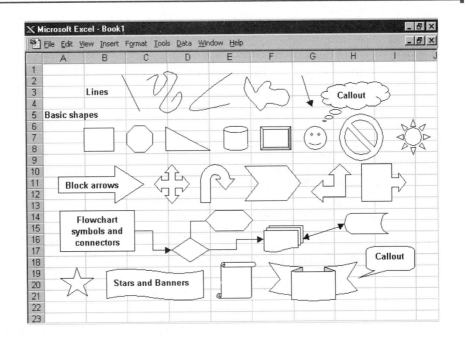

FIGURE 12.6

*Some basic
AutoShapes*

## Rectangles and Ovals

It is difficult, if not impossible, to draw perfect squares and circles freehand. If you
hold down the Shift key while using the Rectangle or Oval tools, you can draw squares
and circles (pressing Shift while drawing an arc will create a 90° arc).

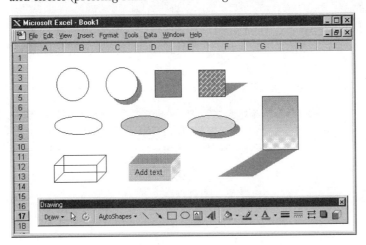

## Lines and Arrows

An arrow is simply a line formatted with an arrowhead (see examples in Figure 12.7). The Format AutoShape dialog box lets you specify the arrowhead type, if you choose to use one:

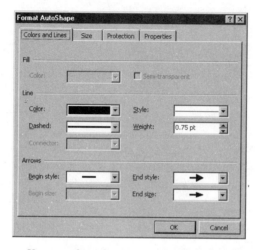

You can draw lines at perfect vertical, horizontal, and 45-degree angles by holding down Shift while drawing.

**FIGURE 12.7**

*Various lines and arrowheads combined to make arrows*

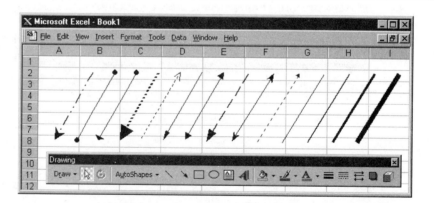

## Text, Text Boxes, and Callouts

A *text box* is a rectangle in which you can enter and format text. It is very useful for adding comments and explanations to worksheets and charts, especially when combined with arrows and circles to point to specific information. A *callout* is an

AutoShape that is really a stylized text box. Callouts are text boxes with pointers that are meant to call attention to a given item, such as a line of text.

After you draw a text box (or a callout), the text-insertion point will blink within the box, ready for you to type text. This is the Text Edit mode. Also notice that the border of the text box has a *hachured* pattern (short parallel lines) rather than the *stippled* (little dots) one of selected objects. Click alternately on the border (where your cursor will change to a four-pointed arrow) and then inside text box to toggle back and forth between these two selection modes; one affects the text within the object, the other the object itself.

You can add text to most drawing objects. To add text to an object, right-click on it to display the shortcut menu, and then choose the Add Text command to access Text Edit mode. Text automatically wraps when you are entering it into an object (press ⏎ to insert a hard break).

**TIP**

The shortcut menu will let you know if the Add Text command is available to the selected object. For example, you cannot add text to arrows.

There are several format settings specific to text objects:

- The Alignment, Margins, and Font tabs are used to format the text.
- The Automatic Size setting on the Alignment tab causes the text box to size automatically based on the text.
- The Lock Text setting on the Protection tab prevents users from changing text. (The worksheet must also be protected for this setting to take effect—see Chapter 11 to learn about sheet protection.)

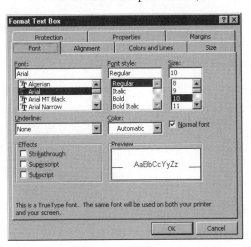

You can also format the text in a text box using tools on the Formatting toolbar.

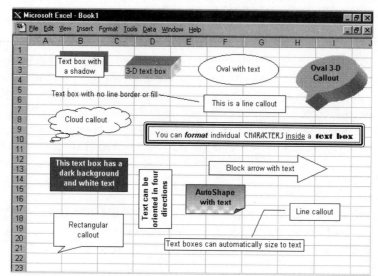

**TIP**

If you are in Edit Text mode, only the font tab will appear on the Format (*Object type*) dialog box.

## Linking Objects to Cells

Suppose you want what appears in a text box to vary according to certain conditions. You can link a text box to a worksheet cell by entering a formula instead of a constant. Try this exercise:

1. On a new worksheet, enter the following formula into cell B2:

   ```
   =IF(ISNUMBER(B3),"You may now save the workbook.","Please enter
   a number into B3.")
   ```

2. Draw a text box.

**3.** Click in the formula bar and type **=B2**, then press ↵ (see Figure 12.8).

**4.** Enter a number in B3 and watch the text box change.

**WARNING**

A common mistake is entering the formula into the text box rather than into the formula bar.

**FIGURE 12.8**

*When a linked text box is selected, the cell reference appears in the formula bar, where the cell reference can be changed.*

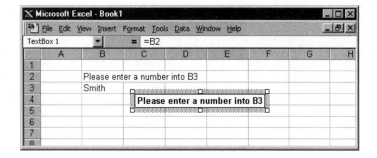

## Creating Linked Pictures

A linked picture is a picture of one or more worksheet cells that remain linked to the source cell(s). Put to creative use, linked pictures can greatly enhance reports and presentations.

The Camera tool is the easiest way to create a linked picture. It is not located on any of the built-in toolbars, so you will have to create a custom toolbar, or add the Camera tool to an existing toolbar, in order to use it. (See Chapter 7 for information on customizing toolbars.)

Here's how to create a linked picture using the Camera tool:

**1.** Select source cell(s).

**2.** Click on the Camera tool.

**3.** Click on a worksheet. A picture of the source cells is created (see Figure 12.9).

Here's how to create a linked picture using menu commands:

**1.** Select the source cell(s).

*FIGURE 12.9*

*When a linked picture is selected, the source cells are displayed on the formula bar.*

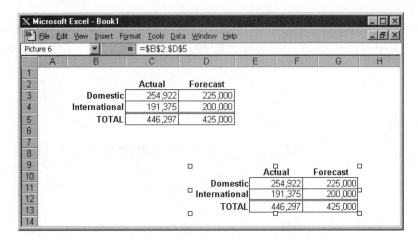

**2.** Choose Edit ➤ Copy.

**3.** Select the place on the worksheet where you want to paste, then hold down the Shift key and choose Edit ➤ Paste Picture Link.

Here are some important properties of linked pictures:

- Any change to the source cells causes a linked picture to update.

- The reference for the source cells displays on the formula bar when a linked picture is selected (see Figure 12.7, earlier in the chapter).

- You can edit (or clear) the reference on the formula bar. If cleared, the link between the picture and the source cell(s) is broken and the picture becomes static.

Application developers can derive two key benefits from linked pictures:

- Pictures can be placed on custom dialog boxes.

- When a linked picture is created, it refers to an absolute cell reference; however, a picture can refer to a named formula (see Chapter 8 to learn about named formulas). This lets user input dynamically change the picture source.

**MASTERING THE OPPORTUNITIES**

### Linking a Picture to a Named Formula

Just as a picture can be linked to a named range, a picture can be linked to a named formula—a name that points to a variable range of cells. For example, suppose you have two named ranges, Sales and Profits. Create a cell named Choice, then create a formula named PictureChoice that points to Sales or Profits based on the value in cell Choice: =IF(Choice=1,Sales,Profits). (See Chapter 8 if you need help naming a formula.) Take

a picture of one of the named ranges (it doesn't matter which), then select the picture and change the formula bar to read =PictureChoice.

Enter a value in cell Choice to see the linked picture work. A value of 1 will display a picture of the Sales range, while any other value will display a picture of the Profits range. Option buttons are a good user interface for entering a value in the Choice cell. See Chapter 23 to learn about option buttons and other worksheet controls.

## Creating Freehand Lines and Freeform Polygons

 To draw a freehand line, choose AutoShapes ➢ Lines from the Drawing command bar and select the Scribble tool. The mouse pointer becomes a pencil while drawing the line. When you release the mouse button, the line is completed.

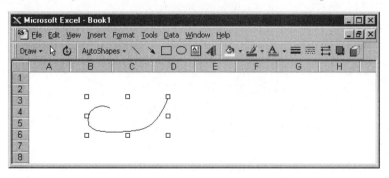

Use the Curve tool to draw smooth curves, curved shapes, and wave patterns. Click to establish the first end point, and again each time you want to make the apex of a curve. To join the end points of a curvilinear object, click to join them. Excel will join them if they are close enough, as shown below.

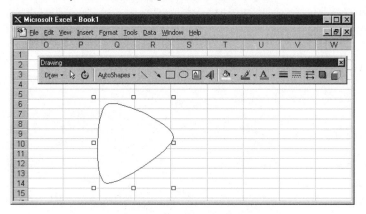

Freeform polygons can combine straight lines and freehand lines. To draw straight lines, click at the end point of the line, or to draw freehand lines in this mode, hold down the left mouse button; the cursor will change from crosshairs to a pencil. You can make a polygon side vertical, horizontal, or a 45-degree angle by holding down Shift while clicking. To stop drawing the polygon, double-click.

To alter the shape of a freehand line after it is drawn, select the line and choose Draw ➤ Edit Points from the Drawing command bar (or use the shortcut menu). Each vertex of the line will have a handle, and you can drag each handle with the crosshairs to reshape the line. To turn the tool off, click on the Edit Points tool again, or click outside the object.

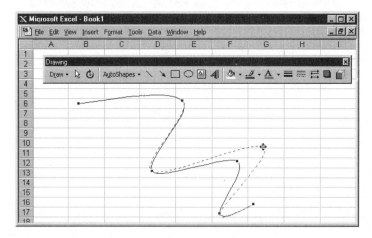

While in Edit Points mode, it is possible to edit the line segments between the points as well as the points themselves. Points and segments have specialized shortcut menus; notice the subtle change in the mouse pointer when you place it over a line segment or point. Right-click on the point or segment to smooth, straighten, add, or delete points or segments; to close a curve; or to format the AutoShape.

## Bringing Text Effects to Your Worksheets with WordArt

WordArt can bring colorful text effects to your worksheets. WordArt allows you to create stylized text objects, similar to poster art. To create a WordArt object, click on the WordArt tool on the Drawing command bar to display a gallery of 30 WordArt styles, select a style, and Excel will display the Edit WordArt Text dialog box.

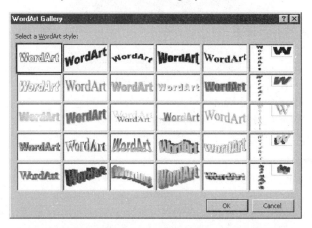

Enter your text, and apply appropriate text formatting (such as font style and size), and click on OK. Excel will place the WordArt object on the worksheet, where you can move, resize, and format it just like any other object. Excel will also display a WordArt toolbar with a selection of formatting tools to accomplish specific WordArt formatting tasks.

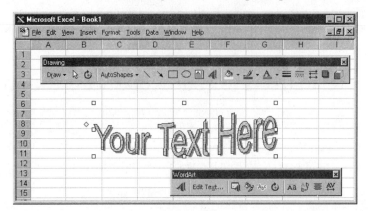

**TIP**

Some WordArt objects, especially curved ones will have a small yellow handle when the object is selected; by clicking on and dragging the handle, you can change the orientation and perspective of the object.

In this chapter you have learned to create, format, and manipulate just a few of the various types of drawing objects and tools. This chapter also demonstrates that Excel's new drawing package is not only a vast improvement over previous versions, but also a lot of fun. Beware of spending too much time on your drawing and not enough on your worksheet data!

In the next few chapters, we'll explain other types of objects, such as those used to create charts.

# Chapter

# 13

## Charting Basics

# Charting Basics

Charts are an effective way to present information: because they present data in a graphical format, they allow the viewer to absorb a lot of information quickly, whereas a traditional columnar report might require considerable study and analysis. Excel includes a powerful built-in charting facility that makes it very easy to create a variety of charts.

This chapter covers all the basics you'll need to know to get busy working with charts. You'll quickly create simple charts both from scratch and using the Chart-Wizard. You'll learn the difference between embedded charts and chart sheets. And, at the end of the chapter, you'll learn about which types of charts are most effective for which kinds of data.

## Charts Made Easy

Before you explore the many charting options covered later in this chapter, here is an exercise that will demonstrate how easy creating charts can be. In this exercise, you'll create a column chart comparing the forecast and actual totals for four geographical regions.

Create the following worksheet:

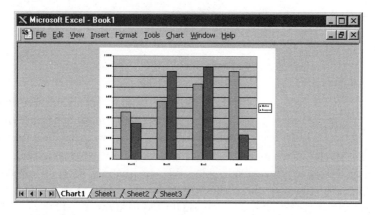

Select a cell within the range B2:D6 and press F11. A chart sheet is created in your workbook.

## Embedding Charts in Worksheets

Charts can be created as chart sheets in a workbook as shown above, or they can be *embedded* in a worksheet. In the example above, we created a simple default column chart and inserted it as a new chart sheet. Sometimes you may want to place a chart on the same worksheet as the source data, or you may want a different type of chart, or to show only a portion of the data. You can use the ChartWizard tool to create a simple embedded column chart, but you can also use it to create more complex and custom charts. Try these steps using the worksheet from the previous example:

1. Select a cell within the range B2:D6.
2. Click on the ChartWizard tool on the Standard toolbar.

**3.** When you release the mouse button, the ChartWizard Step 1 Of 4 dialog box will be displayed (see Figure 13.1).

**FIGURE 13.1**

*At Step 1 of the ChartWizard you choose the chart type. Excel uses the Column type as the default chart.*

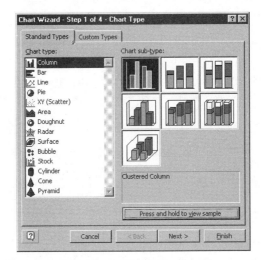

**4.** Click on the Finish button. A chart using the default chart format is drawn on the worksheet (see Figure 13.2).

**FIGURE 13.2**

*A default chart created with the ChartWizard*

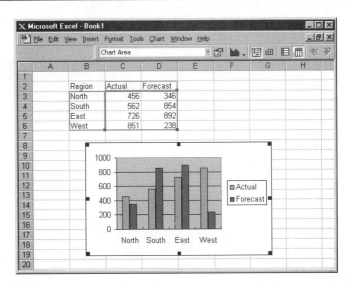

Notice that the chart in Figure 13.2 is selected, as is the original data. Notice that the data is divided into three areas, each bordered with a different color and each showing object resizing handles. While the chart is selected it can be moved, resized, or reformatted just like any graphic object. Select a cell anywhere on the worksheet to deselect chart and source data.

**NOTE**

See Chapter 12 for information on formatting graphic objects in general; formatting charts and chart elements are discussed in Chapter 14.

On an embedded chart, you can add or remove data by using color-coded ranges to

- Add new categories *and* data series (columns and rows of data).
- Add new data series *only* (rows).
- Add new categories and data points (columns).

Select the embedded chart, and click and drag the range selection handles to add data to or remove data from the chart, just like using fill handles on cells. This is done dynamically; by default, charts are *linked* to the worksheet cells—the chart will automatically redraw when changes are made to the source data. Try adding some new categories to the worksheet to see this in action, and dragging the fill handles around the selected cell range as shown below. The new category labels *Southwest* and *Q1* were created and the blue selection handle was dragged to include them (although the data that makes the Southwest data series, and the data points of the new Q1 column have not been entered yet). Chapter 14 will explain data series and data points in greater detail.

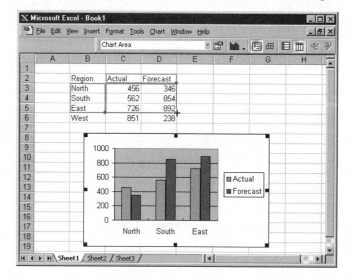

Notice also that when a chart is selected, the menus change. The Data menu is replaced by a Chart menu, and chart-specific commands appear on the View, Insert, and Format menus. In addition, the Chart toolbar may be displayed.

**NOTE**

The Chart toolbar is hidden when you deselect the chart, unless you have displayed it before selecting or displaying the chart.

Table 13.1 describes the tools on the Chart toolbar.

**TABLE 13.1:** TOOLS ON THE CHART TOOLBAR

| Tool Face | Tool | Function |
|---|---|---|
| Chart / Series 1 | Chart Objects Edit Box | Selects individual chart objects |
| | Format Chart Area | Formats selected chart object |
| | Chart Type | Provides a palette of chart types |
| | Legend | Toggles display of legend on/off |
| | Data Table | Toggles attachment of source data to chart |
| | By Row | Displays data series by rows |
| | By Column | Displays data series by columns |

| TABLE 13.1: TOOLS ON THE CHART TOOLBAR (CONTINUED) | | |
|---|---|---|
| **Tool Face** | **Tool** | **Function** |
|  | Angle Text Downward | Angles axis text downward |
| | Angle Text Upward | Angles axis text upward |

# Creating Charts with the ChartWizard

In the previous exercise, you used the ChartWizard to create an embedded chart. But the exercise asked you to immediately click on the Finish button, which skipped over most of the ChartWizard options. In this section, we'll thoroughly explain the four major ChartWizard steps—choosing the chart type, selecting chart source data, entering titles and legends, and orienting the chart.

## Starting the Chart Wizard

Before you can make use of the ChartWizard, you must first select a cell within the data range to be charted, and then do one of the following:

- Click on the ChartWizard tool on the Standard toolbar.
- Choose Insert ➢ Chart.

> **NOTE**
>
> You don't have to select a cell within the data range to start ChartWizard, but if you don't, you have to manually enter the data range later. If you select a cell within the data range, Excel "senses" and includes the adjoining data, including labels. If you select a specific cell range before clicking on ChartWizard, only the selected range will be used to create the chart.

The ChartWizard Step 1 Of 4 dialog box is displayed (see Figure 13.1 earlier in the chapter). The dialog box for each step of the ChartWizard includes Cancel, Back, Next, and Finish buttons:

- Click on Cancel to stop the ChartWizard—no chart will be created.

- Click on Back to go back to the previous step.
- Click on Next to proceed to the next step.
- Click on Finish when you are done specifying chart properties—the chart will be created immediately.

For illustrative purposes, we've created a data sheet that contains quarterly totals for Coffee, Tea, and Cocoa (see Figure 13.3). To follow along with this example, enter the constants shown in Figure 13.3 onto a worksheet of your own.

**FIGURE 13.3**

*Create this sample worksheet to give the ChartWizard something to work with.*

| | A | B | C | D | E | F | G | H |
|---|---|---|---|---|---|---|---|---|
| 1 | | | | | | | | |
| 2 | | | Q1 | Q2 | Q3 | Q4 | | |
| 3 | | Coffee | 770 | 660 | 610 | 840 | | |
| 4 | | Tea | 340 | 270 | 200 | 540 | | |
| 5 | | Cocoa | 170 | 177 | 122 | 420 | | |
| 6 | | | | | | | | |
| 7 | | | | | | | | |
| 8 | | | | | | | | |
| 9 | | | | | | | | |
| 10 | | | | | | | | |

X Microsoft Excel - Book1

File   Edit   View   Insert   Format   Tools   Data   Window   Help

## Selecting a Chart Type

Once you have entered the data, click anywhere within the data area and then click on the Chart Wizard button. Step 1 of the ChartWizard allows you to choose the chart type and subtype either from standard types provided by Excel or from custom types you create, as shown in Figure 13.1. Select the chart type you want, and press the mouse button and hold it on the button in the lower-right corner of the dialog box to preview the chart before creating it. When you have chosen a chart type, click on the Next button.

**NOTE**

You can change the properties of the default chart. This procedure is described in Chapter 15.

## Choosing the Chart's Source Data

The ChartWizard Step 2 Of 4 dialog box is a tabbed dialog box that lets you specify the range of data you want included in the chart, and the ranges for the names and values for each data series (see Figure 13.4).

*FIGURE 13.4*

*Select the data range for your chart from the ChartWizard Step 2 Of 4 dialog box.*

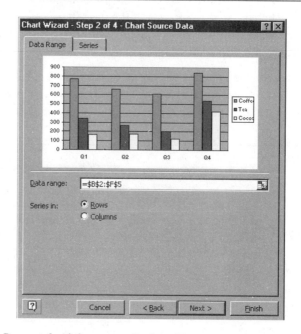

On the Data Range tab, if the range displayed is not correct, change it by typing a new reference or by selecting a different range. The chart data does not have to come from the active worksheet; you can specify a different worksheet, or even a different workbook.

The Series tab allows you to add and remove data series, specify the source ranges for the x-axis labels, and specify the source ranges for the series names and values (e.g., cells C2:F2 are the source of the x-axis labels and *Coffee* in cell B3 is the name for the data series C3:F3, whose cells contain the series values). Chapter 14 further discusses data series and data points.

Clicking on the Collapse Dialog Box button in the Data Range edit box will reduce the ChartWizard Step 2 Of 4 dialog box to a small, toolbar-like dialog box, allowing you to see more of the data range and to select a new range with the mouse, if necessary. Click on the Collapse Dialog Box button again to restore the dialog box.

**Choosing Data from a Different Worksheet** - If the data you want to use is on a different worksheet, display the ChartWizard Step 2 Of 4 dialog box. Select the worksheet, then select the range of cells containing the data. Click on the Next button.

**Choosing Data from a Different Workbook** - If the data you want to use is in a different workbook, be sure the workbook containing the data (Book1, for example) is open and the workbook where the chart will be drawn (Book2) is active. Display the ChartWizard Step 2 Of 4 dialog box. Select Book1 from the Window menu, then select the worksheet and the range of cells containing the data. Click on the Next button.

> **TIP**
>
> At any point in the ChartWizard process, you can click on the Finish button to create the chart; you can always reformat it, change the data range, and add labels later.

When you select a cell range, be sure to include row and column headings if you want them to appear as labels in the chart. When the range is correct, click on Next.

## Choosing Chart Options

The ChartWizard Step 3 Of 4 dialog box, shown in Figure 13.5, lets you choose the chart options. Step 3 is a tabbed dialog box that controls the placement of chart elements; e.g., titles, gridlines, and data labels or values.

**FIGURE 13.5**

*Choose chart options from the Chart- Wizard Step 3 Of 4 dialog box.*

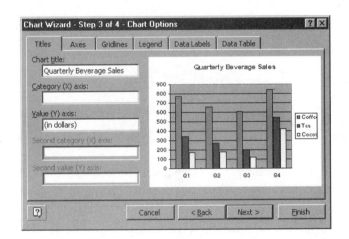

Here is a brief description of the chart option tabs in this dialog box:

**Titles:** Adds or removes titles to chart and chart axes

**Axes:** Toggles axis values on and off

**Gridlines:** Displays major and minor gridlines parallel to x- and y- axes

Graphics and Charts

PART
**IV**

**Legend:** Toggles legend on and off and orients legend to chart

**Data Labels:** Adds or removes labels and values to series

**Data Table:** Attaches source data to or removes it from chart

In this example, we've added the title *Quarterly Beverage Sales* to the chart and the y-value axis title *(in dollars)*.

## Specifying the Chart Location

In the ChartWizard Step 4 Of 4 dialog box, shown in Figure 13.6, you specify the chart location: as an embedded chart on a worksheet or as a chart sheet. Select As Object In, and click on Finish to create the chart. The final chart is shown in Figure 13.7.

**NOTE**

Multiple rows and columns can be selected for x-axis labels and legend text because Excel is capable of charting multilevel categories. To learn more about charting multilevel categories, see Chapter 15.

**FIGURE 13.6**

*Choose either an embedded chart or a chart sheet from the ChartWizard Step 4 Of 4 dialog box.*

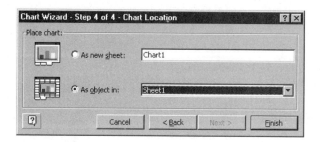

In this example, we've included a legend, added the chart title, and added the y-value axis title *(in dollars)*. The rest of the chart options in this example use Excel default options.

# Changing an Existing Chart with the ChartWizard

You can use the ChartWizard to change an existing chart. To make changes, do the following:

**1.** If the chart is an embedded chart, select it (by clicking on it); if it is a chart sheet, activate the sheet.

**2.** Click on the ChartWizard tool.

**FIGURE 13.7**

*A completed column chart created with ChartWizard*

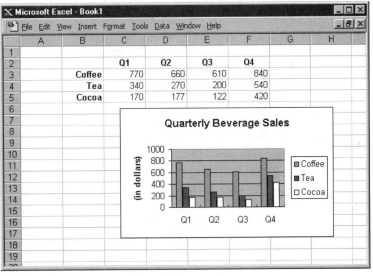

| | A | B | C | D | E | F | G | H |
|---|---|---|---|---|---|---|---|---|
| 1 | | | | | | | | |
| 2 | | | Q1 | Q2 | Q3 | Q4 | | |
| 3 | | Coffee | 770 | 660 | 610 | 840 | | |
| 4 | | Tea | 340 | 270 | 200 | 540 | | |
| 5 | | Cocoa | 170 | 177 | 122 | 420 | | |

Quarterly Beverage Sales

**3.** Move through the same ChartWizard Steps as outlined above to make the necessary changes. Click on Finish when you're through.

## Embedded Charts vs. Chart Sheets

The chart created in the previous exercise is an *embedded* chart. Embedded charts are graphic objects that lie on a worksheet. Charts can also reside on *chart sheets*. Chart sheets are like worksheets, except there are no cells.

You can attach source data to either embedded charts or chart sheets, move and resize the source data along with the attached chart, and format it in the same way as the other chart elements. You can attach source data to the chart in the following ways:

- In the ChartWizard Step 3 Of 4 dialog box, select the Data Table tab and check the Show Data Table check box.
- Select the chart and choose Chart ➢ Chart Options from the main menu.
- Right-click on the chart to select it and display a shortcut menu, and then select Chart Options.

**NOTE** You may notice that commands on the Chart menu and shortcut menu access all of the ChartWizard steps: Chart Type, Chart Source Data, Chart Options, and Chart Location.

## Selecting Chart Objects

Click on the embedded chart to select it, or to select a chart element, depending on where your mouse pointer is. If you click inside the chart, but near the border, the Chart Area will be selected. Likewise, you can select other chart elements by pointing to them, or you can use the Chart objects list box on the Chart toolbar to select different chart elements. You can move the selected chart by dragging it or resize it by dragging one of the handles. (See Chapter 12 for more on graphical objects.) The primary advantage of embedded charts is that they can be viewed (and printed) side by side with the worksheet data. Also, you can place more than one embedded chart on a worksheet.

There is a special command for viewing and resizing an embedded chart and for selecting chart objects independently from the source data. Select the embedded chart and choose View ➤ Chart Window; you can then resize the chart window without affecting the original worksheet layout. This command is especially useful when you want to temporarily resize a chart to format an individual element.

**TIP** If you double-click on a chart or chart object, Excel will display the appropriate formatting dialog box to reformat the object.

## About Chart Sheets

As we discussed previously, a chart sheet is a separate page in a workbook that contains a single chart.

You can rename, move, copy, and delete chart sheets just as you would a worksheet (see Chapter 2). You can also add graphic elements to chart sheets. The primary advantages of chart sheets are that they can be displayed full size without manual sizing, and that when printed, they do not include any extraneous worksheet data.

There is a command that is available only for chart sheets: the View ➤ Sized With Window command controls whether the size of the chart is dependent on the size of the window. By default, this command is unchecked. If checked, the chart is automatically sized to fit the window.

**NOTE**

This setting has no effect on how the chart appears when printed.

## Deleting Embedded Charts and Chart Sheets

Deleting an embedded chart from the worksheet is the same as deleting any other object: select the chart object and press Delete. (Or right-click on the chart and choose Clear from the shortcut menu.) Deleting a chart sheet is just like deleting any other sheet in a workbook: activate the sheet and choose Edit ➤ Delete Sheet. (Or right-click on the sheet tab and choose Delete from the shortcut menu.)

# Choosing a Chart Type

Suppose you are ready to chart data for a presentation. The first question you need to answer is, what kind of chart would be the most effective? Excel offers so many chart types that this may not be an easy question to answer. There are many built-in chart types available in Excel (see Figure 13.1, earlier in the chapter), and there are distinct advantages and disadvantages that you should consider when deciding what type of chart to use.

Within each chart type there are several subtypes. And in addition to the many built-in chart types and subtypes available, you can create hybrid types. For example, you can combine area, line, and column series types in the same chart.

Each chart type is best suited for illustrating specific types of data. To close this chapter, we'll take a look at the different chart types to help you identify which ones are best for your data.

## Comparing Values at Different Points in Time: Column and Bar Charts

You are probably familiar with column and bar charts. They are useful for comparing values at different points in time (for example, quarterly earnings), or making comparisons between items (like total sales for each product line), as you can see in the image just below.

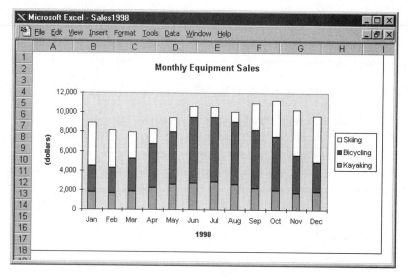

A bar chart is just a column chart tipped on its side (or vice versa), but sometimes a bar chart may give a stronger impression of relative ranking.

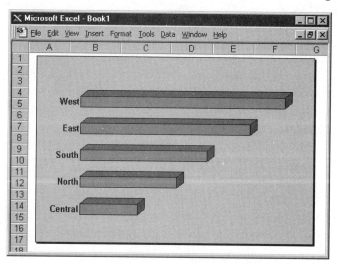

You can create column and bar charts that display negative values below the x-axis (in a column chart) or left of the y-axis (in a bar chart). Or consider stacking series columns or bars to illustrate each data point's relationship to the whole more clearly. You can also display more data in the chart by overlapping the data points in clusters. There are built-in column and bar subtypes for each of these display options, which you can choose from the ChartWizard Step 1 Of 4 dialog box by clicking on the ChartWizard button or by selecting the chart and choosing Chart ➢ Chart Type.

## Illustrating a Trend over Even Intervals of Time: Line Charts

What if you want to illustrate a trend over even intervals of time—for example, daily improvement in air quality after the installation of a smokestack filter? A line chart is the optimum choice.

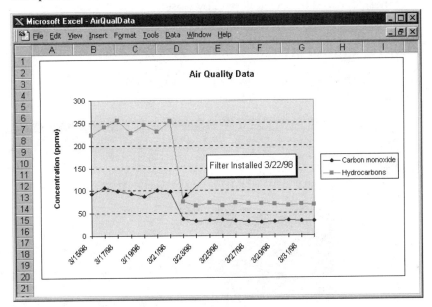

 **TIP**

For uneven time intervals, a scatter chart is better.

With a line chart, you can choose the classic zigzag style, in which points are connected with straight lines, or you can choose a smoothed-out line that emphasizes continuity. You can choose not to connect the data points at all (the chart will resemble a scatter chart). You can also choose between linear and logarithmic scaling. Other variations of the line chart include a subtype for high-low charts (useful for plotting data like high, low, and average daily temperatures).

Suppose you want to chart the performance of stocks or securities? There are two line chart subtypes to be aware of: high-low-close (which charts the high price, low price, and closing price for the day) and open-high-low-close (which charts the opening price, as well as the high, low, and closing prices).

**TIP**

If you want to create a high-low-close or an open-high-low-close chart, your data must be arranged on the worksheet in a specific order. The name of the chart subtype is a good way to remember—the open series first, followed by the high series, followed by low, followed by close.

## Adding Visual Impact with Area Charts

An area chart is just a line chart with the space below the line filled in, yet area charts can have a lot more visual impact than line charts.

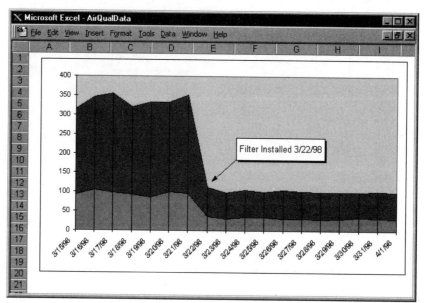

Suppose you want to chart the reduction in forested land in North America over the last 100 years. An area chart would show the reduction in acreage more dramatically than a line chart. You can also use an area chart to advantage by creating a hybrid line-area chart. Suppose you have created a line chart that has four or five series, and the lines are hard to read because they are crowding each other. Or perhaps you want to emphasize a single series apart from the others. You can select a single line and change its chart type to area, which will change the readability and visual impact of the chart considerably.

## Showing Relationships between Data Points: Pie Charts

What is unique about a pie chart is that it can only plot one data series. Although you can plot a single data series in any chart type, a pie chart is especially good at showing the relationship of each data point to the other and to the whole. Also, with Excel, you can emphasize a single point in the series by separating its wedge from the rest of the pie.

Suppose you want to portray this year's expenditures on various office supplies? A pie chart is a great chart for comparing how much of the supplies budget was spent on paper, toner, file folders, etc.

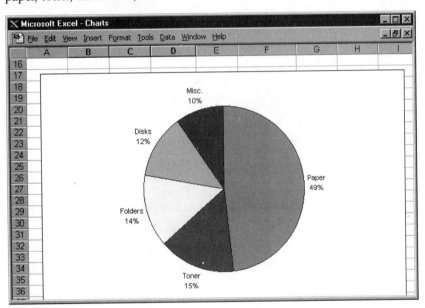

You can label each wedge with total dollars spent on that item, or with percentage of the supplies budget spent on that item. You can emphasize that too much was spent on paper, for example, by separating the Paper wedge from the rest of the chart.

**TIP**

When you create a pie chart, keep in mind that too many data points can make the chart illegible.

## Plotting Multiple Series with Doughnut Charts

A doughnut chart is like a pie chart, but you can plot more than one series using a doughnut chart.

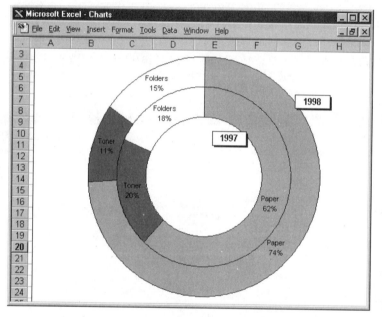

As with pie charts, you can label the data points by value or by percentage of the total series, and you can explode the doughnut into separate wedges or separate a single wedge. Doughnut charts may not be the most effective chart type for all audiences, especially for those who are not used to seeing them.

## Radar Charts

Suppose you own a landscaping business, and you want to chart the seasonal job load for the last five years to determine when you need to hire more employees and when it's safe to schedule vacations. You can use a radar chart to portray seasonal fluctuations, and help you make a decision more quickly than when analyzing tabular data.

In a radar chart, the points in a data series are plotted in a circle around a central point. The central point of the chart represents the y-axis. Each data point has its own spoke, or x-axis, and the value of the data point is displayed by its position on the spoke. Using the landscaping scenario, you would record the number of jobs each month for the last five years, and each year's data would be a data series in the chart.

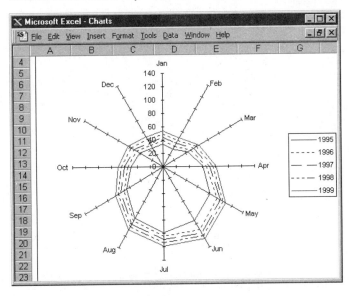

## Showing the Correlation between Two Data Series: Scatter Charts

Suppose you want to show the relationship between the adult heights of women and their mothers. A scatter chart is a good way to display the relationship. Each data point in a scatter chart is a coordinate composed of an x-value (a specific woman's height) and a y-value (her mother's height). If there is a relationship between mother and daughter heights, the coordinate points in the chart will form a straight line or clusters. If there is not a relationship, the coordinate points will be scattered at random in the chart.

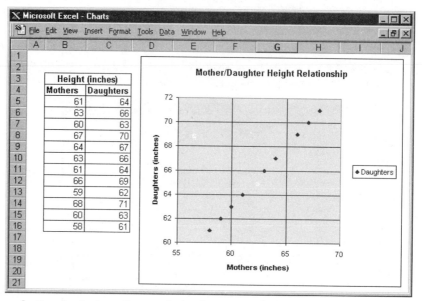

Scatter charts show the correlation between two data series, and are widely used to present scientific data. They are particularly good for value changes over uneven intervals.

**MASTERING THE OPPORTUNITIES**

## Charting Series with Different Value Scales: Combination Charts

Suppose you want to chart the Dow Jones average and the total volume traded every day for a month. You can chart two data series with vastly different value scales on the same chart by using a combination chart. Combination charts are a hybrid of chart types: for example, column and area, or line and column. Combination charts commonly have a secondary axis to display a data series on a different value scale. You can create a combination chart by selecting the combination chart type on the Custom Types tab from the ChartWizard Step 1 (see "Creating Charts with the ChartWizard" in the first part of this chapter). But what if you have already created a chart, and you don't want to recreate it? You can change a chart into a combination chart easily. Chapter 14 describes how to change an individual chart series type, how to add a secondary axis to an existing chart, and how to create combination charts.

# 3-D Charts

There are several 3-D chart formats to choose from: bar, column, pie, etc. Used judiciously, 3-D charts can sometimes represent complex data better than their 2-D counterparts. Often, however, 3-D charts introduce some problems: one data series can obscure another, or the print quality may be unacceptable. Sometimes it is necessary to spin or tilt the chart until you have the best possible viewing angle, or to put the data series in a different order so that all the data markers can be seen. Chapter 16 will discuss 3-D charts in greater detail.

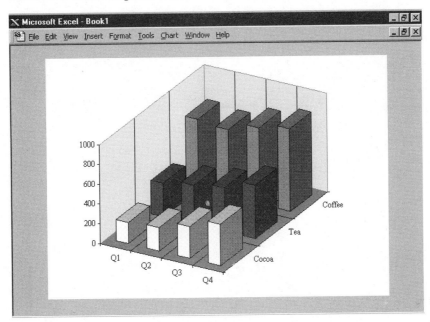

# Surface Charts

Surface charts look like topographical maps. They are unfamiliar to many users, but are extremely useful once you understand how to use and interpret them. In a surface chart, color is used to show value ranges rather than to identify series markers. Surface charts are used to plot data from a continuum (such as temperatures, altitudes, or retail sales prices), rather than discrete data points (such as sales reps or product names). Chapter 16 explains surface charts with a real-world application.

This chapter has introduced you to the fundamentals of creating charts in Excel. In the next three chapters you'll learn more-advanced charting tools, techniques, and tips.

# Chapter

## 14

### Creating Custom Charts

# Creating Custom Charts

**C**hapter 13 covered the basics of working with charts. In this chapter, we'll continue to examine the subject of charts, and we'll introduce the skills you need to create and format many types of custom charts. These skills will help you create the kind of chart you need to emphasize the data you want people to notice.

## Understanding Data Series and Data Points

When working with charts, it's important to understand the difference between a *data series* and *data points*. These concepts are crucial both for understanding how your data is being represented in the chart and for creating a chart that will display your data properly.

### What Is a Data Point?

A *data point* is an individual value that originated in a single worksheet cell. When data points are plotted onto a chart, they are represented by columns, bars, dots, slices, or other shapes called *data markers*. In Figure 14.1, the cell lying at the intersection of

North and Actual is represented in the chart as one data point; the intersection of South and Forecast is another data point.

**FIGURE 14.1**

*Each column represents one data point.*

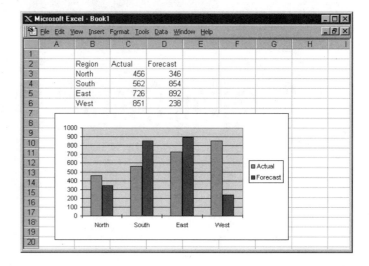

## What Is a Data Series?

A *data series* is a group of related data points that represents a single row or column of data. Each series is distinguished on a chart by a unique color or pattern. In Figure 14.1, Forecast is one data series and Actual is the other data series, each series consisting of four data points.

# Formatting Chart Elements

Formatting chart elements is not difficult. The topic seems complex only because there are so many different elements of a chart, each with unique formatting properties. The various chart elements are identified in Figure 14.2, but if you let the cursor pause on a chart element for a moment, a pop-up note will identify it. You can apply different number formats, fonts, patterns, and colors to the various chart elements.

There are certain procedures that apply to formatting chart elements, regardless of which chart element you are formatting:

• The chart element must be selected in order to format it.

**FIGURE 14.2**

*Chart elements*

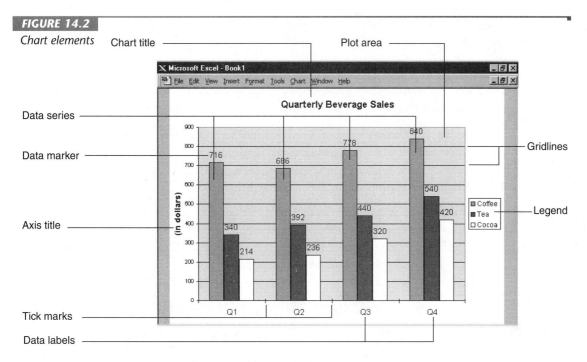

Chart title

Plot area

Data series

Data marker

Axis title

Tick marks

Data labels

Gridlines

Legend

- Double-click on the chart element you want to format to display the Format dialog box (or right-click on the element, and choose the Format command from the shortcut menu). The name of the selected element is displayed in the Name box on the left part of the formula bar.
- Select the formatting options you want, then click on OK.

   Sometimes it is hard to select the right chart element with the mouse. The element you want to select may not be visible, or another element may overlap it. A sure way to select an elusive chart element is via the Chart Objects drop-down list on the Chart command bar. The Chart Objects tool provides a list of the chart objects, allowing you to select a specific object; you can then format it using the adjoining Format (*selected chart object*) button.

**TIP**

To delete a chart element, select the element and press Delete (or choose Clear from the shortcut menu).

# Using Formatting Tools for Quick Chart Element Formatting

You can use most of the tools on the Formatting toolbar to format textual chart elements, such as the chart and axis titles. As an example, follow these steps to apply boldface to the axis text in the Actual-Forecast chart shown in Figure 14.1:

**1.** Be sure the Formatting toolbar is displayed (use the View ➣ Toolbars command).
**2.** Click on the Actual-Forecast chart.
**3.** Select an axis by single-clicking on it.
**4.** Click on the Bold button on the Formatting toolbar.

Normally, you will format chart elements with the Format command for the greatest flexibility; each chart element has a specific formatting dialog box. When you select a chart element, such as a legend, and open the Format menu (or display the shortcut menu), you will find an element-specific command: Format ➣ Selected Legend. When you select this command, the following dialog box appears:

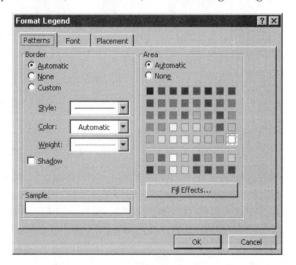

Each dialog box for specific chart elements may also have tabs with controls unique to the selected element; e.g., the Format Gridlines dialog box has a Scale tab, whereas the Format Legend dialog box has a Placement tab.

Figure 14.3 shows several embedded charts with different chart area formatting selected from the Patterns tab of the Format Chart Area dialog box.

Embedded charts with no fill and no border are most effective on a worksheet with no gridlines.

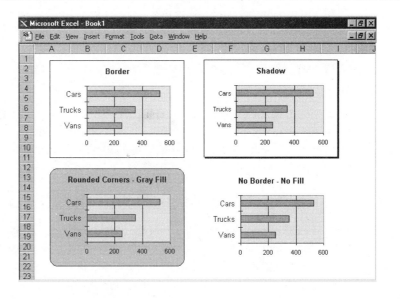

**FIGURE 14.3**

*The only differ-
ence between
these charts is
the formatting of
the chart area.*

# Changing a Chart to a Different Type

You already know from the previous chapter that there are many built-in chart types
from which to choose. Each type of chart has several basic formats, sometimes referred
to by Excel as *subtypes*. For example, a 2-D column chart has three basic subtypes:
columns, stacked columns, and stacked proportional columns.

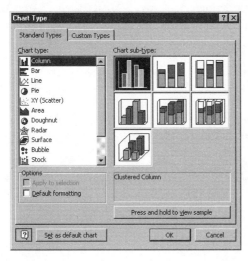

The previous chapter explained how to change a chart using the ChartWizard. There are three other ways to change a chart from one type or subtype to another—from the main or shortcut menus, with the Chart Type tool, or with an AutoFormat.

## Changing the Chart Type Using Menus

When you select a chart element, the Data menu on the main menu is replaced by a Chart menu (right-clicking on the chart also displays the Chart Type option on the shortcut menu). Select the chart, then choose Chart ➤ Chart Type. The Chart Type dialog box displays the types in graphical format. Click on one of the chart types, then click on OK.

## Changing the Chart Type Using the Chart Type Tool

The Chart Type tool (on the Chart toolbar) contains a drop-down palette of chart types. These tools are faster to use than the Chart ➤ Chart Type command, but do not offer the variety of subtypes that the command offers. To use the Chart Type tool, select the chart, then choose a chart type from the palette.

**TIP**

The Chart Type tool has a tear-off palette. See Chapter 1 to learn how to use tear-off palettes.

## Changing the Subtype Using an AutoFormat

You can create your own user-defined chart AutoFormats. A chart AutoFormat is simply a chart with custom formatting that has been saved as a custom chart type. To use an AutoFormat, select the chart, then:

**1.** Choose Chart ➤ Chart Type.
**2.** Click on the Custom Types tab in Chart Types dialog box, and choose the User-Defined option in the Select From area.
**3.** Select a type from the list, then click on OK.
**4.** Choose a format from the Formats options. Click on OK to close the dialog box.

If you don't like the result, choose Edit ➤ Undo Chart Type to undo the AutoFormat, or choose a different chart type. See Chapter 15 to learn how to create AutoFormats.

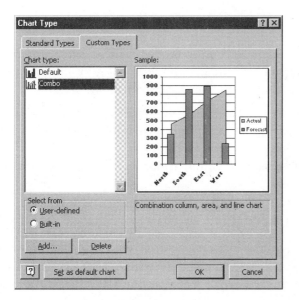

## Copying Chart Formats

Suppose you are looking at a workbook that contains a carefully formatted chart. Perhaps you spent a lot of time formatting it, or maybe someone else created it and you want to "borrow" the formatting to use on one of your charts. You can easily copy and paste the formatting of one chart onto another chart.

To copy and paste formatting, do the following:

1. Select the chart you want to copy.

2. Select the Chart area—the Name box should read *Chart Area*—then choose Edit ➢ Copy.

3. Select the chart where you want to paste the formatting, and choose Edit ➢ Paste Special.

4. In the Paste Special dialog box, select the Formats option. Click on OK.

If you want the format to be readily available in the future, you may want to create a custom AutoFormat (see Chapter 15 for more on AutoFormats).

# Printing Charts

When you print a worksheet with an embedded chart, as you might expect, the printout includes the chart and surrounding worksheet. There may be circumstances where you want to print the worksheet without the chart, or vice versa.

- To print a worksheet without printing a chart embedded in it, select the chart area. Then choose Format ➢ Selected Chart Area, select the Properties tab, and clear the Print Object check box. Click on OK.
- To print an embedded chart without the surrounding worksheet, select it, then choose File ➢ Print.

## Adjusting Print Layout

Whether a chart is embedded or a separate sheet, you can change the printed size and layout of the chart. For example, suppose you want to print a chart on a separate page, but at only half-size, on the top half of the page. To adjust the print size of a chart, do the following:

1. Select the chart area, then choose File ➢ Print Preview.
2. Click on the Margins button so that margin lines are displayed (see Chapter 6 for more information on margins).
3. Drag the margin lines to resize/reposition the chart. Change the orientation of the printed chart to landscape or to portrait by clicking on the Setup button and choosing landscape or portrait.

If you choose File ➢ Page Setup when a chart area is selected, the Page Setup dialog box that appears includes a Chart tab. The Chart tab has settings that control how the chart is resized:

**Use Full Page:** Resizes the chart both horizontally and vertically to margins. The chart may lose its height-to-width ratio, however.

**Scale to Fit Page:** The chart will maintain its height-to-width ratio and expand to nearest margin.

**Custom:** Prints the chart as shown on the worksheet, but chart size is limited by page margins; the chart will still print on one page. For example, if you have a long, skinny chart three pages long, and try to print it using this option, you will print a long, skinny chart that is only one page long. If you print the worksheet, however, you will get a long, skinny chart on three sheets.

### Using Shortcut Menus

Many of the elements within a chart have shortcut menus providing context-sensitive commands. To use a shortcut menu, right-click on the chart element and choose a command. Here is a list of the elements within a chart that can be right-clicked to display a shortcut menu:

| **Chart** | **Plot Area** | **Axis** |
|---|---|---|
| Legend | Legend Entry | Legend Key |
| Data Series | Data Marker | Gridlines |
| Chart Title | Axis Title | Data Label |
| Trendline | Error Bars | Drop lines |
| Series Lines | High-Low lines | Up-Down bars |
| Walls (3-D) | Floor (3-D) | Corner (3-D) |

# Putting a Chart Together: An Exercise

In the following exercise, you will apply many of the skills you've learned in this chapter to create and format a chart.

### Enter Data and Create a Chart

Enter the data shown in Figure 14.4 onto a new worksheet, and use the ChartWizard to create a chart using default formatting (click on Finish in the ChartWizard Step 1 Of 4 dialog box). Move and resize the chart if necessary.

### Change the Colors of the Data Series

**1.** Right-click on one of the data markers. Notice that the whole series is selected, and a shortcut menu is displayed.

**2.** Choose Format ➤ Data Series, then select the Patterns tab.

**3.** Select a different color from the color palette, and click on OK.

**4.** Repeat the process to change the color of the other series.

You can also add various fill effects as well as colors and patterns: from the Format Data Series dialog box, click on the Fill Effects button. See Chapter 12 for more information on fill effects.

**FIGURE 14.4**

*Since the default chart is customizable, your chart may not look identical to this one.*

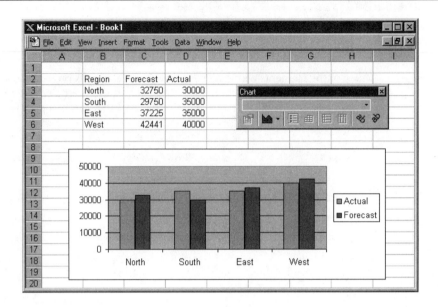

---

**TIP**

The Color tool on the Formatting toolbar can be used to color chart elements. (Use the tear-off Color palette to color chart elements quickly.)

---

## Change the Forecast Series Chart Type from Column to Area

**1.** Right-click on one of the Forecast series markers.

**2.** Choose the Chart Type command, then select Area and click on OK.

## Remove the Plot Area Color

**1.** Right-click on the plot area.

**2.** Select Format Plot Area.

**3.** Select Area—None, then click on OK.

## Change the Chart Area Color

**1.** Right-click near the perimeter of the chart to select the Chart area and display the shortcut menu.

**2.** Choose the Format Chart Area command, then select the Patterns tab.

**3.** Select a gray area color (or some other color), then click on OK.

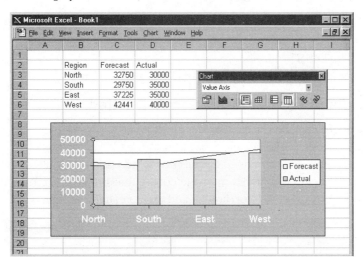

## Change Axis Text Font

**1.** Right-click on one axis and select the Format Axis command.

**2.** Select the Font tab.

**3.** Increase the font size, change the color to white, and click on OK.

**4.** Select the other axis and choose Edit ➤ Repeat Format Axis.

## Format Numbers on the Value Axis to Display in Thousands

**1.** Right-click on the value (y) axis and choose the Format Axis command.

**2.** Select the Number tab, select the Custom category, and select  **#,###,** from the list, or type it in the text box (be sure to include both commas). (See Chapter 5 to learn more about custom number formats.)

**3.** Leave the Format Axis dialog box displayed for the next procedure.

## Change Scale on the Y-Axis to Reduce Gridline Clutter

**1.** Select the Scale tab.

**2.** Type **10000** in the Major Unit text box.

**3.** Click on OK to close the Format Axis dialog box.

**NOTE**

Depending on how large you draw the chart, the default major unit may already be 10,000.

## Format the Legend

**1.** Right-click on the legend and choose the Format Legend command.
**2.** Select the Patterns tab, and select a light gray area color and check the Border Shadow setting.
**3.** Select the Font tab and choose a bold Font Style. Click on OK to close the dialog box.

## Add and Format Chart and Axis Titles

**1.** Right-click on the chart area, and choose Chart Options.
**2.** Select the Titles tab and type **Sales** in the Chart Title text box.
**3.** In the Value (Y) Axis edit, type **thousands**, and click on OK.
**4.** Right-click on the new title and choose the Format Chart Title command.
**5.** Format the title color, border, and text to match the legend, then click on OK.

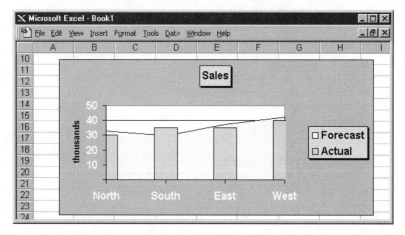

## Reshape the Legend and Plot Area to Reduce Empty Space

**1.** Move the chart title over to the left side of the plot area, and move the legend to the top of the chart by dragging it.
**2.** Reshape the legend (drag handles) to be wide and shallow, with the legend entries side-by-side.
**3.** Select the plot area. Drag the right-side handle to the right side of the chart, to fill in the empty space.

## Apply a Shadowed Border to the Chart

**1.** Right-click on the chart area and choose the Format Chart Area command.
**2.** Select the Patterns tab.

**3.** Select a medium-weight border, check the Shadow setting, then click on OK.

Now, turn off the gridlines on the worksheet, and the chart should look something like this:

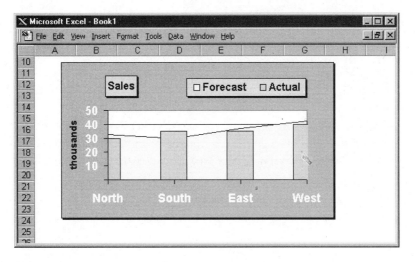

# Adding, Deleting, and Changing Chart Data

Once you've created a chart, you don't need to recreate it in order to add data, delete data, or reorganize the data.

## Adding Data to a Chart

There are several ways to add new data to an existing chart:

- Use drag and drop (embedded charts only).
- Use the Edit ➢ Copy and Edit ➢ Paste commands.
- Drag color-coded ranges.

### Dragging and Dropping New Data onto an Embedded Chart

You can add a new data series, or new data points, using drag and drop:

- To add a new *data series* with drag and drop, select the new row or column of data on the worksheet and drag and drop it onto the chart.
- To add new *data points* to an existing series, select the points and drag and drop them onto the chart.

After you drag and drop, if Excel is unable to determine whether you are adding a series or data points, a dialog box appears where you can specify the type of data being added.

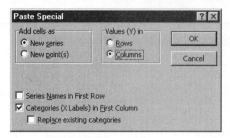

Suppose you have a worksheet that tracks sales by region and charts the data. At the end of each month, data is added to the sheet, and hence must be added to the chart.

Here's how to add the new data for May to the chart shown in Figure 14.5:

1. Select F2:F5.
2. Drag and drop the cells onto the chart. (Drag the cells as if you were moving them, and drop them anywhere on the chart.)

*The new data points are added at the end of each data series—it doesn't matter where on the chart you drop the cells.*

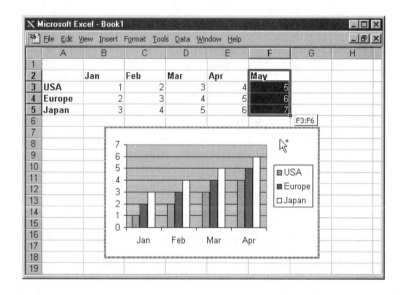

## Adding Data Using Copy and Paste

You can add new data by copying it from the worksheet and pasting it onto the chart. This works for embedded charts and chart sheets:

1. Select the data you are adding to the chart.
2. Choose Edit ➤ Copy.
3. Select the chart.
4. Choose Edit ➤ Paste.

## Adding Data Using Color-Coded Ranges

When a chart is selected, you will notice that the source data and accompanying labels are bounded by colored lines. You can drag the handles on the lines to add (or remove) source data. Using the example above, to add data for May, enter the data onto the worksheet, select the chart, and drag the range handle for the data area to include the new data.

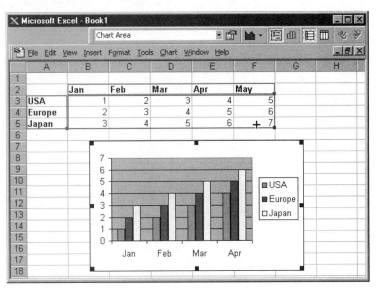

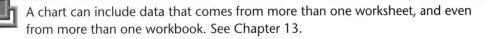

**NOTE** A chart can include data that comes from more than one worksheet, and even from more than one workbook. See Chapter 13.

## Deleting Data from a Chart

You can delete a data series directly from a chart without impacting the underlying worksheet data:

**1.** Select the series you want to delete by clicking on a data marker within the series.

**2.** Choose Edit ➤ Clear ➤ Series (or press Delete).

## Changing Data Orientation

Suppose you want to change the orientation of the chart in Figure 14.5 so that the months are data series (on the legend) and the regions are categories (on the horizontal axis). The ChartWizard makes it easy to change the data orientation:

**1.** Select the chart and click on the ChartWizard tool.

**2.** Click on Next on the ChartWizard Step 1 Of 4 dialog box.

**3.** In the Step 2 Of 4 dialog box, use the Series In options to specify columns instead of rows.

**4.** Click on Finish.

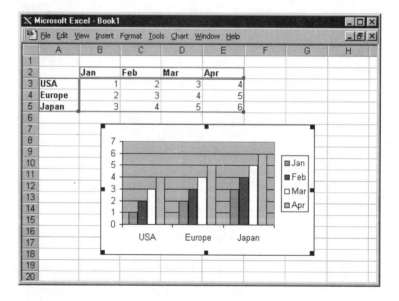

## Changing a Data Series

Suppose that after you create a chart, you want to change the source for one of the data series. In Figure 14.6, the Original budget and Y-T-D columns (C and D) are charted. Revised budget figures have been entered into column F, and the budget data series needs to point to the revised budget instead of the original budget.

**FIGURE 14.6**

*The budget data series points to C3:C4. It needs to be changed to F3:F4.*

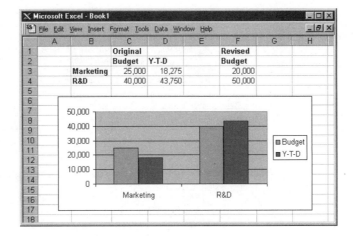

1. Select the budget data series by single-clicking on any data point in the series—in Figure 14.7 the budget data series is selected. Note that the numeric range of the series (C3:C4) is bounded by a blue line.

**TIP**

The first time you click on a data point, the entire data series is selected. If you click the data point a second time, just the single point is selected.

2. Click on and drag the blue border to cells F2:F3. (see Figure 14.8). (Be sure not to drag the handle.)
3. Click on OK.

## Applying Special Formatting

This section will explain how to add special lines, such as drop lines and up-down bars, to your charts, and how to separate pie wedges.

**FIGURE 14.7**

*The series name is shown in the name box on the formula bar.*

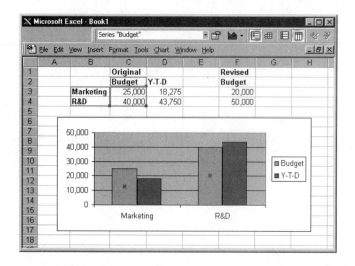

**FIGURE 14.8**

*Dragging the data range to a new location*

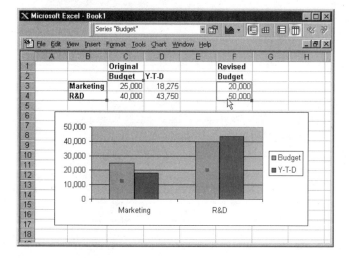

## Adding Lines and Bars

You can add drop lines, high-low lines, and up-down bars to some charts. They are all added the same way:

**1.** Select a data series in a line chart.

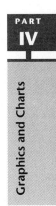

2. Choose the Format ➢ Data Series.

3. Select the Options tab.

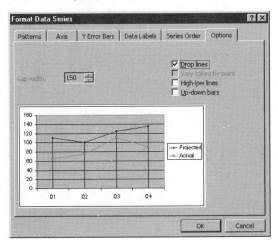

4. Check the setting for Drop Lines, High-Low Lines, or Up-Down Bars.

## Drop Lines

*Drop lines* are vertical lines that emphasize the location of the data point on the x-axis. They are applicable to area and line charts only.

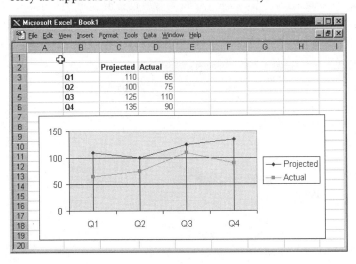

## High-Low Lines

High-low lines emphasize the difference between the high and low data points within each category. They can be applied to line charts only, and are particularly useful on stock market charts.

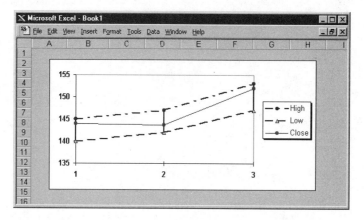

## Up-Down Bars

Up-down bars highlight the performance of one data series relative to another data series. Suppose you have charted forecast vs. actual sales over several periods. In periods where actual sales exceed forecast, the up-down bars display the variance in one color. When actual sales are less than forecast, the up-down bars display the variance in another color. Up-down bars can only be placed on line charts with at least two series.

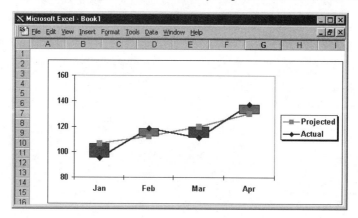

## Series Lines

Series lines connect the series in stacked bar and column charts. They highlight the amount of value change between data points. To add series lines, select a data series, choose Format Data Series, click on the Options tab, and check the Series Lines option.

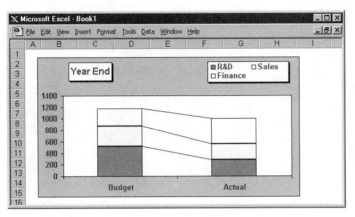

# Changing the Way Data Is Plotted

Once you have created a chart, there are several ways to change how the data is plotted.

## Reversing the Plot Order

There are two common reasons for reversing the plot order for an axis: you may want to look at the data differently, or you may have created the chart incorrectly in the first place. For example, in Figure 14.9, the data in B3:C7 is sorted by sales in descending order. Yet the bar chart presents the data in ascending order.

Follow these steps to reverse the plot order:

**1.** Select the category (y) axis.

**FIGURE 14.9**

*An instance of the data sheet and bar chart being oriented in reverse order*

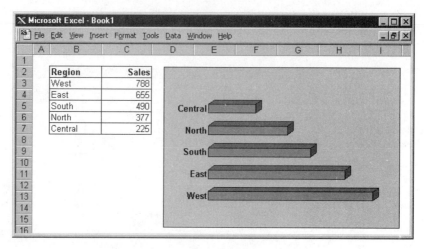

**2.** Choose Format ➤ Axis, then select the Scale tab from the Format Axis dialog box.

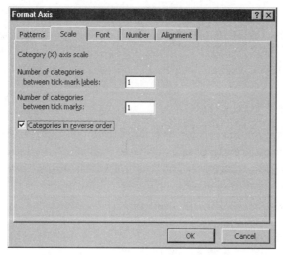

**3.** Activate the Categories In Reverse Order setting, then click on OK.

The reversed chart now appears as shown here:

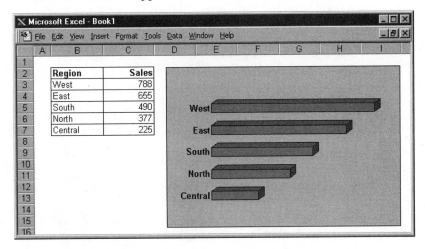

## Changing the Series Order

Suppose you have created a column chart with a data series for year-to-date sales and a data series for prior year sales.

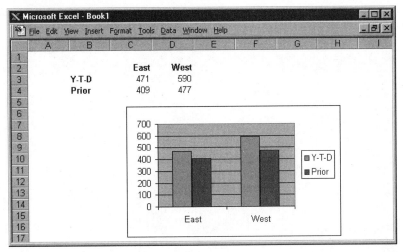

It makes more sense to place Prior to the left of Y-T-D. Follow these steps to do so:

**1.** Select a data series.

**2.** Choose Format ➤ Data Series. Select the Series Order tab from the Format Data Series dialog box.

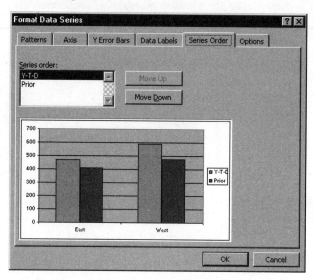

**3.** Select a series in the Series Order box, click on Move Up or Move Down to rearrange the order of the series, then click on OK.

The reformatted chart now appears as shown here:

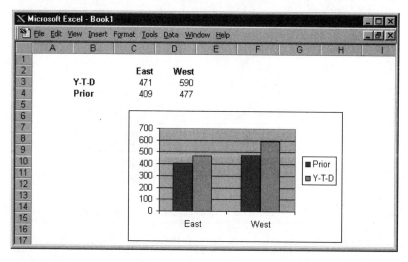

Charting is a remarkably broad topic. Now that you have become familiar with the basics, the next two chapters will discuss intermediate and advanced charting skills, and some advanced techniques for constructing and manipulating complex chart types in Excel.

# Chapter

# 15

## Constructing Complex Charts Using Advanced Techniques

# Constructing Complex Charts Using Advanced Techniques

Chapter 14 demonstrated the endless variety of potential chart types and covered many basic formatting skills. This chapter will introduce some advanced charting skills that will enable you to take full advantage of Excel's versatile charting capabilities.

## Using Custom AutoFormats for Efficiency and Consistency

If you often create charts with similar formatting, you can save a lot of time by creating one or more custom AutoFormats. In addition to saving time, AutoFormats can help you create a consistent, professional look for reports and presentations.

Suppose you frequently chart two types of data—such as budgeted vs. actual expenses, or forecasted vs. actual sales—using the same chart type, with the same colors, fonts, and other formatting. One custom AutoFormat can be used for both of these charts.

Here are the basic steps for creating a custom AutoFormat:

1. Create a chart (embedded chart or chart sheet)—apply all formatting such as fonts, gridlines, color, legend, etc.
2. Select the chart, and choose Chart ➢ Chart Type. The Chart Type dialog box appears.

**3.** Select the Custom Types tab.

**4.** Select the User-Defined option in the Select From area. The User-Defined custom chart types will be displayed.

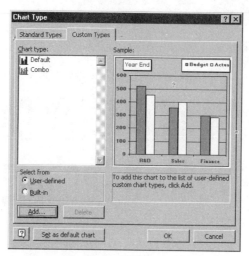

**5.** Click on the Add button. The Add Custom Chart Type dialog box appears.

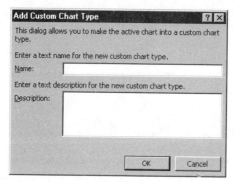

**6.** Type a name for the custom chart (and a brief identifying description, if desired) then click on OK. The name is restricted to 31 characters.

**7.** Click on OK, and on OK again to close the Chart Type dialog box.

## Applying a Custom AutoFormat

Once you have created a custom chart type, follow these steps to apply it:

**1.** Create a new chart using default formats.

**2.** Select the chart.

**3.** Choose Chart ➢ Chart Type to call up the Chart Type dialog box.

**4.** Click on User-Defined to display the custom types that you have defined.

**5.** Select the custom type from the Chart Type list (the custom chart is previewed in the dialog box) and click on OK.

We built and formatted the chart shown in Figure 15.1 and then defined a custom AutoFormat using the newly created chart as the basis.

**FIGURE 15.1**

*The title and legend have shadows and are positioned to allow a large plot area. The fonts are bold-faced, and the colors are customized.*

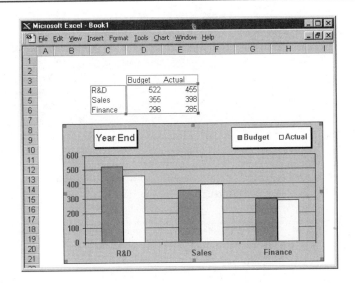

You can apply this AutoFormat to charts that are not necessarily identical to the original chart, as shown in Figure 15.2.

# Changing the Default Chart

The default chart type for Excel is a 2-D column chart. However, you can use one of Excel's built-in chart types as the default type, or you can use one or more custom chart types you have created; it is easy to configure Excel to use one of them as your default chart. To use one of your custom charts as the default type, follow these steps:

**1.** Select any chart you wish to display the Chart menu. Choose Chart ➢ Chart Type, then select the Custom Types tab.

**2.** Click on the User-Defined option, select the chart type from the list, then click on the Set As Default Chart button and click on OK.

PART

IV

Graphics and Charts

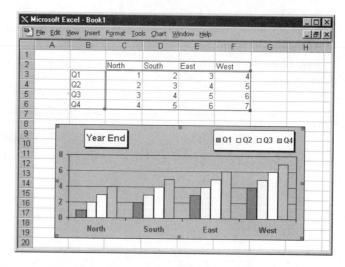

In a similar way, you can use any chart listed in the chart type dialog box as the default type: simply select a built-in or user-defined chart on the Custom Types tab, or one from the Standard Types tab, and click on the Set As Default Chart button.

**NOTE**

If you have not previously saved a chart as a custom type, you may still designate it as the default type. Select the chart, choose Chart ➢ Chart Type to display the dialog box, and click on the Set As Default Chart button. You will be prompted with a message that asks you if you want to use the selected chart as the default, and if you click on Yes, the Add Custom Chart Type dialog box will appear. Enter a name for the chart type and click on OK.

To reset the default chart back to the original default, select a chart to activate the Chart menu, select the Column chart on the Standard Types tab, click on the Set As Default Chart button, and click on OK.

To apply default chart formatting to an existing chart, select the chart, display the Chart Type dialog box, and check Default Formatting in the Options area.

.

## Chart Options

The Active Chart settings, shown in Figure 15.3, are also important to understand. To display this dialog box, choose Tools ➤ Options and select the Chart tab:

**Not Plotted (Leave Gaps):** A gap is left in the chart when a plotted cell is blank.

**Zero:** Blank cells are treated as zero value.

**Interpolated:** Fills in lines by interpolating a value.

**Plot Visible Cells Only:** Visible cells are plotted—hidden cells are ignored (particularly useful in conjunction with outlining).

**Chart Sizes With Window Frame:** This setting pertains to chart sheets—when checked, the chart automatically sizes according to size of the window (same as the View ➤ Sized With Window command).

**FIGURE 15.3**

*The settings inside the Active Chart area are only available when a chart is selected.*

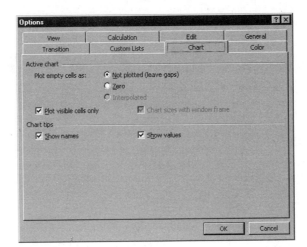

## Drawing inside a Chart

In Chapter 12 you learned how to draw objects on a worksheet. Now suppose that you want an arrow pointing to a certain part of a chart, so you draw an arrow alongside an embedded chart. Unfortunately, the arrow will not retain its precise position relative to the chart when printed. To solve this problem, draw the arrow (or any other drawing object) *inside* the chart—the objects will retain their relative position when printed. The procedure is the same as when you draw on a worksheet, except the chart must be selected:

**1.** Display the Drawing toolbar by clicking on the drawing tool on the Standard toolbar.
**2.** Select the chart.
**3.** Click on a drawing tool, and draw an object directly on the chart.

The objects that you draw in a chart reside inside the chart. If you reposition the chart, the object will stay in the same relative position within the chart. The chart in Figure 15.4 includes a text box and an arrow.

**FIGURE 15.4**

*A text box and an arrow drawn on the chart*

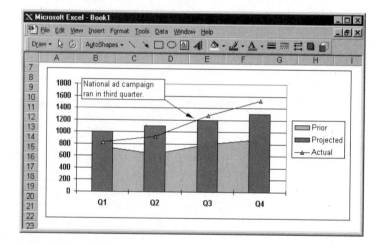

## Copying Objects onto a Chart

You can also copy pictures and objects onto a chart. For example, if you have a company logo as a bitmap file, you can use the Insert ➤ Picture command to insert it into the worksheet:

**1.** Select the chart.
**2.** Choose Insert ➤ Picture ➤ From File to display the Insert Picture dialog box.
**3.** From the dialog box, locate the folder that contains the picture.
**4.** Click on the file, and then click on Insert.

Once the picture is inserted on the chart, you can reposition or resize it accordingly.

## Inserting AutoShapes and WordArt

You can also insert an AutoShape or WordArt object into a chart (see Figure 15.5). Choose Insert ➤ Picture ➤ AutoShape, and click on the AutoShape from an AutoShape palette. Then click on and drag the chart to place the object on the chart and size it appropriately. To insert WordArt, choose Insert ➤ Picture ➤ WordArt, select the desired WordArt format, click on OK, and enter the desired text in the Edit WordArt Text dialog box. Click on OK again, and then move and resize the WordArt object as needed.

**FIGURE 15.5**

*This chart has an inserted WordArt object, a clip art light bulb, and a smiley-face AutoShape.*

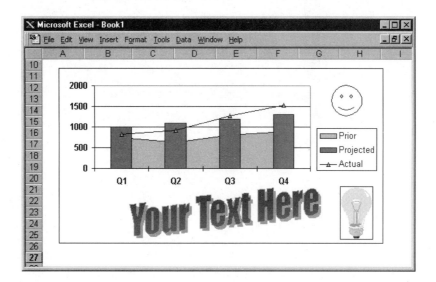

## Charting Discontiguous Ranges

Excel makes it possible to chart selections of cells that do not touch each other, commonly referred to as *discontiguous ranges*. Consider the table shown in the top half of Figure 15.6. Products and services are tracked for goods distributed in two regions. To chart only the TOTAL rows, do the following:

**1.** Enter the constants onto a blank worksheet.
**2.** Select cells C2:F2.
**3.** Hold down Ctrl, then select cells C5:F5 and C9:F9.
**4.** Create the chart with the ChartWizard.

The chart shown in the lower half of Figure 15.6 illustrates charted discontiguous data ranges.

**FIGURE 15.6**

*Only the two TOTAL rows and labels are included in the chart.*

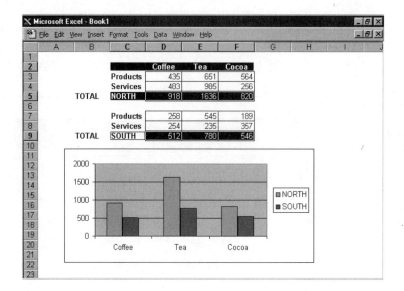

## Using a Secondary Axis to Display Two Value Scales

Suppose you want to chart two series with different value scales on the same chart. For example, one chart needs to show average home sales price and number of homes sold. The average sales price will be over $100,000, whereas the number of homes sold for a given period will be less than 100. Figure 15.7 shows an example of this.

Here's how to create a new chart with a secondary axis using the ChartWizard:

1. Select the built-in Column-Line chart type from the Custom Types tab in the ChartWizard Step 1 Of 4 dialog box.
2. Click on Next and on Next again to go to the Step 3 Of 4 dialog box. Select the Axes tab.

**FIGURE 15.7**

*A secondary axis typically requires a combination chart in order to create a meaningful result.*

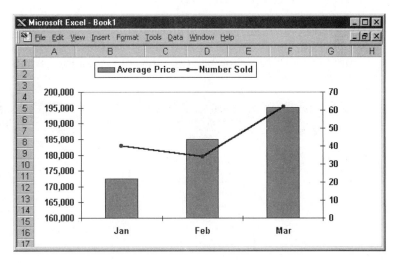

**3.** In the Secondary Axis area of this dialog box, activate the Value (Y) axis setting, and click on Finish.

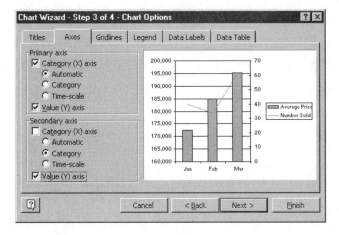

Here's how to add a secondary axis to an existing chart:

**1.** Select the chart.

**2.** Click on and drag the color-coded range to include the new data series that is to be placed on a secondary axis.

**3.** Follow steps 1 through 3 for creating a chart with a secondary axis, previous page.

If you have an existing chart that already contains all the data series you want, but you want to plot one series on a different axis, select the series and choose Format ➢ Data Series, select the Axis tab, and click on the Plot Series On Secondary Axis option.

# Charting Multilevel Categories

You can get more useful information onto a single chart with Excel's multilevel category capability. Suppose you want to chart data on the sales of three products (tennis, running, and hiking shoes), to two different categories of buyers (men and women), in two different regions (east and west).

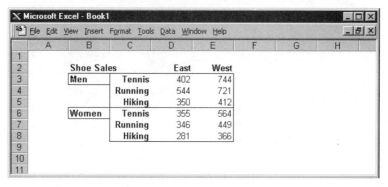

If all of the category labels (columns B and C) are included in the charted range, Excel creates multilevel category labels by default (see Figure 15.8).

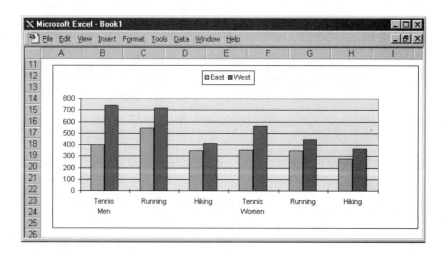

If you want to use only the first column (column B) as category labels, select the chart and click on the ChartWizard button. In the ChartWizard Step 2 Of 4 dialog box, click on the Series tab and enter the revised data label range (B3:B8) in the Category (X) Axis Labels text box.

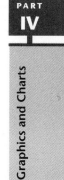

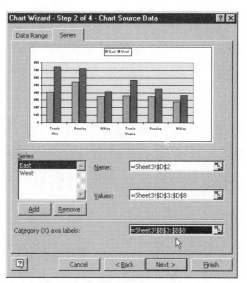

If you are uncertain as to the exact range you want to use, or it is covered by the dialog box, use the Collapse Dialog Box button in the text box to reduce the dialog box, then point to and click on the new range, as shown in Figure 15.9. Click the button again to expand the dialog box.

**FIGURE 15.9**

*The Collapse Dialog Button can help you point to and click on the new range.*

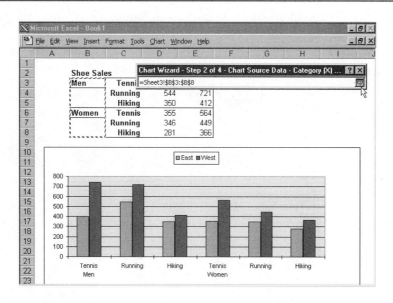

# Changing Worksheet Values by Manipulating the Chart

Some charts let you change underlying worksheet data by manipulating the chart with the mouse. This is a useful technique when doing what-if analysis. Only 2-D bar, 2-D column, and 2-D line charts allow direct manipulation of data markers. Try the following exercise:

**1.** Enter the following onto a worksheet, then create a 2-D column chart:

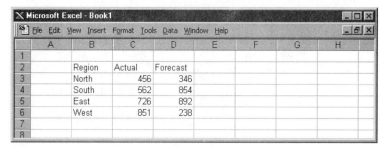

**2.** Select the North Actual marker by single-clicking on it twice (do not double-click).
**3.** Drag the handle on top of the marker up or down (Figure 15.10). Notice that the value in cell C3 changes.

**FIGURE 15.10**

*While dragging the marker, the mouse pointer becomes an up-down arrow. The underlying cell changes as soon as you release the mouse button.*

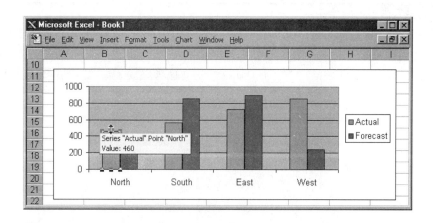

# What If the Chart Is Based on a Cell Containing a Formula?

If you directly manipulate a data marker that points to a cell containing a formula, something different happens. Excel will not change the formula. Rather, it changes one of the cells that the formula depends on. After manipulating a data marker, the Goal Seek dialog box is displayed:

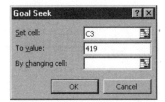

At this point, you are required to enter a cell reference on which the charted cell depends. (See Chapter 27 to learn more about Goal Seek.)

 **MASTERING THE OPPORTUNITIES**

## Charting Data from Multiple Worksheets

Suppose you keep monthly financial data on separate monthly worksheets, yet all the data must be shown in a single chart? You could copy the data from each of the monthly worksheets onto another worksheet, but this is a lot of unnecessary work. Instead, you can create a chart directly from multiple worksheets.

Begin by charting the first month's data. (It doesn't matter where you create the chart—it can be embedded on one of the worksheets, or it can be a separate chart

sheet.) Select the chart, then choose Chart ➤ Source Data to insert data from the second worksheet. To add the new data, you can type the reference into the Source Data dialog box or use the Collapse Dialog Box button to point to and click on the new data. Use the Series list box to add a new series, and use the Name and Values text boxes to add data and series names. Keep in mind that the separate worksheet ranges should be identical—they should all have the same category labels, in the same order (although you don't have to add the labels with each set of data).

# Protecting a Chart

Protecting a chart prevents users from deleting, resizing, or otherwise manipulating the chart. These are the procedures (and implications) for protecting charts:

- Protecting an embedded chart is exactly the same as protecting any graphic object (see Chapter 11). Select the chart, choose Format ➢ Chart Area, select the Properties tab, and check the Locked setting. The lock does not take effect until the worksheet containing the chart is protected.
- Protecting a chart sheet is exactly the same as protecting a worksheet (see Chapter 11). Activate the sheet and choose Tools ➢ Protection ➢ Protect Sheet.

# Charting Data Dynamically

In a spreadsheet environment, there are often many sets of data with a similar structure. For example, you may store budgeting data on a division, department, or cost-center level. The data may be stored in one workbook or many workbooks. But there is always a *budget* column and an *actual* column.

One of the most common design problems is that if you create too many charts, it's hard to be consistent—different budget charts are created for the division, department, cost-center, and so on. This causes a problem in terms of maintenance and consistency. When your organization decides that all budget charts need to be modified to show original and revised budgets, you have a problem on your hands if there are dozens of similar charts floating around.

By applying a variety of Excel skills, you can master what is arguably the most important charting skill: creating a single chart that is capable of charting different sets of data—in other words, dynamically bring data to your chart. This process is illustrated in Figure 15.11, where, instead of "marrying" a given chart to a particular set of data, the worksheet model allows different data to be displayed in the range being charted.

## Tips for Dynamic Charting

Dynamic charting can be accomplished in several ways, involving a variety of Excel skills. Here are some ideas intended to point you in the right direction:

- Use charts to point to cells containing formulas. User input drives the formulas, causing different data sets to be charted (typically, this will entail the use of functions like INDEX, VLOOKUP, OFFSET, MATCH, and SUMIF, which were covered in Chapter 9).

**FIGURE 15.11**

*A well-designed charting model can dynamically chart different sets of data.*

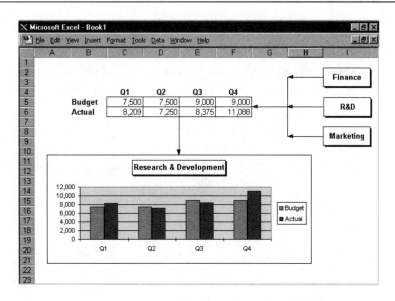

- Use file links (controlled with the Edit ➢ Links command) to link a workbook to different workbooks (see Chapter 4).
- Use dynamic names, covered in Chapter 8, to point to different data sets based on user input.
- Create charts based on pivot tables (see Chapter 21).
- Use workbook templates and chart templates to create reusable models (see Chapter 10).

# Tools Missing from the Built-In Toolbars

There are a number of charting tools that are not on the Chart toolbar. In order to use these tools, you have to add them to a built-in toolbar or create a custom toolbar (see Chapter 7).

Table 15.1 shows just a few of the charting tools available. Most of the tools are AutoFormat shortcuts. These tools, like the Chart Type tools, let you draw a specific type of chart.

The preceding three chapters have provided you with the skills you need to create and manipulate charts, chart objects, and data. In the last of the charting chapters, you will learn about special chart types and scenarios under which a specific chart type may be the most useful to present a given set of data.

**MASTERING THE OPPORTUNITIES**

## Dynamic Charting Using a Named Formula

Charts typically display the values contained in a specific ranges of cells. However, an individual series can dynamically point to different ranges, according to user input. For example, a single chart might display the data for one of several markets, depending on which market the user selects in a list box. The way to accomplish this is to use a named formula in a series name and value.

1. Create a named formula that points dynamically to different ranges according to user input. (See the section on named formulas in Chapter 8 for an example).

2. Create a chart from any one of the ranges.

3. Activate the chart, then right-click on the series you want to make dynamic.

4. Choose Format ➤ Data Series.

5. Select the Name And Values tab.

6. In the Y Values text box, type the name of the named formula, then click on OK.

7. Create a list box (see Chapter 23) to allow the user to choose which range is charted—selecting a choice from the list box causes the worksheet to recalculate and the chart to update.

**TABLE 15.1:** SPECIAL CHARTING TOOLS

| Tool Face | Tool | Function |
| --- | --- | --- |
| | Category Axis Gridlines | Adds/deletes vertical gridlines |
| | Stacked Column Chart AutoFormat | Stacked column chart |
| | 3-D Perspective Column Chart AutoFormat | 3-D perspective column chart |
| | Pie Chart AutoFormat | Pie chart, percentage labels |

**TABLE 15.1:** SPECIAL CHARTING TOOLS (CONTINUED)

| Tool Face | Tool | Function |
| --- | --- | --- |
|  | 3-D Pie Chart AutoFormat | 3-D pie chart, percentage labels |
|  | Doughnut Chart AutoFormat | Doughnut chart, category labels |
|  | Volume/Hi-Lo-Close Chart AutoFormat | Combination chart for stock prices |

# Chapter

# 16

## Special Chart Types

# Chapter 16

# Special Chart Types

**A**s you become more familiar with charting as a tool for data analysis and presentation, you will discover that there are many ways to present data using charts. However, some chart types may be more beneficial than others, depending on what you want to illustrate and who your audience is. Some people may be used to working with only line or column charts, while others may want to use curve-fitting to project market trends. In this chapter you will learn how many of the special chart types provided by Excel can be used to display your data in a more efficient or explanatory way.

Excel has several new chart types and subtypes. You can use cone, pyramid, and cylinder data markers in 2-D and 3-D column and bar charts, and you can create stock charts that show high-low-close stock prices, as well as volume- and open-high-low-close subtypes. You can also create bubble charts, Pie Of Pie, and Bar Of Pie charts. In Step 1 of the ChartWizard, you can peruse the various chart types and subtypes, and also preview them to see which would best display your data.

# Special Types of Charts

In this section, you will learn about some of the more esoteric chart types: picture charts, trendlines, and error bars.

## Adding Visual Appeal: Picture Charts

You can replace the normal data markers used in various 2-D charts with pictures that are imported from a graphics program or drawn with Excel's built-in drawing tools. The result can be very appealing when used in reports and presentations (see Figure 16.1).

**FIGURE 16.1**

*We pasted this picture into the chart from the Microsoft Power-Point clip-art library and then applied the Stretch picture format option to it.*

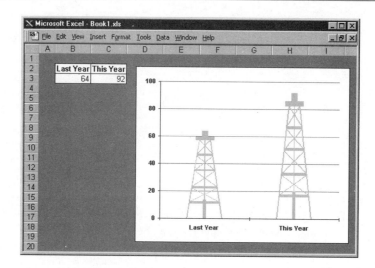

Follow these steps to use a picture in an existing chart:

**1.** Place a picture onto the Clipboard in one of the following ways:

- Copy a graphic from another application.
- Create a picture using Excel's drawing tools, then select it and choose Edit ➤ Copy.

**2.** Select the data series (or individual data point) that you want to replace with a picture.

**3.** Choose Edit ➤ Paste.

## Formatting Picture Markers

You can apply formatting styles for picture markers. To select a picture format, do the following:

**1.** Select the marker, choose Format ➤ Selected Data Series (or if a single point, Format ➤ Selected Data Point), then click on the Patterns tab.

**2.** Click on the Fill Effects button and select the Picture tab.

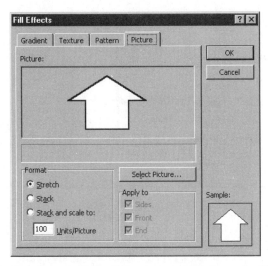

**3.** Choose one of the following options from the Picture Format area and click on OK:

**Stretch:** Causes a single picture to be stretched

**Stack:** Causes the picture to be stacked to the appropriate height (see Figure 16.2)

**Stack And Scale To:** Lets you specify the size of the picture in the same unit of measure as the chart axis

## More Facts about Picture Markers

Here are some important points to keep in mind when working with picture markers:

- More than one picture can be used in a chart (for example, a chart showing statistics for the United States, Mexico, and Canada could use the flag of each nation).
- To remove picture formats from a series, select the series and choose Edit ➤ Clear ➤ Formats—don't accidentally delete the entire data series by using the Edit ➤ Clear Series command on the shortcut menu.
- You can save charts with pictures as custom AutoFormats.

*FIGURE 16.2*

*The picture markers in this figure are stacked rather than stretched.*

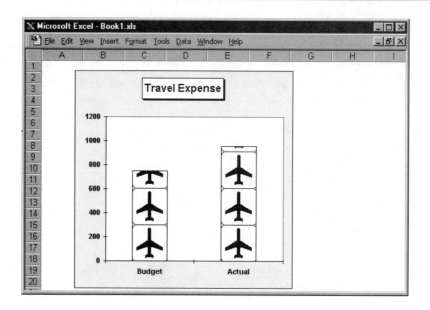

## Presenting Regression with Trendlines

Trendlines are a way of presenting a type of statistical analysis known as *regression*, which is chiefly a forecasting method used to smooth out data and predict trends. If you want to plot a trend, a chart is able to examine a set of data and plot a trendline based on that data—without adding formulas to the worksheet to calculate the trend. Here are some potential applications:

- You could forecast sales for the next 6 months based on the previous 18 months.
- A chemical analysis based on a standard curve can be validated with a linear regression, a statistical method for finding a straight line that best fits two sets of data, establishing a relationship between two variables.
- You could chart the half-life of a radioactive compound into the future.
- You could smooth out the daily fluctuations in stock prices to see performance trends more clearly.

Trendlines can extrapolate data backward as well as forward, and can be based on five different regression equations or on a moving average. Using a moving average, each average is calculated from the specified number of preceding data points.

You can add trendlines to these kinds of 2-D chart:

- Area
- Column
- Line
- Bar
- Scatter

You format and delete trendlines just like other chart elements. You cannot add them to 3-D chart, but you can add multiple trendlines to the same data series.

## Adding a Trendline to a Data Series

Here are the steps to add a trendline to a data series:

1. Right-click on the series to which you want to add the trendline to select it and display the shortcut menu.
2. Choose Add ➢ Trendline.

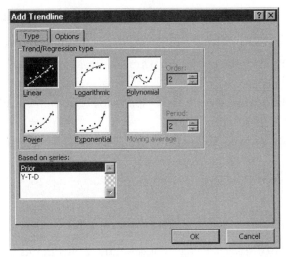

3. Choose from one of the six available statistical methods—linear, logarithmic, polynomial, power, exponential, or moving average.

   - For polynomial regression, specify the highest power for the independent variable in the Order text box (must be an integer between 2 and 6).
   - For a moving average, specify the number of periods the moving average is based on in the Period text box.

**4.** Click on the Options tab.

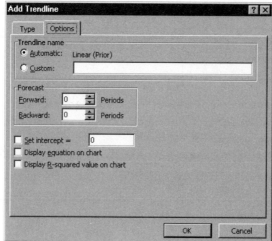

**5.** Set the other trendline options described here, then click on OK:

**Trendline Name:** Displays the name of the trendline in the legend.

**Forecast:** Selects the number of periods forward and backward for trend forecast.

**Display Equation On Chart:** Displays the regression equation (this can be formatted and moved).

**Display R-Squared Value On Chart:** Displays the R-squared value (this can be formatted and moved).

**Set Intercept:** Changes the Y-intercept value.

## Using Error Bars

*Error bars* are used to display a degree of uncertainty (a plus/minus factor) surrounding a given data series, as illustrated in Figure 16.3. You can add error bars to these 2-D chart types:

- Line
- Column
- Area
- Bar
- Scatter

Graphics and Charts

Error bars cannot be used on 3-D charts. In scatter charts, you can add error bars to both axes. If the series values change, the error bars will be automatically adjusted.

*FIGURE 16.3*

*This shows the predicted rate of return for three portfolios, and uses error bars to plot one standard deviation.*

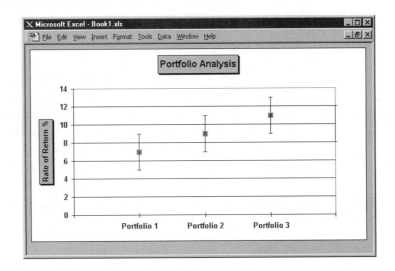

Here are the steps to add an error bar to a data series:

**1.** Click on the data series that you want to add error bars to.
**2.** Choose Format ➢ Selected Data Series. The Format Data Series dialog box appears.
**3.** Select the Y Error Bars tab.

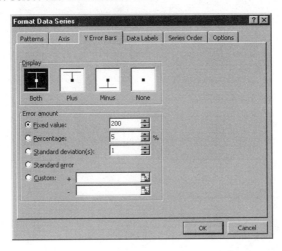

**4.** Choose from the following options, then click on OK:

**Display:** The error bar can display above and/or below the data point.

**Fixed Value:** Specify the constant value used to plot the error bar.

**Percentage:** Error bar is based on percentage calculated from each data point.

**Standard Deviation(s):** Enter the number of standard deviations from the data points.

**Standard Error:** The standard error of the plotted values is displayed as the error amount.

**Custom:** You can enter deviation values in a range of worksheet cells, then enter the worksheet range in the Custom box. The worksheet range must contain the same number of values as there are data points in the series. You can enter positive deviation values, negative deviation values, or both.

# Showing Data to Its Best Advantage: Combination Charts

Suppose you have charted actual and projected sales for a period. A combination chart may emphasize the relationship between the two data series better than a single chart type, as illustrated in Figure 16.4.

**FIGURE 16.4**

*The combination chart, which is easier to understand, combines a column chart and line chart.*

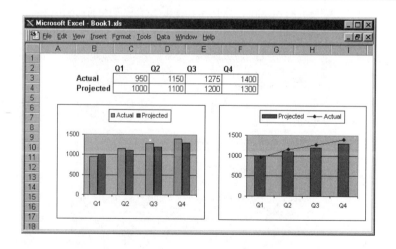

## Creating a Combination Chart

Follow these steps to change a normal chart into a combination chart:

1. Select the data series you want to change.
2. Choose Chart ➤ Chart Type and select a chart type from the Chart Type dialog box, then click on OK. This will be applied only to the selected data series.

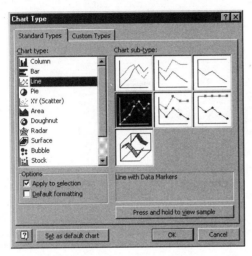

Excel is not limited to two chart types in a combo chart—as you can see in Figure 16.5.

## More on Combination Charts

Here are a few facts to keep in mind when working with combination charts:

- 3-D charts cannot be combined.
- You can create any combination of area, column, line, and scatter charts.
- You can include bar, pie, doughnut, or radar types in a combination chart, but only one series can be formatted using these types.

## Working with 3-D Charts

Three-dimensional charts are a mixed blessing. They are visually appealing, and sometimes allow you to present complex data in a way that is easier to absorb than a 2-D chart. On the other hand, they present certain problems that you don't encounter with 2-D charts. For instance, a data series in a 3-D column chart might obscure another data series. Used judiciously, however, 3-D charts can enhance your reports and presentations.

PART

**IV**

Graphics and Charts

**FIGURE 16.5**

*Combination charts are particularly effective when printed on a black-and-white printer, where it can be difficult to distinguish gray scales.*

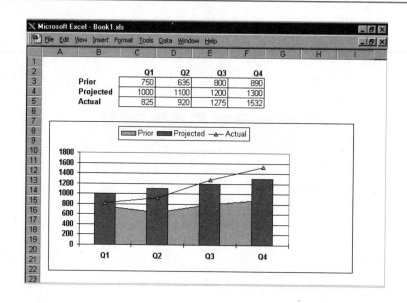

## MASTERING THE OPPORTUNITIES

### Time-Scale Axes

Time-scale axes can be used to chart your data by date, even if the data is not arranged in chronological order. Time-scale axes use increments, or *base units*, based on the shortest interval between any two dates in your data. If you have data points for any two consecutive days, your time axis will be in daily increments.

If the closest two points in your data are two days apart, then your axis will have base units of two days. Once a chart with a time-scale axis has been created, the base unit can be changed to any number of days, or to months or years. You can do this on the Scale tab of the Format Axis dialog box; just click on the axis, and choose Format ➢ Selected Axis.

## Aesthetic and Practical Advantages of 3-D Charts

Some 3-D chart types and formats are essentially the same as their 2-D counterparts. The benefit to going 3-D is visual appeal, as illustrated in Figure 16.6.

**WARNING**

There is a problem with 3-D pie charts, which is often overlooked, and Figure 16.6 shows a good example of it. Most people don't pay attention to the fact that the angles of the corresponding portions in the two pie charts (2-D and 3-D) are not equal. Sure, it's because Excel is putting a bit of perspective on the second pie chart, but it is misleading. Be aware of this fact when working with 3-D pies!

**FIGURE 16.6**

*Sometimes the difference between a 2-D and 3-D chart is purely aesthetic.*

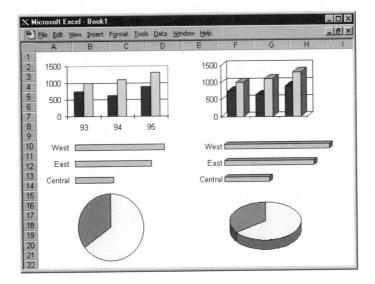

The benefits of 3-D charts are not limited to aesthetics. The 3-D column chart in Figure 16.7 provides a result that would be difficult to achieve using 2-D. Figure 16.7 also illustrates the various components that are unique to certain 3-D charts, such as the chart walls and floor, but more importantly the simultaneous display of three chart axes; value, category, and series.

**FIGURE 16.7**

*Terminology for
3-D column
charts*

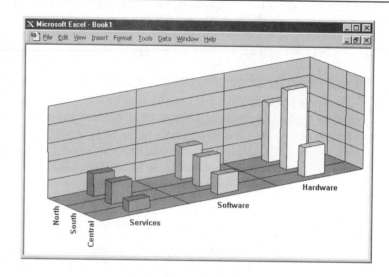

## Viewing a 3-D Chart from Different Angles

For some 3-D chart formats, such as the column chart shown earlier in Figure 16.7, it is possible for a data series to obscure another data series. But you can resolve this problem by changing the angle at which the chart is presented. When a 3-D chart is selected, you can choose Chart ➤ 3-D View to change the view angle.

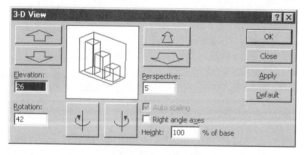

As you click on the elevation, perspective, and spin buttons, the preview box gives you a general idea of how the chart will appear. When you're through adjusting the view angle, do one of the following:

- Click on OK to accept the view.
- Click on Close to cancel the view changes.

- Click on Apply to apply the view settings to the chart but leave the dialog box displayed for more changes.
- Click on Default to go back to the default 3-D view.

Another way to change the 3-D view is by direct manipulation of the chart using the mouse:

**1.** Click on one of the corners of the plot area.

**2.** Click on a corner again and hold down the mouse button until the cursor becomes crosshairs.

When the mouse pointer is on a corner, a pop-up note will display the word *Corners*.

**3.** Drag the corner (hold down Ctrl while dragging the corner if you want to display outlines of the data markers while changing the view, as shown in Figure 16.8). Release the mouse button to redisplay the full chart.

**FIGURE 16.8**

*Hold down Ctrl to display the data marker outlines while you are dragging a corner.*

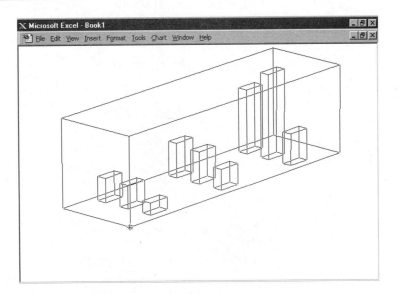

## An Exercise in Creating and Formatting a 3-D Chart

In this exercise, you will create and format a 3-D column chart similar to the one shown in Figure 16.7.

## Enter Data and Create a Chart

**1.** Enter the following onto a new worksheet:

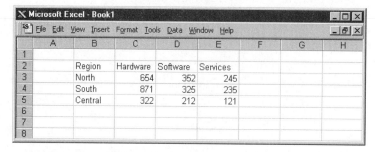

**2.** Select the region B2:E5.

**3.** Choose Insert ➤ Chart to create a chart—choose these options in the ChartWizard:

- Select the column chart type and 3-D column subtype in Step 1.
- Deselect Show legend from the Legend tab in Step 3.
- In Step 4, place the chart as a new sheet in the workbook.
- Click on Finish.
- Choose Chart ➤ 3-D View, set Rotation to 150, Perspective to 25, and Elevation to 15 to best display all the data markers.
- Select the axes and reformat the font size to a more readable size.

Your chart should look like the one shown here:

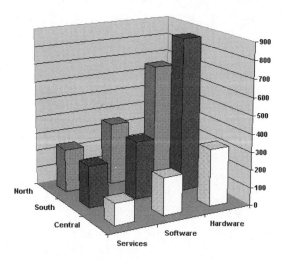

## Change the Floor Color

**1.** Right-click on the floor and choose Format Floor from the shortcut menu.

**2.** Choose a light gray area color from the Format Floor dialog box.

**TIP**

You can change the color of any chart element using the Color tool palette from the Formatting toolbar; use the Font Color tool palette to change text color.

## Change the Size and Spacing of Columns

Now adjust the size and spacing of the columns:

**1.** Select a data series.

**2.** Choose Format ➤ Selected Data Series and click on the Options tab.

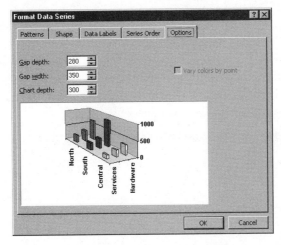

**3.** Change the Gap Depth setting to **280**. As you change the number, a preview appears in the dialog box's preview window.

**4.** Change the Gap Width setting to **350**.

**5.** Change the Chart Depth setting to **300**.

PART

**IV**

Graphics and Charts

**6.** Click on OK.

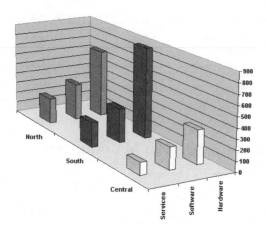

## Separating Pie Slices

As in Excel 7 and previous versions, slices of pie charts can be separated from the rest of the pie for emphasis. You can separate a single slice, or you can separate all of the slices. In Excel 8, you can further divide individual slices of a pie chart into two new subtypes: Pie Of Pie or Bar Of Pie, shown below.

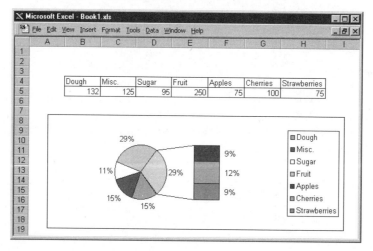

**NOTE**

Note that the data range in the chart above is a single data series; it is an inherent limitation of pie charts that they can only plot one series.

To make the second plot (in this case, a bar), place the elements of the second plot (apples, cherries, and strawberries) at the end of the series, preceded by their general category (fruit). To select the number of data elements for the second plot, double-click on a series and use the Options tab of the Format Data Series dialog box to enter the number of values using the Second Plot Contains The Last option.

Pie slices can also be separated with the mouse:

- To separate all of the slices, select the series (click on any slice) and drag it away from the center of the pie.
- To separate only one slice, select the slice (single-click on the slice, then single-click on it again) and drag it away from the center of the pie.
- To join separated slices, drag the slice(s) back to the center of the pie.

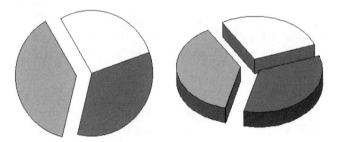

## Using Surface Charts

A surface chart is a graph that shows one variable as a function of two other variables. Surface charts are often used for scientific data, but are also applicable for certain business requirements.

For a surface chart to make sense, the two variables need to represent continuous data. For instance, although an axis may represent temperatures in 10-degree increments, temperature is a continuous measurement—there are temperatures that lie between the 10-degree increments. *Product code* would be an illogical variable—it is not a continuous measurement.

### Surface Chart Case Study

The following case study will use a surface chart to help a company establish a retail price for a new product and establish a marketing budget.

- The company is in the business of making electronic toys. It is introducing a new product with a retail price between $20 and $40.

- The company must establish a marketing budget between $500,000 and $2,500,000.
- Historical sales and profit data have been gathered for similar products where price and marketing expenditures were within the above parameters. (If you want to work along with this example, enter the constants shown here onto a blank worksheet.)

| | Budget (thousands) | 20 | 25 | 30 | 35 | 40 |
|---|---|---|---|---|---|---|
| | 500 | 1,700 | 1,475 | 1,310 | 775 | 507 |
| | 1,000 | 2,300 | 3,444 | 2,590 | 2,530 | 884 |
| | 1,500 | 3,650 | 7,125 | 7,222 | 4,985 | 1,900 |
| | 2,000 | 3,855 | 6,765 | 7,309 | 5,890 | 4,221 |
| | 2,500 | 3,595 | 6,322 | 6,983 | 5,586 | 3,883 |

Historical profits (in thousands) based on retail price and marketing budget — Retail Price

- The historical data will be analyzed to determine a retail price and marketing budget most likely to yield maximum profitability (since marketing expenditures reduce profit, you must determine a point of diminishing returns).

One horizontal axis of the chart will represent list price. The second horizontal axis will represent marketing budget. The two axes define a horizontal plane equivalent to a flat map.

To create a surface chart based on the data from the worksheet shown above, do the following:

1. Select cells C5:H10.
2. Use the ChartWizard to create a chart for the data. Specify Surface as the chart type and 3-D as the subtype at Step 1, then click on Finish.
3. Rotate the chart and reformat the axes as necessary. The result is shown in Figure 16.9.

The contour reveals that a product priced in the $25 to $30 range, with a marketing budget of $1.5 to $2 million, is apt to produce the greatest profitability. As might be expected, a $40 product with a marketing budget under $1 million is apt to fare poorly.

Graphics and Charts

**FIGURE 16.9**

*Elevation and perspective have been adjusted so you can clearly view the most profitable area of the surface. Spinning the chart to change perspective will alter the location of the axes.*

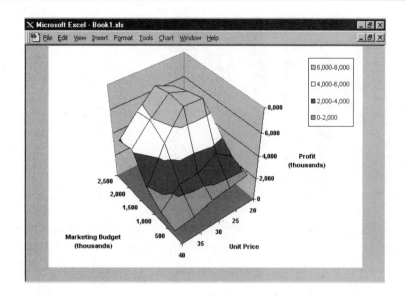

> **TIP**
>
> A printed report of a 3-D surface chart might actually include two or three different charts based on the same data. You could set up each chart from a different angle so that you could view all areas of the contour.

The five chapters you have just finished have presented the major topics of Excel's graphics and charting features. As you can now see, this encompasses a considerable body of knowledge. By using techniques and tools described herein, and applying them to real-world situations, you will soon be on your way to mastering these vital Excel skills.

# PART V

# V

# Working Effectively with Databases

# LEARN TO:

- *Set up worksheet database*

- *Sort and filter database rows*

- *Use the built-in data form*

- *Sort using a custom list*

- *Create criteria ranges and use "D" functions*

- *Use the Query Wizard to access external databases*

- *Use the External Data toolbar*

- *Integrate database queries into your worksheets by setting external data range properties*

- *Work with parameter queries*

# Chapter

# 17

## Working with Internal Databases

# Working with Internal Databases

A s far as Excel is concerned, there are two distinct types of databases—*internal databases*, which reside in worksheets (also called *lists* in Excel); and *external databases*, such as Microsoft Access, dBase, Paradox, FoxPro, SQL Server, and Oracle. This chapter will show you how to work with internal databases. You'll learn the good news and the bad news about internal databases. You'll find out how to sort data and filter a database. And, you'll find out why knowing how to use internal databases is important—even if you don't permanently store databases in Excel.

## Discovering the Advantages of Excel's Database Features

Many users have been put off by Excel's database features simply because the term *database* implies something complex and hard to learn. This perception was reinforced by the fact that database manipulation in early versions of Excel actually *was* hard to learn.

**NOTE**

The extraordinary level of confusion about databases in general, and Excel databases in particular, prompted Microsoft to practically abandon the term *database* altogether. The Excel documentation instead refers extensively to *list management*.

There is another category of users who have avoided internal databases—people who use a "real" database management system (DBMS). An internal Excel database lacks certain features possessed by the simplest DBMS. Knowing this, DBMS aficionados skip over Excel's database features. Just because a range of cells is *treated* as a database doesn't mean that the worksheet is necessarily the permanent home for the data.

Excel is an extraordinary tool for analyzing data stored in a DBMS, however, and the internal database features play an important role in this process. There are many reasons to become familiar with how Excel manages its internal databases.

First, Excel's database functionality is easy to learn, and you can get up and running with it quickly. The functionality is also useful, even if the problems you are solving are not, on the surface, database problems. Excel's database features can help you dissect, analyze, and report, regardless of whether the data is stored in a worksheet or in an external database.

## Limitations of Spreadsheet Databases

Excel provides outstanding facilities for entering, editing, analyzing, and manipulating data. But there are limitations inherent to all spreadsheet programs that you should be aware of before choosing Excel as the place to permanently *store* your data.

- A worksheet is limited to 65,536 rows and 256 columns. While this is huge for a spreadsheet, database tables routinely contain hundreds of thousands of rows.
- Only one user at a time can have write access to an internal database, with the exception of shared workbooks, discussed in Chapter 29.
- Enforcing bulletproof data integrity (disallowing text in numeric columns, for example) requires customization, which can be time consuming and difficult.
- The entire database must be in memory (unless you are accessing an external database—see Chapter 19).
- Data stored on worksheets tends to consume considerably more disk space than data stored in external databases. (A worksheet stores formulas, formatting, graphics, etc.; a DBMS stores raw data.)

### If You Are Upgrading from Excel 4 or Earlier...

Excel 5 made many fundamental changes to the way you work with databases. If you are upgrading from Excel 4 (or earlier) to the new version of Excel, you will notice many important improvements. Many of the old commands are missing from the menu system, which may give you the impression that there has been a loss of functionality. In fact, functionality has been greatly improved. Here are some key differences and similarities between Excel 4 and Excel 8:

- The named ranges Database, Criteria, and Extract are no longer required, which is why the SET DATABASE, SET EXTRACT, and SET CRITERIA commands are no longer on the menu.

- Instead of relying on a named range Database, Excel automatically detects when the active cell is located within a range of data.

- There is a simplified interface for defining simple criteria and performing extracts (covered in this chapter).

- For complex problems, you can still define criteria and perform extracts the old way; see Chapter 18 to learn the nuances.

- Pivot tables, covered in Chapters 20 through 22, are a dramatic improvement over Excel 4 crosstabs.

**PART**

**V**

Working Effectively with Databases

# Setting Up a Database

Setting up a database in Excel is quite simple. But first, it will help if you understand these three terms:

**Field:** A *field* is a column within a database.

**Record:** A *record* is a row within a database.

**Field Name:** The top row of a database usually contains *field names*; a field name consists of unique text describing the field (there is no need to actually name the cells).

In the example in Figure 17.1, there are seven fields and 10 records (B3:H3 is the first record). The field names are contained in cells B2:H2.

Certain database features do not require field names. For example, you can sort a database that does not have field names. But to use all of Excel's database features, you must enter field names. Field names are not limited to alphanumeric characters—they can include spaces, dashes, and other special characters. Each field name should be unique (within the particular data table).

**FIGURE 17.1**

*An internal database consisting of seven fields and 10 records*

| | A | B | C | D | E | F | G | H |
|---|---|---|---|---|---|---|---|---|
| 1 | | | | | | | | |
| 2 | | Client No. | Name | Category | Region | MTD Sales | YTD Sales | Last Year |
| 3 | | 101 | Argus Industries | Mfg | North | 9,569 | 13,775 | 14,723 |
| 4 | | 102 | LEX Software | Services | South | 3,527 | 10,534 | 12,887 |
| 5 | | 103 | National Bank | Financial | South | 1,472 | 8,123 | 10,022 |
| 6 | | 104 | Nelson Group | Services | East | 3,717 | 12,374 | 9,221 |
| 7 | | 105 | Pacific Investments | Financial | North | 3,315 | 18,656 | 11,044 |
| 8 | | 106 | Nica Corporation | Mfg | West | 6,542 | 58,229 | 52,559 |
| 9 | | 107 | MDC Enterprises | Mfg | East | 8,167 | 23,613 | 25,733 |
| 10 | | 108 | Wilson and Roth | Services | West | 4,026 | 11,786 | 9,225 |
| 11 | | 109 | JK Associates | Financial | South | 12,391 | 71,805 | 23,490 |
| 12 | | 110 | T.K. James Inc. | Services | North | 3,146 | 19,104 | 11,373 |
| 13 | | | | | | | | |
| 14 | | | | | | | | |
| 15 | | | | | | | | |

**NOTE**

You may want to create and save the database pictured in Figure 17.1 so you can follow along; this database is referred to throughout this chapter, and in subsequent chapters.

To set up a database in Excel, simply enter field names and data onto a worksheet. You have probably performed this task countless times.

**TIP**

For rapid data entry into a range of cells, select the range, then use the Tab key to navigate the range. (Use Shift+Tab to move backward.)

## Sorting the Database

Sorting data is one of the most common tasks performed with databases. Sorting data allows you to organize the database so that the information you need most is easily accessible. For instance, if you are analyzing the western region using the database shown in Figure 17.1, you would likely sort the database by Region. On the other hand, if you want to see the clients with the most sales, you might sort the database by YTD Sales, in descending order (highest sales to lowest sales). You can sort a database or list by single or multiple fields in the database (e.g., Region, YTD Sales, or both), in ascending or descending order, and by custom sort orders (see Chapter 18 to learn about custom sort orders).

## Sorting by a Single Field

Here's how to sort a database by a single field; (Figure 17.1 was sorted by the Client No. field in Ascending order):

**1.** Select any one cell within the database range.

**2.** Choose Data ➢ Sort. The Sort dialog box appears:

**3.** Choose the field you want to sort by from the Sort By drop-down list.

**4.** Use the option buttons to specify Ascending (a, b, c; 1, 2, 3) or Descending (z, y, x; 10 ,9 ,8) order.

**NOTE**

The two Then By inputs are optional; they allow you to specify two more sort fields (up to three total). We'll cover sorting by multiple fields in the next section.

**5.** Excel tries to determine if the database has a header row (field names), and sets the Header Row or No Header Row setting accordingly in the My List Has area. Override this setting if necessary.

**6.** Click on OK to sort the list.

**WARNING**

If the database has a header row, but you specify no header row, the headings (field names) will be sorted into the database as if the header row was a data record. Excel will make a guess concerning header/no header correctly 99 percent of the time, so users tend not to pay attention to this setting until the first time they sort the header row with the data. Remember, if you sort incorrectly, the sort can be undone using Edit ➢ Undo Sort.

PART

**V**

Working Effectively
with Databases

## Sorting by Multiple Fields

Now let's assume you want to sort the database pictured in Figure 17.1 first by Category, and then by YTD Sales within each category from highest to lowest sales:

**1.** Select a cell inside the database, then choose Data ➢ Sort.

**2.** Select the Category field from the Sort By drop-down list; select Ascending order.

**3.** Select YTD Sales as the second sort field from the Then By drop-down list, and choose Descending order.

**4.** Click on OK. The database will be sorted as shown in Figure 17.2.

 **NOTE**

See Chapter 18 to learn how to sort by more than three fields.

## More Facts about Sorting

Here are a few more important points to know about Excel's sorting feature:

- Sorts are performed according to underlying cell value, not the formatted appearance of the cell.
- Sorts are case-insensitive by default; you can specify case-sensitive sorting by clicking on the Options button on the Sort dialog box and checking the case-sensitive check box.
- The logical value FALSE comes before TRUE in an ascending sort.
- All error values are considered the same.

**FIGURE 17.2**

*The data has
now been
sorted by Cate-
gory and then
by YTD Sales.*

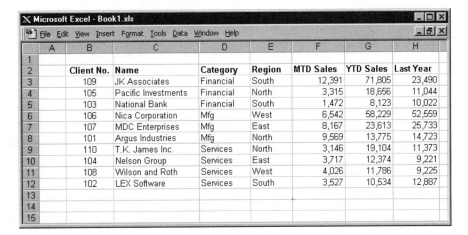

| Client No. | Name | Category | Region | MTD Sales | YTD Sales | Last Year |
|---|---|---|---|---|---|---|
| 109 | JK Associates | Financial | South | 12,391 | 71,805 | 23,490 |
| 105 | Pacific Investments | Financial | North | 3,315 | 18,656 | 11,044 |
| 103 | National Bank | Financial | South | 1,472 | 8,123 | 10,022 |
| 106 | Nica Corporation | Mfg | West | 6,542 | 58,229 | 52,559 |
| 107 | MDC Enterprises | Mfg | East | 8,167 | 23,613 | 25,733 |
| 101 | Argus Industries | Mfg | North | 9,569 | 13,775 | 14,723 |
| 110 | T.K. James Inc. | Services | North | 3,146 | 19,104 | 11,373 |
| 104 | Nelson Group | Services | East | 3,717 | 12,374 | 9,221 |
| 108 | Wilson and Roth | Services | West | 4,026 | 11,786 | 9,225 |
| 102 | LEX Software | Services | South | 3,527 | 10,534 | 12,887 |

- Blanks sort last for both ascending *and* descending sorts.
- Avoid text and numbers in the same field—it is generally a bad practice, and sometimes results in meaningless sorts.

# Filtering Databases

Sometimes it is useful to show only those database records that meet certain criteria. This is accomplished by *filtering* the database. For example, suppose you have a mailing list of names and addresses for clients all over the country, and you want to send letters to only clients with Georgia addresses. You can filter the data so that only the records with Georgia addresses are visible, and then copy the filtered data to another worksheet, a report, or a word processing program. There are two types of filters:

- *AutoFilters*, covered in this chapter
- *Advanced filters*, covered in Chapter 18

An AutoFilter is a simple filter which, with one command, allows you to filter the records in a worksheet database. Advanced filters on the other hand allow you to specify complex filtering criteria.

# Filtering a Database Using AutoFilters

Follow these steps to filter your database with the AutoFilter command:

**1.** Select any cell in the database, then choose Data ➤ Filter ➤ AutoFilter. Drop-down controls are placed on top of the field names, as you can see in Figure 17.3.

*Drop-down controls are placed on top of field names.*

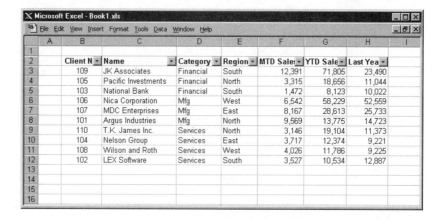

**2.** Click on a drop-down control to apply a filter to the field. The contents of a drop-down list are dictated by the contents of the field. For example, the Category drop-down list will contain each unique data item found in the field, plus five other choices—(All), (Top 10), (Custom), (Blanks), and (NonBlanks):

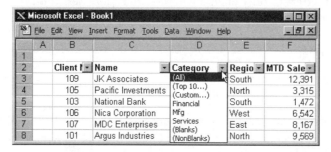

- Select one of the categories, such as Financial, to display only those records where the category is equal to Financial; when the filter is applied, the drop-down control changes color as an indicator that the filter is in effect (the row numbers also change color).

- Select (All) to turn off a filter for a given field (remember, you are turning off the filter for the one field only—filters for other fields are left in place).
- Select (Top 10) to display the Top 10 AutoFilter dialog box. This dialog box allows you to change the number of records you filter and choose the top or bottom number of those records (i.e., the top 10 or bottom 3). You can only filter records that contain numeric values; for example, in Figure 17.2, you can't filter the top 10 records by Region; there is no numeric hierarchy among North, South, East, and West. You can filter the top 10 records by MTD Sales, however. The Top 10 Items command will select the 10 records with the largest MTD Sales, and the Top 10 Percent command will display only those records that are in the top 10 percent.

- Select (Custom) to set a custom AutoFilter. See "Setting Custom AutoFilters" later in this chapter for more details.
- Select (Blanks) to display only those rows where the field is blank.
- Select (NonBlanks) to display only those rows where the field is not blank.

You can filter more than one field at a time. In this example, if you add a filter for Region equals South in addition to Category equals Financial, you will be viewing all records where Category equals Financial *and* Region equals South (a total of two records—clients 103 and 109).

## Setting Custom AutoFilters

The simple filters covered in the previous exercise are based on what a field is *equal* to (i.e., category *equals* Financial, region *equals* South). Custom AutoFilters allow relationships other than *equal* to be specified.

If you choose (Custom) from the AutoFilter drop-down list, the Custom AutoFilter dialog box is displayed.

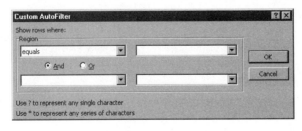

## Using a Filtered List to Find Typos

Picture a worksheet that is used to store payments to suppliers. Each time you make a payment, the supplier's name is typed in, along with other data. The list contains hundreds of rows, and you want to consolidate the data to see how much you have paid to each supplier. However, the consolidation requires that supplier names be typed identically each time they are entered. For example, ABC Corporation must always be entered as ABC Corporation, never as ABC Corp (because ABC Corp would show up in the consolidation as a separate supplier).

How can you check a very long list for typographical errors without tediously looking through the entire list, item by

item? You could add each supplier name to a custom dictionary, then spell check the worksheet. But every time you add a new supplier, you have to add the new name to your custom dictionary. This can be a very tedious process.

There is a quicker way: apply an Auto-Filter to the list. When you click on the AutoFilter arrow for the supplier names column, the drop-down list displays all the unique names in the column, and any misspelled names will be immediately evident. For example, if ABC Corporation has been entered as ABC Corp, both names will show up on the drop-down list. You can select ABC Corp to filter those entries from the list, then quickly change all the ABC Corp entries to ABC Corporation.

The following options are available in the Region area of the Custom AutoFilter dialog box:

- The left drop-down list lets you specify the relational operator (see Table 17.1).
- The right drop-down list lets you specify the field value; you can select an item from the list or type in a value (wildcard characters can be included—use ? for single characters; use * for a series of characters).
- The bottom two drop-down lists are used to specify an optional second comparison criterion.
- Use the And/Or options if you want to apply two comparison criteria. Select And to display rows that meet both criteria; select Or to display rows that meet either criterion.

| **TABLE 17.1:** CUSTOM AUTOFILTER OPERATORS | |
|---|---|
| **Operator** | **Symbol** |
| Equals | = |
| Does not equal | <> |
| Is greater than | > |
| Is greater than or equal to | >= |
| Is less than | < |
| Is less than or equal to | <= |
| Begins with | N/A |
| Does not begin with | N/A |
| Ends with | N/A |
| Does not end with | N/A |
| Contains | N/A |
| Does not contain | N/A |

## Exercise: Setting a Custom AutoFilter

Using the database from Figure 17.1, assume that you want to analyze the North and East regions. Within those regions, you want to display only the larger clients—those with YTD sales greater than $15,000.

**1.** Choose Data ➢ Filter ➢ AutoFilter.

**2.** Choose Custom from the Region AutoFilter drop-down list.

**3.** From the Custom AutoFilter drop-down lists, select Equals North, Or, and Equals East (as pictured below), then click on OK.

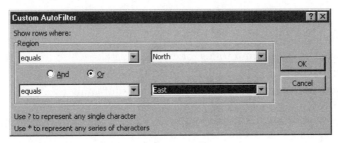

**4.** Next, choose Custom from the YTD Sales AutoFilter drop-down list.

**5.** From the upper drop-down list, choose Is Greater Than and enter **15000** (as pictured below), then click on OK.

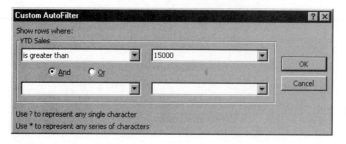

When the filtering exercise is complete, the worksheet will look like Figure 17.4.

| Client I | Name | Categor | Region | MTD Sale | YTD Sale | Last Yea |
|---|---|---|---|---|---|---|
| 105 | Pacific Investments | Financial | North | 3,315 | 18,656 | 11,044 |
| 107 | MDC Enterprises | Mfg | East | 8,167 | 23,613 | 25,733 |
| 110 | T.K. James Inc. | Services | North | 3,146 | 19,104 | 11,373 |

## Removing All Filters at Once

If one or more filters are set, use the Data ➤ Filter ➤ AutoFilter command to remove the filter(s). The command is unchecked, the drop-down controls are removed from the worksheet, and all records are displayed in their original format.

# Totaling Fields of a Filtered Database

If you want to see column totals for a filtered database, use the SUBTOTAL function (covered in Chapter 9) to calculate totals. Unlike SUM, the SUBTOTAL function does *not* include filtered rows (rows hidden as a result of applying a filter) in the calculation. The AutoSum button, used on a cell below a database field, will place a SUBTOTAL function in the cell instead of SUM, but only if the database is filtered.

As a short example of totaling fields of a filtered database, try the following steps, using the worksheet pictured previously in Figure 17.1:

**1.** Filter the database to show region North only.
**2.** Select cells F13:H13.
**3.** Click on the AutoSum button.

The results are shown in Figure 17.5.

**FIGURE 17.5**

*A filtered database with column totals*

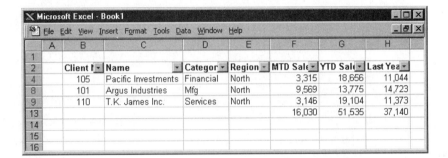

PART

**V**

Working Effectively
with Databases

**TIP**

For clarity and aesthetics, you may be tempted to place the word *TOTALS* in cell C13 or E13. However, this causes Excel to treat row 13 as a database record, and thus hide it when filters are applied. Instead, skip a row, and place the totals on row 14 to prevent it from being treated as a database record. Or, enter the word *TOTALS after* you have subtotaled the filtered database—then Excel will not treat the entry as a record.

# Using the Built-In Data Form

Typically, databases are entered and maintained by typing directly onto a worksheet. When you need a more structured way of performing data entry, Excel's built-in data form may be of use:

- The data form displays one record at a time
- It can be used to add new records and edit existing records.
- It lets you view records matching specified criteria.
- It is used with internal (worksheet) databases only.

**MASTERING TROUBLESHOOTING**

### Implications of a Filtered Database

As you apply AutoFilters to a database, Excel is simply hiding the rows that do not match the filter criteria. However, rows that are hidden as a result of filtering are not the same as rows that are hidden using the Format ➢ Row ➢ Hide command. You should be aware of the following points concerning cells hidden as a result of a filter:

- They are unaffected by AutoFills.

- They are unaffected by formatting commands.

- They are not included in newly created charts (though you can override this on a per-chart basis by clearing the Plot Visible Cells Only setting in the Tools ➢ Options ➢ Chart dialog box).

- They are unaffected by the Clear command.

- They are not copied with the Copy command.

- They are not deleted by the Delete Row command.

- They are unaffected by sorting.

- They are included in SUM functions, but are not included in SUBTOTAL functions.

- They are not printed.

To display a data form, select a cell inside your database, then choose Data ➢ Form. The field names from the database are used as titles inside the form, as you can see in Figure 17.6.

## Adding, Editing, and Deleting Records Using the Data Form

You can use Excel's built-in data form to add records to a worksheet database, edit an existing record, and delete a record:

- To add a new record to a database, display the data form and click on the New button to clear the form—New Record is displayed in the upper-right corner of the dialog box. Fill in the field values (use the Tab key to move between fields), then click on Close to exit the data form.

FIGURE 17.6

*Field names from the database are used as titles inside the form.*

- To edit an existing database record, use the scroll bar on the data form to select the desired record, then edit the field values.
- To delete a database record, use the scroll bar or the Find Prev and Find Next buttons to select the desired record, and then click on the Delete button. A dialog box will appear, allowing you to confirm the deletion.

## Displaying Records Matching Search Criteria

You can also use the data form to search for records that match criteria that you specify:

**1.** Open a data form for the database.

**2.** Click on the Criteria button—the form will clear and *Criteria* is displayed in the upper-right corner of the dialog box.

**3.** Enter criteria in the edit box next to the field or fields you want to filter:

- Enter the value to search for, such as **North**.
- Or, precede the value with a relational operator (see Table 17.1, earlier in the chapter), such as **<>North**.

**4.** Click on the Find Prev or Find Next button.

Using the database pictured in Figure 17.1, the criteria in Figure 17.7 would display every record where region is equal to North, the month-to-date sales total is other than zero, and the year-to-date sales total is greater than 10,000.

To clear the criteria, click on the Criteria button, then manually clear the criteria from specific text boxes (or click on the Clear button to clear all criteria), and click on the Form button.

PART

V

Working Effectively
with Databases

**FIGURE 17.7**

*Using the data
form to search
for criteria
you specify*

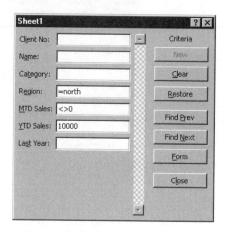

## More Facts about Data Forms

Here are a few important points to keep in mind when working with data forms:

- Values from calculated fields (cells with formulas) are displayed in the form, but cannot be edited.
- Hidden columns are not displayed.
- Suppose that your worksheet contains a database, and several rows beneath the database is another table of data. As new records are added to the database, the data form will not overwrite data located under the database—it will disallow new records from being added.

You have now learned the fundamentals of working with internal databases. The next chapter will cover more advanced aspects of Excel's database features, such as advanced AutoFilters and criteria ranges.

# Chapter

# 18

## Getting More Power from Worksheet Databases

# Getting More Power from Worksheet Databases

Now that you have an understanding of the basics of internal databases, let's turn our attention to some advanced techniques for working with internal (worksheet-based) databases. In this chapter, you'll learn about special database sorts, advanced filters, and embedding totals in a database, among other topics.

## Special Sorting Problems

The previous chapter explained how to address common sorts using up to three fields to sort rows in ascending or descending order. This section covers several other sorting methods.

### Sorting by More Than Three Fields

The more fields (or columns) in your database, the more likely it is that you will encounter instances where sorting by three fields alone is insufficient. Consider the database shown in Figure 18.1.

**FIGURE 18.1**

*This sample database will be in exercises throughout the remainder of this chapter.*

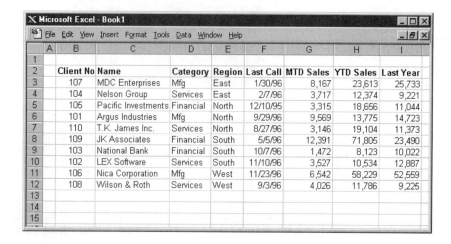

**NOTE** The database in Figure 18.1 is essentially the same database used in Chapter 17, but with the Last Call field inserted. You may want to create this database on your system, as it will be referred to throughout this chapter.

Suppose that you want to sort the database using four fields: Region, Last Call, Category, and Name. There are two ways to work around the three-field limit of the Data ➤ Sort command: sort the data two times, or create a *calculated sort field* (a field that combines other fields). The first method is the most commonly used and the easiest to learn, but it requires at least two passes of the Data ➤ Sort command. The second method requires only one sorting pass, but there is a bit of initial setup involved—this method is more suitable for a database that is re-sorted frequently. Let's take a look at each of these methods.

## Performing Multiple Sorts

Since you are sorting by four fields when you use the multiple sort approach, you will need to sort the data twice, starting with the least significant fields:

1. Select any cell inside the database and choose Data ➤ Sort.
2. Select Last Call from the Sort By drop-down list, then select Category and Name in the two Then By drop-down lists.

3. Click on OK to sort.
4. Choose Data ➢ Sort again.
5. Choose Region from the Sort By drop-down list.
6. Choose (none) as the second and third fields.
7. Click on OK to sort.

**TIP**

Dates and times, when sorted in ascending order, sort from oldest to newest. Sort order is based on the *underlying cell value*, not the formatted appearance.

## Creating Calculated Sort Fields

Another way to get around Excel's limit of three sort fields is to combine multiple fields into a single calculated field. Simple worksheet formulas will *concatenate*, or join, two or more fields into one field.

1. Add a new field in column J using the field name **Region—Last Call**.
2. Place the following formula in cell J3, then fill it down through cell J12:

```
=LEFT(E3&"     ",5)&F3
```

There are five spaces between the quotation marks. The LEFT function is padding the region field to five characters (assuming a maximum region length of five characters). Padding is only required when a field within a calculated sort field is not the last one, and is variable in length.

3. Choose Data ➢ Sort.
4. Choose Region—Last Call as the first sort field.
5. Choose Category and Name as the second and third sort fields.
6. Click on OK to sort.

Note that with calculated sort fields, you lose the ability to specify ascending or descending order for the individual fields within the calculated field. What if you want to combine Region=ascending with YTD Sales=descending in column K? Use a formula in K3 such as this one:

```
=LEFT(E3&"        ",5)&TEXT(1000000-H3,"0000000")
```

## Sorting Columns Instead of Rows

Though sorting columns is not a common need, it can nonetheless be done. In order to perform the exercise below, enter the following constants onto a blank worksheet. Notice that the columns in the following database are sorted alphabetically by region name.

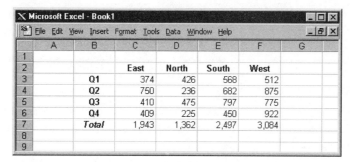

But suppose that you want to sort the columns according to total sales in descending order. Follow these steps to accomplish this:

1. Select cells C2:F7 (to avoid sorting the row labels with the data).
2. Choose Data ➤ Sort to display the Sort dialog box.
3. Click on the Options button to display the Sort Options dialog box.

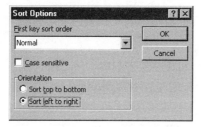

4. Choose the Sort Left To Right option, then click on OK to return to the Sort dialog box.
5. Choose Row 7 from the Sort By list. (This specifies worksheet row number, not row number within database.)
6. Choose the Descending option, then click on OK.

The database will be sorted as in Figure 18.2.

**FIGURE 18.2**

The results of
the column sort

| | | West | South | East | North |
|---|---|---|---|---|---|
| | Q1 | 512 | 568 | 374 | 426 |
| | Q2 | 875 | 682 | 750 | 236 |
| | Q3 | 775 | 797 | 410 | 475 |
| | Q4 | 922 | 450 | 409 | 225 |
| | *Total* | 3,084 | 2,497 | 1,943 | 1,362 |

> **TIP**
>
> The Sort Options dialog box lets you specify case-sensitive sorts. An ascending case-sensitive sort will go *AaBbCc*, etc.

## Using Custom Sort Orders

There are times when you may want to sort data using a sort order that is neither ascending nor descending. For example, your organization may sort regions on printed reports in roughly the order they appear on a map, rather than alphabetically. Or you may want to sort a list of office vendors with the most frequently used vendor on top.

In order to perform the exercise below, enter the following constants onto a blank worksheet. Note that the months are listed in date sequence.

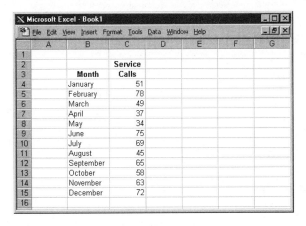

| | Month | Service Calls |
|---|---|---|
| | January | 51 |
| | February | 78 |
| | March | 49 |
| | April | 37 |
| | May | 34 |
| | June | 75 |
| | July | 69 |
| | August | 45 |
| | September | 65 |
| | October | 58 |
| | November | 63 |
| | December | 72 |

Suppose that your company has a fiscal year that begins October 1 and ends September 30. You can cut and paste to get the data in the right sequence, or you can use a custom list to determine the sort order.

## Creating Custom Lists

Follow these steps to create a custom list for an October-through-September fiscal-year sort:

**1.** Enter the data for the custom list onto a worksheet in the desired sequence, as shown below.

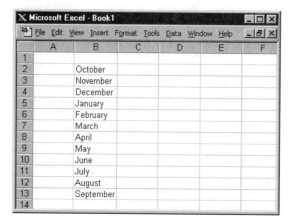

---

**TIP**

To enter the months quickly, you can type in **October**, then use the fill handle to fill in the remaining months. This is an AutoFill, which is discussed in Chapter 7.

---

**2.** Select cells B2:B13.
**3.** Choose Tools ➤ Options, then select the Custom Lists tab (Figure 18.3).
**4.** Click on the Import button, then click on OK.

You only to have to create a custom list once. Since the list is not stored in a workbook, it is available globally.

## Using a Custom List to Drive a Sort

Suppose you have created a custom list using the procedure described above. Here's how to use the list as the basis for sorting a database:

**1.** Select a cell inside the database or list, then choose Data ➤ Sort.

**FIGURE 18.3**

*The Custom
Lists tab in
the Options
dialog box*

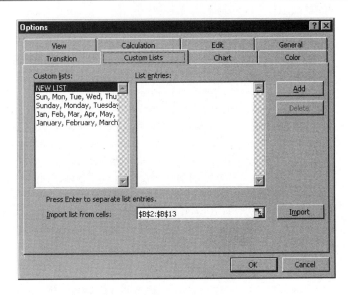

2. Select Month as the Sort By setting.

3. Click on the Options button to display the Sort Options dialog box.

4. Select the item reading October, November, December, etc., from the *First Key Sort
Order* drop-down list.

5. Click on OK to close the Sort Options dialog box, then click on OK again to
perform the sort.

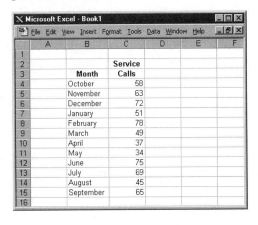

# Working with Criteria Ranges

An age-old spreadsheet construct dating back to early Lotus 1-2-3 days was the *criteria range*—a range of cells that defines a database filter. A criteria range allows you to view and/or perform calculations on a *subset* of rows (records) in a worksheet database (for example, only those customers located in New York).

Since criteria ranges have existed for so long (in Excel and 1-2-3), many advanced users have long struggled with their cumbersome nature. Fortunately, new features have been added to Excel over the past few years that address, in part, the need to filter data. Of most significance are AutoFilters (see Chapter 17) and pivot table page fields (see Chapter 20). Also worth noting is the introduction of the SUMIF function (and its brethren) in Excel 5. These features have *in part* rendered the criteria range obsolete— but not entirely. If you need to perform complex filtering, and your data is *not* stored in an external database, criteria ranges may be part of your solution. (See Chapter 19 to learn how to filter external databases.)

Once you learn how to create a criteria range, you can use it in two ways:

- Use it in conjunction with advanced database filters to display only those records that meet the criteria.
- Use it with *D functions*, a special category of functions that use a criteria range to determine which database records to use in calculations.

**NOTE**

Learning about criteria ranges requires some patience. There is a lot of ground to cover before you will see how to put them to use. In this chapter, we will present the basics of criteria ranges, proceed to the topic of computed criteria, and then move on to advanced filters and D functions. Initially, you might want to read just the basics of criteria ranges and then skip ahead to see how they are used in advanced filters before you finish the presentation of criteria ranges.

## Parts of a Criteria Range

A criteria range consists of two parts: a header row, containing field names that must identically match the database field names, and one or more criteria rows. The following criteria range is used to filter the database in Figure 18.1:

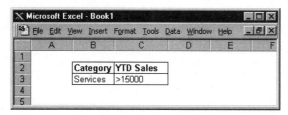

The criteria range in cells B2:C3 means "All records where the Category is equal to Services *and* YTD Sales are greater than 15,000." If this criteria range were used to filter the database shown in Figure 18.1, only the fifth record would display.

**NOTE**  If you are familiar with Structured Query Language (SQL), then you may recognize that a criteria range is the logical equivalent of a simple *where* clause.

## Specifying the Criteria

The criteria specification is identical to criteria entered in a data form. There is an optional relational operator, followed by a value. Table 18.1 defines the relational operators that can be used with criteria ranges.

**TABLE 18.1:** RELATIONAL OPERATORS

| Operator | Meaning |
|---|---|
| = | Equal to |
| > | Greater than |
| < | Less than |
| >= | Greater than or equal to |
| <= | Less than or equal to |
| <> | Not equal to |

Table 18.2 contains examples of criteria as they would be entered into the criteria range.

**NOTE**  The criteria examples in Table 18.2 that begin with an equal sign are not formulas; they are text constants beginning with an equal sign. However, if the first character entered into a cell is an equal sign, Excel assumes the entry is a formula. Precede the equal sign with an apostrophe ('=) to indicate a text entry.

**TABLE 18.2:** CRITERIA EXAMPLES

| Criteria | Meaning |
|---|---|
| =East | Equal to *East* |
| >B | Greater than *B* |
| <Jones | Less than *Jones* |
| >=West | Greater than or equal to *West* |
| <=West | Less than or equal to *West* |
| <>West | Not equal to *West* |
| Smith | Starts with *Smith* (*Smith, Smithe, Smithsonian*) |
| *Smith | Ends with *Smith* (*Jane Smith, John Smith, Smith*) |
| <>*Smith | Every value that does not end with *Smith* |
| *car* | Every value containing *car* (*Carson, scare, car*) |
| ?ON | Finds *Ron* and *Jon*, but not *Stone* |
| =10 | Equal to *10* |
| >100 | Greater than *100* |
| <100 | Less than *100* |
| >=25 | Greater than or equal to *25* |
| <=25 | Less than or equal to *25* |
| <>0 | Not equal to *zero* |
| 100 | Equal to *100* |

## Specifying Multiple Criteria

You can specify multiple criteria in two forms:

AND   Records that match all criteria (e.g., where Region equals west *and* YTD Sales are greater than 15,000). Place the criteria on one row.

OR   Records that match one of several criteria (e.g., where Region equals west *or* Sales are greater than 15,000). Place the criteria on different rows.

The examples shown in Figure 18.4 apply to the database pictured in Figure 18.1.

PART

V

Working Effectively
with Databases

**FIGURE 18.4**

*Examples of
multiple criteria
used with the
database
shown earlier in
the chapter (see
Figure 18.1)*

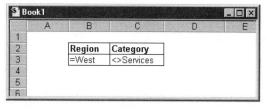

Where Region equals West and Category does not equal Services

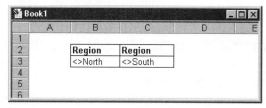

Where MTD Sales does not equal zero and YTD Sales is greater than 20,000

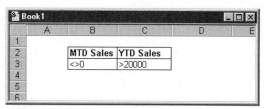

Where Region does not equal North and Region does not equal South

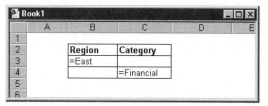

Where Region ends with TH and Category starts with FIN and Last Call is prior to 1/1/97

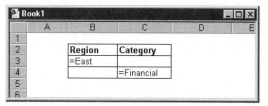

Where Region equals East or Category equals Financial

**FIGURE 18.4**
*Continued*

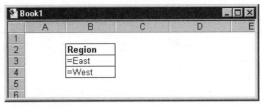

Where Region equals East or Region equals West

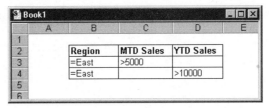

Where Region equals East and MTD Sales > 5000 OR where
Region equals East and YTD Sales > 10,000

> **NOTE**
>
> If you have never used a criteria range before, the topic may seem abstract at this point. This is a good time to jump ahead to advanced filters, where you will learn how to apply criteria ranges. Come back to computed criteria once you have a more solid understanding of the uses of criteria ranges.

## Understanding Computed Criteria

Before Excel had respectable external database connectivity, before there were pivot tables, and before nonprogrammers could use controls such as list boxes and option buttons, developers of advanced worksheet models were forced to use *computed criteria* as a solution for certain advanced problems. Before delving into this preposterously complex topic, consider whether an external database should be used.

Picture a worksheet model with a database, a complex criteria range, and various D functions (covered later in this chapter) that use the criteria range to perform calculations on the database. By changing the data in the criteria range, you can ask different questions of the database. This provides a lot of power, but also presents two problems:

- When you change the criteria, you run the risk of "breaking" the model with a typographical error.

- The model may be intended for use by people in your organization who neither understand criteria ranges nor wish to understand them.

*Computed criteria* can be used to solve these problems. They allow user input to be incorporated into a criteria range without the user of the model knowing about criteria ranges, or even being aware that a criteria range exists. There are several important things to know about computed criteria:

- The term *computed criteria* tends to confuse people because of the unusual use of the word *computed*. Formulas can be entered into a criteria range, and these formulas *calculate* results, just like any formula. A computed criterion is just a criteria range that has formulas in it.
- The topic is widely misunderstood because there are two ways to express computed criteria: the first method—where formulas are used to calculate the criteria—is a logical extension of what you have learned so far; the second method—supporting relative comparisons—is somewhat idiosyncratic.
- The two methods for expressing computed criteria are *not* mutually exclusive. You can employ both techniques in the same criteria range.

## Using Formulas to Calculate Criteria Dynamically

You are *not limited to constant text values* in a criteria range. You can also use formulas that calculate the criteria.

Using the database shown in Figure 18.1, suppose you want to ask the question, "How many clients had YTD Sales exceeding *X* (a user-specified threshold)?" The following exercise explains how to build a criteria range that incorporates variables:

**1.** Create the following worksheet:

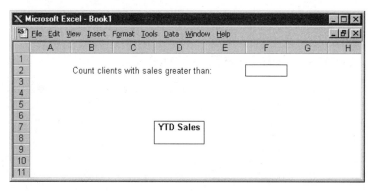

**2.** Enter this formula into D8:

```
=">"&F2
```

**3.** Enter a number into F2; the formula in D8 causes the criteria to change.

**NOTE** Performing the actual count of the database requires the use of a D function in conjunction with the criteria range. This is covered later in this chapter.

Perhaps you also want to count the number of clients with MTD (month-to-date) Sales exceeding a user-specified threshold. Any cell within a criteria range can include a formula instead of a constant. Add the following to your model:

B4    Enter **M** (for MTD) or **Y** (for YTD):

D7    `=IF(F4="M","MTD Sales","YTD Sales")`

Now the criteria range specified in D7:D8 is driven by the variables that the user provides in cells F2 and F4 (see Figure 18.5).

**FIGURE 18.5**

*The user input in cells F2 and F4 is driving the criteria range D7:D8.*

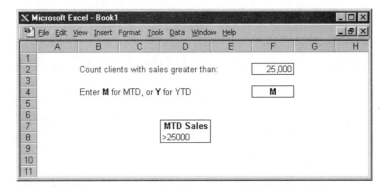

## Performing Relative Comparisons

The second method for expressing computed criteria provides an important capability that cannot be achieved with the first method: the ability to compare a field to one or more fields in the same record.

To illustrate the possible applications of this second method, we've created the database shown in Figure 18.6, which is used to measure the efficiency of regional customer service departments for a fictitious utility company.

Working Effectively with Databases

**FIGURE 18.6**

*The Calls 96 and Calls 97 fields contain the number of incoming calls for 1996 and 1997, respectively. Fields* OK *96 and* OK *97 contain the number of those calls resolved to the customer's satisfaction.*

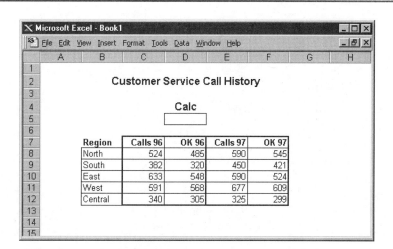

Suppose that you want to create a criteria range that will be used to display only those regions where the number of calls received in 1997 exceeded the number of calls in 1996. Entering the following formula in cell D5:

```
=E8>C8
```

would cause an advanced filter (covered later in this chapter) to display only rows 8, 9, and 11—the rows where 1997 calls exceeded 1996 calls. The rules for constructing this type of relative comparison are as follows:

- The formula must return logical values TRUE or FALSE.
- The field name used in the criteria range (i.e., cell D4 in Figure 18.6) must *not* match a field name in the database—in fact, it can be left blank.
- The cell references in the formula are relative, and point to the first record of the database (you can use absolute references, but not to compare fields within each record).
- Like the first method for computing criteria, the criteria range can contain more than one column.

Here are some more examples of criteria calculated by comparing field content using the database in Figure 18.1. Each formula goes into cell D5.

### Example 1:

Formula    `=C8+E8>1000`

Display    Rows 8, 10, and 11

**Example 2:**

| | |
|---|---|
| Formula | `=(F8/E8)<(D8/C8)` |
| Display | Rows 8 and 11 |

**Example 3:**

| | |
|---|---|
| Formula | `=(F8/E8)<.9` |
| Display | Rows 10 and 11 |

**Example 4:**

| | |
|---|---|
| Formula | `=(D8/C8)>$F$5`  (Note the absolute reference $F$5; it is not contained in the database—an absolute comparison is being performed.) |
| Display | Depends on cell F5—if F5 contains 90%, rows 8 and 11 are displayed |

# Using Advanced Filters

AutoFilters, covered in Chapter 17, allow you to define simple data filters with ease and provide an outstanding interface for specifying filter criteria. Custom AutoFilters provide a little more flexibility, but even they are limited. *Advanced filters* offer all of these benefits:

- They use an unlimited number of criteria per field (using criteria ranges, covered earlier in this chapter).
- They use variables as part of the criteria (using computed criteria, covered earlier in this chapter).

**NOTE**  To remove a filter and display all the data, choose Data ➢ Filter ➢ Show All.

## Filtering "In Place"

When you filter in place, all records that do not meet a criteria specification are hidden, while all other records are displayed (as done with AutoFilters). Here's how to perform an advanced filter in-place:

**1.** Create a criteria range.

2. Select a cell within the database range.
3. Choose Data ➤ Filter ➤ Advanced Filter. The Advanced Filter dialog box appears.

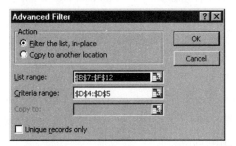

4. Choose the Filter The List In-Place option.
5. Enter the criteria range (you can type a cell reference or point and click on the worksheet).
6. Click on OK to filter.
7. To filter again with new criteria, enter a new value into the criteria range (on worksheet), and then choose Data ➤ Filter ➤ Advanced Filter and click on OK. (The Advanced Filter dialog box remembers the settings from the last Advanced Filter.)

## Copying Records to a New Location

So far, every filter in this chapter (and the previous chapter) has filtered data in place. As an alternative, filtered rows can be copied to a new location. Use the same steps as in the previous exercise, but with the following exceptions:

• In the Advanced Filter dialog box, choose the Copy To Another Location setting—this will make the Copy To setting available.
• Enter a Copy To range (type in a cell reference or point and click on the worksheet).

Every record meeting the criteria specification is copied to the specified location.

Often, when you copy records to a new location, you'll want to copy them to a different worksheet or a different workbook. In order to do this, you must activate the destination workbook or worksheet before choosing Data ➤ Filter ➤ Advanced Filter.

**NOTE**

In Excel 4 and earlier, the process of copying a record to a new location was referred to as a *data extract*.

## Copying Only Specified Fields

If you do not want to extract all fields from a database, you must define an *extract range*. An extract range serves three purposes:

- It specifies which fields to copy.
- It specifies the field order.
- It limits (optionally) the number of rows copied.

An extract range consists of field names that match the field names used in the database. The following exercise will copy records from the database in Figure 18.1:

**1.** Specify the following criteria range:

| Cell | Entry |
|------|-------|
| B14 | Region |
| B15 | North |

**2.** Specify the following extract range:

| Cell | Entry |
|------|-------|
| C17 | Name |
| D17 | YTD Sales |

**3.** Select a cell inside the database range, then choose Data ➤ Filter ➤ Advanced Filter to call up the Advanced Filter dialog box. Excel will automatically detect the list (database) range $B$2:$I$12.

**4.** Choose the Copy To Another Location option.

**5.** Enter a criteria range of **B14:B15**. (If you point and click on the cells on the worksheet, the sheet name is automatically included as part of the range.)

**6.** Enter a Copy To range of **C17:D17**. (If you point and click on the cells on the worksheet, the sheet name is automatically included as part of the range.)

**7.** Click on OK.

The records specified by the criteria range will be copied to the new location beneath the extract range (see Figure 18.7).

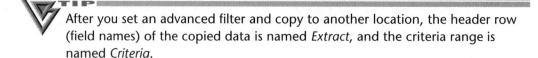

**TIP**

After you set an advanced filter and copy to another location, the header row (field names) of the copied data is named *Extract*, and the criteria range is named *Criteria*.

**FIGURE 18.7**

*The criteria range caused only those records in region North to be copied. The extract range caused only the fields Name and YTD Sales to be copied.*

| | Client No | Name | Category | Region | Last Call | MTD Sales | YTD Sales | Last Year |
|---|---|---|---|---|---|---|---|---|
| 3 | 107 | MDC Enterprises | Mfg | East | 1/30/96 | 8,167 | 23,613 | 25,733 |
| 4 | 104 | Nelson Group | Services | East | 2/7/96 | 3,717 | 12,374 | 9,221 |
| 5 | 105 | Pacific Investments | Financial | North | 12/10/95 | 3,315 | 18,656 | 11,044 |
| 6 | 101 | Argus Industries | Mfg | North | 9/29/96 | 9,569 | 13,775 | 14,723 |
| 7 | 110 | T.K. James Inc. | Services | North | 8/27/96 | 3,146 | 19,104 | 11,373 |
| 8 | 109 | JK Associates | Financial | South | 5/5/96 | 12,391 | 71,805 | 23,490 |
| 9 | 103 | National Bank | Financial | South | 10/7/96 | 1,472 | 8,123 | 10,022 |
| 10 | 102 | LEX Software | Services | South | 11/10/96 | 3,527 | 10,534 | 12,887 |
| 11 | 106 | Nica Corporation | Mfg | West | 11/23/96 | 6,542 | 58,229 | 52,559 |
| 12 | 108 | Wilson & Roth | Services | West | 9/3/96 | 4,026 | 11,786 | 9,225 |

| Region |
|---|
| North |

| Name | YTD Sales |
|---|---|
| Pacific Investments | 18,656 |
| Argus Industries | 13,775 |
| T.K. James Inc. | 19,104 |

# Using the D Functions

The database or list management functions, *D functions*, are different from most other functions in two ways: they perform calculations on a specified column within a specified database (or any range of cells with a header row containing unique field names); and they use a criteria range to determine which records to include in the calculation.

The D functions are all structured identically. We will use the DSUM function here to illustrate the use of D functions. Once you understand DSUM, you will be ready to use all of the D functions.

In addition to the D functions, there is another important list management function: GETPIVOTDATA returns data stored in a pivot table. See Chapter 21 to learn how to retrieve data from pivot tables.

NOTE

For most D functions, there is a nondatabase equivalent. For example, there is a DSUM function and a SUM function.

## DSUM Syntax

The DSUM syntax is as follows:

```
DSUM(DatabaseRange,Field,CriteriaRange)
```

**DatabaseRange:** A range of cells containing a database—must include a header row with unique field names

**Field:** A field within DatabaseRange used in calculation

**CriteriaRange:** A range of cells containing criteria specifications

In Figure 18.8, DSUM is used to calculate MTD Sales for all clients in region North.

**FIGURE 18.8**

*As you can see from the DSUM arguments, the database is at B2:I12, the field being summed is MTD Sales, and the criteria range is at B14:B15.*

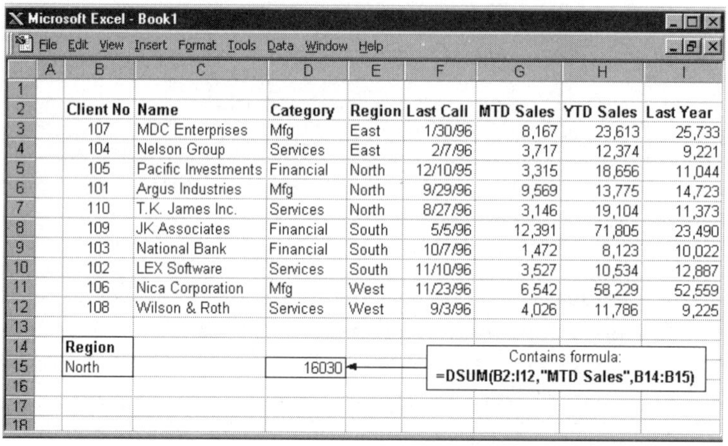

Here are some variations on the DSUM formula in Figure 18.8. Each of these examples is based on the criteria range B14:B15, which specifies region North.

The following formula sums Last Year sales (assuming that the database range is named SalesData, and the criteria range is named SalesCriteria):

```
=DSUM(SalesData,"Last Year",SalesCriteria)
```

Now, assume that the text *"Last Year"* has been entered into C14. The following formula demonstrates that the second argument, *field*, can be a variable:

```
=DSUM(B2:I12,C14,B14:B15)
```

Any worksheet function that requires range arguments can use embedded functions to calculate the range. The D functions are no exception. In the next example, the OFFSET function points to cells B14:B15 (see Chapter 9 for more about OFFSET).

Though the formula does not require the use of the OFFSET function, it still demonstrates a powerful capability. Since the arguments for OFFSET can be variables, user input can be used to dynamically point to different criteria ranges:

```
=DSUM(B2:I12,"MTD Sales",OFFSET(B13,1,0,2,1))
```

## Available D Functions

Table 18.3 presents all of the D functions. They all use the same arguments as DSUM, but perform different types of calculations.

**TABLE 18.3:** AVAILABLE D FUNCTIONS

| Function | Description |
|---|---|
| DAVERAGE | Calculates an average |
| DCOUNT | Counts cells containing numbers |
| DCOUNTA | Counts nonblank cells |
| DGET | Gets a single field from a single record |
| DMAX | Calculates a maximum value |
| DMIN | Calculates a minimum value |
| DPRODUCT | Multiplies values |
| DSTDEV | Estimates standard deviation based on a sample |
| DSTDEVP | Calculates standard deviation based on the entire population |
| DSUM | Sums values |
| DVAR | Estimates variance based on a sample |
| DVARP | Calculates variance based on the entire population |

**TIP**

There are two functions in addition to the D functions that use criteria ranges: SUMIF and COUNTIF. Both are covered in Chapter 9.

PART

**V**

Working Effectively
with Databases

# Inserting Embedded Subtotals into a Database

The ability to embed subtotals into a range of data in a semiautomated fashion is an important Excel feature. This feature (along with pivot tables, the subject of Chapters 20–22) has significantly enhanced Excel's overall capability as a reporting tool.

Using the database pictured in Figure 18.1, assume you want to add subtotals and a grand total for the MTD Sales, YTD Sales, and Last Year fields by region. Here's how you could do it:

**1.** Sort the database by Region.

**2.** Select a cell within the database range.

**3.** Choose Data ➤ Subtotals to display the Subtotal dialog box, shown here:

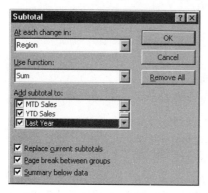

**4.** Choose Region from the At Each Change In list (subtotals will be inserted each time the region changes).

**5.** Select the SUM function from the Use Function list (see SUBTOTAL in Chapter 9 for explanation of each function).

**6.** The Add Subtotal To list is used to specify which fields to subtotal—check MTD Sales, YTD Sales, and Last Year.

**7.** Check the Page Break Between Groups setting to insert a page break after each subtotal.

**8.** If Summary Below Data is checked, the subtotal row is placed beneath the data; otherwise, it is placed on top.

**9.** Click on OK to insert subtotals (see Figure 18.9).

Use Format ➤ AutoFormat to format a range that contains subtotals. The built-in formats detect the subtotals, and format the range accordingly to make it more readable.

*FIGURE 18.9*

*The database
with subtotals,
showing outline
symbols*

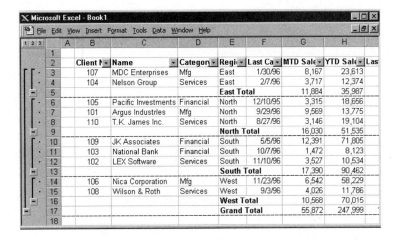

| | Client N | Name | Categon | Regi | Last Ca | MTD Sale | YTD Sale | Las |
|---|---|---|---|---|---|---|---|---|
| 3 | 107 | MDC Enterprises | Mfg | East | 1/30/96 | 8,167 | 23,613 | |
| 4 | 104 | Nelson Group | Services | East | 2/7/96 | 3,717 | 12,374 | |
| 5 | | | | **East Total** | | 11,884 | 35,987 | |
| 6 | 105 | Pacific Investments | Financial | North | 12/10/95 | 3,315 | 18,656 | |
| 7 | 101 | Argus Industries | Mfg | North | 9/29/96 | 9,569 | 13,775 | |
| 8 | 110 | T.K. James Inc. | Services | North | 8/27/96 | 3,146 | 19,104 | |
| 9 | | | | **North Total** | | 16,030 | 51,535 | |
| 10 | 109 | JK Associates | Financial | South | 5/5/96 | 12,391 | 71,805 | |
| 11 | 103 | National Bank | Financial | South | 10/7/96 | 1,472 | 8,123 | |
| 12 | 102 | LEX Software | Services | South | 11/10/96 | 3,527 | 10,534 | |
| 13 | | | | **South Total** | | 17,390 | 90,462 | |
| 14 | 106 | Nica Corporation | Mfg | West | 11/23/96 | 6,542 | 58,229 | |
| 15 | 108 | Wilson & Roth | Services | West | 9/3/96 | 4,026 | 11,786 | |
| 16 | | | | **West Total** | | 10,568 | 70,015 | |
| 17 | | | | **Grand Total** | | 55,872 | 247,999 | |

## Adding Outlining to the Sheet with Subtotals

Take a look at Figure 18.9 and notice the outline symbols located to the left of the row numbers. Outlining is an automatic by-product when you insert subtotals using Data ➤ Subtotals.

• To expand or collapse the outline, click on the outline symbols.
• To hide or unhide outline symbols, choose Tools ➤ Options, select the View tab, then use the Outline Symbols check box.

**NOTE**

Outlining is covered in depth in Chapter 26.

## Removing Embedded Subtotals

There are two ways to remove embedded subtotals inserted via the Data ➤ Subtotals command:

• To remove all embedded subtotals, choose Data ➤ Subtotals, and click on Remove All.
• To add different subtotals to the same range and remove the old subtotals at the same time, activate the Replace Current Subtotals setting in the Subtotal dialog box.

PART

**V**

Working Effectively
with Databases

## Using Multiple Subtotal Formulas

Take a look at Figure 18.9. In this worksheet, subtotals were added that sum sales by region. Suppose you want to show average sales by region, in addition to total sales by region. Adding a second subtotal function is easy. You've learned how to add a first set of subtotals, which in Figure 18.8 used the SUM function to sum both sales fields by region. To average both sales fields by region, repeat the procedure, but do the following in addition:

1. Select AVERAGE from the Use Function drop-down list.
2. Clear the Replace Current Subtotals check box.

Now each region will have two subtotal rows, one for Total and one for Average.

# Creating User-Friendly Databases

Since field names must be unique, you often wind up with field names which, from a user perspective, are not very friendly. The worksheet shown in Figure 18.10 contains two databases, each with different types of problems.

---

**FIGURE 18.10**

*The 1997 database does not have unique field names. The field names in the 1998 database are not user friendly.*

**1997 Budget vs. Actual**

| Division | Q1 Budget | Q1 Actual | Q2 Budget | Q2 Actual | Q3 Budget | Q3 Actual | Q4 Budget | Q4 Actual |
|---|---|---|---|---|---|---|---|---|
| R&D | 7,000 | 7,225 | 7,000 | 6,808 | 8,000 | 7,855 | 8,000 | 8,120 |
| Finance | 3,500 | 3,445 | 3,500 | 3,515 | 3,500 | 3,382 | 4,000 | 4,020 |
| Marketing | 3,000 | 2,830 | 3,500 | 3,667 | 3,500 | 4,210 | 4,000 | 3,831 |

**1998 Budget vs. Actual**

| Division | Q1.Bud | Q1.Act | Q2.Bud | Q2.Act | Q3.Bud | Q3.Act | Q4.Bud | Q4.Act |
|---|---|---|---|---|---|---|---|---|
| R&D | 8,000 | 7,925 | 8,500 | 8,780 | 8,500 | 8,345 | 8,500 | 8,224 |
| Finance | 4,000 | 3,775 | 4,000 | 4,201 | 4,000 | 3,879 | 4,500 | 4,320 |
| Marketing | 4,000 | 3,711 | 4,250 | 4,225 | 4,250 | 4,210 | 4,500 | 4,669 |

- The 1997 database duplicates the field names *Budget* and *Actual*, which causes problems for many database operations.
- The Q1–Q4 descriptive labels above the database confuse Excel—when you sort this database, Excel will attempt to include rows 2 and 3 in the data area.
- The 1998 database uses unique field names—it is perfectly legal, but the field names are aesthetically displeasing and potentially confusing to others.

There is a way to design your databases to combine the friendliness of the 1997 database with the correctness of the 1998 database. Take a look at the database in Figures 18.11 and 18.12.

PART

**V**

Working Effectively with Databases

**FIGURE 18.11**

*The database is at B5:J8. Rows 3 and 4 are for clarity only.*

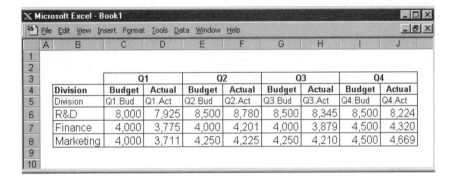

**FIGURE 18.12**

*The first row of the database, containing legal field names, is hidden.*

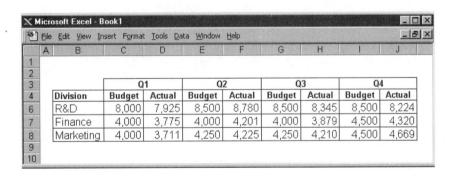

Here is how you can create this database:

**1.** Enter legal field names on the header row of the database.

**2.** Enter field descriptions several rows above the header row.

**3.** Hide the first row of the database (the header row) using Format ➤ Row ➤ Hide.

In this chapter and the previous, we have concerned ourselves with manipulating data from internal databases or lists. In the next chapter, you will learn one of the most important Excel skills: how to retrieve data from external databases, such as Microsoft Access and Oracle.

# Chapter

# 19

## Accessing External Databases

# 19

# Accessing External Databases

n Chapters 17 and 18, you learned how to manage and manipulate databases residing on a worksheet. But in a corporate environment, source data is typically stored in an external database. Such databases include desktop database managers such as Access and dBase, and more robust back-end database servers such as Oracle and SQL Server. Accessing such data is one of the biggest obstacles faced by corporate users, and a lot of time is spent manually entering data into worksheet models when, ideally, data would be imported into worksheets electronically.

---

**NOTE**

Throughout this chapter please do not confuse the word *query* with the program Microsoft Query. Similarly, do not confuse the word *access* with the program Microsoft Access. For the sake of brevity and clarity, the programs will be referred to as *MS Query* and *MS Access*.

---

A program called Microsoft Query comes with Excel. However, MS Query is not automatically installed on your computer when you perform a so-called *typical* installation of Excel. If MS Query is not installed on your system, be sure your install disk is at hand.

# Decoding Database Terminology

As you delve into the subject of external database access, there is a lot of lingo to deal with (some of which only serves to make the topic seem more complex than it really is!). Some of the important terms and concepts are defined here.

**Structured Query Language (SQL)** - There is an industry-standard language used to communicate with databases that is called *Structured Query Language*, or *SQL* (generally pronounced "sequel"). It is not necessary that you know SQL in order to perform queries from Excel, though it is a useful skill to possess.

**Open Database Connectivity (ODBC)** - ODBC is a Microsoft technology that allows different applications, such as Excel and MS Query, to communicate with a variety of database types. ODBC handles the nitty gritty of database interaction on behalf of programs such as Excel, other Microsoft programs, and even many non-Microsoft programs. ODBC stands as the middleman between Excel and a given database, assuming there is the appropriate ODBC *driver*, which is discussed later in this chapter. Once set up properly, ODBC is an invisible component that Excel users need not necessarily be aware of. However, some knowledge of the underpinnings can help you troubleshoot problems, and is vital if you are responsible for creating or maintaining Excel-based reporting systems. Refer to MS Query's online help for more information on this topic.

**ODBC Manager** - Whenever you perform a query from Excel (or another ODBC-aware program), your request is handled by an ODBC subcomponent called the *ODBC manager*. In turn, the ODBC manager dispatches the request to the appropriate *ODBC driver*, discussed in the next section.

**ODBC Driver** - In order to communicate with an external database, you must have the proper ODBC driver. Each type of database (Access, Oracle, etc.) requires its own driver. Included with Excel are drivers for dBase, FoxPro, and Microsoft SQL Server. There are also ODBC drivers for text files and Excel worksheets, allowing them to be queried as if they were databases. In addition, many publishers of database software publish their own drivers. To learn how to install ODBC drivers, refer to MS Query online help.

**TIP**

You don't need Microsoft Access installed on your computer in order to query an MS Access database from Excel. All you need is an MS Access database file (.MDB) and the ODBC driver for MS Access that comes with Excel.

**Data Sources** - When you are performing a query, it is not enough to know what type of database you are accessing. A *data source*, defined in the ODBC manager, specifies the type of data, where to find the database, and in some cases, how to connect to the data. For example, you may have several different *Microsoft Access* databases on your computer, each of which is a discrete data source. You will often see *data source* referred to as *DSN* (data source name).

**Microsoft Query Add-In** - The sole purpose of this Excel add-in, named XLQUERY.XLA, is to provide backward compatibility for programmers who may have utilized it in custom applications created in earlier versions of Excel.

# Overview of Data Access Features

PART

**V**

There are several ways to get external data into your worksheets, which makes the topic somewhat daunting for initiates. Don't be intimidated however—it's not that hard. This section provides an overview of the different data access techniques, explaining where and when each technique is applicable.

## Pivot Tables

Pivot tables, covered in Chapters 20 through 22, provide a powerful, intuitive interface for accessing and viewing external (and internal) databases. Chapter 22 in particular discusses the use of pivot tables with external databases. However, when using pivot tables in this manner, you must first become acquainted with MS Query. Read about MS Query in this chapter before moving to Chapter 22.

## The Data ➤ Get External Data Submenu

The Data ➤ Get External Data submenu contains several important commands that deal principally with creating database queries (using MS Query), and then running these queries. Much of this chapter focuses on these commands, with the exception of *Run Web Query*—this command is discussed in the Internet section of Chapter 29.

## Opening and Editing dBase and FoxPro Files

You can use Excel's standard File ➤ Open command to open a dBase or FoxPro file (referred to collectively as DBF files). The entire file is automatically imported into an Excel worksheet (unlike "real" queries, where you have the ability to retrieve a *subset* of the data—see the sidebar). Once a DBF file is opened, you can edit the data, then save it in its native format using the File ➤ Save command. On the Save As dialog box, pay attention to the Save As Type option.

Working Effectively
with Databases

When you are opening database files in this manner, there are two inherent limitations to be aware of. First, the entire file is loaded into memory. This means the file may not exceed Excel's limit of 65,536 rows and 256 columns.

Second, this is not workable in a multiuser environment. It is impossible for two users on a network to concurrently read and write (open and save) the same disk file without overwriting one another's work.

Fortunately, the ODBC drivers that are included with Excel allow DBF files to be queried in a manner similar to "real" databases.

## Why Can xBase Files Be Opened and Not Oracle?

dBase is a product that has existed for a long time and was once the predominant desktop database program. FoxPro shares a heritage in common, as it was originally a clone of dBase. These (and other) programs came to be know collectively over the years as the *xBase* family. xBase programs have the native ability to create/read/write xBase disk files, generally referred to as DBF files. Each DBF disk file contains a single table of data.

Such is not the case with higher-end relational database management systems (RDBMS), such as Oracle and Microsoft SQL Server, where data is stored in *tables* (the logical equivalent of a single DBF file),

and one or more such tables constitutes a database. An entire database, consisting of many tables and other objects, might be stored in a single disk file (though this is transparent and irrelevant to the Excel user). The RDBMS is the sole proprietor of that data—all requests for data services (queries, updates, etc.) must be handled by the RDBMS. In this capacity, Excel is a *client*, the RDBMS is a database *server*, and thus the term *client/server*.

RDBMSs such as Oracle and SQL Server do not create disk files which can be opened using the File ➢ Open command in Excel (unless specially programmed to *export* disk files). Accessing such databases from Excel involves database *queries*, discussed throughout this chapter.

## Importing Text Files

If your mainframe application is capable of outputting text files, you can import them into Excel with the File ➢ Open command. The same limits as to the number of rows and columns apply as when opening a dBase file. There is one superficial difference: Excel has a built-in wizard—the Text Import Wizard—to walk you through the process. This topic is covered in Chapter 29.

### Exporting Excel Worksheets from a Database Manager

Some database managers, such as Microsoft Access, have the special ability to save data in Excel format. In MS Access, with a database open, use the File ➤ Send command, then choose Excel as the format. If your database does not output Excel format, output a format that Excel can read, such as Lotus 1-2-3 or text. A file output in this manner is opened in Excel just as you would open any Excel file.

Don't overlook an approach where Excel queries the database, using one of the methods discussed in this chapter, rather than outputting XLS files from the database.

### The SQL.REQUEST Worksheet Function

When entered into a range of cells, the SQL.REQUEST worksheet function retrieves data from an external database. This unique worksheet function, introduced with Excel 5, was an honorable attempt by Microsoft to provide something useful. But it was a failed attempt. The primary problem lies with the fact that SQL.REQUEST is a worksheet function which recalculates, thus executing a database query each time the worksheet recalculates, causing unwanted repeat queries. In addition, SQL.REQUEST is not intended to handle a variable number of rows or columns in the query results. For these (and other) reasons, this function is rarely useful, and does not merit further discussion.

## Setting Up Your Computer

Before getting started with database queries, there are several software components that you must install on your computer—MS Query and at least one ODBC driver. Unfortunately, these components are not installed when you perform a so-called *typical* setup. If you know for sure the database access components are not installed on your system, or if in the following tutorial the Data ➤ Get External Data commands fail to operate, you must rerun your setup program and add these components.

## Using the Query Wizard

In this section, you will learn how to create a query using MS Query's wizard. This is not a detailed discussion of MS Query—refer to MS Query's online help to learn more as you go along. Furthermore, readers are expected to understand basic database concepts. Remember, in order to use MS Query, it and at least one ODBC driver must be installed on your system (not to mention an accessible database).

Before beginning, take note of this good news: Excel's usefulness as a tool for accessing external databases has increased significantly. This is because of the simple fact that in Excel 8, a worksheet can hold over 65,000 rows, whereas earlier versions of Excel were limited to 16,000 plus.

PART

**V**

Working Effectively
with Databases

To start the process of creating your first query, from the Excel menu choose Data ➤ Get External Data ➤ Create New Query. The Choose Data Source dialog box appears, as shown in Figure 19.1. Though you may not notice it at first, you are now using MS Query. As you will soon learn, the first time you query a given database, you must define a data source (DSN). Keep in mind that the first time is the hardest—it's all downhill after the first time around.

**NOTE**

On the Choose Data Source dialog box, the Browse button allows you to choose an existing data source (DSN) file from disk. The Options button displays a dialog box allowing you to specify in which folders DSN files reside.

**FIGURE 19.1**

*The Microsoft Query Choose Data Source dialog box. The check box on the bottom determines whether the Query Wizard will be displayed, or the full MS Query interface.*

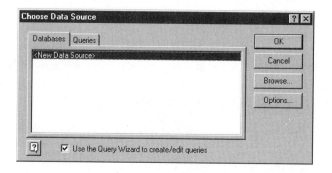

## Defining a New Data Source

A data source (DSN) defines not only the type of database (i.e., MS Access, Oracle, etc.), but also specifies precisely which database (i.e., Inventory, Accounting, etc.). As you learn to define DSNs, there is a vital fact you must know: there is certain basic information that must be provided for each DSN you create, such as the name. However, there is additional information that is *specific to the given ODBC driver*. Setting up a DSN for an MS Access database is different than for an Oracle database, for example.

**NOTE**

In the following tutorial, a sample database is used which is included with MS Access—NorthWind Traders. At press time, it was unknown if this database would also be included with MS Query.

At the Choose Data Source dialog box (see again Figure 19.1) select <New Data Source>, then click on OK. The Create New Data Source dialog box appears.

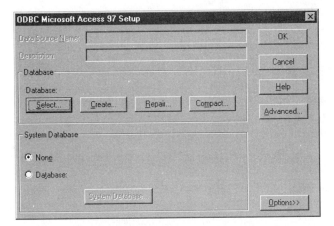

Enter a name and choose an ODBC driver from the drop-down list, then click on the Connect button. At this point, the steps will vary based on the ODBC driver—you must now depend on the online help or other documentation that accompanies the selected driver. In the case of Microsoft Access, the following dialog box appears:

The Select button allows you to locate an existing MS Access file (MDB) on disk. The Create button allows you to create a new MS Access database.

Once you provide the information requested by the ODBC driver, the Create New Data source dialog box is redisplayed, this time with the last two settings available for use. You can specify a default table (or query). This is a useful setting when you actually use one table or query predominantly. You can also choose to save your user ID and password as part of the DSN definition. Be careful—if you do this, anyone who sits at your computer can use this DSN without having to enter a password.

**NOTE**
Microsoft Access uses the term *query* to include a construct referred to in many DBMS programs as a *view*.

Finally, click on OK. The Choose Data Source dialog box is redisplayed. The new DSN will have been added to the list. There is one more vital setting to be aware of—the check box on the bottom of the dialog box determines whether the Query Wizard is to walk you through the query definition. When checked, the Query Wizard walks you through the process of building your query. Otherwise, you must interact with MS Query in much the same way as with earlier versions of the program.

To follow along with this discussion, check this setting, then click on OK. The Query Wizard Choose Column dialog box appears.

## Defining a Query

You have now chosen a data source. As you follow along on the next few pages, using the Query Wizard, you will do the following:

- Add columns (fields) to the query
- Filter the columns (optional)
- Sort the rows (optional)
- Return the data to Excel

### Choosing the Columns

Next, you must specify which columns (often referred to as *fields*) from which tables to include in the query. Notice Figure 19.2. The tables have + buttons, allowing them to be clicked on and expanded, revealing the column (field) names within. Double-click on a column name to add it to the query, or use the > button to add the selected column.

One particularly useful feature is the Preview Now button. When you click on it, it displays a sampling of data from the selected column.

Once you have selected all the columns you wish to include in the query, click on Next to show the Query Wizard Filter Data dialog box.

### Filtering the Rows

Filtering the rows is an optional step; it is also of vital importance. The Query Wizard Filter Data dialog box, shown in Figure 19.3, allows you to filter the database rows. For example, you may want to view only those customers located in California, or only sales orders scheduled for shipment over the next week. If you have the NorthWind

**FIGURE 19.2**

*Each table can be expanded to show the columns. Double-click on column names to add them to the query.*

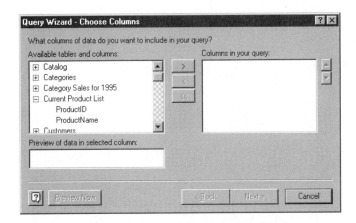

database, and are attempting to follow along, note that Figure 19.3 is using the table named *Orders Qry*. (Orders Qry is actually a query, and not a table. However, that is irrelevant to this discussion.)

**TIP**

Behind the scenes, as you build a query, a SQL statement is being constructed. (SQL is defined at the top of this chapter.) When you add filters to the query, you are adding a WHERE clause to the SQL statement.

**FIGURE 19.3**

*Click on the column you want to filter, then specify the conditions in the right part of the dialog box.*

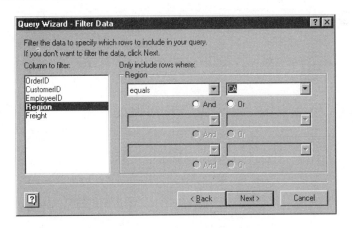

PART

V

Working Effectively with Databases

To add a filter, click on an item in the Column To Filter list. Then specify an operator and a comparison value on the right side of the dialog box. For example, referring to Figure 19.3, suppose you want to retrieve only those rows (records) where region is equal to CA. Here are the steps:

1. Select Region in the Column To Filter list
2. Select *equals* in the leftmost drop-down list (in the Only Include Rows Where section).
3. Choose CA from the rightmost drop-down list (or just type it in). Notice that as soon as something is entered, the And/Or options are activated.

If there is another filter you wish to define for the same column, click on either the And or Or option, then specify the second filter. Logically, the And/Or settings behave in the same manner as Excel's AND/OR worksheet functions. When And is selected, both conditions must be true; when Or is selected, one of the conditions must be true.

Contrary to first appearance, you are *not* limited to three filters per column—once you enter a third filter and click on either And or Or, vertical scroll bars appear, allowing more than three filters per column to be applied.

Refer to the Filter Data dialog box in Figure 19.3. After adding one or more filters for a given column, you can add filters for a different column by selecting the column in the Column To Filter list. After doing so, the filtered, deselected column name becomes boldfaced—this is a visual indicator that filters have been applied to the column. This is incredibly useful when you are editing the query at a later time, when the details of which columns are filtered are long forgotten.

Continue adding filters to columns. When you are done, click on Next. The Query Wizard Sort Order dialog box appears, as shown in Figure 19.4.

**FIGURE 19.4**

*If you specify three sorts, and there are more than three columns in the query, vertical scroll bars appear allowing you to specify more than three sorts.*

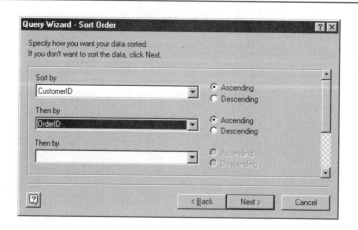

**MASTERING THE OPPORTUNITIES**

## Using MS Query's Full Functionality

Suppose you want to filter a column without including that column in your query—a common requirement. Unfortunately, the Query Wizard has no provision for filtering (or sorting) a column that is not part of the query. To circumvent the Query Wizard, deselect the bottom setting on the Choose Data Source dialog box, shown earlier in Figure 19.1. Or, at the last step of the Query Wizard, choose the View Data Or Edit Query In MS Query option. Both of these actions activate MS Query, sans the Query Wizard, for interactive use.

Remember, MS Query is a stand-alone program (named MSQRY32.EXE) and can be used independent of Excel. Refer to MS Query's online help for more information.

Working Effectively
with Databases

## Sorting the Rows

As you might expect, the Sort Order dialog box, shown in Figure 19.4, allows you to sort the database rows. You are not limited to three fields—after you specify three sort fields, vertical scroll bars automatically appear on the dialog box, allowing you to sort additional fields.

**NOTE**

Pivot table users be aware: there is no benefit whatsoever to sorting a query that is being used for a pivot table. It will needlessly slow down the query.

## Completing the Query Definition

After clicking on Next in the Sort Order dialog box, the Query Wizard Finish dialog box appears (see Figure 19.5). There are some important features to understand on this dialog box.

**Return Data To MS Excel:** When you select this option, the query you just created is run and the query results are retrieved by Excel.

**View Data Or Edit Query In MS Query:** This option causes the full MS Query interface to be exposed, allowing you more control over the construction of the query than the Query Wizard provides.

**Save Query:** Click on this button to save the query definition to disk. Be aware, this does *not* save the query results—just the query definition. The query definition is saved to an MS Query .DQY file. This allows the query to be used in other contexts, and by other users, without being redefined.

In the next section, we assume that you have selected the Return Data To MS Excel option. Click on Finish to return to Excel.

---

**FIGURE 19.5**

*The Save Query button saves the query specification, not the query results.*

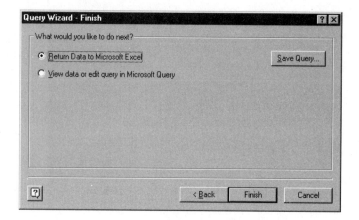

---

## Returning the Data to Excel

You are almost home! After clicking on Finish in the Query Wizard Finish dialog box, the Returning External Data Excel dialog box appears, as shown in Figure 19.6.

---

**FIGURE 19.6**

*The query results are placed in the active workbook—either onto a worksheet or into a pivot table.*

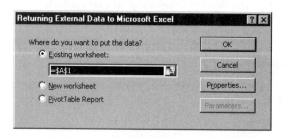

---

In this dialog box, you specify where within the active workbook the query results are to be placed. You can specify an existing worksheet or a new one. If you choose PivotTable Report, the PivotTable Wizard is started.

**NOTE**

The PivotTable Wizard is discussed in Chapters 20 through 22.

Click on OK to close the dialog box. The query is performed, and the query results are placed on the worksheet, as shown in Figure 19.7.

**FIGURE 19.7**

*The query range (sometimes called the data range) is automatically named, as evident in the name box.*

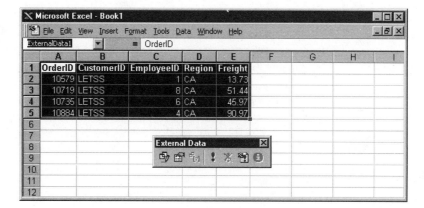

PART

**V**

Working Effectively with Databases

## The External Data Toolbar

This is a good time to discuss the *External Data* toolbar, shown earlier in Figure 19.7. This toolbar automatically appears whenever a worksheet containing a query range is active. (Though like any toolbar, it can be hidden using the View ➢ Toolbars command.) The buttons on this toolbar, explained in Table 19.1, are only available when the active cell is inside the query range.

**TABLE 19.1:** THE EXTERNAL DATA TOOLBAR

| Button | Description |
|---|---|
|  | Starts MS Query for the purpose of changing the query definition (columns, filters, sorting, etc.). |
|  | Displays the External Data Range Properties dialog box, discussed later in the chapter. |

| TABLE 19.1: THE EXTERNAL DATA TOOLBAR (CONTINUED) | |
|---|---|
| **Button** | **Description** |
| | Displays the Query parameters dialog box, discussed later in this chapter. |
| | Refreshes the active query range—the external database is requeried. |
| | Cancels a query in progress. This command is only available when the query in progress is set to enable background refresh (this is covered later in the chapter). |
| | Refreshes all query ranges in the active workbook, and all pivot tables based on external data. |
| | Displays status information about queries in progress. |

## External Data Range Properties

The Returning External Data To Excel dialog box, shown earlier in Figure 19.6, has on it a Properties button. When you click on this button, the External Data Range Properties dialog box is displayed (see Figure 19.8). The settings on this dialog box are of great importance.

**Name:** This is a range name that is automatically applied to the query results on the worksheet.

**Save Query Definition:** When this option is checked, the query definition is stored along with the query results in the active workbook. This allows the query to be refreshed at a later date. This setting is checked by default, and there is no reason to uncheck it unless the query is not intended to be refreshed at a later date. Remember this key fact: this setting has *no relationship* to the Save Query button on the Query Wizard Finish dialog box shown earlier in Figure 19.5.

*These settings are not global— every query range (data range) has its own properties.*

**Save Password:** When this option is checked, the password is saved along with the query, hidden, in the active workbook. Be careful if you select this option: anyone who can open the workbook can refresh the query without a password. This setting is checked by default.

**Enable Background Refresh:** This handy new feature allows you to use Excel while the query executes in the background, rather than watching an hourglass. Since queries can be time consuming, most users will leave this setting checked (the default state).

**Refresh Data On File Open:** When this option is checked, the query automatically refreshes when the workbook is opened. This invaluable new setting will eliminate a vast quantity of custom programming.

**Remove External Data From Sheet Before Saving:** This ill-titled setting is only available when Refresh Data On File Open is checked. It causes the query results *not* to be saved in the workbook. This means that a query refresh must occur when the file is opened in order to view the query results.

**Include Field Names:** When this option is checked, field (column) names are placed at the top of each column.

**Include Row Numbers:** When this setting is checked, the first column of the query results is a sequential row number.

**AutoFormat Data:** When this setting is checked, an AutoFormat is automatically applied to the query results on the worksheet. To specify *which* AutoFormat, use the Format ➢ AutoFormat command *after* the query has been performed.

**Import HTML Table(s) Only:** This setting is discussed in the Internet section of Chapter 29.

The next three options fall under the If The Number Of Rows In The Data Range Changes Upon Refresh heading. When a query refreshes, if the source database has changed, more or fewer rows may be returned by the query. These three options determine whether cells should be inserted, whether entire rows should be inserted, or whether existing cells should be overwritten.

**Fill Down Formulas In Columns Adjacent To Data:** Advanced users will derive tremendous value from this setting. It allows normal worksheet formulas to be placed next to the query results, and when the query is run, the formula is filled down based on the number of rows returned.

## Changing a Query Definition

When you create a query, by default, the query definition is saved in the active workbook—hidden from view. This is controlled by the Save Query Definition setting, shown earlier in Figure 19.8, which is checked by default. When this option is checked, the query definition can be changed.

With the active cell inside of a query range, choose Data ➢ Get External Data ➢ Edit Query. The Query Wizard is displayed, starting with the Choose Columns dialog box shown earlier in Figure 19.2.

## Deleting a Query

As you just learned, the query definition is saved in the workbook hidden from view. As a result, you can not delete a query by simply clearing or deleting the query range. The simplest way to delete a query is to simply delete the worksheet containing the query range. However, when that is not practical, follow these steps:

1. Right-click on any cell inside the query range and choose Data Range Properties from the shortcut menu.
2. Uncheck Save Query Definition, then click on OK.

The query results are still on the worksheet; however, the query definition has been deleted from the workbook.

## Refreshing a Query

Once query results are placed on a worksheet, you may want to refresh the query at a later date. Otherwise, if the source data changes, the worksheet will not be synchronized with the source data. There are two ways to refresh a query: manually or automatically.

**Manually:** With the active cell inside a query range, choose Data ➢ Refresh Data. Or, right-click inside the query range and choose Refresh Data from the shortcut menu.

**Automatically:** Check the setting Refresh Data On File Open on the External Data Range Properties dialog box.

### MASTERING TROUBLESHOOTING

#### Keeping in Synch

Suppose you have an inventory database that is updated nightly. You have created a query that retrieves inventory data, and you have checked the Refresh Data On File Open setting in the External Data Range Properties dialog box (shown earlier in Figure 19.8). As a result, the query is automatically re-executed each time the file is opened. If you open this workbook five times a day, the query will be executed each time, even though the source database is only updated nightly.

If the query is a slow one, this can be a big problem. Unfortunately, there is no easy solution. Custom programming is the only practical way to refresh a query conditionally, triggered by changes to the source database (a topic beyond the scope of this book). This means that keeping worksheet queries in synch with external databases will sometimes entail unnecessary repeated queries.

## Working with Parameter Queries

This is an important feature for advanced readers. Earlier in this chapter, you learned how add one or more filters to a query. A filter allows you, for example, to view only those customers located in California, rather than the entire customer list. A *parameter query* is a special type of query where instead of hard-wiring a comparison value, such as California, you can provide values (parameters) at the time the query is executed.

Creating a parameter query involves using MS Query interactively, rather than using the Query Wizard, the scope of which is beyond this book. In MS Query's online help, search for *parameter query*—there is a thorough, step-by-step explanation.

Once a parameter query has been created, there are some special skills on the Excel end that come into play, and these skills are the focus of the following discussion.

When a query contains parameters, the Data ➢ Get External Data ➢ Parameters command becomes available. It displays the following dialog box:

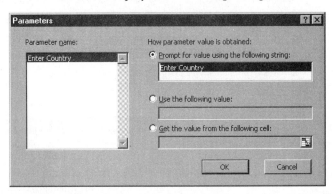

Each parameter defined for the given query appears in the Parameter Name list box. To set how a parameter will be obtained, click on it in the list box. Then choose one of the following three options:

**Prompt For Value Using String:** With this option chosen, the user is prompted to enter the parameter value each time the query is executed. Enter a free-form text string which is used to prompt the user when the query is executed.

**Use The Following Value:** Type in a hard-wired parameter value. (The benefit of this option is elusive, as it defeats the very purpose of the parameter!)

**Get The Value From The Following Cell:** Herein lies one of the most powerful aspects of parameter queries. This is a range edit—the contents of a specified cell can be used to satisfy the parameter.

You have just learned how to use the contents of a cell to satisfy a query parameter. This opens up some powerful options when used in conjunction with other Excel features. For example, you can use custom controls on a worksheet (discussed in Chapter 23), and/or data validation (discussed in Chapter 10) to build a user interface for entering parameters.

# Database Add-Ins

This section briefly covers two database-related features that are not part of the core Excel program; they are *add-ins*. Add-ins are loaded into memory using the Tools ➤ Add-Ins command, which is covered in depth in Chapter 28.

## Template Wizard

First, use the Tools , Add-Ins command to make sure the Template Wizard add-in is loaded.

**NOTE**

Consult Chapter 28 to learn more about working with add-ins.

If the Template Wizard is loaded, start it by choosing Data ➤ Template Wizard. If this command does not appear on your menu, or if it fails to display the Template Wizard, then the add-in is not installed properly.

The Template Wizard is a five-step process that assists you with the task of creating an Excel template that you can use to enter data into an external (or internal) database.

The very nature of Excel add-ins should make users cautious—these external features do not receive the same priority within Microsoft as the core Excel program. Add-ins are sometimes Microsoft's way of testing the water prior to implementing a feature inside core Excel. The Template Wizard is especially suspect; once real-world issues are considered, the add-in is of limited use.

## AccessLinks

The AccessLinks add-in provides integration between Excel and MS Access. It adds two commands to Excel's Data menu:

**MS Access Form:** Displays a wizard that helps you create an MS Access form, the purpose of which is to edit an Excel worksheet database. Before choosing this command, you must activate a worksheet containing a database (list).

**MS Access Report:** Displays a wizard that helps you create an MS Access report, based on data located on a worksheet.

This add-in is of limited use.

You have now learned how to query an external database from Excel using Microsoft Query. Perhaps the most important way to apply this new skill is in conjunction with pivot tables. Chapter 22 explains how to create pivot tables from external databases; the skills you learned in this chapter will serve you well.

# PART VI

## Pivot Tables

## LEARN TO:

- *Use pivot tables as a tool for data analysis and reporting*

- *Create a new pivot table from a worksheet database*

- *Change the layout of a pivot table by dragging and dropping field buttons*

- *Apply special formatting techniques*

- *Group and sort a pivot table*

- *Use the hidden data cache to your advantage*

- *Create charts from pivot tables*

- *Define calculated fields and calculated items*

# Chapter

# 20

## Understanding Pivot Tables

# FEATURING

# Understanding Pivot Tables

One of the biggest real-world challenges when using spreadsheets is the need to derive important *information* from large quantities of raw data. *Pivot tables* provide a way to easily summarize and analyze data using special direct manipulation techniques. They are called pivot tables because you can change their layout by twisting and rearranging, or *pivoting*, the row and column headings quickly and easily.

For many users, pivot tables are the single most important feature in Excel. They are widely applicable, and should not be overlooked by readers who "don't work with databases" per se. After all, a worksheet "database" is merely a range of cells containing data! This chapter is intended to provide a brief overview of pivot tables and to get you started working with them. The following two chapters explore pivot tables in depth.

## How Are Pivot Tables Used?

Pivot tables are used to analyze data in a flexible, ad hoc manner. They are used to summarize, analyze, consolidate, filter, and report:

**Summarizing large databases:** You can use pivot tables to create precise summaries of large quantities of data for data residing on a worksheet or in an external database. (See Chapter 22 to learn how to access an external database with a pivot table.)

**Preparing data for charting:** Many Excel users go to a great deal of trouble preparing charts—much of the effort is spent laying out the data in a manner that allows charts to be created. Pivot tables are ideal for this purpose. Charts based on pivot tables will automatically change as the pivot table changes. For this reason, there are savvy Excel users who rarely create a chart from anything *other* than a pivot table!

**Ad hoc data analysis:** A common use for pivot tables is for ad hoc exploration of a database—looking for trends, exceptions, and problems. You can quickly reorganize the way that data is summarized and presented, and drill-down into a greater level of detail when desired.

**Creating reports:** In general, one of the most common uses for Excel is for creating reports. Think of a pivot table as a report—one that can be interacted with on the screen and/or printed. There is probably no feature in Excel as important as pivot tables when it comes to generating reports.

## Sample Database: Product Sales History

For illustrative purposes throughout this chapter, we've created a sample database, shown in Figure 20.1. To follow along with the subsequent exercises, you may want to create an Excel workbook similar to the one pictured in Figure 20.1.

The database contains sales history for a fictitious company that sells produce and dairy products to supermarkets. Sales are tracked by product category, period (year and month), sales representative, and region.

# Creating a Simple Pivot Table from an Internal Database

You will now learn how to create a pivot table that is based on a worksheet database (versus an external database). This is an important first step toward understanding pivot tables, even if your ultimate goal is to create pivot tables from external databases.

Using the database shown in Figure 20.1, suppose you need to see how each sales representative performed within each region. Since this information is difficult to obtain from a large, detailed database, you can use a pivot table to summarize the data. The following exercise will walk you through the steps required to create a simple pivot table using the Products database.

*Database of sales history. Create a database with the same fields if you want to work along with the exercises in this chapter.*

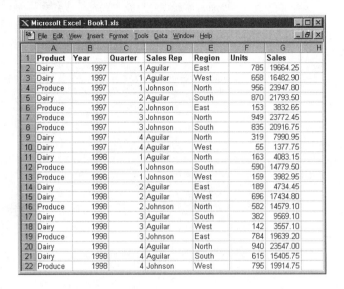

## Starting the PivotTable Wizard

Follow these steps to start the PivotTable Wizard:

**1.** Open the product sales history workbook (shown previously in Figure 20.1)

**2.** Select a cell anywhere inside the database.

**3.** Choose Data ➢ PivotTable Report. The PivotTable Wizard Step 1 Of 4 dialog box appears (see Figure 20.2). This dialog box lets you specify what type of data is to be used as the source for the pivot table.

### Step 1 of the PivotTable Wizard: Identifying the Data Source

Here's how to proceed with the Step 1 dialog box:

**1.** Since the source data is stored in a worksheet database, select the Microsoft Excel List Or Database option.

**2.** Click on Next to proceed to Step 2.

PART

**VI**

Pivot Tables

**FIGURE 20.2**

*The PivotTable Wizard Step 1 Of 4 dialog box lets you specify where the source data for the pivot table is located.*

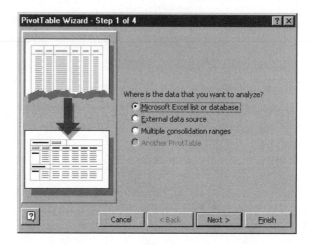

## Understanding the Four Data Sources

In this exercise, you are creating a pivot table based on a worksheet database; this is the simplest way to get acquainted with pivot tables. Here's a brief description of the other three options available at Step 1 of the Wizard: the External Database option is used to create a pivot table using an external database such as Microsoft Access, dBase, or Oracle as your data source (this is discussed in Chapter 22). The Multiple Consolidation Ranges option is also discussed in Chapter 22; this option is used to consolidate data that is located in more than one worksheet range. The Another PivotTable option is an important way to optimize your computer's memory for situations where you want to create several pivot tables using the same data set—this vital feature is discussed in Chapter 21.

## Step 2 of the PivotTable Wizard: Confirming the Database Range

In the PivotTable Wizard Step 2 Of 4 dialog box, shown in Figure 20.3, you confirm the database range.

**FIGURE 20.3**

*Confirm the database range that the pivot table will be based on.*

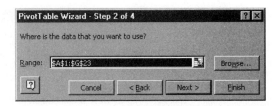

If the active cell is inside a worksheet database when you choose Data ➤ PivotTable, the Wizard automatically detects the boundaries of the database. You can enter a different range, or you can use the mouse to point, click, and drag a range of cells. Here's how to handle three common exceptions:

- If the source data is on a different worksheet, click on the sheet tab, then select the database range.
- If the source data is in a different (open) workbook, use the Window menu to activate the workbook, then select the database range.
- If the source data is stored in a workbook that is not open, click on the Browse button to choose the workbook, then select the database range.

Once you have confirmed the database range, click on Next to proceed to the Pivot-Table Wizard Step 3 Of 4 dialog box.

## Step 3 of the PivotTable Wizard: Laying Out the Pivot Table

Step 3 of the PivotTable Wizard (see Figure 20.4) is the heart of the pivot table. At this point, you specify the layout of the table.

The data fields are represented by a set of buttons at the right of the dialog box. You can select whichever buttons you want as row and column fields—and whichever one you want as the data inside the pivot table. You create the desired layout by dragging and dropping the field buttons onto the pivot table. There are four places where you can drop a field button:

| | |
|---|---|
| **Row** | Field(s) used as row titles |
| **Column** | Field(s) used as column titles |
| **Page** | Field(s) used to filter the database, allowing the data to be viewed one *page* at a time |
| **Data** | The actual data that will be inside the pivot table (typically numeric fields)—at least one field *must* be placed in the data area |

PART

**VI**

Pivot Tables

*FIGURE 20.4*

*The database fields are displayed as buttons on the right part of the dialog box. The pivot table in the dialog box is a preview of the actual table that will be placed on a worksheet.*

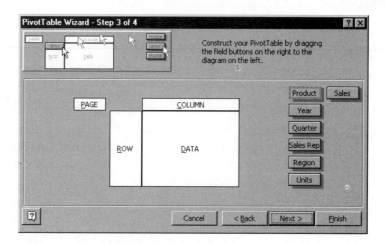

Follow the steps below to arrange the pivot table so that it displays the names of the sales reps that are selling certain products. Use Figure 20.5 as a guide.

**1.** Drag the Sales Rep field into the Row area.
**2.** Drag the Region field into the Column area.
**3.** Drag the Product field into the Page area.
**4.** Drag the Sales field into the Data area (the label changes to *Sum of Sales*—the next chapter will explain how to change this title).
**5.** Click on Next to proceed to the last step.

**WARNING**
Don't be alarmed if the Sales field calculation defaulted to Count rather than Sum. The field summarization type is supposed to default to Sum for numeric fields, and to Count for non-numeric fields. This is a long-standing Excel anomaly. You can change it by double-clicking on the field button and selecting a different calculation type in the list box.

This example positions one data field at each of the four places that a field can be positioned: row field, column field, page field, and data field. Bear in mind you are not limited to one field per location—you can place more than one field at each of the four areas. Nor must there be a page, row, or column field. However, there must be at least one data field.

**TIP**
If you place the wrong field onto the pivot table, you can removed it by dragging it anywhere outside of the table.

Drag and drop
field buttons
onto the pivot
table.

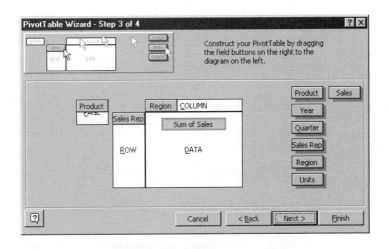

## Step 4 of the PivotTable Wizard: Finishing the Pivot Table

The PivotTable Wizard Step 4 Of 4 dialog box, shown in Figure 20.6, lets you specify
where the pivot table will be placed.

Step 4 allows
you to specify
where the pivot
table is placed.

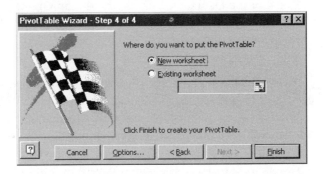

**PART**

**VI**

Pivot Tables

1. Specify where the pivot table goes by entering a cell reference into the PivotTable
   Starting Cell:

   • If you specify New Worksheet, a worksheet is added to the active workbook,
     and the pivot table is placed in the upper-left corner, starting at cell A1.
   • If you specify Existing Worksheet, you must then click on the worksheet tab
     where the table is to be placed, then click on the target cell. (To place the pivot

table on an open workbook other than the active workbook, use the Window menu to activate the book, click on a tab, and select a cell.)

**2.** Click on Finish. Figure 20.7 shows the finished pivot table.

**FIGURE 20.7**

*You can change the table layout by dragging the field buttons on the worksheet, without using the PivotTable Wizard.*

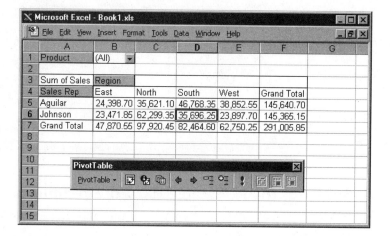

At Step 4 of the PivotTable Wizard, there is an Options button which, when clicked, displays a dialog box containing a number of advanced settings discussed in the following two chapters.

The pivot table in Figure 20.7 shows how each salesperson performed within each region. The layout, specified in Step 3 of the PivotTable Wizard, determines the level of summarization. In this example, a database containing many records (rows) can be summarized into an informative, concise format.

You cannot edit the cells inside a pivot table as you would "normal" cells. However, in the following two chapters, you will learn how to format pivot tables and how to add custom formulas. In a subsequent section, you will learn how to change the layout of a pivot table using special direct manipulation techniques.

**NOTE**

There is no limit, other than available memory, to the number of pivot tables that can be defined in the same workbook—or even on the same worksheet.

# Refreshing a Pivot Table

Here's a vital piece of information: pivot tables do not automatically recalculate when the source data changes. For example, if you create a pivot table from the products database shown in Figure 20.1, then edit the database in any manner (add rows, delete rows, change numbers, etc.), the change will *not* automatically appear in the pivot table. To refresh a pivot table, select any cell inside the table, then choose Data ➤ Refresh Data. (This is also the case when a pivot table is based on an external database, which is discussed in Chapter 22.)

**NOTE**  The PivotTable Options dialog box, discussed in the next chapter, allows a pivot table to be automatically refreshed when the workbook is opened.

# Changing the Layout of a Pivot Table

Once you have created a pivot table, there are two ways to change the layout: by using the PivotTable Wizard, or by direct interaction with the table on the worksheet. The Wizard is an easy way to change the layout, but once users learn how to change a pivot table interactively, using drag and drop techniques, this becomes hands-down the method of choice—there are fewer steps involved.

## Changing a Pivot Table Interactively

One of the best aspects of pivot tables is that you can manipulate them directly on the worksheet, without having to restart the PivotTable Wizard. Most users are of the opinion that this method is the most intuitive—once you become familiar with pivot tables, the interaction becomes second nature.

### Using Page Fields to Filter Data

The pivot table shown previously in Figure 20.7 has a page field drop-down list box for Product that lets you filter the data displayed in the pivot table. By default, when a pivot table is first created, the page field will be set to (All)—in the products database, a combination of dairy *and* produce products. Suppose you only want to view information pertaining to dairy products. Click on the drop-down arrow and select Dairy from the list. The data in the table changes accordingly. (This is one case where direct interaction is the only way to go—the Wizard provides no mechanism for changing the selection in a page field.)

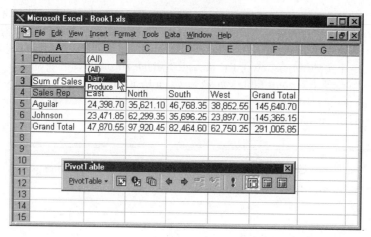

## Changing the Layout by Dragging Field Buttons

As shown previously in Figure 20.7, after you create the pivot table using the Wizard, the field buttons are placed on the worksheet. This allows you to change your view of the data by dragging the buttons on the sheet, without having to redisplay the Wizard. For instance, using the pivot table in Figure 20.7, suppose you want to see sales by region for each sales rep—just click on the Region button, and drag it just under the Sales Rep button. The new layout is shown in Figure 20.8. It is this type of ad hoc manipulation of the pivot table layout that provides extraordinary analytical capabilities.

The best way to learn about pivot tables is through experimentation. Try positioning each button as a row category, column category, and page field—the pivot table will reveal different information about the underlying data with each layout.

## Removing a Field

To remove a field from a pivot table, simply drag the field button outside the pivot table range. When a large × appears, as shown in Figure 20.9, release the mouse button. Remember, removing a field from a pivot table does not affect the underlying data. (In fact, the pivot table *never* affects the underlying data.)

**NOTE**

You can add fields to a pivot table without using the Wizard. This topic is discussed in the next chapter.

**FIGURE 20.8**

*Sales by region by product by salesperson*

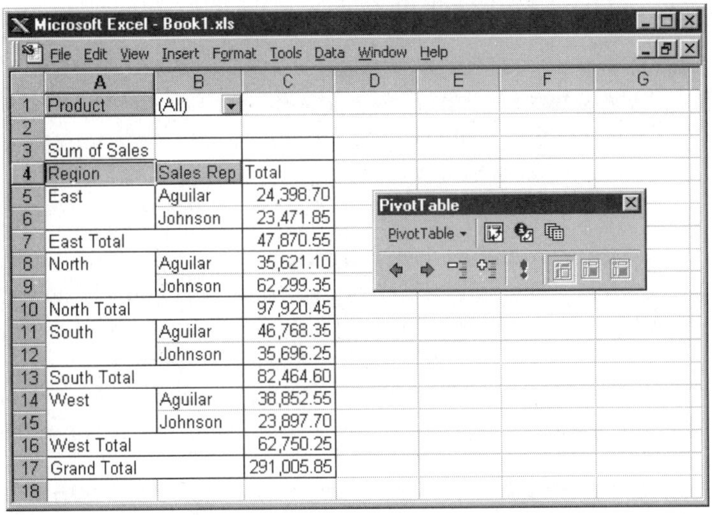

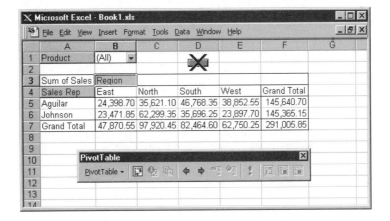

**FIGURE 20.9**

*Drag a field button outside of the pivot table to remove it from the table. Release the mouse button when the large x appears.*

## Changing the Pivot Table Layout Using the Wizard

Another way to change a pivot table is with the PivotTable Wizard. As you might expect, this process is similar to the process you used when you first created the pivot table. Follow these steps:

**1.** Select a cell inside the pivot table.

PART

**VI**

Pivot Tables

**2.** Start the PivotTable Wizard by choosing Data ➢ PivotTable Report or by clicking on the PivotTable tool on the PivotTable toolbar.

**NOTE** If the active cell is not inside the pivot table when you choose Data ➢ PivotTable, Excel assumes that you want to create a new pivot table. There can be more than one pivot table on a worksheet.

The Wizard is displayed starting at Step 3 (as shown earlier in Figure 20.4). The procedure for changing the layout is the same as when you first created the pivot table—simply drag and drop the field buttons to the desired location. To remove a field from the pivot table, drag and drop it outside of the table.

Just because the Wizard starts at Step 3 doesn't mean you can't go backward. Click on the Back button to navigate back to Step 2 or Step 1, if desired.

**NOTE** Behind every pivot table is a hidden data cache. This cache is what allows the extraordinarily rapid response when a pivot table is manipulated. The cache is discussed in the next chapter, under the section entitled "Understanding the Cache." This is a vitally important topic if your use of pivot tables is more than casual.

# Deleting and Copying Pivot Tables

Pivot table cells are unique animals. In certain respects, the cells inside a pivot table behave quite differently than normal cells. In particular, there are some nuances involved when it comes to copying and deleting pivot tables.

## Deleting Pivot Tables

There are two ways to delete a pivot table. The first method is obvious—you can delete the entire worksheet containing the pivot table. However, if don't want to delete the entire worksheet, you can clear or delete the pivot table cells, in a similar manner as you would clear or delete normal cells. (Chapter 3 covers these skills.) There's one important caveat, however: you must clear or delete the *entire* pivot table, including the page field(s), if any. If you attempt to clear or delete just a portion of a pivot table, an error message appears, and the operation is disallowed.

# Copying Pivot Tables

The obvious way to copy a pivot table is to copy the entire worksheet (a skill discussed in Chapter 2). But if you don't want to copy the entire sheet, then copy and paste the cell contents. While you can copy just a portion of a pivot table, the result, once pasted, will be normal cells rather than an actual pivot table. To get a real pivot table, you must copy/paste the *entire* pivot table, including any page fields.

You have now learned the rudimentary aspects of creating a pivot table and changing its layout. These skills are enough to get started with, and will allow you to derive some real value from pivot tables. The next two chapters will explore this vital feature in greater depth.

PART

**VI**

Pivot Tables

# Chapter

## 21

### Mastering Pivot Tables

# FEATURING

# Mastering Pivot Tables

ivot tables are an easy win. In return for a nominal learning investment, there is a significant gain in productivity to be realized. Chapter 20 scratched the surface of the pivot table feature set—it is important that you have a firm grasp of the topics covered in Chapter 20 before proceeding. In this chapter and the next, we'll go into depth on this important Excel functionality.

## Getting the Lay of the Land

Before we start in on substance, it will be useful to understand where various commands and settings pertaining to pivot tables are located, and to examine the terminology for the different elements of a pivot table. In the last chapter, you learned how to display the PivotTable Wizard using the Data ➤ PivotTable Report command. In this section, the shortcut menu, the PivotTable toolbar (*a.k.a.* command bar), and the PivotTable Options dialog box will be introduced. Subsequently, these items will be referenced throughout this chapter and the next. First, examine Figure 21.1. This screen, from Excel's online help, points out the different elements of a pivot table.

**FIGURE 21.1**

*This pivot table contains one page field (Region), one column field (Quarters), two row fields (Product and Sold By), and one data field (Sum of Order Amount). Remember, there must be at least one data field, but the other fields are optional.*

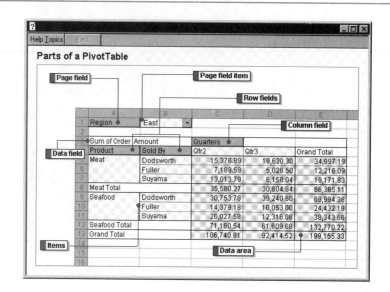

## Locating Pivot Table Commands and Dialog Boxes

When you right-click anywhere inside of a pivot table, the pivot table shortcut menu appears.

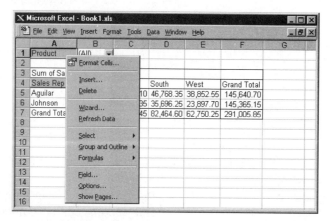

In addition, by default, whenever a worksheet containing a pivot table is activated, the PivotTable command bar appears.

All of the commands found on the PivotTable toolbar, shown above, can also be found on the shortcut menu. The method you choose is one of personal preference. Since you can always rely on the shortcut menu to be available, whereas the command bar can be hidden, this chapter will refer to shortcut menus as the primary way of accessing pivot table commands. The equivalent toolbar button will be pictured in the margin as each command is discussed.

## The Pivot Table Options Dialog Box

At Step 4 of the PivotTable Wizard (see Chapter 20, Figure 20.6), there is an Options button which, when clicked on, displays the PivotTable Options dialog box (see Figure 21.2). This dialog box provides several advanced settings, which span a wide range of functionality. The settings on this dialog box will be referenced throughout this chapter. You can also display this dialog box by right-clicking anywhere within a pivot table, then selecting the Options command from the shortcut menu.

**FIGURE 21.2**

*The PivotTable Options dialog box includes many disparate settings.*

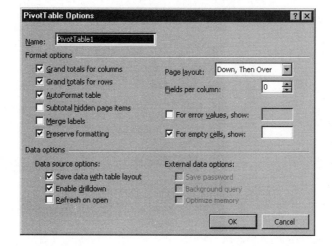

**PART**

**VI**

Pivot Tables

## Working with Data Fields

In this section you will learn several important skills related to *data fields*—fields that are placed in the data area of a pivot table.

## Changing Data Field Orientation

When multiple data fields are placed in a pivot table, they are oriented vertically by default. Notice how in Figure 21.3, the Units and Dollars fields are in the same column, rather than side by side. While sometimes this may be desirable, usually it is not. To compound this problem, the method used to change the data field orientation is obscure.

**TIP**

You can double-click on any data cell in a pivot table in order to view the detail behind that cell; a new worksheet containing the additional data is created and added to the workbook.

**FIGURE 21.3**

*Multiple data fields are oriented vertically by default.*

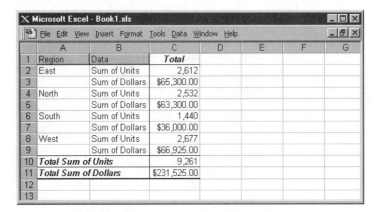

To change the data fields to horizontal orientation, click on the Data button and drag it to the right. As soon as you start dragging, the mouse pointer changes—it shows a vertically oriented rectangle. As you drag a little bit further to the right, the rectangle changes to horizontal, as shown below. Release the button now. Figure 21.4 shows the resulting layout.

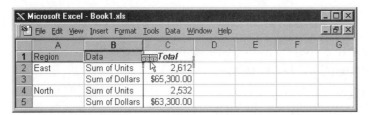

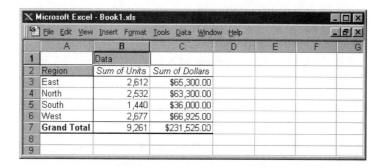

**FIGURE 21.4**

By dragging the
Data button to
the right, the
data fields are
changed to
horizontal
orientation.

## Changing How Data Fields Summarize

When a data field inside a pivot table is numeric, by default, the summarization performed by the pivot table is a *sum*. This is why the data field names are prefaced with *Sum of*. (Field names can be changed—see below.) Conversely, if a data field is not numeric, the calculation defaults to a *count*. There are many other ways to summarize a data field, as listed in Table 21.1.

**TABLE 21.1:** DIFFERENT WAYS TO SUMMARIZE A PIVOT TABLE DATA FIELD

| Use... | To Calculate... |
| --- | --- |
| Sum | Sum (total) of the values |
| Count | Number of records (rows) |
| Average | Average value in underlying data |
| Max | Maximum value in underlying data |
| Min | Minimum value in underlying data |
| Product | Product of the underlying data |
| Count Nums | Number of records (rows) containing numbers |
| StdDev | Estimated standard deviation of population where the underlying data represents the sample |
| StdDevp | Standard deviation of population where the underlying data represents the entire population |

PART
VI

Pivot Tables

| **TABLE 21.1:** DIFFERENT WAYS TO SUMMARIZE A PIVOT TABLE DATA FIELD (CONTINUED) | |
| --- | --- |
| **Use...** | **To Calculate...** |
| Var | Variance of population where underlying data represents the sample |
| Varp | Variance of population where underlying data represents the entire population |

Here's how to change the way a data field summarizes: right-click on any cell belonging to a given data field, then choose Field from the shortcut menu. The dialog box pictured in Figure 21.5 appears. Select a summarization method from the list, and click on OK.

Alternatively, you can display the PivotTable Field dialog box from the Wizard by double-clicking on the field button(s) at Step 3.

**NOTE** Chapter 22 explains how to define more complex custom calculations, and how to create calculated fields. To see how to format a data field, read the formatting section later in this chapter.

## Performing Two Calculations on One Data Field

Suppose that you want to calculate the sum of a data field and calculate the average of the same field. The same field can be placed into the data area more than once. Then, they are treated as separate fields. One can be set to sum, and the other to average.

## Changing Field Names

After creating a pivot table, the first thing most users want to change are the field names—particularly the data field names. The vast majority of data fields are performing a summation. Therefore, the *Sum of* prefix automatically added to the field name adds little value in most users' minds, and makes for an awful visual presentation. Not the least of the problems is the ridiculously wide columns that result from these long field names. Fortunately, changing field names is a simple task: just select the cell and enter a new field name. Unfortunately, there's a pitfall lurking around the corner.

Consider this scenario: suppose there is a field in the source database named *Units*. When you place Units in the pivot table as a data field, the field is renamed *Sum of Units*—as far as Excel is concerned, *Sum of Units* is now a field name. Typically, you will want to change it back to its original name, *Units*. However, behind the scenes, the field Units did not go away. Excel will not allow a field name conflict, thus it will not allow *Sum of Units* to be changed to *Units*. The following error message will appear:

If you're determined for the field to be named Units, here's a trick to get around the problem: you can place a space before or after the word *Units*. (This trick is offered with the full realization that leading or trailing spaces in field names can cause confusion later on, when you forget the space is there!)

**TIP**

The procedure for renaming a field directly in the pivot table is not limited to data fields. The same steps are used to change Row, Column, or Page field names.

# Working with Page Fields

In Chapter 20, you learned how to create a simple pivot table containing a page field. A *page field* is a drop-down list box located at the top of the pivot table (see Chapter 20, Figure 20.7). It lets you *filter* the data being displayed in the pivot table by allowing individual pages to be selected. A pivot table can have no page fields, one page field, or many page fields. Some interesting, useful aspects of page fields are discussed below.

PART

**VI**

Pivot Tables

## Showing Pages

As you have already learned, a page field allows you to view data pertaining to any one page by selecting an item from the drop-down list box. Or, when (All) is selected from the list box, all of the pages are summarized together as one virtual page. However, suppose you want to print out each individual page. It is a tedious process to manually select the first page, print it, then repeat this process for each subsequent page. There's a far better way to go about it! From the pivot table shortcut menu, choose the Show Pages command. The following dialog box is displayed.

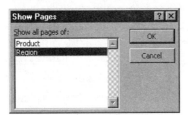

Suppose the Region page field, shown above, consists of pages North, South, East, and West. By simply selecting the Region field and clicking on OK, four new pages are added to the workbook—one for each region (see Figure 21.6). The new worksheets are named according to the names of the pages (in this case, regions).

**WARNING**

Be careful when showing pages for a field consisting of a large number of pages. Since a new worksheet will be added to the active workbook for each page, you may run out of memory.

**FIGURE 21.6**

*A new worksheet has been inserted into this workbook for each page of the Region field.*

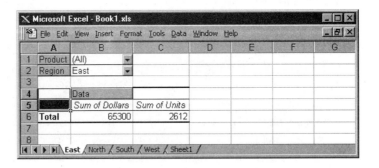

## Customizing the Page Field Layout

NEW

By default, page fields are stacked one on top of another. Figure 21.7 shows a pivot table with four page fields. This layout causes the data to begin at row eight, which in turn causes the data not to fit on the screen—you must scroll down in order to see the grand total. Fortunately, the PivotTable Options dialog box (shown earlier in Figure 21.2) has two settings which allow you to customize this layout. (Remember, this dialog box is displayed by right-clicking anywhere in the pivot table, then selecting Options from the shortcut menu.) Of primary importance is the Fields Per Column settings, which allows page fields to be placed in more than one column. When this setting is 0 (the default), all of the page fields are placed in one column. By changing Fields Per Column to 2, for example, the grand total will fit on the screen. Figure 21.8 illustrates this point.

**FIGURE 21.7**

*By having four page fields, the user must scroll down in order to see the grand total.*

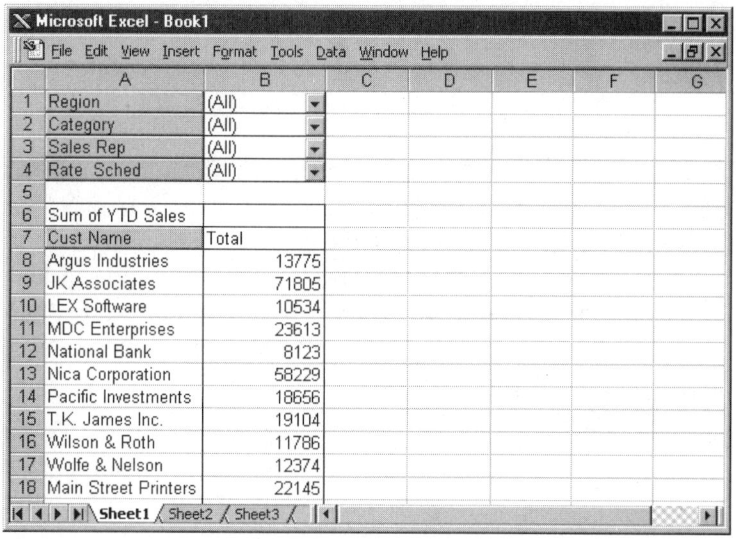


The second relevant setting is Page Layout. This esoteric setting provides the following two choices. Assume for a moment that Fields Per Column is set to 2, and the pivot table begins at A1.

**Down Then Over:** The first page field is placed in A1, the second in A2, the third in C1, the fourth in C2, and so on.

**Over Then Down:** The first page field is placed in A1, the second in C1, the third in A2, the fourth in C2, and so on.

**FIGURE 21.8**

*The Fields Per Column setting on the PivotTable Options dialog box controls the layout of the page fields. By changing this setting to 2, more data is viewable without scrolling.*

| | A | B | C | D | E | F | G |
|---|---|---|---|---|---|---|---|
| 1 | Region | (All) | | Sales Rep | (All) | | |
| 2 | Category | (All) | | Rate Sched | (All) | | |
| 3 | | | | | | | |
| 4 | Sum of YTD Sales | | | | | | |
| 5 | Cust Name | Total | | | | | |
| 6 | Argus Industries | 13775 | | | | | |
| 7 | JK Associates | 71805 | | | | | |
| 8 | LEX Software | 10534 | | | | | |
| 9 | MDC Enterprises | 23613 | | | | | |
| 10 | National Bank | 8123 | | | | | |
| 11 | Nica Corporation | 58229 | | | | | |
| 12 | Pacific Investments | 18656 | | | | | |
| 13 | T.K. James Inc. | 19104 | | | | | |
| 14 | Wilson & Roth | 11786 | | | | | |
| 15 | Wolfe & Nelson | 12374 | | | | | |
| 16 | Main Street Printers | 22145 | | | | | |
| 17 | Ruiz Machine | 12770 | | | | | |
| 18 | Grand Total | 282914 | | | | | |

**NOTE**
Another important aspect of page fields comes into play when creating pivot tables based on *external* databases: the ability to automatically requery the database each time a new page is selected. This feature allows larger volumes of data to be analyzed while avoiding memory overflow. This topic is discussed in Chapter 22.

# Formatting a Pivot Table

As you have probably discovered by this time, cells occupied by a pivot table differ significantly from "normal" cells. One area of considerable difference is formatting. In this section, you will learn the various techniques, tips, and traps when it comes to formatting pivot tables. Don't be disheartened by the many nuances involved—the old 80/20 rule is at play. You are likely to find that 80% of your formatting needs are quite easy to accomplish. For the other 20%, brace yourself for some initial confusion!

## Applying an AutoFormat

Perhaps the easiest way to create a professional-looking pivot table is by using *Auto-Formats*. AutoFormats are not limited to pivot tables—this general-purpose table formatting feature is discussed in Chapter 5. However, there are a couple of simple nuances to be aware of when applying AutoFormats to pivot tables. In fact, if you have already created your first pivot table, the odds are you have already used an AutoFormat. This is because, by default, pivot tables are formatted using the AutoFormat named *Classic 1*.

There are two dialog boxes that control AutoFormat settings. First, there is the AutoFormat Table setting, which specifies whether or not the pivot table is to have an AutoFormat at all. This setting is found on the PivotTable Options dialog box, shown previously in Figure 21.2. (Remember, to display this dialog box click on the Options button at Step 4 of the Wizard. Or without the Wizard, right-click anywhere in the pivot table and select Options from the shortcut menu.) When it comes right down to it, the rationale for deselecting this setting is fairly trivial: it is minutely faster to manipulate the pivot table when there is no AutoFormat, and minutely less memory is consumed.

As you now know, Classic 1 is the default AutoFormat for a pivot table. To change to a different AutoFormat, select any cell inside the table, then choose Format ➤ AutoFormat. Pick one of the formats from the list, then click on OK. Here's the good news: when the size of the pivot table is changed (by pivoting, refreshing, picking a different page field, or whatever), the AutoFormat automatically adjusts to the table's new boundaries.

> **TIP**
>
> The Options button on the AutoFormat dialog box exposes additional settings that provide more control over your formatting. Of particular interest when working with pivot tables is the Width/Height setting. When deselected, the pivot table will no longer adjust the column widths every time the table is manipulated. This overcomes the sometimes annoying tendency for pivot table column widths to be ridiculously large.

## Data Field Formatting

Suppose you have a pivot table with two data fields, and the fields need to be formatted differently. Consider Figure 21.9: both data fields need to be formatted with commas. However, just one of the fields requires currency formatting. AutoFormats will *not* do the trick. Rather, you must format the fields individually. As you read on, you will learn that these cells *can* be formatted like normal cells, but there are caveats galore. Instead, you should format these cells using a special pivot table field formatting technique.

Here's how you would typically format the Dollars field shown in Figure 21.9 for a currency format:

**1.** Select any cell(s) in the Dollars data field (C2:C7).

**FIGURE 21.9**

*This pivot table contains two data fields. The Units field needs to be formatted with a comma, whereas the Dollars field must be formatted as dollars.*

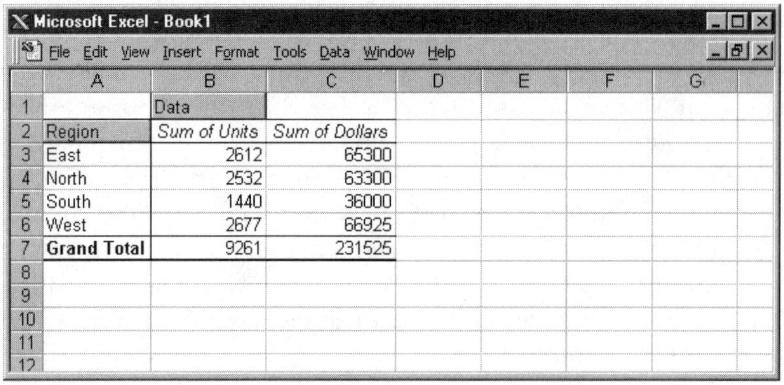

2. Right-click, and select Field from the shortcut menu—this displays the PivotTable Field dialog box shown earlier in Figure 21.5.
3. Click on the Number button to display the Format Cells dialog box. (This is the standard number formatting dialog box discussed in Chapter 5.) Choose the Currency format, click on OK, then click on OK again. The *entire field* is formatted.

Repeat this process for the Units field, choosing an appropriate format. Now, even when you manipulate the table, each field will retain its new number format. Figure 21.10 shows the same pivot table with a column field added. Notice that the fields retained their numeric formatting in spite of the changed layout.

**FIGURE 21.10**

*Different number formats have been applied to the two data fields.*

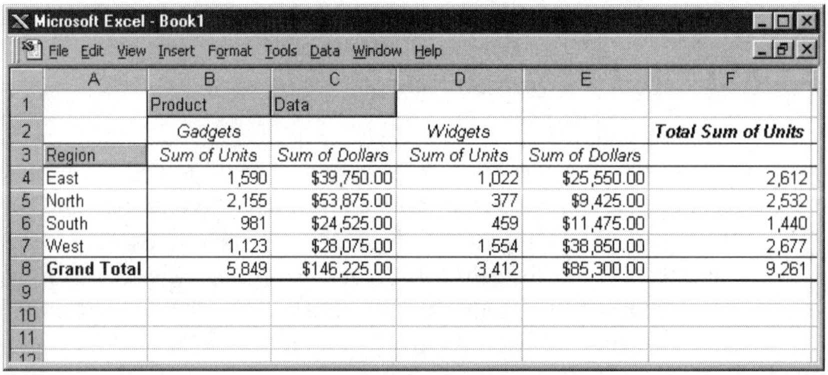

## Merging Labels

Here's a feature that may not be high in substance, but is nifty nonetheless: merging labels in a pivot table. There is a setting on the PivotTable Options dialog box, shown earlier in Figure 21.2, called Merge Labels. This setting is used to improve the visual appearance of pivot tables that have more than one row field or more than one column field. Examine Figure 21.11: notice that the Product labels are left-aligned over each set of Region labels (i.e., Gadgets is directly above East).

**FIGURE 21.11**

*This pivot table has two column fields—Product and Region. The Product labels are left-aligned over each set of Region labels.*

| | A | B | C | D | E | F | G | H |
|---|---|---|---|---|---|---|---|---|
| 1 | | Product | Region | | | | | |
| 2 | | Gadgets | | | Gadgets Total | Widgets | | |
| 3 | Data | East | West | Central | | East | West | Central |
| 4 | Sum of Units | 1590 | 2155 | 981 | 4726 | 1022 | 377 | 459 |
| 5 | Sum of Dollars | 39750 | 53875 | 24525 | 118150 | 25550 | 9425 | 11475 |
| 6 | | | | | | | | |
| 7 | | | | | | | | |
| 8 | | | | | | | | |
| 9 | | | | | | | | |
| 10 | | | | | | | | |

By checking the Merge Labels setting on the PivotTable Options dialog box, the inner column field (Product) is centered over the outer field (Region). This is shown in Figure 21.12.

> **TIP**
>
> Behind the scenes, the PivotTable Merge Labels feature makes use of the Merge Cells feature, which is discussed in Chapter 5. To transform a range of cells into one large virtual cell, choose Format ➢ Cells, click on the Alignment tab, and check the Merge Cells setting.

## Structured Selection

Before peeling the next layer of the pivot table formatting onion, there's an important feature you must first grasp—*structured selection*. Structured selection allows you to easily select different parts of a pivot table. On the surface, structured selection has little to do with formatting. But in fact, one of the primary functions of structured selection is to aid and abet the task of pivot table formatting.

**FIGURE 21.12**

*The Merge Labels setting on the PivotTable Options dialog box causes inner column fields to be centered over outer fields. This works for row fields as well.*

| | A | B | C | D | E | F | G | H |
|---|---|---|---|---|---|---|---|---|
| 1 | | Product | Region | | | | | |
| 2 | | | Gadgets | | Gadgets Total | | Widgets | |
| 3 | Data | East | West | Central | | East | West | Central |
| 4 | Sum of Units | 1590 | 2155 | 981 | 4726 | 1022 | 377 | 459 |
| 5 | Sum of Dollars | 39750 | 53875 | 24525 | 118150 | 25550 | 9425 | 11475 |
| 6 | | | | | | | | |
| 7 | | | | | | | | |
| 8 | | | | | | | | |
| 9 | | | | | | | | |
| 10 | | | | | | | | |

Remember this vital fact: structured selection is a feature that can be turned off and on. Pivot tables behave differently in several ways, depending on the on/off status of structured selection. (This is particularly true of the formatting discussion that follows this section.) Structured selection is turned on and off by choosing the Select command from the pivot table shortcut menu, then selecting the Enable Selection command. This is a global setting—it affects your subsequent interaction with all pivot tables, not just the active one.

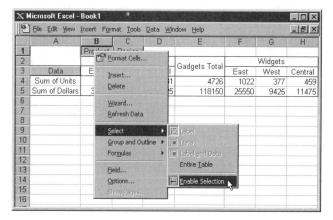

When structured selection is turned on and you click on a row or column label, you have a surprise in store. All data pertaining to the clicked-on label is selected, not just the one cell. Look at Figure 21.13: when we clicked on B3, all of the Gadgets rows were selected. Experiment for yourself. Create a relatively complex pivot table, turn on structured selection, and click everywhere. Try clicking on row fields, columns fields, page fields, and data fields. Click on subtotals and grand totals. Making use of structured selection is the first step when applying advanced formatting to a pivot table.

**FIGURE 21.13**

With structured
selection turned
on, clicking on
B3 causes all of
the Gadgets
cells to be
selected.

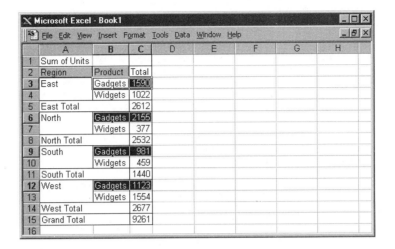

**NOTE**

You can also use structured selection to help create calculated fields. This topic is
discussed in the next chapter.

## Structured Selection Commands

There are three commands that are available only when structured selection is turned
on, as shown in Table 21.2. These commands provide additional flexibility for structured selection.

**TABLE 21.2:** STRUCTURED SELECTION COMMANDS

| Button | Description |
| --- | --- |
| | Select label only |
| | Select data only |
| | Select label and data |

PART

VI

Pivot Tables

## Data-Aware Cell Formatting

This section covers a very useful way to format pivot table cells—a technique that transcends superficial formatting and actually helps you analyze data more effectively. Before you proceed with this section, it is important that you understand *structured selection*, discussed above. It is also worth mentioning again that you can handle most day-to-day formatting needs using the simpler formatting techniques previously discussed.

Here's the good news for pivot table devotees: you can now format the cells in a pivot table just as you would format normal cells. But it's even better than that. The formatting you apply to pivot table cells is smart indeed—the formatting is *data-aware*. Consider the following pivot table:

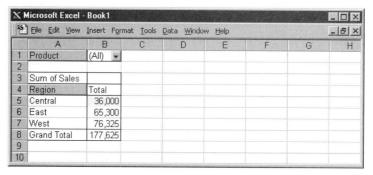

Cell B5—Sales for the Central region—has been formatted in order to emphasize sales below expectations. (This format was manually applied to the one cell with standard formatting techniques, using the Format ➢ Cells command discussed in Chapter 5.) Now, suppose you want to view additional details by Product. One way to accomplish this is by dragging the Product page field to a row field. In Figure 21.14, the Central region is still formatted, in spite of the revised layout. This is why we refer to this formatting feature as *data-aware*—the cell formatting is actually applied to the data, and it moves as the data moves.

Naturally, there are some pitfalls involved. In order for this feature to work properly, there are two settings to be concerned with:

- The Preserve Formatting check box on the PivotTable Options dialog box (shown previously in Figure 21.2) must be checked. (It is checked by default.) If this setting is unchecked, formatting is lost whenever the pivot table is manipulated.
- Structured selection must be turned on. If you turn off structured selection, then manipulate the pivot table, cell formatting will be lost. (It is turned on by default.) Remember, since structured selection is a global setting, if you turn it off, it can come back to haunt you unexpectedly at a later time.

**FIGURE 21.14**

*Cell formatting inside of a pivot table is data aware. When the pivot table layout is changed, the formatting moves accordingly.*

| | A | B | C | D | E | F | G | H |
|---|---|---|---|---|---|---|---|---|
| 1 | | | | | | | | |
| 2 | | | | | | | | |
| 3 | Sum of Sales | | | | | | | |
| 4 | Product | Region | Total | | | | | |
| 5 | Gadgets | Central | 24,525 | | | | | |
| 6 | | East | 39,750 | | | | | |
| 7 | | West | 53,875 | | | | | |
| 8 | Gadgets Total | | 118,150 | | | | | |
| 9 | Widgets | Central | 11,475 | | | | | |
| 10 | | East | 25,550 | | | | | |
| 11 | | West | 22,450 | | | | | |
| 12 | Widgets Total | | 59,475 | | | | | |
| 13 | Grand Total | | 177,625 | | | | | |
| 14 | | | | | | | | |

Unlike cell formatting, field formatting (discussed earlier in this chapter) is not affected by these settings. Field formatting will work correctly regardless of any other settings, even when the pivot table is manipulated.

## Sorting a Pivot Table

Data in a pivot table is automatically sorted according to label, in ascending order. This is true of both rows and columns. Figure 21.14 is a good example—the inner row field, Product, is sorted alphabetically. The outer row field, Region, is sorted alphabetically within each Region. Prior to Excel 8, changing the sort order was a thorny problem—pivot tables had a frustrating tendency to "forget" the sort order as the table was manipulated or refreshed. Users who grappled with this problem will be pleased to learn that Excel 8 pivot tables are a lot smarter than their ancestors when it comes to sorting. Take a look at this pivot table:

| | A | B | C | D | E | F | G | H |
|---|---|---|---|---|---|---|---|---|
| 1 | Sum of Sales | | | | | | | |
| 2 | Region | Total | | | | | | |
| 3 | Central | 36000 | | | | | | |
| 4 | East | 111966 | | | | | | |
| 5 | North | 67675 | | | | | | |
| 6 | South | 35025 | | | | | | |
| 7 | West | 110880 | | | | | | |
| 8 | Grand Total | 361546 | | | | | | |
| 9 | | | | | | | | |
| 10 | | | | | | | | |

PART

**VI**

Pivot Tables

As you can see, the regions are sorted by name alphabetically, in ascending order. Suppose, however, you need to sort the regions by sales in descending order—the region with the highest sales first. Here's how:

**1.** Double-click on the Region button to display the dialog box shown below:

**2.** Click on the Advanced button. This displays the PivotTable Field Advanced Options dialog box shown in Figure 21.15.

**FIGURE 21.15**

*To display this dialog box, click on the Advanced button on the PivotTable Field dialog box.*

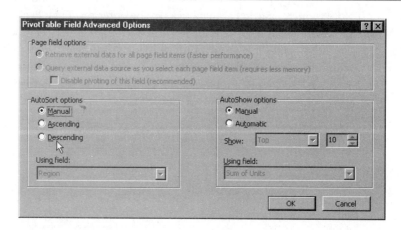

**3.** Select the AutoSort Descending option.

**4.** From the Using Field list, choose the field you wish to sort by—in this case, Sum of Sales. Click on OK to close the dialog box, then click on OK once again to close the PivotTable Field dialog box.

Figure 21.16 shows the result. The new sort order will persist when the pivot table is refreshed or otherwise manipulated.

**FIGURE 21.16**

*The regions are sorted by Sales, in descending order. This sort order will persist even when the pivot table is manipulated.*

| | A | B | C | D | E | F | G | H |
|---|---|---|---|---|---|---|---|---|
| 1 | Sum of Sales | | | | | | | |
| 2 | Region | Total | | | | | | |
| 3 | East | 111966 | | | | | | |
| 4 | West | 110880 | | | | | | |
| 5 | North | 67675 | | | | | | |
| 6 | Central | 36000 | | | | | | |
| 7 | South | 35025 | | | | | | |
| 8 | Grand Total | 361546 | | | | | | |
| 9 | | | | | | | | |
| 10 | | | | | | | | |

## Using a Custom Sort Order

It is a common requirement in the corporate world for items on a report to be sorted in a specific sort order that is not logical from a software standpoint. For example, suppose the regions in Figure 21.16 absolutely have to be sorted North, South, East, West, Central. (Perhaps if the true cost of this type of reporting requirement, measured in work hours, were better understood by management, this idiosyncratic practice would be less pervasive. Oh well.) Fortunately, Excel's Custom List feature can be used to impose a custom sort order on a pivot table.

**TIP**

Custom lists are created by choosing Tools ➢ Options, then clicking on the Custom List tab. The list can be typed into the List Entries box, or can be imported from a range. This feature is discussed in Chapter 18.

Assuming that the custom lists already exist, using it with a pivot table is simple. In fact, it's so simple that it's automatic! If the items in a row, column, or page field precisely match an existing custom list, then the custom list automatically determines the sort order at the time the pivot table is created. However, there is one important

PART

**VI**

Pivot Tables

caveat: the custom sort order takes effect only when the pivot table is initially created. If you create a pivot table, and then create the custom list, the custom sort will have no effect, even when the table is refreshed.

Remember, all of the sorting techniques discussed in this section apply to column (and page) fields, not just rows.

> **WARNING**
>
> Try not to get too euphoric about sorting with custom lists. Indeed, if the requirement exists, this feature is a boon to productivity. But remember, the custom list is just one more thing that has to be maintained when a new region, for example, is added. Furthermore, when you define a custom list, it is defined only on your computer—it does not travel with the workbook. Thus, the custom list on every desktop in your organization must be maintained.

## Grouping Data

There may be times when your source database is structured such that it does not fit the way you want to present data in the pivot table. This problem often occurs with the use of dates in databases. We'll use the database shown in Figure 21.17 to illustrate this point.

**FIGURE 21.17**

*The Invoice Database to be used as the source for a pivot table, intended to show how each rep performed by month*

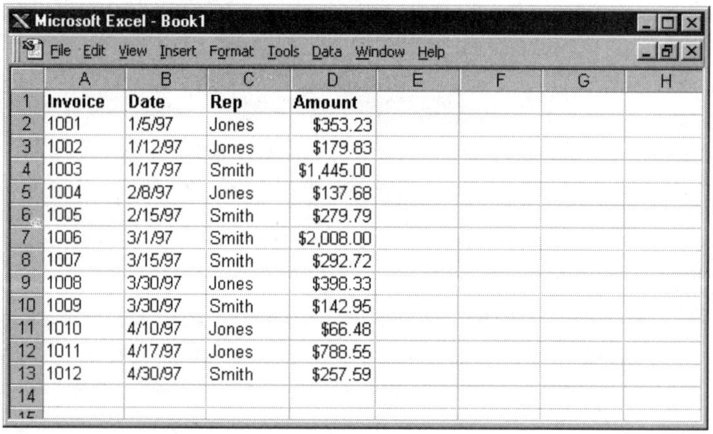

## Grouping in Action

Suppose you want to design a pivot table that shows the sales reps, Smith and Jones, on separate rows, and their total sales for each month in columns. To create the pivot table shown in Figure 21.18, use *Rep* as a row category, *Date* as a column category, and *Amount* as a data value. As you can see, each discrete date in the source database occupies a separate column.

**FIGURE 21.18**
*The date columns are too detailed—the goal is to see totals for each month.*

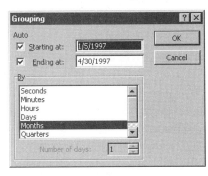

The date information is too detailed for our purposes, however. The solution to this problem is to roll up, or *group*, the dates by month. Follow these simple steps:

1. Right-click on any of the date-column heading cells (i.e., B2), and from the shortcut menu choose Group And Outline ➤ Group. The Grouping dialog box appears.

2. Choose Months, then click on OK. The date columns are rolled up into months, as shown in Figure 21.19.

PART
**VI**

Pivot Tables

**FIGURE 21.19**

You can group
dates by any
number of
days (such
as weeks),
months, quar-
ters, or years.

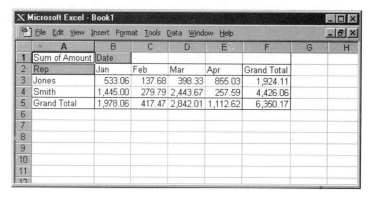

As you might expect, Excel uses the oldest date to determine the first column, and the most recent date to determine the last column. Suppose there were no invoices in January. The pivot table would show only February through April. This would likely cause confusion were this report distributed to other people in your organization— why no January? Notice the Starting At and Ending At settings in the Grouping dialog box shown above—these allow you to override Excel and specify a range of dates. If a starting data of 1/1/97 were entered, the pivot table would include a January column with no data in it.

Here is the procedure for ungrouping the columns: right-click on any of the date (month) column heading cells, and from the shortcut menu choose Group And Outline ➤ Ungroup.

## Understanding the Hidden Data Cache

Behind every newly created pivot table is a hidden *cache* of data. The cache stores data in what is known as a *multidimensional format*. In simplified terms, all of the potential layouts for the pivot table are precalculated in the cache. This provides the rapid response time you've come to expect when pivoting or otherwise manipulating a pivot table. It is not essential to understand the cache, or even know that it exists, to be productive with pivot tables. But some basic understanding will prove invaluable if your use of pivot tables goes beyond dabbling. Figure 21.20 illustrates the flow of data. In between the source data and the pivot table lies the hidden data cache.

**FIGURE 21.20**

A hidden data cache stores pre-calculations, making pivot tables very fast when they are pivoted or otherwise manipulated.

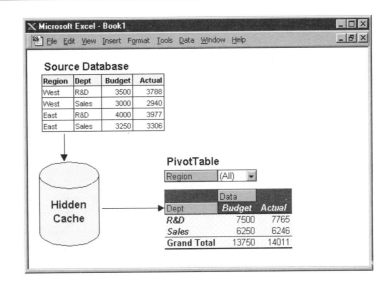

## Advanced Uses of Grouping

Suppose that you have a database that contains three years' worth of sales data by date. If you use the dates as a row field or column field in a pivot table, Excel recognizes dates and makes it easy for you to group them into several kinds of date groups. For example, you can group the dates into months, the months into quarters, and the quarters into years. The user can then show or hide the monthly, quarterly, or yearly figures by double-clicking on the fields. To create multiple-level group dates, right-click on a date cell in the pivot table, then choose Group And Outline ➢ Group. The By list is a multiselect list. This means you can choose Months, Quarters, and Years, then click on OK.

Now let's assume that you have data of a different kind—perhaps sales figures by city. The cities are a row field in the pivot table, and you want to group the cities in the pivot table by state. If you select a city cell and attempt to group, Excel will display the alert "Cannot group that selection." In this case you have to create the group definition explicitly: select all the cities to be grouped into one state. (Hold down Ctrl to select noncontiguous cells.) Then choose Data ➢ Group And Outline ➢ Group. The selected cities will be grouped together as Group 1. Finish grouping the cities, then change the newly created group field names to state names.

PART

**VI**

Pivot Tables

## Saving Data with Table Layout

The cache plays an integral role when a pivot table is based on another pivot table, as you will read about soon. It also plays an important role when working with external databases, as is discussed in the next chapter. In addition, now that you know about the cache, there is an important setting that can be accurately explained. Examine the PivotTable Options dialog box, shown earlier in Figure 21.2. There is a Data Options setting called Save Data With Table Layout. When checked, the cache is saved (albeit hidden) inside the workbook. (This setting is checked by default.) As you can likely guess, if you uncheck the Save Data With Table Layout setting, the cache is not saved to disk inside the workbook. Here are the implications of checking and unchecking this setting:

- When checked, you can manipulate the pivot table without having to requery the source data—a key factor when creating pivot tables from external databases. This is because the pivot table is driven by the cache, not the source data directly.
- When a pivot table is based on a worksheet database, and the setting is checked, you can delete the source data from the workbook and still manipulate the pivot table. However, you cannot refresh it in this circumstance, since the source data will be missing.
- Immediately after the setting is unchecked, there is no noticeable effect on the pivot table. The implications of unchecking the setting will not be apparent until you save, close, then reopen the workbook.
- When unchecked, the workbook saved to disk will be smaller than otherwise—perhaps considerably so, depending on the quantity of source data.
- When you open a workbook containing a pivot table, and the setting was previously unchecked, you can view and print the pivot table. But you cannot otherwise manipulate it—it will (for the moment) be strictly static. The cache must be present in order to manipulate the table. If you attempt to manipulate the table, the following error message appears:

Here is a key fact: when you open a workbook containing a pivot table, and the setting was previously unchecked, you can restore the cache by refreshing the table. (Simply choose Data ➤ Refresh Data.) Refreshing the pivot table causes the cache to be reconstructed in memory, and in turn, the table can be manipulated. Keep in mind that refreshing the table does not change the Save Data With Table Layout setting. The workbook will still have to be refreshed each time it is opened in order to manipulate the table. (The Refresh On Open setting, found on the PivotTable Options dialog box, comes in handy in this case.)

Once you learn about creating pivot tables using external databases as their source, in Chapter 22, you will realize another key benefit provided by the cache: it is not limited to 65,536 rows, as is a worksheet. Depending on a variety of factors, such as the number of fields being analyzed and the amount of memory in your computer, the cache is capable of storing hundreds of thousands of data rows.

# Creating a Pivot Table from Another Pivot Table

So far, you have learned how to create pivot tables based on a worksheet database. However, you have no doubt observed that Step 1 of the PivotTable Wizard provides three other possible choices. External databases and multiple consolidation ranges are discussed in the next chapter. In this section, you will read about an all-important option: creating a pivot table from another pivot table. The importance of this feature cannot be overemphasized if you seek mastery of pivot tables. Before we delve into this topic, you must first understand a key behind-the-scenes aspects of pivot tables—the hidden data cache that is behind every newly created pivot table. (The cache is discussed above.) Once you understand the cache, the concept of basing a pivot table on another pivot table is a slam-dunk!

## The Cache Is the Driving Force

Here's the bottom-line: at Step 1 of the Wizard, when you choose to use an existing pivot table as the data source, you are in fact using the *cache behind that existing pivot table* as the data source, not the pivot table itself. There must be at least one pivot table in the active workbook in order for this option to be available, although it does not have to reside on the active worksheet. Here are the steps involved:

1. Activate a cell that lies outside of the existing pivot table, then choose Data ➢ PivotTable Report to display the PivotTable Wizard Step 1 Of 4 dialog box. (If the active cell is inside an existing pivot table when the Wizard is displayed, Excel assumes you are changing the existing table.)

> **NOTE**
> Generally, it's *not* a good practice to place multiple pivot tables on the same worksheet. Since the boundaries of a pivot table can change as the table is manipulated, positioning multiple tables on one sheet can be a dicey proposition.

**2.** Choose the Another PivotTable option, and then click on Next to proceed to Step 2 of the Wizard.

**3.** Select the pivot table that you want to use from the list, and then click on Next to proceed to Step 3.

From this point on, the procedure is the same as when creating any other pivot table. Follow the standard procedures for Steps 3 and 4 of the PivotTable Wizard, as covered in Chapter 20, to complete the pivot table.

> **TIP**
>
> The PivotTable Options dialog box, shown earlier in Figure 21.2, lets you override the default name assigned by the Wizard. Meaningful names can come in handy if you create more than one pivot table in a workbook, then create a new pivot table based on an existing table. With meaningful names, it is easier to distinguish the tables from one another.

There is one obvious benefit to this technique: by creating pivot tables based on other pivot tables (caches), you are using less memory and consuming less disk space than if each table had its own cache. There is one other nifty benefit too: assuming there are three pivot tables based on the same cache, when you refresh any one of them, the other two will refresh automatically.

## Dynamic Charting Using Pivot Tables

Pivot tables play an important role when it comes to charting. This is because charts have special pivot table-awareness. A chart created from a pivot table will automatically change as the pivot table changes—this is what we mean by the term *dynamic charting*. (There's more discussion of dynamic charting in Chapter 15.)

Pivot tables can help you overcome one of the most common real-world inefficiencies—the profusion of (nearly identical) charts, when in fact one dynamic chart will do the job. There are plenty of workbooks in plenty of corporations where there resides one chart for each region, or one chart for each period, or one chart for each whatever. The maintenance chore involved when a simple formatting change needs to be implemented is obvious. For these reasons, there are savvy Excel users who rarely create charts from anything *other* than a pivot table.

## A Dynamic Charting Example

For example, look at the worksheet shown in Figure 21.21. This sheet contains a pivot table and a chart. Suppose different regions have different lists of categories associated with them. When you pick a different region from the page field, there may be five items in the Category row field, rather than three: the chart will automatically expand. The fact that a chart will react to a new item chosen in a page field in and of itself is worth the price of admission. But read on: it gets even better!

**FIGURE 21.21**

**FIGURE 21.21**

*When a different region is selected from the page field, the chart redraws accordingly, even when there are more or fewer Categories in different regions. Even the chart title can be dynamic, by l inking it to cell C2.*

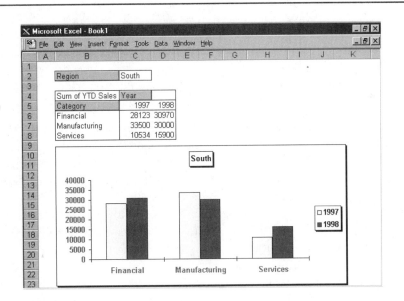

Figure 21.22 is the same worksheet as Figure 21.21. However, the pivot table layout has been changed. The Year field has been repositioned as a page field. The Region field has been repositioned as a column field. Again, the chart has dynamically adjusted to the changed table layout.

## But Watch Your Step...

Now the gotchas: there are two key points to remember when charting a pivot table. To achieve a successful result, you *must* chart the entire data area of the pivot

**FIGURE 21.22**

*Charts linked to pivot tables automatically adjust to changes in the pivot table layout.*

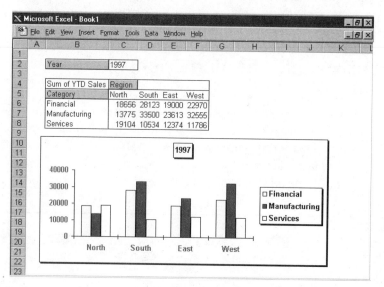

table. Accordingly, the pivot table should not include totals. Here are expanded explanations of these two salient issues:

- In order for the chart to be pivot table-aware, you must chart the entire data area of the table. This range must include the row and column labels, but not the page fields. In Figure 21.22, the range you would select before clicking on the Chart-Wizard tool is B4:F8. (A shortcut for selecting this range is to click on any cell in the pivot table, then press Ctrl+Shift+*.)

- Typically, you should *not* include totals in a pivot table intended for charting. Remember, the entire data area must be charted. Thus, if there are totals, you will wind up with a scaling problem, where the totals dwarf the detail. To remove totals from a pivot table, uncheck the row/column totals settings on the Pivot-Table Options dialog box, shown earlier in Figure 21.2. In summary, you can chart a pivot table with totals; the result may not be desirable, however.

To learn more about charting, see Chapters 12 through 15.

This chapter may have given you considerable food for thought. However, pivot table devotees should not stop here. Chapter 22 discusses some of the most important new Excel pivot table features—calculated items and calculated fields. It also discusses a key skill for corporate Excel citizens: how to work with pivot tables that use an external database as the data source.

# Chapter

## 22

### Advanced Pivot Tables

# Advanced Pivot Tables

In the past two chapters, you have had a chance to get familiar with the basics of what you can accomplish with pivot tables. In this chapter, pivot table aficionados will learn a variety of advanced skills. Creating pivot tables from external databases is a vital skill for corporate citizens, where indeed, most data resides in external databases. You will also read about two particularly important new features—*calculated fields* and *calculated items*.

## Using Pivot Tables with External Databases

In the last two chapters, you learned how to create pivot tables using worksheet databases as their source. You also learned how to create a pivot table using another pivot table (actually, the cache) as the data source. In this section, we will discuss what is arguably the most important mode for pivot tables in corporations and other large organizations—analyzing data stored in external databases.

> **NOTE**
> Creating pivot tables using external databases involves the use of a program called Microsoft Query. This program comes on the Excel (or Office) setup disk; however, it is an optional component at the time you install Excel. If you are unfamiliar with Microsoft Query or how to install it, please read Chapter 19 before you proceed with this section. Also of importance is the discussion of the hidden data cache in Chapter 21.

Before beginning, let's deal with some semantics. When many corporate Excel users are asked "Do you create pivot tables from external databases?" they answer yes. When asked to show an example, they often show a pivot table that is based on a worksheet database. Why? Because, explain these users, the worksheet database is actually the result of a query to an external database (a skill that is discussed in Chapter 19). In this example, though the pivot table is based *indirectly* on external data, the source data is nonetheless a *range*. There's nothing wrong with this approach per se. However, these users are not realizing some of the benefits that pivot tables provide when based directly on external data.

The key benefit is this: a pivot table based on external data is capable of analyzing far greater volumes of data than one based on a worksheet database. This is because the hidden data cache (discussed in Chapter 21) is not limited to 65,536 rows, as is a worksheet. But don't let this be the sole determining factor. Suppose you are analyzing just 10,000 rows. A worksheet database is still massively inefficient. When a pivot table is based on a worksheet database, the data resides in memory in *two places*: the worksheet database *and* the cache. Such is not the case when an external database is the source, and accordingly, there are considerable memory efficiencies to be realized.

## Creating the Pivot Table

To create a pivot table using an external database, at Step 1 of the Wizard, choose the option External Data Source. After clicking on Next, you will see that Step 2 is completely different from what you are accustomed to.

Notice that the Next button is unavailable, and there is a statement "No data fields have been retrieved." You cannot proceed to Step 3 until you click on the Get Data button. When you click on Get Data, Microsoft Query is started. It is within Microsoft Query that you specify which database you are querying, which tables, fields, etc. (These topics are discussed at length in Chapter 19.) After creating a query in Microsoft Query and choosing to Return Data To Microsoft Excel, Step 2 of the Pivot-Table Wizard is redisplayed, with two differences. The Next button is now available, and the message inside the dialog box reads "Data Fields Have Been Retrieved."

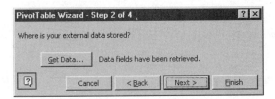

Now the easy part: Steps 3 and 4 of the PivotTable Wizard are exactly the same (on the surface) as when you created pivot tables using worksheet databases.

## Optimizing Page Fields

There are some special features pertaining to page fields that come into play only when the data source is an external database. Before explaining these features, let's discuss the real-world problems they address. A query to an external database can be time-consuming. It might take seconds, minutes, or under the most extreme circumstances, hours. In addition, keep in mind that large databases can be very large indeed, and you may need to analyze so many rows of data that it is impractical (from a performance standpoint), or even impossible (from a capacity standpoint), to retrieve the data into the pivot table cache. Accordingly, there are page field settings that are used to optimize database access.

Assume you are at Step 3 of the Wizard, or viewing a worksheet with an existing pivot table. (Again, the pivot table must be based on an external database.) Here are the steps for accessing the page field optimization settings:

1. Double-click on the page field button to display the PivotTable Field dialog box. (This button is available on either the Wizard or the worksheet.)
2. Click on the Advanced button to display the PivotTable Field Advanced Options dialog box shown in Figure 22.1.

In short, the page field options boil down to this trade-off: retrieve all of the data from the external database when the pivot table is created and refreshed. Or, retrieve smaller subsets of the data each time an item is selected from the page field. Before

PART

**VI**

Pivot Tables

**FIGURE 22.1**

*The page fields options are only available when the pivot table uses an external database as its source.*

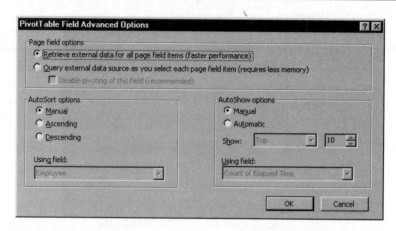

reading the detailed pros and cons below, remember this fact: the parenthetical *faster performance* comment (shown earlier in Figure 22.1) is potentially misleading. In reality, it makes certain operations faster and other operations slower.

**Retrieve External Data For All Page Field Items:** Retrieves all data when the pivot table is created or refreshed. When this option is checked, these are the pros and cons:

**PROS:** Since the cache is fully populated with all page field items, page field manipulation (selecting a new item from the list box, or pivoting) is typically orders of magnitude faster than otherwise (though no faster than an equivalent worksheet database).

**CONS:** Creating and refreshing the pivot table will be slower—perhaps by an order of magnitude. Far more memory is consumed because of the larger cache.

**Query External Data Source As You Select Each Page Field Item:** Database is requeried each time a page field is manipulated. In general, use this option when you are working with very large volumes of data. When selected, these are the pros and cons:

**PROS:** Creating and refreshing pivot table is (much?) faster. Less memory is used because of smaller cache.

**CONS:** Each time a page field is changed or pivoted, the database is requeried.

**Disable Pivoting Of This Field:** This setting is only available when the Query External Data Source option is selected. If this check box were unchecked, you would be able to drag the page field to a row or column position. However, this would produce the very scenario you are trying to avoid—issuing a query that returns a huge volume of data. This is because all field items have to be retrieved in order to display a field as a row or column field. For this reason, it is highly recommended that you check this setting.

There is no substitute for a solid understanding of databases, and of Microsoft Query. Make your query do as much work for you as possible. If your pivot table is intended to analyze only the region West, for instance, make sure only West data is returned to the pivot table cache. This is accomplished by filtering the Region field, in this quasi-example, for West only.

## Deciding How to Optimize Page Fields

There are no fixed rules for performance and memory optimization. However, here are three important considerations:

1. With the Retrieve External Data option selected, is the query result set simply too large for the cache, or too slow for the user(s)? Try it and see.

2. Count the unique items in the page field. The higher the number, the better candidate the page field is for the Query External Data Source option. (Sorry, there are too many variables to define "higher" in this case—which database, database schema, computer memory, speed of network connection, etc.)

3. How likely are the users of the pivot table to change the page field? With what frequency? The more the page field is interacted with, the more benefit to the Retrieve External Data option.

## External Data Options

The PivotTable Options dialog box, shown in Figure 22.2, has five settings that are of great importance when a pivot table uses an external database as its source.

**Save Data With Table Layout:** When selected, the pivot table cache is saved inside the workbook. This setting pertains to all pivot tables, not just ones based on external databases. (The implications of the setting are discussed in depth in Chapter 21.) If you are distributing the workbook to other users who do not have access to the source database, and you want these users to be able to pivot, this setting *must* be checked.

PART VI

Pivot Tables

*The PivotTable Options dialog box is displayed by clicking on the Options button at Step 4 of the Wizard, or by selecting the Options command from the shortcut menu.*

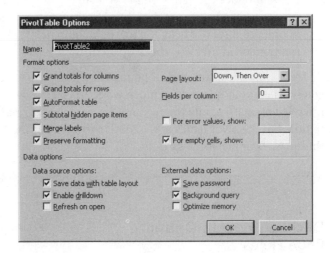

**Refresh On Open:** Again, this setting is not specific to pivot tables based on external data, but it does take on special meaning in this context. When selected, the pivot table automatically refreshes when the workbook is opened. Remember, when the table is based on external data, a database query will occur each time the workbook is opened.

**NOTE**

Though Excel allows the above two settings to both be checked, in many cases it would be illogical to do so. When a pivot table is refreshed, the cache also refreshes. Thus, if set to refresh on open, a previously saved cache would be over-written. The only benefit of checking both settings is as follows: if you open the workbook and are unable to refresh the pivot table (because of a database problem, for example), the cache would still be present and the pivot table available for manipulation.

**Save Password:** When checked, and if the external database requires a password, the password will be saved in the workbook so that the user doesn't have to reenter it later. In organizations where data security is a concern, this is a dangerous setting to check. Anyone with access to the workbook would have access to the source data.

**Background Query:** When checked, the query will run in the background, allowing you to continue to work with Excel before the query is finished.

**Optimize Memory:** Check this setting if you get an out-of-memory error message when creating the pivot table. It sacrifices performance in exchange for greater memory efficiency.

# Using Multiple Consolidation Ranges

There are four possible pivot table data source options available on Step 1 of the Wizard., and we have already discussed three of them. The last one, Multiple Consolidation Ranges, comes last (in this book, not in the dialog box itself) for good reason: this feature is obscure and difficult to use. That doesn't mean, however, that it has no merit. This feature allows you to consolidate data that resides in multiple worksheet ranges.

Here's an example: suppose your organization, a distributor of electronic goods, has several regional offices, and each office submits a sales forecast by product. It is your job to create a report that consolidates these forecasts. In the next section, you will learn how to create a pivot table that consolidates these multiple ranges. Consider the workbooks shown in Figure 22.3. (If you would like to work along with the following exercise, enter the constants shown here onto four separate workbooks.)

**FIGURE 22.3**

*Four regional sales forecasts that need to be consolidated*

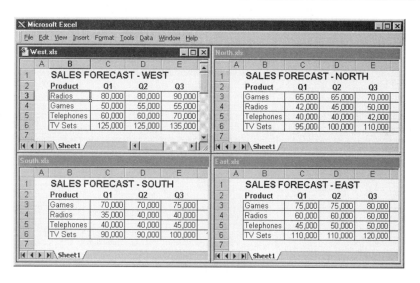

With the four workbooks open, follow these steps to consolidate the information onto a new workbook:

1. Create a new workbook. Choose Data ➢ PivotTable Report, and Step 1 of the PivotTable Wizard appears.

**2.** Select the Multiple Consolidation Ranges option, then click on Next. Step 2a of the PivotTable Wizard, shown in Figure 22.4, appears.

**FIGURE 22.4**

*Step 2a is a special step that applies only when consolidating multiple consoli-dation ranges.*

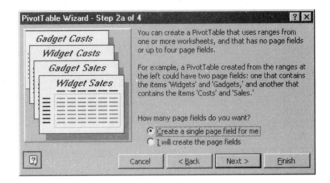

**3.** Select the option Create A Single Page For Me, then click on Next to proceed to Step 2b of the PivotTable Wizard, shown in Figure 22.5.

> **NOTE**
> When you select the option Create A Single Page Field For Me, the Wizard creates a separate page for each consolidated range. The option I Will Create The Page Fields lets you override the default pagination.

**FIGURE 22.5**

*Step 2b lets you specify the ranges to be consolidated.*

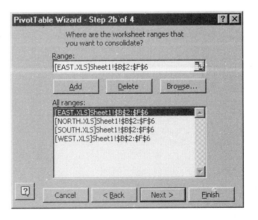

**4.** Enter the range by pointing and clicking on the workbooks—for instance, click on WEST and select cells B2:E6, then click on Add.

**5.** Repeat step 4 above for EAST, NORTH, and SOUTH, then click on Next to proceed to Step 3 of the PivotTable Wizard (Figure 22.6).

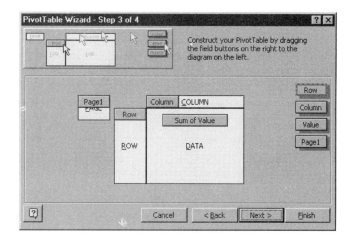

**FIGURE 22.6**

*Double-click on the field buttons to customize them. For aesthetic reasons only, you may want to change the name Page1 to Region, Row to Product, etc.*

**6.** The field button in the data area will likely read *Sum of Value*. (The PivotTable Wizard occasionally defaults to *Count of*.) If it doesn't, double-click on the button and select Sum from the Summarize By list.

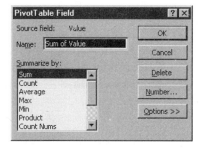

**7.** Click on Next to proceed to Step 4, then click on Finish. The final pivot table is shown in Figure 22.7.

There is one key fact to keep in mind when creating a pivot table from multiple consolidation ranges: the consolidation is based on the column labels (field names) and the row labels (the values in the first column of each range). Matching labels are consolidated, though the position of the label within the range is not a factor.

PART

**VI**

Pivot Tables

**FIGURE 22.7**

*The four regions are consolidated. The drop-down list lets you select any of the four regions, or all of them (All is chosen by default). The column and row field buttons have been renamed, and the word forecast was entered in cell B3.*

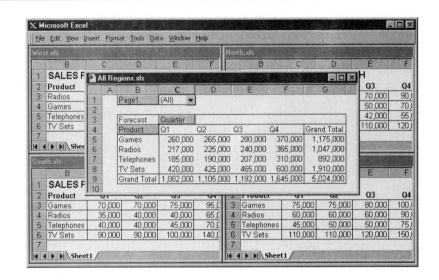

# Introducing Calculated Fields and Items

This section discusses two special new pivot table features—*calculated fields* and *calculated items*. For pivot table devotees, there is perhaps no new feature in Excel 8 of greater significance.

## Using Calculated Fields

Suppose you have a database with a Budget field and an Actual field. It might be nice, in a pivot table, to show the variance (Budget minus Actual). Until Excel 8, this was impossible. To the great happiness of pivot table aficionados, *calculated fields* provide this capability, and much more. Consider the pivot table shown in Figure 22.8. It includes two data fields, Budget and Actual, just as previously discussed.

Naturally, you could place normal cell formulas into column E that subtract Actual from Budget. However, column E would not be part of the pivot table, and accordingly, would not pivot. Calculated fields provide the solution. To add a calculated field for variance, follow these steps:

1. Select any cell inside the data area of the pivot table (in this example, any cell in C2:D15), then select Insert ➢ Calculated Field. The dialog box shown in Figure 22.9 appears.

**FIGURE 22.8**

*The database behind this pivot table contains a Budget field and an Actual field, but no Variance field (Budget minus Actual).*

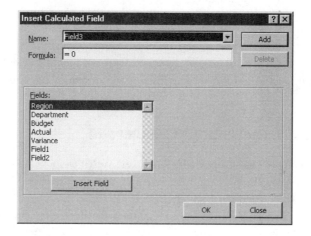

| | A | B | C | D |
|---|---|---|---|---|
| 1 | | | Data | |
| 2 | Region | Department | Sum of Budget | Sum of Actual |
| 3 | North | Manufacturing | 50000 | 51200 |
| 4 | | Warehouse | 34000 | 33952 |
| 5 | North Total | | 84000 | 85152 |
| 6 | South | Manufacturing | 45000 | 41090 |
| 7 | | Warehouse | 31000 | 34225 |
| 8 | South Total | | 76000 | 75315 |
| 9 | East | Manufacturing | 72500 | 69900 |
| 10 | | Warehouse | 43500 | 39750 |
| 11 | East Total | | 116000 | 109650 |
| 12 | West | Manufacturing | 75000 | 81125 |
| 13 | | Warehouse | 48000 | 50190 |
| 14 | West Total | | 123000 | 131315 |
| 15 | Grand Total | | 399000 | 401432 |
| 16 | | | | |

**FIGURE 22.9**

*Calculated fields can use other fields as part of the calculation. To display this dialog box, select any cell inside the pivot table, and select Insert ≻ Calculated Field.*

2. Optionally, enter a meaningful name for the field (i.e., Variance).
3. For the formula, enter **=Budget-Actual**, click on Add, then click on OK. Figure 22.10 shows the result.

**TIP**

You don't have to type field names when entering the formula for a calculated field. As you enter the formula, when a field name needs to be inserted, click on the desired field from the list, then click on the Insert Field button.

PART

**VI**

Pivot Tables

**FIGURE 22.10**

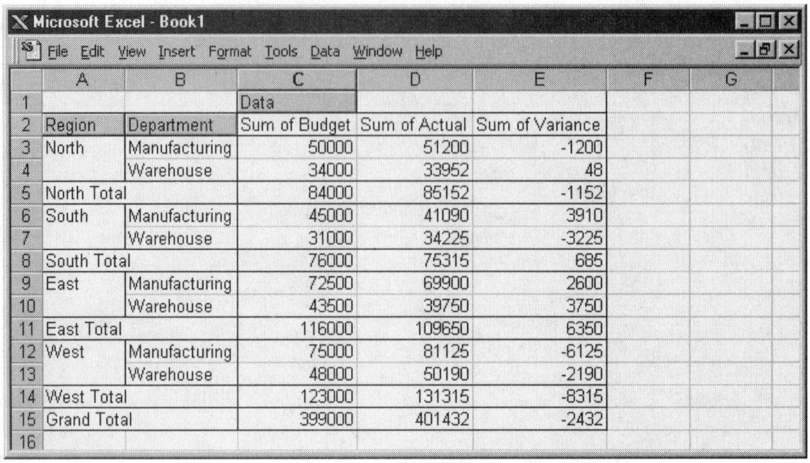

*A calculated field, Sum of Variance, has been added to the pivot table.*

| | A | B | C | D | E | F | G |
|---|---|---|---|---|---|---|---|
| 1 | | | Data | | | | |
| 2 | Region | Department | Sum of Budget | Sum of Actual | Sum of Variance | | |
| 3 | North | Manufacturing | 50000 | 51200 | -1200 | | |
| 4 | | Warehouse | 34000 | 33952 | 48 | | |
| 5 | North Total | | 84000 | 85152 | -1152 | | |
| 6 | South | Manufacturing | 45000 | 41090 | 3910 | | |
| 7 | | Warehouse | 31000 | 34225 | -3225 | | |
| 8 | South Total | | 76000 | 75315 | 685 | | |
| 9 | East | Manufacturing | 72500 | 69900 | 2600 | | |
| 10 | | Warehouse | 43500 | 39750 | 3750 | | |
| 11 | East Total | | 116000 | 109650 | 6350 | | |
| 12 | West | Manufacturing | 75000 | 81125 | -6125 | | |
| 13 | | Warehouse | 48000 | 50190 | -2190 | | |
| 14 | West Total | | 123000 | 131315 | -8315 | | |
| 15 | Grand Total | | 399000 | 401432 | -2432 | | |
| 16 | | | | | | | |

The formula entered in the prior exercise is based on two other data fields. Be aware that these formulas can also include constants. For example, using the Budget/Actual example above, suppose you want to use the same pivot table for budgeting purposes the following year. Cost-cutting measures in your organization require a 5 percent across-the-board budget decrease. You could create a calculated field, Next Year Budget, using the following formula which includes the constant 95%:

```
= Budget * 95%
```

## More Facts about Calculated Fields

- **You can delete a calculated field:** Display the Insert Calculated Fields dialog box (shown earlier in Figure 22.9). Select the field from the Name drop-down list box, then click on the Delete button.
- **You can modify a calculated field:** Display the Insert Calculated Fields dialog box (shown earlier in Figure 22.9). Select the field from the Name drop-down list box. Modify the formula, then click on OK.
- **Calculated fields pivot like "normal" fields:** When the layout of the pivot table is changed, the field moves just as you would expect a normal field to move.
- **Calculated fields exist in the cache:** This is a critical, and very useful, aspect of calculated fields. If you create a calculated field in PivotTable1, for example, then create PivotTable2 using PivotTable1 as its source, the calculated field will appear on the list, at Step 3 of the Wizard, along with the all the "normal" fields. (The hidden data cache is discussed in depth in Chapter 21.)

- **The summarization type cannot be changed:** Calculated fields *sum* the underlying data. Unlike "real" fields, this cannot be changed.

Last but not least, note that a calculated field can be referenced by another calculated field.

> **TIP**
>
> If your pivot table uses an external database as its source, and you need a calculated field, don't overlook this fact: when defining the query in Microsoft Query, you can create calculated fields as part of the query definition. And, since these queries can be saved, the calculated field can be reused in different pivot tables (and other contexts) without having to redefine the calculation over and over again.

## Using Calculated Items

In the last section, you learned about calculated fields. Now, you will learn the feature which, for advanced users, is the ultimate icing on the cake—*calculated items*. This feature dramatically enhances the analytical and reporting capabilities of pivot tables. As the name implies, a calculated item is a new item that, once defined, becomes a member of a specified field.

For example, look again at Figure 22.8. Suppose the company is planning to start operating in a new region—Central. Since the Central operation is not under way yet, it has yet to appear in your corporate database. It is your job to forecast the Central region based on data from an existing region. During the Central region's first year of operation, for instance, it might be forecast as 60 percent of the West region. In the following discussion, using the pivot table in Figure 22.8, you will learn how to add a *calculated item* to the Region field.

Right-click on any cell belonging to the field for which you are creating a new item—in this case, the Region field. Then select Formulas ➢ Calculated Item. The dialog box shown in Figure 22.11 appears. Typically, you will enter a meaningful name—*Central*. Enter the following formula, then click on OK.

```
= West * 60%
```

Notice in Figure 22.12 that the Central item has been added to the pivot table. As you pivot or otherwise manipulate the pivot table, this calculated item will move just as you would expect from "real" items. As with calculated fields, behind-the-scenes, calculated items are actually added to the hidden cache (discussed in depth in Chapter 21). Accordingly, if a pivot table (Table1) has a calculated item, then a new pivot table that uses Table1 as its source will also contain the calculated item (assuming that the field containing said item is placed in the new table).

**FIGURE 22.11**

*A calculated item is usually based on other items within the same field.*

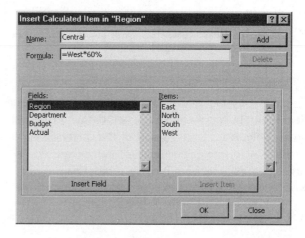

**FIGURE 22.12**

*The calculated item—Central—looks no different than the other items. It will move as expected when the pivot table is manipulated.*

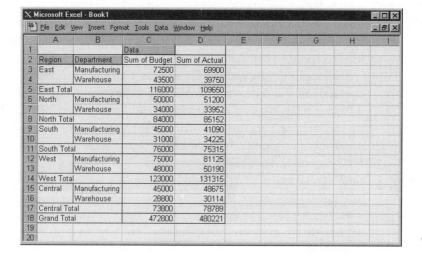

## Overriding a Calculated Item

You have learned how to create a simple calculated item. In this section, you will learn two new skills: first, you will discover how to override a calculated item for a given cell or range of cells. This is accomplished via direct worksheet interaction. Within that task, you will learn a second new skill—using structured selection as a way to simplify the process. (You might want to first go back and read the structured selection discussion in Chapter 21 before proceeding with the exercise.)

Referring again to Figure 22.12, consider this business scenario: remember that Central was defined as equal to 60 percent of West. This calculation was defined in such a way that the calculation applied to both departments—Manufacturing and Warehousing. Suppose however, that Warehousing requires a different factor, say 55 percent of West. No problem! Select the data for Central-Warehousing—cells C16:D16. Notice the formula displays in the formula bar, just like the good old cell formulas.

Now, click inside the formula bar to edit the formula. In this case, change 60% to **55%**, then press ↵. The new formula is entered into both cells automatically (unlike normal cells, where you must press Ctrl+↵ to place a formula into a range). As you might assume, it was not required that both C16 and D16 (Budget and Actual) be changed. You can override the formula for just one cell, or for multiple cells.

## Using Structured Selection When Entering Formulas

Examine the pivot table in Figure 22.13. Region has been pivoted; it is no longer the outer row field. Accordingly, the data for our calculated item—Central—is now broken down by Department. Here's the problem: in order to change a formula for all cells within a calculated field, these cells must all be selected. This is where structured selection enters the equation (in addition to its role in pivot table formatting, discussed in Chapter 21).

PART

**VI**

Pivot Tables

***FIGURE 22.13***

*In this example, Central is a calculated item. Structured selection simplifies the entry of formulas when the cells are noncontiguous.*

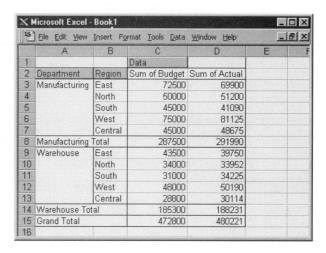

First, make sure that structured selection is turned on (which it is by default). From the pivot table shortcut menu, use the Select ➤ Enable Selection command to toggle structured selection. Referring to Figure 22.13, follow these steps:

**1.** Click on B7. Structured selection causes all Central rows—labels and data—to be selected.

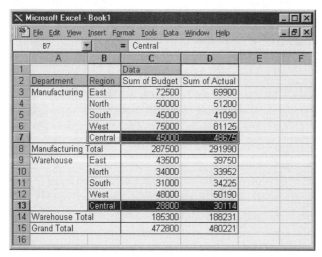

**2.** Click on the Select Data tool. (Or from the pivot table shortcut menu, choose Select ➤ Data.) This causes the labels to be deselected.

**3.** You can now edit the formula on the formula bar.

---

**TIP**

At step 1 of the exercise above, structured selection allows you to click on a row field and automatically select all rows belonging to the clicked field. You may have already guessed that this skill applies to column fields as well, but it also applies to page fields.

---

## Using Functions in a Calculated Field

You can use built-in Excel functions, such as SUM and AVERAGE, in a formula for a calculated field. For example, referring back to the pivot table in Figure 22.12, suppose you want to calculate the Central budget as the average of East and West. Simply select C15:C16, and enter this formula:

```
=AVERAGE(East, West)
```

This is but one simple example of using a built-in function for a calculated field. Excel has hundreds of built-in functions, allowing as many types of calculations to be performed as your imagination will allow.

## Setting the Solve Order

In a pivot table where you are performing complex analysis, you might have many calculated items belonging to various fields at various levels of summary. It is quite possible to create a model where the order of calculation, or *solve order*, has a vast impact on

PART

**VI**

Pivot Tables

the result one way or the other. To override the default solve order, from the pivot table shortcut menu, select Formulas ➣ Solve Order.

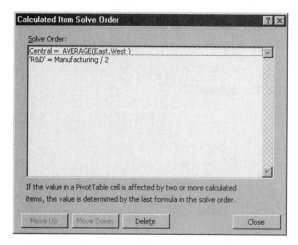

Select an item from the list, and use the Move Up or Move Down buttons to change its position within the list.

## Documenting Field and Item Calculations

You have learned how to create calculated fields and calculated items. Further, you have learned that these calculations actually reside in the hidden data cache. Consider this implication: using the Wizard or via direct manipulation, you can remove fields from a pivot table—a fundamental pivot table skill. Such fields may be calculated fields, or fields containing calculated items. *Removing* them from the pivot table isn't the same as *deleting* them, and they will continue to exist in the cache. Accordingly, it is easy to lose track of them.

Here is the solution: from the pivot table shortcut menu, select Formulas ➣ List Formulas. A new worksheet is added to the active workbook, documenting the calculated fields and items. Once you have viewed and/or printed this sheet, you probably want to delete it. Calculations that are added after the documentation sheet is generated are not automatically added to the sheet—you must issue the List Formulas command again to get updated documentation.

# Referencing Cells with the GETPIVOTDATA Function

Suppose you have an existing pivot table and wish to reference one or more cells in that table from a different worksheet. A normal cell reference won't work in the long run. If the table is pivoted, the cell reference will be rendered incorrect, since the data will have moved to a different location.

The GETPIVOTDATA function is intended to solve this problem. It allows you to reference cells logically, rather than by cell address. The function takes two arguments, referred to cryptically in online help as *Pivot_Table* and *Name*.

**Pivot_Table:** This argument serves to identify which pivot table is the source. Specify a cell reference that points to *any cell* in the source pivot table.

**Name:** This text argument specifies the field(s). One field can be specified (i.e., "Sum of Sales"), or you can specify more than one field (i.e., "North Sum of Sales"). Notice that a space serves to separate the field names. This can be confusing since a field name can contain spaces.

In this chapter you learned about using pivot tables with external databases. You learned about calculated fields and calculated items. Once you master this powerful feature, you will have learned a set of skills arguably as complex as entire spreadsheet programs were ten years ago! In the next chapter, you will learn how to incorporate custom controls, such as list boxes and check boxes, into your worksheet models.

# PART VII

# Customizing Excel

## LEARN TO:

- *Create and format controls*

- *Link controls to cells*

- *Use the macro recorder*

- *Create and run macros*

- *Assign macros to objects*

- *Customize command bars*

- *Build data-driven workbook models*

- *Maintain workbook integrity by bulletproofing*

# Chapter

# 23

## Using Custom Controls on Worksheets

# Using Custom Controls on Worksheets

**U**sers are drawn to spreadsheet products in large part because of the openness of the spreadsheet environment. However, this same openness is one of the biggest obstacles when you are trying to deploy bulletproof solutions. Validating user input and performing certain actions based on user input are among the most common development tasks. This chapter shows the nonprogrammer how to use *custom controls*, such as list boxes and option buttons, to simplify the use of a worksheet model.

Professionally crafted custom applications often include custom dialog boxes, a topic beyond the scope of this book, as it involves considerable VBA programming knowledge. However, even professional programmers should be aware of what can be accomplished nonprogrammatically.

## Working with Custom Controls

A *custom control* is a special type of object that is placed on a worksheet to facilitate user input. A list box, for example, allows you to make selections from a list rather than typing in a response. You place controls on worksheets by drawing them, just as you would draw a graphic object such as a rectangle. (See Chapter 12 to learn about graphic objects.) Accordingly, custom controls share many properties in common with drawing objects, and in fact can be thought of as interactive drawing objects. They are drawn, moved, and deleted in much the same way as with other drawing objects, with one important difference we'll tell you about in just a minute.

Incidentally, don't allow the words *user input* to limit your thinking as to when to use custom controls—they are not limited to classical data entry applications. In fact, an important use of custom controls is for gathering user input, which in turn is used to recalculate a worksheet model. For example, the user may need to produce a chart for any one of several regions, and a list box may be the mechanism for selecting which region. Once the user clicks on a region, good old worksheet formulas do the rest of the work. (This is an example of user input that you don't intend to save.)

 **TIP**

A topic that goes hand in hand with custom controls is data validation, a feature that is accessed using the Data ➤ Validation command. Data validation is covered in Chapter 10.

## The Forms Toolbar

The tools that you use to draw controls are on the Forms toolbar. Use the View ➤ Toolbars command to display the Forms toolbar.

Once you display the toolbar, you will notice that several of the controls are unavailable; these controls are limited to custom dialog boxes, sometimes referred to as *forms*, and cannot be placed on worksheets. Table 23.1 describes the drawing tools for custom controls on the Forms toolbar, and indicates which of them can be used on a worksheet. Also, the table specifies which controls are *passive*. There is generally no direct user interaction with passive controls—nothing happens when you click on them.

## Placing a Control on a Worksheet

Follow these steps to draw a control on a worksheet:

**1.** Display the Forms toolbar using View ➤ Toolbars.
**2.** Click on a tool (control) on the Forms toolbar (one of the tools designated in Table 23.1 as usable on worksheets)—the mouse pointer becomes crosshairs.
**3.** Draw the object on the worksheet using the mouse (as you would draw any graphic object).

**TABLE 23.1:** DRAWING TOOLS ON THE FORMS TOOLBAR

| Tool | Description | Usable On Worksheets? | Passive? |
|------|-------------|----------------------|----------|
| | Label (text) | Yes | Yes |
| | Edit box | No | No |
| | Group box | Yes | Yes |
| | Button | Yes | No |
| | Check box | Yes | No |
| | Option button | Yes | No |
| | List box | Yes | No |
| | Drop-down list box | Yes | No |
| | Combo list/edit | No | No |
| | Combo drop-down/ edit | No | No |
| | Scroll bar | Yes | No |
| | Spinner | Yes | No |

**NOTE** Excel will not let you to draw a control on a worksheet if the particular control is not allowed there—these buttons are dimmed and thus unavailable.

Suppose you need to move or resize a check box control. When you click on the check box, it is checked and unchecked. You must right-click on the control in order to select it. Then, it can be moved and resized the same way as any graphical object. See Chapter 12 to learn about drawing and graphics.

## Linking Controls to Cells

There is one important property shared by *some* of the controls—they can be linked to worksheet cells. This facilitates the use of these controls without the need for custom programming. For worksheet developers, particularly those who are not hard-core VBA programmers, this is the key to deriving the maximum benefit from custom controls. These are the controls that can be linked to cells:

List Box          Option Button

Drop-Down List Box     Scroll Bar

Check Box        Spinner

Suppose one of the above controls already has been placed on a worksheet. To link the control to a cell, right-click on the control, select Format ➢ Control, then select the Control tab. But before we explain the settings available from the Control tab in more depth, there are several important things you should understand about linking controls to cells:

- When you click a control that is linked to a cell, a value is placed in the linked cell.
- Clicking a control can only output to one cell. However, a cell can have multiple controls linked to it.
- Controls are typically linked to a cell in the same workbook, but can also be linked to a cell in a different one (in which case the workbook must be open for the control to work).
- Cells that are written to from a control typically are referred to by other cells—clicking the control causes a recalculation.

# Formatting Controls

The term *format*, when applied to controls, encompasses all of the control's properties, not just the visual format. Here's how to access the formatting dialog box for worksheet controls:

**1.** Right-click on the control.

**2.** Select Format ➤ Control from the context-sensitive menu.

In the next few sections, we'll explain the settings that are available in this dialog box.

## Setting Control Options

Active controls have *control options*. This is where cell linkage is defined, as well as other behavioral settings. Regardless of the type of control, there are two ways to access the control options:

- Follow the procedures for displaying the Format Control dialog box (described above), then select the Control tab.
- Or, select the control and click on the Control Properties tool on the Forms toolbar.

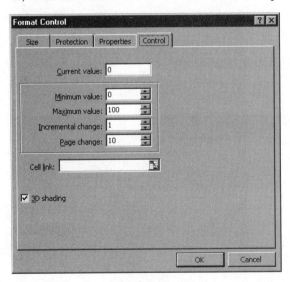

The contents of this dialog box differ, based on the type of control. Each control is discussed below.

**NOTE**
The Current Value setting in the Control tab of the Format Control dialog box is not particularly useful for controls on worksheets; it is used to set default values for controls on custom forms, which requires programming to implement. This is true of all the controls that allow an initial value to be set.

# Using Each Type of Control

In this section, you will learn the nuances of each type of control. Only those controls which can be used on worksheets are discussed.

## Labels

Use labels for text. They are passive and are of little value on worksheets because they are less flexible than text boxes. Unlike a text box, you cannot format a label, nor can you use a formula. There is one benefit to labels: the text format is dictated by a setting accessed via Windows' Control Panel Display settings.

## Check Boxes

Use check boxes to toggle between logical values TRUE and FALSE (for inputs that require a yes/no answer). Here's how to create a check box linked to a cell:

1. Draw a check box on a worksheet.
2. With the check box object still selected, select Format ➤ Control, then select the Control tab.

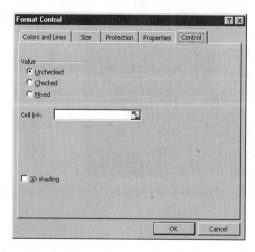

**3.** Enter a cell reference or cell name into the Cell Link text box (this is a range text box—you can point and click on the worksheet to specify the cell). Click on OK.

**4.** Optionally, with the control still selected, change the text next to the check box—click inside it and edit as you would a text box.

Test the check box by clicking on it. It should enter TRUE or FALSE into the linked cell (see Figure 23.1).

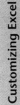

Customizing Excel

---

**FIGURE 23.1**

*The check box is linked to cell B6. When checked, B6 is set to TRUE. When unchecked, B6 is set to FALSE.*

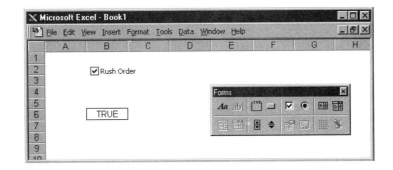

Remember, it is often helpful for the linked cell to be located out of view, often on a separate worksheet within the same workbook. (You may not want users of the worksheet to see the cryptic TRUE/FALSE value, for instance.) Rather, cells that are in view might reference the linked cell, performing calculations that are dependent on the user input.

## Scroll Bars

Scroll bars are used to control an integer value in a cell:

- Minimum and Maximum values in the Format Control dialog box constrain the cell value—these values can be no less than zero and no greater than 30,000 (meaning that the cell must contain a number from 0 to 30,000).
- Incremental Change is controlled by clicking on the up or down arrows.
- Page Change is controlled by clicking on the scroll bar itself, or by dragging the scroll box—the box between the up and down arrows.
- Enter the cell reference (or cell name) in Cell Link.

The scroll bar settings in Figure 23.2 would add or subtract 1 from the cell it is linked to when the arrows are clicked, and add or subtract 10 when the bar is clicked.

The cell will not go below 0 or above 100. Scroll bars can be oriented vertically or horizontally (Figure 23.3).

**FIGURE 23.2**

*Scroll bars control the integer value in a cell.*

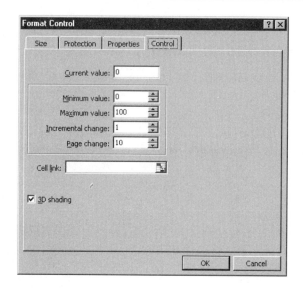

**FIGURE 23.3**

*Scroll bars can be oriented vertically or horizontally.*

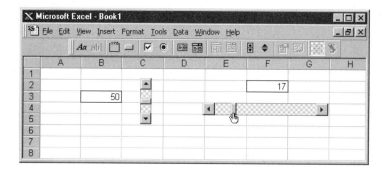

## Spinners

Spinners are identical to scroll bars, except the Page Change setting is no longer available from the Control tab of the Format Control dialog box. Spinners can only be oriented vertically.

## Option Buttons and Group Boxes

Option buttons are used to select one option from a list of two or more exclusive choices. Option buttons are sometimes called *radio buttons* because they work the same way as the buttons on a car radio—since you can only listen to one station at a time, the choices are mutually exclusive.

The worksheet shown in Figure 23.4 includes three option buttons, all linked to the same cell. However, you only need to set the linkage for one of the option buttons—the other buttons are automatically linked.

**FIGURE 23.4**

*All of the option buttons are linked to cell D5. When the first button is chosen, D5 is set to 1. When the second button is chosen, D5 is set to 2, etc.*

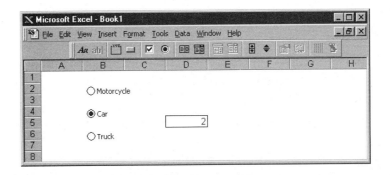

Option buttons can be placed inside of a group box. The group box groups the buttons not only visually, but logically as well (see Figure 23.5).

**FIGURE 23.5**

*The option buttons in the Media group box are linked to B11. The option buttons in the Category group box are linked to E11.*

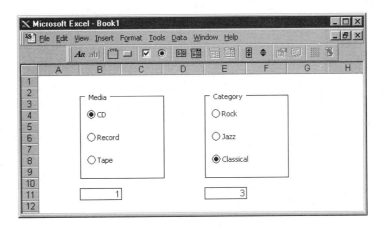

Here are some important facts to remember about the behavior of option buttons and group boxes:

- All option buttons on a worksheet that are *not* inside a group box are part of the same logical group. When you link any of them to a cell, all of the others are automatically linked to the same cell.

- All options buttons within a group box are part of the same logical group. When you link any of them to a cell, all of the others are automatically linked to the same cell.
- There can be more than one group box on a sheet containing option buttons. And, on the same sheet, there can be option buttons that are not inside a group box.
- If you resize a group box so that an option button that was previously not inside the box is then inside, the new member automatically becomes part of the logical group. Conversely, if you resize a group box so that one of the option buttons is no longer in the box, the "orphaned" option button ceases to be a member of the logical group.

You can place other controls, such as check boxes and list boxes, inside a group box (see Figure 23.6). The sole purpose is aesthetics—there is no logical side effect.

**FIGURE 23.6**

Controls other than option buttons, such as the check box shown here, can be placed in a group box, with no effect on the behavior of the controls. Group boxes only affect the behavior of option buttons.

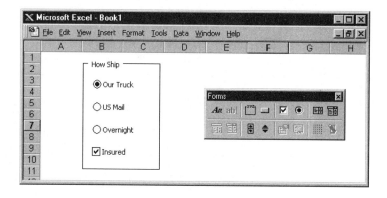

## List Boxes

List boxes let the user select an item from a list and place a number in a linked cell based on the item clicked on by the user. For example, if the second item in the list is clicked on, the number *2* is placed in the linked cell. List boxes are the only type of control that use two separate cell linkages:

- An input range—the range of cells that contains the list of choices.
- A cell link—when an item is selected in the list box, this cell contains the position within the list of the selected item.

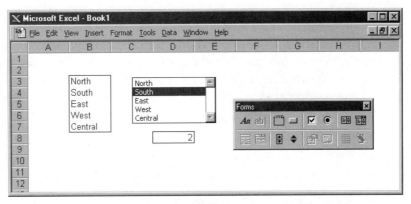

Figure 23.7 shows a list box (top) and the control properties associated with it (bottom).

**FIGURE 23.7**

*The input range for the list box (top) is B3:B7 and the cell link is D8 (bottom). Since the second item in the list is selected, D8 contains the number 2.*

You can use names in place of cell addresses for the list box cell linkages. For example, for the list box shown in Figure 23.7, you could name B3:B7 **Regions**, then enter **Regions** as the input range. The Selection Type setting on the Control tab allows you to control the way users select items:

**Single:** Allows the user to make one selection at a time.

**Multi:** Allows the user to select and deselect multiple items in the list by clicking on them. You cannot have a cell link when Multi is chosen.

**Extend:** Allows the user to select a contiguous range of items by holding down the Shift key (like in the File ➤ Open dialog box). You cannot have a cell link when Extend is chosen.

**TIP**

For *all* controls that are linked to cells, a cell name can be entered for the link. When the control and the linked cell are in the same workbook, the benefit is clarity. But if the control and linked cell are on separate workbooks, the benefit is integrity, and in this type of case, it is very important to refer to cells by name.

## Drop-Down-List Boxes

Drop-down-list boxes are identical to standard list boxes, except you can specify how high the list box is, measured in lines, when dropped down. The primary benefit of drop-down-list boxes is they consume less space.

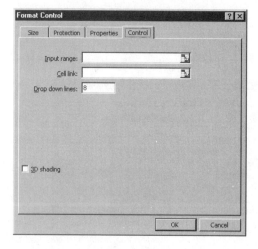

## Buttons

Buttons are not linked to cells—their sole purpose is to run a macro. When you draw a button, the Assign Macro dialog box is displayed.

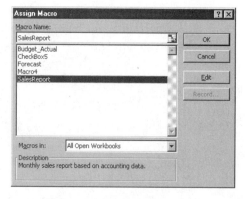

At this stage, there are two ways to assign a macro:

- Select an existing macro from the list.
- Click on Record to record a macro—the Record New Macro dialog box appears.

Chapter 24 provides more information on how to assign macros to buttons, and how to record macros.

**TIP**

Any graphic object can be assigned to a macro, not just "official" buttons. Just select the object and select Tools ➤ Assign Macro. As with official buttons, when the object is clicked on, the macro is run.

In terms of formatting, buttons are similar to text boxes (see Chapter 12). You can format the font and set the text alignment. Figure 23.8 shows some buttons with different formatting.

**FIGURE 23.8**

*Examples of buttons with different formatting*

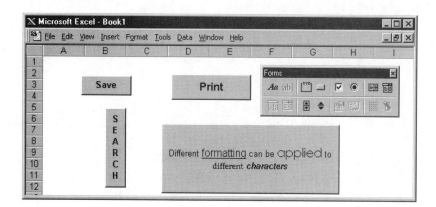

By default, buttons do not print (whereas by default, all other controls do). You can change this by activating the Print Object setting on the Properties tab of the Format Control dialog box.

**MASTERING TROUBLESHOOTING**

### Controls Won't Work if Linked Cells Are Locked and Protected

Here's a frustrating problem: you're developing a worksheet that uses controls to facilitate various kinds of user input. The worksheet is intended to be used by many nontechnical users, and needs to be reasonably bulletproof. When you are done, you protect the worksheet so that users will not be able to delete objects or edit certain locked cells. But now, when you click on controls that are linked to cells, you get an error message. Remember, all cells are locked by default, so after the worksheet was protected, the control was trying to place data into a locked cell.

You can get around this problem without sacrificing the security afforded by cell and worksheet protection. The linked cell does not have to be on the same worksheet as the control—it can be placed on a separate, hidden worksheet. But how does the user know what's happening when the cell is out of view? A locked cell on the visible sheet can refer to the unlocked cell on the hidden sheet using standard worksheet formulas. In fact, using a hidden worksheet for all of the behind-the-scenes machinery in your model is a very good way to build applications.

# Using Controls Effectively

Here are some tips to help you design effective user interfaces using controls.

## Option Buttons vs. List Boxes

Use option buttons when there are only a few choices, and when the choices are relatively static. Otherwise, a list box is probably a better bet. Adding more choices to a list box only involves expanding the input range, as opposed to redesigning the sheet to accommodate more option buttons. Figures 23.9 and 23.10 show some examples using option buttons and list boxes.

## Check Boxes vs. Option Buttons

Technically, one check box can serve the same purpose as a group of two option buttons. But sometimes two option buttons provide more clarity, as shown in Figure 23.11.

**FIGURE 23.9**

*List boxes require less maintenance than option buttons when the contents of the list change, since they are data driven. And when the list is long, list boxes are more aesthetically pleasing.*

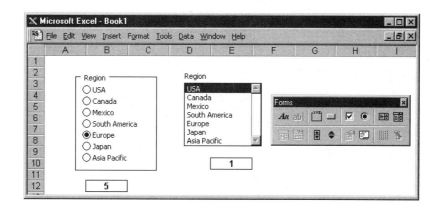

**FIGURE 23.10**

*Option buttons are very effective when there are few choices and the choices are relatively static. List boxes with only two or three choices are not aesthetically appealing.*

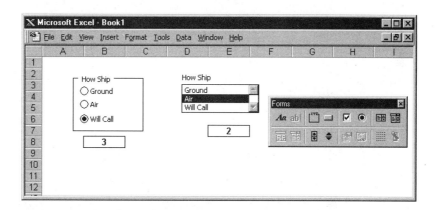

**FIGURE 23.11**

*The single check box can perform the same logical function as the two option buttons. But in this example, the option buttons provide more clarity because the meaning of each choice is spelled out.*

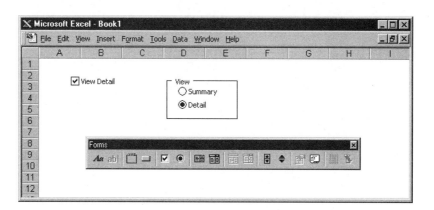

## Emulating a Dialog Box on a Worksheet

You can make a worksheet look similar to a "real" custom dialog box. Color the cells gray and remove gridlines from the sheet, as pictured in Figure 23.12.

**FIGURE 23.12**

A worksheet formatted to look like a dialog box. The controls are formatted with 3-D shading.

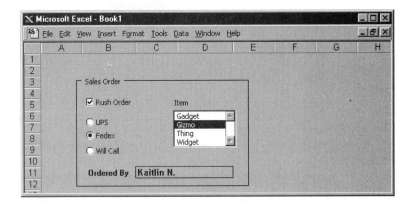

# Dynamic List Boxes

Here is an advanced technique that combines named formulas (covered in Chapter 8) with list boxes. This exercise illustrates how you can use named formulas to dynamically change the contents of a list box—without having to write custom macros.

**1.** On a new worksheet, enter the values shown in range B2:D15:

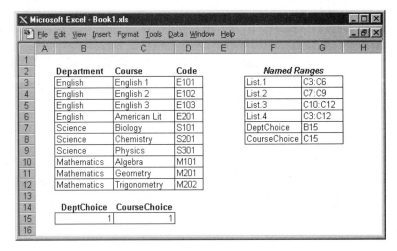

**2.** Name the ranges indicated on the right side of the worksheet.

**3.** Define the name CourseList referring to the following formula:

```
=INDIRECT("List."&DeptChoice)
```

This formula will cause the list to be dynamic. (See Chapter 9 for more information on INDIRECT.)

**4.** Add grouped option buttons to the worksheet:

- Draw a group box.
- Draw four option buttons inside the group box, and link one of them to the cell named DeptChoice (the rest will be linked automatically).

**5.** Add a list box to the worksheet:

- Input range: **CourseList**
- Cell link: **CourseChoice**

Now, when you click on an option button, the contents of the list change automatically.

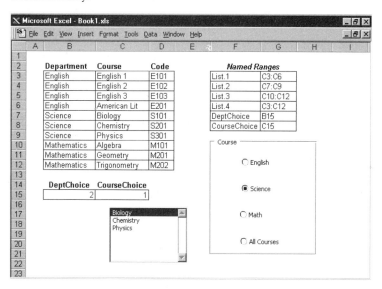

**TIP**

The formula =INDEX(CourseList,CourseChoice) will return the code for the course selected in the list box.

Another common problem is a list with a variable number of rows. For example, a list may be built by querying an external database, and the number of rows may vary from time to time. The standard approach to this problem is to programmatically (or manually!) define a named range after performing the query. Alternatively, the list box can use a name that dynamically calculates the number of rows in the list. Consider the following worksheet:

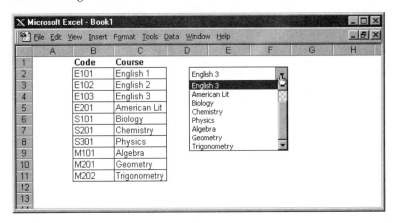

- The name CourseList is defined as

  ```
  =OFFSET($C$2,1,0,COUNTA(OFFSET($C$2,1,0,999,1)),1)
  ```

- This formula assumes a maximum of 999 rows.
- The Input range for the list box is CourseList.
- If new rows of data are added to bottom of list, the drop-down list box automatically includes the new rows.

You have now learned about the custom controls found on the forms toolbar. You have learned how to incorporate controls by linking them to cells. In the next chapter, you will learn more about customizing Excel. In addition, data validation, covered in Chapter 10, goes hand in hand with custom controls.

# Chapter

## 24

### Effectively Using the Macro Recorder

# Effectively Using the Macro Recorder

There are two types of people who create macros: everyday users (non-programmers) who can use the *macro recorder* to automate simple tasks; and application developers, who create complete custom applications. This chapter does not attempt to teach you how to program—that is a very broad topic, requiring an entire book to do it justice. Rather, this chapter focuses on teaching the nonprogrammer how to reap considerable benefit from the macro recorder. Refer to the *Visual Basic User's Guide* and to Excel's online help for in-depth treatment of VBA and other developer-related information.

Once you learn how to record macros, you will learn how to run them using buttons, menus, and toolbars.

## What Is VBA?

Excel was the first application to support VBA—Microsoft's *Visual Basic for Applications*—a language based on the popular Visual Basic programming language. VBA is the programming language that is used in all of the Microsoft Office applications, making it strategically important for software developers. Upon the release of Office 97, VBA is the programming language for Excel, Word, Access, PowerPoint, and Project.

VBA code (and knowledge) is easily transferable between Microsoft applications—a benefit that helps justify the investment in learning VBA.

> **NOTE**
>
> The skills discussed in this chapter do not require that you know VBA. If you want to learn more about it, there is a wealth of information to be found in Excel's online help.

# Working with the Macro Recorder

The *macro recorder* is a tool that translates your actions into VBA macros, without requiring that you understand the underlying language syntax. It works like a tape recorder: when you turn the recorder on, it "records" everything you do. Later, you can play back (run) the macro, and the actions that you previously recorded are repeated. The macro recorder provides two primary benefits:

- You can automate simple, repetitive tasks without the need to know VBA.
- The recorder is an excellent tool for learning VBA.

Here is the most important fact you should know about recorded macros: there are considerable limitations. Yes, you can automate simple tasks. No, you can not write bulletproof applications. Those who become frustrated with the macro recorder are those who attempt to push it beyond its capabilities.

## What Tasks Can Be Automated?

When used in conjunction with general Excel know-how, you can automate surprisingly complex tasks. But using the recorder *effectively* requires that you understand its limitations, and carefully plan a course of action before you start recording. Here are some typical tasks that could be automated with recorded macros:

- Formatting a range of cells
- Opening a workbook, printing it, then closing it
- Opening a text file that was output by a mainframe application, sorting the data, inserting subtotals and grand totals, then printing the report
- Opening several workbooks, consolidating information onto a new workbook, then saving the new workbook
- Performing a query, then charting the results

As you can see from these examples, creating reports is a task that is ideally suited for automation by recording macros.

## Starting to Record a Macro

Before you start, you should carefully plan exactly what you want to accomplish and how to go about it. In fact, you should run through the precise keystrokes that you plan on recording before actually recording them. It can be a frustrating experience to make a minor mistake and have to start over again.

To start recording, choose Tools ➢ Macro ➢ Record New Macro. The Record Macro dialog box, shown in Figure 24.1, appears.

**FIGURE 24.1**

*It is not necessary to know how to program in VBA to make effective use of the macro recorder.*

### Naming the Macro

Enter a meaningful name for your macro into this dialog box. The name can be up to 255 characters long and can consist of letters, numbers, and underscores. There can be no spaces or other punctuation marks—including hyphens. (If you need to separate words, use underscores.) The name must begin with a letter. The list below shows a sampling of valid and invalid macro names.

| Valid Names | Invalid Names | Reason |
|---|---|---|
| MyMacro | My Macro | Contains a space |
| Sales_Report | Sales.Report | Contains a period |
| Summary97 | 97Summary | Starts with a number |
| Get_YTD_Info | Y-T-D | Contains illegal characters |

### Assigning a Shortcut Key

Optionally, you can assign a shortcut key for the macro you are about to record. The shortcut key can be any letter, lowercase or uppercase. If you specify a lowercase letter, once the macro is recorded, you can run it by pressing Ctrl and the shortcut key. If you specify an uppercase letter, you can run the macro by pressing Ctrl and Shift and the shortcut key. Be careful: if you choose a shortcut that is already used by Excel, the macro will take precedence over Excel's built-in shortcut.

### Storing Your Macros

You can select one of three locations from the Store Macro In list box where you can place the recorded macro:

**Personal Macro Workbook:** This workbook, named PERSONAL.XLS, is automatically opened and hidden each time you start Excel. It is located in the XLSTART folder. This is a good place to store macros that you want available at all times. (The Personal Macro Workbook is discussed later in this chapter.)

**This Workbook:** Places the macro in the active workbook.

**New Workbook:** A new workbook will be created, and the macro will be recorded in it.

## Recording Your Actions

After filling in the inputs on the Record Macro dialog box and then clicking on OK, the recording process begins. Behind the scenes, every action you take is translated into a VBA procedure (macro)—including mistakes! The word *Recording* is displayed on the status bar, and a Stop tool is displayed (see Figure 24.2). At this point, you simply perform the actions that you want to record. For example, you might open a workbook, create a chart, and then print the workbook.

> **NOTE**
>
> The recorder tries not to record wasted actions. Suppose you select cell A2, then realize you made a mistake, and then immediately select B2. The selection of cell A2 will not be recorded. Or, suppose you display the wrong dialog box. If you click on Cancel, the action will not be recorded.

## Stopping the Recorder

Once you have completed all the necessary actions for the macro, you can stop recording in two ways:

- Click on the Stop tool.
- Choose Tools ➤ Macro ➤ Stop Recording.

Customizing Excel

**FIGURE 24.2**

*Click on the Stop tool to stop recording. The tool also serves as a visual reminder that you are recording a macro.*

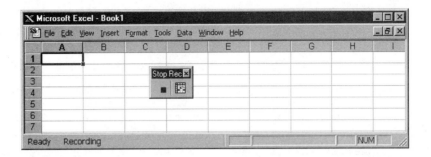

 **WARNING**

Don't forget to stop recording when you've finished your macro. Many users forget to do this and unwittingly record a huge, useless macro. As the macro becomes larger and larger, your computer will start to slow down.

## Recording a Macro from Start to Finish

The following exercise will walk you through the steps of recording a macro and then running the newly recorded macro. You'll enter data onto a worksheet and format it.

1. Choose Tools ➤ Macro ➤ Record New Macro to display the Record New Macro dialog box. Enter a name for your macro.
2. Assign **m** as the shortcut key. Store the macro in a new workbook (so as not to pollute your personal workbook with this learning exercise). Click on OK to start recording.
3. Perform the following actions:

   • Create a new workbook using the File ➤ New command.
   • Enter some data onto the new workbook.
   • Apply some formatting.

4. Stop the recorder by choosing Tools ➤ Macro ➤ Stop Recording.

Before running the macro, close the workbook where you entered and formatted data (no need to save it). Then, press Ctrl+m to run the macro. Just like the first time, a new workbook is created, data is entered, and formatting is applied.

> **TIP**
>
> It is wise to save your work, including the workbook containing the newly recorded macro, before running the macro. Until a macro is tested, consider it capable of unpredictable consequences.

## Recording in Relative or Absolute Reference Mode

By default, the macro recorder records absolute cell references. Sometimes, however, you will want to record using relative references. (Absolute and relative cell references are discussed in Chapter 4.) The second tool on the Stop Recording toolbar, pictured in the margin, is used to toggle between absolute and relative reference mode. The following example illustrates the usefulness of this option.

Suppose you want to record a macro that adds a number in the active cell to the number above the active cell. The macro will place a formula in the cell beneath the active cell (see Figure 24.3).

**FIGURE 24.3**

*The macro needs to act relative to the active cell at the time the macro is run. If B3 is active, the formula should be placed in B4. If D3 is active, the formula should be placed in D4.*

| | A | B | C | D | E | F | G | H | I |
|---|---|---|---|---|---|---|---|---|---|
| 1 | | | | | | | | | |
| 2 | | 10 | | 15 | | | | | |
| 3 | | 20 | | 25 | | | | | |
| 4 | | | | | | | | | |
| 5 | | | | | | | | | |
| 6 | | | | | | | | | |
| 7 | | | | | | | | | |
| 8 | | | | | | | | | |

*Microsoft Excel - Book1 — File Edit View Insert Format Tools Data Window Help*

Create the worksheet shown in Figure 24.3. First, you will record a macro in absolute reference mode. Follow these steps:

1. Select B3. Choose Tools ➢ Macro ➢ Record New Macro.
2. Name the macro. Assign a shortcut key. Store the macro in the active workbook. Click on OK to start recording.
3. Select B4. Enter the formula **=B2+B3**.
4. Stop recording.

To see how it worked, clear cell B4. Then select D3 and run your new macro using the shortcut key. Since you were in Absolute reference mode as the macro was recorded, the formula is placed in B4, not in D4. Regardless of which cell is active, the macro will always place the formula in B4.

Now, record the same macro again. This time switch to relative reference mode before you do step 3. After you are done recording, test the new macro:

1. Clear B4 and D4.
2. Select B3 and run the macro.
3. Select D3 and run the macro.

Since you recorded the macro in relative reference mode, the macro enters formulas relative to the active cell.

**TIP**

You can switch back and forth between absolute reference mode and relative reference mode at any time while recording a macro.

Here are the two key facts to remember about recording macros in absolute or relative reference mode:

- When you record in absolute reference mode, Excel records the absolute reference of every cell you select.
- When you record in relative reference mode, and you select one or more cells, Excel records the selection relative to the previously selected cell.

# Recording Macros That Work

Learning to use the macro recorder is one thing. But creating a successful result is quite another. In this section, you will learn about some of the common problems that occur with recorded macros, and some techniques for solving them.

## What Can Go Wrong with Recorded Macros?

The initial feeling of empowerment provided by the macro recorder can quickly vanish as you try to solve real-world problems. Here are four common ways you might get into trouble:

**Ambiguous Intent** - Many actions you record can be interpreted in several ways by the macro recorder. For example, assume cell B2 is the active cell, the macro recorder is on, and you select cell B3. Do you really mean B3? Or did you mean to move down one row relative to the active cell?

**Conditions May Change** - Picture an automobile with a trip recorder. You want to automate the task of getting to work each day, so you get in the car, turn on the recorder, drive to work, then turn off the recorder. But everything goes wrong when the "macro" is played back the next morning. The problem stems from the fact that things are different when you play back the macro: a bike is in the driveway, the traffic light is red, and there is a traffic jam. Similarly, obstacles may arise unexpectedly when you play back your recorded VBA macros.

**Over-Recording** - Many recorded macros start out with a blank slate—unnecessarily! By using templates (covered in Chapter 10) you can simplify macro recording. Templates can be preformatted, and they can contain predefined names, styles, and formulas that make the job easier.

**Inherent Limitations** - The macro recorder is pretty good at automating everyday tasks. But if you want to create serious applications, you will need to learn how to write macros yourself.

## Selecting Variable Size Ranges

Suppose that every month you are responsible for creating a report based on data that is output from a mainframe. (See Chapter 29 to learn more about importing data.) The mainframe outputs a text file in CSV format (comma separated values). You need to copy the data into another workbook, which contains related information. Figure 24.4 shows the text file, opened in Excel.

**FIGURE 24.4**

*Sales data output as text file from mainframe. The number of rows varies from month to month.*

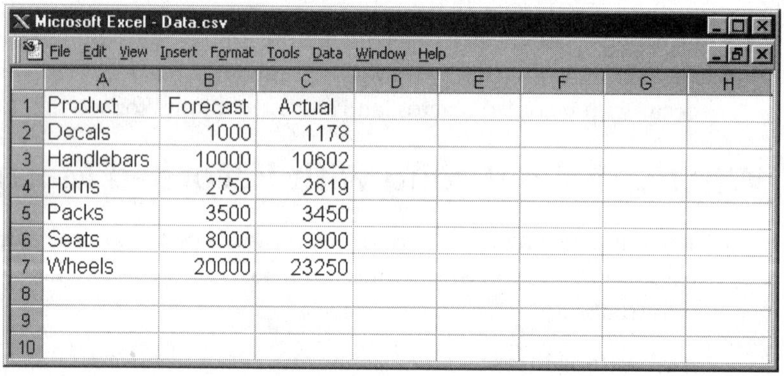

This is plan of action for recording the macro:

1. Start recording.
2. Open the workbook where you want to copy the source data (REPORT).
3. Open the text file—by default, A1 is the active cell.

Customizing Excel

4. Select the data, and copy it to the Clipboard.
5. Activate the REPORT workbook and select the destination cell.
6. Paste the data onto the active worksheet.
7. Print the worksheet.
8. Stop recording.

There is one small, yet typical, problem that you must deal with: remember, the number of rows in the text file is variable. It does no good to record the selection of A1:C7 as an absolute reference, because next month the data may reside in A1:C10. Therefore, the task of selecting the data to be copied (step 4) presents a problem.

The solution is to use a command that selects the *current region*, rather then using the mouse to select A1:C7. (The current region is a rectangular range of data bordered by any combination of blank rows or blank columns.) At step 4, instead of selecting the range using the mouse, press Ctrl+Shift+*. A1:C7 is selected, but the recorded macro is different than if you had selected A1:C7 with the mouse.

## Formatting a Column of Numbers

The database shown in Figure 24.5 is a slight variation of that from Figure 24.4. There is a column for units (an integer value), and dollars (currency).

*The recorded macro must apply a currency format to the values in the Dollars column. The number of rows varies from month to month.*

| | A | B | C |
|---|---|---|---|
| 1 | Product | Units | Dollars |
| 2 | Decals | 320 | 1178.55 |
| 3 | Handlebars | 299 | 10602.2 |
| 4 | Horns | 266 | 2619.75 |
| 5 | Packs | 309 | 3450.03 |
| 6 | Seats | 245 | 9900.8 |
| 7 | Wheels | 504 | 23250.32 |

Microsoft Excel - Data.csv
File Edit View Insert Format Tools Data Window Help

The recorded macro must apply a currency format to the Dollars column. Again, the number of rows is variable from month to month—formatting C2:C7 won't work when next month there are more rows. Nor can you select the *current region*, as in the previous problem, because you would mistakenly format the Units column. The solution is simple: select the entire column C before applying the currency format. It doesn't matter that a number format will be applied to C1—the format has no effect on text.

## Charting a Variable Number of Rows

Suppose that you want to record a macro that charts the data in Figure 24.4. Remember, the number of rows varies from month to month. Don't use the ChartWizard to create the chart—no matter how you go about it, recording the ChartWizard results in a macro that charts an absolute range. Here is a procedure that works:

1. Start recording.
2. Open the file.
3. Make sure the active cell is positioned within the data. Press Ctrl+Shift+* to select the current region.
4. Create the chart using one of these techniques:

   - Press F11 to create a chart sheet.
   - Use the default Chart tool (not the ChartWizard) to draw an embedded chart.

5. Stop recording.

The Chart Wizard thwarts the use of current region by converting it to an absolute range, a problem overcome by using the Chart tool.

## Summing a Column with a Variable Number of Rows

Using the data in Figure 24.5, suppose that your recorded macro must add a total to the bottom of column C. This presents two problems:

- How do you select the cell at the bottom of column C? (Remember, the number of rows is variable.)
- How do you write the formula? Regardless of the reference mode, the AutoSum tool will record the wrong formula.

Follow these steps to record a macro that will sum a column with a variable number of rows, regardless of the number of rows:

1. Start recording.
2. Open the file.
3. Select C1.
4. Hold down the End key, then press ↓ (selects the last number in the column).
5. Switch to relative reference mode.
6. Press ↓ (moving the active cell to C8).
7. Enter the formula **=SUM(OFFSET($C$1,1,0,ROW()-2))**.
8. Stop recording.

In plain language, the formula reads, "Sum the range of cells beginning one cell beneath C1, and include the number of rows equal to the row number containing the formula, minus two (accounting for the header row)." The OFFSET and ROW functions are among the most useful worksheet functions—they are both covered in Chapter 9.

## Be Aware of the Active Cell When You Start Recording

Suppose you want record a macro to enter a formula into cell A5 that sums cells A1:A4. You enter your numbers into cells A1:A4, then select cell A5. You turn on the macro recorder, enter your sum formula, and stop recording. To test the macro you clear cell A5 and run the macro, and it works fine. Later you run the macro again—but this time cell D6 is the active cell. The macro enters the formula **=SUM(D2:D5)** into cell D6—not at all what you intended.

The problem is that your macro does not have a defined starting position. You have

recorded a macro that sums the four cells above the active cell, wherever the active cell happens to be. Fixing the problem is simple—for the first step of the macro, you must record the selection of the cell where you want to enter the formula (in this example, cell A5). So, start the macro recorder, click on the cell where you want the macro to begin, then record the rest of the macro. If the starting cell is already selected when you begin recording, click on it anyway. You can also begin a macro by going to a named range using the Edit ➤ Go To command (or the Name box), and the macro will record the selection by name.

# Working with the Personal Macro Workbook

Earlier in this chapter, you learned how to record macros into a *personal macro workbook* named PERSONAL.XLS. When you first install Excel, the personal macro workbook does not exist. PERSONAL.XLS is created the first time you record a macro into it. It is stored in the XLSTART folder (located in the folder where you installed Excel).

**TIP**

All workbooks in the XLSTART folder are automatically opened each time you start Excel. You can also place templates in XLSTART, which is covered in Chapter 10.

PERSONAL.XLS is a good place to store macros that are used on an everyday basis. Here are some important things you should know about it:

- PERSONAL.XLS is automatically opened each time you start Excel; however, it is automatically hidden.
- If you know VBA, you can manually edit PERSONAL.XLS. Use the Window ➤ Unhide command to view it.
- Since it is opened every time you start Excel, you may want to avoid placing large macros on it that you don't regularly use.

# Running Macros

There are several ways to run a macro. Earlier in this chapter, you learned how to assign a shortcut key to a recorded macro. In this section, you will learn how to run a macro in several ways:

- Using the Excel menu
- From a button
- Automatically when a workbook is opened or closed
- From a toolbar and menu bar

## Running a Macro from the Excel Menu

To run a macro from the Excel menu, choose Tools ➤ Macro ➤ Macros to display the Macro dialog box.

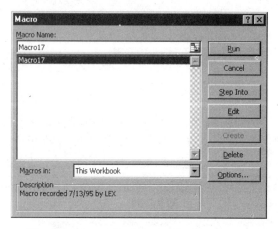

The drop-down-list box on the bottom of the dialog box determines which macros are listed. By default, all macros in all open workbooks are listed. You can choose to list only those macros that reside in a particular workbook by selecting the workbook from the Macros In list. To run a macro, select it from the list and click on Run. The Macro dialog box provides several additional capabilities:

**Step Into:** Click on this button to run the macro step-by-step. For programmers, this is a useful debugging tool.

**Edit:** The module containing the macro is activated, and the macro is displayed for editing purposes.

**Delete:** Deletes the selected macro.

**Options:** Lets you change the shortcut key and macro description.

## Assigning a Macro to a Button

It is a simple task to place a button on a worksheet, and assign a macro to it which will run when the button is clicked on. Here's how:

**1.** Display the Forms toolbar using the View ➢ Toolbars command. (The Forms toolbar is discussed in depth in Chapter 23.)

**2.** Click on the Button tool, then draw the button on the worksheet. (Drawing a button is just like drawing other objects—see Chapter 12 to learn about graphic objects and drawing tools.) The Assign Macro dialog box appears.

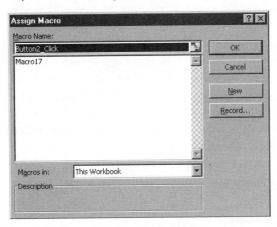

**3.** Select a macro from the list, and click on OK.

If the macro doesn't yet exist, you can click on the Record button, which will display the Record Macro dialog box. The macro you record is automatically assigned to the button. To change the macro assignment for a button, right-click on the button, then choose Assign Macro from the shortcut menu.

## Running Macros Automatically When a Workbook Is Opened or Closed

You can create special macros that run automatically when a workbook is opened or closed. This is accomplished by placing macros in the workbook that are given one of the following special reserved names:

**Auto_Open**   A macro named Auto_Open in a workbook will run automatically when the workbook is opened.

**Auto_Close**   A macro named Auto_Close in a workbook will run automatically *before* the workbook is closed.

### Suppressing Auto_Open or Auto_Close Macros

Suppose that you want to suppress an Auto_Open or Auto_Close macro from running. How do you do it? Just hold down the Shift key while you open or close the workbook.

# Building Command Bars

As we explained earlier in this book, prior to Excel 8, toolbars and menu bars were different animals entirely. Toolbars consisted of buttons and other icons. Menu bars, such as the default worksheet menu bar (containing the File, Edit, and other menus) consisted of text. Both objects served the same purpose—providing an interface for issuing commands. Now, they have converged into *command bars*. A command bar may contain icons, text, and drop-down menus. This provides not only a more flexible interface, but there is also less to learn—when learning to build command bars, one set of skills replaces what used to require two different skills. In the following discussion, the term *command bar* is used to describe both menu bars and toolbars.

Whereas a macro that is assigned to a button on a worksheet is only available when the worksheet is active, macros assigned to command bars are available whenever the command bar is displayed, regardless of the active worksheet. This is a logical approach when the macro is not specific to one worksheet.

## Creating a New Command Bar

In this section, you will learn how to create a new command bar. First, choose Tools ➢ Customize. (If the Toolbars tab is not active, click on it.) The Customize dialog box appears, shown in Figure 24.6.

**FIGURE 24.6**

*The Toolbars tab of the Customize dialog box lets you hide and unhide existing command bars and create new command bars.*

> **NOTE**
>
> A simple service provided by the Toolbars tab, shown in Figure 24.6, is the ability to hide or unhide command bars (toolbars) using the check boxes appearing next to each command bar.

Click on the New button and enter a name for your new command bar. Then click on OK.

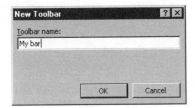

At this point, a new, blank command bar will have been created and displayed.

## Adding Commands to a Command Bar

You just learned how to create a new command bar. Next, you will learn how to add commands. On the Customize dialog box pictured in Figure 24.6, click on the Commands tab. The dialog box is shown in Figure 24.7.

**FIGURE 24.7**

*The Commands tab lists all Excel commands by category. Notice the blank command bar to the right of the dialog box.*

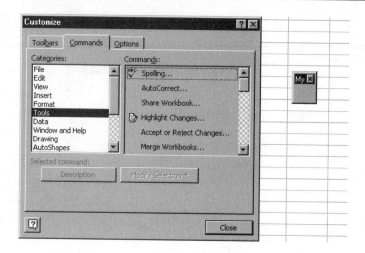

> **NOTE**
>
> Adding a command to a newly created command bar is no different than adding a command to an existing command bar. After all, when you create a new command bar, it exists, even though it has no commands on it!

First, let's add a built-in command—the spell check command, for instance. Referring to Figure 24.7, select the Commands tab and click on Tools in the Category list. Then, drag the Spelling icon from the Commands list, and drop it onto your blank command bar. It's that simple. Removing an item entails dragging it away from the command bar, and dropping it somewhere other than on top of another command bar.

Earlier in this chapter, you learned how to record a macro. Suppose there is a macro that you recorded in the personal macro workbook. In the following discussion you will learn how to place a command on your command bar that will run your recorded macro. The starting point is the Commands tab of the Customize dialog box, shown in Figure 24.7.

In the Categories list, scroll down and click on the Macros category. Drag the Custom Button (yes, that confounded smiley face!), and drop it on top of your new command bar. Now, here's the key: right-click on the smiley-face icon and choose Assign Macro from the shortcut menu (see Figure 24.8). This shortcut menu is only available if the Customize dialog box is showing—it will *not* appear if you right-click on a command icon otherwise. Choose your macro from the list, and click on OK.

Customizing Excel

**FIGURE 24.8**

*Choose Assign Macro from the shortcut menu to add a command to your command bar.*

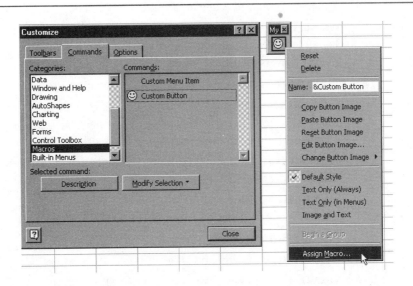

## You Don't Have to Use the Smiley Face!

You can use any of Excel's myriad of built-in icons on a custom command bar and override the icon's default behavior by assigning a macro to it. In fact, the steps are exactly the same as with the smiley face.

For example, suppose you have recorded a macro that opens a certain workbook,

prints it, then closes it. You can use the built-in Print icon, then assign a macro to it by choosing Assign Macro from the shortcut menu. Or, if there are no icons that suit your purpose (and you are artistically inclined), pick one that is close, then choose the Edit Button Image command from the shortcut menu. This displays a dialog box that allows you to edit the bitmap image.

Here is a brief explanation of the other commands found on the shortcut menu pictured above. Keep in mind that this menu is displayed when you right-click on a specific command on a command bar *only* while the Customize dialog box is showing.

**Reset:** If you assign a macro to a built-in Excel command, this command unassigns the macro and resets the command to its default behavior.

**Delete:** Command is deleted from command bar.

**Name:** For a text command, this is the text that will appear on the command bar. For an icon, this text appears in a yellow pop-up help box when the mouse pointer hovers over the command.

**Copy Button Image:** Copies the icon bitmap to the Clipboard.

**Paste Button Image:** Pastes a graphic image from the Clipboard, which replaces the icon graphic. (The image must have been previously copied to the Clipboard from a graphics program or some other source.)

**Reset Button Image:** If you modify a built-in icon, this resets it back to its default appearance.

**Edit Button Image:** Displays a bitmap editor, allowing you to edit the graphic image. (See the sidebar on this topic earlier in this chapter.)

**Change Button Image:** Presents a palette of canned images to choose from.

**Default Style:** Command shown in default style.

**Text Only (Always):** Command always shown as text.

**Text Only (In Menus):** Command shown as text only in menus.

**Image and Text:** Both icon and text shown.

**Begin A Group:** Inserts a gap before the selected command, thus allowing related command to be visually grouped together.

**Assign Macro:** Displays a list of macros to assign to the command.

You have now learned how to record macros, and how to add your macros to the command system. Worksheet developers should also be aware of custom controls, covered in Chapter 23, and data validation, covered in Chapter 10. In the next chapter, you'll learn how to create a custom application from start to finish using many of the skills you learned in this chapter.

# Chapter

## 25

### Building a Data-Driven Model

# Building a Data-Driven Model

T his chapter will walk you through all the steps to create a workbook model intended to analyze the performance of a fictitious company that sells bicycle parts. You will utilize skills that have been discussed throughout the book, and several new techniques will be introduced along the way. Be forewarned—this is an *advanced* chapter. To get the most out of it, there are certain core skills you should possess:

- You should know how to work with pivot tables, covered in Chapter 20.
- You should understand names (particularly named formulas), covered in Chapter 8.
- You should have charting experience—charting is covered in Chapters 13 through 16.
- You should be familiar with custom controls, covered in Chapter 23.

## Data-Driven Modeling

At times, you will be asked to approach problems in a way seemingly more complex than need be. Here's why:

In the real world, rare is the worksheet model that is *data-driven*. Most semi-complex models are built making certain hard-wired assumptions as to the number of items in various lists (i.e., regions, customers, products, etc.). As a result, such models require considerable maintenance each time, for example, when a new product line is introduced. In a perfect world, the new product line would be entered once, into a central database, and all of your models/reports would automatically adjust. (In this regard, it is certainly worth considering Excel's capabilities for accessing external databases, which is discussed in Chapter 19.)

> **NOTE**
> There is no formal definition as to what is *data-driven* and what is not. Rather, the term implies a flexible, adaptive approach to model design and construction, where, to some extent, the model responds appropriately to data changes.

But even without a central database, it is entirely possible to construct models that do not require time-consuming modification with each addition or deletion of an item. Data-driven modeling takes more time and requires a higher skill level. Obviously, you must consider the volatility of a given list when deciding how flexible of a design should be implemented. No need to allow for more than 12 months per year, for example. (Unless your organization uses 13 accounting periods!) On the other hand, who would have thought that the Soviet Union would break up?

## The Business Requirement

The remainder of this chapter is a multipart tutorial. (Don't be intimidated—many of the steps are optional.) In this tutorial, you will construct a workbook for a fictitious company named *Western BikeStuff* used to analyze sales. Management needs to track actual sales performance against forecast.

- The company carries four product lines: helmets, handlebars, seats, and racks. More may be added in the future, so the model must be insensitive to the number of product lines (data-driven).
- Products are sold in two markets: the United States and Europe. Even if new markets are added in the future, management will combine all foreign markets into one for analysis purposes (not data-driven).
- Sales and forecast data is tracked per market, per product, per month.
- The program must start off by displaying a high-level summary, and then allow the users to "drill down" to a greater level of detail.

## Getting Started

This tutorial does not instruct you to save your work. Needless to say, however, you should save the workbook periodically. In addition, bear in mind that every keystroke is not provided—you are expected to possess the base skills itemized at the top of the chapter.

Create a new workbook, and save it as **INFO.XLS**. Rename the first worksheet *Data*. For simplicity, delete all other worksheets.

# Building the Database

The first step is to build the worksheet database which will be analyzed by the model. Tedious though this task may be, it is often the first step in a modeling project. Fortunately, there are some shortcuts along the way that should be useful to you now and in the future.

**1.** On the Data worksheet, enter the following information:

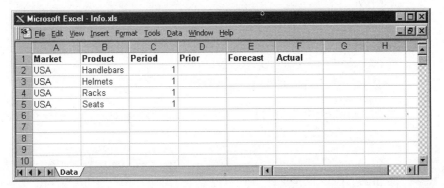

## Understanding the Database Fields

Here are descriptions for the six database fields (columns):

**Market:** geographic marketing region—United States or Europe (model is *not* being designed to be adaptive to added or deleted markets)

**Product:** company sells four product lines—handlebars, helmets, racks, and seats (model will adapt if new product lines are added)

**Period:** 1 through 12, representing month of the year

**Prior:** sales for the prior year (dollars)

**Forecast:** sales forecast for the current year (dollars)

**Actual:** sales for the current year (dollars)

**2.** Copy the range A2:C5, and paste it at the bottom of the data (A6). Then change the number in C6:C9 to a **2** (for period 2).

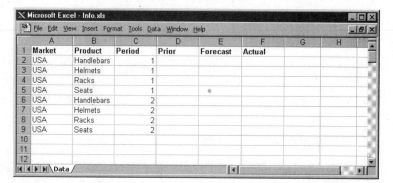

**3.** Repeat step 2 above 10 more times, for periods 3 through 12. (When this step is complete, the data will extend to row 49.)

**4.** Copy the range A2:C49, and paste it starting at A50. Then change the contents of A50:A97 to **Europe**.

**5.** Select D2:F97 and enter: **=INT(RAND()*10000)** into the range. Enter the formula into the selected range by pressing Ctrl+↵.

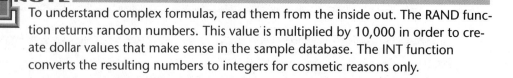

**NOTE**

To understand complex formulas, read them from the inside out. The RAND function returns random numbers. This value is multiplied by 10,000 in order to create dollar values that make sense in the sample database. The INT function converts the resulting numbers to integers for cosmetic reasons only.

**6.** With D2:F97 still selected, choose Edit ➤ Copy, then Edit ➤ Paste Special. Choose Values on the Paste Special dialog box. (This replaces the formulas with the underlying values, so that the random numbers don't constantly recalculate.)

## Naming the Database Using a Dynamic Range Name

You have already created a database on the Data worksheet. Soon, you will create pivot tables using this data. However, if you build a pivot table based on the range A1:F97, then add rows to the bottom of the database later, the new rows will not be reflected in the pivot tables. For this reason, we are going to name the database using a *dynamic named range*—a special named range that dynamically expands or contracts based on the number of data rows. (This skill is explained in Chapter 8.) This special named range will allow the pivot tables to automatically stay in synch when rows are added to the database.

With the Data worksheet active, choose Insert ➤ Name ➤ Define. Create the name **Database** that refers to the following:

```
=OFFSET(Data!$A$1,0,0,COUNTA(Data!$A:$A),6)
```

> **TIP**
>
> The name Database will automatically expand or contract based on the number of values in column A. Since a named formula is not a "real" named range, it will not display in the Name box. To test the name, press F5 and type **Database**—the range A1:F97 should be selected. Bear in mind this formula requires that the Market field must contain a value, and there can be no information located in column A outside of the database range.

## Setting Up the Globals

Most moderately complex workbooks include various settings and calculations that are used by worksheets throughout the workbook. You can save a lot of time by defining such settings one time only on a worksheet, the sole purpose of which is to store *global* settings. The BikeStuff information system, as designed, has only two such settings. Still, it is worthwhile to set up a globals worksheet as a learning exercise.

Insert a new worksheet, and name it *Settings*—it will be used to store global settings that will be referred to by other worksheets. With Settings active, follow these steps:

1. Name cell B1 **Current.Year**. (Optionally, place the text **Current.Year** in cell A1 as a visual reminder.)
2. Enter the formula **=YEAR(TODAY())** into cell B1 to calculate the current year.
3. Name cell B3 **View.Choice**. (Optionally, place the text **View.Choice** in cell A3 as a visual reminder.)

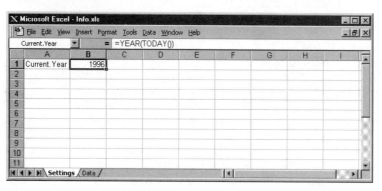

# Building the Home Worksheet

The worksheet named Home will be the first sheet displayed when the workbook is opened. It provides a very high-level summary, from which the user can *drill down* into a greater level of detail. This summary information will be presented in the form of a chart. (Charting is covered in Chapters 13 through 16.) Again, a pivot table will do most of the work for you.

## The Basic Home Worksheet

In this series of exercises, you will build a basic version of the Home worksheet. It will contain a pivot table and a linked chart. Pivot table page fields will be used to filter the data and to redraw the chart accordingly. (The finished worksheet is shown later in the chapter.)

To start with, insert a new worksheet and name it **Home**. Choose Data ➢ PivotTable Report to display the PivotTable Wizard, then follow these steps:

**1.** At Step 1 of the Wizard, choose Microsoft Excel List or Database.

**2.** At Step 2 of the Wizard, enter the range name **Database**. (The Wizard will automatically default to Database.)

**3.** At Step 3 of the Wizard, drag the Market and Product fields into the page area, then drag Prior, Forecast, and Actual fields into the data area, as shown below.

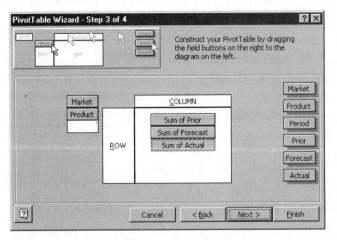

**4.** *Optional*: The data field labels in your pivot table all begin with a *Sum of* prefix. While still at Step 3 of the Wizard, double-click on the three data field buttons, and change the names to **Prior**, **Forecast**, and **Actual**, respectively, with one special caveat: since these names can't conflict with database field names, place a trailing space at the end of each word.

**5.** At Step 4 of the Wizard, check the Existing Worksheet option and enter **B5** as the starting cell.

**6.** Still at Step 4 of the Wizard, click on the Options button. Check the Refresh On Open setting. Click on OK, then finish the Wizard. This will cause the pivot table to automatically refresh when the workbook is opened.

## Creating the Home Worksheet Chart

**1.** Select the data area of the pivot table (range B8:C11). If you are unable to select this range, you must first turn off *structured selection* (a pivot table feature discussed in Chapter 21). From the pivot table shortcut menu, choose Select ➢ Enable Selection to turn on/off structured selection.

**2.** With B8:C11 selected, use the ChartWizard to create a column chart from this data. Do not include a legend in the chart.

**3.** Size and position the chart so that it completely obscures the data area of the pivot table, but not its page field drop-down menus.

**4.** *Optional*: Format the chart to have no border and to not move or size with cells.

**5.** *Optional*: Select the y-axis of the chart with your mouse. Choose Format ➢ Selected Axis ➢ Number. Choose the Custom category from the Category list box. Enter the following custom number format into the Type edit box: **#,##0,** (the purpose of this formatting code is to show the values in thousands).

To finish up, choose Tools ➢ Options ➢ View to turn off the display of gridlines and row and column headers on the Home worksheet. A completed example is shown in Figure 25.1. Remember, since the data is based on random numbers, the values on your chart will differ from Figure 25.1.

**NOTE**

When you pick a new item from one of the page fields, the column resizes, which in turn causes the chart to resize. To suppress this behavior, right-click on a cell inside the pivot table and choose Options from the shortcut menu. Uncheck the AutoFormat Table setting and click on OK. Then, set column C to the desired width using Format ➢ Column ➢ Width.

# Adding Charting Options to the Home Worksheet

This exercise is optional, and requires good charting skills (Chapters 13 through 16), a solid understanding of named ranges and named formulas (Chapter 8), and familiarity

**FIGURE 25.1**

*The chart is lying on top of the data area of the pivot table. The pivot table page fields are left showing.*

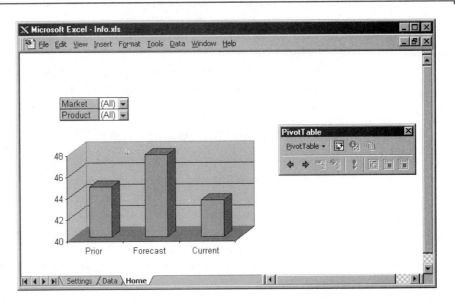

with custom controls (Chapter 23). If you'd like, you can skip ahead to the section entitled "Comparing Actual to Prior," then come back here later. In this exercise, on the Home sheet, you will allow the user to choose the type of chart, using option buttons.

## Placing the Supporting Charts and Data on a Separate Worksheet

In order to create a chart on the Home worksheet where the chart type can be manipulated using controls, several items of background "plumbing" need to be created. These will be placed on a separate sheet that will eventually be hidden from view.

Insert a new worksheet, and name it **Home_Charts**. This name will serve as a reminder that the sheet contains charts supporting the Home worksheet. This sheet can be hidden later.

Activate the **Home_Charts** worksheet and follow these steps:

1. Using Format ➢ Column ➢ Width, set the width of column D to **50** or so. Using Format ➢ Row ➢ Height, set the height of rows 2 and 4 to **125** or so.
2. Name these three cells:

    D2    **Chart.1**

    D4    **Chart.2**

    B1    **Chart.Choice**

**3.** Now you will move the chart from the home sheet to Home_Charts. Activate the Home worksheet and select the chart that you created earlier. Choose Edit ➤ Cut from the menu. Now activate the Home_Charts worksheet and select cell D2. Choose Edit ➤ Paste from the menu. Your chart will be pasted into cell D2. Move and/or resize the chart so that it fits completely within the boundaries of cell D2.

**TIP**

To resize the chart (or any object) so that it fits precisely on a cell or range of cells, hold down the Alt key while you move and resize it. This causes the object to move and size with the gridlines.

**4.** Select your chart and choose Format ➤ Selected Chart Area ➤ Patterns from the menu. Choose None under the Area option. Click on OK.

**5.** Select the chart in cell D2 and choose Edit ➤ Copy from the menu. Then select cell D4 and choose Edit ➤ Paste. Move and/or resize the chart if necessary to make it fit completely within cell D4. With the chart in cell D4 selected, choose Chart ➤ Chart Type from the menu. Change the chart type of this chart to a 2-D Bar. Click on OK.

**6.** Use the Tools ➤ Options ➤ View menu to turn off the display of gridlines on the Home_Charts worksheet.

The Home_Charts worksheet is shown here:

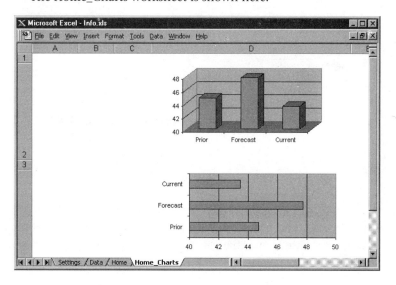

## Adding the Option Buttons

Now that you have prepared the two charts on the Home_Charts worksheet, you can add the option buttons that will control the chart display on the Home worksheet.

Activate the Home worksheet and follow these steps:

1. Using the Forms toolbar, place two option buttons on the Home worksheet.
2. Change the caption of the first option button to **Column** and the caption of the second option button to **Bar**.

**NOTE**

To edit the text of any control, right-click on the control and choose Edit Text from the shortcut menu.

3. Right-click on the **Column** option button and choose Format Control from the shortcut menu. Choose the Control tab from the Format Control dialog box. In the Cell Link text box enter **Chart.Choice**.

This causes the two option buttons, when clicked on, to place the value 1 or 2, respectively, into the cell named Chart.Choice (located on Home_Charts).

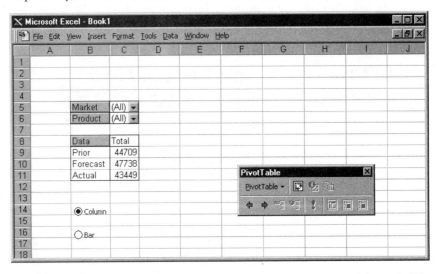

Next, you will create a picture object that is linked to a named formula. The named formula, in turn, causes one chart or the other to be displayed on the home view, based on which option button is clicked on.

## Creating the Picture Control and Title

With the supporting structures in place, you can now add the picture control that will display the charts on the Home worksheet and the Home worksheet title to complete the view.

1. Activate Home_Charts, and select one of the large cells with a chart. Choose Edit ➤ Copy. Activate Home, select cell A7, and while holding down the Shift key, choose Edit ➤ Paste Picture Link. You have created a picture object that is linked to the cell on Home_Charts.

2. Position the picture so that it completely covers the data area of the pivot table but not the page field drop-downs or the option buttons.

3. Next, you will create a named formula referring to the cell underneath one chart or the other, based on the value in Chart.Choice. Create a named formula using the name **Chart.Range.Choice**, referring to the following:

```
=IF(Chart.Choice=1,Chart.1,Chart.2)
```

4. Select the picture and replace the contents of the formula bar with the formula **=Chart.Range.Choice**. Notice that selecting between the two option buttons now changes the chart displayed in the picture control.

5. In cell B2 of the Home worksheet, enter the following formula. (Optionally, format the title with a large, boldfaced font.)

```
="Western BikeStuff - "&Current.Year
```

6. If necessary, use the Tools ➤ Options ➤ View menu to turn off the display of gridlines and column headers on the Home worksheet. An example of the completed Home worksheet is shown below.

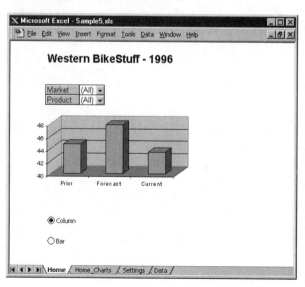

# Comparing Actual to Prior Year

The Home sheet displays a high-level summary. Now, you will build the Comparison worksheet, which uses a line chart that compares the current year's actual sales to one of two values, based on user input: forecast or prior. Again, we'll use a pivot table to organize the data for charting.

## Creating the Pivot Table

In this exercise you will create a new worksheet with a pivot table. To begin, insert a worksheet into INFO.XLS and name it **Comparison**.

1. Choose Data ➤ PivotTable Report from the menu. In Step 1 of the PivotTable Wizard, choose Another PivotTable.

### Why Use Another PivotTable as the Data Source?

Behind a pivot table lies a hidden data cache, sometimes referred to as a *multidimensional cache.* The cache is the reason that pivot tables respond quickly as you pivot them—all of the data combinations are precalculated.

When you use an existing pivot table (Table1) as the data source for a new pivot table (Table2), here's what is really happening behind the scenes: Table2 uses Table1's *cache* as its data source. A single workbook can have many pivot tables, all based on one cache. This is a very memory efficient technique. Another benefit is that when you refresh any one of these tables, all other tables based on the same cache refresh automatically. The cache is discussed further in Chapter 21.

2. In Step 2 of the Wizard, select the first pivot table. This causes the new pivot table to share a cache with the original table (see the sidebar "Why Use Another Pivot-Table as the Data Source").
3. In Step 3, drag the **Market** and **Product** fields into the Page area, the **Period** field into the Column area and the **Prior**, **Forecast**, and **Actual** fields into the Data area.

4. *Optional*: The data field labels in your pivot table all begin with a *Sum of* prefix. As with the pivot table created on the Home sheet, change the field names to **Prior**, **Forecast**, and **Actual**, respectively, each with a trailing space.

5. In Step 4, click on the Options button and uncheck the Grand Totals For Rows and the Grand Totals For Columns options, then click on OK.

6. Still at Step 4 of the Wizard, choose Existing Worksheet, and cell B2 as the starting cell. Then click on Finish (see Figure 25.2).

**FIGURE 25.2**

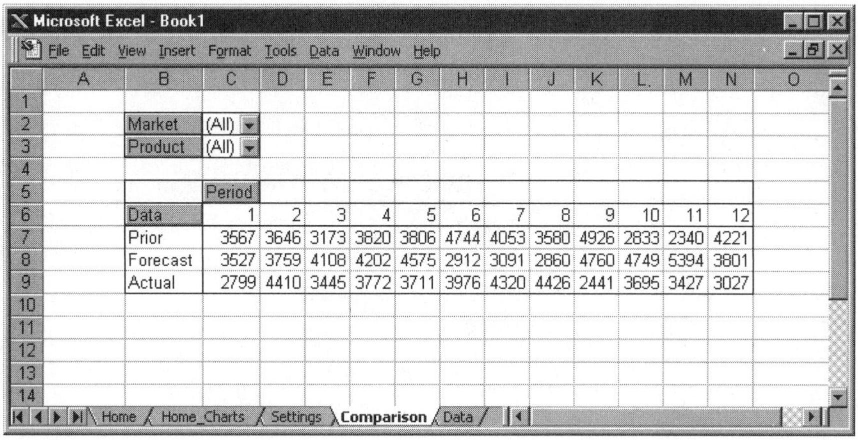

*The finished pivot table. Don't worry about the appearance— the chart is going to obscure most of the pivot table.*

## Adding the Controls and Names

In the following exercise, you will add option buttons to the worksheet. Later, these buttons will allow the user to chart either Prior or Forecast.

1. Using the Forms toolbar, place a group box on the Comparison worksheet. Place it approximately over cells C17:F21. Change the caption of the group box to **Compare Actual to:**. It doesn't matter where you place the group box. A range is specified only so that you will achieve a result similar to the worksheets pictured in the accompanying figures.

2. Add two option buttons inside the group box. Make the caption of the upper option button **Prior Year** and the caption of the lower option button **Current Year Forecast**.

3. Right-click on the **Prior Year** option button and choose Format Control from the shortcut menu. Choose the Control tab from the Format Control dialog box

and in the Cell Link edit box, enter **View.Choice** (a name you defined when you built the Globals sheet). Click on OK.

4. Test the option buttons. When you click them, the two option buttons should place the numbers 1 and 2, respectively, into the cell View.Choice.

5. Select the range of cells containing the Period field headings in the pivot table (range C6:N6). Name this range **Period**. Name cell B6 (in the pivot table) **Series.Label**.

6. Define a named formula **Data.Choice** referring to the following:

   =OFFSET(Period,View.Choice,0)

7. Define a named formula **Series.Choice** referring to the following:

   =OFFSET(Series.Label,View.Choice,0)

Your worksheet should now appear similar to this one.

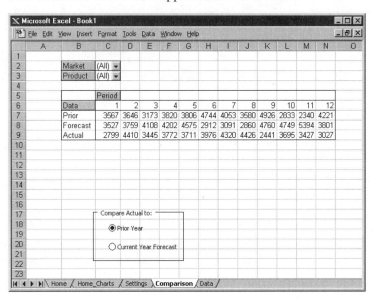

## Creating the Chart

In the next exercise, you will create a chart based on the pivot table.

1. Select the data area of the pivot table (range B6:N9). Then use the ChartWizard to create a line chart from this data. Include a legend.

2. Size and position the chart so that it completely obscures the data area of the pivot table, but not its page field drop-downs or the group box.

**3.** Activate the chart. Use your mouse to select the data series labeled Prior Year (or Prior) and then press Delete on your keyboard. This will remove the Prior Year data series from the chart.

**4.** Use your mouse to select the data series labeled Forecast. Modify the SERIES equation in the formula bar as follows:

```
=SERIES(Info.xls!Series.Choice,Info.xls!Period,
Info.xls!Data.Choice,1)
```

**5.** *Optional*: Format the Comparison worksheet to have no gridlines and no row or column headers. Format the chart to have no border and to not move or size with cells.

The completed line chart is shown in Figure 25.3.

**FIGURE 25.3**

*The completed Comparison sheet. The user is discouraged (though not completely prevented) from changing the pivot table layout.*

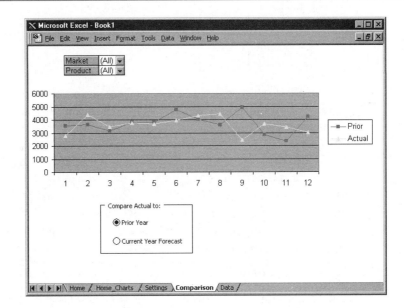

Test it out. Click on the option buttons—the chart should reflect your choice.

# Putting on the Finishing Touches

There are a few more steps required to complete the workbook.

**1.** Hide the worksheets that are not supposed to be seen. Select each sheet, and choose Format ➤ Sheet ➤ Hide.

**TIP**

By grouping the sheets, they can be hidden with one command (see Chapter 2).

2. Remove gridlines and remove row and column headings (on all the visible sheets) by using Tools ≻ Options, then selecting the View tab. You can also remove the horizontal and vertical scroll bars, since the information on each sheet fits in the window.

**NOTE**

The scroll bar settings are not specific to a given worksheet. They apply to the entire workbook.

3. Activate Home, and save the workbook.

# Bulletproofing the Workbook

The more people who use a workbook, the more important it is for it to be *bulletproof*. In other words, no matter what the users do, they cannot cause errors, harm the data, or change the program.

**NOTE**

Bulletproofing is a matter of degree. It is kind of like the temperature absolute zero—you can get very close, but it is ultimately unachievable. You need to weigh the development cost of each bulletproofing measure against the benefits realized (reduced support cost and overall user satisfaction).

Here are some things you could do to bulletproof the workbook:

**Create a Custom Command Bar** - A workbook is not even remotely bulletproof if the built-in menus are displayed. There are too many commands that permit the user(s) to do damage.

**Protecting the Worksheets** - Minimally, the worksheets should be protected so that users cannot delete the objects (embedded charts and controls). You can also protect cells, but this has many side-effects that you should be aware of. For instance, you can't manipulate a pivot table on a worksheet where the cells are protected, nor can macros write data to cells that are protected. Also, certain worksheet controls (i.e., list boxes, check boxes, and option buttons) won't work if the cells they are linked to are locked and protected.

**Protecting the Workbook** - If you protect the workbook structure, users will not be able to unhide hidden worksheets, or delete worksheets. (See Chapter 11 to read more about this topic.)

**Save the File as Read-Only** - With the data stored in an external database, there is no reason for users to be able to change the workbook. Use File ➢ Save As, then click on Options to save the workbook as a read-only file (using the write-reservation password).

In this chapter, you have seen firsthand the usefulness of pivot tables. You have also experienced the importance of an obscure feature—named formulas. Finally, you have learned to use custom controls to simplify user interaction. Visit one of the following Web sites to find more examples of data-driven Excel modeling:

- **http://www.sybex.com**
- **http://www.lexsoft.com**

# PART VIII

# Solving Real-World Problems

## LEARN TO:

- *Consolidate data and create workbook outlines*

- *Perform predictive, or what-if, analysis*

- *Install and configure Excel add-ins*

- *Convert files from other programs to Excel 8 workbook format*

- *Link workbooks locally, or through the Internet*

- *Import external text and graphics files*

- *Share workbooks among users*

# Chapter

## 26

### Consolidating and Outlining

# Consolidating and Outlining

onsolidating information from multiple sources is a task often performed using spreadsheet software. Consolidation gives an overall view of data that may come from many workbooks. This chapter will show you how to use Excel's consolidation features to create a multilevel budgeting model.

We'll also cover Excel's outlining features. Outlining works much like consolidation, but on the worksheet level. Outlining also works in conjunction with consolidation; several commands in Excel, such as Consolidate, create worksheet outlines as an automatic by-product, but you can also create your own outlines.

## Consolidating Data

In a sense, many of the formulas placed on a worksheet serve to consolidate data, using a broad definition for this term. But this section covers a specific command: Data ➤ Consolidate.

Data consolidations are used to roll up, or bring together, and summarize data from more than one source. For example, suppose that you have workbooks storing population statistics for each county within a state, with one workbook for each county. You need to take the information from the county workbooks and create a statewide report that summarizes all of the counties. You *could* painstakingly open each workbook, copy the information to a new workbook, and then write formulas to summarize the information. But, there's a better way: you can use Excel's built-in consolidation capabilities to simplify this process. Using the DataConsolidate command, you can do all of the following:

- Consolidate information stored on different worksheets within the same workbook
- Consolidate information stored on different workbooks (without the need to open the workbooks)
- Consolidate multiple ranges on the same worksheet
- Consolidate data on the basis of row and column labels, regardless of position on the worksheet
- Use different calculations when you consolidate, such as sum, count, and average
- Link the consolidation to the source data

**NOTE**

Pivot tables, covered in Chapters 20, 21, and 22, provide a powerful, flexible way to analyze data. They can consolidate data from multiple sources, summarize detailed data, and create multilevel outlines. If you need to perform consolidations, pivot tables are a *must learn* topic.

## Solving a Business Problem

In this section, you will learn how to perform a two-level consolidation for a fictitious company, Electronic Gizmos Corporation (EGC), that distributes electronic products nationwide.

- EGC has four distribution centers, which are designated as A, B, C, and D.
- Two distribution centers, A and B, are in the eastern region. Centers C and D are in the western region. There is a regional manager for each of the two regions.
- Every year, during the fourth quarter, the distribution centers prepare a proposed budget for the following year and submit it to the regional manager for approval.
- The regional managers submit consolidated budgets for their respective regions to the VP of Finance for approval.

### Using a Template for Conformity

To simplify the consolidation process, we'll use a template to ensure that the distribution centers enter data in the same format. The budget template is shown in Figure 26.1.

PART

**VIII**

Solving Real-World
Problems

**FIGURE 26.1**

*Budgets are sub-
mitted for four
departments.
Notice that the
row labels
(B6:B10) and
column labels
(C5:F5) are
unique.*

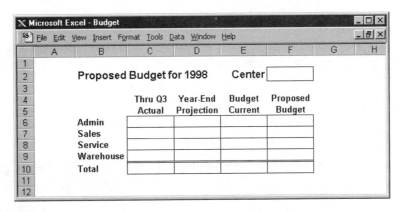

Follow these steps to create the template pictured in Figure 26.1:

**1.** Create a new workbook—delete every worksheet except Sheet1.

**2.** Enter the row and column labels shown in Figure 26.1.

**3.** Hide the gridlines (using View tab on the Tools ➤ Options dialog box).

**4.** Apply borders as shown in Figure 26.1. (See Chapter 5 to learn about cell formatting.)

**TIP**

Place the double border on the top of row 10 rather than the bottom of row 9. Later, when you copy D6 to D7:D9, the double border won't get overwritten.

**5.** Enter the following formulas into the indicated cells:

| | |
|---|---|
| D6 | **=C6*1.33** |
| C10 | **=SUM(C6:C9)** |

**NOTE**

The distribution centers submit budget proposals for the upcoming year during the fourth quarter—before fourth quarter data is available. The formula in D6 is intended to predict fourth quarter expenses on the basis of the previous three quarters.

**6.** Copy the formula in D6 to D7:D9. Use the fill handle to AutoFill D6 down through D9. (AutoFill is discussed in Chapter 7.)

**7.** Copy the formula in C10 to D10:F10.

**8.** Name the range B5:F10 **Budget_Area**. Note that the column titles in row 4 are superfluous and are not part of the consolidation.

**TIP**

To suppress the display of zero values, choose Tools ➤ Options, click on the View tab, and uncheck the Zero Values option.

**9.** Choose File ➤ Save As, and enter the file name **BUDGET**. From the Save File As Type drop-down list, choose Template (*.xlt).

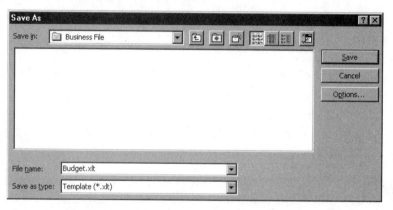

**TIP**

If you want to prevent users from overwriting formulas, all cells where data entry is allowed should be unlocked, and all other cells should be locked. (All cells are locked by default). The cell lock takes effect when the worksheet cells are protected using Tools ➤ Protection ➤ Protect Worksheet. (See Chapter 11 for more on protecting worksheets.)

The template is complete. When you close it and then reopen it using the File ➤ New command, a copy of the template is loaded into memory, instead of the original. (See Chapter 10 for more information on templates.)

**TIP**

To open an original template rather than a copy, hold down the Shift key while you open the template.

## Using a File Naming Convention

For reasons you will discover later, a file naming convention is vitally important when performing workbook consolidations. EGC has chosen the following conventions:

- Distribution center workbook names begin with the name of the parent region, followed by an underscore, followed by the one-character distribution center ID. For example, center C, which is in the western region, will create a budget workbook named WEST_C. Center A, in the eastern region, will create a workbook named EAST_A, and so on.
- The regional managers create workbooks beginning with REG, followed by an underscore, followed by the region. These two workbooks will be named REG_EAST and REG_WEST.
- The corporate summary workbook will be named CORP, though the name of this workbook is not as critical as are the names of the lower-level workbooks.

PART
**VIII**

Solving Real-World
Problems

## Consolidating by Position or Category

Before creating a consolidation, there is an important issue to consider: the Data ➤ Consolidate command lets you consolidate on the basis of position or on the basis of row/column categories.

**Consolidating by Position** - Consolidation based on position requires that the data be structured identically, relative within each data source.

- Each cell being consolidated must reside in the same relative position within the source range, as is the case with the EGC model. The Data ➤ Consolidate command lets you consolidate multiple ranges from the same worksheet. Therefore, the *relative* position of cells within each range is critical—not the absolute position on the worksheet. (See Figure 26.2)
- The row and column heading in the source range(s) are ignored, even if they are included as part of the consolidation range. Since the row and column headings are not part of the source data (and are not copied to the consolidation even if included), the source data and the consolidation are often based on a template.

Generally, consolidating by position is a risky proposition. A minor change to source data can cause erroneous results.

**Consolidating by Category** - When you consolidate on the basis of category, the row and/or column labels are used to determine how to perform the consolidation. Accordingly, the source data ranges do not have to be structured identically.

- The source ranges can contain a varying number of rows or columns and must include the row and/or column labels.

*FIGURE 26.2*

*F7:G8 is a consolidation of the two source ranges, C4:D5 and C11:D12.*

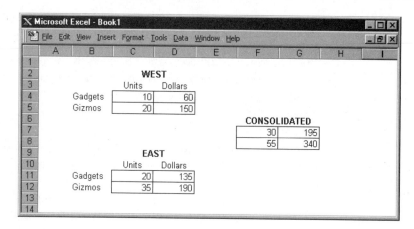

- The sequence of the row and/or column labels doesn't matter.

To perform a consolidation by category, check the Top Row and/or Left Column check boxes in the Data ➤ Consolidate dialog box. Figure 26.3 shows a consolidation by category, with the source ranges and the consolidation located on the same worksheet.

*FIGURE 26.3*

*F7:H10 is a consolidation of the two source ranges, B3:D6 and B12:D14. Consolidation by category allows the source ranges to differ.*

Consolidating by category provides greater data integrity and more flexibility than consolidating by position.

## To Link or Not to Link

The second major choice you are presented with when consolidating is whether to link the consolidation to the source data ranges.

**When to Link** - A consolidation that is linked to source data recalculates automatically when links are refreshed. Linking is a good idea if the source data is subject to change, and if the consolidation needs to stay in sync with the source data. For instance, using the EGC model, suppose that the budgeting process is iterative. A distribution center submits a proposal. The manager reviews the numbers and sends it back for revision. The center makes changes, the manager reviews again, and so on. In this scenario, the workbooks will remain in sync without manual effort.

**When Not to Link** - You should not link if the consolidation is a one-time process—the consolidation will be a "frozen" report, with no formulas pointing back to the source data. Otherwise, you run the risk of the consolidation inadvertently changing because of a change in the source.

## Step One—The Distribution Center Budget

Now it's time to begin the task of consolidating the budget information for the Electronic Gizmos Corporation. Suppose you are the controller for distribution center C. Follow these steps to prepare a budget proposal:

1. Choose File ➤ New to open the BUDGET template created in the previous exercise. (Notice that a copy of the template, named Budget1, is loaded into memory—not the original.)
2. Enter **C** into F2. Enter numbers into C6:C9, E6:E9, and F6:F9 as shown in Figure 26.4.

PART

**VIII**

Solving Real-World Problems

---

**FIGURE 26.4**

*The completed budget proposal for distribution center C.*

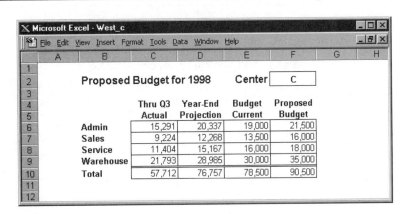

Proposed Budget for 1998    Center   C

| | Thru Q3 Actual | Year-End Projection | Budget Current | Proposed Budget |
|---|---|---|---|---|
| Admin | 15,291 | 20,337 | 19,000 | 21,500 |
| Sales | 9,224 | 12,268 | 13,500 | 16,000 |
| Service | 11,404 | 15,167 | 16,000 | 18,000 |
| Warehouse | 21,793 | 28,985 | 30,000 | 35,000 |
| Total | 57,712 | 76,757 | 78,500 | 90,500 |

**3.** Choose File ➢ Save As, and name the file **WEST_C**.

In the next step, the western region manager will consolidate centers C and D. You can repeat the previous steps for center D, or take a shortcut: save WEST_C as **WEST_D**, then change a few numbers so that the workbooks can be distinguished later, then save again. When you're through, close WEST_C and WEST_D.

## Step Two—The Regional Consolidation

Now suppose you are the western regional manager for EGC. It is your job to consolidate the proposed budgets submitted by the distribution centers within your region. The structure of the template will allow a consolidation by position. However, the personnel at center D are known to break the rules from time to time, so the safest bet is a consolidation by category.

**TIP**

The source workbooks do not have to be open in order to perform a consolidation. This is an important feature, especially when there are dozens of source workbooks instead of only two.

Follow these steps to perform the regional consolidation:

**1.** Create a new workbook, and save it as **Western Region**.

**NOTE**

When performing a consolidation by category, the row and column headings are part of the source data ranges. As such, the template provides marginal value, as the consolidation process will copy row and column headings for you.

**2.** Select B2 (the upper-left corner of the consolidation range) and choose Data ➢ Consolidate. The Consolidate dialog box appears.

**3.** Enter **WEST_?.XLS!Budget_Area** in the Reference box, then click on Add.

**4.** Check Top Row and Left Column in the Use Labels In area. This causes the consolidation to be based on category, rather than position. Check Create Links To Source Data.

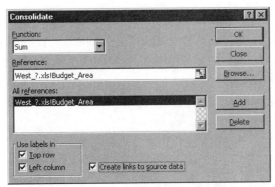

**5.** Click on OK to perform the consolidation. The result is shown in Figure 26.5.

**FIGURE 26.5**

*Note that when
you create links
to the source
data, the sheet
is automatically
outlined.*

| | | | Actual | Projection | Current | Budget | | |
|---|---|---|---|---|---|---|---|---|
| Admin | | | 31,513 | 41,912 | 37,500 | 43,500 | | |
| Sales | | | 19,230 | 25,576 | 27,500 | 32,500 | | |
| Service | | | 23,968 | 31,877 | 33,500 | 37,000 | | |
| Warehouse | | | 44,585 | 59,298 | 65,000 | 75,000 | | |
| Total | | | 119,296 | 158,664 | 163,500 | 188,000 | | |

**6.** Name the range B2:G17 **Budget_Area** (this will be used for the corporate consolidation).

Notice that the name Budget_Area is used in the Western Region workbook as well as the source workbooks, even though the named ranges are of different sizes. Using a single name simplifies the task of consolidating similar data from various sources. The data consolidated on Western Region can now be consolidated with the data from other regions to form a corporate consolidation.

**NOTE**

You do not have to use the .XLS file extension when typing a file reference in the Consolidate dialog box; however, it is a good practice to do so. It is important to note that Excel still uses file extensions to distinguish files of different types—.XLT, .XLK, etc.—although they may be hidden (see Chapter 2).

# Refreshing a Linked Consolidation

A linked consolidation behaves just like any workbook that is linked to one or more source workbooks. When the file is opened, a dialog box is displayed to confirm that you want to reestablish links.

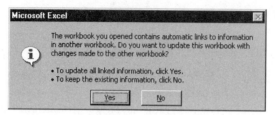

Click on Yes to recalculate the links. New values are retrieved from the source workbooks, even if they are closed.

**TIP** If you want dependent workbooks to update links without a prompt, choose Tools ➢ Options, click on the Edit tab, and uncheck Ask To Update Automatic Links. This is a global setting that pertains to all workbooks.

# Using Wildcards and Named Ranges

Two vitally important techniques were used in the previous exercise—including wildcards in filenames and referring to named ranges. The benefits of these techniques cannot be overestimated if you intend to perform, and rely upon, consolidations.

## Using Wildcards in the Filename

You can include asterisks and question marks in the file name as wildcard characters. The use of wildcards adheres to software conventions: the asterisk is used as a place marker for any number of characters, and the question mark is used as a place marker for any one character. The EGC file naming convention, discussed earlier in this chapter, is intended to support this wildcard-based consolidation methodology.

The file name WEST_?.XLS will consolidate data from all workbooks in the current folder with a prefix of WEST_, and any character in the sixth position (i.e., WEST_C, WEST_D, WEST_X). The benefit may not be obvious with the EGC budget model, consisting of two source workbooks, but consider the following:

- Consolidations can be performed on a large number of workbooks, without the tedious effort of specifying each source range.

- If a new workbook is added to the directory and the name of the workbook matches the wildcard specification, it will be included automatically the next time the consolidation workbook recalculates.

## Referring to the Source Data by Name

The second vital technique, the reference to a named range, Budget_Area, is also extremely useful when performing consolidations. (The name Budget_Area was defined when the template was created.) Consider the following benefits of using a name:

- When creating links to source data, the name helps ensure the integrity of the external reference. (Refer to Chapter 8 to learn more about names.)
- New categories can be inserted into one or more source data ranges. The name expands automatically, and the next time the consolidation recalculates, everything stays in sync.

# Automatic Outlining

The worksheet shown in Figure 26.6 contains outline symbols, which are an automatic by-product when you create links to source data. When you click on the outline symbols in the left margin, the outline expands. (Outlining is covered in depth later in this chapter.)

PART

**VIII**

Solving Real-World
Problems

**FIGURE 26.6**

*Rows 3 and 4 have been expanded. On the detail rows, Column C contains the workbook prefix indicating which row comes from which source.*

| | | | Actual | Projection | Current | Budget | | |
|---|---|---|---|---|---|---|---|---|
| | | West_D | 16,222 | 21,575 | 18,500 | 22,000 | | |
| | | West_C | 15,291 | 20,337 | 19,000 | 21,500 | | |
| | Admin | | 31,513 | 41,912 | 37,500 | 43,500 | | |
| | Sales | | 19,230 | 25,576 | 27,500 | 32,500 | | |
| | Service | | 23,968 | 31,877 | 33,500 | 37,000 | | |
| | Warehouse | | 44,585 | 59,298 | 65,000 | 75,000 | | |
| | Total | | 119,296 | 158,664 | 163,500 | 188,000 | | |

The numbers on the detail rows contain formulas that refer to the source workbooks.

## Entering Source References

In the EGC budget exercise, the source reference was entered manually. But there are several other ways to enter this information.

- If the source workbook is open, you can point and click on the source range.

**TIP**

It is especially useful to use the Collapse Dialog Box button on the right side of the Reference text box to point and click on source ranges; see Chapter 7 for an explanation of the Collapse Dialog Box button.

- Click on the Browse button in the Consolidate dialog box to select a closed workbook, then click on the file name in the Browse dialog box and the source range will be entered into the Reference edit box.
- Use a single 3-D reference to consolidate source areas that are identically positioned on different sheets in the same workbook. (See Chapters 4 and 8 for more on 3-D references.)

## Using Category Labels in the Consolidation Range

In the previous exercise, one cell (B2) was selected when the Data ➤ Consolidate command was chosen. However, if you select more than one cell when you choose Data ➤ Consolidate, and the range contains category labels, the labels control what data is consolidated. The following exercise demonstrates the technique:

**1.** On a new workbook, build the worksheet shown in Figure 26.7.

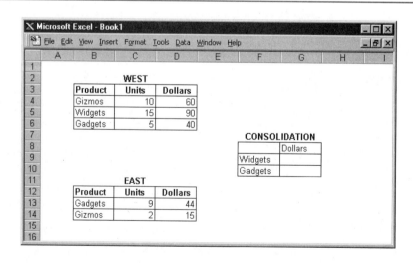

**2.** Select F8:G10 and choose Data ➤ Consolidate.

**3.** With the Consolidate dialog box displayed, select B3:D6 (which enters the range into the Reference in the consolidate dialog box), then click on Add.

**4.** Add the second source range: Select B12:D14 and click on Add.

**5.** Check both Top Row and Left Column options.

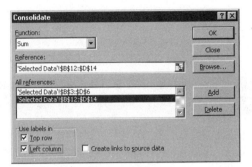

 **NOTE**
When the consolidation is on the same sheet as the source data, you cannot create a link to the source.

Click on OK to perform the consolidation. Figure 26.8 shows the result.

**FIGURE 26.8**

*Product* Gizmos
*and column*
Units *were*
*excluded*
*from the*
*consolidation.*

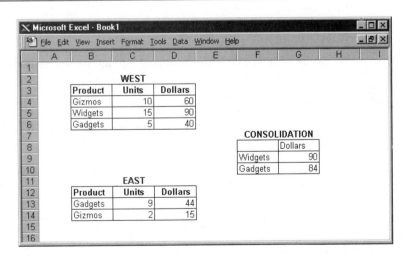

Since category labels were included in the selected range when Data ➤ Consolidate was chosen, the labels controlled which data was consolidated.

## Using Wildcards in the Categories

There is an interesting and powerful variation to the technique described above. If the categories in the consolidation range include wildcards, all categories matching the wildcard are summarized. Consider the worksheet in Figure 26.9.

**FIGURE 26.9**

*Category labels inside the consolidation range can include wildcard characters.*

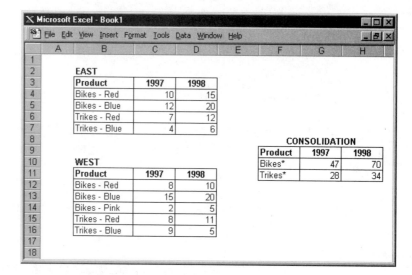

When the consolidation in Figure 26.9 was created, F9:H11 was selected. The asterisks in cells F10 and F11 caused all bikes, and all trikes, to be summarized.

## Consolidation Functions

While consolidation is most often performed to sum data, you can also perform consolidations that use other functions:

| | |
|---|---|
| Count | Counts cells containing a value—text or number (equivalent to COUNTA function) |
| Average | Calculates average |
| Max | Finds the maximum value |
| Min | Finds the minimum value |
| Product | Calculates the product |

| Count Nums | Counts numbers (equivalent to COUNT function) |
| StDev | Calculates the standard deviation of a sample |
| StDevP | Calculates the standard deviation of the population |
| Var | Calculates the variance of a sample |
| VarP | Calculates the variance of the population |

## Multilevel Consolidations

There are some important things to understand about multilevel consolidations. To illustrate these points, it will be helpful to revisit the EGC budget model.

At step 2, the western region consolidation was completed and saved as Western Region. Suppose that the eastern region consolidation was also performed and saved as Eastern Region. (Remember, both of these consolidations are linked to the distribution center source data.) Consolidating the two regions into a corporate total involves the same basic procedure as when the regional consolidations were created (the only difference is the file name). Here are the implications of EGC's two-level linked model:

- The regional budgets are linked to the distribution center budgets. When the regional budgets are opened, the links are (optionally) recalculated.
- The corporate budgets are linked to the regional budgets. When the corporate budget is opened, the links are (optionally) recalculated.
- Link recalculation only goes down one level. Suppose a change is made to a distribution center (bottom-level) budget. Then, the corporate (top-level) workbook is opened. The change at the bottom level will not flow to the top level. The workbooks must be recalculated in reverse order of the hierarchy.

## Worksheet Outlining

An outlined worksheet lets you easily and quickly view various levels of detail—for rows and/or columns. There are several operations in Excel that create outlines for you automatically:

- Data ➤ Subtotals (see Chapter 18)
- Data ➤ Consolidate, when the Link To Source option is chosen (covered earlier in this chapter)
- A summary report created with Solver (see Chapter 27)

This section will explain how to create your own outlines and how to use outlining symbols, regardless of how the outline was created.

## More Facts about Consolidation

Here are some additional points to keep in mind when performing consolidations:

- You can only define one consolidation on a (destination) worksheet (you can perform many consolidations on the same worksheet, but only the most recent consolidation will remain defined in the Data ➤ Consolidate dialog box as a reusable model).

- Consolidation dialog box settings are persistent—you can use the same consolidation model repeatedly without setting it up from scratch each time.

- Destination cells are formatted using the number formats in the first source selected for consolidation.

- You can reverse an unlinked consolidation by choosing Edit ➤ Undo immediately following the consolidation.

- A linked consolidation cannot be reversed with Edit ➤ Undo. (It can only be reversed by closing the workbook without saving the consolidation.)

- If the source and destination areas are on the same worksheet, you cannot create a linked consolidation.

## Creating Automatic Outlines

The easiest way to create an outline is with the Data ➤ Group And Outline ➤ Auto Outline command. Excel looks for formulas on the active sheet, and on the basis of the formulas, determines where the summary and detail rows/columns are located. Consider the outlined worksheet in Figure 26.10.

The outline symbols in the left and top margins indicate where the summary rows and columns are located. Since row 5 sums rows 2 through 4, it becomes a summary row in the outline. Since column G sums columns D through F, it becomes a summary column.

## Expanding and Collapsing Outlines

You can expand or collapse an outline to show different details—for instance, you may want to see just totals from all regions, or quarterly instead of monthly sales. You can do this using the margin outline symbols.

**FIGURE 26.10**

*Automatic outlining was applied to this worksheet.*

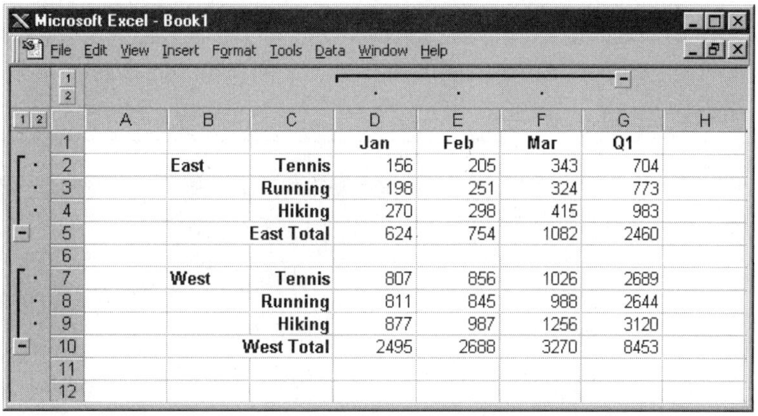


## Using the Outline Symbols

The plus and minus symbols in the top and left margins of an outlined worksheet are used to expand or collapse sections of the outline selectively. Using the worksheet pictured in Figure 26.10, suppose that you want to collapse the data for region East. Figure 26.11 shows the sheet after the symbol to the left of row 5 is clicked on—rows 2 through 4 are hidden.

**FIGURE 26.11**

*The symbols in the top and left margins are used to collapse sections of the outline selectively.*

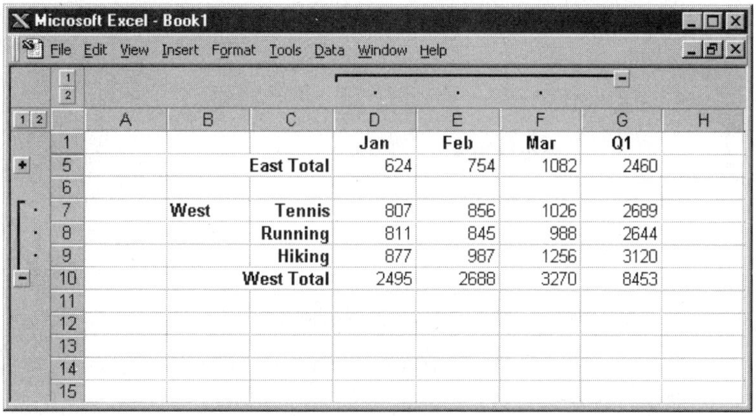


The symbols in the upper-left corner of the sheet are used to expand and collapse the entire outline at once. Figure 26.11 shows two numbered buttons for changing the row outline and two numbered buttons for changing the column outline. The number of buttons depends upon the number of levels in the outline.

Figure 26.12 shows the same worksheet, after both of the level one (1) buttons in the corner of the sheet have been clicked on.

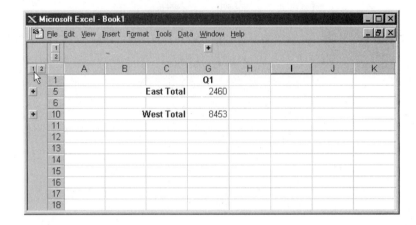

## Using Menu Commands

You can use menu commands in lieu of the outline symbols to expand or collapse an outline. Follow these steps to collapse a section of an outline using menu commands:

**1.** Select a summary cell for the group you want to collapse (e.g., monthly total or quarterly total), such as cell D10 in Figure 26.11.

**2.** Choose Data ➤ Group And Outline ➤ Hide Detail.

Here's how to expand an outline group (display details) using menu commands:

**1.** Select a summary cell for the group you want to expand.

**2.** Choose Data ➤ Group And Outline ➤ Show Detail.

# Hiding the Outline Symbols

Suppose you are distributing an outlined worksheet to co-workers, and you do not want the outline symbols displayed. Follow these steps to hide the symbols:

**1.** Choose Tools ➤ Options and select the View tab.

**2.** Uncheck the Outline Symbols setting and click on OK.

You can also use the Show Outline Symbols tool to toggle outline symbols, or from the keyboard, press Ctrl+8. Hiding the outline symbols does not remove the underlying outline from the worksheet. The outline is still in place, and can still be manipulated with menu commands.

## Creating Manual Outlines

Automatic outlining is convenient because it does all the work for you. But sometimes you may want more control over the outline, in which case you must define the outline manually. Here are several scenarios in which you might use manual outlining:

- If there are no formulas on the worksheet (for example, data downloaded from a mainframe)
- If you want to outline just a portion of the worksheet
- If the data is not organized for automatic outlining (for instance, one section has summary data above detail data, and another section has summary data below detail data)

Consider the worksheet in Figure 26.13. Suppose you want the ability to collapse just the East section.

PART

**VIII**

Solving Real-World Problems

---

**FIGURE 26.13**

*You can outline just the East section of the worksheet by creating a manual outline.*

| | A | B | C | D | E | F | G | H | I |
|---|---|---|---|---|---|---|---|---|---|
| 1 | | | | | | | | | |
| 2 | | | | 1997 | 1998 | | | | |
| 3 | | East | Wages | 120000 | 120000 | | | | |
| 4 | | | Rent | 5000 | 5000 | | | | |
| 5 | | | Utilities | 450 | 450 | | | | |
| 6 | | | Insurance | 300 | 300 | | | | |
| 7 | | | Advertising | 200 | 200 | | | | |
| 8 | | | Supplies | 250 | 270 | | | | |
| 9 | | | Repairs | 50 | 75 | | | | |
| 10 | | | **Total East** | 126250 | 126295 | | | | |
| 11 | | | | | | | | | |
| 12 | | West | Wages | 50000 | 50000 | | | | |
| 13 | | | Utilities | 450 | 300 | | | | |
| 14 | | | **Total West** | 50450 | 50300 | | | | |
| 15 | | | | | | | | | |
| 16 | | | **Grand Total** | 176700 | 176595 | | | | |
| 17 | | | | | | | | | |
| 18 | | | | | | | | | |

Microsoft Excel - Book1

File  Edit  View  Insert  Format  Tools  Data  Window  Help

**1.** Select the rows you want to outline (rows 3:9).

**2.** Choose Data ➤ Group And Outline ➤ Group (or click on the Group tool on the PivotTable toolbar).

The East section will be outlined and can then be collapsed, as shown in Figure 26.14.

**FIGURE 26.14**

*The manual outline created for Region East has been collapsed.*

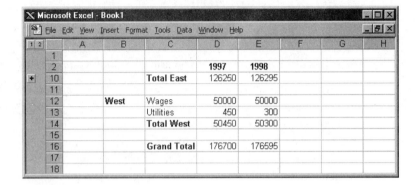

## Formatting Worksheet Outlines

You can manually format an outline, as you would any range of cells. But there are two more effective techniques: styles and table AutoFormats.

### Applying Styles to Outlines

You can apply built-in styles to different levels of an outline, as shown in Figure 26.15. As with cell styles, if you change a style definition, every outline level using the given style will be automatically reformatted.

To apply automatic styles to an outline, the Automatic Styles option must be selected before you create the outline:

**1.** Choose Data ➤ Group And Outline ➤ Settings.

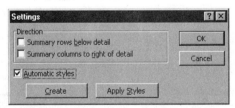

**2.** Check the Automatic Styles setting. Click on OK.

**FIGURE 26.15**

*Outline with
styles defined
for each of
three levels*

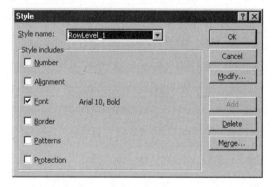

Now, when an automatic outline is created, the outline styles are automatically applied. Here's how to change the definition of a style:

**1.** Choose Format ➢ Style.

Now, when an automatic outline is created, the outline styles are automatically applied. Here's how to change the definition of a style:

**2.** Select the style from the Style Name drop-down list (the styles are named RowLevel_1, ColumnLevel_1, and so on).

**3.** Click on the Modify button and make your changes, then click on OK to close the Format Cells dialog box. Click on OK again to close the Style dialog box.

The new style definition is automatically applied. (See Chapter 5 to learn more about styles.)

## Applying Table AutoFormats to Outlines

You can apply AutoFormats to a worksheet before or after outlining the data. The AutoFormat feature is "smart"—it detects summary and detail levels using the formulas. Follow these steps to apply an AutoFormat:

1. Select a cell within the data range.
2. Choose Format ➤ AutoFormat.
3. Select an AutoFormat from the list of Table Formats.
4. Click on OK.

**MASTERING TROUBLESHOOTING**

### Creating Charts from Outlines

Suppose you have a large table of sales data, and you have outlined it so that the data can be easily viewed on a summary or detail level. Now, you want to chart the sales data. By default, charting is based on visible data only, so that as the outline is collapsed and expanded, the chart changes accordingly. However, an expanded outline can result in a chart with so many data series that the chart becomes unreadable. So another option is to create a chart that is based on the summary level, even if the outline is expanded to a detail level. To create a chart that will not expand, begin by collapsing the outline to a summary level. Select the entire table, then select only the visible cells in the table by choosing Edit ➤ Go To, clicking on the Special button, and selecting Visible Cells Only. Now, when you create the chart, it will not expand when the outline is expanded.

Consider the opposite scenario: suppose you want the chart to always show detail, even when the outline is collapsed. Select all of the data in the expanded outline and create the chart. With the chart active, choose Tools ➤ Options and select the Chart tab. Clear the Plot Visible Cells Only check box.

If only one cell is selected when you choose Format ➤ AutoFormat, the format will be applied to all contiguous data. If the range you want to AutoFormat contains blank rows or columns, you must select the entire range before choosing the command.

# Removing an Outline

You can remove outlining from an entire worksheet or from selected rows or columns. To remove outlining from the entire worksheet, do the following:

**1.** Select any cell on the worksheet.

**2.** Choose Data ➢ Group And Outline ➢ Clear Outline.

To remove outlining from a group of rows or columns, do the following:

**1.** Select the rows or columns you want to remove outlining from.

**2.** Choose Data ➢ Group And Outline ➢ Ungroup (or click on the Ungroup tool).

Excel's consolidating and outlining features are important tools for data organization and interpretation, and extremely useful for data presentation. The next chapter will introduce some of Excel's powerful predictive tools: Goal Seek, Solver, and Scenario Manager.

PART

**VIII**

Solving Real-World Problems

# Chapter

## 27

### What-If Analysis

# What-If Analysis

Generally, a worksheet with simple SUM functions is capable of performing simple *what-if* analysis. When you change a cell, you can see what happens as a result. This means that almost everything you do with worksheets can be characterized as what-if analysis, using a broad definition of the term. This chapter, however, explains three specific tools to help with complex what-if analysis:

- Goal Seek, which determines the input required to produce a desired result
- Solver, which finds the optimum solution to complex problems involving multiple variables and constraints
- Scenario Manager, which allows you to create and save sets of input values that produce different results

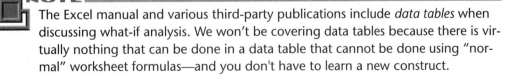

**NOTE** The Excel manual and various third-party publications include *data tables* when discussing what-if analysis. We won't be covering data tables because there is virtually nothing that can be done in a data table that cannot be done using "normal" worksheet formulas—and you don't have to learn a new construct.

# Solving Simple Problems Using Goal Seek

Essentially, *Goal Seek* solves formulas backwards. Use Goal Seek when you know the result you want, but need to determine how much to change a single input to get that result. For example, here are two typical problems that you can solve with Goal Seek:

- You want to take out a loan to buy a car, but the maximum payment your budget will allow is $300 per month. What is the most expensive car can you afford?
- You are taking a course in biology, and the final grade is based on the weighted average of six exams. You have taken five of the six exams, and want to know the minimum score you need on the sixth exam in order to get a B for the course.

You will learn to solve these two problems in the following pages.

## Starting Goal Seek

To start Goal Seek, select a cell containing a formula, then choose Tools ➤ Goal Seek. The Goal Seek dialog box is displayed.

Three text boxes allow you to specify which cell value you want to remain constant and which you want to vary to meet that goal.

**Set Cell:** Must be a cell that contains a formula—it defaults to the active cell.

**To Value:** Must be a constant value (not a cell reference).

**By Changing Cell:** Must be a cell containing a constant value, and must be directly or indirectly referenced by the cell specified in Set Cell. The reference can be several levels away, and can be located in another worksheet or another workbook.

Goal Seek is a graphical representation of an algebraic function with two variables, an independent one $x$, and a dependent one $y$. For any given function of $x$ (e.g., $3x = y$), the value of $y$ is said to be *dependent* on the value of $x$. Goal Seek allows you to set your dependent value (or goal) and find the value of $x$ that meets that goal.

## Goal Seek—Case One

Suppose you want to buy a new car. Here's what you know:

- You can get a bank loan at 9% annual interest rate.
- The term of loan is 36 months.
- The loan requires a 20% down payment.
- The maximum monthly payment you can afford is $300.

What's the most expensive car you can afford? Follow this exercise, using the PMT function and Goal Seek, to find out:

**1.** Enter the following onto a new worksheet:

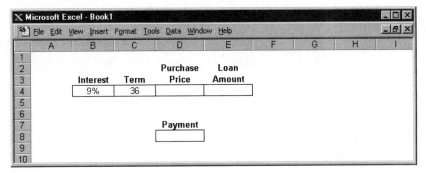

**2.** In cell E4, enter the formula **=D4\*0.8** (the loan amount is 80% of the purchase price).

**3.** Enter the formula **=PMT(B4/12,C4,-E4)** into cell D8 (the PMT function calculates the monthly payment, where B4/12 is the interest rate per period, C4 is the number of periods and E4 is the total amount of the loan.

**4.** Select cell D8, then choose Tools ➢ Goal Seek. Fill in the dialog box as shown below.

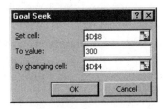

**5.** Click on OK. Goal Seek finds the answer and displays it in the Goal Seek Status dialog box.

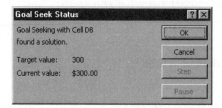

**6.** To keep the answer (and change the values in the worksheet), click on OK on the Goal Seek Status dialog box. Figure 27.1 shows the completed worksheet.

**FIGURE 27.1**

*Goal seek has determined the maximum purchase price.*

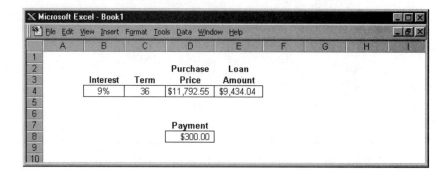

## Goal Seek—Case Two

You are taking a course in biology, and you want to know what grade you have to get on the final exam in order to get a B for the course.

- There are six exams given during the course, and you have taken five of them— you scored 75, 80, 95, 76, and 62.
- The exams scores are weighted. Exams #1, #2, #4, and #5 are each worth 10% of the final grade, exam #3 is worth 20%, and exam #6 is worth 40%.
- The final score is calculated from the average of the six weighted exam scores.

Goal Seek will change an indirectly referenced value (the sixth exam score) to reach a final weighted average of 80% (which will give you a final grade of B).

**1.** Enter the following on a new worksheet:

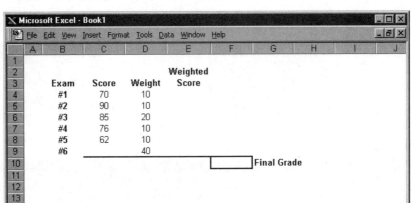

**2.** In cell E4, enter the formula **=C4*D4**, then copy it down to E5:E9.

**3.** In cell D10, enter the formula **=SUM(D4:D9)**, then copy it to E10. In cell F10, enter the formula **=E10/D10**.

**4.** With F10 selected, choose Tools ➢ Goal Seek. Fill in the dialog box as shown below.

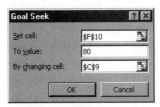

**5.** Click on OK. Again, Goal Seek finds the answer and displays it in the Goal Seek Status dialog box.

**6.** To keep the new values in the worksheet, click on OK on the Goal Seek Status dialog box. Figure 27.2 shows the completed worksheet.

## If You Make a Mistake

Here are some of the error messages you'll see if you enter invalid information in the Goal Seek dialog box.

PART

VIII

Solving Real-World
Problems

If the By Changing Cell contains a formula, you'll see this message:

If the cell entered in Set Cell contains a constant, you'll see this message:

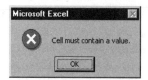

**FIGURE 27.2**

*Goal Seek has determined the score required on the final exam (C9) in order to get a B for the course.*

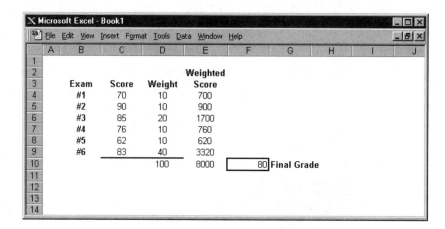

## Goal Seeking using a Chart

Experienced charting users are aware that you can drag a data point using the mouse, and as a result, the underlying cell value is changed. This skill is explained in Chapter 15. This same feature can be used in conjunction with goal seek. Here's how:

Suppose you have created a chart which is based on cells that contain formulas.

You then select one of the data points using the mouse, and drag it to change the value. Excel recognizes that the cell contains a formula. Rather than change the cell, the goal seek dialog box is automatically displayed. This allows you to specify which cell (referenced by the formula) to change in order to reach the desired goal, just as when you use goal seek normally.

# Solving Complex Problems with Solver

Solver is used to find solutions to problems involving multiple variables and constraints—problems that are more complex than Goal Seek can handle. While Goal Seek finds a specific solution, Solver finds the best, or optimal, solution.

> **NOTE**
>
> Solver is not part of the core Excel program—it is an add-in. If the Solver add-in is configured properly on your computer, a Solver command will display on the Tools menu. If the Solver command does not display, choose Tools ➤ Add-Ins. Check Solver in the list of available add-ins. If Solver does not display in the list, it must be installed from the Excel setup disk. See Chapter 28 to learn more about working with add-ins.

**PART**

**VIII**

Solver is a complex tool, but is worth the time to learn if you must find optimal solutions to complex problems. Solver can save money and resources for your business by finding better, more efficient ways to allocate resources. It can also save you the time spent finding solutions by trial and error. Solver can help you to solve problems such as these:

- Finding the optimal allocation of parts inventory to minimize production costs
- Creating the most efficient personnel schedule to minimize costs while meeting business needs and individual scheduling requests
- Optimizing allocation of funds in an investment portfolio to minimize risk and maximize return

There may be different optimal solutions to a problem, depending on the mathematical techniques Solver uses to solve the problem. The default Solver settings are appropriate for many problems, but experimentation with the different Solver Options settings (see Figure 27.3) may yield better results.

## Types of Problems Solver Can Analyze

Solver can analyze and solve three types of problems:

**Linear Problems** - A problem in which the variables are related through linear functions of the type $y = mx + b$—where $x$ and $y$ are the variables and $m$ and $b$ are constants. If you know that your problem is linear, place a check in the Assume Linear Model setting on the Solver Options dialog box (Figure 27.3) to speed up the calculation. This is especially important if the data model is large.

Solving Real-World
Problems

*FIGURE 27.3*

*In the Solver Options dialog box, you can change the allowable time and number of iterations and experiment with different mathematical techniques.*

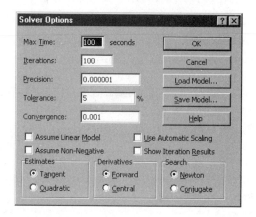

**Nonlinear Problems** - A problem in which the variables cannot all be related through linear functions. Examples include polynomials, exponential functions, and sine waves.

**Integer Problems** - A problem in which any of the variables is constrained to an integer value. Solver takes a longer time to solve integer problems.

## Sample Business Case

Suppose you are the manager of a dairy farm, and one of your responsibilities is to determine a livestock feed mixture that meets certain protein requirements but is still cost effective. Ingredient costs are continually changing, and as they change, you must recalculate the ingredient mix to minimize cost. Here's what you know:

- The feed mixture is composed of oats, corn, and barley.
- The final mix must have a protein content of between 9.2% and 9.5%.

Finding a solution to this kind of problem can be a lengthy trial and error process if you use conventional methods. Instead, Solver can find a solution for you.

First, you must understand three definitions:

**Target cell:** The *target cell* is the specific objective of the problem—the cell whose value Solver will set to be a minimum, maximum, or a specific value. In this problem, the target cell is the cost (which is to be minimized) of the final mix.

**Changing cells:** *Changing cells* are cells whose values Solver will manipulate to meet the target cell objective. In this problem, the changing cells are the proportions of each ingredient in the final mix.

**Constraints:** *Constraints* are the limits set on the values in any of these cells—there can be constraints on changing cells, the target cell, or any cells involved in the calculations. In this problem, these are the constraints:

- The final protein concentration must be between 9.2% and 9.5%.
- The amount of each ingredient must be at least 0 lbs. (This constraint prevents Solver from using a negative value.)
- The total of the ingredients must equal 100%.

To determine the optimum solution for the problem above, do the following:

**1.** Make sure the Solver add-in is loaded, then enter the following on a new worksheet:

|  | feed | % protein | price/lb | lbs feed in 100 lbs mix | cost per 100 lbs mix | lbs protein/ 100 lbs mix |  |
|---|---|---|---|---|---|---|---|
|  | oats | 9.50% | 0.23 |  |  |  |  |
|  | corn | 8.50% | 0.08 |  |  |  |  |
|  | barley | 9.00% | 0.14 |  |  |  |  |
|  |  |  |  |  |  |  | % protein |

**2.** Enter these formulas:

| Cell | Formula |
|---|---|
| E7 | =SUM(E4:E6) |
| F4 | =E4*D4 |
| G4 | =E4*C4 |

PART
**VIII**

Solving Real-World Problems

**3.** Copy the formulas:

- Copy the formula in E7 to F7 and G7.
- Copy the formula in F4 to F5 and F6.
- Copy the formula in G4 to G5 and G6.

**4.** Choose Tools ➤ Solver. The Solver Parameters dialog box is displayed.

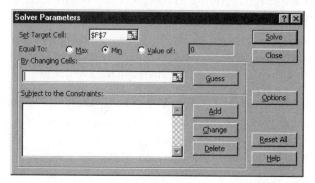

**5.** Enter cell **F7** into the Set Target Cell text box, and set the Equal To setting to Min.

**6.** In the By Changing Cells range edit box, enter E4:E6.

**7.** Click on the Add button to display the Add Constraint dialog box:

**8.** Add the following constraints. Click on the Add button between each entry:

| Cell | Operator | Constraint |
| --- | --- | --- |
| E7 | = | **100** |
| G7 | >= | **9.2** |
| G7 | <= | **9.5** |
| E4:E6 | >= | **0** |

**9.** Click on OK after you add the last constraint. (Verify the constraints in the Solver Parameters dialog box.) Use the Add, Change, and Delete buttons to make corrections as needed (see Figure 27.4).

**10.** Click on the Solve button to start Solver. Figure 27.5 shows the results.

**FIGURE 27.4**

*The Solver Parameters dialog box is set up to find the lowest-cost mixture of feeds within the constraints allowed.*

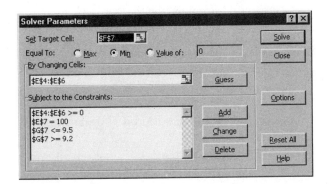

**FIGURE 27.5**

*Solver has found the lowest-cost mixture that meets the protein requirements.*

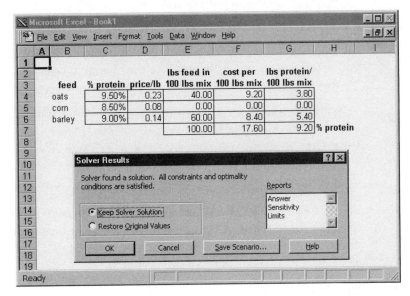

**11.** Select the Keep Solver Solution option and click on OK to keep the new values in the worksheet. At this point, you can also save the solution as a named scenario by clicking on the Save Scenario button and entering a name for the scenario in the Save Scenario dialog box. (Scenarios are covered later in this chapter.)

Solver works by trying different values in the changing cells and observing the results. By default, Solver is allowed 100 seconds and 100 tries, or *iterations*, to solve the problem. Complex problems (or slower computers) may require more time or iterations to reach a solution. If Solver runs out of time before reaching a solution, a dialog box will be displayed informing you that the maximum time limit was reached.

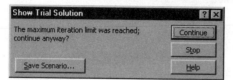

Click on the Continue button if you want to disregard the limit and continue the process.

To change the time or number of iterations allowed, click on the Options button on the Solver Parameters dialog box (shown earlier in Figure 27.4) to display the Solver Options dialog box (shown in Figure 27.3). Enter new numbers in the Max Time and/ or Iterations text boxes, and click on OK.

**TIP**

Although you can start Solver with the changing cells blank, Solver works faster if you enter some rough estimates into the changing cells.

The Solver settings are saved with the worksheet. When the price of corn changes and the feed mix must be recalculated, all you need to do is open the workbook, change the price on the worksheet, choose Tools ➢ Solver, and click on the Solve button.

# Solver Reports

The Solver Results dialog box provides three reports to choose from—Answer, Sensitivity, and Limits. To produce any of these reports, select the report(s) from the list (hold down Ctrl while clicking to select more than one) and click on OK. The reports will be added to the workbook as new worksheets.

## The Answer Report

The Answer report (Figure 27.6) displays the starting and final values of the target and changing cells, and an analysis of the constraint cells (whether the constraint could be met, and how much difference, or *slack*, there is between the constraints and the final values). If a constraint is *binding*, the final value of the cell is limited by the constraint. (Notice that where a constraint is binding, the final value of the cell equals the constraint.)

**PART**

**VIII**

Solving Real-World
Problems

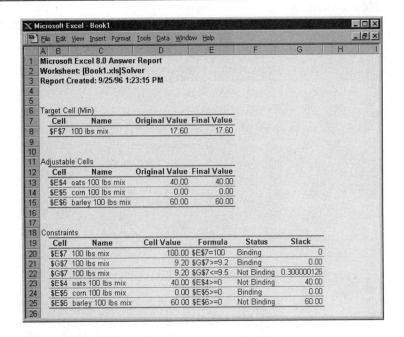

**FIGURE 27.6**

*The Answer
report displays
an analysis of
the constraints
used to solve the
problem.*

## The Sensitivity Report

The Sensitivity report (see Figure 27.7) tells you how much of a difference changes in the changing cells (or constraints) would make in the target cell.

> **NOTE**
> A different version of the Sensitivity report is created if you checked the Assume Linear Model setting in the Solver Options dialog box.

## The Limits Report

The Limits report (see Figure 27.8) lists the values of the target and changing cells, and their upper and lower limits (as specified by the constraints). Essentially, this report shows the margin of variation for each changing cell.

## More Facts about Solver

Here are a few more important points to remember when working with Solver:

- Up to 200 changing cells can be specified in a single problem.

*FIGURE 27.7*

*The Sensitivity report tells you how sensitive the target value is to changes in constraints or changing values.*

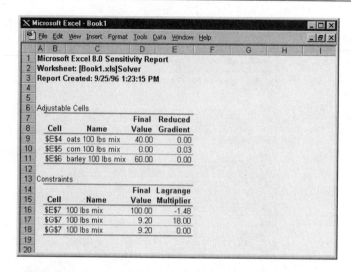

*FIGURE 27.8*

*The Limits report shows the margin for variation in the changing cells.*

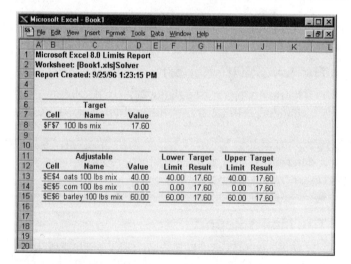

- Solver settings (parameters and options) are persistent and are saved on the worksheet. To save different settings on the same worksheet, save the settings as a *model*. To save a model, click on the Save Model button in the Solver options dialog box.
- If you want to watch the values on the worksheet change as Solver tries different values, check the Show Iteration Results setting on the Solver Options dialog box.

Each major change in values will be displayed on the worksheet, and a dialog box will ask if you want to continue the process after each change.

- Excel includes a sample Solver problem in the EXCEL\EXAMPLES\SOLVER file.

# Using Scenario Manager

Scenario Manager lets you create and save different sets of input values, with their results, as *scenarios*. In Excel, a scenario is a group of input values (called *changing cells*) saved with a name. Each scenario represents a set of what-if assumptions that you can apply to a workbook model to see the effects on other parts of the model.

Use the scenario manager to do the following:

- Create multiple scenarios with multiple sets of changing cells.
- View the results of each scenario on your worksheet.
- Create a summary report of all input values and results.

## A Sample Business Case with Scenario Manager

Suppose you have been looking for a new home, and have narrowed your choices down to two: one for $200,000, the other for $300,000. The following information will apply to either home:

- The interest rate is 7%, and a 20% down payment is required.
- The term of the loan can be either 15 years or 30 years.

There are four different scenarios: either the $300,000 house or the $200,000 house, with either the 15-year or 30-year loan. Scenario manager can help organize, manage, and summarize these scenarios.

Begin by creating a scenario for the $300,000 home, with a 15-year loan.

**1.** Enter the following on a new worksheet:

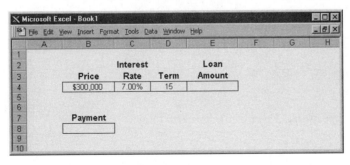

**2.** Name cells B4:E4 and B8 according to their respective column labels in cells B3:E3 and B7.

**3.** Enter the following formulas:

| Cell | Formula |
| --- | --- |
| E4 | **=Price\*.8** (The loan amount is 80% of the purchase price.) |
| B8 | **=PMT(Rate/12,Term\*12,-Amount)** |

**4.** Choose Tools ➢ Scenarios. The Scenario Manager dialog box appears.

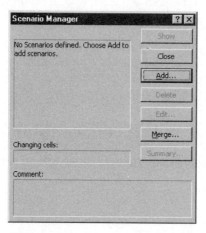

**5.** Click on the Add button to display the Add Scenario dialog box.

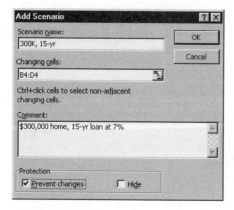

**6.** Type **300K, 15-yr** as the scenario name.

7. Double-click on the Changing Cells text box (to highlight it), then select cells B4:D4 and click on OK. The Scenario Values dialog box will be displayed, with the names of the changing cells and their values.

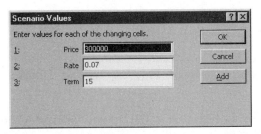

8. Since the values for the first scenario are already entered, click on Add to return to the Add Scenario dialog box and set up the next scenario.
9. Type **300K, 30-yr** in the Scenario Name text box to create (and name) the second scenario, and click on OK.
10. In the Scenario Values dialog box, change the Term value to **30**.
11. Repeat steps 8, 9, and 10 to set up the two remaining scenarios, changing both the Term and Price values, being sure to change the 300,000 to 200,000 in the Scenario Values dialog box.

   • **200K, 15-yr** with values of **$200,000** and **15**
   • **200K, 30-yr** with values of **$200,000** and **30**

12. Click on OK after creating the fourth scenario. The Scenario Manager dialog box now contains your list of four scenarios.

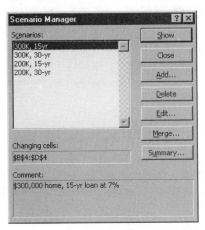

PART VIII

Solving Real-World Problems

To see any single scenario displayed on the worksheet, select the name of the scenario and click on the Show button. The worksheet values will change according to the selected scenario.

## Scenario Summary Reports

One of the best parts of Scenario Manager is its ability to summarize all of the scenarios in a single report. Once you have created your scenarios, follow these steps to create a scenario summary report:

1. Choose Tools ➢ Scenarios to display the Scenario Manager dialog box.
2. Click the Summary button on the Scenario Manager dialog box. The Scenario Summary dialog box will appear.

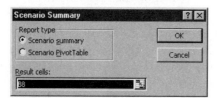

3. Select the Scenario Summary option, and be sure the Result_Cell is $B$8 (the cell displaying the payment).
4. Click on OK.

A new sheet named *Scenario Summary* (Figure 27.9) will be added to the workbook.

> **NOTE**
> The PivotTable option on the Scenario Summary dialog box creates a pivot table based on the scenario. See Chapters 20, 21, and 22 to learn more about pivot tables.

## Merging Scenarios

Suppose that you have created a number of budget scenarios based on revenue forecasts, and someone else in your department has created other budget scenarios based on different assumptions. The scenarios, defined in two separate workbooks, can be merged into a single model so that you can have all scenarios on a single list for ease of comparison.

FIGURE 27.9

The Scenario Summary is an outlined report of all the scenarios you created.

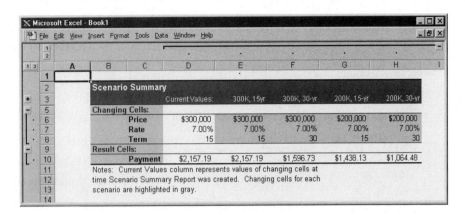

Follow these steps to merge scenarios:

1. Open the workbooks that contain the scenarios you want to merge (for example, HIS_BOOK and MY_BOOK). Make sure the worksheet that will contain the merged scenarios is active.
2. Choose Tools ➤ Scenarios, and click on the Merge button on the Scenario Manager dialog box. The Merge Scenarios dialog box will be displayed, with a drop-down list of all open workbooks and a list of the worksheets in each workbook.
3. Select the workbook (HIS_BOOK) and worksheet (Sheet1) you want to merge from, then click on OK. This will add the scenarios from the other workbook into the active workbook.

## Deleting Scenarios

Here's how to delete a scenario:

1. Choose Tools ➤ Scenarios.
2. Select the scenario to be deleted.
3. Click on the Delete button.

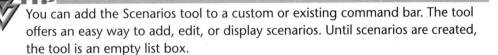

You can add the Scenarios tool to a custom or existing command bar. The tool offers an easy way to add, edit, or display scenarios. Until scenarios are created, the tool is an empty list box.

PART

VIII

Solving Real-World Problems

## Protecting Scenarios

You can protect scenarios using the Prevent Changes setting on the Add Scenario and Edit Scenario dialog boxes. By default, this setting is checked, and takes effect when the worksheet is protected.

The Tools ➤ Protection ➤ Protect Sheet dialog box also has a Scenarios setting that prevents changes to the definition of a scenario when the sheet is protected. See Chapter 11 to learn more about worksheet protection.

## More Facts about Scenario Manager

Here are a few more important points to remember when working with Scenario Manager:

- Up to 32 changing cells can be defined per scenario.
- Scenario Manager can be used to save scenarios created with Solver (click on the Save Scenario button in the Solver Results dialog box).
- When a scenario is created or edited, the user name and date are recorded by Scenario Manager. This information is displayed in the Scenario Manager dialog box and in the first outline level of the Summary report.

In this chapter you have learned about several important tools for what-if analysis. Another feature used for advanced analysis you may want to explore is *pivot tables*—this topic is covered in Chapters 20 through 22.

# Chapter

## 28

### Using Excel Add-Ins

# Using Excel Add-Ins

**A**s the name implies, add-ins are not part of the Excel core program—they are separate components which, if designed properly, seamlessly extend the power of Excel. There are a number of add-ins that come with Excel, and some are included automatically when you set up Excel on your hard drive. You may have already used one or more of them without realizing what they were. In addition, there are a number of Excel add-ins produced by independent software manufacturers. View Manager, formerly an add-in, is now a full-fledged feature of Excel called *Custom Views* in the View menu. This chapter describes some of the more commonly used add-ins that come with Excel and several new ones.

You can use Report Manager, together with Custom Views and Scenario Manager, to generate and print separate reports based on specific data ranges from different areas on the same worksheets, or different worksheets within a workbook. This allows the user to synthesize large amounts of widely separated information without having to create separate workbooks.

# Installing and Configuring Add-Ins

This section explains how to configure Excel so that the add-ins you want available at all times will open automatically. As you read this section, keep this fact in mind: there are two steps involved for making an add-in available for use:

- The add-in must be installed onto your computer (using the Excel or Office setup program).
- The add-in must be configured to automatically load every time you start Excel, or else you must manually load it.

## Installation Issues

When you first install Excel, there are a number of optional components that you can choose to install, many of which are add-ins. During setup, users typically install only those add-ins with which they are familiar, such as AutoSave, and later install other add-ins as they become familiar with them or as the need to use them arises.

Something happens when you install add-ins that is very important to understand: in some cases, the Excel setup program not only copies the add-in to your hard disk, but also configures Excel to load the add-in automatically. (Or, in some cases, a small part of the add-in is loaded automatically which, when evoked, opens the entire add-in.) This introduces two problems:

- It takes longer to start Excel when lots of add-ins are automatically loaded.
- Add-ins consume memory.

Don't be surprised if, when you first use the add-in configuration utility, you find that a handful of add-ins are being automatically opened every time you start Excel—including some obscure ones that you may never use.

**NOTE** The Excel (or Office) setup program can be used to install components that were not installed when you first set up Excel on your system.

## How Add-Ins Behave

Different add-ins add different commands. Analysis ToolPak adds a Data Analysis command to your Tools menu and provides special worksheet functions. Report Manager adds a command to the View menu.

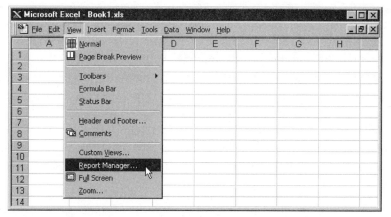

An add-in can also be a custom application that takes over the Excel workspace and displays a custom menu system (though none of the add-ins that come with Excel behave this way).

## Loading an Add-In into Memory

Remember, installing an add-in program from the Excel setup disk is not the same thing as loading the add-in into memory. In this section, you will learn how to automatically load an add-in each time you start Excel. You will also learn how to load an add-in manually.

To set which add-ins you want Excel to load automatically, choose the Tools ➤ Add-Ins command to display the Add-Ins dialog box.

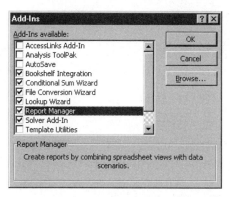

In the Add-Ins Available list box, check the add-ins you want Excel to load automatically. Uncheck the ones you will never (or seldom) use.

PART

**VIII**

Solving Real-World
Problems

**NOTE**
The Add-Ins dialog box only lists the add-ins that you chose to install during setup. When you uncheck an add-in, it is *not* removed from your disk. You can always recheck and reactivate an add-in later.

Suppose there is an add-in that you seldom use. It has been installed onto your computer using the Excel (or Office) setup program. However, since it is rarely used, it is undesirable to load it automatically, as this causes Excel to take longer to start up, and it consumes memory. For these reasons, you may want to uncheck seldom-used add-ins in the Add-Ins dialog box. There are two ways to load such an add-in into memory on the fly:

- Use the File ➤ Open command and open the add-in as you would open any Excel file. Add-ins typically end with an XLA suffix, instead of the default XLS suffix.
- Choose Tools ➤ Add-Ins and check the add-in (as explained in the prior section). Then, when done, choose Tools ➤ Add-Ins again, and uncheck the add-in.

# AutoSave—Saving Your Files Automatically

The AutoSave add-in automatically saves your work at specified time intervals. The add-in file is named AUTOSAVE.XLA. Choose Tools ➤ AutoSave to display the AutoSave dialog box.

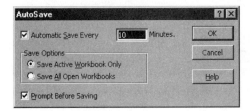

## Setting Up AutoSave

In the AutoSave dialog box, you can select from the following options:

- Place a check in the check box to activate AutoSave, or clear it to deactivate the feature.
- Enter the number of minutes between AutoSaves.
- Specify whether you want to save just the active workbook, or all open workbooks.
- Check Prompt Before Saving if want the chance to confirm or cancel the save.

Once you have loaded AutoSave, you can change the settings at any time by choosing Tools ➤ AutoSave.

> Saving files automatically, without the option to confirm, can be a risky proposition. Just imagine that the save occurs right after you make a serious mistake, and just before you are about to choose the Edit ➤ Undo command.

# Custom Views—Defining Views on a Worksheet

Before Excel 8, the Custom Views feature (formerly called *View Manager*) was courtesy of an add-in. In Excel 8, Custom Views is no longer an add-in—it has been built into the core Excel program. Why is it discussed in this chapter? Because Custom Views works hand in hand with Report Manager, which *is* an add-in.

The View ➤ Custom Views command is a tool that lets you define different *views* on a worksheet and display them with ease. For example, you may want to view only a small part of a large worksheet, view hidden rows or columns, or just view a different format. Custom views and combinations of custom views and scenarios can be extracted and are often used to prepare reports. A view definition consists of the following:

- A view name
- A range of cells
- Display settings such as gridlines, scroll bars, and row and column headings
- Print settings (optional)
- Hidden row and column settings (optional)

## Defining a View

To define a new view with Custom Views, do the following:

**1.** Select the cells or sheet you want to view.

**2.** Choose the View ➤ Custom Views command. The Custom Views dialog box is displayed.

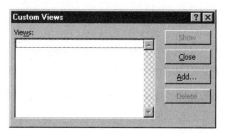

**3.** Click on the Add button. The Add View dialog box is displayed.

**4.** Enter a view name in the Name text box. The rules for the view name are the same as those for a cell name: it has to start with a letter; it cannot contain spaces; it can contain only letters, numbers, periods, and underscores; and it can't exceed 255 characters.

**5.** Choose from the following options and click on OK:

**Print Settings:** Stores the current print settings as part of the view definition.

**Hidden Rows & Columns:** Tracks which rows or columns are hidden. When you add a new view, the current status of the workspace (e.g., gridlines, scroll bars) is stored as part of the view definition.

## Showing a View

Here's how to show a view:

**1.** Choose View ➤ Custom Views to call up the Custom Views dialog box.
**2.** Select a view from the Views list.
**3.** Click on Show.

## Deleting a View

Here's how to delete a view:

**1.** Choose View ➤ Custom Views to open the Custom Views dialog box.
**2.** Select a view from the list.
**3.** Click on Delete.

## Real-World Application of Custom Views

Custom Views is especially useful when it is used on an outlined worksheet (see Chapter 26). You can define different views for different outline levels. Try this brief exercise to get a better feel for how Custom Views works:

**1.** On a new worksheet, select B2:D5 and choose View ➤ Custom Views.

**2.** Click Add in the Custom Views dialog box.

**3.** Enter a name—View1 for example—and check both settings, then click on OK.

> **NOTE**
>
> View settings are stored as a hidden name on the active worksheet.

**4.** Next, choose Tools ➤ Options, click on the View tab, and uncheck the Gridlines setting. Click on OK.

**5.** Hide column B.

**6.** Select D4:D9 and choose View ➤ Custom Views. Click on Add.

**7.** Enter a name (for example, View2), check both settings, then click on OK.

Now, show the two views to see how they work:

**8.** Choose View ➤ Custom Views, choose View1 as defined at step 3, and click on Show.

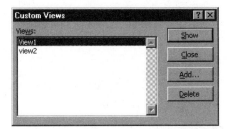

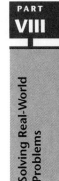

**9.** Choose View ➤ Custom Views, choose View2, and click on Show.

As you show each view, the workspace is changed according to the settings at the time the view was defined.

# Report Manager: Defining Custom Reports

The Report Manager add-in lets you define one or more custom *reports* that are stored in the active workbook. A report consists of one or more sections that will be printed as separate pages in the report. In each section you specify the following:

- The name of the worksheet
- Optionally, one scenario on that worksheet (see Chapter 27 to learn about Scenario Manager)
- Optionally, one view that has been defined on the worksheet (see the preceding section on Custom Views in this chapter)

Here are some typical problems that can be solved with Report Manager:

- A workbook contains numerous worksheets. When you print the workbook, you want to print only three of the sheets, in a specified sequence.
- A worksheet contains three scenarios created with Scenario Manager: Optimistic, Pessimistic, and Realistic. When you print the sheet, you want to print each scenario separately.
- A worksheet contains two noncontiguous ranges that you want to print on the same report, using the same page number sequence. (Each range is setup as a view using Custom Views.)

You can create more than one report per workbook.

The Report Manager add-in file is named REPORTS.XLA.

## Creating a Report

Here's how to create a new report:

**1.** Activate the desired workbook, then choose View ➤ Report Manager. The Report Manager dialog box appears:

**2.** Click on the Add button. The Add Report dialog box appears (see Figure 28.1).

**3.** Enter a report name consisting of letters, numbers, and spaces. Special characters are not permitted.

**4.** Add sheets to the report by selecting sheet names from the drop-down list. Click on the Add button as you select each sheet. You can add the same sheet to the report more than once.

**5.** Choose from the following options in the Section To Add area:

**View:** Include a view (defined by Custom Views) as part of the definition for each section of the report. Only the view range will print on the page (including all of the view settings). Choose the view from the drop-down list.

**FIGURE 28.1**

*The Add Report dialog box*

**Scenario:** Include a scenario (created by Scenario Manager) as part of the section definition. Choose the scenario from the drop-down list.

**6.** The Sections In This Report (views and/or scenarios) displayed in the list box determine their print order. Use the Move Up and Move Down buttons to change the order of the sections within the list.

**7.** If necessary, click on Delete to remove a selected section from the report. Click on OK when finished.

**NOTE**

When the Use Continuous Page Numbers option is checked, the entire report uses the same page number sequence.

## Editing, Printing, and Deleting Reports

For each of these procedures (editing, printing, and deleting), start by choosing View ➤ Report Manager to display the Report Manager dialog box. Select a report from the list of reports. Then,

- To edit a report, click on Edit. The Edit Report dialog box works the same way as the Add Report dialog box.
- To print a report, click on Print.
- To delete a report, click on Delete.

PART

**VIII**

Solving Real-World Problems

# Analysis ToolPak: Adding Special Worksheet Functions

The Analysis ToolPak adds the Data Analysis command to the Tools menu, and adds a wide variety of special worksheet functions. When the add-in is loaded, the functions are available for use just like built-in functions, such as SUM.

The functions included in the ToolPak are in the following general categories:

- Engineering functions
- Functions for statistical analysis
- Financial functions

You'll find a listing of the worksheet functions provided by the Analysis ToolPak in Appendix A.

# Writing Lookup Formulas Using the Lookup Wizard

The Lookup Wizard is a special wizard that helps you write a certain type of complex formula. Specifically, it helps you write a formula that performs a table lookup using the MATCH and INDEX functions (both of which are discussed in Chapter 9). The Lookup Wizard walks you through the process of creating a lookup formula without having to learn how to use these two powerful functions.

## Using the Lookup Wizard

Consider the following example:

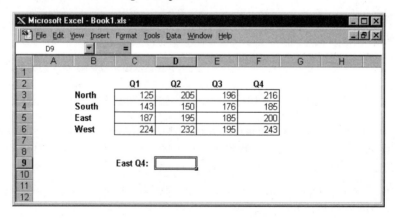

In cell D9, we want to place a formula that points to a specific value within the range B2:F6, in this case cell F5, or Q4 East. Select Tools ➤ Wizard ➤ Lookup to start the Lookup Wizard and display the Lookup Wizard Step 1 Of 4 dialog box.

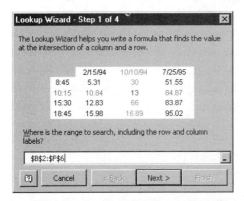

Insert the data range $B$2:$F$6 in the range edit and click on Next to move to Step 2.

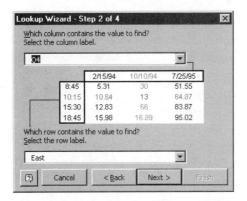

Specify the row and column label for the value in cell F5, Q4 and East, and click on Next. In the Lookup Wizard Step 3 Of 4 dialog box, you are given two options for how the formula will be written. If you select the Copy Just The Formula To A Single Cell option and then click on Next, you display the Step 4 Of 4 dialog box and can specify the location of the target cell for the formula, as shown on the next page. If you select the Copy The Formula And Lookup Parameters option and click on Next, the Lookup Wizard adds two more steps that allows you to place the lookup parameters,

Q4 and East, in separate cells. (See the sidebar "The Benefit of Placing Arguments in Discrete Cells" later in the chapter.)

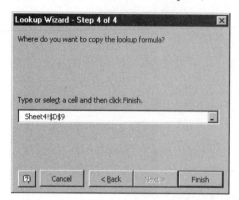

## The Benefit of Placing Arguments in Discrete Cells

At Step 3 of the Lookup Wizard, there is an option called Copy The Formula And Lookup Parameters. Choose this option to realize the full benefit of the Lookup Wizard. (This is also true of the similar Conditional Sum Wizard, discussed below.)

When chosen, this option causes the function arguments, sometimes referred to as *parameters*, to be placed in separate cells, rather than embedding them in the formula. Later, this makes it much easier to change an argument. All you have to do is enter a different value into a cell, rather than edit a complex formula. If you don't want users of the worksheet to see the argument(s), you can hide the row or column containing the argument(s), or even place them on a separate worksheet.

Arguments placed in discrete cells facilitate the use of custom controls, such as list boxes and scroll bars. Controls can be used to implement a friendly interface, where you click a control in order to change an argument. (Custom controls are discussed in Chapter 23.)

When you click on Finish, the target cell for the formula will display the value from the referenced cell, but will actually contain the formula pointing to that cell, the intersection of column Q4 and row East, as shown in the Formula bar in Figure 28.2.

**FIGURE 28.2**

The target cell
for the formula
(D9) shows the
value in cell F5,
but the Formula
bar displays
the underlying
formula.

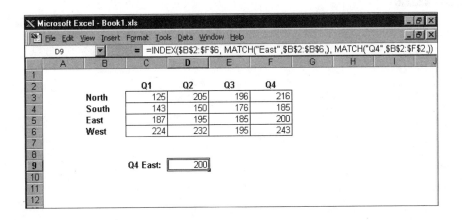

# The Conditional Sum Wizard

Like the Lookup Wizard, the Conditional Sum Wizard is a wizard that's sole purpose is to help you write a certain type of complex worksheet formula. (The name of the add-in file is SUMIF.XLA.) In this case, the formula performs summation conditionally, based on criteria you specify. For example, you could use this wizard to write a formula which, given a database of customers nationwide, calculates the total sales for customers located in Florida.

## Using the Conditional Sum Wizard

In Figure 28.3, a group of accounts earn a higher rate of interest if the balance is over $10,000, and a lower rate if the balance is $10,000 or less.

Suppose you want to sum the total dollars at each different rate. Choose Tools ➤ Wizard ➤ Conditional Sum to display the Conditional Sum Wizard Step 1 Of 4 dialog box. Here is where you select the list of values you want to apply your conditions to. In this case we want to sum values from the range labeled *Balance*, $C$3:$C$13. Notice that the label must be included in this range, unlike a normal SUM function (see Figure 28.4).

In Step 2, specify the conditions under which you want to sum the values in the source range. In this case, we sum the Balance column in the Column To Sum list box based on values within the same column in the Column list box. For the total sum that earned a higher rate, select the greater than symbol in the Is list box and enter **10,000** in the This Value text box (see Figure 28.5).

PART

**VIII**

Solving Real-World
Problems

**FIGURE 28.3**

*A group of accounts earn a higher rate of interest if the balance is over $10,000 and a lower rate if the balance is $10,000 or less.*

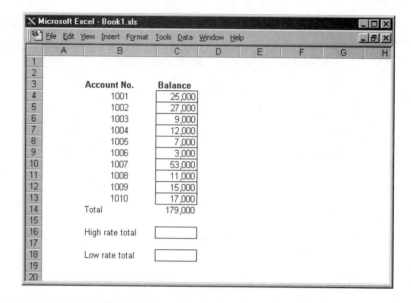

**FIGURE 28.4**

*The label must be included in this range.*

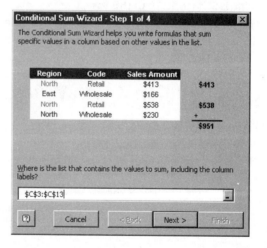

Click on Add Condition and click on Next to display Step 3. Step 3 allows you the option to just copy the formula into a single cell, or to place the condition (10,000) into a separate cell as well (which adds another step). Select the first option and click on Next (see Figure 28.6).

**FIGURE 28.5**

*Enter the information shown in Step 2.*

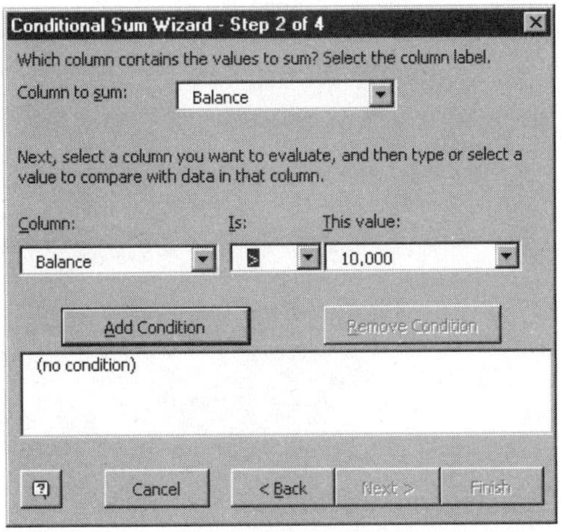

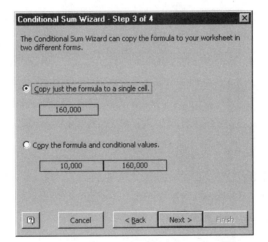

**FIGURE 28.6**

*Select the first option and click on Next.*

Select cell C16 as the target cell for your formula and click on Finish (see Figure 28.7). Cell C16 now contains the sum of all accounts in the range C3:C13 that are greater than $10,000. The underlying formula in cell C16 is displayed in the formula bar when the cell is selected, as shown in Figure 28.8.

You can run the Lookup Wizard again to calculate the sum of accounts less than or equal to $10,000, except select the less-than-or-equal-to sign (< =) in the Is list box in Step 2, and select C18 as the target cell for your formula in Step 4. The finished worksheet is shown in Figure 28.8.

**FIGURE 28.7**

Select C16 as the target cell for your formula and click on Finish.

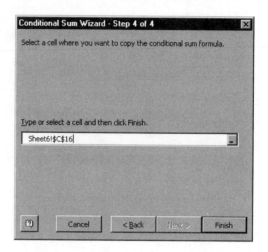

**FIGURE 28.8**

The finished worksheet

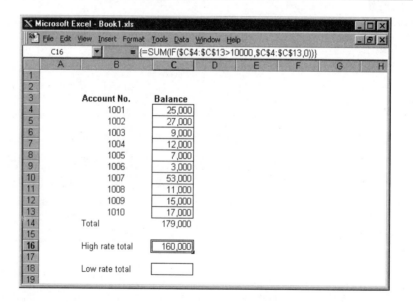

## Using the File Conversion Wizard

The File Conversion Wizard is a three-step process that converts files in other formats to Excel 8 workbook format. You can convert Lotus 1-2-3 files and dBase files, as well as Quattro Pro/DOS, Microsoft Works, SYLK, and Data Interchange Format files. See

Chapter 29 for information on working with other programs. You can also convert earlier Excel file formats to the current workbook format.

You can convert files in batches with the File Conversion Wizard, as long as you heed two conditions:

- Place all the files to be converted in the same folder.
- Make sure all the files are in the same file format; e.g., don't try to convert Lotus and Quattro Pro files to Excel workbook format at the same time.

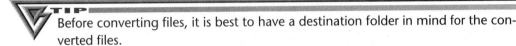

Before converting files, it is best to have a destination folder in mind for the converted files.

To start the file conversion, choose Tools ➢ Wizard ➢ File Conversion to display the Step 1 Of 3 dialog box.

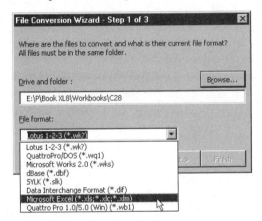

In Step 1, specify the drive and folder for the files you want to convert, specify their file format, and click on Next. If necessary, use the Browse button to find files.

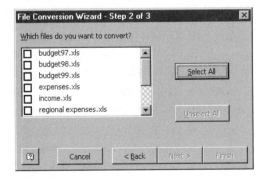

Step 2 is where you select the individual files that you want to convert from within the folder. Put a check next to the files and click on Next to display Step 3.

In Step 3 you specify the destination folder for the converted files. Click on Finish to make the file conversion.

**NOTE**

The File Conversion Wizard does not permanently convert your original files, it only makes converted copies of them.

The File Conversion add-in file name is FILECONV.XLA.

# Miscellaneous Add-Ins

There are several other add-ins that come with Excel, available following either the Typical or Custom installation. If you don't see them in your Tools ➢ Add-Ins dialog box, rerun the Excel setup. Here's an overview of some miscellaneous add-ins:

**Access Links Add-In:** Creates data links between Microsoft Access and Excel, allowing you to import Excel data into Access, and to create Access forms and reports from Excel data. External databases are covered in Chapter 19.

**Template Wizard With Data Tracking:** Tracks worksheet data that is used in databases; see Chapter 19.

**Template Utilities:** A collection of utilities for Excel's built-in templates.

**Bookshelf Integration:** Adds the Tools ➢ Lookup Reference command, and allows you to search available references in the Microsoft Bookshelf and copy data to Excel.

**Update Add-In Links:** Updates links from older Excel documents to new built-in features; an example is the Custom Views feature, which replaces View Manager (VIEWS.XLA). Update Add-In Links helps you to update your workbooks to use the new built-in Custom View feature, in place of the old add-in.

The following two utilities are installed when you install the Web Page Authoring component during setup; both are discussed in Chapter 29:

**Excel Internet Assistant Wizard:** Converts Excel data to HTML page files.

**Web Form Wizard:** Creates a form for funneling data from a Web server to a database.

In this chapter, you learned about many of the add-in programs that come with Excel. There are also a wide variety of third-party Excel add-ins available. You can download many add-ins from Microsoft's Web site: **http://www.microsoft.com**.

PART

**VIII**

Solving Real-World
Problems

# Chapter

## 29

### Excel and the World Outside

Chapter 29

# Excel and the World Outside

No software program is an island. The ability to work with other programs— and the data created by them—is an important feature in any modern software package. Excel is an outstanding citizen in this regard, providing a variety of ways to interact with other programs, import data, and utilize a host of new Internet-related features.

This chapter covers important new features such as Internet operability and shared workbooks. It also covers mundane topics like the Windows Clipboard—and everything in between.

 **NOTE**
One critical aspect of "the world outside" is querying external databases. This topic is covered in Chapter 19.

## Excel and the Internet

Make no mistake, Microsoft has embraced the Internet. A number of new features have been added in Excel 8 to enhance its operability with the Internet, both from the standpoint of Web browsing and of Web authoring. Some familiarity with the Internet, especially the Web, will be useful in order to get the most from this information.

## Using Hyperlinks

One of the most appealing features of the Web is the ability to navigate documents using *hyperlinks*. When you click on a hyperlink (usually consisting of one or more distinctively formatted words), the screen jumps to a different spot in the same document, or to a different document. Now, in Excel 8, you can add such hyperlinks to Excel worksheets—without programming. A hyperlink on an Excel worksheet can link to the following:

- another worksheet/range in the same workbook
- a different workbook
- any file on your local hard drive or network file server (as long as the file type is known to Windows)
- an Internet/intranet address or file

As you might expect, Microsoft has implemented hyperlinks throughout Office, allowing users and organizations to build internal webs based on Office documents (Excel, Word, etc.) that are navigable much like the Internet. In fact, for organizations that have standardized on Microsoft Office, a web based on a combination of HTML and Microsoft Office documents has much to offer, given Excel's rich, interactive environment (in contrast with the still-primitive nature of HTML).

**NOTE**

Suppose you want to publish Microsoft Office documents on the Internet or your organization's intranet. However, you can not rely on every user having Microsoft Office installed on their computers. (On the Internet this problem is a given.) Microsoft publishes so-called *viewer* programs free of charge, which allow you to view files, but not edit them. There are viewers for Excel, Word, and PowerPoint.

To place a hyperlink on a worksheet, enter some text into a cell. With the cell selected, choose Insert ➤ Hyperlink. Figure 29.1 shows the Insert Hyperlink dialog box.

**Link to File or URL** - As the onscreen prompt indicates, this can be a file name on your local hard drive, or on a networked drive. Optionally, use the Browse button to locate the file, or enter an Internet address (URL). See Table 29.1 for a list of sample entries. If you are creating a hyperlink to another range in the same workbook, bypass this setting.

**Path** - The path is a text string that specifies the precise location of a the file, whether that file is located on your hard drive, or on the Internet. The path is for display

**FIGURE 29.1**

*A hyperlink can link to a disk file, or to an Internet address (URL).*

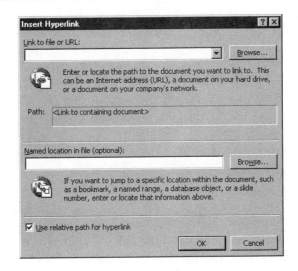

| Insert Hyperlink | ? X |
|---|---|
| **Link to file or URL:** | |
| [ ] ▼  Browse... | |
| Enter or locate the path to the document you want to link to. This can be an Internet address (URL), a document on your hard drive, or a document on your company's network. | |
| **Path:**  &lt;Link to containing document&gt; | |
| **Named location in file (optional):** | |
| [ ]  Browse... | |
| If you want to jump to a specific location within the document, such as a bookmark, a named range, a database object, or a slide number, enter or locate that information above. | |
| ☑ Use relative path for hyperlink | |
| OK  Cancel | |

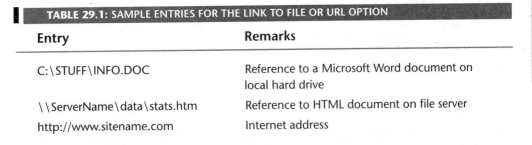

**TABLE 29.1:** SAMPLE ENTRIES FOR THE LINK TO FILE OR URL OPTION

| Entry | Remarks |
|---|---|
| C:\STUFF\INFO.DOC | Reference to a Microsoft Word document on local hard drive |
| \\ServerName\data\stats.htm | Reference to HTML document on file server |
| http://www.sitename.com | Internet address |

only—it cannot be directly edited. However, pay careful attention to it—the path is a vital consideration if you plan on deploying the workbook to others. Look at the discussion of the Use Relative Path For Hyperlink option that follows.

**Location In File** - This optional qualifier, applicable only for Office files, allows you to link to a specific location within a file. When linking to an Excel workbook, for example, you can specify a worksheet, a range, or a name. When linking to a Word document, specify a bookmark. For PowerPoint, specify a slide within the presentation. When linking to an Access file, specify a database object such as a form or report. The Browse button displays a list of choices that depend upon the type of file being linked to.

**Use Relative Path For Hyperlink** - Checking this setting changes the path, discussed above. When checked, the path is stored relative to the path of the linking document. When unchecked, the absolute path is stored. Here's an example:

Assume the full path of the document you are linking from is named C:\MYWEB\ HOME.XLS, and the full path of the document you are linking to is C:\MYWEB\FILES\ MOREINFO.XLS. In this case, the relative path to MOREINFO.XLS (in relation to HOME.XLS) is FILES\MOREINFO.XLS.

The Use Relative Path For Hyperlink setting is useful when you are organizing files in folders below the main linking document in the directory structure. It allows you to easily move the whole set of linked documents without adjusting each link. This setting is only enabled when creating links to disk files—it is not available for Internet addresses.

On the Insert Hyperlink dialog box, once you click on OK, a hyperlink is added to the active cell as a formatted text string. When you click on this text string, the linked document is opened. If you opt not to place anything in the cell before creating the link, the file name, including the full path, is the default text, as you can see in Figure 29.2.

**TIP**

Worksheet hyperlinks are not text-only—you can use graphic objects as well. Place a picture or other graphic object on a worksheet. Then, with the object selected, choose Insert ➢ Hyperlink.

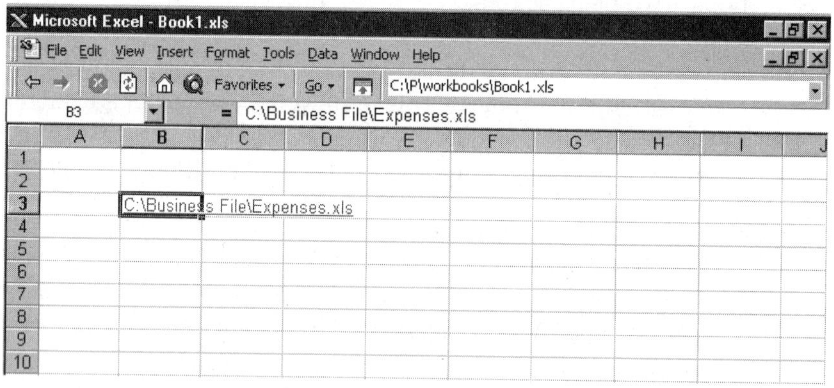

**FIGURE 29.2**

*When you click on the hyperlink, the linked document is activated. Notice the Web toolbar, which Excel displays automatically when hyperlinks are used.*

## Changing a Hyperlink

There are three properties of a hyperlink you can change:

- The text that displays on the worksheet (the friendly name)
- The format of the friendly name
- The file name/URL being linked to

**Changing the Friendly Name** - Since when you click on a hyperlink a jump occurs, editing a friendly name requires a special procedure:

1. Right-click on the cell containing the hyperlink.
2. Click on Cancel to close the shortcut menu.
3. Type a new value into the cell (or press F2 to edit it).

**Changing the Text Format** - Hyperlinks change color after being clicked on. The text formatting, before and after being clicked on, is changeable. Here's how:

There is a new built-in style called *Hyperlink*. (Read about *styles* in Chapter 5.) To change your hyperlink formatting, select a hyperlink cell, then choose Format ➢ Style. Click on the Modify button, and off you go. Refer to Chapter 5 for more information on modifying styles.

While you can format a hyperlink cell using the Format ➢ Cells command, the hyperlink will always be the same format as a result—its format won't change when clicked on.

Remember this key fact: when you change the Hyperlink style (or any style, for that matter), the change impacts only the active workbook.

**Changing the Link** - To change the link, right-click on the cell, then choose Hyperlink ➢ Edit Hyperlink. The Edit Hyperlink dialog box appears—it is nearly identical to the Insert Hyperlink dialog box. One difference is the Remove Link button at the bottom of the dialog box—this button causes the hyperlink to be removed (though it leaves the text label in the cell).

# The HYPERLINK Function

To get the most from this discussion, you should have a solid understanding of worksheet formulas and functions, covered in Chapters 4 and 9. You should also read the preceding section on hyperlinks.

There is a new worksheet function in Excel 8—the *HYPERLINK* function. It provides functionality similar to the Insert ➢ Hyperlink command, discussed earlier. It has an important capability in addition: since the link is an argument, it can be formulated

## Building a Web of Office Documents

Hyperlinks in Microsoft Office work similarly to World Wide Web hyperlinks. They change color once they are clicked on. In addition, the Web toolbar, shown in Figure 29.2, contains buttons (home/ forward/back), which let you navigate a web of Office documents the same way you navigate the World Wide Web. This same toolbar displays in other Office 97 programs, too.

Remember that you can create a hyperlink to an Internet address. When you click on this type of hyperlink, your Web browser is started automatically. This allows organizations that have standardized on Office to setup up a semi-seamless web consisting of both HTML and Office documents.

dynamically. We will demonstrate this concept in a moment. First, here are the two arguments used by the HYPERLINK function:

```
=HYPERLINK(Link Location, Friendly Name)
```

> **Link Location:** File name including path

> **Friendly Name:** Text that displays on the worksheet for the hyperlink

Consider the following example:

```
=HYPERLINK("c:\files\Sales1997.xls", "Display 1997 Sales Data")
```

The second argument (friendly name) displays on the worksheet, whereas the first argument (link location) is the file name that is opened when the hyperlink is clicked on. This hyperlink is not functionally different than one created with the Insert ➢ Hyperlink command—the information is hard-wired. However, as is the case with most arguments, the value can be dynamically formulated.

To appreciate the concept of formulating these two arguments dynamically, consider this example: every year, an Excel file named SALES*YYYY*.XLS is saved in a certain folder, where *YYYY* is the current year. Another Excel file, HOME.XLS, is the start page for an intranet. HOME.XLS will have a hyperlink to SALES*YYYY*.XLS, and perhaps other documents.

If the link is hard-wired, HOME.XLS must be modified every year when the new sales workbook is published. The solution involves built-in worksheet functions, used in conjunction with the HYPERLINK function. Here is a formula that will calculate the link location and friendly name using the current year:

```
=HYPERLINK("c:\files\Sales" & YEAR(NOW()) & ".xls" , "Display " &
YEAR(NOW()) & " Sales Data")
```

To simplify the reading of this formula, here are the two arguments broken down:

**Link Location:**

```
"c:\files\Sales" & YEAR(NOW()) & ".xls"
```

**Friendly Name:**

```
"Display " & YEAR(NOW()) & " Sales Data"
```

Now, rather than hard-wiring the year, it is being calculated using the YEAR and NOW functions. As used together in this example, YEAR and NOW return the current year. Notice that the friendly name is also being calculated using similar logic. Try entering this formula on a worksheet—it doesn't matter if the linked files don't exist (until you click on the hyperlink, that is).

**TIP**

When you are typing a formula with nested functions, and aren't quite getting it, work from the inside out. For instance, to better understand the complex HYPER-LINK formula above, enter =NOW(). Then enter =YEAR(NOW()), and so on.

The examples above are all based on disk files. Remember, however, that HYPER-LINK can also reference Internet addresses/documents (UNC address or URL path).

## The Web Toolbar

Excel's Web toolbar looks a lot like the toolbar found in Microsoft Internet Explorer. This is no accident. With the rising popularity of the Internet, Microsoft seeks to provide a Web-like interface for navigating and browsing Office documents. The Web toolbar is also a part of Word, PowerPoint, and other Office programs. This allows users to navigate all Office documents using techniques familiar to Web surfers.

The toolbar displays automatically when you add a hyperlink to a worksheet, though you can show it at any time using the View ➢ Toolbars command. Table 29.2 describes the commands available on Excel's Web toolbar.

PART

**VIII**

Solving Real-World Problems

| TABLE 29.2: EXCEL'S WEB TOOLBAR | |
| --- | --- |
| **ICON** | **DESCRIPTION** |
| ← | Jumps back to the last active page (range, worksheet, or file other than an Excel file). |
| → | Jumps ahead to the next page (somewhere you came back from using the back arrow). |
| ⊗ | If a jump to a new page is in process, click on this icon to stop the jump. |
| ⟳ | Refreshes the active page by reloading it into memory. |
| 🏠 | Displays your Web browser's default startup page. |
| 🔍 | Activates a Microsoft Internet Web page for searching the Internet—this page links to several popular search engines. |
| Favorites ▾ | Displays a menu allowing you to jump to a favorite Web site, or add/delete items from the favorites list. |
| Go ▾ | Displays a menu that allows you to set your start page and search page. |
| ⊡ | This is a shortcut for hiding all toolbars other than the Web toolbar (making Excel look a little more like a Web browser). |

## The Internet Assistant

There is an add-in program that is included with Office—the *Internet Assistant*—which extends Excel's Internet capabilities. If there is no Save As HTML command on Excel's File menu, either the add-in is not installed on your computer, or else it is not loaded into memory.

Use the Tools ➢ Add-Ins command to display a list of add-ins. The Internet Assistant must be checked. If it's not on the list, it probably needs to be installed using your Excel (or Office) setup disk. (See Chapter 28 to learn about setting up add-ins.) Here are two features that the add-in provides:

**Saving HTML Format:** By choosing the File ➤ Save As HTML command, you can save a table or chart to HTML format. The entire worksheet is *not* saved—just the active table of data or chart. Remember, the Internet Assistant add-in must be loaded in order for the File ➤ Save AS HTML command to appear.

**The Web Form Wizard:** This wizard walks you through the process of creating input forms for Web publication, intended for input to a database. To display the wizard, choose the Tools ➤ Wizard ➤ Web Form command.

## Opening Excel Files from an Internet Server

Excel, and other Office programs, are able to directly access files located on HTTP and FTP servers (Internet file servers). This allows you to open and save Excel files using the standard File ➤ Open and File ➤ Save commands (as opposed to the age-old download, open, save, upload routine). Before you can save a workbook to an FTP site, you must have write permission to the site, and you must add the FTP site to your list of Internet sites—refer to Excel's online help for more information. In the File ➤ Open dialog box, you must enter the full path/address of the file.

# Exchanging Data Using the Clipboard

Excel has several powerful facilities for importing and exporting data, such as object linking and embedding (OLE). But for everyday manual tasks, the Clipboard is a convenient way to move information in and out of Excel. Most Windows programs are capable of using the Clipboard, and you can use it to copy both text and graphics.

## Copying Text into Excel

Here is an exercise that demonstrates how to copy text from Notepad (the ASCII text editor that comes with Windows 95) into Excel:

1. Start Notepad, and enter some text. (You can start Notepad using the Windows Start button.)
2. Select the text, and choose Edit ➤ Copy (this copies the text to the Clipboard).
3. Activate Excel, select a target cell, and choose Edit ➤ Paste (this pastes the text from the Clipboard onto the worksheet).

The text is placed into one or more cells. It's that simple. Every other use of the Clipboard is simply a variation on the above exercise.

## Copying Graphics into Excel

The procedure for copying graphics into Excel is very similar. Follow these steps:

1. Use a program such as Paintbrush to create your own graphic.
2. Select the graphic with the mouse, then choose the Edit ➢ Copy command to copy a graphic to the Clipboard.
3. Activate Excel, select the cell where you want to paste the graphic, and choose Edit ➢ Paste.

The graphic is placed on the worksheet as a graphic object, as shown in Figure 29.3.

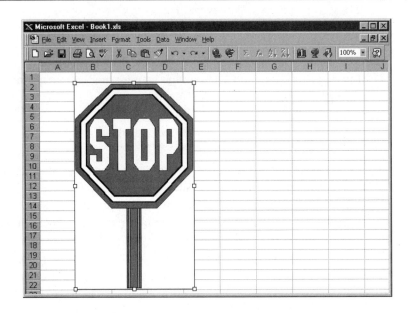

Graphics copied into Excel can be moved, resized, and deleted just like any other graphic object. (See Chapter 12 for a review of working with graphic objects.)

## Copying Data Out of Excel

Copying data (text or graphics) out of Excel involves the same procedure used to copy into Excel, but in the opposite direction. Follow this exercise to copy some information from Excel into WordPad (the word processor that comes with Windows 97).

1. Enter some data onto a blank worksheet.

**2.** Select a range of cells that contains the data, and choose Edit ➤ Copy.

**3.** Activate WordPad, and choose Edit ➤ Paste.

Figure 29.4 shows a WordPad file where two different paste operations have occurred.

---

**FIGURE 29.4**

*The same data from Excel was pasted two times, using different paste options available in WordPad.*

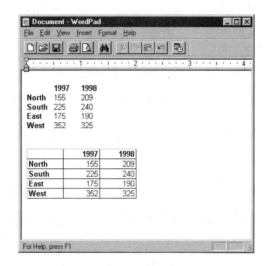

The first table of numbers in Figure 29.4 is formatted text. The second table is a graphic image (bitmap). WordPad can import the data in different formats, using its Edit ➤ Paste Special command. This illustrates an important point: the type of data that pastes into the other program is dependent on that program's capabilities. For example, Notepad is not capable of importing graphics. If you wanted to paste the data pictured in Figure 29.4 into Notepad, the only option would be to paste text.

# Using Object Linking and Embedding

*Object Linking and Embedding* (OLE) is a technology that allows different applications to communicate and share data with one another. OLE has become a popular buzzword, though few really understand it. It's actually quite simple. The term *OLE* is derived from the fact that a piece of data, called an *object,* which is created in one application can be *embedded* in another. And the embedded object can be *linked* to the source document.

**NOTE** OLE is not limited to Microsoft products. It is an important part of the Windows operating system, and many non-Microsoft applications support OLE, including most major word processing and graphics applications.

The ultimate purpose of OLE (from a user's perspective, as opposed to a programmer's) is to remove barriers between programs. It allows users to focus on *their information*, rather than the program that created the information. In this section, you will walk through a simple exercise to see how OLE works. The following examples will use Excel and Word for Office 97.

## Copying an Excel Object into Word

Suppose you are writing a business plan in Word, and that you have built a worksheet in Excel that contains supporting data. The following exercise shows you how to copy part of the worksheet to the Word document.

**1.** Enter the following onto a blank Excel worksheet.

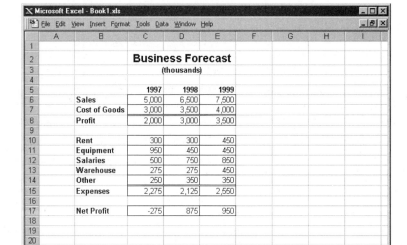

**2.** Select the range of cells that contains the data, then choose Edit ➢ Copy.

**3.** Activate Word. Place the cursor at the place where you want to paste the object.

**4.** Choose Edit ➢ Paste Special. The Paste Special dialog box is displayed.

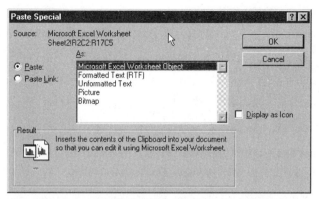

**5.** Select Microsoft Excel Worksheet Object from the list, and select how you want to paste:

**Paste:** Places an embedded object into Word. The Excel object then "lives" inside the Word document, with no link to the original Excel document. (You will still be able to edit the Excel object using Excel, as you will soon see.)

**Paste Link:** Links the object to the original Excel document. Changes to the original Excel document will cause the linked object to update.

**6.** Click on OK. The Word document is shown in Figure 29.5.

---

**FIGURE 29.5**

*The Excel infor-
mation is
pasted into the
Word document
as an Excel
object.*

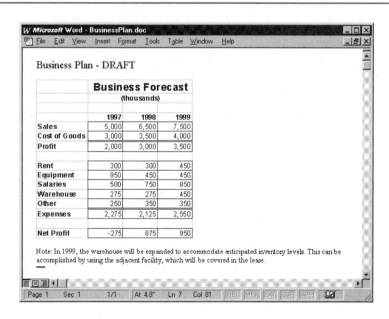

### Using Drag and Drop

Instead of using menu commands, you can drag and drop information from Excel to Word. Arrange your workspace so that you can see both applications at once. Activate Excel, and follow these steps:

**1.** Select the cell(s) you want to copy.

**2.** Click on the outermost border of the selected range, and while holding down the mouse button, use one of the following methods:

- Drag the cells onto the Word document to *cut and paste.*
- Hold down Ctrl while dragging to *copy and paste.*

**TIP**
You are not limited to cells when copying Excel objects to other applications. You can also copy Excel charts and other graphic objects. Just drag and drop the chart onto a Word document, for instance, to embed the chart in Word.

## Understanding How Embedded Objects Work

As mentioned earlier, when you select the Paste option in the Paste Special dialog box, the copied Excel object is *embedded* in the Word document, where it is physically stored. The following points apply to embedded objects:

- There is no link between the embedded object and the original Excel worksheet. A change to the original Excel worksheet has no effect on the embedded object.
- If you double-click on the embedded object (in the Word document), Excel is activated and takes control—even though you do not leave the Word document. (See Figure 29.6). At this point, you are using Excel, but within the context of the Word document. This is called *in-place editing.*
- If you edit the embedded Excel object, there is no effect on the original Excel worksheet, since there is no link.
- When you click outside the embedded object (within the Word document), Word assumes control again.

## Understanding How Linked Objects Work

When, on the other hand, you select the Paste Link option in the Paste Special dialog box, the Excel object is *linked* to the original worksheet—it is simply a copy of the worksheet cells. The following points apply to linked objects:

- When you make changes to the worksheet, the linked object changes.

**FIGURE 29.6**

The Excel object
on the Word
document has
been double-
clicked on. The
Excel menu
takes over, and
the object
becomes an
editable Excel
worksheet.

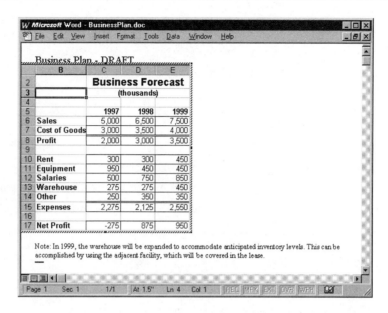

- If you double-click on the linked object (in the Word document), the original worksheet is loaded into Excel (unlike the in-place editing that occurs for embedded objects).

## Placing a Word Object into Excel

Placing OLE objects into Excel involves identical concepts and procedures to the previous exercises—but in reverse. Since Word and Excel are both Microsoft products, even the dialog boxes are similar. Figure 29.7 shows Excel's Edit ➤ Paste Special dialog box.

**NOTE**

Excel's Edit ➤ Paste Special dialog box is different, depending on the contents of the Clipboard at the time the command is chosen. If the Clipboard contains data from another application (non-Excel data), it looks like Figure 29.7. If, however, the Clipboard contains Excel data, the dialog box provides different options, such as the choice to paste formulas, values, formatting, etc.

**FIGURE 29.7**

*Excel's Edit ➤ Paste Special dialog box is similar to the Word dialog box.*

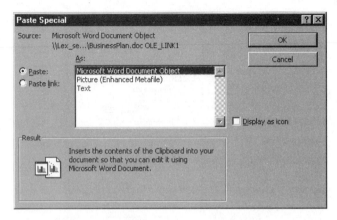

Figure 29.8 shows an Excel worksheet with an embedded Word object.

## Linking a Word Object into Excel with an Icon

Suppose you have information in a Word document that is supplemental to your Excel report, and you don't want the information displayed unless the user specifically asks to see it. If the report is going to be used primarily in electronic format, you can display the Word object as an icon on the worksheet. When the user double-clicks on the icon, the Word document is opened.

Both embedded and linked objects can be displayed as icons. To display an embedded or linked object as an icon, check the Display As Icon setting on the Paste Special dialog box.

## Embedding an Object in Excel Using the Excel Menu

You have seen how to copy objects from one application to another when both applications are running. You can also insert OLE objects into Excel by starting out with a command on the Excel menu. Choose Insert ➤ Object to display the Object dialog box pictured in Figure 29.9.

**FIGURE 29.8**

*A Word object embedded in Excel*

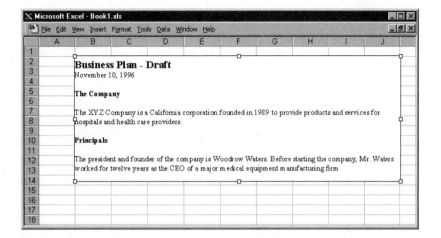

**FIGURE 29.9**

*The Object dialog box lets you create a new object or import one from an existing file.*

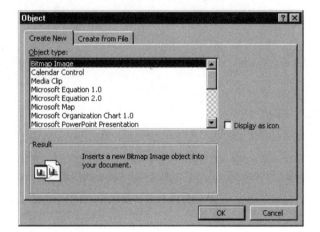

## Inserting a New Object

The Create New tab (see Figure 29.9) lists the different types of OLE objects that you are able to create. Choose an object from the list, then click on OK. The program that is responsible for the given object is started. When you finish creating the object and quit the program, the object is placed on the worksheet. (The precise behavior depends on the individual program.)

### Inserting an Object from an Existing File

The Create From File tab (see Figure 29.10) lets you insert an existing file (object) into the active worksheet. Type in a file name, or click on Browse to locate a file on your system. Check Link To File to link the object to the file. Check Display As Icon to place an icon on the worksheet representing the object.

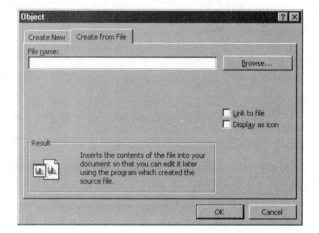

# Importing Text Files

Since most applications are able to export data in text format, importing text files is usually fairly easy. Unfortunately, however, there are several different text file formats—something that has confounded users of earlier Excel versions. To avoid confusion, Excel employs a Text Import Wizard to simplify the job of importing text files.

**NOTE**

This discussion is based on text files that contain data oriented as records, with each record containing fields of data, as opposed to random text. Random textual data can easily be copied into Excel using the Clipboard, from a text program such as Notepad.

The first step to import a text file is to choose the File ➢ Open command. Select Text Files from the list of file types, then open the desired file.

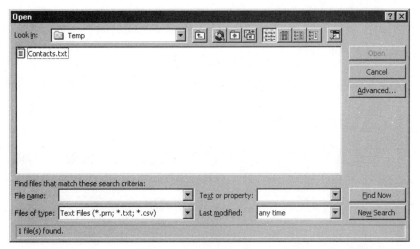

What happens next depends on the format, and file name suffix, of the text file.

## Text Files with Delimiters

*Delimiters* are special characters that separate fields, allowing Excel to place each field into a new column on the worksheet. When a text file is delimited, importing it into Excel is easy.

### Working with Comma Delimited Text Files

There are several delimiters that are frequently used. Perhaps the most common one is *comma delimited,* referred to as CSV (for *comma separated values*). Figure 29.11 shows a CSV file that has been opened using Notepad.

**FIGURE 29.11**

*This comma-delimited text file contains four rows (records) and five columns (fields).*

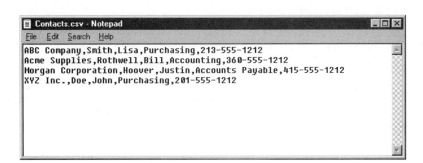

PART

**VIII**

Solving Real-World Problems

If you import a certain text file on a regular basis, and have any control of the file format, use CSV format. When you open a CSV file, the data is automatically placed into rows and columns. However, you must adhere to one rule: the file name must have an extension of .CSV. This extension causes Excel to *not* display the Text Import Wizard. This is true even if Office 97 is set up to hide file extensions. Figure 29.12 shows the same text file opened in Excel.

**FIGURE 29.12**

*When a CSV file is opened in Excel, and the file is named with a .CSV extension, the data is automatically placed in rows and columns without manual intervention.*

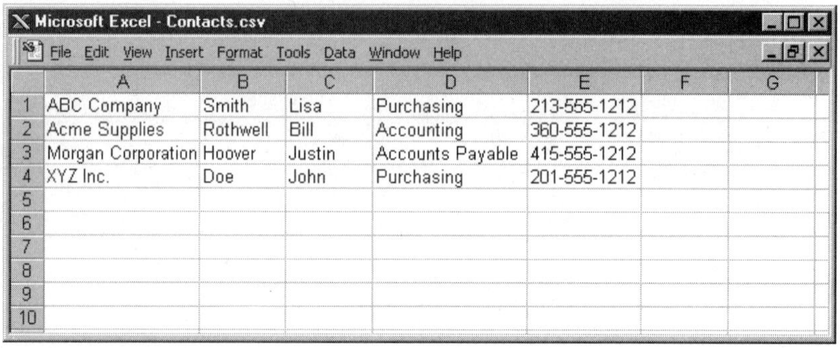

**Working with Delimiters Other than Commas**

When other types of delimiters are used (tabs, for instance), the Text Import Wizard verifies the delimiter before placing the data onto the worksheet. After you check Delimited in the Text Import Wizard Step 1 dialog box, you can choose from a variety of delimiters in the Step 2 dialog box. When the correct delimiter is selected, the preview in the Step 2 dialog box will display the data in columns. The following section gives a step-by-step overview of the Text Import Wizard.

# Using the Text Import Wizard for Fixed-Width Files

If your text file does not use delimiters, then the fields must be fixed-width. This, too, is a very common format, and has historically caused users the most trouble. Figure 29.13 shows a text file with fixed-field widths, opened in Notepad.

The Text Import Wizard makes it relatively easy to import fixed-width text files. The following section describes the steps required to import the text file pictured in Figure 29.13.

**FIGURE 29.13**

*The fields of a
fixed-width text
file are typically
padded with
spaces. The
fourth field of
the third row,
containing
Accounts Pay-
able, is the max-
imum width for
the fourth field,
and thus has no
trailing spaces.*

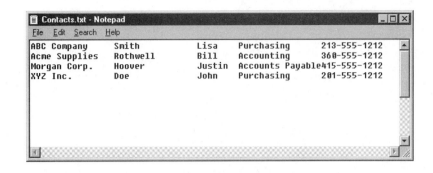

## Starting the Text Import Wizard

To start the Text Import Wizard, choose File ➢ Open, and open the file as usual. The
Text Import Wizard—Step 1 Of 3 dialog box appears, as shown in Figure 29.14.

**FIGURE 29.14**

*Step 1 lets you
confirm the text
file format.*

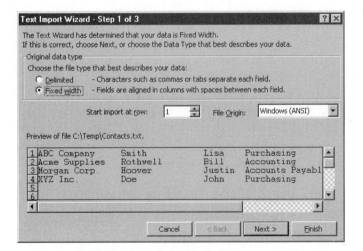

## Step 1 of 3 of the Text Import Wizard: Confirming the Text File Format

Step 1 of the Text Import Wizard lets you confirm the format of the text file you wish to import. The following options and features are available in the Step 1 dialog box:

**Original Data Type:** In this case, the Wizard detects that the file is fixed width, though you can override this option if the Wizard is wrong.

**Start Import At Row:** This lets you specify the starting row number. This setting is useful if the file contains a header row, and you don't want to import it.

**File Origin:** There are slight differences between files originated on different platforms (i.e., the character that indicates a new row). The Wizard will usually determine this setting correctly, but you can select from the drop-down list to override the choice.

**Preview Area:** This scrollable part of the dialog box lets you examine the file.

After you have finished selecting the desired options, click on Next to move to Step 2.

## Step 2 of 3 of the Text Import Wizard: Specifying the Column Breaks

Step 2 of the Wizard (Figure 29.15) lets you specify where the column breaks are located. You can create, delete, and move break lines using this dialog box. The Text Import Wizard tries to determine the column breaks for you, and usually does a pretty good job. But as you can see in Figure 29.15, the column breaks are incorrect. Fixed-width fields are typically padded with spaces. The first row was a space in the middle of the first fields—between the words ABC and Company. Accordingly, Excel has incorrectly guessed that there is a column break at position 4. As the text on the top of the dialog box states, you can create a new column break by single-clicking anywhere, remove an existing column break by double-clicking on it, or move a column break by dragging and dropping it with the mouse.

## Step 3 of 3 of the Text Import Wizard: Formatting the Columns

Step 3 of the Wizard (Figure 29.16) lets you format columns, or exclude them from being imported entirely.

To format a column, click on it with the mouse. Then choose the appropriate column format option from the Column Data Format area.

**General:** If a column is formatted as General, Excel will automatically determine the data type.

**FIGURE 29.15**

*Step 2 provides thorough instruction on how to set the column breaks.*

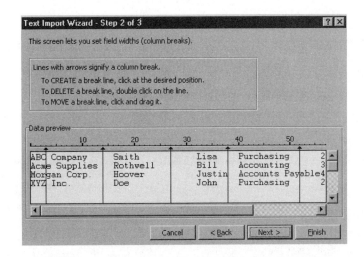

**FIGURE 29.16**

*Step 3 is used to format the columns.*

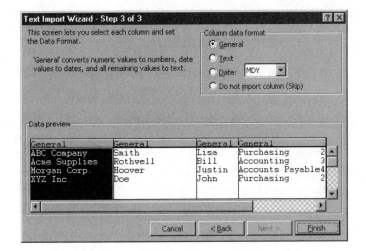

**Text:** Select this option when a column contains numeric values that should be text; e.g., zip codes or social security numbers.

**Date:** Select the date option (and the associated drop-down list) to format a column as dates.

**Do Not Import Column (Skip):** Select this option to exclude the column entirely.

PART

VIII

Solving Real-World Problems

When you click on Finish, the text file is imported onto the active worksheet into rows and columns.

TIP

Suppose that you create reports each month based on a fixed-width text file that is output by a mainframe application. You can automate this task by recording a macro.

**MASTERING TROUBLESHOOTING**

## Correcting Data Parsing Problems

Suppose you routinely download tab-delimited data from a mainframe, and it is always imported into Excel with columns parsed appropriately. One day you open a text file that is comma delimited, and because the file has a .TXT extension, Excel automatically displays the Text Import Wizard to guide you in selecting the correct delimiter for the text file. You select the comma delimiter and open the text file, and the data parses correctly into columns.

Next, you download the data from the mainframe as usual, but the data appears on the worksheet all in a single column. It might even have garbage characters mixed in with it. What happened?

The problem is that Excel tried to import the tab-delimited mainframe data using a comma delimiter, because you set the delimiter to comma when you imported the text file. Delimiter settings are persistent, and Excel will keep using the comma delimiter until you change it. If you happen to be importing data that is tab-delimited (or uses any delimiter other than a comma), the data will be imported entirely into one column. You can fix any data parsing problem using the Text Import Wizard. To parse the imported data into columns correctly, select a single data cell in the column of data, then press Ctrl+Shift+* to select the entire data region. Then choose Data ➢ Text To Columns. The Text Import Wizard dialog box will be displayed. In Step 2 of the dialog box, specify the correct delimiter. Look at the Data Preview window to be sure you've selected the correct delimiter—when you've got the right delimiter, the preview data will be in columns.

# Switching from Lotus 1-2-3

Excel has many features to help out Lotus 1-2-3 users.

**Opening 1-2-3 Files** - Lotus 1-2-3 spreadsheets can be opened using the File ➤ Open command, and saved using the File ➤ Save command (though Excel-specific information cannot be saved). You can build Excel models that use 1-2-3 sheets and even refer to names defined on them.

**Running Macros** - You can run 1-2-3 macros under Excel, without having to translate them.

**Getting Help** - The Help ➤ Lotus 1-2-3 command provides detailed help for Lotus users.

**Special Transition Settings** - Choose Tools ➤ Options, then click the Transition tab. Select the Lotus 1-2-3 Help option. The slash key (/) will then help you write formulas using 1-2-3 syntax.

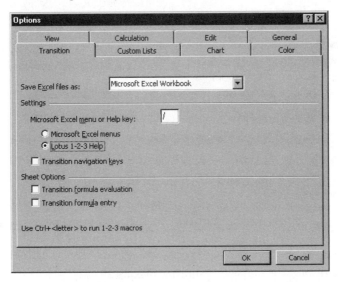

# Working with Shared Workbooks

As the name implies, a shared workbook is an Excel 8 file that has been set up to be shared by multiple networked users. This allows more than one person to have read/write access to an Excel workbook simultaneously.

Consider the budgeting process for a large organization. Invariably, this involves a lot of people, and a lot of data passing from user to user—often, up and down the organization's management hierarchy. The shared workbook feature can be an important tool for managing this sort of data flow.

When a workbook is shared, the following is true:

- More than one user can revise the workbook simultaneously.
- Inputs made by different people can be merged into a "master" copy (in an automated manner).

**MASTERING THE OPPORTUNITIES**

### Using Them Is Easy—Knowing When Is the Hard Part

Used judiciously, shared workbooks can play a key role for many collaborative activities. However, you must consider how important the data is, and whether a database management system should also be employed.

As you read about sharing workbooks, you will quickly discover that using this set of features is not particularly difficult. Knowing *when* to use sharing, however, is a different issue entirely. In some applications, at some point, the data integrity of a shared workbook must be considered, in comparison to an industrial-strength database management system. It's not a simple choice of technology A versus technology B. Both could have a role to play solving a given problem.

## Sharing a Workbook

Before sharing your first workbook, make sure that your name has been entered correctly. Choose Tools ➢ Options ➢ General—on the bottom of the dialog box is a place to change your name. With this detail aside, choose the Tools ➢ Share Workbook command to display the dialog box shown in Figure 29.17.

The check box at the top of the dialog box is *the* setting that determines if a workbook is shared. The dialog box also lists all of the people who currently have the workbook open. If you are setting up a workbook for sharing the first time, only your name will be listed. To enable sharing, check the setting at the top of the dialog box.

**FIGURE 29.17**

*The Share Work-
book dialog box*

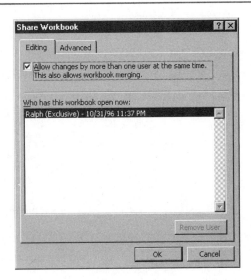

When you click on the Advanced tab, located on the top of the dialog box, the dialog box pictured in Figure 29.18, is displayed. This dialog box is explained in the following paragraphs.

**Track Changes:** Determines if a history of changes should be retained, and if
yes, for how many days. By default, change history is retained for 30 days.

**Update Changes:** Changes from other users can be updated every time you save
the file, or at a time interval you specify. (In either case, you must have the shared
workbook open.)

**Conflicting Changes Between Users:** A conflict occurs when two people
revise the same cell(s). You can choose to manually resolve such conflicts—when
this option is chosen, a dialog box automatically displays whenever a conflict
occurs, allowing you to specify which change takes precedence. Or, choose The
Changes Being Saved Win to automatically accept the last change.

**Include In Personal View:** Each user of the shared workbook can include print
settings and/or filter settings in his or her personal view of the shared book. Filter
settings pertain to database filtering, discussed in Chapter 17.

Once a workbook is shared, you are prominently reminded of this fact—**[Shared]**
appears next to the file name on the window title bar.

**FIGURE 29.18**

*Multiple users
can revise
shared
workbooks
simultaneously.*

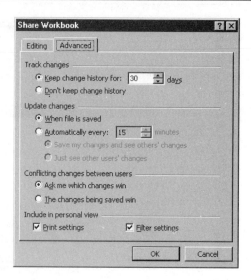

## Reviewing Changes

The Share Workbook dialog box, shown in Figure 29.18, allows you to keep a history of changes. When Keep Change History For N Days is chosen, you can view the history of changes to the workbook using the Tools ➤ Track Changes ➤ Highlight Changes command. The following dialog box appears:

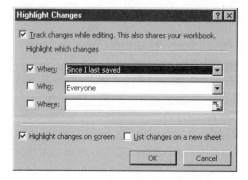

**Track Changes While Editing:** This check box determines if the workbook is shared. If the workbook is already shared, and you uncheck this setting, the change history is lost.

**When:** You can view all changes, only changes that occurred since you last saved the file, only changes that have not been reviewed, or only changes that occurred since a given date.

**Who:** You can view changes made by all users, or specified users.

**Where:** Enter a range if you want to view changes only for a certain range of cells.

**Highlight Changes On Screen:** When selected, a colored border appears around each cell that has been changed. When you point to a changed cell with the mouse, an audit trail of changes displays in the form of a cell comment. (See Chapter 11 to learn more about cell comments.)

**List Changes On A New Sheet:** When selected, a new worksheet named History is added to the workbook containing a detailed list of changes.

## Accepting and Rejecting Changes

Again, suppose you have a shared workbook, and you are keeping a change history. The Tools ➤ Track Changes ➤ Accept Or Reject Changes command allows you to, as you might expect, accept or reject the changes that have been made to the workbook by you and/or others. When the command is chosen, the following dialog box is displayed. Responding to this dialog box is the first step.

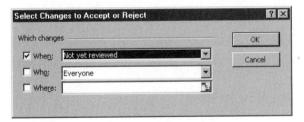

**When:** You can view all changes which have not been reviewed yet, or all changes since a specified date.

**Who:** You can view changes made by all users, or specified users.

**Where:** Enter a range if you want to accept/reject changes only for a certain range of cells.

When you click on OK on the Select Changes To Accept Or Reject dialog box, the Accept Or Reject Changes dialog box is displayed. It displays the change history one cell at a time.

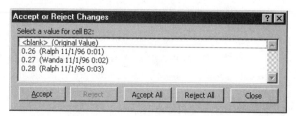

Here are descriptions for the buttons on the Accept or Reject Changes dialog box:

**Accept:** The change is accepted. If there have been multiple inputs made to a cell, you must select which input you want to accept before clicking on Accept.

**Reject:** The change is rejected, and the cell is restored to its original value.

**Accept All:** Click on this button to accept all of the changes.

**Reject All:** Click on this button to reject all of the changes.

## Protecting a Shared Workbook

There is a special protection setting for shared workbooks, which you access by choosing Tools ➢ Protection ➢ Protect Shared Workbook. When workbooks are protected in this manner, users of the workbook are unable to delete the change history. Nor are they permitted to "unshare" the workbook, since this action automatically deletes the change history.

Unless you use a password, protecting a shared workbook is based on the honor system, as anyone who can open the workbook can also unprotect it. Therefore, to establish viable security, you should use a password. There is one special caveat to keep in mind, however: you cannot assign a password for a workbook that has already been shared—you should assign the password before the workbook is shared. If the workbook has already been shared, you must set the workbook to not be shared before assigning a password. Choose Tools ➢ Share Workbook ➢ Editing, and uncheck the Allow Changes setting. Then, protect the workbook, assign a password, and set the workbook to be shared again.

Arguably the most important aspect of working with data external to Excel is the ability to query external databases. Read Chapter 19 to learn about this key feature. Appendix A follows. It is an A-to-Z function reference, covering the hundreds of built-in worksheet functions.

# Appendix

# A

## Alphabetical List of Worksheet Functions

# Alphabetical List of Worksheet Functions

This appendix has complete descriptions of the Excel functions, including both the built-in worksheet functions and the functions that are contained in the Analysis ToolPak add-in. For more information about using functions, see Chapter 4.

## Built-In Worksheet Functions

### ABS

The ABS function returns the absolute value of a number.

#### Syntax

```
ABS(number)
```

**Number** is the real number for which you want the absolute value.

#### Examples

`ABS(43)` returns 43—43 is the absolute value of 43.

`ABS(-105)` returns 105—105 is the absolute value of –105.

### ACOS

Returns the arccosine of a number. The returned angle is given in radians in the range 0 to pi.

#### Syntax

```
ACOS(number)
```

**Number** is the cosine of the angle you want, and must be between –1 and 1. If you want to convert the result from radians to degrees, multiply the result by 180/PI().

### Examples

ACOS(-0.5) returns 2.094395 ($2\pi/3$ radians).

ACOS(-0.5)*180/PI() returns 120 (degrees).

## ACOSH

Returns the inverse hyperbolic cosine of a number (number must be greater than or equal to 1).

### Syntax

ACOSH(number)

**Number** is any real number equal to or greater than 1.

### Examples

ACOSH(10) returns 2.993223.

## ADDRESS

Creates a cell address as text, given specified row and column numbers.

### Syntax

ADDRESS(row_num,column_num,abs_num,a1,sheet_text)

**Row_num** is the row number to use in the cell reference.

**Column_num** is the column number to use in the cell reference.

**Abs_num** specifies the type of reference to return. If abs_num is 1 or omitted, an absolute reference is returned; if abs_num is 2, an absolute row/relative column reference is returned; if abs_num is 3, a relative row/absolute column reference is returned; if abs_num is 4, a relative reference is returned.

**A1** is a logical value that specifies the A1 or R1C1 reference style. If A1 is TRUE or omitted, ADDRESS returns an A1-style reference; if FALSE, ADDRESS returns an R1C1-style reference.

**Sheet_text** is text specifying the name of the worksheet or macro sheet to be used as the external reference. If sheet_text is omitted, no sheet name is used.

### Examples

ADDRESS(2,3) returns "$C$2."

ADDRESS(2,3,2,FALSE) returns "R2C[3]."

APDX

**A**

Alphabetical List of
Worksheet Functions

## AND

The AND function joins test conditions. Returns TRUE if all its logical arguments are TRUE; returns FALSE if one or more logical arguments is FALSE. Logical arguments are statements that return a value of true or false.

### Syntax

```
AND(logical1,logical2,...)
```

**Logical1,logical2,...** are conditions you want to test; conditions can be either TRUE or FALSE. Up to 30 arguments can be tested.

### Examples

AND(TRUE,TRUE) returns TRUE.

AND(TRUE,FALSE) returns FALSE.

AND(2+2=4,2+3=5) returns TRUE.

## AREAS

Returns the number of areas in a reference. An area is a single cell or a range of contiguous cells.

### Syntax

```
AREAS(reference)
```

**Reference** is a reference to a cell or range of cells and can refer to multiple areas. If you want to specify several references as a single argument, then you must include extra sets of parentheses so that Excel will not interpret the comma as a field separator (see the second example).

### Examples

AREAS(B2:D4) returns 1.

AREAS((B2:D4,E5,F6:I9)) returns 3.

## ASIN

Returns the arcsine of a number. To express the arcsine in degrees, multiply the result by 180/PI().

### Syntax

```
ASIN(number)
```

**Number** is the sine of the angle you want and must be from –1 to 1.

**Examples**

ASIN(-0.5) returns –0.5236 (-π/6 radians).

ASIN(-0.5)*180/PI() returns –30 (degrees).

# ASINH

Returns the inverse hyperbolic sine of a number.

## Syntax
ASINH(number)

**Number** is any real number.

## Examples

ASINH(-2.5) returns –1.64723.

# ATAN

Returns the arctangent of a number. To express the arctangent in degrees, multiply the result by 180/PI().

## Syntax
ATAN(number)

**Number** is the tangent of the angle you want.

## Examples

ATAN(1) returns 0.785398 (π/4 radians).

ATAN(1)*180/PI() returns 45 (degrees).

# ATAN2

Returns the arctangent from x- and y-coordinates. To express the arctangent in degrees, multiply the result by 180/PI().

## Syntax
ATAN2(x_num,y_num)

**X_num** is the x-coordinate of the point.

**Y_num** is the y-coordinate of the point.

APDX

**A**

Alphabetical List of Worksheet Functions

### Examples

ATAN2(1,1) returns 0.785398 ($\pi/4$ radians).

ATAN2(-1,-1) returns –2.35619 (-3$\pi$/4 radians).

ATAN2(-1,-1)*180/PI() returns –135 (degrees).

# ATANH

Returns the inverse hyperbolic tangent of a number.

### Syntax

ATANH(number)

**Number** is any real number between 1 and –1.

### Examples

ATANH(0.76159416) returns 1 (approximately).

ATANH(-0.1) returns –0.10034.

# AVEDEV

Returns the average of the absolute deviations of data points from their mean.

### Syntax

AVEDEV(number1,number2,...)

**Number1,number2,...** are 1 to 30 arguments for which you want the average of the absolute deviations. You can also use a single array or a reference to an array instead of arguments separated by commas.

### Examples

AVEDEV(4,5,6,7,5,4,3) returns 1.020408.

# AVERAGE

Returns the average of its arguments.

### Syntax

AVERAGE(number1,number2,...)

**Number1,number2,...** are 1 to 30 numeric arguments for which you want the average.

When averaging cells, bear in mind the difference between empty cells and cells containing the value zero, especially if you have cleared the Zero Values check box in the View tab of the Tools ➢ Options dialog box. Empty cells are not included in the average, but zero values are.

### Examples

If A1:A5 is named Scores and contains the numbers 10, 7, 9, 27, and 2, then:

    AVERAGE(A1:A5) returns 11.

    AVERAGE(Scores) returns 11.

## AVERAGEA

Returns the average of the values in a range of cells. Whereas the AVERAGE function ignores cells containing text and logical values (TRUE and FALSE), AVERAGEA calculates a text value as zero, FALSE as zero, and TRUE as 1. The syntax for AVERAGEA is the same as for AVERAGE.

## BETADIST

Returns the cumulative beta probability density function.

### Syntax

    BETADIST(x,alpha,beta,A,B)

**X** is the value between A and B at which to evaluate the function.

**Alpha** is a parameter to the distribution.

**Beta** is a parameter to the distribution.

**A** is an optional lower bound to the interval of x.

**B** is an optional upper bound to the interval of x.

### Examples

    BETADIST(2,8,10,1,3) returns 0.685470581.

## BETAINV

Returns the inverse of the cumulative beta probability density function.

APDX

A

Alphabetical List of Worksheet Functions

### Syntax

```
BETAINV(probability,alpha,beta,A,B)
```

**Probability** is a probability associated with the beta distribution.

**Alpha** is a parameter to the distribution.

**Beta** is a parameter to the distribution.

**A** is an optional lower bound to the interval of x.

**B** is an optional upper bound to the interval of x.

### Examples

```
BETAINV(0.685470581,8,10,1,3)
```
returns 2.

# CEILING

Rounds a number away from zero to the nearest integer or to the nearest multiple of significance.

For example, if you want to avoid using pennies in your prices and your product is priced at $5.47, use the formula =CEILING(5.47,0.05) to round prices up to the nearest nickel.

### Syntax

```
CEILING(number,significance)
```

**Number** is the value you want to round.

**Significance** is the multiple to which you want to round.

### Examples

```
CEILING(2.5,1)
```
returns 3.

```
CEILING(0.234,0.01)
```
returns 0.24.

# CELL

Returns information about the formatting, location, or contents of a cell. The CELL function is provided for compatibility with other spreadsheet programs.

### Syntax

```
CELL(info_type,reference)
```

**Info_type** is a text value that specifies what type of cell information you want.

**Reference** is the cell that you want information about.

See the Online Help worksheet function reference for a listing of info types.

### Examples

CELL("row",A20) returns 20.

If A3 contains TOTAL, then CELL("contents",A3) returns "TOTAL."

## CHAR

Returns the character specified by the code number. You can use CHAR to translate code numbers you might get from files on other types of computers into characters.

### Syntax

CHAR(number)

**Number** is a number between 1 and 255 specifying which character you want. The character is from the character set used by your computer (e.g., Windows 95 uses the ANSI character set).

### Examples

CHAR(65) returns "A."

CHAR(33) returns "!."

## CHIDIST

Returns the one-tailed probability of the chi-squared distribution.

### Syntax

CHIDIST(x,degrees_freedom)

**X** is the value at which you want to evaluate the distribution.

**Degrees_freedom** is the number of degrees of freedom.

### Examples

CHIDIST(18.307,10) returns 0.050001.

## CHIINV

Returns the inverse of the chi-squared distribution. CHIINV uses an iterative technique for calculating the function. Given a probability value, CHIINV iterates until the result is accurate to within $\pm 3 \times 10^{-7}$. If CHIINV does not converge after 100 iterations, the function returns the #N/A error value.

APDX

**A**

Alphabetical List of
Worksheet Functions

### Syntax

```
CHIINV(probability,degrees_freedom)
```

**Probability** is a probability associated with the chi-squared distribution.

**Degrees_freedom** is the number of degrees of freedom.

### Examples

```
CHIINV(0.05,10)
```
returns 18.30703.

## CHITEST(actual_range,expected_range)

Returns the test for independence.

### Syntax

```
CHITEST(actual_range,expected_range)
```

**Actual_range** is the range of data that contains observations to test against expected values.

**Expected_range** is the range of data that contains the ratio of the product of row totals and column totals to the grand total.

See the Online Help worksheet function reference for information about the equation used to calculate CHITEST and an example.

## CHOOSE

Uses the argument index_num to choose a value from the list of value arguments. You can use CHOOSE to select one of up to 29 values based on the index number. For example, if value1 through value7 are the days of the week, CHOOSE returns one of the days if index_num is a number between 1 and 7.

### Syntax

```
CHOOSE(index_num,value1,value2,...)
```

**Index_num** specifies which value argument is selected. Index_num must be a number between 1 and 29, or a formula or reference to a cell containing a number between 1 and 29.

- If index_num is 1, CHOOSE returns value1; if it is 2, CHOOSE returns value2; and so on.
- If index_num is less than 1 or greater than the number of the last value in the list, CHOOSE returns the #VALUE! error value.

- If index_num is a fraction, it is truncated to the lowest integer before being used.

**Value1,value2,...** are up to 29 value arguments from which CHOOSE selects a value or an action to perform based on index_num. The arguments can be numbers, cell references, defined names, formulas, macro functions, or text.

### Examples

CHOOSE(2,"1st","2nd","3rd","Finished") returns "2nd."

## CLEAN

Removes all nonprintable characters from text. You can use CLEAN on text imported from other applications which contains characters that may not print with your operating system. For example, you can use CLEAN to remove some low-level computer code that is frequently at the beginning and end of data files and cannot be printed.

### Syntax

CLEAN(text)

**Text** is any worksheet information from which you want to remove nonprintable characters.

### Examples

CHAR(7) returns a nonprintable character.

CLEAN(CHAR(7)&"text"&CHAR(7)) returns "text."

## CODE

Returns a numeric code for the first character in a text string. The character is from the character set used by your computer. (e.g., Windows 95 uses the ANSI character set).

### Syntax

CODE(text)

**Text** is the text for which you want the code of the first character.

### Examples

CODE("A") returns 65.

CODE("Alphabet") returns 65.

APDX

**A**

Alphabetical List of
Worksheet Functions

## COLUMNS

Returns the number of columns in a reference or array. (See Chapter 9 for in-depth coverage and examples of COLUMNS.)

### Syntax

COLUMNS(array)

**Array** is an array, array formula, or reference to a range of cells for which you want the number of columns.

## COLUMN

Returns the column number of the reference. (See Chapter 9 for in-depth coverage and examples of COLUMN.)

### Syntax

COLUMN(reference)

**Reference** is the cell or range of cells for which you want the column number.

## COMBIN

Returns the number of combinations for a given number of objects.

### Syntax

COMBIN(number,number_chosen)

**Number** is the number of objects.

**Number_chosen** is the number of objects in each combination.

### Examples

Suppose you want to know the odds of winning a lottery in which each entry is a combination of 6 numbers between 1 and 49.

COMBIN(49,6) returns 13,983,816 possible combinations.

## CONCATENATE

Joins several text items into one text item. The "&" operator can be used instead of CONCATENATE to join text items.

### Syntax
```
CONCATENATE (text1,text2,...)
```

**Text1,text2,...** are up to 30 text items to be joined into a single text item. The text items can be text strings, numbers, or single-cell references.

### Examples
```
CONCATENATE("Total ","Value")
```
returns "Total Value".

## CONFIDENCE

Returns a confidence interval for a population.

### Syntax
```
CONFIDENCE(alpha,standard_dev,size)
```

**Alpha** is the significance level used to compute the confidence level. The confidence level equals 100(1 – alpha)%, or in other words, an alpha of 0.05 indicates a 95% confidence level.

**Standard_dev** is the population standard deviation for the data range, and is assumed to be known.

**Size** is the sample size.

See the Online Help worksheet function reference for information about the equation used to calculate CONFIDENCE and an example.

## CORREL

Returns the correlation coefficient between two data sets.

### Syntax
```
CORREL(array1,array2)
```

**Array1** is a cell range of values.

**Array2** is a second cell range of values.

### Examples
```
CORREL({3,2,4,5,6},{9,7,12,15,17})
```
returns 0.997054.

## COS

Returns the cosine of the given angle. If the angle is in degrees, multiply it by PI()/180 to convert it to radians.

### Syntax

```
COS(number)
```

**Number** is the angle (in radians) for which you want the cosine.

### Examples

`COS(1.047)` returns 0.500171.

`COS(60*PI()/180)` returns 0.5, the cosine of 60 degrees.

## COSH

Returns the hyperbolic cosine of a number.

### Syntax

```
COSH(number)
```

**Number** is the number for which you want the hyperbolic cosine.

### Examples

`COSH(4)` returns 27.30823.

`COSH(EXP(1))` returns 7.610125, where EXP(1) is e, the base of the natural logarithm.

## COUNT

Counts how many numbers are in the list of arguments. (See Chapter 9 for in-depth coverage and examples of COUNT.)

### Syntax

```
COUNT(value1,value2,...)
```

**Value1,value2,...** are up to 30 arguments that can contain or refer to a variety of data types, but only numbers are counted.

## COUNTA

Counts the number of nonblank values in the list of arguments. Use COUNTA to count the number of cells with data in a range or array. (See Chapter 9 for in-depth coverage and examples of COUNTA.)

### Syntax

```
COUNTA(value1,value2,...)
```

**Value1,value2,...** are up to 30 arguments representing the values you want to count. In this case, a value is any type of information, including empty text ("") but not including empty cells. If an argument is an array or reference, empty cells within the array or reference are ignored.

## COUNTBLANK

Counts the number of blank cells within a single range. (See Chapter 9 for in-depth coverage and examples of COUNTBLANK.)

### Syntax

```
COUNTBLANK(range)
```

**Range** is the range within which you want to count the blank cells.

## COUNTIF

Counts the number of nonblank cells within a range that meet the given criteria. (See Chapter 9 for in-depth coverage and examples of COUNTIF.)

### Syntax

```
COUNTIF(range,criteria)
```

**Range** is the range of cells from which you want to count cells.

**Criteria** is the expression that defines which cells will be counted.

## COVAR

Returns covariance, the average of the products of paired deviations. Covariance helps to determine the relationship between two data sets (for example, whether greater income accompanies greater levels of education).

### Syntax

```
COVAR(array1,array2)
```

**Array1** is the first cell range of integers.

**Array2** is the second cell range of integers.

### Examples

```
COVAR({3,2,4,5,6},{9,7,12,15,17}) returns 5.2.
```

## CRITBINOM

Returns smallest value for which cumulative binomial distribution is less than or equal to criterion value.

### Syntax

`CRITBINOM(trials,probability_s,alpha)`

**Trials** is the number of Bernoulli trials.

**Probability_s** is the probability of a success on each trial.

**Alpha** is the criterion value.

### Examples

`CRITBINOM(6,0.5,0.75)` returns 4.

## DATE

Returns the serial number of a particular date. (See Chapter 9 for in-depth coverage and examples of DATE.)

### Syntax

`DATE(year,month,day)`

**Year** is the year number 1900 or larger.

**Month** is a number representing the month of the year.

**Day** is a number representing the day of the month.

## DATEVALUE

Converts a date in the form of text to a serial number.

### Syntax

`DATEVALUE(date_text)`

**Date_text** is text that returns a date in a Microsoft Excel date format.

### Examples

`DATEVALUE("8/22/55")` returns 20323 in the 1900 date system.

## DAVERAGE

Returns the average of selected database entries.

### Syntax

`DAVERAGE(database,field,criteria)`

**Database** is the range of cells that make up the database.

**Field** indicates which field is used in the function.

**Criteria** is the range of cells that contains the database criteria.

## DAY

Converts a serial number to a day of the month. (See Chapter 9 for in-depth coverage and examples of DAY.)

### Syntax

`DAY(serial_number)`

**Serial_number** is the date-time code used by Microsoft Excel for date and time calculations.

## DAYS360

Calculates the number of days between two dates on the basis of a 360-day year.

### Syntax

`DAYS360(start_date,end_date,method)`

**Start_date,end_date** are the two dates between which you want to know the number of days (can be either text strings using numbers to represent the month, day, and year, or they can be serial numbers representing the dates).

**Method** is a logical value that specifies whether the European or US method should be used in the calculation.

- **FALSE or omitted**—US (NASD). If the starting date is the 31st of a month, it becomes equal to the 30th of the same month. If the ending date is the 31st of a month and the starting date is less than the 30th of a month, the ending date becomes equal to the 1st of the next month, otherwise the ending date becomes equal to the 30th of the same month.
- **TRUE**—European method. Starting dates or ending dates which occur on the 31st of a month become equal to the 30th of the same month.

### Examples

`DAYS360("1/30/93","2/1/93")` returns 1.

**TIP**
To determine the number of days between two dates in a normal year, you can use normal subtraction—for example, "12/31/93"-"1/1/93" equals 364.

## DB

Returns the depreciation of an asset for a specified period using the fixed-declining balance method.

### Syntax

`DB(cost,salvage,life,period,month)`

**Cost** is the initial cost of the asset.

**Salvage** is the value at the end of the depreciation (sometimes called the salvage value of the asset).

**Life** is the number of periods over which the asset is being depreciated (sometimes called the useful life of the asset).

**Period** is the period for which you want to calculate the depreciation. Period must use the same units as life.

**Month** is the number of months in the first year. If month is omitted, it is assumed to be 12.

### Examples

Suppose a factory purchases a new machine. The machine costs $1,000,000 and has a lifetime of six years. The salvage value of the machine is $100,000. The following examples show depreciation over the life of the machine (the results are rounded to whole numbers).

`DB(1000000,100000,6,1,7)` returns $186,083.

## DCOUNT

Counts the cells containing numbers from a specified database using a criteria range.

### Syntax

`DCOUNT(database,field,criteria)`

**Database** is the range of cells that make up the database.

**Field** indicates which field is used in the function.

**Criteria** is the range of cells that contains the database criteria.

## DCOUNTA

Counts nonblank cells from a specified database using a criteria range.

### Syntax

DCOUNTA(database,field,criteria)

**Database** is the range of cells that make up the database.

**Field** indicates which field is used in the function.

**Criteria** is the range of cells that contains the database criteria.

## DDB

Returns the depreciation of an asset for a specified period using the double-declining balance method.

### Syntax

DDB(cost,salvage,life,period,factor)

**Cost** is the initial cost of the asset.

**Salvage** is the value at the end of the depreciation (sometimes called the salvage value of the asset).

**Life** is the number of periods over which the asset is being depreciated (sometimes called the useful life of the asset).

**Period** is the period for which you want to calculate the depreciation. Period must use the same units as life.

**Factor** is the rate at which the balance declines. If factor is omitted, it is assumed to be 2 (the double-declining balance method).

All five arguments must be positive numbers.

### Examples

Suppose a factory purchases a new machine. The machine costs $2400 and has a lifetime of 10 years. The salvage value of the machine is $300. The following examples show depreciation over several periods. The results are rounded to two decimal places.

DDB(2400,300,3650,1) returns $1.32, the first day's depreciation (Excel automatically assumes that factor is 2).

DDB(2400,300,120,1,2) returns $40.00, the first month's depreciation.

## DEGREES

Converts radians to degrees.

### Syntax

```
DEGREES(angle)
```

**Angle** is the angle in radians that you want to convert.

### Examples

DEGREES(PI()) returns 180.

## DEVSQ

Returns the sum of squares of deviations.

### Syntax

```
DEVSQ(number1,number2,...)
```

**Number1,number2,...** are up to 30 arguments for which you want to calculate the sum of squared deviations. You can also use a single array or a reference to an array instead of arguments separated by commas. The arguments should be numbers, or names, arrays, or references that contain numbers. If an array or reference argument contains text, logical values, or empty cells, those values are ignored; however, cells with the value zero are included.

### Examples

DEVSQ(4,5,8,7,11,4,3) returns 48.

## DGET

Extracts from a database a single record that matches the specified criteria.

### Syntax

```
DGET(database,field,criteria)
```

**Database** is the range of cells that make up the database.

**Field** indicates which field is used in the function.

**Criteria** is the range of cells that contains the database criteria.

## DMAX

Returns the maximum value from selected database entries using a criteria range.

### Syntax

`DMAX(database,field,criteria)`

**Database** is the range of cells that make up the database.

**Field** indicates which field is used in the function.

**Criteria** is the range of cells that contains the database criteria.

## DMIN

Returns the minimum value from selected database entries using a criteria range.

### Syntax

`DMIN(database,field,criteria)`

**Database** is the range of cells that make up the database.

**Field** indicates which field is used in the function.

**Criteria** is the range of cells that contains the database criteria.

## DOLLAR

Converts a number to text, using currency format.

### Syntax

`DOLLAR(number,decimals)`

**Number** is a number, a reference to a cell containing a number, or a formula that evaluates to a number.

**Decimals** is the number of digits to the right of the decimal point. If decimals is negative, number is rounded to the left of the decimal point. If you omit decimals, it is assumed to be 2.

**NOTE** The difference between formatting a cell with the Format ➢ Cell command and formatting a number directly with the DOLLAR function is that the result of the DOLLAR function is text, while a number in a formatted cell is still a number. You can use numbers formatted with DOLLAR in formulas, because numbers entered as text are converted to numbers when Excel calculates.

### Examples

DOLLAR(1234.567,2) returns "$1234.57."

DOLLAR(1234.567,-2) returns "$1200."

# DPRODUCT

Multiplies the values in a particular field of records using a criteria range.

### Syntax

DPRODUCT(database,field,criteria)

**Database** is the range of cells that make up the database.

**Field** indicates which field is used in the function.

**Criteria** is the range of cells that contains the database criteria.

# DSTDEV

Estimates the standard deviation on the basis of a sample of selected database entries.

### Syntax

DSTDEV(database,field,criteria)

**Database** is the range of cells that make up the database.

**Field** indicates which field is used in the function.

**Criteria** is the range of cells that contains the database criteria.

# DSTDEVP

Calculates the standard deviation on the basis of the entire population of selected database entries.

### Syntax

DSTDEVP(database,field,criteria)

**Database** is the range of cells that make up the database.

**Field** indicates which field is used in the function.

**Criteria** is the range of cells that contains the database criteria.

# DSUM

Adds the numbers in the field column of records in the database using a criteria range.

### Syntax
```
DSUM(database,field,criteria)
```

**Database** is the range of cells that make up the database.

**Field** indicates which field is used in the function.

**Criteria** is the range of cells that contains the database criteria.

## DVAR

Estimates variance on the basis of a sample from selected database entries.

### Syntax
```
DVAR(database,field,criteria)
```

**Database** is the range of cells that make up the database.

**Field** indicates which field is used in the function.

**Criteria** is the range of cells that contains the database criteria.

## DVARP

Calculates variance on the basis of the entire population of selected database entries.

### Syntax
```
DVARP(database,field,criteria)
```

**Database** is the range of cells that make up the database.

**Field** indicates which field is used in the function.

**Criteria** is the range of cells that contains the database criteria.

## EVEN

Rounds a number up to the nearest even integer.

### Syntax
```
EVEN(number)
```

**Number** is the value to round.

### Examples
```
EVEN(1.5)
```
returns 2.
```
EVEN(3)
```
returns 4.

APDX

**A**

Alphabetical List of
Worksheet Functions

# EXACT

Checks to see if two text values are identical (it is case sensitive). You can use EXACT to test text entries.

### Syntax

```
EXACT(text1,text2)
```

**Text1** is the first text string.

**Text2** is the second text string.

### Examples

```
EXACT("word","word")
```
 returns TRUE.

```
EXACT("Word","word")
```
 returns FALSE.

# EXP

Returns e raised to the power of a given number.

### Syntax

```
EXP(number)
```

**Number** is the exponent applied to the base e.

### Examples

```
EXP(2)
```
 returns e2, or 7.389056.

```
EXP(LN(3))
```
 returns 3.

# EXPONDIST

Returns the exponential distribution.

### Syntax

```
EXPONDIST(x,lambda,cumulative)
```

**X** is the value of the function.

**Lambda** is the parameter value.

**Cumulative** is a logical value that indicates which form of the exponential function to provide.

### Examples

```
EXPONDIST(0.2,10,TRUE)
```
 returns 0.864665.

```
EXPONDIST(0.2,10,FALSE)
```
 returns 1.353353.

# FACT

Returns the factorial of a number.

### Syntax

`FACT(number)`

> **Number** is the nonnegative number you want the factorial of. If number is not an integer, it is truncated.

### Examples

`FACT(1)` returns 1.

`FACT(1.9)` returns FACT(1) equals 1.

# FALSE

Returns the logical value FALSE.

### Syntax

`FALSE()`

You can also type the word FALSE directly into the worksheet or formula, and Excel interprets it as the logical value FALSE.

# FDIST

Returns the F probability distribution.

### Syntax

`FDIST(x,degrees_freedom1,degrees_freedom2)`

> **X** is the value at which to evaluate the function.

> **Degrees_freedom1** is the numerator degrees of freedom.

> **Degrees_freedom2** is the denominator degrees of freedom.

### Examples

`FDIST(15.20675,6,4)` returns 0.01.

# FIND

Finds one text value within another (case sensitive). (See Chapter 9 for in-depth coverage and examples of FIND.)

### Syntax

```
FIND(find_text,within_text,start_num)
```

**Find_text** is the text you want to find.

**Within_text** is the text containing the text you want to find.

**Start_num** specifies the character at which to start the search. The first character in within_text is character number 1. If you omit start_num, it is assumed to be 1.

## FINV

Returns the inverse of the F probability distribution. FINV uses an iterative technique for calculating the function. Given a probability value, FINV iterates until the result is accurate to within $\pm 3 \times 10^{-7}$. If FINV does not converge after 100 iterations, the function returns the #N/A error value.

### Syntax

```
FINV(probability,degrees_freedom1,degrees_freedom2)
```

**Probability** is a probability associated with the F cumulative distribution.

**Degrees_freedom1** is the numerator degrees of freedom.

**Degrees_freedom2** is the denominator degrees of freedom.

### Examples

```
FINV(0.01,6,4)
```
returns 15.20675.

## FISHER

Returns the Fisher transformation.

### Syntax

```
FISHER(x)
```

**X** is a numeric value for which you want the transformation.

### Examples

```
FISHER(0.75)
```
returns 0.972955.

## FISHERINV

Returns the inverse of the Fisher transformation.

### Syntax

```
FISHERINV(y)
```

**Y** is the value for which you want to perform the inverse of the transformation.

### Examples

FISHERINV(0.972955) returns 0.75.

# FIXED

Formats a number as text with a fixed number of decimals.

### Syntax

FIXED(number,decimals,no_commas)

**Number** is the number you want to round and convert to text.

**Decimals** is the number of digits to the right of the decimal point.

**No_commas** is a logical value that, if TRUE, prevents FIXED from including commas in the returned text. If no_commas is FALSE or omitted, then the returned text includes commas as usual.

### Examples

FIXED(1234.567,1) returns "1234.6."

FIXED(1234.567,-1) returns "1230."

# FLOOR

Rounds a number down, toward zero.

### Syntax

FLOOR(number,significance)

**Number** is the numeric value you want to round.

**Significance** is the multiple to which you want to round.

### Examples

FLOOR(2.5,1) returns 2.

FLOOR(-2.5,-2) returns –2.

# FORECAST

Returns a value along a linear trend.

### Syntax

FORECAST(x,known_y's,known_x's)

**X** is the data point for which you want to predict a value.

APDX

**A**

Alphabetical List of
Worksheet Functions

**Known_y's** is the dependent array or range of data.

**Known_x's** is the independent array or range of data.

### Examples

```
FORECAST(30,{6,7,9,15,21},{20,28,31,38,40}) returns 10.60725.
```

# FREQUENCY

Returns a frequency distribution as a vertical array.

### Syntax

```
FREQUENCY(data_array,bins_array)
```

**Data_array** is an array of or reference to a set of values for which you want to count frequencies. If data_array contains no values, FREQUENCY returns an array of zeros.

**Bins_array** is an array of or reference to intervals into which you want to group the values in data_array. If bins_array contains no values, FREQUENCY returns the number of elements in data_array.

### Examples

Suppose a worksheet lists scores for a test. The scores are 79, 85, 78, 85, 83, 81, 95, 88, 97, and are entered into cells A1:A9. The data_array would contain a column of these test scores. The bins_array would be another column of intervals by which the test scores are grouped. In this example, bins_array would be C4:C6 and would contain the values 70, 79, 89. When entered as an array, you can use FREQUENCY to count the number of scores corresponding to the letter grade ranges 0–70, 71–79, 80–89, and 90–100 (this example assumes all test scores are integers). The following formula is entered as an array formula after selecting four vertical cells adjacent to your data.

```
FREQUENCY(A1:A9,C4:C6) returns {0;2;5;2}.
```

# FTEST

Returns the result of an F-test.

### Syntax

```
FTEST(array1,array2)
```

**Array1** is the first array or range of data.

**Array2** is the second array or range of data.

## Examples

FTEST({6,7,9,15,21},{20,28,31,38,40}) returns 0.648318.

## FV

Returns the future value of an investment.

### Syntax

FV(rate,nper,pmt,pv,type)

**Rate** is the interest rate per period.

**Nper** is the total number of payment periods in an annuity.

**Pmt** is the payment made each period; it cannot change over the life of the annuity. Typically, pmt contains principal and interest but no other fees or taxes. Payment arguments are entered as negative numbers.

**Pv** is the present value, or the lump-sum amount that a series of future payments is worth right now. If pv is omitted, it is assumed to be 0.

**Type** is the number 0 or 1 and indicates when payments are due. If type is 0, payments are due at the end of the period; if type is 1, payments are due at the beginning of the period. If type is omitted, it is assumed to be 0.

### Examples

FV(0.5%,10,-200,-500,1) returns $2581.40.

FV(11%/12,35,-2000,,1) returns $82,846.25.

Suppose you want to save money for a special project occurring a year from now. You deposit $1000 into a savings account that earns 6 percent annual interest compounded monthly (monthly interest of 6%/12, or 0.5%). You plan to deposit $100 at the beginning of every month for the next 12 months. How much money will be in the account at the end of 12 months?

FV(0.5%,12,-100,-1000,1) returns $2301.40.

## GAMMADIST

Returns the gamma distribution.

### Syntax

GAMMADIST(x,alpha,beta,cumulative)

**X** is the value at which you want to evaluate the distribution.

**Alpha** is a parameter to the distribution.

**Beta** is a parameter to the distribution. If beta=1, GAMMADIST returns the standard gamma distribution.

**Cumulative** is a logical value that determines the form of the function. If cumulative is TRUE, GAMMADIST returns the cumulative distribution function; if FALSE, it returns the probability mass function.

### Examples

GAMMADIST(10,9,2,FALSE) returns 0.032639.

GAMMADIST(10,9,2,TRUE) returns 0.068094.

## GAMMAINV

Returns the inverse of the gamma cumulative distribution. GAMMAINV uses an iterative technique for calculating the function. Given a probability value, GAMMAINV iterates until the result is accurate to within $\pm 3 \times 10^{-7}$. If GAMMAINV does not converge after 100 iterations, the function returns the #N/A error value.

### Syntax

GAMMAINV(probability,alpha,beta)

**Probability** is the probability associated with the gamma distribution.

**Alpha** is a parameter to the distribution.

**Beta** is a parameter to the distribution. If beta=1, GAMMAINV returns the standard gamma distribution.

### Examples

GAMMAINV(0.068094,9,2) returns 10.

## GAMMALN

Returns the natural logarithm of the gamma function, G(x).

### Syntax

GAMMALN(x)

**X** is the value for which you want to calculate GAMMALN.

### Examples

GAMMALN(4) returns 1.791759.

EXP(GAMMALN(4)) returns 6 or (4–1)!

## GEOMEAN

Returns the geometric mean.

### Syntax

GEOMEAN(number1,number2,...)

**Number1,number2,...** are up to 30 arguments for which you want to calculate the mean. You can also use a single array or a reference to an array instead of arguments separated by commas.

### Examples

GEOMEAN(4,5,8,7,11,4,3) returns 5.476987.

## GETPIVOTDATA

Returns data stored in a pivot table. You can use GETPIVOTDATA to retrieve summary data from a pivot table, provided the summary data is visible in the pivot table. This function is discussed in Chapter 22.

### Syntax

GETPIVOTDATA(pivot_table, name)

**Pivot_Table** refers to any cell(s) in a pivot table. The purpose of this argument is to identify which pivot table is the basis for the calculation. It does not matter which cell(s) within the pivot table are referenced.

**Name** is a text string containing one or more field names, separated by spaces.

### Examples

GETPIVOTDATA(A1, "East Sales")

GETPIVOTDATA(MyPivotTable, "South Widgets Forecast")

## GROWTH

Returns values along an exponential trend. See the Online Help worksheet function reference for more information and examples.

### Syntax

GROWTH(known_y's,known_x's,new_x's,const)

**Known_y's** is the set of y-values you already know in the relationship $y=b*m^x$.

**Known_x's** is an optional set of x-values that you may already know in the relationship $y=b*m^x$.

**New_x's** are new x-values for which you want GROWTH to return corresponding y-values.

**Const** is a logical value specifying whether to force the constant b to equal 1.

# HARMEAN

Returns the harmonic mean.

### Syntax

```
HARMEAN(number1,number2,...)
```

**Number1,number2,...** are up to 30 arguments for which you want to calculate the mean. You can also use a single array or a reference to an array instead of arguments separated by commas.

### Examples

```
HARMEAN(4,5,8,7,11,4,3)
```
returns 5.028376.

# HLOOKUP

Looks in the top row of an array and returns the value of the indicated cell.

### Syntax

```
HLOOKUP(lookup_value,table_array,row_index_num,range_lookup)
```

**Lookup_value** is the value to be found in the first row of the table.

**Table_array** is a table of information in which data is looked up. Use a reference to a range or a range name.

**Row_index_num** is the row number in table_array from which the matching value should be returned. A row_index_num of 1 returns the first row value in table_array, a row_index_num of 2 returns the second row value in table_array, and so on.

**Range_lookup** is a logical value that specifies whether you want HLOOKUP to find an exact match or an approximate match. If TRUE or omitted, an approximate match is returned (if an exact match is not found, the next largest value that is less than lookup_value is returned). If FALSE, HLOOKUP will find an exact match. If one is not found, the error value #N/A is returned.

### Examples

Suppose you have an inventory worksheet of auto parts. Cells A1:A4 contain "Axles," 4, 5, 6. Cells B1:B4 contain "Bearings," 4, 7, 8. Cells C1:C4 contain "Bolts," 9, 10, 11.

```
HLOOKUP("Axles",A1:C4,2,TRUE) returns 4.
HLOOKUP("Bearings",A1:C4,3,FALSE) returns 7.
```

# HOUR

Converts a serial number to an hour. (See Chapter 9 for in-depth coverage and examples of HOUR.)

### Syntax
```
HOUR(serial_number)
```

**Serial_number** is the date-time code used by Excel for date and time calculations. You can give serial_number as text, such as "16:48:00" or "4:48:00 PM," instead of as a number (the text is automatically converted to a serial number).

# HYPERLINK

Creates a hyperlink to another range, file, or Internet address. This function is discussed in depth in Chapter 29.

# HYPGEOMDIST

Returns the hypergeometric distribution.

### Syntax
```
HYPGEOMDIST(sample_s,num_sample,population_s,num_population)
```

**Sample_s** is the number of successes in the sample.

**Num_sample** is the size of the sample.

**Population_s** is the number of successes in the population.

**Num_population** is the population size.

### Examples
A sampler of chocolates contains 20 pieces. Eight pieces are caramels, and the remaining 12 are nuts. If a person selects 4 pieces at random, the following function returns the probability that exactly 1 piece is a caramel:

```
HYPGEOMDIST(1,4,8,20) returns 0.363261.
```

APDX

**A**

Alphabetical List of
Worksheet Functions

## IF

Specifies a logical test to perform.

### Syntax

```
IF(logical_test,value_if_true,value_if_false)
```

**Logical_test** is any value or expression that can be evaluated to TRUE or FALSE.

**Value_if_true** is the value that is returned if logical_test is TRUE. If logical_test is TRUE and value_if_true is omitted, TRUE is returned.

**Value_if_false** is the value that is returned if logical_test is FALSE. If logical_test is FALSE and value_if_false is omitted, FALSE is returned.

Up to seven IF functions can be nested as value_if_true and value_if_false arguments to construct more elaborate tests.

### Examples

See Chapter 10 for several examples of IF functions.

## INDEX

Uses an index to choose a value from a reference or array. (See Chapter 9 for in-depth coverage and examples of INDEX.)

### Syntax 1

```
INDEX(array,row_num,column_num)
```

### Syntax 2

```
INDEX(reference,row_num,column_num,area_num)
```

**Reference** is a reference to one or more cell ranges.

**Row_num** is the row number within the range.

**Column_num** is the column number within the range.

**Area_num** is the specific area from a multiple-area range reference.

## INDIRECT

Returns a reference indicated by a text value. (See Chapter 9 for in-depth coverage and examples of INDIRECT.)

### Syntax

```
INDIRECT(ref_text,a1)
```

**Ref_text** is a reference to a cell that contains an A1- style reference, an R1C1-style reference, or a name defined as a reference.

**A1** is a logical value that specifies what type of reference is contained in the cell ref_text.

## INFO

Returns information about the current operating environment. See the On-line Help worksheet function reference for information about INFO, examples, and a list of type_text arguments.

### Syntax

```
INFO(type_text)
```

**Type_text** is text specifying what type of information you want returned.

## INT

Rounds a number down to the nearest integer.

### Syntax

```
INT(number)
```

**Number** is the real number you want to round down to an integer.

### Examples

INT(8.9) returns 8.

INT(-8.9) returns –9.

## INTERCEPT

Returns the intercept of the linear regression line.

### Syntax

```
INTERCEPT(known_y's,known_x's)
```

**Known_y's** is an array of the dependent set of observations or data.

**Known_x's** is the independent set of observations or data, expressed as an array.

### Examples

INTERCEPT({2,3,9,1,8},{6,5,11,7,5}) returns 0.0483871.

## IPMT

Returns the interest payment for an investment for a given period.

Alphabetical List of
Worksheet Functions

### Syntax

`IPMT(rate,per,nper,pv,fv,type)`

**Rate** is the interest rate per period.

**Per** is the period for which you want to find the interest, and must be in the range 1 to nper.

**Nper** is the total number of payment periods in an annuity.

**Pv** is the present value, or the lump-sum amount that a series of future payments is worth right now.

**Fv** is the future value, or a cash balance you want to attain after the last payment is made. If fv is omitted, it is assumed to be 0 (the future value of a loan, for example, is 0).

**Type** is the number 0 or 1 and indicates when payments are due. Type 0 means payments are due at the end of the period; type 1 means payments are due at the beginning of the period. If type is omitted, it is assumed to be 0.

### Examples

The following formula calculates the interest due in the first month of a three-year $8000 loan at 10 percent annual interest:

`IPMT(0.1/12,1,36,8000)` returns –$66.67.

The following formula calculates the interest due in the last year of a three-year $8000 loan at 10 percent annual interest, where payments are made yearly:

`IPMT(0.1,3,3,8000)` returns –$292.45.

## IRR

Returns the internal rate of return for a series of cash flows. Excel uses an iterative technique for calculating IRR. Starting with guess, IRR cycles through the calculation until the result is accurate within 0.00001 percent. If IRR can't find a result that works after 20 tries, the #NUM! error value is returned.

### Syntax

`IRR(values,guess)`

**Values** is an array or a reference to cells that contain numbers for which you want to calculate the internal rate of return.

**Guess** is a number that you guess is close to the result of IRR.

### Examples

Suppose you want to start a restaurant business. You estimate it will cost $70,000 to start the business and expect to net the following income in the first five years: $12,000, $15,000, $18,000, $21,000, and $26,000. B1:B6 contain the following values: –$70,000, $12,000, $15,000, $18,000, $21,000 and $26,000, respectively.

To calculate the investment's internal rate of return after four years:

`IRR(B1:B5)` returns –2.12%.

To calculate the internal rate of return after five years:

`IRR(B1:B6)` returns 8.66%.

To calculate the internal rate of return after two years, you need to include a guess:

`IRR(B1:B3,-10%)` returns –44.35%.

## ISBLANK

Returns TRUE if the value is blank.

### Syntax

`ISBLANK(value)`

**Value** is the value you want tested. Value can be a blank (empty cell), error, logical, text, number, or reference value, or name referring to any of these, that you want to test.

## ISERR

Returns TRUE if the value is any error value except #N/A.

### Syntax

`ISERR(value)`

**Value** is the value you want tested. Value can be a blank (empty cell), error, logical, text, number, or reference value, or name referring to any of these, that you want to test.

## ISERROR

Returns TRUE if the value is any error value.

APDX

**A**

Alphabetical List of
Worksheet Functions

### Syntax

```
ISERROR(value)
```

**Value** is the value you want tested. Value can be a blank (empty cell), error, logical, text, number, or reference value, or name referring to any of these, that you want to test.

## ISLOGICAL

Returns TRUE if the value is a logical value.

### Syntax

```
ISLOGICAL(value)
```

**Value** is the value you want tested. Value can be a blank (empty cell), error, logical, text, number, or reference value, or name referring to any of these, that you want to test.

## ISNA

Returns TRUE if the value is the #N/A error value.

### Syntax

```
ISNA(value)
```

**Value** is the value you want tested. Value can be a blank (empty cell), error, logical, text, number, or reference value, or name referring to any of these, that you want to test.

## ISNONTEXT

Returns TRUE if the value is not text.

### Syntax

```
ISNONTEXT(value)
```

**Value** is the value you want tested. Value can be a blank (empty cell), error, logical, text, number, or reference value, or name referring to any of these, that you want to test.

## ISNUMBER

Returns TRUE if the value is a number.

### Syntax

```
ISNUMBER(value)
```

**Value** is the value you want tested. Value can be a blank (empty cell), error, logical, text, number, or reference value, or name referring to any of these, that you want to test.

# ISREF

Returns TRUE if the value is a reference.

### Syntax
```
ISREF(value)
```

**Value** is the value you want tested. Value can be a blank (empty cell), error, logical, text, number, or reference value, or name referring to any of these, that you want to test.

# ISTEXT

Returns TRUE if the value is text.

### Syntax
```
ISTEXT(value)
```

**Value** is the value you want tested. Value can be a blank (empty cell), error, logical, text, number, or reference value, or name referring to any of these, that you want to test.

# KURT

Returns the kurtosis of a data set.

### Syntax
```
KURT(number1,number2,...)
```

**Number1,number2,...** are 1 to 30 arguments for which you want to calculate kurtosis. You can also use a single array or a reference to an array instead of arguments separated by commas.

### Examples
```
KURT(3,4,5,2,3,4,5,6,4,7) returns –0.1518.
```

# LARGE

Returns the *k*th largest value in a data set.

### Syntax

```
LARGE(array,k)
```

**Array** is the array or range of data for which you want to determine the *k*th largest value.

**K** is the position (from the largest) in the array or cell range of data to return.

### Examples

```
LARGE({3,4,5,2,3,4,5,6,4,7},3) returns 5.
LARGE({3,4,5,2,3,4,5,6,4,7},7) returns 4.
```

## LEFT

Returns the leftmost characters from a text value. (See Chapter 9 for in-depth coverage and examples of LEFT.)

### Syntax

```
LEFT(text,num_chars)
```

**Text** is the text string containing the characters you want to extract.

**Num_chars** specifies how many characters you want LEFT to return.

## LEN

Returns the number of characters in a text string. (See Chapter 9 for in-depth coverage and examples of LEN.)

### Syntax

```
LEN(text)
```

**Text** is the text whose length you want to find. Spaces count as characters.

## LINEST

Uses the "least squares" method to calculate a straight line that best fits your data and returns an array that describes the line. The equation for the line is $y=mx+b$. LINEST is often unnecessary in Excel because of the trendline capability in charts. See the Online Help worksheet function reference for detailed information about LINEST and examples.

### Syntax

```
LINEST(known_y's,known_x's,const,stats)
```

**Known_y's** is the set of y-values you already know in the relationship y=mx+b.

**Known_x's** is an optional set of x-values that you may already know in the relationship y=mx+b.

**Const** is a logical value specifying whether to force the constant *b* to equal 0.

**Stats** is a logical value specifying whether to return additional regression statistics.

# LN

Returns the natural logarithm of a number.

## Syntax
```
LN(number)
```

**Number** is the positive real number for which you want the natural logarithm.

## Examples

LN(86) returns 4.454347.

LN(2.7182818) returns 1.

# LOG

Returns the logarithm of a number to a specified base.

## Syntax
```
LOG(number,base)
```

**Number** is the positive real number for which you want the logarithm.

**Base** is the base of the logarithm. If base is omitted, it is assumed to be 10.

## Examples

LOG(10) returns 1.

LOG(8,2) returns 3.

# LOG10

Returns the base-10 logarithm of a number.

## Syntax
```
LOG10(number)
```

**Number** is the positive real number for which you want the base-10 logarithm.

**APDX**

**A**

**Alphabetical List of Worksheet Functions**

### Examples

LOG10(86) returns 1.934498451.

LOG10(10) returns 1.

LOG10(10^5) returns 5.

# LOGEST

Returns the parameters of an exponential trend. See the Online Help worksheet function reference for detailed information about LOGEST and examples. LOGEST is often unnecessary in Excel because of the trendline capability in charts.

### Syntax

LOGEST(known_y's,known_x's,const,stats)

**Known_y's** is the set of y-values you already know in the relationship y=b*m^x.

**Known_x's** is an optional set of x-values that you may already know in the relationship y=b*m^x.

**Const** is a logical value specifying whether to force the constant b to equal 1.

**Stats** is a logical value specifying whether to return additional regression statistics.

# LOGINV

Returns the inverse of the lognormal distribution.

### Syntax

LOGINV(probability,mean,standard_dev)

**Probability** is a probability associated with the lognormal distribution.

**Mean** is the mean of ln(x).

**Standard_dev** is the standard deviation of ln(x).

### Examples

LOGINV(0.039084,3.5,1.2) returns 4.000014.

# LOGNORMDIST

Returns the cumulative lognormal distribution.

### Syntax

LOGNORMDIST(x,mean,standard_dev)

**X** is the value at which to evaluate the function.

**Mean** is the mean of ln(x).

**Standard_dev** is the standard deviation of ln(x).

### Examples

    LOGNORMDIST(4,3.5,1.2) returns 0.039084.

# LOOKUP (vector form)

Looks up values in a vector (an array that contains only one row or one column). The vector form of LOOKUP looks in a vector for a value, moves to the corresponding position in a second vector, and returns this value. Use this form of the LOOKUP function when you want to be able to specify the range that contains the values you want to match. See the Online Help worksheet function reference for examples of LOOKUP.

### Syntax

    LOOKUP(lookup_value,lookup_vector,result_vector)

**Lookup_value** is a value that LOOKUP searches for in the first vector. Lookup_value can be a number, text, a logical value, or a name or reference that refers to a value.

**Lookup_vector** is a range that contains only one row or one column. The values in lookup_vector can be text, numbers, or logical values.

**Result_vector** is a range that contains only one row or column. It should be the same size as lookup_vector.

# LOOKUP (array form)

Looks up values in an array. The array form of LOOKUP looks in the first row or column of an array for the specified value, moves down or across to the last cell, and returns the value of the cell. Use this form of LOOKUP when the values you want to match are in the first row or column of the array. See the Online Help worksheet function reference for examples of LOOKUP.

**TIP** In general, it's best to use the HLOOKUP or VLOOKUP function instead of the array form of LOOKUP. This form of LOOKUP is provided for compatibility with other spreadsheet programs.

### Syntax

```
LOOKUP(lookup_value,array)
```

> **Lookup_value** is a value that LOOKUP searches for in an array. Lookup_value can be a number, text, a logical value, or a name or reference that refers to a value.

> **Array** is a range of cells that contains text, numbers, or logical values that you want to compare with lookup_value.

## LOWER

Converts text to lowercase.

### Syntax

```
LOWER(text)
```

> **Text** is the text you want to convert to lowercase. LOWER does not change characters in text that are not letters.

### Examples

```
LOWER("E. E. Cummings") returns "e. e. cummings."
```

```
LOWER("Apt. 2B") returns "apt. 2b."
```

## MATCH

Looks up values in a reference or array. (See Chapter 9 for in-depth coverage and examples of MATCH.)

### Syntax

```
MATCH(lookup_value,lookup_array,match_type)
```

> **Lookup_value** is the value you use to find the value you want in a table.

> **Lookup_array** is a contiguous range of cells containing possible lookup values. Lookup_array can be an array or an array reference.

> **Match_type** is the number –1, 0, or 1. Match_type specifies how Microsoft Excel matches lookup_value with values in lookup_array.

## MAX

Returns the maximum value in a list of arguments.

### Syntax

```
MAX(number1,number2,...)
```

> **Number1,number2,...** are 1 to 30 numbers for which you want to find the maximum value.

### Examples

If A1:A5 contains the numbers 10, 7, 9, 27, and 2, then:

MAX(A1:A5) returns 27.

MAX(A1:A5,30) returns 30.

## MAXA

Returns the maximum value in a list of arguments. Whereas the MAX function ignores cells containing logical values (TRUE and FALSE), MAXA calculates FALSE as zero and TRUE as 1. The syntax for MAXA is the same as MAX.

## MDETERM

Returns the matrix determinant of an array.

### Syntax

MDETERM(array)

**Array** is a numeric array with an equal number of rows and columns.

### Examples

MDETERM({1,3,8,5;1,3,6,1;1,1,1,0;7,3,10,2}) returns 88.

MDETERM({3,6,1;1,1,0;3,10,2}) returns 1.

## MEDIAN

Returns the median of the given numbers.

### Syntax

MEDIAN(number1,number2,...)

**Number1,number2,...** are up to 30 numbers for which you want the median.

### Examples

MEDIAN(1,2,3,4,5) returns 3.

MEDIAN(1,2,3,4,5,6) returns 3.5 (the average of 3 and 4).

## MID

Returns a specific number of characters from a text string starting at the position you specify. (See Chapter 9 for in-depth coverage and examples of MID.)

### Syntax
```
MID(text,start_num,num_chars)
```

**Text** is the text string containing the characters you want to extract.

**Start_num** is the position of the first character you want to extract in text. The first character in text has start_num 1, and so on.

**Num_chars** specifies how many characters to return from text.

## MIN

Returns the minimum value in a list of arguments.

### Syntax
```
MIN(number1,number2,...)
```

**Number1,number2,...** are up to 30 numbers for which you want to find the minimum value.

### Examples
If A1:A5 contains the numbers 10, 7, 9, 27, and 2, then:

```
MIN(A1:A5)
```
returns 2.

```
MIN(A1:A5,0)
```
returns 0.

## MINA

Returns the minimum value in a list of arguments. Whereas the MIN function ignores cells containing logical values (TRUE and FALSE), MINA calculates FALSE as 0 and TRUE as 1. The syntax for MINA is the same as MIN.

## MINUTE

Converts a serial number to a minute. (See Chapter 9 for in-depth coverage and examples of MINUTE.)

### Syntax
```
MINUTE(serial_number)
```

**Serial_number** is the date-time code used by Microsoft Excel for date and time calculations.

## MINVERSE

Returns the matrix inverse of an array.

### Syntax

`MINVERSE(array)`

**Array** is a numeric array with an equal number of rows and columns.

### Examples

`MINVERSE({4,-1;2,0})` returns {0,0.5;–1,2}

`MINVERSE({1,2,1;3,4,-1;0,2,0})` returns {0.25,0.25,–0.75;0,0,0.5;0.75, –0.25,–0.25}

## MIRR

Returns the internal rate of return where positive and negative cash flows are financed at different rates.

### Syntax

`MIRR(values,finance_rate,reinvest_rate)`

**Values** is an array or a reference to cells that contain numbers. These numbers represent a series of payments (negative values) and income (positive values) occurring at regular periods.

**Finance_rate** is the interest rate you pay on the money used in the cash flows.

**Reinvest_rate** is the interest rate you receive on the cash flows as you reinvest them.

### Examples

Suppose you're a commercial fisher just completing your fifth year of operation. Five years ago, you borrowed $120,000 at 10 percent annual interest to purchase a boat. Your catches have yielded $39,000, $30,000, $21,000, $37,000, and $46,000. During these years you reinvested your profits, earning 12% annually. In a worksheet, your loan amount is entered as -$120,000 in B1, and your five annual profits are entered in B2:B6. To calculate the investment's modified rate of return after five years:

`MIRR(B1:B6,10%,12%)` returns 12.61%.

To calculate the modified rate of return after three years:

`MIRR(B1:B4,10%,12%)` returns –4.80%.

APDX

**A**

Alphabetical List of Worksheet Functions

## MMULT

Returns the matrix product of two arrays.

### Syntax

```
MMULT(array1,array2)
```

**Array1,array2** are the arrays you want to multiply.

### Examples

```
MMULT({1,3;7,2},{2,0;0,2}) returns {2,6;14,4}.
```

```
MMULT({3,0;2,0},{2,0;0,2}) returns {6,0;4,0}.
```

## MOD

Returns the remainder from division.

### Syntax

```
MOD(number,divisor)
```

**Number** is the number for which you want to find the remainder.

**Divisor** is the number by which you want to divide number. If divisor is 0, MOD returns the #DIV/0! error value.

### Examples

```
MOD(3,2) returns 1.
```

## MODE

Returns the most common value in a data set.

### Syntax

```
MODE(number1,number2,...)
```

**Number1,number2,...** are up to 30 arguments for which you want to calculate the mode. You can use a single array or a reference to an array instead of arguments separated by commas.

### Examples

```
MODE({5.6,4,4,3,2,4}) returns 4.
```

## MONTH

Converts a serial number to a month. (See Chapter 9 for in-depth coverage and examples of MONTH.)

### Syntax

```
MONTH(serial_number)
```

**Serial_number** is the date-time code used by Excel for date and time calculations.

## N

Returns a value converted to a number. This function is provided for compatibility with other spreadsheet programs.

### Syntax

```
N(value)
```

**Value** is the value you want converted. If value is a number, N returns the number; if value is a date (in an Excel date format), N returns the serial number of the date; if value is TRUE, N returns 1; if value is anything else, N returns 0.

### Examples

If A1 contains "7," A2 contains "Even," and A3 contains "TRUE," then:

```
N(A1) returns 7.
```

```
N(A2) returns 0, because A2 contains text.
```

```
N(A3) returns 1, because A3 contains TRUE.
```

## NA

Returns the error value #N/A. You can also type the value #N/A directly into a cell. The NA function is provided for compatibility with other spreadsheet programs.

### Syntax

```
NA()
```

## NEGBINOMDIST

Returns the negative binomial distribution.

### Syntax

```
NEGBINOMDIST(number_f,number_s,probability_s)
```

**Number_f** is the number of failures.

**Number_s** is the threshold number of successes.

**Probability_s** is the probability of a success.

### Examples

NEGBINOMDIST(10,5,0.25) returns 0.055049.

## NORMDIST

Returns the normal cumulative distribution.

### Syntax

NORMDIST(x,mean,standard_dev,cumulative)

**X** is the value for which you want the distribution.

**Mean** is the arithmetic mean of the distribution.

**Standard_dev** is the standard deviation of the distribution.

**Cumulative** is a logical value that determines the form of the function.

### Examples

NORMDIST(42,40,1.5,TRUE) returns 0.908789.

## NORMINV

Returns the inverse of the normal cumulative distribution.

### Syntax

NORMINV(probability,mean,standard_dev)

**Probability** is a probability corresponding to the normal distribution.

**Mean** is the arithmetic mean of the distribution.

**Standard_dev** is the standard deviation of the distribution.

### Examples

NORMINV(0.908789,40,1.5) returns 42.

## NORMSDIST

Returns the standard normal cumulative distribution.

### Syntax

NORMSDIST(z)

**Z** is the value for which you want the distribution.

### Examples

NORMSDIST(1.333333) returns 0.908789.

## NORMSINV

Returns the inverse of the standard normal cumulative distribution.

### Syntax

NORMSINV(probability)

**Probability** is a probability corresponding to the normal distribution.

### Examples

NORMSINV(0.908789) returns 1.3333.

## NOT

Reverses the logic of its argument.

### Syntax

NOT(logical)

**Logical** is a value or expression that can be evaluated to TRUE or FALSE. If logical is FALSE, NOT returns TRUE; if logical is TRUE, NOT returns FALSE.

### Examples

NOT(FALSE) returns TRUE.

NOT(1+1=2) returns FALSE.

## NOW

Returns the serial number of the current date and time. (See Chapter 9 for in-depth coverage and examples of NOW.)

### Syntax

NOW()

## NPER

Returns the number of periods for an investment.

### Syntax

NPER(rate,pmt,pv,fv,type)

**Rate** is the interest rate per period.

**Pmt** is the payment made each period; it cannot change over the life of the annuity. Typically, pmt contains principal and interest but no other fees or taxes.

**Pv** is the present value, or the lump-sum amount that a series of future payments is worth right now.

**Fv** is the future value, or a cash balance you want to attain after the last payment is made. If fv is omitted, it is assumed to be 0 (the future value of a loan, for example, is 0).

**Type** is the number 0 or 1 and indicates when payments are due. A return of 0 or omitted means payments are due at the end of the period; 1 means payments are due at the beginning of the period.

### Examples

NPER(12%/12,-100,-1000,10000,1) returns 60.

NPER(1%,-100,-1000,10000) returns 60.

## NPV

Returns the net present value of an investment on the basis of a series of periodic cash flows and a discount rate.

**WARNING**
The NPV function is actually a present value function, but there are a couple of methods of using NPV as a true net present value function. The first method is to not include the initial cash flow in the list of cash flows; instead, add the initial cash flow to the NPV function result. The second method is to include the initial cash flow in the list of cash flows, then multiply the NPV result by 1+I (I is the discount rate).

### Syntax

NPV(rate,value1,value2,...)

**Rate** is the rate of discount over the length of one period.

**Value1,value2,...** are 1 to 29 arguments representing the payments and income.

### Examples

Suppose you're considering an investment in which you pay $10,000 one year from today and receive an annual income of $3000, $4200, and $6800 in the three years that follow. Assuming an annual discount rate of 10 percent, the net present value of this investment is

NPV(10%,-10000,3000,4200,6800)

which returns $1188.44.

## ODD

Rounds a number up to the nearest odd integer.

### Syntax

`ODD(number)`

**Number** is the value to round.

### Examples

`ODD(1.5)` returns 3.

`ODD(3)` returns 3.

`ODD(2)` returns 3.

## OFFSET

Returns a reference offset from a given reference. (See Chapter 9 for in-depth coverage and examples of OFFSET.)

### Syntax

`OFFSET(reference,rows,cols,height,width)`

**Reference** is the reference from which you want to base the offset.

**Rows** is the number of rows, up or down, that you want the upper-left cell to refer to.

**Cols** is the number of columns, to the left or right, that you want the upper-left cell of the result to refer to.

**Height** is the height, in number of rows, that you want the returned reference to be.

**Width** is the width, in number of columns, that you want the returned reference to be.

## OR

Returns TRUE if any argument is TRUE.

### Syntax

`OR(logical1,logical2,…)`

**Logical1,logical2,…** are 1 to 30 conditions you want to test that can be either TRUE or FALSE.

### Examples

OR(1+1=1,2+2=5) returns FALSE.

If A1:A3 contains the values TRUE, FALSE, and TRUE, then OR(A1:A3) returns TRUE.

## PEARSON

Returns the Pearson product moment correlation coefficient, which reflects the extent of a linear relationship between two data sets.

### Syntax

PEARSON(array1,array2)

**Array1** is a set of independent values.

**Array2** is a set of dependent values.

### Examples

PEARSON({9,7,5,3,1},{10,6,1,5,3}) returns 0.699379.

## PERCENTILE

Returns the *k*th percentile of values in a range. You can use PERCENTILE, for example, to examine candidates that score above the 90th percentile.

### Syntax

PERCENTILE(array,k)

**Array** is the array or range of data that defines relative standing.

**K** is the percentile value in the range 0..1, inclusive.

### Examples

PERCENTILE({1,2,3,4},0.3) returns 1.9.

## PERCENTRANK

Returns the percentage rank of a value in a data set. You can use PERCENTRANK, for example, to evaluate the standing of a test score among a population of test scores.

### Syntax

PERCENTRANK(array,x,significance)

**Array** is the array or range of data with numeric values that defines relative standing.

**X** is the value for which you want to know the rank.

**Significance** is an optional value that identifies the number of significant digits for the returned percentage value. If omitted, PERCENTRANK uses three digits (0.xxx%).

### Examples

PERCENTRANK({1,2,3,4,5,6,7,8,9,10},4) returns 0.333.

## PERMUT

Returns the number of permutations for a given number of objects. You can use PERMUT for lottery-style probability calculations.

### Syntax

PERMUT(number,number_chosen)

**Number** is an integer that describes the number of objects.

**Number_chosen** is an integer that describes the number of objects in each permutation.

### Examples

Suppose you want to calculate the odds of selecting a winning lottery number. Each lottery entry contains three numbers, each of which can be between 0 and 99, inclusive. The following function calculates the number of possible permutations.

PERMUT(100,3) returns 970,200.

## PI

Returns the value of pi (3.14159265358979), accurate to 15 digits.

### Syntax

PI()

### Examples

PI()/2 returns 1.57079…

SIN(PI()/2) returns 1.

## PMT

Returns the periodic payment for an annuity based on constant payments and a constant interest rate.

Be consistent about the units used for rate and nper. For example, if you make monthly payments on a four-year loan at 12 percent annual interest, use 12%/12 for rate and 4*12 for nper; to make annual payments on the same loan, use 12% for rate and 4 for nper.

### Syntax

```
PMT(rate,nper,pv,fv,type)
```

**Rate** is the interest rate per period.

**Nper** is the total number of payment periods in an annuity.

**Pv** is the present value, the total amount that a series of future payments is worth now.

**Fv** is the future value, or a cash balance you want to attain after the last payment is made. If fv is omitted, it is assumed to be 0 (the future value of a loan, for example, is 0).

**Type** is the number 0 or 1 and indicates when payments are due. If type is 0 or omitted, payments are due at the end of the period; If type is 1, payments are due at the beginning of the period.

### Examples

The following formula returns the monthly payment on a $10,000 loan at an annual rate of 8% that you must pay off in 10 months:

```
PMT(8%/12,10,10000) returns –$1037.03.
```

For the same loan, if payments are due at the beginning of the period, the payment is

```
PMT(8%/12,10,10000,0,1)
```

which returns –$1030.16.

TIP

To find the total amount paid over the duration of the annuity, multiply the returned PMT value by nper.

## POISSON

Returns the Poisson distribution.

### Syntax

```
POISSON(x,mean,cumulative)
```

**X** is the number of events.

**Mean** is the expected numeric value.

**Cumulative** is a logical value that determines the form of the probability distribution returned. If cumulative is TRUE, POISSON returns the cumulative Poisson probability that the number of random events occurring will be between zero and x inclusive; if FALSE, it returns the Poisson probability mass function that the number of events occurring will be exactly x.

### Examples

POISSON(2,5,FALSE) returns 0.084224.

POISSON(2,5,TRUE) returns 0.124652.

## POWER

Returns the result of a number raised to a power.

### Syntax

POWER(number,power)

**Number** is the base number. It can be any real number.

**Power** is the exponent, to which the base number is raised.

### Examples

POWER(5,2) returns 25.

POWER(98.6,3.2) returns 2401077.

POWER(4,5/4) returns 5.656854.

## PPMT

Returns the payment on the principal for a given period for an investment based on periodic, constant payments and a constant interest rate.

Be consistent about the units used for rate and nper. For example, if you make monthly payments on a four-year loan at 12 percent annual interest, use 12%/12 for rate and 4*12 for nper; to make annual payments on the same loan, use 12% for rate and 4 for nper.

### Syntax

PPMT(rate,per,nper,pv,fv,type)

**Rate** is the interest rate per period.

**Per** specifies the period and must be in the range 1 to nper.

**Nper** is the total number of payment periods in an annuity.

**Pv** is the present value, the total amount that a series of future payments is worth now.

**Fv** is the future value, or a cash balance you want to attain after the last payment is made. If fv is omitted, it is assumed to be 0 (the future value of a loan, for example, is 0).

**Type** is the number 0 or 1 and indicates when payments are due. If type is 0 or omitted, payments are due at the end of the period; if type is 1, payments are due at the beginning of the period.

## Examples

The following formula returns the principal payment for the first month of a two-year $2000 loan at 10% annual interest:

    PPMT(10%/12,1,24,2000) returns –$75.62.

The following function returns the principal payment for the last year of a 10-year $200,000 loan at 8% annual interest:

    PPMT(8%,10,10,200000) returns –$27,598.05.

# PROB

Returns the probability that values in a range are between two limits.

## Syntax

    PROB(x_range,prob_range,lower_limit,upper_limit)

**X_range** is the range of numeric values of x with which there are associated probabilities.

**Prob_range** is a set of probabilities associated with values in x_range.

**Lower_limit** is the lower bound on the value for which you want a probability.

**Upper_limit** is the optional upper bound on the value for which you want a probability.

## Examples

    PROB({0,1,2,3},{0.2,0.3,0.1,0.4},2) returns 0.1.
    PROB({0,1,2,3},{0.2,0.3,0.1,0.4},1,3) returns 0.8.

## PRODUCT

Multiplies its arguments.

### Syntax

PRODUCT(number1,number2,…)

**Number1,number2,…** are up to 30 numbers that you want to multiply.

### Examples

If cells A2:C2 contain 5, 15, and 30:

PRODUCT(A2:C2) returns 2250.

PRODUCT(A2:C2,2) returns 4500.

## PROPER

Capitalizes the first letter in each word of a text value.

### Syntax

PROPER(text)

**Text** is text enclosed in quotation marks, a formula that returns text, or a reference to a cell containing the text you want to partially capitalize.

### Examples

PROPER("this is a TITLE") returns "This Is A Title."

PROPER("2-cent's worth") returns "2-Cent'S Worth."

PROPER("76BudGet") returns "76Budget."

## PV

Returns the present value of an investment (the total amount that a series of future payments is worth now). For example, when you borrow money, the loan amount is the present value to the lender.

Be consistent about the units used for rate and nper. For example, if you make monthly payments on a four-year loan at 12 percent annual interest, use 12%/12 for rate and 4*12 for nper; to make annual payments on the same loan, use 12% for rate and 4 for nper.

For all the arguments, cash you pay out (e.g., deposits to savings) is represented by negative numbers; cash you receive (e.g., dividend checks) is represented by positive numbers.

## Syntax

`PV(rate,nper,pmt,fv,type)`

**Rate** is the interest rate per period.

**Nper** is the total number of payment periods in an annuity.

**Pmt** is the payment made each period and cannot change over the life of the annuity.

**Fv** is the future value, or a cash balance you want to attain after the last payment is made. If fv is omitted, it is assumed to be 0. The future value of a loan is 0; however, if you want to save $50,000 to pay for a special project in 18 years, then $50,000 is the future value.

**Type** is the number 0 or 1 and indicates when payments are due. If type is 0 or omitted, payments are due at the end of the period; If type is 1, payments are due at the beginning of the period.

## Examples

Suppose you're thinking of buying an insurance annuity that pays $500 at the end of every month for the next 20 years. The cost of the annuity is $60,000 and the money paid out will earn 8%. You want to determine whether this would be a good investment. Using the PV function you find that the present value of the annuity is

PV(0.08/12,12*20,500,,0)

which returns –$59,777.15.

# QUARTILE

Returns the quartile of a data set. You can use QUARTILE, for example, to find the top 25% of incomes in a population.

## Syntax

`QUARTILE(array,quart)`

**Array** is the array or cell range of numeric values for which you want the quartile value.

**Quart** indicates which value to return. If quart equals 0, QUARTILE returns the minimum value; if quart equals 1, QUARTILE returns the first quartile (25th percentile); if quart equals 2, QUARTILE returns the median value (50th percentile); if quart equals 3, QUARTILE returns the third quartile (75th percentile); if quart equals 4, QUARTILE returns the maximum value.

## Examples

QUARTILE({1,2,4,7,8,9,10,12},1) returns 3.5.

# RADIANS

Converts degrees to radians.

### Syntax

RADIANS(angle)

**Angle** is an angle in degrees that you want to convert.

## Examples

RADIANS(270) returns 4.712389 (3p/2 radians).

# RAND

Returns a random number between 0 and 1. The random number will recalculate every time the worksheet recalculates—to freeze the random values, copy the numbers, then choose Edit ➢ Paste Special ➢ Values.

### Syntax

RAND( )

TIP

To generate a random number between a and b, use the formula **=RAND()*(b-a)+a**.

## Examples

To generate a random number greater than or equal to 0 but less than 100:

RAND()*100 returns a random number between 0 and 100.

INT(RAND()*100) returns a random integer between 0 and 100.

RAND()*(49-2)+2 returns a random number between 2 and 49.

# RANK

Returns the rank of a number in a list of numbers.

### Syntax

```
RANK(number,ref,order)
```

**Number** is the number whose rank you want to find.

**Ref** is an array of, or a reference to, a list of numbers (non-numeric values in ref are ignored).

**Order** is a number specifying how to rank number.

### Examples

If A1:A5 contain the numbers 7, 3.5, 3.5, 1, and 2, respectively, then:

```
RANK(A2,A1:A5,1)
```
returns 3.

```
RANK(A1,A1:A5,1)
```
returns 5.

## RATE

Returns the interest rate per period of an annuity.

### Syntax

```
RATE(nper,pmt,pv,fv,type,guess)
```

**Nper** is the total number of payment periods in an annuity.

**Pmt** is the payment made each period and cannot change over the life of the annuity.

**Pv** is the present value (the total amount that a series of future payments is worth now).

**Fv** is the future value, or a cash balance you want to attain after the last payment is made. If fv is omitted, it is assumed to be 0 (the future value of a loan, for example, is 0).

**Type** is the number 0 or 1 and indicates when payments are due. If type is 0 or omitted, payments are due at the end of the period; if type is 1, payments are due at the beginning of the period.

**Guess** is your guess for what the rate will be.

### Examples

To calculate the monthly rate of a four-year, $8000 loan with monthly payments of $200:

```
RATE(48,-200,8000)
```
returns 0.77%.

## REPLACE

Replaces characters within text.

### Syntax

```
REPLACE(old_text,start_num,num_chars,new_text)
```

**Old_text** is text in which you want to replace some characters.

**Start_num** is the position of the character in old_text that you want to replace with new_text.

**Num_chars** is the number of characters in old_text that you want to replace with new_text.

**New_text** is the text that will replace characters in old_text.

### Examples

The following formula replaces the last two digits of 1990 with 91:

```
REPLACE("1990",3,2,"91") returns "1991."
```

If cell A2 contains "123456," then:

```
REPLACE(A2,1,3,"@") returns "@456."
```

# REPT

Repeats text a given number of times.

### Syntax

```
REPT(text,number_times)
```

**Text** is the text you want to repeat.

**Number_times** is a positive number specifying the number of times to repeat text. If number_times is 0, REPT returns "" (empty text). If number_times is not an integer, it is truncated. The result of the REPT function cannot be longer than 255 characters.

### Examples

```
REPT("*-",3) returns "*-*-*-."
```

If A3 contains "Sales", then REPT($A$3,2.9) returns "SalesSales."

# RIGHT

Returns the rightmost characters from a text value. (See Chapter 9 for in-depth coverage and examples of RIGHT.)

APDX

**A**

Alphabetical List of
Worksheet Functions

### Syntax

```
RIGHT(text,num_chars)
```

**Text** is the text string containing the characters you want to extract.

**Num_chars** specifies how many characters you want to extract.

# ROMAN

Converts an Arabic numeral to Roman, as text.

### Syntax

```
ROMAN(number,form)
```

**Number** is the Arabic numeral you want converted.

**Form** is a number specifying the type of Roman numeral you want. The Roman numeral style ranges from Classic (form 0, TRUE, or omitted) to Simplified (form 4 or FALSE), becoming more concise as the value of form increases.

### Examples

```
ROMAN(499,0)
```
 returns "CDXCIX."

```
ROMAN(499,1)
```
 returns "LDVLIV."

```
ROMAN(499,2)
```
 returns "XDIX."

# ROUND

Rounds a number to a specified number of digits.

### Syntax

```
ROUND(number,num_digits)
```

**Number** is the number you want to round.

**Num_digits** specifies the number of digits to which you want to round number. If num_digits is greater than 0, then number is rounded to the specified number of decimal places; if num_digits is 0, then number is rounded to the nearest integer; if num_digits is less than 0, then number is rounded to the left of the decimal point.

### Examples

```
ROUND(2.149,1)
```
 returns 2.1.

```
ROUND(-1.475,2)
```
 returns –1.48.

```
ROUND(21.5,-1)
```
 returns 20.

## ROUNDDOWN

Rounds a number down, toward zero.

### Syntax

```
ROUNDDOWN(number,num_digits)
```

**Number** is any real number that you want rounded down.

**Num_digits** is the number of digits (to the right of the decimal point) to which you want to round number.

### Examples

```
ROUNDDOWN(3.2,0) returns 3.
```

```
ROUNDDOWN(76.9,0) returns 76.
```

```
ROUNDDOWN(3.14159,3) returns 3.141.
```

## ROUNDUP

Rounds a number up, away from zero.

### Syntax

```
ROUNDUP(number,num_digits)
```

**Number** is any real number that you want rounded up.

**Num_digits** is the number of digits (to the right of the decimal point) to which you want to round number.

### Examples

```
ROUNDUP(3.2,0)  returns 4.
```

```
ROUNDUP(76.9,0) returns 77.
```

```
ROUNDUP(-3.14159,1) returns –3.2.
```

## ROW

Returns the row number of a reference. (See Chapter 9 for in-depth coverage and examples of ROW.)

### Syntax

```
ROW(reference)
```

**Reference** is the cell or range of cells for which you want the row number.

# ROWS

Returns the number of rows in a reference. (See Chapter 9 for in-depth coverage and examples of ROWS.)

### Syntax

ROWS(array)

> **Array** is an array, an array formula, or a reference to a range of cells for which you want the number of rows.

# RSQ

Returns the square of the Pearson product moment correlation coefficient.

### Syntax

RSQ(known_y's,known_x's)

> **Known_y's** is an array or range of data points.
>
> **Known_x's** is an array or range of data points.

### Examples

RSQ({2,3,9,1,8,7,5},{6,5,11,7,5,4,4}) returns 0.05795.

# SEARCH

Finds one text value within another. (See Chapter 9 for in-depth coverage and examples of SEARCH.)

### Syntax

SEARCH(find_text,within_text,start_num)

> **Find_text** is the text you want to find. You can use the wildcard characters, question mark (?) and asterisk (*), in find_text.
>
> **Within_text** is the text in which you want to search for find_text.
>
> **Start_num** is the character number in within_text, counting from the left, at which you want to start searching.

# SECOND

Converts a serial number to a second.

### Syntax

SECOND(serial_number)

> **Serial_number** is the date-time code used by Excel for date and time calculations.

### Examples

SECOND("4:48:18 PM") returns 18.

SECOND(0.01) returns 24.

SECOND(4.02) returns 48.

# SIGN

Determines the sign of a number. Returns 1 if number is positive, 0 if number is 0, and –1 if number is negative.

### Syntax

SIGN(number)

**Number** is any real number.

### Examples

SIGN(10) returns 1.

SIGN(4-4) returns 0.

SIGN(-0.00001) returns –1.

# SIN

Returns the sine of the given angle.

### Syntax

SIN(number)

**Number** is the angle in radians for which you want the sine. If your argument is in degrees, multiply it by PI()/180 to convert it to radians.

### Examples

SIN(PI()) returns 1.22E-16, which is approximately zero.

SIN(PI()/2) returns 1.

SIN(30*PI()/180) returns 0.5, the sine of 30 degrees.

# SINH

Returns the hyperbolic sine of a number.

### Syntax

SINH(number)

**Number** is any real number.

APDX
A

Alphabetical List of
Worksheet Functions

### Examples

SINH(1) returns 1.175201194.

SINH(-1) returns –1.175201194.

## SKEW

Returns the skewness of a distribution.

### Syntax

SKEW(number1,number2,…)

**Number1,number2…** are 1 to 30 arguments for which you want to calculate skewness.

### Examples

SKEW(3,4,5,2,3,4,5,6,4,7) returns 0.359543.

## SLN

Returns the straight-line depreciation of an asset for one period.

### Syntax

SLN(cost,salvage,life)

**Cost** is the initial cost of the asset.

**Salvage** is the value at the end of the depreciation (sometimes called the salvage value of the asset).

**Life** is the number of periods over which the asset is being depreciated (sometimes called the useful life of the asset).

### Examples

Suppose you've bought a truck for $30,000 that has a useful life of 10 years and a salvage value of $7500. The depreciation allowance for each year is:

SLN(30000,7500,10)

which returns $2250.

## SLOPE

Returns the slope of the linear regression line.

### Syntax

SLOPE(known_y's,known_x's)

**Known_y's** is an array or cell range of numeric dependent data points.

**Known_x's** is the set of independent data points.

### Examples

SLOPE({2,3,9,1,8,7,5},{6,5,11,7,5,4,4}) returns 0.305556.

# SMALL

Returns the *k*th smallest value in a data set.

### Syntax

SMALL(array,k)

**Array** is an array or range of numerical data for which you want to determine the *k*th smallest value.

**K** is the position (from the smallest) in the array or range of data to return.

### Examples

# SQRT

SMALL({3,4,5,2,3,4,5,6,4,7},4) returns 4.

SMALL({1,4,8,3,7,12,54,8,23},2) returns 3.

Returns a positive square root.

### Syntax

SQRT(number)

**Number** is the number for which you want the square root. If number is negative, SQRT returns the #NUM! error value.

### Examples

SQRT(16) returns 4.

SQRT(-16) returns #NUM!.

SQRT(ABS(-16)) returns 4.

# STANDARDIZE

Returns a normalized value.

### Syntax

STANDARDIZE(x,mean,standard_dev)

**X** is the value you want to normalize.

APDX

**A**

Alphabetical List of
Worksheet Functions

**Mean** is the arithmetic mean of the distribution.

**Standard_dev** is the standard deviation of the distribution.

### Examples

STANDARDIZE(42,40,1.5) returns 1.333333.

## STDEV

Estimates standard deviation based on a sample.

### Syntax

STDEV(number1,number2,…)

**Number1,number2,...** are 1 to 30 number arguments corresponding to a sample of a population. You can also use a single array or a reference to an array instead of arguments separated by commas.

### Examples

Suppose 10 tools stamped from the same machine during a production run are collected as a random sample and measured for breaking strength. The sample values (1345, 1301, 1368, 1322, 1310, 1370, 1318, 1350, 1303, 1299) are stored in A2:E3, respectively. STDEV estimates the standard deviation of breaking strengths for all the tools.

STDEV(A2:E3) returns 27.46.

## STDEVA

Estimates standard deviation based on a sample. Whereas the STDEV function ignores cells containing text and logical values (TRUE and FALSE), STDEVA calculates text as zero, FALSE as zero, and TRUE as one. The syntax for STDEVA is the same as STDEV.

## STDEVP

Calculates standard deviation on the basis of the entire population.

### Syntax

STDEVP(number1,number2,…)

**Number1,number2,...** are 1 to 30 number arguments corresponding to a population. You can also use a single array or a reference to an array instead of arguments separated by commas.

### Examples

Using the same data from the STDEV example and assuming that only 10 tools are produced during the production run, STDEVP measures the standard deviation of breaking strengths for all the tools.

STDEVP(A2:E3) returns 26.05.

## STDEVPA

Calculates standard deviation on the basis of the entire population. Whereas the STDEVP function ignores cells containing text and logical values (TRUE and FALSE), STDEVA calculates text as zero, FALSE as zero, and TRUE as one. The syntax for STDEVPA is the same as STDEVP.

## STEYX

Returns the standard error of the predicted y-value for each x in the regression.

### Syntax

STEYX(known_y's,known_x's)

**Known_y's** is an array or range of dependent data points.

**Known_x's** is an array or range of independent data points.

### Examples

STEYX({2,3,9,1,8,7,5},{6,5,11,7,5,4,4}) returns 3.305719.

## SUBSTITUTE

Substitutes new text for old text in a text string.

### Syntax

SUBSTITUTE(text,old_text,new_text,instance_num)

**Text** is the text or the reference to a cell containing text for which you want to substitute characters.

**Old_text** is the text you want to replace.

**New_text** is the text you want to replace old_text with.

**Instance_num** specifies which occurrence of old_text you want to replace with new_text. If you specify instance_num, only that instance of old_text is replaced. Otherwise, every occurrence of old_text in text is changed to new_text.

**Examples**

```
SUBSTITUTE("Sales Data","Sales","Cost") returns "Cost Data."
SUBSTITUTE("Quarter 1, 1991","1","2",1) returns "Quarter 2, 1991."
SUBSTITUTE("Quarter 1 1991","1","2",3) returns "Quarter 1, 1992."
```

# SUBTOTAL

Returns a subtotal in a list or database. (See Chapter 9 for in-depth coverage and examples of SUBTOTAL.)

### Syntax

```
SUBTOTAL(function_num,reference)
```

**Function_num** is the number 1 to 11 that specifies which function to use in calculating subtotals within a list.

**Ref** is range or reference for which you want the subtotal.

# SUM

Adds its arguments.

### Syntax

```
SUM(number1,number2,…)
```

**Number1,number2,…** are 1 to 30 arguments for which you want the sum.

### Examples

```
SUM(3,2) returns 5.
```

If cells A2:C2 contain 5, 15, and 30, then `SUM(A2:C2)` returns 50.

# SUMIF

Adds the cells specified by a given criteria. (See Chapter 9 for in-depth coverage and examples of SUMIF.)

### Syntax

```
SUMIF(range,criteria,sum_range)
```

**Range** is the range of cells you want evaluated.

**Criteria** is the criteria in the form of a number, expression, or text that defines which cells will be added. For example, Criteria can be expressed as 32, "32", ">32", "apples."

**Sum_range** are the actual cells to sum. The cells in sum_range are summed only if their corresponding cells in range match the criteria.

# SUMPRODUCT

Returns the sum of the products of corresponding array components.

### Syntax
```
SUMPRODUCT(array1,array2,array3,…)
```

**Array1,array2,array3,...** are 2 to 30 arrays whose components you want to multiply and then add.

See the Online Help worksheet function reference for an example.

# SUMSQ

Returns the sum of the squares of the arguments.

### Syntax
```
SUMSQ(number1,number2,…)
```

**Number1,number2,...** are 1 to 30 arguments for which you want the sum of the squares.

### Examples
```
SUMSQ(3,4)
```
returns 25.

# SUMX2MY2

Returns the sum of the difference of squares of corresponding values in two arrays.

### Syntax
```
SUMX2MY2(array_x,array_y)
```

**Array_x** is the first array or range of values.

**Array_y** is the second array or range of values.

### Examples
```
SUMX2MY2({2,3,9,1,8,7,5},{6,5,11,7,5,4,4})
```
returns –55.

## SUMX2PY2

Returns the sum of the sum of squares of corresponding values in two arrays.

### Syntax

```
SUMX2PY2(array_x,array_y)
```

**Array_x** is the first array or range of values.

**Array_y** is the second array or range of values.

### Examples

```
SUMX2PY2({2,3,9,1,8,7,5},{6,5,11,7,5,4,4})
```
returns 521.

## SUMXMY2

Returns the sum of squares of differences of corresponding values in two arrays.

### Syntax

```
SUMXMY2(array_x,array_y)
```

**Array_x** is the first array or range of values.

**Array_y** is the second array or range of values.

### Examples

```
SUMXMY2({2,3,9,1,8,7,5},{6,5,11,7,5,4,4})
```
returns 79.

## SYD

Returns the sum-of-years' digits depreciation of an asset for a specified period.

### Syntax

```
SYD(cost,salvage,life,per)
```

**Cost** is the initial cost of the asset.

**Salvage** is the value at the end of the depreciation (sometimes called the salvage value of the asset).

**Life** is the number of periods over which the asset is being depreciated (sometimes called the useful life of the asset).

**Per** is the period and must use the same units as life.

### Examples

If you've bought a truck for $30,000 that has a useful life of 10 years and a salvage value of $7500, the yearly depreciation allowance for the first year is

```
SYD(30000,7500,10,1)
```

which returns $4090.91.

The yearly depreciation allowance for the 10th year is

```
SYD(30000,7500,10,10)
```

which returns $409.09.

## T

Returns the text referred to by value. You do not generally need to use the T function in a formula since Excel automatically converts values as necessary (this function is provided for compatibility with other spreadsheet programs).

### Syntax
```
T(value)
```

**Value** is the value you want to test. If value is or refers to text, T returns value. If value does not refer to text, T returns "" (empty text).

### Examples

If B1 contains the text "Rainfall", then T(B1) returns "Rainfall".

If B2 contains the number 19, then T(B2) returns "".

## TAN

Returns the tangent of a number. If your argument is in degrees, multiply it by PI()/180 to convert it to radians.

### Syntax
```
TAN(number)
```

**Number** is the angle in radians for which you want the tangent.

### Examples

TAN(0.785) returns 0.99920.

TAN(45*PI()/180) returns 1.

## TANH

Returns the hyperbolic tangent of a number.

### Syntax
```
TANH(number)
```

**Number** is any real number.

APDX
**A**

Alphabetical List of
Worksheet Functions

### Examples

TANH(-2) returns –0.96403.

TANH(0.5) returns 0.462117.

# TDIST

Returns the Student's t-distribution.

### Syntax

TDIST(x,degrees_freedom,tails)

**X** is the numeric value at which to evaluate the distribution.

**Degrees_freedom** is an integer indicating the number of degrees of freedom.

**Tails** specifies the number of distribution tails to return. If tails=1, TDIST returns the one-tailed distribution. If tails=2, TDIST returns the two-tailed distribution.

### Examples

TDIST(1.96,60,2) returns 0.054645.

# TEXT

Formats a number and converts it to text.

### Syntax

TEXT(value,format_text)

**Value** is a numeric value, a formula that evaluates to a numeric value, or a reference to a cell containing a numeric value.

**Format_text** is a number format in text form from the Number tab in the Cell Properties dialog box.

### Examples

TEXT(2.715,"$0.00") returns "$2.72."

TEXT("4/15/91","mmmm dd, yyyy") returns "April 15, 1991."

# TIME

Returns the serial number of a particular time.

### Syntax

TIME(hour, minute, second)

**Hour** is a number from 1 to 23 that represents the hour.

**Minute** is a number from 0 to 59 that represents the minute.

**Second** is a number from 0 to 59 that represents the second.

### Examples

TIME(13, 50, 27) returns 0.57670389, which is equivalent to 1:50:27 PM.

## TIMEVALUE

Converts a time in the form of text to a serial number.

### Syntax

TIMEVALUE(time_text)

**Time_text** is a text string that gives a time in any one of the Microsoft Excel time formats. Date information in time_text is ignored.

### Examples

TIMEVALUE("2:24 AM") returns 0.1.

TIMEVALUE("22-Aug-55 6:35 AM") returns 0.274305556.

## TINV

Returns the inverse of the Student's t-distribution.

### Syntax

TINV(probability,degrees_freedom)

**Probability** is the probability associated with the two-tailed Student's t-distribution.

**Degrees_freedom** is the number of degrees of freedom to characterize the distribution.

### Examples

TINV(0.054645,60) returns 1.96.

## TODAY

Returns the serial number of today's date. (See Chapter 9 for in-depth coverage and examples of TODAY.)

### Syntax

TODAY()

APDX

**A**

Alphabetical List of Worksheet Functions

# TRANSPOSE

Returns the transpose of an array.

## Syntax

```
TRANSPOSE(array)
```

> **Array** is an array on a worksheet or macro sheet that you want to transpose. Array can also be a range of cells.

## Examples

Suppose A1:C1 contain 1, 2, 3, respectively. When the following formula is entered as an array into cells A3:A5:

> `TRANSPOSE($A$1:$C$1)` returns the same respective values, but in A3:A5.

# TREND

Returns values along a linear trend.

## Syntax

```
TREND(known_y's,known_x's,new_x's,const)
```

> **Known_y's** is the set of y-values you already know in the relationship y=mx+b.

> **Known_x's** is an optional set of x-values that you may already know in the relationship y=mx+b.

> **New_x's** are new x-values for which you want TREND to return corresponding y-values.

> **Const** is a logical value specifying whether to force the constant b to equal 0. If const is TRUE or omitted, b is calculated normally. If const is FALSE, b is set equal to 0 and the m-values are adjusted so that y=mx.

## Examples

Suppose a business wants to purchase a tract of land in July, the start of the next fiscal year. The business collected cost information that covers the most recent 12 months for a typical tract in the desired area. Known_y's contains the set of known values ($133,890, $135,000, $135,790, $137,300, $138,130, $139,100, $139900, $141,120, $141,890, $143,230, $144,000, $145,290), and are stored in B2:B13, respectively.

When entered as a vertical array in the range C2:C6, the following formula returns the predicted prices for March, April, May, June, and July:

> `TREND(B2:B13,,{13;14;15;16;17})` returns {146172;147190;148208;149226;150244}.

## TRIM

Removes spaces from text. Use TRIM to remove extra spaces when downloading fixed-width data from a mainframe.

### Syntax

```
TRIM(text)
```

**Text** is the text from which you want spaces removed.

### Examples

```
TRIM(" First    Quarter    Earnings    ")
```
returns "First Quarter Earnings."

## TRIMMEAN

Returns the mean of the interior of a data set. TRIMMEAN calculates the mean taken by excluding a percentage of data points from the top and bottom tails of a data set. Use this function when you want to exclude outlying data from your analysis.

### Syntax

```
TRIMMEAN(array,percent)
```

**Array** is the array or range of values to trim and average.

**Percent** is the fractional number of data points to exclude from the calculation. For example, if percent=0.2, 4 points are trimmed from a data set of 20 points $(20 \times 0.2)$, 2 from the top and 2 from the bottom of the set.

### Examples

```
TRIMMEAN({4,5,6,7,2,3,4,5,1,2,3},0.2)
```
returns 3.777778.

## TRUE

Returns the logical value TRUE.

### Syntax

```
TRUE()
```

## TRUNC

Truncates a number to an integer.

### Syntax

```
TRUNC(number,num_digits)
```

**Number** is the number you want to truncate.

**Num_digits** is a number specifying the precision of the truncation. The default value for num_digits is zero.

### Examples

TRUNC(8.9) returns 8.

TRUNC(-8.9) returns –8.

TRUNC(PI()) returns 3.

# TTEST

Returns the probability associated with a Student's t-Test.

### Syntax

TTEST(array1,array2,tails,type)

**Array1** is the first data set.

**Array2** is the second data set.

**Tails** specifies the number of distribution tails. If tails=1, TTEST uses the one-tailed distribution. If tails=2, TTEST uses the two-tailed distribution.

**Type** is the kind of t-test to perform. If type equals 1, a paired test is performed; if type equals 2, a two-sample equal variance (homoscedastic) test is performed; if type equals 3, a two-sample unequal variance (heteroscedastic) test is performed.

### Examples

TTEST({3,4,5,8,9,1,2,4,5},{6,19,3,2,14,4,5,17,1},2,1) returns 0.196016.

# TYPE

Returns a number indicating the data type of a value.

### Syntax

TYPE(value)

**Value** can be any Microsoft Excel value, such as a number, text, logical value, and so on. If value is a number, TYPE returns 1; If value is text, TYPE returns 2; If value is a logical value, TYPE returns 4; If value is a formula, TYPE returns 8; If value is an error value, TYPE returns 16; If value is an array, TYPE returns 64.

**Examples**

If A1 contains the text "Smith", then:

TYPE(A1) returns 2.

TYPE("MR. "&A1) returns 2.

## UPPER

Converts text to uppercase.

### Syntax

UPPER(text)

**Text** is the text you want converted to uppercase (text can be a reference or text string).

### Examples

UPPER("total") returns"TOTAL."

If E5 contains "yield," then UPPER(E5) returns "YIELD."

## VALUE

Converts a text argument to a number. This function is provided for compatibility with other spreadsheet programs.

### Syntax

VALUE(text)

**Text** is the text enclosed in quotation marks or a reference to a cell containing the text you want to convert. Text can be in any of the constant number, date, or time formats recognized by Excel. If text is not in one of these formats, VALUE returns the #VALUE! error value.

### Examples

VALUE("$1,000") returns 1,000.

VALUE("16:48:00")-VALUE("12:00:00") returns 0.2, the serial number equivalent to 4 hours and 48 minutes.

## VAR

Estimates variance on the basis of a sample. If your data represents the entire population, you should compute the variance using VARP.

APDX

**A**

Alphabetical List of
Worksheet Functions

### Syntax

```
VAR(number1,number2,…)
```

**Number1,number2,...** are 1 to 30 number arguments corresponding to a sample of a population.

### Examples

Suppose 10 tools stamped from the same machine during a production run are collected as a random sample and measured for breaking strength. The sample values (1345, 1301, 1368, 1322, 1310, 1370, 1318, 1350, 1303, 1299) are stored in A2:E3, respectively. VAR estimates the variance for the breaking strength of the tools.

```
VAR(A2:E3) returns 754.3.
```

## VARA

Estimates variance on the basis of a sample. If your data represents the entire population, you should compute the variance using VARPA. Whereas the VAR function ignores cells containing text and logical values (TRUE and FALSE), VARA calculates text as zero, FALSE as zero, and TRUE as one. The syntax for VARA is the same as VAR.

## VARP

Calculates variance on the basis of the entire population. If your data represents a sample of the population, you should compute the variance using VAR.

### Syntax

```
VARP(number1,number2,…)
```

**Number1,number2,...** are 1 to 30 number arguments corresponding to a population.

### Examples

Using the data from the VAR example and assuming that only 10 tools are produced during the production run, VARP measures the variance of breaking strengths for all the tools.

```
VARP(A2:E3) returns 678.8.
```

## VARPA

Calculates variance on the basis of the entire population. If your data represents a sample of the population, you should compute the variance using VARP. Whereas the VARP function ignores cells containing text and logical values (TRUE and FALSE),

VARPA calculates text as zero, FALSE as zero, and TRUE as one. The syntax for VARPA is the same as VARP.

## VDB

Returns the depreciation of an asset for a specified or partial period using a declining balance method.

### Syntax
```
VDB(cost,salvage,life,start_period,end_period,factor,no_switch)
```

**Cost** is the initial cost of the asset.

**Salvage** is the value at the end of the depreciation (sometimes called the salvage value of the asset).

**Life** is the number of periods over which the asset is being depreciated (sometimes called the useful life of the asset).

**Start_period** is the starting period for which you want to calculate the depreciation. Start_period must use the same units as life.

**End_period** is the ending period for which you want to calculate the depreciation. End_period must use the same units as life.

**Factor** is the rate at which the balance declines. If factor is omitted, it is assumed to be 2 (the double-declining balance method). Change factor if you do not want to use the double-declining balance method.

**No_switch** is a logical value specifying whether to switch to straight-line depreciation when depreciation is greater than the declining balance calculation.

### Examples
Suppose a factory purchases a new machine. The machine costs $2400 and has a lifetime of 10 years. The salvage value of the machine is $300. The following examples show depreciation over several periods. The results are rounded to two decimal places.

`VDB(2400,300,3650,0,1)` returns $1.32, the first day's depreciation. Excel automatically assumes that factor is 2.

`VDB(2400,300,120,0,1)` returns $40.00, the first month's depreciation.

`VDB(2400,300,10,0,1)` returns $480.00, the first year's depreciation.

## VLOOKUP

Looks in the first column of an array and moves across the row to return the value of a cell. (See Chapter 9 for in-depth coverage and examples of VLOOKUP.)

APDX

**A**

Alphabetical List of Worksheet Functions

### Syntax

```
VLOOKUP(lookup_value,table_array,col_index_num,range_lookup)
```

**Lookup_value** is the value to be found in the first column of the array.

**Table_array** is the table of information in which data is looked up.

**Col_index_num** is the column number in table_array from which the matching value should be returned.

**Range_lookup** is a logical value that specifies whether you want VLOOKUP to find an exact match or an approximate match. If TRUE or omitted, an approximate match is returned (values must be sorted in ascending order).

## WEEKDAY

Converts a serial number to a day of the week. (See Chapter 9 for in-depth coverage and examples of WEEKDAY.)

### Syntax

```
WEEKDAY(serial_number,return_type)
```

**Serial_number** is the date-time code used by Excel for date and time calculations.

**Return_type** is a number that determines the type of return value.

## WEIBULL

Returns the Weibull distribution.

### Syntax

```
WEIBULL(x,alpha,beta,cumulative)
```

**X** is the value at which to evaluate the function.

**Alpha** is a parameter to the distribution.

**Beta** is a parameter to the distribution.

**Cumulative** determines the form of the function.

### Examples

```
WEIBULL(105,20,100,TRUE) returns 0.929581.
```

```
WEIBULL(105,20,100,FALSE) returns 0.035589.
```

## YEAR

Converts a serial number to a year. (See Chapter 9 for in-depth coverage and examples of YEAR.)

### Syntax

```
YEAR(serial_number)
```

**Serial_number** is the date-time code used by Excel for date and time calculations.

## ZTEST

Returns the two-tailed P-value of a z-test.

### Syntax

```
ZTEST(array,x,sigma)
```

**Array** is the array or range of data against which to test x.

**X** is the value to test.

**Sigma** is the population (known) standard deviation. If omitted, the sample standard deviation is used.

### Examples

```
ZTEST({3,6,7,8,6,5,4,2,1,9},4) returns 0.090574.
```

# Analysis ToolPak Functions

The following functions are contained in the Analysis ToolPak add-in (see Chapter 28).

## ACCRINT

Returns the accrued interest for a security that pays periodic interest.

### Syntax

```
ACCRINT(issue,first_interest,settlement,rate,par,frequency,basis)
```

**Issue** is the security's issue date, expressed as a serial date number.

**First_interest** is the security's first interest date, expressed as a serial date number.

**Settlement** is the security's settlement date, expressed as a serial date number.

**Rate** is the security's annual coupon rate.

Alphabetical List of Worksheet Functions

**Par** is the security's par value. If you omit par, ACCRINT uses $1000.

**Frequency** is the number of coupon payments per year. For annual payments, frequency=1; for semiannual, frequency=2; for quarterly, frequency=4.

**Basis** is the type of day count basis to use. If basis is 0 or omitted, day count basis is US (NASD) 30/360; If basis is 1, day count basis is Actual/actual; If basis is 2, day count basis is Actual/360; If basis is 3, day count basis is Actual/365; If basis is 4, day count basis is European 30/360.

### Examples

A Treasury bond has the following terms: February 28, 1993 issue date; May 1, 1993 settlement date; August 31, 1993 first interest date; 10.0% coupon; $1000 par value; Frequency is semiannual; 30/360 basis. The accrued interest (in the 1900 Date System) is:

```
ACCRINT(34028,34212,34090,0.1,1000,2,0)
```

which returns 16.94444.

## ACCRINTM

Returns accrued interest for a security that pays interest at maturity.

### Syntax

```
ACCRINTM(issue,maturity,rate,par,basis)
```

**Issue** is the security's issue date, expressed as a serial date number.

**Settlement** is the security's maturity date, expressed as a serial date number.

**Rate** is the security's annual coupon rate.

**Par** is the security's par value. If you omit par, ACCRINTM uses $1000.

**Basis** is the type of day count basis to use. If basis is 0 or omitted, day count basis is US (NASD) 30/360; If basis is 1, day count basis is Actual/actual; If basis is 2, day count basis is Actual/360; If basis is 3, day count basis is Actual/365; If basis is 4, day count basis is European 30/360.

### Examples

A note has the following terms: April 1, 1993 issue date; June 15, 1993 maturity date; 10.0% coupon; $1000 par value; Actual/365 basis. The accrued interest (in the 1900 Date System) is:

```
ACCRINTM(34060,34135,0.1,1000,3)
```

which returns 20.54795.

## AMORDEGRC

Returns the depreciation for each accounting period.

### Syntax

AMORDEGRC(cost,date_purchased,first_period,salvage,period,rate,basis)

**Cost** is the cost of the asset.

**Date_purchased** is the date of the purchase of the asset.

**First_period** is the date of the end of the first period.

**Salvage** is the salvage value at the end of the life of the asset.

**Period** is the period.

**Rate** is the rate of depreciation.

**Basis** is the year_basis to be used. If basis is 0, date system is 360 days (NASD method); if basis is 1, date system is Actual; if basis is 3, date system is 365 days in a year; if basis is 4, date system is 360 days in a year (European method).

### Examples

Suppose a machine bought on August 19, 1993 costs $2400 and has a salvage value of $300, with a 15% depreciation rate. December 31, 1993 is the end of the first period.

AMORDEGRC(2400,34199,34334,300,1,0.15,1) returns a first period depreciation of $775.

## AMORLINC

Returns the depreciation for each accounting period.

### Syntax

AMORLINC(cost,date_purchased,first_period,salvage, period,rate,basis)

**Cost** is the cost of the asset.

**Date_purchased** is the date of the purchase of the asset.

**First_period** is the date of the end of the first period.

**Salvage** is the salvage value at the end of the life of the asset.

**Period** is the period.

**Rate** is the rate of depreciation.

**Basis** is the year_basis to be used. If basis is 0, date system is 360 days (NASD method); if basis is 1, date system is Actual; if basis is 3, date system is 365 days in a year; if basis is 4, date system is 360 days in a year (European method).

### Examples

Suppose a machine bought on August 19, 1993 costs $2400 and has a salvage value of $300, with a 15% depreciation rate. December 31, 1993 is the end of the first period.

**AMORLINC(2400,34199,34334,300,1,0.15,1)** returns a first period depreciation of $360.

## BESSELI

Returns the modified Bessel function In(x). (See the Online Help worksheet function reference for information about the equation used to calculate BESSELI.)

### Syntax

BESSELI(x,n)

**X** is the value at which to evaluate the function.

**N** is the order of the Bessel function. If n is not an integer, it is truncated.

### Examples

BESSELI(1.5,1) returns 0.981666.

## BESSELJ

Returns the Bessel function Jn(x). (See the Online Help worksheet function reference for information about the equation used to calculate BESSELJ.)

### Syntax

BESSELJ(x,n)

**X** is the value at which to evaluate the function.

**N** is the order of the Bessel function. If n is not an integer, it is truncated.

### Examples

BESSELJ(1.9,2) returns 0.329926.

## BESSELK

Returns the modified Bessel function Kn(x). (See the Online Help worksheet function reference for information about the equation used to calculate BESSELK.)

### Syntax

BESSELK(x,n)

**X** is the value at which to evaluate the function.

**N** is the order of the Bessel function. If n is not an integer, it is truncated.

### Examples

BESSELK(1.5,1) returns 0.277388.

## BESSELY

Returns the Bessel function $Y_n(x)$. (See the Online Help worksheet function reference for information about the equation used to calculate BESSELY.)

### Syntax

BESSELY(x,n)

**X** is the value at which to evaluate the function.

**N** is the order of the Bessel function. If n is not an integer, it is truncated.

### Examples

BESSELY(2.5,1) returns 0.145918.

## BIN2DEC

Converts a binary number to decimal.

### Syntax

BIN2DEC(number)

**Number** is the binary number you want to convert.

### Examples

BIN2DEC(1100100) returnsls 100.

BIN2DEC(1111111111) returns –1.

## BIN2HEX

Converts a binary number to hexadecimal.

### Syntax

BIN2HEX(number,places)

**Number** is the binary number you want to convert.

**Places** is the number of characters to use. If places is omitted, BIN2HEX uses the minimum number of characters necessary.

APDX

**A**

Alphabetical List of
Worksheet Functions

### Examples

BIN2HEX(11111011,4) returns 00FB.

BIN2HEX(1110) returns E.

## BIN2OCT

Converts a binary number to octal.

### Syntax

BIN2OCT(number,places)

**Number** is the binary number you want to convert.

**Places** is the number of characters to use. If places is omitted, BIN2OCT uses the minimum number of characters necessary.

### Examples

BIN2OCT(1001,3) returns 011.

BIN2OCT(01100100) returns 144.

## BINOMDIST

Returns the individual term binomial distribution probability.

### Syntax

BINOMDIST(number_s,trials,probability_s,cumulative)

**Number_s** is the number of successes in trials.

**Trials** is the number of independent trials.

**Probability_s** is the probability of success on each trial.

**Cumulative** is a logical value that determines the form of the function. If cumulative is TRUE, then BINOMDIST returns the cumulative distribution function, which is the probability that there are at most number_s successes; if FALSE, it returns the probability mass function, which is the probability that there are number_s successes.

### Examples

The flip of a coin can only result in heads or tails. The probability of the first flip being heads is 0.5, and the probability of exactly 6 of 10 flips being heads is

BINOMDIST(6,10,0.5,FALSE)

which returns 0.205078.

## COMPLEX

Converts real and imaginary coefficients into a complex number.

### Syntax
```
COMPLEX(real_num,i_num,suffix)
```

**Real_num** is the real coefficient of the complex number.

**i_num** is the imaginary coefficient of the complex number.

**Suffix** is the suffix for the imaginary component of the complex number. If omitted, suffix is assumed to be "i."

### Examples

COMPLEX(3,4) returns 3 + 4I.

COMPLEX(3,4,"j") returns 3 + 4j.

COMPLEX(0,1) returns i.

## CONVERT

Converts a number from one measurement system to another.

### Syntax
```
CONVERT(number,from_unit,to_unit)
```

**Number** is the value in from_units to convert.

**From_unit** is the units for number.

**To_unit** is the units for the result.

## COUPDAYBS

Returns the number of days from the beginning of the coupon period to the settlement date.

### Syntax
```
COUPDAYBS(settlement,maturity,frequency,basis)
```

**Settlement** is the security's settlement date, expressed as a serial date number.

**Maturity** is the security's maturity date, expressed as a serial date number.

**Frequency** is the number of coupon payments per year. For annual payments, frequency=1; for semiannual, frequency=2; for quarterly, frequency=4.

**Basis** is the type of day count basis to use. If basis is 0 or omitted, day count basis is US (NASD) 30/360; if basis is 1, day count basis is Actual/actual; if basis is 2, day count basis is Actual/360; if basis is 3, day count basis is Actual/365; if basis is 4, day count basis is European 30/360.

### Examples

A bond has the following terms: January 25, 1993 settlement date; November 15, 1994 maturity date; Semiannual coupon; Actual/actual basis. The number of days from the beginning of the coupon period to the settlement date (in the 1900 Date System) is

```
COUPDAYBS(33994,34653,2,1)
```

which returns 71.

## COUPDAYS

Returns the number of days in the coupon period that contains the settlement date.

### Syntax

```
COUPDAYS(settlement,maturity,frequency,basis)
```

**Settlement** is the security's settlement date, expressed as a serial date number.

**Maturity** is the security's maturity date, expressed as a serial date number.

**Frequency** is the number of coupon payments per year. For annual payments, frequency=1; for semiannual, frequency=2; for quarterly, frequency=4.

**Basis** is the type of day count basis to use. If basis is 0 or omitted, day count basis is US (NASD) 30/360; if basis is 1, day count basis is actual/actual; if basis is 2, day count basis is actual/360; if basis is 3, day count basis is actual/365; if basis is 4, day count basis is European 30/360.

### Examples

A bond has the following terms: January 25, 1993 settlement date; November 15, 1994 maturity date; Semiannual coupon; Actual/actual basis. The number of days in the coupon period that contains the settlement date (in the 1900 Date System) is

```
COUPDAYS(33994,34653,2,1)
```

which returns 181.

## COUPDAYSNC

Returns the number of days from the settlement date to the next coupon date.

### Syntax

```
COUPDAYSNC(settlement,maturity,frequency,basis)
```

**Settlement** is the security's settlement date, expressed as a serial date number.

**Maturity** is the security's maturity date, expressed as a serial date number.

**Frequency** is the number of coupon payments per year. For annual payments, frequency=1; for semiannual, frequency=2; for quarterly, frequency=4.

**Basis** is the type of day count basis to use. If basis is 0 or omitted, day count basis is US (NASD) 30/360; if basis is 1, day count basis is Actual/actual; if basis is 2, day count basis is Actual/360; if basis is 3, day count basis is Actual/365; if basis is 4, day count basis is European 30/360.

### Examples

A bond has the following terms: January 25, 1993 settlement date; November 15, 1994 maturity date; Semiannual coupon; Actual/actual basis. The number of days from the settlement date to the next coupon date (in the 1900 Date System) is

```
COUPDAYSNC(33994,34653,2,1)
```

which returns 110.

## COUPNCD

Returns the next coupon date after the settlement date.

### Syntax

```
COUPNCD(settlement,maturity,frequency,basis)
```

**Settlement** is the security's settlement date, expressed as a serial date number.

**Maturity** is the security's maturity date, expressed as a serial date number.

**Frequency** is the number of coupon payments per year. For annual payments, frequency=1; for semiannual, frequency=2; for quarterly, frequency=4.

**Basis** is the type of day count basis to use. If basis is 0 or omitted, day count basis is US (NASD) 30/360; if basis is 1, day count basis is actual/actual; if basis is 2, day count basis is actual/360; if basis is 3, day count basis is actual/365; if basis is 4, day count basis is European 30/360.

### Examples

A bond has the following terms: January 25, 1993 settlement date; November 15, 1994 maturity date; Semiannual coupon; Actual/actual basis. The next coupon date after the settlement date (in the 1900 Date System) is

```
COUPNCD(33994,34653,2,1)
```

which returns 34104 or May 15, 1993.

APDX
**A**

Alphabetical List of
Worksheet Functions

## COUPNUM

Returns the number of coupons payable between the settlement date and maturity date.

### Syntax

```
COUPNUM(settlement, maturity, frequency, basis)
```

> **Settlement** is the security's settlement date, expressed as a serial date number.
>
> **Maturity** is the security's maturity date, expressed as a serial date number.
>
> **Frequency** is the number of coupon payments per year. For annual payments, frequency=1; for semiannual, frequency=2; for quarterly, frequency=4.
>
> **Basis** is the type of day count basis to use. If basis is 0 or omitted, day count basis is US (NASD) 30/360; if basis is 1, day count basis is actual/actual; if basis is 2, day count basis is actual/360; if basis is 3, day count basis is actual/365; if basis is 4, day count basis is European 30/360.

### Examples

A bond has the following terms: January 25, 1993 settlement date; November 15, 1994 maturity date; Semiannual coupon; Actual/actual basis. The number of coupon payments (in the 1900 Date System) is

```
COUPNUM(33994,34653,2,1)
```

which returns 4.

## COUPPCD

Returns the previous coupon date before the settlement date.

### Syntax

```
COUPPCD(settlement,maturity,frequency,basis)
```

> **Settlement** is the security's settlement date, expressed as a serial date number.
>
> **Maturity** is the security's maturity date, expressed as a serial date number.
>
> **Frequency** is the number of coupon payments per year. For annual payments, frequency=1; for semiannual, frequency=2; for quarterly, frequency=4.
>
> **Basis** is the type of day count basis to use. If basis is 0 or omitted, day count basis is US (NASD) 30/360; if basis is 1, day count basis is actual/actual; if basis is 2, day count basis is actual/360; if basis is 3, day count basis is actual/365; if basis is 4, day count basis is European 30/360.

## Examples
A bond has the following terms: January 25, 1993 settlement date; November 15, 1994 maturity date; semiannual coupon; actual/actual basis. The previous coupon date before the settlement date (in the 1900 Date System) is

```
COUPPCD(33994,34653,2,1)
```

which returns 33923 or November 15, 1992.

## CUMIPMT
Returns the cumulative interest paid between two periods.

### Syntax
```
CUMIPMT(rate,nper,pv,start_period,end_period,type)
```

**Rate** is the interest rate.

**Nper** is the total number of payment periods.

**Pv** is the present value.

**Start_period** is the first period in the calculation. Payment periods are numbered beginning with 1.

**End_period** is the last period in the calculation.

**Type** is the timing of the payment. If type is 0, payments are due at the end of the period; If type is 1, payments are due at the beginning of the period.

### Examples
A home mortgage loan has the following terms: Interest rate, 9.00% per annum (rate=9.00%/12=0.0075); term, 30 years (nper=30*12=360); present value, $125,000. The total interest paid in the second year of payments (periods 13 through 24) is

```
CUMIPMT(0.0075,360,125000,13,24,0)
```

which returns -11135.23.
   The interest paid in a single payment, in the first month, is

```
CUMIPMT(0.0075,360,125000,1,1,0)
```

which returns –937.50.

## CUMPRINC
Returns the cumulative principal paid on a loan between two periods.

APDX
**A**

Alphabetical List of Worksheet Functions

### Syntax

`CUMPRINC(rate,nper,pv,start_period,end_period,type)`

**Rate** is the interest rate.

**Nper** is the total number of payment periods.

**Pv** is the present value.

**Start_period** is the first period in the calculation. Payment periods are numbered beginning with 1.

**End_period** is the last period in the calculation.

**Type** is the timing of the payment. If type is 0, payments are due at the end of the period; if type is 1, payments are due at the beginning of the period.

### Examples

A home mortgage loan has the following terms: Interest rate, 9.00% per annum (rate= 9.00%/12=0.0075); Term, 30 years (nper=30*12=360); Present value, $125,000. The total principal paid in the second year of payments (periods 13 through 24) is

`CUMPRINC(0.0075,360,125000,13,24,0)`

which returns –934.1071.

The principal paid in a single payment in the first month is

`CUMPRINC(0.0075,360,125000,1,1,0)`

which returns –68.27827.

# DEC2BIN

Converts a decimal number to binary.

### Syntax

`DEC2BIN(number,places)`

**Number** is the decimal integer you want to convert.

**Places** is the number of characters to use. If places is omitted, DEC2BIN uses the minimum number of characters necessary.

### Examples

`DEC2BIN(9,4)` returns 1001.

`DEC2BIN(-100)` returns 1110011100.

## DEC2HEX

Converts a decimal number to hexadecimal.

### Syntax

`DEC2HEX(number,places)`

**Number** is the decimal integer you want to convert.

**Places** is the number of characters to use. If places is omitted, DEC2HEX uses the minimum number of characters necessary.

### Examples

`DEC2HEX(100,4)` returns 0064.

`DEC2HEX(-54)` returns FFFFFFFFCA.

## DEC2OCT

Converts a decimal number to octal.

### Syntax

`DEC2OCT(number,places)`

**Number** is the decimal integer you want to convert.

**Places** is the number of characters to use. If places is omitted, DEC2OCT uses the minimum number of characters necessary.

### Examples

`DEC2OCT(58,3)` returns 072.

`DEC2OCT(-100)` returns 7777777634.

## DELTA

Tests whether two values are equal.

### Syntax

`DELTA(number1,number2)`

**Number1** is the first number.

**Number2** is the second number. If omitted, number2 is assumed to be zero.

APDX

**A**

Alphabetical List of
Worksheet Functions

### Examples

DELTA(5,4) returns 0.

DELTA(5,5) returns 1.

DELTA(0.5,0) returns 0.

# DISC

Returns the discount rate for a security.

### Syntax

DISC(settlement,maturity,pr,redemption,basis)

**Settlement** is the security's settlement date, expressed as a serial date number.

**Maturity** is the security's maturity date, expressed as a serial date number.

**Pr** is the security's price per $100 face value.

**Redemption** is the security's redemption value per $100 face value.

**Basis** is the type of day count basis to use. If basis is 0 or omitted, day count basis is US (NASD) 30/360; if basis is 1, day count basis is actual/actual; if basis is 2, day count basis is actual/360; if basis is 3, day count basis is actual/365; if basis is 4, day count basis is European 30/360.

### Examples

A bond has the following terms: February 15, 1993 settlement date; June 10, 1993 maturity date; $97.975 price; $100 redemption value; actual/360 basis. The bond discount rate (in the 1900 Date System) is

DISC(34015,34130,97.975,100,2)

which returns 0.063391 or 6.3391%.

# DOLLARDE

Converts a dollar price expressed as a fraction into a dollar price expressed as a decimal number.

### Syntax

DOLLARDE(fractional_dollar,fraction)

**Fractional_dollar** is a number expressed as a fraction.

**Fraction** is the integer to use in the denominator of the fraction.

### Examples

DOLLARDE(1.02,16) returns 1.125.

DOLLARDE(1.1,8) returns 1.125.

## DOLLARFR

Converts a dollar price expressed as a decimal number into a dollar price expressed as a fraction.

### Syntax

DOLLARFR(decimal_dollar,fraction)

**Decimal_dollar** is a decimal number.

**Fraction** is the integer to use in the denominator of a fraction.

### Examples

DOLLARFR(1.125,16) returns 1.02.

DOLLARFR(1.125,8) returns 1.1.

## DURATION

Returns the annual duration of a security with periodic interest payments.

### Syntax

DURATION(settlement,maturity,coupon,yld,frequency,basis)

**Settlement** is the security's settlement date, expressed as a serial date number.

**Maturity** is the security's maturity date, expressed as a serial date number.

**Coupon** is the security's annual coupon rate.

**Yld** is the security's annual yield.

**Frequency** is the number of coupon payments per year. For annual payments, frequency=1; for semiannual, frequency=2; for quarterly, frequency=4.

**Basis** is the type of day count basis to use. If basis is 0 or omitted, day count basis is US (NASD) 30/360; if basis is 1, day count basis is actual/actual; if basis is 2, day count basis is actual/360; if basis is 3, day count basis is actual/365; if basis is 4, day count basis is European 30/360.

Alphabetical List of Worksheet Functions

### Examples

A bond has the following terms: January 1, 1986 settlement date; January 1, 1994 maturity date; 8% coupon; 9.0% yield; frequency is semiannual; actual/actual basis. The duration (in the 1900 Date System) is

    DURATION(31413,34335,0.08,0.09,2,1)

which returns 5.993775.

## EDATE

Returns the serial number of the date that is the indicated number of months before or after the start date.

### Syntax

    EDATE(start_date,months)

**Start_date** is a serial date number that represents the start date.

**Months** is the number of months before or after start_date. A positive value for months yields a future date; a negative value yields a past date.

### Examples

    EDATE(DATEVALUE("01/15/91"),1) returns 33284 or 02/15/91.

    EDATE(DATEVALUE("03/31/91"),-1) returns 33297 or 02/28/91.

## EFFECT

Returns the effective annual interest rate.

### Syntax

    EFFECT(nominal_rate,npery)

**Nominal_rate** is the nominal interest rate.

**Npery** is the number of compounding periods per year.

### Examples

    **EFFECT(5.25%,4)** returns 0.053543 or 5.3543%.

## EOMONTH

Returns the serial number of the last day of the month before or after a specified number of months.

### Syntax

```
EOMONTH(start_date,months)
```

**Start_date** is a serial date number that represents the start date.

**Months** is the number of months before or after start_date. A positive value for months yields a future date; a negative value yields a past date.

### Examples

```
EOMONTH(DATEVALUE("01/01/93"),1) returns 34028 or 2/28/93.

EOMONTH(DATEVALUE("01/01/93"),-1) returns 33969 or 12/31/92.
```

## ERF

Returns the error function integrated between lower_limit and upper_limit.

### Syntax

```
ERF(lower_limit,upper_limit)
```

**Lower_limit** is the lower bound for integrating ERF.

**Upper_limit** is the upper bound for integrating ERF. If omitted, ERF integrates between zero and lower_limit.

### Examples

```
ERF(0.74500) returns 0.70793.

ERF(1) returns 0.84270.
```

## ERFC

Returns the complementary error function integrated between x and infinity.

### Syntax

```
ERFC(x)
```

**X** is the lower bound for integrating ERF.

### Examples

```
ERFC(1) returns 0.1573.
```

APDX
**A**

Alphabetical List of
Worksheet Functions

## FACTDOUBLE

Returns the double factorial of a number.

### Syntax

```
FACTDOUBLE(number)
```

**Number** is the value for which to return the double factorial. If number is not an integer, it is truncated.

### Examples

```
FACTDOUBLE(6) returns 48.
```

```
FACTDOUBLE(7) returns 105.
```

## FVSCHEDULE

Returns the future value of an initial principal after applying a series of compound interest rates.

### Syntax

```
FVSCHEDULE(principal,schedule)
```

**Principal** is the present value.

**Schedule** is an array of interest rates to apply.

### Examples

```
FVSCHEDULE(1,{0.09,0.11,0.1}) returns 1.33089.
```

## GCD

Returns the greatest common divisor.

### Syntax

```
GCD(number1,number2,…)
```

**Number1, number2,...** are up to 29 values. If any value is not an integer, it is truncated.

### Examples

```
GCD(5,2) returns 1.
```

```
GCD(24,36) returns 12.
```

```
GCD(7,1) returns 1.
```

## GESTEP

Tests whether a number is greater than a threshold value.

### Syntax

```
GESTEP(number,step)
```

**Number** is the value to test against step.

**Step** is the threshold value. If you omit a value for step, GESTEP uses zero.

### Examples

```
GESTEP(5,4) returns 1.
GESTEP(5,5) returns 1.
```

## HEX2BIN

Converts a hexadecimal number to binary.

### Syntax

```
HEX2BIN(number,places)
```

**Number** is the hexadecimal number you want to convert.

**Places** is the number of characters to use. If places is omitted, HEX2BIN uses the minimum number of characters necessary.

### Examples

```
HEX2BIN("F",8) returns 00001111.
HEX2BIN("B7") returns 10110111.
```

## HEX2DEC

Converts a hexadecimal number to decimal.

### Syntax

```
HEX2DEC(number)
```

**Number** is the hexadecimal number you want to convert.

### Examples

```
HEX2DEC("A5") returns 165.
HEX2DEC("FFFFFFFF5B") returns –165.
```

APDX
**A**

Alphabetical List of
Worksheet Functions

## HEX2OCT

Converts a hexadecimal number to octal.

### Syntax

```
HEX2OCT(number,places)
```

**Number** is the hexadecimal number you want to convert.

**Places** is the number of characters to use. If places is omitted, HEX2OCT uses the minimum number of characters necessary.

### Examples

```
HEX2OCT("F",3) returns 017.
HEX2OCT("3B4E") returns 35516.
```

## IMABS

Returns the absolute value (modulus) of a complex number.

### Syntax

```
IMABS(inumber)
```

**Inumber** is a complex number for which you want the absolute value.

### Examples

```
IMABS("5+12i") returns 13.
```

## IMAGINARY

Returns the imaginary coefficient of a complex number.

### Syntax

```
IMAGINARY(inumber)
```

**Inumber** is a complex number for which you want the imaginary coefficient.

### Examples

```
IMAGINARY("3+4i") returns 4.
IMAGINARY("0-j") returns -1.
```

## IMARGUMENT

Returns the argument theta, an angle expressed in radians.

### Syntax

```
IMARGUMENT(inumber)
```

**Inumber** is a complex number for which you want the argument.

### Examples

IMARGUMENT("3+4i") returns 0.927295.

## IMCONJUGATE

Returns the complex conjugate of a complex number.

### Syntax

```
IMCONJUGATE(inumber)
```

**Inumber** is a complex number for which you want the conjugate.

### Examples

IMCONJUGATE("3+4i") returns 3 – 4i.

## IMCOS

Returns the cosine of a complex number.

### Syntax

```
IMCOS(inumber)
```

**Inumber** is a complex number for which you want the cosine.

### Examples

IMCOS("1+i") returns 0.83373 – 0.988898i.

## IMDIV

Returns the quotient of two complex numbers.

### Syntax

```
IMDIV(inumber1,inumber2)
```

**Inumber1** is the complex numerator or dividend.

**Inumber2** is the complex denominator or divisor.

### Examples

IMDIV("-238+240i","10+24i") returns 5 + 12i.

APDX

**A**

Alphabetical List of
Worksheet Functions

## IMEXP

Returns the exponential of a complex number.

### Syntax

```
IMEXP(inumber)
```

**Inumber** is a complex number for which you want the exponential.

### Examples

`IMEXP("1+i")` returns 1.468694 + 2.287355i.

## IMLN

Returns the natural logarithm of a complex number.

### Syntax

```
IMLN(inumber)
```

**Inumber** is a complex number for which you want the natural logarithm.

### Examples

`IMLN("3+4i")` returns 1.609438 + 0.927295i.

## IMLOG10

Returns the base-10 logarithm of a complex number.

### Syntax

```
IMLOG10(inumber)
```

**Inumber** is a complex number for which you want the common logarithm.

### Examples

`IMLOG10("3+4i")` returns 0.69897 + 0.402719i.

## IMLOG2

Returns the base-2 logarithm of a complex number.

### Syntax

```
IMLOG2(inumber)
```

**Inumber** is a complex number for which you want the base-2 logarithm.

### Examples

IMLOG2("3+4i") returns 2.321928 + 1.337804i.

## IMPOWER

Returns a complex number raised to an integer power.

### Syntax

IMPOWER(inumber,number)

**Inumber** is a complex number you want to raise to a power.

**Number** is the power to which you want to raise the complex number.

### Examples

IMPOWER("2+3i",3) returns –46 + 9i.

## IMPRODUCT

Returns the product of two complex numbers.

### Syntax

IMPRODUCT(inumber1,inumber2,…)

**inumber1,inumber2,…** are 1 to 29 complex numbers to multiply.

### Examples

IMPRODUCT("3+4i","5-3i") returns 27 + 11I.

IMPRODUCT("1+2i",30) returns 30 + 60i.

## IMREAL

Returns the real coefficient of a complex number.

### Syntax

IMREAL(inumber)

**Inumber** is a complex number for which you want the real coefficient.

### Examples

IMREAL("6-9i") returns 6.

## IMSIN

Returns the sine of a complex number.

### Syntax
`IMSIN(inumber)`

**Inumber** is a complex number for which you want the sine.

### Examples

`IMSIN("3+4i")` returns 3.853738 - 27.016813i.

## IMSQRT

Returns the square root of a complex number.

### Syntax
`IMSQRT(inumber)`

**Inumber** is a complex number for which you want the square root.

### Examples

`IMSQRT("1+i")` returns 1.098684 + 0.45509i.

## IMSUB

Returns the difference of two complex numbers.

### Syntax
`IMSUB(inumber1,inumber2)`

**Inumber1** is the complex number from which to subtract inumber2.

**Inumber2** is the complex number to subtract from inumber1.

### Examples

`IMSUB("13+4i","5+3i")` returns 8 + i.

## IMSUM

Returns the sum of complex numbers.

### Syntax
`IMSUM(inumber1,inumber2,...)`

**Inumber1,inumber2,...** are 1 to 29 complex numbers to add.

### Examples

`IMSUM("3+4i","5-3i")` returns 8 + i.

# INTRATE

Returns the interest rate for a fully invested security.

### Syntax

`INTRATE(settlement,maturity,investment,redemption,basis)`

**Settlement** is the security's settlement date, expressed as a serial date number.

**Maturity** is the security's maturity date, expressed as a serial date number.

**Investment** is the amount invested in the security.

**Redemption** is the amount to be received at maturity.

**Basis** is the type of day count basis to use. If basis is 0 or omitted, day count basis is US (NASD) 30/360; if basis is 1, day count basis is actual/actual; if basis is 2, day count basis is actual/360; if basis is 3, day count basis is actual/365; If basis is 4, day count basis is European 30/360.

### Examples

A bond has the following terms: February 15, 1993 settlement (issue) date; May 15, 1993 maturity date; 1,000,000 investment; 1,014,420 redemption value; Actual/360 basis. The bond discount rate (in the 1900 Date System) is

`INTRATE(34015,34104,1000000,1014420,2)`

which returns 0.058328 or 5.8328%.

# ISEVEN

Returns TRUE if the number is even.

### Syntax

`ISEVEN(value)`

**Value** is the value you want tested.

# ISODD

Returns TRUE if the number is odd.

### Syntax

`ISODD(value)`

**Value** is the value you want tested.

APDX

**A**

Alphabetical List of
Worksheet Functions

## LCM

Returns the least common multiple.

### Syntax

```
LCM(number1,number2,…)
```

**Number1,number2,…** are 1 to 29 values for which you want the least common multiple. If value is not an integer, it is truncated.

### Examples

```
LCM(5,2) returns 10.
```

```
LCM(24,36) returns 72.
```

## MDURATION

Returns the Macauley modified duration for a security with an assumed par value of $100.

### Syntax

```
MDURATION(settlement,maturity,coupon,yld,frequency,basis)
```

**Settlement** is the security's settlement date, expressed as a serial date number.

**Maturity** is the security's maturity date, expressed as a serial date number.

**Coupon** is the security's annual coupon rate.

**Yld** is the security's annual yield.

**Frequency** is the number of coupon payments per year. For annual payments, frequency=1; for semiannual, frequency=2; for quarterly, frequency=4.

**Basis** is the type of day count basis to use. If basis is 0 or omitted, day count basis is US (NASD) 30/360; if basis is 1, day count basis is actual/actual; if basis is 2, day count basis is actual/360; if basis is 3, day count basis is actual/365; if basis is 4, day count basis is European 30/360.

### Examples

A bond has the following terms: January 1, 1986 settlement date; January 1, 1994 maturity date; 8.0% coupon; 9.0% yield; frequency is semiannual; actual/actual basis. The modified duration (in the 1900 Date System) is

```
MDURATION(33239,36631,0.08,0.09,2,1)
```

which returns 5.73567.

## MROUND

Returns a number rounded to the desired multiple.

### Syntax

MROUND(number,multiple)

**Number** is the value to round.

**Multiple** is the multiple to which you want to round number.

### Examples

MROUND(10,3) returns 9.

MROUND(-10,-3) returns –9.

## MULTINOMIAL

Returns the multinomial of a set of numbers.

### Syntax

MULTINOMIAL(number1,number2,...)

**Number1,number2,...** are 1 to 29 values for which you want the multinomial.

### Examples

MULTINOMIAL(2,3,4) returns 1260.

## NETWORKDAYS

Returns the number of whole workdays between two dates.

### Syntax

NETWORKDAYS(start_date,end_date,holidays)

**Start_date** is a serial date number that represents the start date.

**End_date** is a serial date number that represents the end date.

**Holidays** is an optional set of one or more serial date numbers to exclude from the working calendar, such as state and federal holidays and floating holidays.

### Examples

NETWORKDAYS(DATEVALUE("10/01/91"),DATEVALUE("12/01/91"), DATEVALUE("11/28/91")) returns 43.

APDX

**A**

Alphabetical List of
Worksheet Functions

# NOMINAL

Returns the annual nominal interest rate.

## Syntax

```
NOMINAL(effect_rate,npery)
```

**Effect_rate** is the effective interest rate.

**Npery** is the number of compounding periods per year.

## Examples

```
NOMINAL(5.3543%,4) returns.
```

# OCT2BIN

Converts an octal number to binary.

## Syntax

```
OCT2BIN(number,places)
```

**Number** is the octal number you want to convert.

**Places** is the number of characters to use. If places is omitted, OCT2BIN uses the minimum number of characters necessary.

## Examples

```
OCT2BIN(3,3) returns 011.
```

```
OCT2BIN(7777777000) returns 1000000000.
```

# OCT2DEC

Converts an octal number to decimal.

## Syntax

```
OCT2DEC(number)
```

**Number** is the octal number you want to convert.

## Examples

```
OCT2DEC(54) returns 44.
```

```
OCT2DEC(7777777533) returns –165.
```

# OCT2HEX

Converts an octal number to hexadecimal.

### Syntax

```
OCT2HEX(number,places)
```

> **Number** is the octal number you want to convert.
>
> **Places** is the number of characters to use. If places is omitted, OCT2HEX uses the minimum number of characters necessary.

### Examples

> OCT2HEX(100,4) returns 0040.
>
> OCT2HEX(7777777533) returns FFFFFFFF5B.

## ODDFPRICE

Returns the price per $100 face value of a security with an odd first period.

### Syntax

```
ODDFPRICE(settlement,maturity,issue,first_coupon,rate,yld,redemption,
frequency,basis)
```

> **Settlement** is the security's settlement date, expressed as a serial date number.
>
> **Maturity** is the security's maturity date, expressed as a serial date number.
>
> **Issue** is the security's issue date, expressed as a serial date number.
>
> **First_coupon** is the security's first coupon date, expressed as a serial date number.
>
> **Rate** is the security's interest rate.
>
> **Yld** is the security's annual yield.
>
> **Redemption** is the security's redemption value per $100 face value.
>
> **Frequency** is the number of coupon payments per year. For annual payments, frequency=1; for semiannual, frequency=2; for quarterly, frequency=4.
>
> **Basis** is the type of day count basis to use. If basis is 0 or omitted, day count basis is US (NASD) 30/360; if basis is 1, day count basis is actual/actual; if basis is 2, day count basis is actual/360; if basis is 3, day count basis is actual/365; if basis is 4, day count basis is European 30/360.

**APDX**

**A**

Alphabetical List of Worksheet Functions

### Examples

A treasury bond has the following terms: November 11, 1986 settlement date; March 1, 1999 maturity date; October 15, 1986 issue date; March 1, 1987 first coupon date; 7.85% coupon; 6.25% yield; $100 redemptive value; frequency is semiannual;

actual/actual basis. The price per $100 face value of a security having an odd (short or long) first period (in the 1900 date system) is

```
ODDFPRICE(31727,36220,31700,31837,0.0785,0.0625,100,2,1)
```

which returns 113.597717.

## ODDFYIELD

Returns the yield of a security with an odd first period.

### Syntax
```
ODDFYIELD(settlement,maturity,issue,first_coupon,rate,
pr,redemption,frequency,basis)
```

**Settlement** is the security's settlement date, expressed as a serial date number.

**Maturity** is the security's maturity date expressed as a serial date number.

**Issue** is the security's issue date, expressed as a serial date number.

**First_coupon** is the security's first coupon date, expressed as a serial date number.

**Rate** is the security's interest rate.

**Pr** is the security's price.

**Redemption** is the security's redemption value per $100 face value.

**Frequency** is the number of coupon payments per year. For annual payments, frequency=1; for semiannual, frequency=2; for quarterly, frequency=4.

**Basis** is the type of day count basis to use. If basis is 0 or omitted, day count basis is US (NASD) 30/360; if basis is 1, day count basis is actual/actual; if basis is 2, day count basis is actual/360; if basis is 3, day count basis is actual/365; If basis is 4, day count basis is European 30/360.

### Examples
A bond has the following terms: January 25, 1991 settlement date; January 1, 1996 maturity date; January 18, 1991 issue date; July 15, 1991 first coupon date; 5.75% coupon; $84.50 price; $100 redemptive value; frequency is semiannual; 30/360 basis. The yield of a security that has an odd (short or long) first period is

```
ODDFYIELD(33263,35065,33256,33434,0.0575,084.50,100,2,0)
```

which returns .09758 or 9.76%.

## ODDLPRICE

Returns the price per $100 face value of a security with an odd last period.

### Syntax

```
ODDLPRICE(settlement,maturity,last_interest,rate,yld,redemption,
frequency,basis)
```

**Settlement** is the security's settlement date, expressed as a serial date number.

**Maturity** is the security's maturity date, expressed as a serial date number.

**Last_interest** is the security's last coupon date, expressed as a serial date number.

**Rate** is the security's interest rate.

**Yld** is the security's annual yield.

**Redemption** is the security's redemption value per $100 face value.

**Frequency** is the number of coupon payments per year. For annual payments, frequency=1; for semiannual, frequency=2; for quarterly, frequency=4.

**Basis** is the type of day count basis to use. If basis is 0 or omitted, day count basis is US (NASD) 30/360; if basis is 1, day count basis is actual/actual; if basis is 2, day count basis is actual/360; if basis is 3, day count basis is actual/365; if basis is 4, day count basis is European 30/360.

### Examples

A bond has the following terms: February, 7, 1987 settlement date; June 15, 1987 maturity date; October 15, 1986 last interest date; 3.75% coupon; 4.05% yield; $100 redemptive value; frequency is semiannual; 30/360 basis. The price per $100 of a security having an odd (short or long) last coupon period is

```
ODDLPRICE(31815,31943,31700,0.0375,0.0405,100,2,0)
```

which returns 99.87829.

## ODDLYIELD

Returns the yield of a security with an odd last period.

### Syntax

```
ODDLYIELD(settlement,maturity,last_interest,rate,pr,redemption,
frequency,basis)
```

**Settlement** is the security's settlement date, expressed as a serial date number.

**Maturity** is the security's maturity date, expressed as a serial date number.

**Last_interest** is the security's last coupon date, expressed as a serial date number.

**Rate** is the security's interest rate.

**Pr** is the security's price.

APDX
A

Alphabetical List of
Worksheet Functions

**Redemption** is the security's redemption value per $100 face value.

**Frequency** is the number of coupon payments per year. For annual payments, frequency=1; for semiannual, frequency=2; for quarterly, frequency=4.

**Basis** is the type of day count basis to use. If basis is 0 or omitted, day count basis is US (NASD) 30/360; if basis is 1, day count basis is actual/actual; if basis is 2, day count basis is actual/360; if basis is 3, day count basis is actual/365; if basis is 4, day count basis is European 30/360.

## Examples

A bond has the following terms: April 20, 1987 settlement date; June 15, 1987 maturity date; October 15, 1986 last interest date; 3.75% coupon; $99.875 price; $100 redemptive value; Frequency is semiannual; 30/360 basis. The yield of a security that has an odd (short or long) first period is

```
ODDLYIELD(31887,31943,31770,0.0375,99.875,100,2,0)
```

which returns 0.044873.

# PRICEDISC

Returns the price per $100 face value of a discounted security.

## Syntax

```
PRICEDISC(settlement,maturity,discount,redemption,basis)
```

**Settlement** is the security's settlement date, expressed as a serial date number.

**Maturity** is the security's maturity date, expressed as a serial date number.

**Discount** is the security's discount rate.

**Redemption** is the security's redemption value per $100 face value.

**Basis** is the type of day count basis to use. If basis is 0 or omitted, day count basis is US (NASD) 30/360; if basis is 1, day count basis is actual/actual; if basis is 2, day count basis is actual/360; if basis is 3, day count basis is actual/365; if basis is 4, day count basis is European 30/360.

## Examples

A bond has the following terms: February 15, 1993 settlement date; March 1, 1993 maturity date; 5.25% discount rate; $100 redemption value; Actual/360 basis. The bond price (in the 1900 Date System) is

```
PRICEDISC(34015,34029,0.0525,100,2)
```

which returns 99.79583.

## PRICEMAT

Returns the price per $100 face value of a security that pays interest at maturity.

### Syntax

`PRICEMAT(settlement,maturity,issue,rate,yld,basis)`

**Settlement** is the security's settlement date, expressed as a serial date number.

**Maturity** is the security's maturity date, expressed as a serial date number.

**Issue** is the security's issue date, expressed as a serial date number.

**Rate** is the security's interest rate at date of issue.

**Yld** is the security's annual yield.

**Basis** is the type of day count basis to use. If basis is 0 or omitted, day count basis is US (NASD) 30/360; if basis is 1, day count basis is actual/actual; if basis is 2, day count basis is actual/360; if basis is 3, day count basis is actual/365; If basis is 4, day count basis is European 30/360.

### Examples

A bond has the following terms: February 15, 1993 settlement date; April 13, 1993 maturity date; November 11, 1992 issue date; 6.1% semiannual coupon; 6.1% yield; 30/360 basis. The price (in the 1900 Date System) is

`PRICEMAT(34015,34072,33919,0.061,0.061,0)`

which returns 99.98449888.

## PRICE

Returns the price per $100 face value of a security that pays periodic interest.

### Syntax

`PRICE(settlement,maturity,rate,yld,redemption,frequency,basis)`

**Settlement** is the security's settlement date, expressed as a serial date number.

**Maturity** is the security's maturity date, expressed as a serial date number.

**Rate** is the security's annual coupon rate.

**Yld** is the security's annual yield.

**Redemption** is the security's redemption value per $100 face value.

**Frequency** is the number of coupon payments per year. For annual payments, frequency=1; for semiannual, frequency=2; for quarterly, frequency=4.

**Basis** is the type of day count basis to use. If basis is 0 or omitted, day count basis is US (NASD) 30/360; if basis is 1, day count basis is actual/actual; if basis is 2, day count basis is actual/360; if basis is 3, day count basis is actual/365; if basis is 4, day count basis is European 30/360.

### Examples

A bond has the following terms: February 15, 1991 settlement date; November 15, 1999 maturity date; 5.75% semiannual coupon; 6.50% yield; $100 redemption value; frequency is semiannual; 30/360 basis. The bond price (in the 1900 Date System) is

```
PRICE(33284,36479,0.0575,0.065,100,2,0)
```

which returns 95.04287.

## QUOTIENT

Returns the integer portion of a division.

### Syntax

```
QUOTIENT(numerator,denominator)
```

**Numerator** is the dividend.

**Denominator** is the divisor.

### Examples

```
QUOTIENT(5,2) returns 2.
```

```
QUOTIENT(4.5,3.1) returns 1.
```

## RANDBETWEEN

Returns a random number between two specified numbers.

### Syntax

```
RANDBETWEEN(bottom,top)
```

**Bottom** is the smallest integer RANDBETWEEN will return.

**Top** is the largest integer RANDBETWEEN will return.

**TIP**

You can get the same result without loading the Analysis ToolPak by using the RAND function. To generate random numbers between a and b, where a is the bottom number and b is the top number, use the formula **RAND()\*(b-a)+a**.

## RECEIVED

Returns the amount received at maturity for a fully invested security.

### Syntax
```
RECEIVED(settlement,maturity,investment,discount,basis)
```

**Settlement** is the security's settlement date, expressed as a serial date number.

**Maturity** is the security's maturity date, expressed as a serial date number.

**Investment** is the amount invested in the security.

**Discount** is the security's discount rate.

**Basis** is the type of day count basis to use. If basis is 0 or omitted, day count basis is US (NASD) 30/360; if basis is 1, day count basis is actual/actual; if basis is 2, day count basis is actual/360; if basis is 3, day count basis is actual/365; if basis is 4, day count basis is European 30/360.

### Examples
A bond has the following terms: February 15, 1993 settlement (issue) date; May 15, 1993 maturity date; 1,000,000 investment; 5.75% discount rate; Actual/360 basis. The total amount to be received at maturity (in the 1900 Date System) is

```
RECEIVED(34015,34104,1000000,0.0575,2)
```

which returns 1,014,420.266.

## SERIESSUM

Returns the sum of a power series on the basis of the formula.

### Syntax
```
SERIESSUM(x,n,m,coefficients)
```

**X** is the input value to the power series.

**N** is the initial power to which you want to raise x.

**M** is the step by which to increase n for each term in the series.

APDX

**A**

Alphabetical List of
Worksheet Functions

**Coefficients** is a set of coefficients by which each successive power of x is multiplied. The number of values in coefficients determines the number of terms in the power series. For example, if there are three values in coefficients, then there will be three terms in the power series.

See Excel's Online Help worksheet function reference for an example of SERIESSUM.

# SQRTPI

Returns the square root of (number*PI).

### Syntax
```
SQRTPI(number)
```

**Number** is the number by which pi is multiplied.

### Examples
```
SQRTPI(1) returns 1.772454.
```
```
SQRTPI(2) returns 2.506628.
```

# TBILLEQ

Returns the bond-equivalent yield for a Treasury bill.

### Syntax
```
TBILLEQ(settlement,maturity,discount)
```

**Settlement** is the Treasury bill's settlement date, expressed as a serial date number.

**Maturity** is the Treasury bill's maturity date, expressed as a serial date number.

**Discount** is the Treasury bill's discount rate.

### Examples
A Treasury bill has the following terms: March 31, 1993 settlement date; June 1, 1993 maturity date; 9.14% discount rate. The bond equivalent yield for a treasury bill (in the 1900 Date System) is

```
TBILLEQ(34059,34121,0.0914)
```

which returns 0.094151 or 9.4151%.

# TBILLPRICE

Returns the price per $100 face value for a Treasury bill.

## Syntax

`TBILLPRICE(settlement,maturity,discount)`

**Settlement** is the Treasury bill's settlement date, expressed as a serial date number.

**Maturity** is the Treasury bill's maturity date, expressed as a serial date number.

**Discount** is the Treasury bill's discount rate.

## Examples

A Treasury bill has the following terms: March 31, 1993 settlement date; June 1, 1993 maturity date; 9% discount rate. The Treasury bill price (in the 1900 Date System) is

`TBILLPRICE(34059,34121,0.09)`

which returns 98.45.

# TBILLYIELD

Returns the yield for a Treasury bill.

## Syntax

`TBILLYIELD(settlement,maturity,pr)`

**Settlement** is the Treasury bill's settlement date, expressed as a serial date number.

**Maturity** is the Treasury bill's maturity date, expressed as a serial date number.

**Pr** is the Treasury bill's price per $100 face value.

## Examples

A Treasury bill has the following terms: March 31, 1993 settlement date; June 1, 1993 maturity date; 98.45 price per $100 face value. The Treasury bill yield (in the 1900 Date System) is

`TBILLYIELD(34059,34121,98.45)`

which returns 9.1417%.

APDX

**A**

Alphabetical List of Worksheet Functions

# WORKDAY

Returns the serial number of the date before or after a specified number of workdays.

## Syntax

`WORKDAY(serial_number,return_type)`

**Serial_number** is the date-time code used by Excel for date and time calculations. You can give serial_number as text, such as "15-Apr-1993" or "4-15-93," instead of as a number. The text is automatically converted to a serial number.

**Return_type** is a number that determines the type of return value. If Return_type is 1 or omitted, the number returned is 1 (Sunday) through 7 (Saturday) (behaves like previous versions of Microsoft Excel); if Return-_type is 2, the number returned is 1 (Monday) through 7 (Sunday); if Return-_type is 3, the number returned is 0 (Monday) through 6 (Sunday).

### Examples

WORKDAY("2/14/90") returns 4 (Wednesday).

WORKDAY(29747.007) returns 4 (Wednesday) in the 1900 date system.

# XIRR

Returns the internal rate of return for a schedule of cash flows. Excel uses an iterative technique for calculating XIRR. Using a changing rate (starting with guess), XIRR cycles through the calculation until the result is accurate within 0.000001%. If XIRR can't find a result that works after 100 tries, the #NUM! error value is returned.

### Syntax

XIRR(values,dates,guess)

**Values** is a series of cash flows that correspond to a schedule of payments in dates. The first payment is optional, and corresponds to a cost or payment that occurs at the beginning of the investment. All succeeding payments are discounted based on a 365-day year.

**Dates** is a schedule of payment dates that corresponds to the cash flow payments. The first payment date indicates the beginning of the schedule of payments. All other dates must be later than this date, but they may occur in any order.

**Guess** is a number that you guess is close to the result of XIRR.

### Examples

Consider an investment that requires a $10,000 cash payment on January 1, 1992; and returns $2750 on March 1, 1992; $4250 on October 30, 1992; $3250 on February 15, 1993; and $2750 on April 1, 1993. The internal rate of return (in the 1900 Date System) is

XIRR({10000,2750,4250,3250,2750},{33604,33664,33907,34015,34060},0.1)

which returns 0.373363 or 37.3363%.

## XNPV

Returns the net present value for a schedule of cash flows.

### Syntax

```
XNPV(rate,values,dates)
```

**Rate** is the discount rate to apply to the cash flows.

**Values** is a series of cash flows that correspond to a schedule of payments in dates. The first payment is optional, and corresponds to a cost or payment that occurs at the beginning of the investment. All succeeding payments are discounted based on a 365-day year.

**Dates** is a schedule of payment dates that corresponds to the cash flow payments. The first payment date indicates the beginning of the schedule of payments. All other dates must be later than this date, but they may occur in any order.

### Examples

Consider an investment that requires a $10,000 cash payment on January 1, 1992; and returns $2750 on March 1, 1992; $4250 on October 30, 1992; $3250 on February 15, 1993; and $2750 on April 1, 1993. Assume that the cash flows are discounted at 9%. The net present value is

```
XNPV(0.09,{10000,2750,4250,3250,2750},{33604,33664,33907,34015,34060})
```

which returns 2086.647602.

## YEARFRAC

Returns the year fraction representing the number of whole days between start_date and end_date.

### Syntax

```
YEARFRAC(start_date,end_date,basis)
```

**Start_date** is a serial date number that represents the start date.

**End_date** is a serial date number that represents the end date.

**Basis** is the type of day count basis to use. If basis is 0 or omitted, day count basis is US (NASD) 30/360; if basis is 1, day count basis is actual/actual; if basis is 2, day count basis is actual/360; if basis is 3, day count basis is actual/365; if basis is 4, day count basis is European 30/360.

### Examples

YEARFRAC(DATEVALUE("01/01/93"),DATEVALUE("06/30/93"),0) returns 0.5.

YEARFRAC(DATEVALUE("01/01/93"),DATEVALUE("07/01/93"),3) returns 0.49863.

## YIELD

Returns the yield on a security that pays periodic interest. If there is more than one coupon period until redemption, YIELD is calculated through a hundred iterations. The resolution uses the Newton method based on the formula used for the function PRICE. The yield is changed until the estimated price given the yield is close to price.

### Syntax

YIELD(settlement,maturity,rate,pr,redemption,frequency,basis)

**Settlement** is the security's settlement date, expressed as a serial date number.

**Maturity** is the security's maturity date, expressed as a serial date number.

**Rate** is the security's annual coupon rate.

**Pr** is the security's price per $100 face value.

**Redemption** is the security's redemption value per $100 face value.

**Frequency** is the number of coupon payments per year. For annual payments, frequency=1; for semiannual, frequency=2; for quarterly, frequency=4.

**Basis** is the type of day count basis to use. If basis is 0 or omitted, day count basis is US (NASD) 30/360; if basis is 1, day count basis is actual/actual; if basis is 2, day count basis is actual/360; if basis is 3, day count basis is actual/365; if basis is 4, day count basis is European 30/360.

### Examples

A bond has the following terms: February 15, 1991 settlement date; November 15, 1999 maturity date; 5.75% coupon; 95.04287 price; $100 redemption value; frequency is semiannual; 30/360 basis. The bond yield (in the 1900 Date System) is

YIELD(33284,36479,0.0575,95.04287,100,2,0)

which returns 0.065 or 6.5%.

## YIELDDISC

Returns the annual yield for a discounted security.

### Syntax

`YIELDDISC(settlement,maturity,pr,redemption,basis)`

**Settlement** is the security's settlement date, expressed as a serial date number.

**Maturity** is the security's maturity date, expressed as a serial date number.

**Pr** is the security's price per $100 face value.

**Redemption** is the security's redemption value per $100 face value.

**Basis** is the type of day count basis to use. If basis is 0 or omitted, day count basis is US (NASD) 30/360; if basis is 1, day count basis is actual/actual; if basis is 2, day count basis is actual/360; if basis is 3, day count basis is actual/365; if basis is 4, day count basis is European 30/360.

### Examples

A bond has the following terms: February 15, 1993 settlement date; March 1, 1993 maturity date; 99.795 price; $100 redemption value; Actual/360 basis. The bond yield (in the 1900 Date System) is

`YIELDDISC(34015,34029,99.795,100,2)`

which returns 5.2823%.

## YIELDMAT

Returns the annual yield of a security that pays interest at maturity.

### Syntax

`YIELDMAT(settlement,maturity,issue,rate,pr,basis)`

**Settlement** is the security's settlement date, expressed as a serial date number.

**Maturity** is the security's maturity date, expressed as a serial date number.

**Issue** is the security's issue date, expressed as a serial date number.

**Rate** is the security's interest rate at date of issue.

**Pr** is the security's price per $100 face value.

**Basis** is the type of day count basis to use. If basis is 0 or omitted, day count basis is US (NASD) 30/360; if basis is 1, day count basis is actual/actual; if basis is 2, day count basis is actual/360; if basis is 3, day count basis is actual/365; if basis is 4, day count basis is European 30/360.

### Examples

A bond has the following terms: March 15, 1993 settlement date; November 3, 1993 maturity date; November 8, 1992 issue date; 6.25% semiannual coupon; 100.0123 price; 30/360 basis. The yield (in the 1900 Date System) is

```
YIELDMAT(34043,34276,33916,0.0625,100.0123,0)
```

which returns 0.060954 or 6.0954%.

# Appendix B

## Keyboard Shortcuts

# KEYBOARD SHORTCUTS

This appendix contains 14 tables, summarizing the usage of shortcut keys in Excel.

**NOTE**  For keyboards with only ten function keys, use Alt+F1 for F11. Use Alt+F2 for F12.

## Entering and Editing Cells

| | |
|---|---|
| F2 | Edit active cell |
| Esc | Cancel entry |
| Backspace | Delete character to left of insertion point, or delete selection |
| Shift+F2 | Edit cell note |
| F3 | Paste name into formula |
| Shift+F3 | Display Function Wizard |
| Ctrl+A | After typing valid function name in formula, display Step 2 of Function Wizard |
| Ctrl+Shift+A | After typing valid function name in formula, insert argument names for the function |
| Alt+= | Insert AutoSum formula |
| Ctrl+semicolon | Enter date in cell or formula bar |
| Ctrl+Shift+colon | Enter time in cell or formula bar |
| Ctrl+D | Fill down |
| Ctrl+R | Fill right |
| Ctrl+Del | Delete text to end of line |
| Alt+↵ | Insert carriage return |

| | |
|---|---|
| Ctrl+Alt+Tab | Insert tab |
| Arrow keys | Move one character up, down, left, or right |
| Ctrl+Shift+" | Copy value from cell above the active cell |
| Ctrl+' (apostrophe) | Copy formula from cell above the active cell |
| Ctrl+` | Alternate between displaying values or formulas |
| Ctrl+↵ | Fill a selection of cells with current entry |
| Ctrl+Shift+↵ | Enter array formula |
| F4 | Change cell reference type (absolute-relative-mixed) |

## Command Keys

| | |
|---|---|
| Ctrl+N | New workbook |
| Ctrl+O (or Ctrl+F12) | Open |
| Ctrl+S (or Shift+F12) | Save |
| F12 | Save As |
| Ctrl+P (or Ctrl+Shift+F12) | Print |
| Alt+F4 | Close Excel |
| Ctrl+Z (or Alt+Backspace) | Undo |
| F4 | Repeat |
| Ctrl+X (or Shift+Delete) | Cut |
| Ctrl+C (or Ctrl+Insert) | Copy |
| Ctrl+V (or Shift+Insert) | Paste |
| Del | Clear contents (in worksheet); clear selected item (in chart) |
| Ctrl+F | Display Find dialog box |
| Ctrl+H | Display Replace dialog box |
| Shift+F4 | Find next |
| Ctrl+Shift+F4 | Find previous |
| F5 | Go To |

| | |
|---|---|
| Ctrl+minus sign | Display Delete dialog box |
| Ctrl+Shift+plus sign | Display Insert dialog box |
| Shift+F11 | Insert new worksheet |
| F11 | Insert new chart sheet |
| Ctrl+F3 | Display Define Name dialog box |
| F3 | Display Paste Name dialog box (if names are defined) |
| Ctrl+Shift+F3 | Display Create Names dialog box |
| Alt+' | Display Style dialog box |
| Ctrl+1 | Display Format Cells dialog box |
| Ctrl+9 | Hide rows |
| Ctrl+Shift+( | Unhide rows |
| Ctrl+0 (zero) | Hide columns |
| Ctrl+Shift+) | Unhide columns |
| F7 | Check spelling |
| Ctrl+F6 | Next window |
| Ctrl+Shift+F6 | Previous window |
| F6 | Next pane |
| Shift+F6 | Previous pane |
| F1 | Help Contents screen |
| Shift+F1 | Show Help Pointer |
| Ctrl+7 | Show or hide Standard toolbar |
| F9 or Ctrl+= | Calculate all open workbooks |
| Shift+F9 | Calculate active sheet |

## Function Keys

| | |
|---|---|
| F1 | Help Contents screen |
| Shift+F1 | Display help pointer |
| F2 | Activate formula bar |
| Shift+F2 | Insert note |
| Ctrl+F2 | Display Info window |
| F3 | Display Paste Name dialog box (if names are defined) |

| | |
|---|---|
| Shift+F3 | Display Function Wizard |
| Ctrl+F3 | Display Define Name dialog box |
| Ctrl+Shift+F3 | Display Create Names dialog box |
| F4 | When editing a formula, change cell reference type (absolute-relative-mixed); when not editing a formula, repeat last action |
| Ctrl+F4 | Close window |
| Alt+F4 | Close Excel |
| Ctrl+F5 | Restore window size |
| F6 | Next pane |
| Shift+F6 | Previous pane |
| Ctrl+F6 | Next window |
| Ctrl+Shift+F6 | Previous window |
| F7 | Check spelling |
| Ctrl+F7 | Move command (document Control menu) |
| F8 | Turn Extend mode on or off |
| Shift+F8 | Turn Add mode on or off |
| Ctrl+F8 | Size command (document Control menu) |
| F9 | Calculate all sheets in all open workbooks |
| Shift+F9 | Calculate active sheet |
| Ctrl+F9 | Minimize workbook |
| F10 | Activate menu bar |
| Shift+F10 | Activate shortcut menu |
| Ctrl+F10 | Maximize workbook |
| F11 | Insert new chart sheet |
| Shift+F11 | Insert new worksheet |
| Ctrl+F11 | Insert new Excel 4.0 macro sheet |
| F12 | Save As |
| Shift+F12 | Save |
| Ctrl+F12 | Open |
| Ctrl+Shift+F12 | Print |

# Moving and Selecting in Worksheets and Workbooks

| | |
|---|---|
| ↵ | Move down through selected cells |
| Shift+↵ | Move up through selection |
| Tab | Move right through selection; move among unlocked cells in protected worksheet |
| Shift+Tab | Move left through selection |
| Ctrl+Backspace | Scroll to display active cell |
| Arrow key | Move by one cell in direction of arrow |
| Shift+any arrow key | Extend selection by one cell |
| Ctrl+↑ or Ctrl+↓ | Move up or down to edge of current data region |
| Ctrl+← or Ctrl+→ | Move left or right to edge of current data region |
| Ctrl+Shift+any arrow key | Extend selection to edge of current data region (in direction of arrow) |
| Home | Move to beginning of row |
| Shift+Home | Extend selection to beginning of row |
| Ctrl+Home | Move to beginning of worksheet |
| Ctrl+Shift+Home | Extend selection to beginning of worksheet |
| Ctrl+End | Move to last cell in worksheet (lower-right corner) |
| Ctrl+Shift+End | Extend selection to last cell in worksheet (lower-right corner) |
| Ctrl+spacebar | Select entire column |
| Shift+spacebar | Select entire row |
| Ctrl+A | Select entire worksheet |
| Shift+Backspace | Collapse selection to active cell |
| PgDn | Move down one screen |
| PgUp | Move up one screen |
| Alt+PgDn | Move right one screen |
| Alt+PgUp | Move left one screen |
| Ctrl+PgDn | Move to next sheet in workbook |
| Ctrl+PgUp | Move to previous sheet in workbook |
| Shift+PgDn | Extend selection down one screen |

| | |
|---|---|
| Shift+PgUp | Extend selection up one screen |
| Ctrl+Shift+* | Select current region |
| Ctrl+Shift+spacebar | When an object is selected, select all objects on sheet |
| Ctrl+6 | Alternate between hiding objects, displaying objects, and displaying placeholders for objects. |

If ↵ does not move to the next cell, choose Tools ➤ Options, then select the Edit tab and check the Move Selection After Entry setting.

If the selection is one column, pressing either ↵ or Tab moves you down (Shift+↵ and Shift+Tab both move up). If the selection is one row, pressing either ↵ or Tab moves you right (Shift+↵ and Shift+Tab both move left).

## Moving and Selecting While in End Mode

| | |
|---|---|
| End | Turn End mode on/off |
| End, arrow key | Move by one block of data within a row or column |
| End, Shift+arrow key | Extend selection to end of data block in direction of arrow |
| End, Home | Move to last cell in worksheet (lower-right corner) |
| End, Shift+Home | Extend selection to last cell in worksheet (lower-right corner) |
| End, ↵ | Move to last cell in current row |
| End, Shift+↵ | Extend selection to last cell in current row |

End, ↵ and End, Shift+↵ are unavailable if you have selected the Transition Navigation Keys setting on the Transition tab in the Tools ➤ Options dialog box.

## Moving and Selecting with Scroll Lock

| | |
|---|---|
| Scroll Lock | Turn scroll lock on/off |
| ↑ or ↓ | Scroll screen up or down one row |
| ← or → | Scroll screen left or right one column |
| Home | Move to upper-left cell in window |
| End | Move to lower-right cell in window |
| Shift+Home | Extend selection to upper-left cell in window |
| Shift+End | Extend selection to lower-right cell in window |

## Selecting Special Cells

| | |
|---|---|
| Ctrl+Shift+? | Select all cells containing a note |
| Ctrl+Shift+* | Select rectangular range of cells around the active cell—range selected is an area enclosed by any combination of blank rows and blank columns |
| Ctrl+/ | Select entire array, if any, to which active cell belongs |
| Ctrl+\ | Select cells whose contents are different from the comparison cell in each row |
| Ctrl+Shift+| | Select cells whose contents are different from the comparison cell in each column |
| Ctrl+[ | Select only cells directly referred to by formulas in selection |
| Ctrl+Shift+{ | Select all cells directly or indirectly referred to by formulas in selection |
| Ctrl+] | Select only cells with formulas that refer directly to active cell |
| Ctrl+Shift+} | Select all cells within formulas that directly or indirectly refer to active cell |
| Alt+semicolon | Select only visible cells in current selection |

## Formatting

| | |
|---|---|
| Alt+' (apostrophe) | Display Style dialog box |
| Ctrl+Shift+~ | General number format |
| Ctrl+Shift+$ | Currency format with two decimal places (negative numbers appear in parentheses) |
| Ctrl+Shift+% | Percentage format with no decimal places |
| Ctrl+Shift+^ | Exponential number format with two decimal places |
| Ctrl+Shift+# | Date format with day, month, and year |
| Ctrl+Shift+@ | Time format with hour and minute (indicate AM or PM) |
| Ctrl+Shift+! | Two-decimal-place format with commas |
| Ctrl+Shift+& | Apply outline border |
| Ctrl+Shift+_ (underscore) | Remove all borders |

| Ctrl+B | Apply or remove bold (toggle) |
|---|---|
| Ctrl+I | Apply or remove italic (toggle) |
| Ctrl+U | Apply or remove underline (toggle) |
| Ctrl+5 | Apply or remove strikethrough (toggle) |
| Ctrl+9 | Hide rows |
| Ctrl+Shift+( | Unhide rows |
| Ctrl+0 (zero) | Hide columns |
| Ctrl+Shift+) | Unhide columns |

## Outlining

| Alt+Shift+← | Ungroup a row or column |
|---|---|
| Alt+Shift+→ | Group a row or column |
| Ctrl+8 | Display or hide outline symbols |
| Ctrl+9 | Hide selected rows |
| Ctrl+Shift+( | Unhide selected rows |
| Ctrl+0 (zero) | Hide selected columns |
| Ctrl+Shift+) | Unhide selected columns |

## Print Preview Mode

| Arrow keys | Move around page when zoomed in |
|---|---|
| ↑, ↓ | Move by one page when zoomed out |
| PgUp, PgDn | Move by one page when zoomed out; move around page when zoomed in |
| Ctrl+↑ or Ctrl+← | Move to first page when zoomed out |
| Ctrl+↓ or Ctrl+→ | Move to last page when zoomed out |

## Selecting Chart Items When Chart Is Active

| ↓ | Select previous group of items |
|---|---|
| ↑ | Select next group of items |
| → | Select next item within group |
| ← | Select previous item within group |

## Using AutoFilter

| | |
|---|---|
| Alt+↓ | Display drop-down list for selected column label |
| Alt+↑ | Close drop-down list for selected column label |
| ↑ | Select previous item in list |
| ↓ | Select next item in list |
| Home | Select first item in list (All) |
| End | Select last item in list (Nonblanks) |
| Enter | Filter worksheet list using selected item |

## Window Commands

| | |
|---|---|
| Ctrl+F4 | Close window |
| Ctrl+F5 | Restore window size |
| Ctrl+F6 or Ctrl+Tab | Next window |
| Ctrl+Shift+F6 or Ctrl+Shift+Tab | Previous window |
| Ctrl+F7 | Move command (Control menu) |
| Ctrl+F8 | Size command (Control menu) |
| Ctrl+F9 | Minimize window |
| Ctrl+F10 | Maximize window |

## Switching Applications

| | |
|---|---|
| Alt+Esc | Next application |
| Alt+Shift+Esc | Previous application |
| Alt+Tab | Next Windows application |
| Alt+Shift+Tab | Previous Windows application |
| Ctrl+Esc | Display Task List dialog box |

# Appendix

# C

Numeric Formatting Symbols

# NUMERIC FORMATTING SYMBOLS

This appendix documents the symbols you can use as part of a numeric formatting code (discussed in Chapter 5 under the section "Understanding Format Symbols"). To define a number format using these symbols, choose Format ➣ Cells ➣ Number, then select Custom from the Category list.

**TABLE C.1:** NUMBER FORMAT SYMBOLS

| Symbol | Function | Remarks |
| --- | --- | --- |
| 0 | Digit placeholder | Determines number of decimal places displayed; rounds to number of zeros right of decimal point; displays leading and trailing zeros |
| # | Digit placeholder | Same as 0, but doesn't display leading or trailing zeros |
| ? | Digit placeholder | Same as 0, but insignificant zeros removed; spaces inserted to align numbers correctly |
| . (period) | Decimal point | Marks location of decimal point |
| % | Percent | Displays % sign and treats number as percent |
| , (comma) | Thousands separator | Marks thousands position |
| _ (underscore) | Alignment feature | Skips width of character following underscore; aligns positives with negatives enclosed in () so that numbers and commas remain aligned |

**TABLE C.1:** NUMBER FORMAT SYMBOLS (CONTINUED)

| Symbol | Function | Remarks |
|---|---|---|
| E- E+ e- e+ | Exponent indicator | Displays number in scientific format |
| : $ _ + ( ) - / | Characters | These characters displayed |
| / | Fraction separator | Indicates fraction |
| \ | Text indicator | Character following is text |
| " " | Text indicator | Entry within quotes is text |
| * | Fill indicator | Fills remaining cell width with character following asterisk |
| @ | Format code | Indicates where user-input text will appear |
| [color] | Color indicator | Displays characters in indicated color (black, blue, white, green, cyan, magenta, red, yellow) |
| [color n] | Color indicator | Displays characters in corresponding color from color palette (n is number from 0–56) |
| [condition value] | Conditional statement | Sets criteria for each section of number format; uses conditions <,>,=,<=,>=,<>, and numeric values |

**APDX**
**C**

Numeric Formatting Symbols

**TABLE C.2:** DATE AND TIME FORMAT SYMBOLS

| Symbol | Display | Remarks |
|---|---|---|
| yyyy | 1997 | Year—four digits |
| yy | 97 | Year—two digits |
| mmmm | January | Month—full name |
| mmm | Jan | Month—abbreviated to three characters |

**TABLE C.2:** DATE AND TIME FORMAT SYMBOLS (CONTINUED)

| Symbol | Display | Remarks |
| --- | --- | --- |
| mm | 01 | Month—number, leading zeros |
| m | 1 | Month—number, no leading zeros |
| dd | 07 | Day—number, leading zeros |
| d | 7 | Day—number, no leading zeros |
| h | 1 | Hour |
| mm | 01 | Minute—displays leading zeros |
| ss | 01 | Second—displays leading zeros |
| AM/PM | AM | AM or PM for 12-hour time format |

**TABLE C.3:** FORMATTING EXAMPLES

| Value | Format | Display |
| --- | --- | --- |
| 1234.335 | 0 | 1234 |
| 1234.335 | #,##0 | 1,234 |
| 1234.335 | #,##0.00 | 1,234.34 |
| 1234 | 0.00 | 1234.00 |
| 1234.335 | # ?/? | 1234 1/3 |
| .1234 | 0% | 12% |
| 1234.335 | 0.00E+00 | 1.23E+03 |
| June 11, 1998 | m/d/yy | 6/11/98 |
| June 11, 1998 | d-mmm-yy | 11-Jun-98 |
| June 11, 1998 | mmm-yy | Jun-98 |

**TABLE C.3**: FORMATTING EXAMPLES (CONTINUED)

| Value | Format | Display |
|---|---|---|
| 8:07 PM | h:mm AM/PM | 8:07 PM |
| 8:07 PM | h:mm | 20:07 |
| 8:07:32 | h:mm:ss | 8:07:32 |

**TABLE C.4**: SPECIAL FORMATTING SYMBOLS

| Symbol | Function |
|---|---|
| ;; | Hides all numbers (but not text) |
| ;;; | Hides all values (including text) |
| 0;0; | Displays both positive and negative values as whole positive numbers; zero values as blank cells; text as entered |

# Master's Reference

# MASTER'S REFERENCE

## Add-Ins

An *add-in* is an Excel file that expands the scope of operations you can perform in workbooks. Excel comes with a library of add-ins designed to provide you with special-purpose functions and menu commands.

### To Install Add-Ins

1. Choose Tools ➢ Add-Ins. The Add-Ins dialog box contains a list of the available add-ins, each represented as a check box.

2. Click on the name of the add-in you want to install. A check mark appears in the corresponding check box. Repeat this step for any combination of add-ins in the list.

3. When all the add-ins you want are checked, click on OK.

When you use the Tools ➢ Add-Ins command to install an add-in, the corresponding menu commands and/or functions will be available in the current session and all subsequent sessions with Excel, unless you later remove the add-in.

### To Remove an Add-In

1. Choose Tools ➢ Add-Ins. The Add-In dialog box appears on the screen.

2. In the Add-Ins Available list, click on the name of the add-in that you want to remove. The check mark is cleared from the corresponding check box.

3. Click on OK. The next time you start Excel, the features of this add-in will be removed.

## Alignment

Excel offers a variety of horizontal and vertical alignments and diagonal orientations for displaying text and numeric entries in a cell or range. You can also change the alignment and orientation of attached text in a chart.

### To Change the Alignment of Entries in a Cell or Range

1. Select the cell or range of cells that you want to realign.

2. Choose Format ➢ Cells. In the Format Cells dialog box, click on the Alignment tab.

3. Pull down the Horizontal list and select the Left, Center, or Right option to change the alignment of text and numeric entries within the current column-width settings. The General option represents the default alignment settings: left-alignment for text entries, right-alignment for numeric entries, and centering for logical and error values.

4. Optionally, pull down the Vertical list and choose Top, Center, Justify, or Bottom to adjust the placement of entries within the current row height. Click on OK.

### To Rotate Entries within Cells

1. Select the cell or range of cells that you want to rotate.

2. Choose Format ➢ Cells, and click on the Alignment tab. In the Orientation frame, a half-circle of small black markers represents the range of available rotations.

3. Click on one of the markers in the half-circle. (Alternatively, change the numeric setting in the Degrees box to a value between -90 to 90.) Click on OK.

## To Justify a Long Text Entry within Its Cell

1. Select the cell.

2. Choose Format ➢ Cells and click on the Alignment tab.

3. Pull down the Horizontal list and choose Justify. Then click on OK. Excel wraps the text within the cell, increasing the row height as necessary. To the extent possible, the text is aligned along the left and right sides of the cell.

4. Optionally, adjust the column width and row height at the cell's location to achieve the justified text arrangement that you want.

## To Break and Realign Long Text Entries within a Range of Cells

1. Select a range consisting of a column of long text entries and the adjacent columns (to the right) within which you want to realign the text.

2. Choose Edit ➢ Fill ➢ Justify. Excel redistributes the text contained in the first column of the range selection, resulting in lines of text that are roughly the same length.

## To Change the Alignment of Titles or Labels in a Chart

In a chart window, select the title or axis containing the text that you want to realign, and choose Format ➢ Selected Chart Title, Format ➢ Selected Axis Title, or Format ➢ Selected Axis. In the resulting dialog box, click on the Alignment tab, and then select any combination of alignment and orientation options. Click on OK.

# Analysis Tools

The Analysis ToolPak add-in supplies tools for engineering and statistical applications. Given the input of relevant worksheet data, the components of this add-in are designed to perform specific statistical and engineering analyses. In order to use these features, you must first choose Tools ➢ Add-Ins to install the add-in. (See "Add-Ins" for more information.)

## To Use a Tool from the Analysis ToolPak

1. Create or open a worksheet containing the data that you want to analyze.

2. Choose Tools ➢ Data Analysis. The Data Analysis dialog box appears on the screen.

3. Select the analysis you want to perform and click on OK. The dialog box for the corresponding analysis tool appears on the screen.

4. In the Input Range box enter a reference to the range of data to be analyzed.

5. In the Output Range text box, enter a reference to the location where you want Excel to display the results of the analysis. (You can enter a reference to a single cell to specify the upper-left corner of the output range.) Respond to the other options that appear in the dialog box (different for each analysis tool). Click on Help if you need more information about a particular analysis tool.

6. Click on OK to perform the analysis. The results appear in the selected output range.

The following tools are available in the Analysis ToolPak:

**Anova: Single-Factor** produces an analysis of variance for an input range that contains two or more data samples.

**Anova: Two-Factor With Replication** produces an analysis of variance for two or more groups of samples.

**Anova: Two-Factor Without Replication** produces an analysis of variance for two or more data samples.

**Correlation** calculates the statistical correlation between two sets of data.

**Covariance** calculates the statistical relationship between two sets of data.

**Descriptive Statistics** supplies a table of statistical measurements, including mean, standard deviation, minimum, maximum, and so on.

**Exponential Smoothing** implements a mathematical forecasting technique.

**F-Test: Two-Sample For Variances** produces a comparison of variances, given an input range containing two columns or rows of data.

**Fourier Analysis** calculates the coefficients of a periodic function.

**Histogram** calculates frequency distributions, given an input range of numeric data and a range of bins in which to perform the distribution.

**Moving Average** supplies a forecasting tool.

**Random Number Generation** produces an output range of random numbers; optionally, the numbers can match a particular distribution scheme that you specify in this tool's dialog box.

**Rank And Percentile** determines the ordinal and percentile rank of each value in an input range, in relation to the other values in the range.

**Regression** performs a linear regression analysis, calculating the best straight-line fit through a data sample.

**Sampling** produces a representative data sample from a larger population in the input range.

**t-Test** calculates the correlation between paired sets of measurements in an input range. (Three variations of this test are available.)

**z-Test** compares two sets of measurements in the input range.

# Arithmetic Operations

Along with the four most familiar arithmetic operations—addition, subtraction, multiplication, and division—Excel supports exponentiation and percentage operations for use in arithmetic formulas.

## To Write an Arithmetic Formula

Use any combination of the following operands:

| | |
|---|---|
| + | Addition |
| - | Subtraction |
| * | Multiplication |
| / | Division |
| % | Percent |
| ^ | Exponentiation |

In a formula that contains more than one arithmetic operand, Excel performs operations in this order: percent, exponentiation, multiplication, and division from left to right, addition and subtraction from left to right. Use parentheses in a formula to override this default order of operations.

# Array Formulas

An array formula can be an efficient and economical way to perform an operation involving multiple rows and columns of data, or to enter the same formula into multiple cells in a range. In addition, several of Excel's built-in functions take arrays as arguments or return array results.

## To Enter an Array Formula

1. Select the cell or cells where you want the formula to appear.

2. Enter the elements of the formula. To include a range as an operand in the formula, point to the range with the mouse or enter the range reference directly from the keyboard.

3. Press Ctrl+Shift+↵ to complete the formula. In response, Excel encloses the array formula in braces, { and }.

You can include an *array constant* as an operand in an array formula. An array constant is a sequence of numeric or text values enclosed in braces. Within the braces, the sequence of constant values requires specific punctuation:

commas to separate columns of data, and semicolons to separate rows. For example, in the following array formula, each value in the five-column by three-row range A1:E3 is multiplied by the corresponding value in a five-by-three array constant:

```
{=A1:E3*{1,2,3,4,5;2,2,2,2,2;9,8,7,6,5}}
```

When you enter this array formula into a worksheet range of the appropriate size, the result is an array consisting of five columns and three rows.

## To Select the Range of an Array Formula

Select any cell within the range where the array formula is entered, and press Ctrl+/. (Alternatively, choose Edit ➢ Go To, click on the Special button, and select the Current Array option in the Go To Special dialog box. Then click on OK.)

## To Edit an Array Formula

1. Select the entire array range or any cell within the range, and press F2. (The braces around the formula disappear.)

2. Edit the formula—either in the formula bar or in the active cell—and then press Ctrl+Shift+↵ to reenter the array formula.

# Auditing

The commands in the Auditing submenu allow you to trace *precedents* and *dependents* on a worksheet. A precedent is a cell that is referenced in the formula of the active cell. A dependent is a cell containing a formula that refers to the active cell. By selecting the Trace commands in the Auditing submenu, you can visually examine a cell's precedents or dependents.

## To Trace a Cell's Precedents

1. Select a cell that contains a formula referring to other cells.

2. Choose Tools ➢ Auditing and then choose Trace Precedents from the Auditing sub-

menu. Excel displays one or more tracer arrows from the precedent cells to the active cell.

## To Trace the Cells That Refer to the Active Cell

1. Select a cell that appears in one or more formulas elsewhere on the active worksheet or another worksheet.

2. Choose Tools ➢ Auditing and then choose Trace Dependents in the Auditing submenu. Excel displays one or more tracer arrows from the active cell to its dependent cells.

## To Trace an Error Value

Select a cell that contains an error value and choose Tools ➢ Auditing ➢ Trace Error.

## To Remove Tracer Arrows

Choose Tools ➢ Auditing ➢ Remove All Arrows.

# AutoCalculate

The AutoCalculate panel, located near the center of the status bar, displays a value that Excel calculates from a selected range of entries on the current sheet. You can choose among the following six calculations: the average of the numeric values in the range, the count of all entries in the range, the count of numbers in the range, the largest numeric value in the range, the smallest numeric value in the range, or the sum of numeric values in the range.

## To Display a Calculation on the Status Bar

1. Click on any position on the status bar with the right mouse button. A pop-up menu of calculation options appears.

2. Select one of the six options in the menu: Average, Count, Count Nums, Max, Min, or Sum.

**3.** On the current sheet, select a range of two or more cells containing text or numeric entries. The status bar displays the calculation you've selected.

# AutoFill

By dragging the fill handle—the small black box at the lower-right corner of a selected cell or range—you can easily create a series, copy data, or replicate formulas across rows or down columns in a worksheet.

Excel also defines built-in lists of labels that you can enter into a worksheet range by entering the first couple of entries and dragging the fill handle. These include the days of the week (Sunday to Saturday, or Sun to Sat) and the names of the months (January to December, or Jan to Dec). You can define your own custom lists of commonly used labels; when you do so, the AutoFill feature is available for entering these lists into a worksheet.

## To Create a Series by Dragging the Fill Handle

**1.** Enter the first elements of the series in consecutive cells in a column or adjacent cells in a row, and then select the range of cells containing these entries.

**2.** Position the mouse pointer over the fill handle for the current selection. The pointer changes to a crosshair shape.

**3.** Drag the mouse down or across to the cells where you want to extend the series. As you perform the drag operation, a small box shows the value that will be entered into each cell in turn. When you release the mouse button, Excel fills the selection with sequential elements of the series you defined in the initial cell entries.

## To Create a Custom List of AutoFill Labels

**1.** Choose Tools ➢ Options. In the Options dialog box, click on the Custom Lists tab.

**2.** The NEW LIST entry is selected in the Custom lists box. Activate the List Entries box and begin typing the labels of your custom list. Press ↵ after each label in the list.

**3.** When you finish typing your list, click on the Add button to copy the list to the Custom Lists box.

**4.** If you want to create an additional list, select NEW LIST in the Custom Lists box, and repeat steps 2 and 3.

**5.** Click on OK to close the Options dialog box.

# AutoFormat

In the AutoFormat command, Excel offers a variety of predesigned table formats from which you can choose. These designs include specific selections from Excel's border, font, pattern, alignment, and numeric formatting options, as well as adjustments in column widths and row heights. If one of the available designs suits the data you have entered into a given worksheet, you can save time by selecting the format directly from the Auto-Format dialog box, rather than applying formats individually.

## To Use the AutoFormat Feature

**1.** Select the table of data to which you want to apply a predesigned format. (Alternatively, select a single cell within the data table, and Excel will select the contiguous table range.)

**2.** Choose the Format ➢ AutoFormat command. The AutoFormat dialog box appears on the screen.

**3.** Select the name of a predesigned table format in the Table format list, and preview the selected format that appears in the Sample box.

4. Repeat step 3 until you find a format that suits the current data table. Then click on OK to apply this format to your data.

# Borders

Using the Borders command, you can draw a border around the perimeter of a selected range of cells in a worksheet, or around the individual cells within a range selection. Alternatively, you can draw borders along specified sides of cells in a range. You can select from a variety of border styles and colors.

## To Draw Borders

1. Select the range of cells for which you want to create a border.

2. Choose the Format ➢ Cells command, and then click on the Border tab.

3. From the Style options, select a border style for a particular location. A variety of dotted, dashed, and solid borders are available in light and bold styles.

4. Optionally, pull down the Color list and select a color for the border style.

5. In the Border box, click on any combination of buttons representing the locations where you want to apply the current border style and color. You can choose vertical, horizontal, and diagonal border locations. Alternatively, click on one of the Presets buttons to apply a combination of borders.

6. Repeat steps 3 to 5 for each additional location where you want to apply a border. Note that you can apply different border styles and colors to particular locations within the current range of cells.

7. Click on OK to apply the borders you have selected.

## To Remove a Border

1. Select the range of cells that contain the border you want to remove.

2. Choose Format ➢ Cells and then click on the Border tab.

3. In the Style frame, select the None option. Then, in the Border frame, select each of the locations where you want to remove the border. Click on OK.

# Centering across a Row

Worksheet titles and other text or numeric entries can be centered across a horizontal range of cells.

## To Center an Entry across a Row of Cells

1. Starting from the cell that contains a text or numeric entry, select a horizontal range of cells. The selected cells to the right of the entry should be blank.

2. Choose Format ➢ Cells and click on the Alignment tab. Pull down the list of Horizontal options and choose Center Across Selection. Then click on OK. Excel centers the entry across the range you have selected.

# Charting

A chart in Excel is created from—and linked to—a table of worksheet data. You can create a chart as an embedded graphic object in a worksheet, or as a separate sheet in a workbook. Either way, the ChartWizard guides you easily through the steps of designing your chart.

## To Use the ChartWizard

1. Select the worksheet data from which you want to create your chart. Then choose Insert ➢ Chart or click on the ChartWizard button on the Standard toolbar.

2. Excel displays the first of four dialog boxes, ChartWizard Step 1 Of 4. Select one of the listed chart types, and then click on one of the subtypes, illustrated individually by large icons displayed just to the right of the Chart Type list. For a preview of the chart you're actually creating, position the mouse pointer over the command button labeled Press And Hold To View Sample and hold down the left mouse button. Click on Next to continue to the next step in the process.

3. In the second ChartWizard dialog box, Excel displays the data range you've selected for this chart. (You can change the range if necessary at this point; click on the range button at the right side of the Data range box, and select a new range.) Select one of the two Series In options, Rows or Columns. The illustration in the upper half of the dialog box shows you what your chart will look like under either of these options. Click on Next to continue.

4. In the six tabbed sections of the third dialog box, you can refine the appearance of your chart by selecting among a variety of options. In the Titles section, enter a chart title and optional axis titles. In the Axes section, check or uncheck the axes that you want included in your chart. In the Gridlines section, specify which gridlines you want to see. In the Legend section, select the placement of the legend box. In the Data Labels section, select any labels that you want displayed along with the graphic elements of your chart. And in the Data Table section, check the Show Data Table option if you want to display a grid of data values beneath the chart itself. As you make selections among these options, the resulting chart is displayed at the right side of the dialog box. Click on Next to continue.

5. In the fourth ChartWizard dialog box, choose between creating a new sheet for your chart or embedding the chart as an object on an existing sheet.

6. Click on Finish. Excel creates a chart, following the specifications you have supplied in the ChartWizard dialog boxes.

## To Edit and Reformat a Chart

1. Activate the chart. To activate an embedded chart, click on inside the chart area; Excel displays selection handles around the perimeter of the chart frame. To activate a chart sheet, click on the sheet's tab in the active workbook. By default, Excel displays the Chart toolbar; if this toolbar does not appear, you can choose View ➢ Toolbars ➢ Chart to display it.

2. Optionally, choose commands from the Chart menu to review and revise the four dialog boxes corresponding to the ChartWizard steps: Chart ➢ Chart Type, to select a new type or subtype; Chart ➢ Source Data, to adjust the range to which the chart is linked; Chart ➢ Chart Options, to make changes in specific elements of the chart; or Chart ➢ Location, to switch between a chart sheet and an embedded chart.

3. Select a specific part of the chart by clicking on the item or area with the mouse; Excel displays selection handles around or within the element you select. Then choose the corresponding Selected command from the top of the Format menu, or click on the Selected button in the Chart toolbar. In response, Excel displays a dialog box with specific formatting options for the chart element you've selected. You can open format dialog boxes for the chart area, the plot area, the axes, the legend, the gridlines, the data series, and the chart title.

When you select a series in the chart—that is, the chart markers representing a particular range of numbers from the source worksheet range—the formula bar shows the series formula that links the series to the corresponding worksheet range. The series formula consists of a call to Excel's built-in SERIES function.

To delete a series from a chart, select the series and press Delete. To insert a new series into an embedded chart, select the range of worksheet data for the new series, and drag the range to the chart object. To insert a series into a chart sheet, choose Chart ➢ Add Data. In the Add Data dialog box, enter the worksheet range into the Range box (or point to the range in the source worksheet) and click on OK.

## To Change Series from Rows to Columns or Columns to Rows

1. Activate the chart. If the Chart toolbar is not in view, choose View ➢ Toolbars ➢ Chart to open it.

2. Click on the By Column or the By Row button on the toolbar.

## To Change a Chart's Location Property

1. Activate the chart and choose Chart ➢ Location.

2. In the Chart Location dialog box, choose As New Sheet to change an embedded chart to a chart sheet; or As Object In to change a chart sheet to an embedded chart.

# Clearing Worksheet Cells

The Edit ➢ Clear command allows you to clear the contents, formats, or comments in a range of worksheet cells. Clearing data is not the same as deleting cells. See "Deleting" for details.

## To Clear Data with the Edit ➢ Clear Command

1. Select the range of worksheet data that you want to clear.

2. Choose Edit ➢ Clear, and select one of the four options from the Clear submenu:
   - All removes all entries, formats, and comments
   - Formats removes formatting only
   - Contents removes text, numbers, and formula entries
   - Comments removes any comments you have saved in the worksheet range. (See the "Comments" entry.)

## To Use the Dragging Technique for Clearing Data

1. Select the range of data that you want to clear.

2. Position the mouse pointer over the fill handle (the small black square located at the lower-right corner of the selection). The mouse pointer is displayed as a crosshair shape.

3. Drag the fill handle up or to the left, over the data that you want to delete. (Optionally, hold down the Ctrl key while you drag if you want to delete data, formats, and comments.) The range that you drag over is displayed in gray.

4. Release the mouse button. Excel clears the data from the range.

# Colors

Several formatting commands in Excel provide color palettes from which you can select the colors for worksheets and charts. For worksheets, the color selections appear in the Font, Border, and Patterns tabs of the Format ➢ Cells command. For charts, color selections are available on the Patterns tab (and where appropriate, the

Font tab) of the Format ➤ Selected commands—for example, Format ➤ Selected Chart Area, Format ➤ Selected Plot Area, Format ➤ Selected Series, and so on. You can use the Color tab of the Tools ➤ Options command to customize the color palette for a given workbook.

## To Display Worksheet Entries in Color

1. Select the range of worksheet data and choose Format ➤ Cells. Click on the Font tab in the Format Cells dialog box.

2. Click on the arrow at the right side of the Color box to view the available colors.

3. Select a color and click on OK.

## To Change the Cell Color of a Worksheet Range

1. Select the worksheet range and choose the Format ➤ Cells command. Click on the Patterns tab in the Format Cells dialog box.

2. Select a color in the Color palette.

3. Optionally, click on the down arrow next to the Pattern box and make a selection in the resulting palette. The Sample box shows what your combined color and pattern selections will look like.

4. Click on OK to apply these selections to the current range.

## To Change the Border Color in a Worksheet Selection

1. Select the worksheet range and choose Format ➤ Cells. Then click on the Border tab.

2. Click on the arrow at the right of the Color box and select a color for the border.

3. Select a border style and location. (See the "Borders" entry for details.) Then click on OK.

## To Change the Color of Gridlines

1. Activate a sheet in a workbook.

2. Choose the Tools ➤ Options command. Then click on the View tab.

3. Click on the arrow at the right side of the Color box, just beneath the Gridlines check box.

4. Select a color. (Make sure the Gridlines option is checked.) Then click on OK.

## To Change the Color of a Text Item in a Chart

1. In a chart window, select a text item (a title, label, axis title, legend, or text box).

2. Choose the appropriate Format ➤ Selected command (Selected Chart Title, Selected Data Labels, Selected Axis Title, and so on). Click on the Font tab.

3. Select a color from the Color list, and then click on OK.

## To Change the Color of a Chart Area or Chart Item

1. In a chart window, select the chart area, plot area, series, or other item whose color you want to change, and choose the corresponding Format ➤ Selected command. Click on the Patterns tab on the Format dialog box.

2. On the Patterns dialog box, choose a color from the palette or Color list and click on OK.

## To Customize a Color in a Workbook's Color Palette

1. Switch to the workbook in which you want to customize the color.

2. Choose the Tools ➤ Options command, and then click on the Color tab in the Options dialog box.

3. In any one of the color categories, select the color that you want to customize. Then click on the Modify button. The Colors dialog box appears.

4. Select a new color in the Colors box and click on OK.

5. Repeat steps 3 and 4 to change any other colors in the palette for the active document.

6. Click on OK in the Options dialog box to apply the new color palette to the workbook.

# Column Widths

Adjusting the widths of worksheet columns allows you to display large amounts of data as effectively as possible.

## To Change the Width of a Single Column

1. Select a cell in the column, or click on the column heading to select the entire column.

2. Choose Format ➤ Column ➤ Width.

3. Enter a new value in the Column Width text box. (This value is the width of the column in characters, in the standard font and point size.) Then click on OK.

Alternatively, you can use a mouse technique to change column widths. Position the mouse pointer over the line just to the right of the column's heading, and drag the line to the right for a wider column or to the left for a narrower one. Double-click on the line to adjust the column width to the best fit for the current contents, or choose Format ➤ Column ➤ AutoFit Selection.

## To Change the Width of Multiple Columns

To change the widths of a group of columns, select the columns and choose Format ➤ Column ➤ Width. Then enter a new column width.

All columns that you have not adjusted individually use the standard column width for a worksheet. To change the standard width setting, choose Format ➤ Column ➤ Standard Width. Enter a new value in the Standard Column Width text box, and click on OK.

# Comments

A comment is a text annotation that you can attach to a cell in a worksheet.

## To Annotate a Cell

Select the cell and choose Insert ➤ Comment. Type the text of your comment in the box that appears next to the cell. Word wrap takes place automatically as you type your comment. You can use standard Windows editing features—including cut and paste and copy and paste—inside the box. Click off to another cell when finished writing the comment.

A cell that contains a comment has a special marker that is displayed at the upper-right corner of the cell. On a color monitor, the marker appears as a small red arrowhead.

## To View the Comment in a Cell

Position the mouse pointer over any cell that contains a comment marker. Excel immediately displays the comment box. To view all comments at once, choose View ➤ Comments. (Choose the same command again to hide the comments.)

## To Edit a Comment

Select the cell that contains the comment, and choose Insert ➤ Edit Comment. Change the contents of the comment box in any way you wish.

## To Copy Comments

1. Select the cell or range containing the comments you want to copy, and choose

Edit ➤ Copy. A moving border appears around the selection.

2. Select the cell or the upper-left corner of the range to which you want to copy the notes.

3. Choose Edit ➤ Paste Special. In the Paste Special dialog box, select the Comments option, and click on OK. Excel copies the comment or comments from the source range to the destination.

## To Print Comments

1. Choose File ➤ Page Setup and click on the Sheet tab on the Page Setup dialog box.

2. Pull down the Comments list and choose one of the options: At End Of Sheet to print all comments together on a separate page; or As Displayed On Sheet to print comments as they appear on the sheet. Click on OK.

3. Choose File ➤ Print. Click on OK to begin printing.

## To Delete Comments from a Range of Cells

1. Select the range from which you want to delete notes.

2. Choose Edit ➤ Clear ➤ Comments.

# Consolidating Data

The Data ➤ Consolidate command provides flexible techniques for combining data from multiple worksheet sources in a single destination worksheet. By default, the Consolidate command uses the Sum function to combine the corresponding values from source worksheets; but you can choose from 11 different functions—including Average, Count, Max, Min, Product, and others—to perform the consolidation. Optionally, you can create links between the source worksheets and the destination worksheet, so that the destination is updated whenever the data changes in any one of the sources.

## To Consolidate Data from Multiple Sheets

1. Activate the destination worksheet and select the location in which you want to consolidate data. You can specify the destination area by selecting the upper-left corner cell, the top-row range, the left-column range, or the entire range. (During the consolidation process, Excel expands the destination area accordingly.)

2. Choose Data ➤ Consolidate. The Consolidate dialog box contains boxes labeled Function, Reference, and All references, along with several buttons and check boxes. The Reference text box is active when you open the dialog box.

3. Optionally, click on the Browse button if your source workbooks are not currently open. In the resulting dialog box, find and select the name of a source workbook, and click on OK. Back in the Consolidate dialog box, Excel enters a reference to the source workbook.

4. If the source area is not on the same worksheet as the destination area, type the name of the worksheet followed by an exclamation point. Then type a range name or range reference identifying the data that you want to consolidate from the source worksheet. (If the source worksheet is in the active workbook or another open workbook, you can select the source area with the mouse or the keyboard. Excel enters a reference to your selection in the Reference text box.) The source area may contain numeric entries alone, from a worksheet range that matches the size and shape of other source areas you are including in the consolidation; in this case, Excel consolidates by position. Alternatively, the source area may include an identifying row and/or column of labels, and the data may be arranged differently in other source areas; in this case, Excel consolidates by category.

5. Click on the Add button. Excel adds the current source area reference to the All

references list, and reactivates the Reference text box.

6. Repeat steps 3, 4, and 5 for all the source areas that you want to include in the consolidation.

7. If you are performing a consolidation by category, click on one or both of the Use Labels In options: Top Row if the category labels are at the top of each source area; Left Column if the category labels are at the left side of each source area. (In response, Excel will copy the selected category labels to the destination area.)

8. Optionally, pull down the Functions list and select an entry other than the default Sum function.

9. Optionally, select the Create Links To Source Data check box, if you want Excel to create external references to the source.

10. Click on OK. Excel consolidates the data and displays it in the destination area you have selected.

If you have created the source worksheets in a consistent format—placing the source data in the same rectangular arrangement in each worksheet—you can consolidate the data by position. When you consolidate by position, Excel does not copy labels from the source worksheets to the destination area. You should therefore begin your work by entering any necessary labels at the top row or left column of the destination area, and formatting the area appropriately.

On the other hand, if you are consolidating data from diverse arrangements in the source worksheets, the source areas should include consistent category labels that identify particular rows or columns of data. When you consolidate by category, Excel copies the category labels from the source to the destination.

The Function list in the Consolidation dialog box offers 11 functions: Sum, Count, Average,

Max, Min, Product, Count Nums, StdDev, StdDevp, Var, and Varp.

If you select the Create Links To Source Data option, Excel reorganizes the destination area as an outline and inserts rows into the area for references to the source data. You can then expand the outline to view the source data along with the consolidated data, or collapse the outline to view the consolidated data alone.

You can revise the consolidation at any time—adding new source areas, deleting source areas, or changing the references to source areas—by activating the destination worksheet and choosing Data ➤ Consolidate again.

# Copying Data

Along with the familiar Copy and Paste commands available in most Windows applications, Excel has a simple drag-and-drop operation that you can use to copy a range of data from one worksheet area to another.

## To Copy Data Using the Copy and Paste Commands

1. Select the range of data that you want to copy, and choose Edit ➤ Copy. Excel displays a moving border around the range, and copies the data to the Clipboard.

2. Select a cell or range for the destination, and choose Edit ➤ Paste. Excel copies the data to the paste range.

## To Insert Data during a Copy-and-Paste Operation

1. Select the range of data that you want to copy, and choose Edit ➤ Copy.

2. Select a cell or range for the destination, and choose the Insert ➤ Copied Cells command. (This command is available only when a source copy range is marked with a moving border.)

**3.** In the Insert Paste dialog box, select the Shift Cells Right or Shift Cells Down option and click on OK. Excel pastes the data and moves existing entries into the cells to the right or the cells below the paste area.

## To Copy a Selection to Multiple Locations

**1.** Select the copy range and choose Edit ➢ Copy.

**2.** Select the first paste range, then hold down Ctrl as you select each additional range.

**3.** Choose Edit ➢ Paste. Excel copies the data to all of the paste ranges at once.

## To Copy Only the Cells That Are Visible

**1.** Select a range of cells that includes hidden or collapsed ranges.

**2.** Choose Edit ➢ Go To, and click on the Special button on the Go To dialog box.

**3.** In the Go To Special dialog box, select the Visible Cells Only option, and click on OK. This step results in a multiple range selection consisting of the visible cells.

**4.** Choose Edit ➢ Copy. A moving border appears around the copy range.

**5.** Select a cell or range for the paste area, and choose Edit ➢ Paste.

## To Copy Data Using the Drag-and-Drop Technique

**1.** Select the range of data that you want to copy.

**2.** Position the mouse pointer along the border of the selection. The pointer shape changes to an arrow.

**3.** Hold down Ctrl and the left mouse button, and drag the mouse pointer to the location where you want to copy the data. A gray frame representing the data follows the mouse pointer as you drag.

**4.** Release the mouse button. Excel copies the range to its new destination.

Alternatively, you can hold down the *right* mouse button and drag a range to a new location. When you release the mouse button, a pop-up menu provides a list of useful options, including Move Here, Copy Here, Copy Here As Values Only, Copy Here As Formats Only, and so on.

# Copying Formats

You can use the Edit ➢ Paste Special command, the Format Painter button, or the drag-and-drop action to copy formats from one worksheet range to another without changing the data values in the destination range. This operation copies alignments, fonts, borders, colors, patterns, and number formats.

## To Copy Formats from One Range to Another

**1.** Select the range from which you want to copy the formats, and choose Edit ➢ Copy. A moving border appears around the copy range.

**2.** Select a cell or range to which you want to copy the formatting.

**3.** Choose Edit ➢ Paste Special. In the Paste Special dialog box, select the Formats option and click on OK. In response, Excel applies all the formats from the copy range to the paste range.

## To Copy Formats Using the Format Painter Button

**1.** Select the cell or range that contains the formats you want to copy.

**2.** Click on the Format Painter button in the Standard toolbar. When you move the mouse pointer into the worksheet area, the

COPYING FORMULAS | **905**

pointer appears as a cross with an animated paintbrush icon.

3. Select the area that you want to format, or click on the upper-left corner cell of the area. Excel copies the formats from the source range to the destination.

If you want to copy the formats to more than one range, double-click on the Format Painter button. Then select each of the destination ranges in turn. When you are finished, click on the Format Painter button once to turn the feature off.

## To Copy Formats Using the Drag-and-Drop Technique

1. Select the range of data from which you want to copy the formats.

2. Position the mouse pointer along the border of the selection. The pointer shape changes to an arrow.

3. Click on the *right* mouse button and drag the mouse pointer to the location where you want to paste the data. A gray frame representing the copy area follows the mouse pointer as you drag.

4. Release the mouse button. A pop-up menu shows the available paste options.

5. Select Copy Here As Formats Only. Excel copies the formats from the copy range to the paste range.

## To Clear Formats from a Range

1. Select the range from which you want to clear the formats.

2. Choose Edit ➤ Clear ➤ Formats. Excel clears all formats from the range you have selected.

# Copying Formulas

When you copy a formula from one location to another in a worksheet, the result depends on

the types of references included in the original formula:

- An absolute reference is copied verbatim from the original formula to the copy; each copy refers to a fixed location on the worksheet.

- A relative reference is adjusted according to the location of the copy, so that the row and/or column portions of the reference may be different for each copy of the formula.

- A mixed reference contains a combination of absolute and relative elements.

You can use copy-and-paste, AutoFill, or drag-and-drop operations to copy formulas from one location to another. In addition, you can use the Copy and Paste Special commands to copy a range of formulas to itself, converting all the formulas to fixed values.

## To Create and Copy a Formula

1. While you enter the first instance of a formula, decide whether each reference should be absolute, relative, or mixed—depending on how you want the reference to be copied across rows and/or down columns. Enter a reference into the formula bar by pointing with the mouse or by typing the reference directly from the keyboard, and then press F4 repeatedly to step through the possible reference types: relative, absolute, or mixed. Excel inserts a dollar sign ($) before the absolute portions of the reference.

2. After you complete the original formula, use any of the techniques available in Excel for copying an entry from one location to another. (See "AutoFill" and "Copying Data" to learn about these various techniques.)

## To Convert Formulas to Values in a Range

1. Select the range of cells containing the formulas you want to convert, and choose Edit ➤ Copy.

2. Without changing the range selection, choose Edit ➤ Paste Special.

3. In the Paste Special dialog box, select the Values option and click on OK. Excel converts each formula entry in the range to its current value. In other words, the range now contains only constant entries; the formulas are lost.

# Custom Number Formats

The Number tab of the Format ➤ Cells command provides dozens of built-in numeric display formats in several categories: Number, Currency, Accounting, Date, Time, Percentage, Fraction, Scientific, Text, and Special (such as Zip Code). You can add your own custom formats to these built-in ones by editing an existing format or by devising an entirely new format.

## To Create a Custom Number Format

1. Select the cell or range of cells to which you want to apply the custom format, and choose Format ➤ Cells. Click on the Number tab. In the Category list, choose Custom.

2. Optionally, select a starting format from the Type list. This format appears in the text box above the list.

3. Activate the text box. Edit or enter the code for the custom format you want to create. Use new combinations of the same formatting symbols that are used in the built-in format codes.

4. Click on OK. Excel applies the new format to the current selection of worksheet cells, and adds the custom format to the Type list. You can reuse this custom format at other locations.

A custom format is defined for the current workbook, although you can copy it to other open workbooks. When you close all the workbooks

for which the custom format is defined, it is no longer available.

## To Delete a Custom Number Format

1. Choose Format ➤ Cells and click on the Number tab.

2. In the Category list, choose Custom. In the Format Codes list, select the custom format that you want to delete.

3. Click on the Delete button. Click on OK.

# Data Form

A *data form* is a dialog box designed to simplify your work with lists and databases. (See the "Database" and "Lists" entries for more information.) A data form is useful for examining and editing the fields of individual records, scrolling through the list one record at a time, adding new records to the list, deleting records from the list, and searching for records that match specific criteria.

## To Open a Data Form for Viewing Records

1. Activate a worksheet that contains a list. Select any cell within the range of the list.

2. Choose Data ➤ Form. The data form for the list appears on the screen. At the left side of the form are labels identifying the fields of the list and text boxes showing the field entries for the first record. At the right side is a column of command buttons that you can use to perform specific operations on your list.

3. Use the vertical scroll bar in the middle of the data form to scroll one record at a time through the list or to move quickly from one position to another in the list. (Alternatively,

press ↓ to move to the next record in the list, or ↑ to move to the previous record.) At the upper-right corner of the data form, Excel displays the current record number and the total number of records.

**4.** Click on the Close button to close the data form when you are finished viewing the records of the list.

## To Edit a Record in the Data Form

**1.** Choose Data ➢ Form to open the data form for the current list.

**2.** Scroll to the record that you want to edit, and make changes in any of the text boxes displaying the fields of the record.

**3.** Scroll to a different record. Excel copies the changes in the edited record to the list itself.

Before scrolling to a different record, you can click on the Restore button to bring back the original unedited version of the current record. Once you scroll to a different record any changes you have made are copied to the list.

## To Add New Records to the List in the Data Form

**1.** Choose Data ➢ Form to open the data form for the current list.

**2.** Click on the New button. The data form displays blank text boxes for all of the fields that can be edited. The words *New Record* appear at the upper-right corner of the data form.

**3.** Enter a data item for each of the fields of the new record.

**4.** Press ↵ to add the new record to the list. The data form displays blank fields for the next new record.

**5.** Repeat steps 3 and 4 for each new record you want to add to the list.

**6.** Click on the Close button to close the data form.

The data form always appends new records to the end of the list, regardless of the current order of other records. Choose Data ➢ Sort or click on the Sort Ascending or the Sort Descending button on the Standard toolbar to rearrange the list after you have added one or more records.

## To Delete a Record in the Data Form

**1.** Choose Data ➢ Form to open the data form for the current list.

**2.** Scroll to the record that you want to delete.

**3.** Click on the Delete button. A message box appears on the screen asking you to confirm the deletion.

**4.** Click on OK to delete the record from the list, or click on Cancel to back out of the deletion.

## To Search for Records in the Data Form

**1.** Choose Data ➢ Form to open the data form for the current list.

**2.** Click on the Criteria button. The data form displays a blank text box for each of the fields in the list, including calculated fields. The word *Criteria* appears in the upper-right corner of the data form, and the scroll bar is temporarily removed.

**3.** Enter a comparison criterion into a field box. The criterion can be any text or numeric entry that you want to search for. Alternatively, you can begin the criterion expression with one of Excel's six comparison operators (=, <, >, <=, >=, <>), or you can include wildcard characters (* or ?) to search for variations of matching text. (See "Database Criteria" for more information about criteria expressions.)

**4.** Repeat step 3 for each field in which you want to include a criterion. If you enter multiple criteria into the data form, Excel reads them as "and" conditions—that is, a record must meet all of the criteria to be selected as a match.

5. Click on the Find Next and/or Find Prev buttons repeatedly to find and scroll through the records that match your criteria. Excel beeps in response to either button when there are no more matching records in the specified direction.

6. Click on Close to close the data form when you have finished examining the matching records.

## Data Tables

In a data table, Excel calculates multiple results from a formula that contains one or two variables. A one-input data table includes a column or a row of values to be substituted into a single variable. A two-input table has both a column and a row of values to be substituted into two variables.

### To Create a One-Input Data Table with One Formula

1. Enter a single column of values, and then enter a target formula in the cell one row above and one column to the right of the values. Or, enter a single row of values and a target formula just below and to the left. The formula includes a direct or indirect reference to an input cell elsewhere on the worksheet; this is the formula's *variable*.

2. Select the two-column or two-row range that includes the values and the formula.

3. Choose Data ➢ Table. In the resulting dialog box, enter a reference to the input cell into the Column input cell box for a column-oriented table, or into the Row input cell box for a row-oriented table. Click on OK, and Excel fills in the table.

### To Create a Two-Input Data Table

1. Enter the target formula into the upper-left corner cell of the range where you want to create the data table. The formula includes

direct or indirect references to two input cells elsewhere on the worksheet; these are the formula's two *variables*.

2. Enter a column of input values beneath the formula, and a row of input values to the right of the formula.

3. Select the two-dimensional range of cells that includes the formula and the row and column of input values.

4. Choose Data ➢ Table. Enter references to the two input cells into the Row Input Cell and Column Input Cell text boxes. Click on OK, and Excel fills in the data table.

## Data Validation

When you are designing a worksheet that will ultimately be used by people other than yourself, you may want to build safeguards against inappropriate data entries. For example, if your worksheet contains formulas that depend on numeric input within a specific scope, an invalid entry may generate confusing and erroneous results. The Data ➢ Validation command allows you to define appropriate validation criteria for a cell or a range of cells. Using the same command, you can design messages that provide input guidance and error alerts for invalid entries.

### To Design a Data Validation Scheme

1. Select the cell or cells where you want to impose a particular data validation scheme.

2. Choose Data ➢ Validation. In the Data Validation dialog box, click on the Settings tab.

3. Pull down the Allow list and select the type of value you want the user to enter into the current cell or cells. If you choose one of the numeric types (including Whole Number, Decimal, Date, and Time), the dialog box displays three new boxes labeled Data, Minimum, and Maximum.

4. Pull down the Data list and choose a condition that describes the data input requirement. For example, choose Between if you want to enter a minimum and maximum value for the input; or choose Greater Than or Less Than if you want to supply only a minimum or only a maximum.

5. If applicable, fill in the Minimum and Maximum boxes with numeric entries to establish the scope of the input validation.

6. Optionally, click on the Input Message tab. Enter a title and a message to explain the input requirements to the user. A message box displaying this information will appear on the desktop whenever the user selects the current cell or cells.

7. Optionally, click on the Error Alert tab. Select one of the three alert styles—Stop, Warning, or Information. (Each of these has a distinct icon, as shown on the dialog box itself.) Then enter a title and a message to explain the error. A warning box displaying this information will appear on the desktop whenever the user enters an invalid or inappropriate value into the cell or cells.

8. Click on OK to complete the validation scheme. You should now try it out by selecting the target cell (or one of the cells) and entering a variety of valid and invalid test values.

# Database

In a worksheet, a database contains rows of consistently arranged information. The columns in the database range are known as fields, and the rows are records. The top row of the database contains the field names. In Excel, a database is one kind of *list* you can create to keep records in a worksheet. After you create a list—whether you think of your list as a database or not—you can perform a variety of operations, such as searching for records that match specified criteria, copying selected records to a new location, and sorting the database. In addition, Excel provides a special

data form dialog box that simplifies several basic database operations. (See "Data Form" for details.)

## To Create a Database

1. In a worksheet, enter a row of field names at the top of the range in which you plan to create the database. Enter a unique field name in each cell.

2. Use formatting options of your choice to give the field names a distinctive appearance from the rest of the database. For example, select the row of field names and click on the Bold button on the Formatting toolbar.

3. Enter one record in each row after the field names. A field entry may be text, a number, a date, a time value, or even a formula, but the entries in a given field column should all contain the same type of data. Do not leave any rows blank between records.

# Database Criteria

One way to find database records that meet certain conditions is to create a *criteria range*, consisting of field names and search expressions. Excel uses the expressions in the range to determine whether a given record matches your selection criteria. In the criteria range you can write comparison criteria to find records that contain a certain value or range of values; or computed criteria to find records based on a formula. Once you have created a criteria range, you can use the Data ➤ Filter ➤ Advanced Filter command to find matching records or copy matching records to a separate location.

Creating a criteria range is an awkward database technique. But it has the advantage of familiarity, since it has been available since the first version of Excel. A more elegant Excel technique known as AutoFilter can often simplify your work with lists and databases. (See the "Filters" entry for more information.)

## To Create a Criteria Range

1. Select a location for the criteria range. In general, it's best to use the rows *above* your database for this purpose. (Insert new rows if necessary, using the Insert ➢ Rows command. Note that a criteria range located in the rows beneath the database range might limit the growth of the database itself. A criteria range next to the database might be hidden when the database is filtered.)

2. Enter a row of field names for the criteria range. The row may contain all of the field names from the database or only a selection of names. (For a computed criterion, enter a name that is not the same as any field name in the database.)

3. In the row or rows beneath the field names, enter the criteria expressions. Multiple criteria in the same row denote an "and" condition—that is, a record must match all of the criteria in the row to be selected. Multiple criteria in different rows denote an "or" condition; a record is selected if it matches all the criteria in any one row.

A comparison criterion consists of a simple text or numeric entry, or an expression that begins with one of Excel's six comparison operators: =, <, >, <=, >=, or <>. In addition, comparison criteria can use the wildcard characters * and ? to search for patterns of text entries.

A computed criterion is a formula that includes a relative reference to at least one of the fields in the database. The reference may appear as a field name, whether or not you have actually defined field names as range names in your worksheet. (See "Names" for information about defining range names.) For example, in a database of salespeople you might use the computed criterion

```
=Sales*CommRate>5000
```

to find all records in which the product of the Sales field and the commission rate is greater than 5000. (The name CommRate could be

either a field name or a range name defined elsewhere on the worksheet.)

Once you've created a criteria range, you're ready to choose the Data ➢ Filter ➢ Advanced Filter command to begin the record search. In the Advanced Filter dialog box you identify the database (or list) range and the criteria range. You can choose between filtering the list in place or copying the matching records to another range. (See the "Filters" entry for details.)

# Database Functions

Excel provides a set of statistical and arithmetic functions that operate on selected records in a database. In general, these functions take three arguments: a database range, a target field name enclosed in quotes, and a criteria range. Given a selection of records that match the criteria, each function performs a particular calculation on the data in the target field.

## To Use the Database Functions

On a worksheet that contains a database and criteria range, enter any of the following functions at an appropriate location on the worksheet:

- DAVERAGE finds the average of the target numeric field entries in the records that match the criteria.

- DCOUNT counts the numeric entries in the target field of the selected records.

- DCOUNTA counts the nonblank entries in the target field of the selected records.

- DGET reads a field value from a single record that matches the criteria. (DGET returns the error value #NUM! if there are multiple records that match the criteria, or #VALUE! if no record matches the criteria.)

- DMAX returns the largest of the target numeric field values in the selected records.

- DMIN returns the smallest of the target numeric field values in the selected records.

- DPRODUCT finds the product of the target numeric field values in the selected records.

- DSTDEV calculates the standard deviation of the target numeric field values in the selected records. (The DSTDEVP function performs the same statistical calculation based on an entire "population.")

- DSUM returns the sum of the target numeric field values in the selected records.

- DVAR calculates the variance of the target numeric field values in the selected records. (The DVARP function performs the same statistical calculation based on an entire population.)

The second argument can appear either as a field name in quotation marks or a field number. For example, the following function returns the average of the numeric entries in the sixth field:

```
=DAVERAGE(Database,6,Criteria)
```

The database fields, left to right, are numbered consecutively from 1 up to the number of fields.

# Date and Time Functions

Excel provides a useful collection of date and time functions that you can use to enter the current date and time into a cell, convert values between various date and time formats; perform date arithmetic for special business applications, and read specific calendar or chronological information from a serial number.

## To Enter the Current Date and Time into a Cell

Use one of these functions:

- NOW( ) returns a numeric value representing the current date and time. (The integer portion of the number is the date, and the fractional portion represents the time. When you enter this function, Excel automatically applies a date-and-time format to the cell. For more information about the numeric representation of date and time

values, see "Date Entries" and "Time Entries.")

- TODAY( ) returns an integer representing the current date.

## To Convert between Formats

Use these functions:

- DATE(yy,mm,dd) returns an integer representing the specified date.
- DATEVALUE("DateString") returns the integer equivalent of a date string.
- TIME(hh,mm,ss) returns a decimal fraction representing the specified time value.
- TIMEVALUE("TimeString") returns the decimal fraction equivalent of a time string.

## To Perform Date Arithmetic

Use one of these functions:

- DAYS360(date1,date2,method) returns the number of days between the two dates, based on a 360-day business year. The optional *method* argument is 1 (or omitted) for the US method, or 2 for the European method of calculation.
- NETWORKDAYS(date1,date2,holidays) returns the number of business days between the two dates, not including weekends or specified holidays.
- YEARFRAC(date1,date2,basis) returns the fraction of the year represented by the difference between the two dates. (Basis is used much like "method" in the DAYS360 function.)
- EDATE(date,months) returns the date that is a specified number of months from the given date.
- EOMONTH(date,months) returns the date at the end of the month, a specified number of months from the given date.
- WORKDAY(date,workdays,{holidays}) returns the date that is a specified number of work days from the given date, not counting the holidays listed in the array.

912 | DATE ENTRIES

## To Read Date or Time Information

Use these functions:

- YEAR(date) returns the year from a serial date.
- MONTH(date) returns the month, from 1 to 12.
- WEEKNUM(date,method) returns the week number, from 1 to 52.
- DAY(date) returns the day of the month, from 1 to 31.
- WEEKDAY(date) returns the day of the week from 1 to 7, where 1 is Sunday.
- HOUR(date) returns the hour, from 0 to 23, from a serial time value.
- MINUTE(date) returns the minute, from 0 to 59.
- SECOND(date) returns the second, from 0 to 59.

# Date Entries

You can enter a date value into a worksheet cell in any of several date formats that Excel recognizes. In response, Excel applies a date format to the cell, but stores the date itself as a special type of numeric value known as a *serial number*. The serial number format allows you to perform date arithmetic operations in a worksheet.

## To Enter a Date into a Worksheet Cell

Select the cell and type the date in a recognizable format. Here are some examples of date-entry formats that Excel recognizes:

3/14/97
3-14-97
March 14, 1997
14 Mar 1997

In response to these entries, Excel applies one of its built-in date formats to the cell and displays

the date either as 3/14/97 or 14-Mar-97. Excel stores the date internally as 35503, which is the serial number for March 14, 1997.

## To Find the Difference between Two Dates

Enter a formula that subtracts one date from the other. Suppose you have entered date values in cells B1 and C1. The following formula gives the difference between the two dates:

```
=C1-B1
```

Internally, Excel subtracts one date's serial number from the other, resulting in the difference in days between the dates.

To include a date in a formula, enclose the date in double quotation marks and use a date format that Excel recognizes. For example, the formula

```
="3/14/97"+90
```

adds 90 days to the date 3/14/97. The result is the serial number for the date 6/12/97.

## To View the Serial Number for a Date Entry

1. Select the cell that contains the entry displayed in a date format.

2. Choose Format ➤ Cells, and click on the Number tab on the resulting dialog box.

3. Select General in the Category box. Click on OK.

# Deleting

You can use either the Delete command or a special dragging technique to delete rows, columns, or a selection of cells from a worksheet. When you do so, Excel shifts other cells up or to the left to fill in the deleted area. (See "Clearing Worksheet Cells" for a description of special dragging techniques.)

## To Delete Entire Rows or Columns

1. Select the rows or columns by dragging the mouse along the appropriate row or column headings. (To select a single row or column, click on the row or column heading.)

2. Choose Edit ➢ Delete. Or, hold down the Shift key and drag the fill handle up (for rows) or to the left (for columns).

Alternatively, select the rows or columns and press Ctrl+− (minus sign), or, point to the selected rows or columns, and hold down the right mouse button to view the shortcut menu; choose the Delete command to finish.

When you select entire rows, the fill handle is located at the lower-left corner of the selection. When you select entire columns, the fill handle is at the upper-right corner of the selection.

## To Delete a Range of Cells

1. Select the range you want to delete.

2. Choose Edit ➢ Delete.

3. In the Delete dialog box, select either the Shift Cells Left or Shift Cells Up option, depending on how you want Excel to fill in the empty area. Click on OK.

# Editing

You can edit the contents of a cell either in the formula bar or in the cell itself.

## To Edit the Contents of a Cell

1. Double-click on the cell whose contents you want to edit. A flashing insertion bar appears inside the cell.

2. Use the keyboard to insert, delete, or revise any part of the cell's contents.

3. Press ↵ to complete the revision. To cancel an entry without changing the contents of the current cell, click on the cancel box, or press Esc.

Alternatively, press F2 to switch to the Edit mode for the active cell. In this mode, press Home to move the insertion point to the beginning of the entry or to the beginning of the current line in a multiline entry. Press End to move to the end of the current entry or line. Press ← or → to move the insertion point left or right by one character.

Press Alt+↵ to enter a carriage return into a text entry in the Formula bar. This results in a multiple-line entry in the current cell. Press Ctrl+Tab to enter a tab character into a cell.

# Engineering Functions

The Analysis ToolPak add-in supplies a library of mathematical and technical functions suitable for engineering applications. If you have installed the add-in, you can either enter these functions directly into worksheets or select them from the Paste Function dialog box. (See "Functions" for details.)

The engineering function category includes the following groups of tools:

- Base conversion functions for converting between binary, octal, decimal, and hexadecimal numbers (BIN2DEC, BIN2HEX, BIN2OCT, DEC2BIN, DEC2HEX, DEC2OCT, HEX2BIN, HEX2DEC, HEX2OCT, OCT2BIN, OCT2DEC, OCT2HEX).

- Bessel functions (BESSELI, BESSELJ, BESSELK, BESSELY).

- Complex number functions (COMPLEX, IMABS, IMAGINARY, IMARGUMENT, IMCONJUGATE, IMCOS, IMDIV, IMEXP, IMLN, IMLOG2, IMLOG10, IMPOWER, IMPRODUCT, IMREAL, IMSIN, IMSQRT, IMSUB, IMSUM).

- The double factorial function (FACT-DOUBLE).

- Error functions (ERF, ERFC).
- A measurement conversion function (CONVERT).
- Number comparisons (DELTA, GESTEP).

## Exiting Excel

Choose File ➤ Exit. For each unsaved document, Excel displays a prompt asking you for instructions: Click on Yes to save the document to disk, or click on No to abandon the changes in the document. Click on Cancel to return to the Excel application window.

## File Conversion Wizard

Use the File Conversion Wizard to convert a group of files from an external format (Lotus 1-2-3, QuattroPro, Microsoft Works, dBase, SYLK, DIF, or a previous version of Excel) to the current Excel format.

### To Convert a Batch of Files

1. Choose Tools ➤ Wizard ➤ File Conversion.

2. In the first dialog box, specify the folder where the target files are located. Then pull down the format list, and choose the format in which the files are currently saved. Click on Next to continue.

3. Select the files that you want to convert. Then click on Next.

4. Finally, specify the folder where you want to save the converted files. (The original files will remain unchanged in their own folder.) Click on Finish. The File Conversion Wizard creates a worksheet to report the results of the batch conversion.

Note that you can use the File ➤ Open command to convert files individually. See the "File Formats" entry for details.

## File Formats

You can use the File ➤ Save As command to save files in the formats used by software other than Excel. Likewise, the File ➤ Open command allows you to open files created in other programs and convert those files into Excel workbooks.

### To Save a File in a Selected Format

1. Activate the workbook that you want to save in a new format, and choose File ➤ Save As. The Save As dialog box appears. Optionally, enter a new name into the File name text box and select a path in the Save In box.

2. Click on the down arrow at the right side of the box labeled Save As Type. A scrollable list of available file formats appears.

3. Select the format in which you want to save the file. In the File Name text box, Excel supplies the appropriate extension name for the file. Click on OK to save the file.

The Save As Type list includes the following file formats:

- Microsoft Excel Workbook is the default for Excel 97.

- Template is the format for template files. (See "Templates" for details.)

- Formatted Text, Text, and CSV save the active sheet in delimited text formats.

- Microsoft Excel 5.0/95 Workbook is the format for the previous two versions of Excel.

- Microsoft Excel 97 & 5.0/95 Workbook is a special dual-format file that allows you to share Excel 97 files conveniently with users of the previous versions. (Excel 5.0 and Excel for Windows 95 users should open the files in read-only mode.)

- Microsoft Excel 4.0, 3.0 and 2.1 Worksheet are formats for early versions of Excel; they save the active sheet only.

- Microsoft Excel 4.0 Workbook saves worksheets, charts, and Excel 4 macro sheets in a workbook.
- WKS, WK1, WK3, and WK4 are formats for versions of Lotus 1-2-3. (Excel can also create an associated format file with an extension name of FMT or FM3.)
- WQ1 is the format for QuattroPro for DOS.
- DBF 2, DBF 3, and DBF 4 are formats for the dBase II, III, and IV database-management programs.
- Text and CSV (Macintosh, OS/2, or MS-DOS) are text formats for transferring a file to other operating environments.
- DIF (Data Interchange Format) is a data transfer format that many applications can read and write. (It was introduced with VisiCalc, the first popular spreadsheet program for personal computers.)
- SYLK (Symbolic Link) is another data transfer format.
- Microsoft Excel Add-In is the format for creating new add-in files.

## To Open a File in a Selected Format

1. Choose File ➢ Open. The Open dialog box appears. Optionally, use the Look in box to select the folder of the file you want to open.

2. Click on the down-arrow next to the Files of type box. A drop-down list of readable formats appears.

3. Select the format of the file you want to open. In the File Name text box, Excel enters a pattern for the corresponding extension name or names, and the file list displays only the files that match the pattern.

4. Select a file name, and click on OK to open the file.

# File Searches

The File ➢ Open command helps you find the files you want to work with, even if those files are located deep within the layers of folders and subfolders on a disk. You can look in multiple locations for files that meet a variety of criteria. You can also save a search definition for future use.

## To Find a File

1. Choose File ➢ Open. In the Open dialog box, the default search is for worksheet files with extensions of XLS. If you want to search for some other type of file, pull down the Files Of Type list, and select the file type.

2. To look for a specific file, or for files with similar names, enter an identifier into the File Name box. You can include wildcard characters (* and ?) in this box.

3. To search for files that contain particular text contents, make an entry in the Text Or Property box.

4. To search for files that have been modified within a certain time period, make a selection from the Last modified list. The default selection is Any Time.

5. Pull down the Look In list and select the drive or other location where you want to look for files. You can then navigate through the resulting list of folders and open the folder where your file is located. Double-click on any folder to open it and list its contents. (Notice that you can select Internet Locations (FTP) in the Look In list to find a file at an Internet or intranet location.)

6. If you want to look in all the subfolders of a selected location, click on the Commands And Settings button (the last button on the toolbar at the top of the Open dialog box) and select the Search Subfolders command on the resulting menu list. The search begins immediately, and the resulting file names appear in the list beneath the Look In box.

7. To change the view of the target files, click on one of the four view buttons on the toolbar. The List button shows only the file

names and their icons. The Details button shows the Size, Type, and Modified date for each file. The Properties button displays a box of properties for a selected file; properties may include the title, subject, author, comments, and other information about the file. The Preview button displays a preview box for a selected file; this box shows a graphic view of the actual file contents.

### To Use the Advanced Find Features

1. Choose File ➢ Open.

2. Click on the Advanced button in the Open dialog box. In the Advanced Find dialog box, use the Define More Criteria options to define specific criteria for the file search. For each new criterion, choose a file property, select a condition, and enter a search value. Select And or Or, and then click on Add To List to include this criterion in the search definition.

3. Optionally, click on the Save Search button and type a name to save your search criteria for future use.

4. Click on the Find Now button to start the search. The results of the search are shown in the Open dialog box.

## Filling Ranges

The Edit ➢ Fill commands are designed to fill a range of cells by copying the contents of a single cell located at the beginning or end of the range. (In addition, the Edit ➢ Fill ➢ Across Worksheets command copies the contents of a range across a group of sheets. See "Group Editing" for details.) Alternatively, you can fill all the cells of a range by selecting the range before you begin an entry.

### To Use the Fill Commands to Copy Entries

1. Enter a number, text entry, or formula into the beginning or ending cell of the range

you want to fill. Optionally, apply formats to the entry.

2. Starting from the cell containing the entry, select the row or column range that you want to fill.

3. Choose Edit ➢ Fill. From the Fill submenu, choose Right or Left to fill a row, or Down or Up to fill a column. Excel copies the entry and formats in the first or last cell to all the cells in the range.

Alternatively, the fill handle is often an ideal tool for filling a range of cells. See "AutoFill" for details.

### To Enter Data or Formulas into a Range

1. Select the range into which you want to enter the data or formulas.

2. Type the entry into the formula bar.

3. Press Ctrl+↵ to complete the entry. Excel copies the entry into each cell of the range.

## Filters

Filters allow you to work with selected rows of information in any list, including a list that you have organized as a database. (See the "Database" and "Lists" entries for background information.) Excel gives you two ways to filter a list or database—AutoFilter and Advanced Filter.

### To Filter a List or Database with AutoFilter

1. Activate the worksheet that contains your list or database. Select the entire range or any cell within the range of data.

2. Choose Data ➢ Filter ➢ AutoFilter. In response, Excel displays drop-down arrows in the first row of your database, where the field names are located.

3. Click on the drop-down arrow at the top of any column. The resulting list shows all

the unique data entries in the column, along with several other options. Select an entry. Excel immediately hides all the records that do not match your selection.

4. Repeat step 3 in other columns to apply additional filters to your database. To be displayed in the filtered database, a record must match *all* of the selections that you make in the drop-down lists.

In addition to the unique data entries in a given column, each drop-down list contains three additional options that you can use for special purposes:

- Choose (All) to cancel the filter defined for the current column. (Filters in other columns remain in effect.)

- Choose (Top 10…) to apply criteria based on the values in the cells of the current column. For example, you can display the 10 records with the highest values or 50 cells with the lowest values. You can also select the top or bottom values by percent.

- Choose (Custom…) to apply complex or compound criteria to your database. (See instructions in the next part of this entry.)

## To Apply Custom Criteria to a Filtered Database

1. Select a cell in the database, and choose Data ➢ Filter ➢ AutoFilter. Drop-down arrows appear at the top of the database.

2. Click on the arrow next to any field name and choose the Custom entry. The Custom AutoFilter dialog box appears on the screen. It contains four boxes in which you can develop one or two criteria to apply to the current column. Each criterion consists of a condition and a data item.

3. Click on the arrow next to the first box. Select one of the operators in the resulting list; these include conditions such as Equals, Does Not Equal, Is Greater Than, Is Less Than, and so on.

4. Click on the arrow for the adjacent box. The list contains all the unique data entries in the current column. Select an entry to complete the criterion. (Alternatively, enter a new value into this box, a value that does not necessarily appear in the database column.)

5. Optionally, repeat steps 3 and 4 to develop another criterion in the second row of text boxes. If you do so, select either the And or the Or option button to connect the two criteria. The And option means that a record must match *both* criteria to be selected. The Or option means that a record will be selected if it matches one or both criteria.

6. Click on the OK button to apply the custom criteria you have developed. In response, Excel hides all records that do not match your criteria.

## To Display All the Records in a List or Database

Choose Data ➢ Filter ➢ Show All. In response, Excel redisplays all the hidden records in the database.

## To Remove a Filter from a List Database

Choose Data ➢ Filter ➢ AutoFilter. Excel removes the arrows from the top of the database, and redisplays any hidden records.

## To Use a Criteria Range to Filter a Database

1. Develop a criteria range in the rows above your database, as described in the Database Criteria entry.

2. Select any cell within the database range, and choose Data ➢ Filter ➢ Advanced Filter. In the List range text box of the Advanced Filter dialog box, Excel automatically enters the range of your database.

**3.** Activate the Criteria range text box, and enter a reference to the criteria range you have developed on the worksheet. (Alternatively, use the mouse to point to the range.)

**4.** Make sure that the option labeled Filter The List, In-Place is selected in the Action group, and click on OK. Excel filters the database in place, temporarily hiding all records that do not match the criteria you have expressed in the criteria range.

## To Copy Selected Records to a New Location

**1.** In a worksheet that contains a database and a criteria range, select a cell in the database range. Then choose Data ➤ Filter ➤ Advanced Filter.

**2.** In the Action group of the Advanced Filter dialog box, click on the option labeled Copy To Another Location.

**3.** Make sure that the database range is entered correctly into the List range box. Enter the criteria range into the Criteria range box.

**4.** Activate the Copy To box, and enter a reference to the upper-left corner of the range (on the current sheet) where you want to copy the records that match your criteria. Alternatively, point to the location with the mouse.

**5.** Click on OK. Excel copies the matching records to the location you have specified.

# Financial Functions

Excel provides a library of financial functions in several categories. Many of these are supplied as part of the Analysis ToolPak add-in. Once this add-in is installed and enabled, you can enter these functions directly into worksheets or select them from the Paste Function dialog box. (See the "Add-Ins" and "Functions" entries for details.) The financial function category includes the following groups of tools:

- Conversion functions (DOLLARDE, DOLLARFR).

- Coupon functions (COUPDAYBS, COUPDAYS, COUPDAYSNC, COUPNCD, COUPNUM, COUPPCD).

- Depreciation functions (AMORDEGRC, AMORLINC, DB, DDB, SLN, SYD, VDB).

- Internal rate of return functions (IRR, MIRR, XIRR).

- Loan payment calculation functions (CUMIPMT, CUMPRINC, EFFECT, IPMT, NOMINAL, NPER, PMT, PPMT, RATE).

- Net present value, present value, and future value functions (FV, FVSCHEDULE, NPV, PV, XNPV).

- Security functions for calculating interest, discount rate, duration, price, yield, and amount received at maturity (ACCRINT, ACCRINTM, DISC, DURATION, INTRATE, MDURATION, ODDFPRICE, ODDFYIELD, ODDLPRICE, ODDLYIELD, PRICE, PRICEDISC, PRICEMAT, RECEIVED, YIELD, YIELDDISC, YIELDMAT).

- Treasury bill functions (TBILLEQ, TBILLPRICE, TBILLYIELD).

# Finding Data

The Edit ➤ Find command allows you to search for text or numeric data on a sheet. The Find command operates on the active sheet, not through all the sheets of a workbook. (Excel also has a find-and-replace operation; see the "Replacing Data" entry for details.)

## To Search for Information

**1.** Activate the sheet in which you want to perform the search, and choose Edit ➤ Find. Alternatively, press Shift+F5 or Ctrl+F to open the Find dialog box.

**2.** In the Find what box, enter the information that you want to search for. You can use wildcard characters in the search text: ? stands for a single character, and * stands for a string of characters.

3. In the Search box, select By Rows to search from the top to the bottom of the sheet, or By Columns to search from left to right.

4. In the Look In box, select the kind of cell contents that you want to search through: Formulas, Values, or Comments.

5. Check the Match Case option if you want Excel to search for the text in the exact uppercase and lowercase combinations you entered into the Find What box.

6. Check the Find Entire Cells Only option if the text you have entered in the Find What box represents an entire cell entry. Leave this option unchecked if you want to search for the text as a portion of a cell entry.

7. Click on the Find Next button to begin the search.

## Fonts

You can display and print worksheet data in any of the fonts available in your installation of Windows. You can also select a point size and any combination of styles—including boldface, italics, underlining, and others. In addition, Excel allows you to apply different formats to individual characters within a text entry in a cell.

### To Change the Font in a Cell or Range

1. Select the target data, choose Format ➤ Cells, and click on the Font tab. The resulting dialog box has Font, Font Style, Size, Underline, Color, and Effects options.

2. Select a font name from the Font box and a numeric setting from the Size box.

3. Select any of the Font style options: Regular, Italic, Bold, or Bold Italic. Optionally, select an Underline option and/or a Color option. Click on any combination of check boxes in the Effects group.

4. Click on OK to apply the font to the current selection of cells.

A variety of shortcuts are available. Press Ctrl+B, Ctrl+I, or Ctrl+U to apply boldface, italics, or underlining to the current selection. Alternatively, select the font, point size, and style properties from the Formatting toolbar.

### To Apply Fonts and Styles to Characters in an Entry

1. Double-click on the cell that contains the text entry. A flashing insertion bar appears in the entry.

2. Use the mouse or the keyboard to highlight the characters whose font or style you want to change.

3. Click on buttons in the Formatting toolbar to make changes in the selected text—for example, click on the Bold, Italic, or Underline buttons, or make a selection from the Font list. Alternatively, choose Format ➤ Cells and select options from the Font tab.

4. Press ↵ to confirm the changes.

## Formatting Worksheet Cells

The format properties of a cell or range in a worksheet include the numeric display format, the alignment of data within the cell, the font and style selections, the borders, patterns, and the optional cell protection scheme. In addition, Excel's *conditional formatting* feature allows you to apply formats to a cell if the contents meet certain conditions that you specify.

### To Change the Format in a Range of Cells

Select the range, choose Format ➤ Cells, and click on one of the tabs along the top of the Format Cells dialog box:

• **Number**: Changes the display format of numeric values in the range. (See "Number Formats" and "Custom Number Formats" for details.)

- **Alignment**: Determines the horizontal, vertical, and diagonal alignment of entries in their cells. (See "Alignment.")
- **Font**: Provides fonts, sizes, styles, and display colors for the data in a range. (See "Fonts.")
- **Border**: Displays borders in several styles along selected sides of cells in a range. (See "Borders.")
- **Patterns**: Changes the background pattern and color of a range of cells. (See the "Patterns" and "Colors" entries.)
- **Protection**: Creates a protection scheme of locked cells and/or hidden formulas. (See "Protecting Cells in a Worksheet.")

## To Apply Conditional Formatting

1. Select the target cell or range and choose Format ➤ Conditional Formatting.

2. The first list box in the Conditional Formatting dialog box offers two types of conditions, described as Cell Value Is and Formula Is. Under the default Cell Value Is option, you define a condition by choosing an operator (between, equal to, greater than, less than, etc.) and entering a value or range of values. Alternatively, choose the Formula Is condition and enter a formula that evaluates to True or False for the cell contents.

3. Click on the Format button. In the resulting Format Cells dialog box, select any combination of available options in the Font, Border, and Patterns tabs. Then click on OK.

4. Optionally, click on the Add button to define another conditional format. Repeat steps 2 and 3 to complete the condition and the corresponding format. You can define as many as three conditional formats for a given cell or range of cells.

5. Click on OK. To test the conditional formatting you've defined, try entering different values into the range, and note the formats that Excel applies in response.

## Formulas

A *formula* in Excel is an entry that performs a calculation or other operation on one or more operands. A formula begins with an equal sign (=) and may include values, references, names, functions, and operations. In a worksheet, the formula's result is displayed in the cell where you enter the formula; the formula itself appears in the formula bar when you select the cell. In a *natural language formula*, the labels in a sheet stand for specific data.

### To Enter a Formula into a Cell

1. Type = to begin the formula.

2. Enter an operand. To enter a reference as the operand, type the reference directly from the keyboard, or point to the cell or range with the mouse or the keyboard. Alternatively, enter a name you have defined to represent a range, or choose Insert ➤ Name ➤ Paste and select a name from the Paste Name list.

3. Optionally, enter an arithmetic operator (+, –, *, /, ^, or %), a comparison operator (<, >, <=, >=, <>, or =), or a text operator (&).

4. Optionally, enter a function by typing the function name and arguments directly from the keyboard, or by clicking on the Paste Function button.

5. Repeat any combination of steps 2, 3, and 4 to complete the formula, and then press ↵.

In a formula that you intend to copy to other cells, it's important to enter cell references appropriately in *relative*, *absolute*, or *mixed* formats. To step through the available reference formats press F4 repeatedly while the cursor is positioned next to a reference in the formula bar. (See "Copying Formulas" for more information.)

To replace a formula with its current value while the formula bar is active, press F9.

In a natural language formula, you can use headings and labels from your worksheet to refer to corresponding data values. (The headings and labels need not be defined as names on the sheet.) This feature may require some testing and verification to make sure you've created the formula you want.

You can enter formulas into each cell of a selected range in a single entry operation. See "Array Formulas" and "Filling Ranges" for details.

## Functions

A function performs a predefined calculation or operation in Excel. Each function has a name and may require one or more arguments. Excel has many built-in functions for specific categories of applications (such as statistics, engineering, date and time operations, and so on). The Paste Function dialog box helps you enter functions and their arguments correctly into a worksheet.

### To Enter a Function

1. Select the cell where you want to enter the function, and click on the Paste Function button on the Standard toolbar (or choose Insert ➤ Function or press Shift+F3). The resulting Paste Function dialog box has a list of function categories and a Function name box that lists all the functions in a selected category.

2. Select a function category. Then, from the Function Name list, select the function that you want to enter into the active cell. At the bottom of the dialog box you can read a brief description of the function you have selected.

3. Click on OK. Excel displays a new dialog box designed to guide you in the process of entering the arguments for the function you've selected. You'll see text boxes for each of the required arguments. As you select each argument text box, the dialog box supplies a brief description of the information required in the argument. Type a value or an expression for each required argument; the resulting value is displayed just to the right of the text box.

4. When you complete all the required arguments, the resulting value of the function is displayed on the bottom line of the dialog box. Click on OK to enter the function and arguments into the current cell.

## Goal Seek

The Tools ➤ Goal Seek command adjusts the value of an existing entry in order to achieve a specific result from a target formula.

### To Change the Result of a Formula

1. Select the cell containing the formula whose result you want to change, and choose Tools ➤ Goal Seek. The Goal Seek dialog box has three text boxes labeled Set Cell, To Value, and By Changing Cell. The Set Cell box shows a reference to the cell containing the formula.

2. In the To Value text box, enter the end result that you want to produce from the selected formula.

3. In the By changing cell box, enter a reference to a cell that the formula depends on. The cell must contain a numeric entry.

4. Click on OK. The Goal Seek Status dialog box appears on the screen, and Excel finds the target solution.

5. Click on OK to accept the solution. Excel records the new data value in the worksheet.

## Graphic Objects

Using the buttons on the Drawing toolbar, you can add a variety of two- or three-dimensional graphic objects to a worksheet. These objects include lines, arrows, geometric shapes, and a great variety of drawings known as AutoShapes. You can also use the WordArt button to create banners and other text graphics. All of these objects can be moved, resized, and formatted.

## To Add a Graphic Object to a Worksheet

1. If the Drawing toolbar is not currently displayed, choose View ➤ Toolbars ➤ Drawing.

2. Activate the sheet on which you want to display graphic objects.

3. Click on the button representing the object you want to add. To use the AutoShape feature, click on the AutoShape button, select a category of shapes from the resulting menu, and then choose the shape that you want to draw.

4. Drag the mouse over the worksheet area where you want the object to be displayed. When you release the mouse button, Excel displays this object with selection handles around it.

5. To display a label inside the shape, simply enter the text while the shape is selected.

6. To change the colors and properties of the shape, make selections from the Fill Color, Line Color, Font Color, and Line Style lists, represented by buttons on the Drawing toolbar.

7. Click on elsewhere on the worksheet or press Escape to deselect the object.

Click on a graphic object to reselect it; the selection handles reappear around the object. Move a selected object by dragging it with the mouse. Change its size and shape by dragging individual selection handles. To copy a selected object, choose Edit ➤ Copy (or press Ctrl+C), then select a location for the copy and choose Edit ➤ Paste (or press Ctrl+V). To delete an object, select it and press the Delete key.

## To Select Multiple Graphic Objects

Click on the border of one object to select it, and then hold down the Shift key while you click on the borders of other objects. By selecting multiple objects, you can change the patterns or properties of all the objects at once.

# Gridlines

Gridlines are the lines that delineate rows, columns, and cells on a sheet. The Tools ➤ Options command gives you control over the appearance and color of gridlines.

## To Hide or Change the Appearance of Gridlines

1. Choose Tools ➤ Options. In the Options dialog box, click on the View tab.

2. To hide gridlines on the current sheet, remove the check from the Gridlines check box. To display the gridlines, restore the check in the Gridlines check box.

3. To display gridlines in a new color, click on the button at the right side of the Color box and choose a color from the resulting palette.

4. Click on OK to confirm your new options.

## To Include Gridlines on a Printed Sheet

1. Choose File ➤ Page Setup. In the Page Setup dialog box, click on the Sheet tab.

2. Click on the Gridlines option, placing a check in the corresponding check box.

3. Click on OK.

4. Choose File ➤ Print (or click on the Print button on the Standard toolbar) to print the sheet.

# Group Editing

Group editing allows you to enter and format data on multiple sheets in a workbook at the same time.

## To Edit Sheets in a Group

1. Open the workbook in which you want to perform group editing. Click on the tab of the worksheet from which you want to control the editing.

2. Hold down the Ctrl key and click on the tabs for the other worksheets that you want to include in the group. (To select several worksheets in a row, hold down Shift—without the Ctrl key—and click on the last worksheet in the group.) The notation [Group] appears in the title bar, after the name of the workbook.

3. On the active sheet, perform the operations that you want to complete on all the documents of the group: you can enter new data, edit existing data, format the worksheet, print the worksheet, and so on. During group editing, Excel treats each document in the group identically.

4. To end group editing, click on the tab for any sheet other than the active one.

## To Copy Data to Worksheets in a Group

1. Activate the sheet that contains the data you want to copy to other worksheets.

2. Hold down the Ctrl key and click on the tabs of other worksheets that you want to include in the group.

3. On the active worksheet, select the range of data that you want to copy to the other worksheets in the group.

4. Choose Edit ➢ Fill ➢ Across Worksheets. In the Fill Across Worksheets dialog box, select one of the three option buttons—All to copy data and formats, Contents to copy data alone, or Formats to copy formats alone.

5. Click on OK. Excel copies the selection to the other worksheets in the group.

# Headers and Footers

A *header* is a block of text that appears at the top of every page in a printed document. A *footer* is text that appears at the bottom of every page. If you're planning to print many pages of workbook data, headers and footers can provide the page numbers, the date and time, the source document, the author's name, and other relevant information.

## Creating Headers and Footers

1. Activate the sheet where you want to create the header or footer. (To create the same header or footer for several sheets, select a group of sheets in the active workbook; see "Group Editing" for details.) Choose File ➢ Page Setup, and click on the Header/Footer tab.

2. The Header and Footer lists provide a selection of built-in header and footer suggestions, combining information such as the sheet name, the workbook name, the page number, the date, and the user's name. To use one of these suggestions, click on the arrow next to the Header or Footer box and select an item from the resulting list. The sample box shows what the header or footer will look like. Notice that the built-in entries are divided by commas for the left, center, and right sections of the header or footer.

3. To create a custom header or footer, click on the Custom Header or Custom Footer button. The resulting dialog box divides the header or footer into three side-by-side sections labeled Left Section, Center Section, and Right Section.

4. Enter text into any or all of the three text boxes. To change the font or style, select the text and click on the Font button (labeled A) on the Header or Footer dialog

box. Make selections on the resulting Font dialog box, and click on OK.

5. To include special information in a text box, click on the Page Number button, the Total Pages button, the Date button, the Time button, the File Name button, or the Sheet Name button. In response, Excel enters the appropriate code into the current section box.

6. Click on OK to record your entries for the header or footer, and then click on OK on the Page Setup dialog box.

You can enter multiple lines into any of the sections in the Header or the Footer dialog box. To start a new line, simply press ↵. When you save a worksheet, the header and footer text is saved in the file, along with other settings in the Page Setup dialog box. To edit existing headers or footers, activate the target sheet or sheets, choose File ➤ Page Setup, and click on the Header/Footer tab.

# Help

Excel 97 provides help in a variety of forms, including the Help Topics window; the amusing and useful Office Assistant; the What's This? feature, for identifying objects on the desktop; and links to several support pages on the World Wide Web.

## To Use the Help Topics Window

1. Choose Help ➤ Contents and Index.

2. Click on the Contents tab for information organized by general and introductory categories. Open a category by double-clicking on the corresponding book icon. Most categories are further organized into subcategories, represented by additional book icons; double-click on the icon for the category you want to open. Individual help topics are represented by page icons with question marks. Double-click on a page icon to open a topic.

3. Click on the Index tab to search for information by specific entries. Type the topic you want to look for; then select an entry in the index list and click on Display. If a Topics Found dialog box appears, select a topic and click on Display to open the help topic.

4. Click on the Find tab for more detailed word searches within all help topics. The first time you click on the Find tab, be prepared to wait while Excel prepares a database for this help feature. Subsequently you can use this tab to search for all the help topics that contain a word that you enter.

## To Use the Office Assistant

1. Choose Help ➤ Microsoft Excel Help, or click on the Office Assistant button on the Standard toolbar. An animated Office Assistant appears on the desktop, with a box of options for you to choose from. (The default Office Assistant, named Clippit, is an animated paper clip character; you can choose a different Assistant if you wish. See the next topic in this section for details.)

2. If necessary, drag the Office Assistant to a convenient location on the desktop.

3. Under the question "What would you like to do?" enter a brief description of the activity or topic you want help with. Then click on Search.

4. Select a topic from the list that the Office Assistant displays in response to your request. Alternatively, enter a new request and click on Search again.

5. To close the Office Assistant's help box, click on the Close button. To remove the assistant itself from the screen, click on the × box at the upper-right corner of the assistant box.

## To Choose a New Office Assistant

1. Open the current Office Assistant.

2. Click on the Assistant box with the right mouse button, and select the Choose Assistant command.

3. In the Gallery tab of the Office Assistant dialog box, click on the Next and Back buttons to preview all the available Office Assistant characters. These include Clippit, the Dot, the Genius, the Hoverbot, the Office logo, Mother Nature, the Power Pup, Scribble the cat, and Will (as in Shakespeare).

4. Select the Assistant you like and click on OK. If your Microsoft Office CD is not currently in the CD-ROM drive, you'll be prompted to insert it.

The new Office Assistant character appears next time you use this help feature.

## To Use the "What's This?" Help Feature

In any dialog box, click on the question mark button located at the right side of the title bar. (Alternatively, choose Help ➢ What's This? for general help about the Excel desktop.) The mouse pointer becomes an arrow with a bold-faced question mark. Click on any control or object to open a help box that describes the item. After you've read the description, click elsewhere to close the box.

## To Connect to the Internet for Online Help

Choose Help ➢ Microsoft On The Web and then select any of the topics listed in the resulting menu. In response, Excel activates your Web browser and connects to the page you've requested. (To use this feature, your system needs a modem, a Web browser, and a host networking connection such as the Microsoft Network.)

# Hiding

You can hide workbooks, worksheets, rows, and columns so that you can focus more easily on other parts of your work.

## To Hide or Display an Open Workbook

Activate the workbook that you want to hide, and choose Window ➢ Hide. To display the workbook again, choose Window ➢ Unhide, select the name of the workbook you want to unhide, and click on OK.

## To Hide a Worksheet

Click on the tab of the sheet you want to hide, and choose Format ➢ Sheet ➢ Hide. To redisplay a hidden sheet, choose Format ➢ Sheet ➢ Unhide. Choose the sheet you want to redisplay, and click on OK.

## To Hide Rows or Columns

Select the columns or rows that you want to hide, and choose Format ➢ Column ➢ Hide or Format ➢ Row ➢ Hide. To redisplay the columns or rows, choose Format ➢ Column ➢ Unhide or Format ➢ Row ➢ Unhide.

# Hyperlinks

A *hyperlink* is a graphic or text item that a user can click on in order to jump to a new location. The destination of the hyperlink can be a sheet in the current workbook, a file stored on disk, a shared network file, or a page on the Web. Using the Insert ➢ Hyperlink command, you can create a hyperlink on any Excel worksheet. If you want the hyperlink to be represented by a graphic object, draw the object first and then select it before choosing the Hyperlink command. (See the "Graphic Objects" entry for details.)

## To Create a Hyperlink

1. Select the cell or graphic where you want to insert the hyperlink, and choose Insert ➢ Hyperlink.

2. If a message box prompts you to save the current file before creating a hyperlink, click on the Yes button. Enter a name for the file in the Save As dialog box, and click on Save.

**3.** The Insert Hyperlink dialog box appears next. In the text box labeled Link To File Or URL, enter a file name or an Internet address. (Click on the Browse button if you want to select the destination by searching through folders.) If you leave this text box blank, the default destination is a location in the current workbook.

**4.** In the text box labeled Named Location In File, enter a specific location in the destination file or address. (Click on the Browse button to select from a list of possible locations.)

**5.** Click on OK.

If the hyperlink is attached to a graphic, you can now deselect the graphic by clicking elsewhere on your sheet. If your hyperlink is at a cell location, Excel displays the link as an underlined text reference to the destination.

## To Jump to a Hyperlink Destination

Move the mouse pointer over the text or graphic that represents the hyperlink. The mouse pointer becomes a hand with an upward-pointing index finger. Click on the left mouse button to jump to the linked destination. At the destination, the Web toolbar appears above the file or page. To return to the location of the hyperlink, click on the Back button at the beginning of the Web toolbar.

## To Change the Destination of a Hyperlink

**1.** Click on the hyperlink (text or graphic) with the right mouse button.

**2.** On the resulting shortcut menu, choose Hyperlink ➢ Edit Hyperlink.

**3.** In the Edit Hyperlink dialog box, change the name of the destination in the text box labeled Link To File Or URL.

**4.** Change the entry in the text box labeled Named Location In File.

**5.** Click on OK to confirm the change.

To delete a hyperlink from a cell or graphic, click on the Remove Link button on the Edit Hyperlink dialog box.

## To Change the Appearance of Hyperlink Text

**1.** Activate a workbook containing one or more hyperlinks. The changes you make in these steps apply to all text hyperlinks in the current workbook.

**2.** Choose Format ➢ Style.

**3.** Pull down the Style Name list. To change the appearance of hyperlink text before a jump, choose Hyperlink. To change the appearance of the text after a jump has taken place, choose Followed Hyperlink.

**4.** Click on the Modify button. In the resulting dialog box, make any combination of formatting changes in the available tabs (Number, Alignment, Font, Border, Patterns, Protection.) Then click on OK.

**5.** Back on the Style dialog box, check any style categories that you want included in the hyperlink style. Then click on OK.

# Information Functions

The information functions are designed to identify cell properties and data types in a worksheet. In addition, one function, INFO, provides information about the current operating system and memory environment. You can enter these functions directly from the keyboard, or you can use the Paste Function dialog box. (See the "Functions" entry for details.) The information functions include the following:

- Cell information function (CELL).

- Data-type functions, which identify the type of entry in a cell (ISBLANK, ISEVEN, ISLOGICAL, ISNONTEXT, ISNUMBER, ISODD, ISREF, ISTEXT, TYPE).

- Error functions (ERROR.TYPE, ISERR, ISERROR, ISNA, NA).

- Numeric conversion function (N).

- Operating system function (INFO).

Functions whose names begin with IS all return logical values of either TRUE or FALSE.

# Inserting

You can use the Rows, Columns, or Cells commands from the Insert menu to make insertions into a sheet. Alternatively, you can use a special dragging technique with the mouse to achieve the same effects. Either way, Excel shifts other cells down or to the right to make room for the insertion.

## To Insert Entire Rows or Columns

1. Select a cell, a range of cells, or a range of rows or columns at the position where you want to perform the insert operation. (To select a single row or column, click on the row or column heading. To select more than one row or column, drag the mouse along the appropriate row or column headings.)

2. Choose Insert ➤ Rows or Insert ➤ Columns.

Alternatively, use one of the following shortcuts:

- Select the rows or columns and press Ctrl+Shift++ (plus sign).

- Point to the selected rows or columns, and click on the right mouse button to view the shortcut menu; then choose Insert.

## To Insert a Range of Cells

1. Select the range at the position where you want to insert cells.

2. Choose Insert ➤ Cells.

3. On the Insert dialog box, select Shift Cells Right or Shift Cells Down, depending on how you want Excel to make room for the new blank cells.

4. Click on OK.

## To Insert Rows, Columns, or Cells by Dragging

1. Select the cell, range, row, or column located above or to the left of the position where you want to perform the insert operation.

2. Hold down the Shift key and drag the selection's fill handle down or to the right. The size of the insertion depends on how far you drag the fill handle.

The fill handle for a cell or a range selection is located at the lower-right corner of the selection. By contrast, the fill handle for a selection of rows is at the lower-left corner, and for a selection of columns, at the upper-right corner of the selection.

# Iteration

Iteration is the process of resolving a circular reference by recalculating a worksheet multiple times. A formula that depends directly or indirectly on its own result contains a circular reference. In its default calculation mode, Excel cannot resolve circular references. To find a result from a circular reference, you must activate the Iteration option.

## To Resolve a Circular Reference

1. Choose Tools ➤ Options. In the Options dialog box, click on the Calculation tab.

2. Click on the Iteration option. A check mark appears in the corresponding check box.

3. Optionally, enter new values for the maximum number of iterations and for the maximum change.

4. Click on OK.

On a sheet that contains a circular reference, Excel begins the iterative calculation in an attempt to find a solution. The iterations continue until one of the following conditions is met:

- The number of iterations reaches the value entered in the Maximum iterations box.
- The difference in the result of the circular formula from one iteration to the next is less than the Maximum change value.

If the Iteration option is turned off, Excel displays an error message in response to a circular formula. The Circular Reference toolbar contains buttons that will help you trace the structure of a circular reference.

# Links and 3-D References

You can use link formulas to share and automatically update data between two worksheets. Several kinds of links are possible in Excel:

- You can create a link between worksheets stored in different workbooks. In this case, the link is created by an *external reference* that identifies the source workbook and the location of the information within the workbook.
- You can also link worksheets that are stored within the same workbook. In this case, a reference identifies the source worksheet and range.
- You can use *3-D references* to consolidate data from multiple sheets within a workbook. This kind of link is a convenient way to summarize large amounts of data stored in related sheets.

To create a link, either enter a reference directly from the keyboard or use the mouse to point to the source location. Or, if you want Excel to create the link formula for you, click on the

Paste Link button in the Edit ➢ Paste Special command.

## To Create a Link between Two Workbooks

1. Open the source and destination workbooks and activate the target sheets. To view both workbooks at the same time, choose Window ➢ Arrange, select the Tiled option, and click on OK.

2. In the source workbook, select the data that will become the object of the link, and choose Edit ➢ Copy.

3. Activate the target sheet in the destination workbook and select the cell where you want to create the link.

4. Choose Edit ➢ Paste Special. In the Paste Special dialog box, click on the Paste Link button. Excel enters an external reference into the destination worksheet.

To create a link between two sheets in the same workbook, follow similar steps: select the source data on one sheet, and choose Edit ➢ Copy. Then activate the destination sheet, choose Edit ➢ Paste Special, and click on the Paste Link button.

## Creating a 3-D Formula

1. Within a workbook, develop two or more adjacent worksheets containing related data. These worksheets will be the source of the data in the 3-D formula; they must be organized identically, with data entered into the same range on each sheet.

2. Activate the worksheet in which you want to summarize the data in the source worksheets. Select the cell in which you'll enter the 3-D formula.

3. Type an equal sign (=) and any other elements you want to include at the beginning of the formula. For example, enter the name of a function such as SUM, AVERAGE, MIN, or MAX and then enter the opening parenthesis for the function. (In

this case, the 3-D reference will become the argument of the function.)

4. Click on the tab of the first source worksheet, and then hold down Shift and click on the tab of the last worksheet in the group. In the formula bar, Excel enters a sheet range such as Sheet2:Sheet4!.

5. On the first source worksheet, click on the cell or range containing the data you want the 3-D formula to operate on. After the exclamation point in the formula bar, Excel enters a reference to the cell or range that you've selected.

6. Complete the formula (for example, by entering the closing parenthesis to complete a function) and press ↵ to enter the formula into the cell of the destination worksheet. Your 3-D formula is complete. You can copy this formula to other locations in the destination worksheet.

## Lists

A list is a table of data stored in a worksheet. The top row of a list contains labels identifying the contents of each column. Subsequent rows in the column contain data, all arranged in the same way. A list can also be thought of as a database table. Excel provides a variety of operations that you can perform on the data:

- You can open a special *data form* dialog box designed to simplify several basic database operations. (See the "Data Form" entry for more information.)

- You can use a *filter* to isolate rows of data that match specific criteria. (See the "Database Criteria" and "Filters" entries.)

- You can quickly rearrange the rows in a list. (See "Sorting" for details.)

- You can employ a special set of worksheet tools known as *database functions* to calculate statistical values on records that match certain criteria. (See "Database Functions" for a list of the tools available in this category.)

As you type data into a column of a list or database, the Pick From List command and the AutoComplete feature are convenient shortcuts for making duplicate text entries. For example, suppose you are entering data into a column named Department in a Personnel database. Although you may be entering records for dozens or hundreds of employees, they all belong to a limited number of departments. Once the column contains at least one entry for each department, you can begin using Pick From List or AutoComplete to make subsequent entries in the column.

### To Use the Pick From List Feature

1. Begin developing a list by entering a sequence of complete records.

2. For a new entry in a text column, click on the next blank cell with the right mouse button, and choose Pick From List. Excel displays a list of all the unique entries you've made in the column so far.

3. Click on one of the entries in the list. Your selection is entered into the current cell.

### To Use the AutoComplete Feature

Type the first letter or letters of the text item you want to enter. If there is already a list item that matches those letters, Excel copies the entire matching text entry. To accept this copy, press ↵.

## Logical Functions

Using Excel's six logical functions, you can introduce various decision-making formulas into a worksheet. Several of these functions take logical arguments—that is, expressions that result in values of TRUE or FALSE. All logical functions except IF return logical results. You can use the Paste Function dialog box to enter a logical function into a cell, or you can type the function directly from the keyboard.

(See the "Functions" entry for details.) The logical functions include the following:

- The decision function (IF).
- The functions that represent logical operations (AND, OR, and NOT).
- Functions that return logical values (TRUE and FALSE).

## Lookup and Reference Functions

Excel's lookup functions provide a variety of techniques for reading individual data values from lookup tables. The reference functions return range references from specific arguments, or, conversely, provide information about ranges. You can enter one of these functions directly from the keyboard, or you can make use of the Paste Function dialog box. (See the "Functions" entry for details.) The lookup and reference functions can be grouped into the following categories:

- Lookup functions that read a value from a worksheet table, a list, or an array (CHOOSE, HLOOKUP, INDEX, LOOKUP, MATCH, VLOOKUP).
- Functions that return information about a reference or an array (AREAS, COLUMN, COLUMNS, ROW, ROWS).
- Functions that return a reference or an array (ADDRESS, INDIRECT, OFFSET, TRANSPOSE).
- A function that creates a shortcut to a link (HYPERLINK).

## Lookup Wizard

The Lookup Wizard is designed to help you develop complex lookup formulas, for finding data from the intersection of a row and a column in a list or table. The resulting formula employs a combination of Excel's lookup functions. (See the "Lookup and Reference Functions" entry.) If the Lookup Wizard is not

available, it can be installed as an add-in. (See the "Add-Ins" entry for details.)

### To Use the Lookup Wizard

1. Develop a lookup table containing data items to be retrieved from the intersections of rows and columns. The rows and columns should begin with labels or values that serve as references in the lookup process.

2. Select the range of the lookup table, and choose Tools ➤ Wizard ➤ Lookup.

3. The first dialog box of the Lookup Wizard shows a range reference for the lookup table. Confirm that this is correct, and click on the Next button.

4. The next dialog box contains two pull-down lists from which you can choose the column label and the row label corresponding to the value you want to find. Make a selection from each list, and click on Next.

5. The next step is to decide how you want the Lookup Wizard to organize its output. You can copy the lookup formula alone to a cell on your worksheet, or you can copy the target column and row labels (the "parameters") in addition to the formula. If you copy the parameters, you'll be able to change them directly on your worksheet and immediately see the change in the result of the lookup formula. Select one of the two options, then click on Next.

6. Finally, the Lookup Wizard next asks you to indicate cell locations for the parameters and/or the lookup formula. Enter a reference or point to a cell for each item requested, and then click on Finish. The Wizard copies the lookup formula to your sheet.

## Mapping

The Insert ➤ Map command creates maps depicting geographically oriented data. As the basis for a map, you begin by developing a list of place names (states or countries) and a corresponding collection of numeric data. For example, you might use a map to compare population levels, economic data, natural resources, or any other numeric data organized by geographic regions.

## To Create a Map from Geographical Data

1. Develop a table of geographical data on a worksheet. Then select the entire range of the table.

2. Click on the Map button on the Standard toolbar, or choose Insert ➢ Map.

3. Hold down the left mouse button and drag the mouse through the worksheet area where you want to display the map.

4. Release the mouse button. If a dialog box named Multiple Maps Available appears, select the map that you want to use and click on OK.

In the resulting map, the states or countries represented in your data table are color coded according to the range of their corresponding numeric data. A key to the color coding appears at the lower-right corner of the map. While the map is selected, you can use commands from the Map menu or buttons on the Map toolbar to make changes in the content and appearance of your map.

## Mathematical Functions

Excel's library of mathematical functions includes several categories of tools, including trigonometric, logarithmic, exponential, integer and rounding, random-number, summation, matrix, and calculation functions. To enter one of these functions, you can choose Insert ➢ Function and select the Math & Trig category in the Paste Function dialog box. Then select a function from the resulting list. Here is a list of the mathematical functions available:

- Absolute value and sign (ABS, SIGN)
- Algebraic (MULTINOMIAL)
- Common divisor and multiple (GCD, LCM)
- Counting and combinations (COUNT-BLANK, COUNTIF, COMBIN, SUBTOTAL)
- Factorial (FACT)
- Integer and rounding (CEILING, EVEN, FLOOR, INT, MROUND, ODD, ROUND, ROUNDDOWN, ROUNDUP, TRUNC)
- Inverse trigonometric (ACOS, ACOSH, ASIN, ASINH, ATAN, ATAN2, ATANH)
- Logarithmic, exponential, and powers (EXP, LN, LOG, LOG10, POWER)
- Matrix (MDETERM, MINVERSE, MMULT)
- Products, quotients, and remainders (MOD, PRODUCT, QUOTIENT)
- Random number (RAND, RANDBETWEEN)
- Arabic numeral to Roman numeral conversion (ROMAN)
- Square roots (SQRT, SQRTPI)
- Summation (SERIESSUM, SUM, SUMIF, SUMPRODUCT, SUMSQ, SUMX2MY2, SUMX2PY2, SUMXMY2)
- Trigonometric and degree/radian conversion (COS, COSH, DEGREES, PI, RADIANS, SIN, SINH, TAN, TANH)

## Moving Data

You can move data from one range of worksheet cells to another either with the familiar Cut and Paste commands or by dragging the range with the mouse.

### To Move Data Using Cut and Paste

1. Select the range of data you want to move.

2. Choose Edit ➢ Cut. A moving border appears around the selection.

3. Select the upper-left corner of the location where you want to move the data.

4. Choose Edit ➤ Paste.

## To Move a Range by Dragging

1. Select the range that you want to move.

2. Position the mouse pointer along the border of the selection. The pointer becomes an arrow.

3. Drag the selection to its new position in the worksheet. While you drag, an empty frame represents the selection that you are moving, and a small box shows the new destination range reference.

4. Release the mouse button. The entire selection moves to its new location.

# Names

A *name* is an identifier that represents a cell or a range. You can define names to represent data in formulas; this results in formulas that are easier to read, understand, and maintain. To define a name, use either the Insert ➤ Name ➤ Define command, or the Name Box, a tool located just to the left of the formula bar.

Excel 97 also allows the use of worksheet labels in formulas, even if those labels have not been defined as names. In this context, a label might be any text heading that you've entered at the top of a column or the beginning of a row to describe the data that follows. (See the "Formulas" entry for more information.) Because of this new feature, defining names for cells and ranges on a worksheet is sometimes optional. But names still prove useful for a variety of purposes:

- Identifying a cell or range that has no corresponding label entry.

- Clarifying ambiguities when a label entry doesn't precisely represent a target cell or range that you want to include in a formula.

- Developing a list of identifiers in the Name Box at the left side of the Formula bar. This box is a convenient tool for quickly selecting cells or ranges that are represented by names.

- Adding to the cell and range locations that are accessible from the Edit ➤ Go To command.

## To Define a Name

1. Select the cell or range to which you want to assign a name.

2. Choose Insert ➤ Name ➤ Define. The Define Name dialog box appears on the screen.

3. Enter a name into the Names in workbook box, and click on OK.

A name begins with a letter or an underscore character, and may contain a combination of letters, digits, backslashes, underscores, question marks, and periods. Spaces are not allowed. In the Refers To box of the Define Name dialog box, you can enter any cell or range reference, beginning with an equal sign (=). The default entry is a reference to the selected cell or range.

You can also enter a numeric or text value into the Refers to box. Doing so creates a "constant"—that is, a name that refers to a specific value rather than a cell or range. Another option is to type a formula into the Refers To box, starting with an equal sign (=); in this case, the defined name becomes a shorthand tool for entering the complete formula into a cell.

## To Define a Name in the Name Box

1. Select the cell or range to which you want to assign a name.

2. Click on inside the name box, located at the left side of the formula bar.

3. Enter a name for the selected range, and press ↵.

## To Create Names from Text Entries

1. Select a range that includes both the text entries that you want to assign as names, and the cells, rows, or columns that the names will represent. The text entries can appear on the top row, bottom row, first column, or last column of the range selection.

2. Choose Insert ➢ Name ➢ Create.

3. In the Create Names dialog box, select any combination of the four check box options: Top Row, Left Column, Bottom Row, and Right Column. Then click on OK. Excel assigns names from the text in the indicated rows and columns to the corresponding adjacent cells in the range.

## To Go to a Named Cell or Range

Choose Edit ➢ Go To, select a name from the list of defined names, and click on OK. Alternatively, pull down the Name Box list at the left side of the formula bar, and choose a name in the list.

## To Paste a Name into a New Formula Entry

Choose Insert ➢ Name ➢ Paste. In the Paste Name dialog box, select a name from the list of defined names, and click on OK. Excel enters the name as an operand in the current formula.

## To Apply Names to an Existing Formula

1. Select a range of formulas that contain A1-style references to named cells.

2. Choose Insert ➢ Name ➢ Apply. In the Apply Names list, select all the names that you want to apply to the selected formulas.

3. Click on OK. Excel replaces A1-style references with names.

## To Create a List of Names and Their References

1. Select a cell at the upper-left corner of an empty range on a sheet.

2. Choose Insert ➢ Name ➢ Paste.

3. Click on the Paste List button. Excel creates a list of all the names you've defined on the active workbook.

# Number Formats

Excel provides several categories of display formats for numeric values; for example, you can choose among currency, date and time, percentage, scientific, and special formats. (If none of the predefined formats suit your requirements, you can create your own custom formats; see the "Custom Number Formats" entry for details.)

## To Apply a Built-in Number Format

1. Select the cell or range of values that you want to format.

2. Choose Format ➢ Cells. Click on the Number tab on the Format Cells dialog box.

3. Select an entry in the Category list.

4. Select among the options that are displayed for the format category you've chosen. For example, if a Type list appears, highlight one of the available format types from the list.

5. Click on OK to apply the format.

If you use one of the built-in date or time formats when you enter a date or time value in a cell, Excel recognizes the value as a chronological entry and automatically applies the appropriate format to the cell. (See "Date Entries" and "Time Entries" for details.)

# Object Linking and Embedding (OLE)

Object linking and embedding is a technique for sharing information and features between Excel and other Windows applications that support OLE. Using OLE, you can embed or link documents:

- When you embed a document from another application into an Excel worksheet, the embedded document appears as an object that you can move and resize to suit your presentation. To edit the contents, you double-click on the embedded object; this action starts the application in which the object was originally created.

- In a link between two files, information from the source document is inserted into the destination document. As a result of the link, data in the destination document is updated whenever a change occurs in the source.

## To Embed an Object in a Worksheet

1. Activate the sheet where you want to display an embedded object.

2. Choose Insert ➢ Object. In the Object dialog box, click on the Create New tab.

3. Select an application from the Object type list, and click on OK. Excel starts the selected application.

4. Use the embedded object to develop the document that you want to display in the Excel worksheet. Then click elsewhere inside the sheet to deactivate the object.

Another way to embed an object is to open the source application and develop the graphics or data that you want to embed. Then select the information and press Ctrl+C to copy it to the Clipboard. Return to Excel and choose Edit ➢ Paste Special. In the As list of the Paste Special dialog box, select the format in which you want to paste the object, and click on OK.

## To Insert or Link a Document File

1. Activate the sheet where you want to link a document.

2. Choose Insert ➢ Object, and then click on the Create From File tab on the Object dialog box.

3. Type the file name for the document file you want to link. Alternatively, use the Browse button to search for the file.

4. To establish a link to the source file, check the Link To File option. Click on OK.

## To Edit an Embedded Object

1. Double-click on the object. In response, Excel starts the source application; the program's menus and other features appear on the desktop.

2. Use the source application to complete any changes you want to make.

3. Click on elsewhere on the current worksheet. The edited document appears once again as an embedded object on the sheet.

## To Embed an Excel Object in Another Application

1. Select the worksheet range or the chart that you want to embed, and choose Edit ➢ Copy.

2. Start the other application, and open the document in which you want to embed the Excel object.

3. In the menu system of the host application, choose Edit ➢ Paste Special, select Paste Link, and click on OK.

# Opening Files

Use the File ➢ Open command to open existing workbooks from disk. Use File ➢ New to create a new workbook.

## To Open Workbooks from Disk

1. Choose File ➢ Open.

2. If necessary, use the Look In box to select the location of the file you want to open. (Alternatively, use the Find Now or Advanced Find features; see the "Finding Data" entry for details.)

3. Select a document from the list. To open two or more documents in one operation, hold down the Ctrl key while you click on the names of other documents that you want to open.

4. Click on OK.

If you want to examine an open document but not change its contents, click on the Commands And Settings button (the last button in the toolbar at the top of the Open dialog box) and choose the Open Read Only command.

## To Open a New Workbook

1. Choose File ➢ New.

2. In the General tab of the New dialog box, select the Workbook icon, and click on OK.

Alternatively, click on the New button on the Standard toolbar.

## To Connect to a Web Site

Choose File ➢ Open and enter the destination address (URL) into the File name box. Then click on Open. See the "World Wide Web" entry for more information.

# Outlines

You can create an outline in any worksheet that is organized in sections with subtotals and totals. To simplify your work with the outline,

Excel displays Row- and Column-Level symbols, Show Detail symbols, and Hide Detail symbols just to the left and/or just above the outlined worksheet. Using these symbols, you can select levels of the outline to view and hide—that is, you can focus either on the whole worksheet or on selected levels of subtotals and totals.

## To Create an Outlined Worksheet

1. Develop a worksheet in which numeric data is divided into sections, with levels of subtotals and totals at the end of each section. The subtotals can be in rows, columns, or both.

2. Select the range of data that you want to outline, if less than the entire worksheet. Otherwise, Excel will attempt to determine the data to be outlined.

3. Choose the Data ➢ Group And Outline ➢ Auto Outline command. Excel creates the outline and displays special symbols along the left and upper borders of the worksheet.

Excel determines the levels of the outline from the way you have organized subtotals and totals (or other summary-type formulas) at the end of each section of your worksheet. If the Auto Outline command does not produce the results you want, you can regroup the outline using the Group and Ungroup commands in the Group And Outline submenu. Select the rows or columns that you want to regroup, choose Data ➢ Group And Outline, and choose the Group command or the Ungroup command.

Another way to plan or modify an outline is to choose Data ➢ Group And Outline ➢ Settings. The Settings dialog box contains check boxes for selecting row or column outline organization and for automatic styles.

## To Collapse or Expand the Outline

Click on one of the numbered outline level symbols that Excel displays for the row levels or the column levels. Excel temporarily hides all levels of the worksheet *after* the level that you click on. You can also collapse or expand individual sections of the outline by clicking the hide detail symbols (minus signs) or the show detail symbols (plus signs). You can hide the outline level and detail symbols if you wish. Choose Tools ➢ Options, click on the View tab, and clear the Outline symbols check box. Then click on OK.

## To Clear an Outline

Choose Data ➢ Group and Outline ➢ Clear Outline. Excel removes the outline symbols and displays the entire worksheet.

# Page Setup

The Page Setup command helps you plan the appearance of a printed document. Select options from the Page Setup dialog box before you choose the Print command.

## To Prepare a Workbook for Printing

Activate a worksheet, choose File ➢ Page Setup, and select options from any of the tabs that appear on the Page Setup dialog box:

- Click on the Page tab. Select Portrait to print the document from the top to the bottom of the paper, or Landscape to print the document sideways. In the Scaling box, enter a value less than 100% to reduce the size of a printed document, or a value greater than 100% to enlarge the printed document. Alternatively, click on the Fit To option button if you want Excel to scale the document automatically to fit the number of pages you specify. Select an option from the Paper Size list. The sizes include standard paper dimensions such as letter, legal, and executive, along with standard envelope sizes. Select a Print

Quality option. Finally, if you want the page numbering to start at some point other than 1, enter a value in the First Page Number box. (By default, page numbers are printed in the footer. See the "Headers and Footers" entry for details.)

- Click on the Margins tab. Enter measurements for the top, bottom, left, and right margins, and for the positions of the header and footer. To center the document on the page, click on one or both of the Center On Page check boxes, labeled Horizontally and Vertically.

- Click on the Header/Footer tab, and enter information about the header and footer you want printed on each page. (See the "Headers and Footers" entry for details.)

- Click on the Sheet tab. Optionally, enter a reference in the Print Area box. (Alternatively, you can select a Print What option in the Print dialog box. See "Printing Worksheets" for details.) If you want to print certain rows or columns of information as "titles" on each page, select the Rows To Repeat At Top and/or Columns To Repeat At Left boxes and point to the rows or columns that contain the titles. Select any combination of options in the Print Group: check the Gridlines box if you want to print the gridlines, select the Black And White check box for black-and-white printing, select Draft Quality for faster printing, select the Row And Column headings check box if you want to print the sheet's row numbers and column letters, and select an option from the Comments box the printout to include comments you have stored in worksheet cells. In the Page Order box, select one of the two options—Down, Then Over; or Over, Then Down—to specify how the pagination should be organized in a multi-page document.

A column of command buttons appears on the right side of the Page Setup dialog box. Click on the Print button to open the Print dialog box and print the document. Click on Print Preview to preview your document before printing it. Click on Options to open the Setup dialog box for your printer.

# Panes

By dividing a worksheet into panes, you can view two or four different parts of the sheet at once.

## To Divide a Sheet into Panes

Select the row, column, or cell at which you want to divide the sheet, and choose Window ➤ Split. This command creates two or four panes, depending on the range or cell you select before choosing the command:

- To create two panes that are split vertically, select an entire column or a single cell in row 1 (other than cell A1).
- To create two panes split horizontally, select an entire row or a single cell in column A (other than cell A1).
- To create four panes, select any cell except in row 1 or column A.
- To create four panes of approximately equal size, select cell A1.

Scrolling is synchronized in the panes of a split sheet. With a horizontal split, the two panes stay together during horizontal scrolling; and with a vertical split, the two panes stay together during vertical scrolling.

## To Freeze the Panes

Choose Window ➤ Freeze Panes. This command prevents the top pane from scrolling vertically, or the left pane from scrolling horizontally. Choose Window ➤ Unfreeze Panes to return the panes to their original scrolling capabilities.

## To Remove Panes from a Sheet

Choose Window ➤ Remove Split.

# Parsing

*Parsing* is the process of separating long lines of text into individual data items and entering each item into a separate cell on a worksheet. You may need to parse data that you have copied into Excel from another application.

## To Convert Text to Columns

1. Select a column range (one column wide) in which each cell contains a similarly formatted line of text.

2. Choose Data ➤ Text To Columns. A dialog box named Convert Text To Columns Wizard appears on the screen. The Text Wizard is designed to guide you through the steps required for a successful parse.

3. In Step 1, the Text Wizard determines whether the selected data is *delimited*—that is, individual data items are separated by special characters like commas or semicolons; or *fixed width*—that is, arranged in columns. Click on the Next button to move to the next step of the procedure.

4. The next step depends on whether the data is delimited or fixed width:

   - For delimited data, select the relevant character in the Delimiters box (Tab, Semicolon, Comma, Space, or Other), and select the single-quote, double-quote, or {none} option in the Text qualifier box. Check the Treat Consecutive Delimiters As One option if you want Excel to assume a blank data field is not desired. The Data Preview box shows how your selection will be parsed into columns.

   - For fixed width data, drag the column break lines to their correct positions in the Data Preview box. Click at a position to create a new break line. Double-click on a break line to remove it.

   Click on Next when the columns of data are arranged the way you want them.

5. In the final step of the Text Wizard, you define the data type of each column of parsed data. Select a column in the Data Preview box and then select the correct data type in the Column Data Format group. Repeat this step for each column of data.

6. Click on the Finish button. Excel copies the parsed data into the appropriate number of columns on your worksheet.

# Passwords

You can use passwords to restrict access to an Excel workbook that is saved on disk. Two kinds of passwords are available. If you create an *open* password, a user must supply the password correctly in order to open the workbook file from disk. If you create a *modify* password, it must be supplied in order to make changes to the workbook; without this password, a user is allowed to open the file in read-only mode. (In addition, a password is an optional tool for protecting the contents of a worksheet and the structure of a workbook. See the "Protecting Cells in a Worksheet" and "Protecting Workbooks" entries for details.)

## To Save a File with Passwords

1. Activate the file you want to save, and choose File ➢ Save As.

2. In the Save As dialog box, enter a name for the file and then click on the Options button.

3. In the Save Options dialog box, enter a password in the text box labeled Password To Open. Excel displays an asterisk for each character you type. (Press the Backspace key to erase any character that you want to retype.)

4. Optionally, enter a second password in the text box labeled Password To Modify.

5. Click on OK when you complete the password entries. A Confirm Password dialog box appears for each password you've

entered. Retype each password and click on OK.

6. Click on OK on the Save Options dialog box, and click on Save on the Save As dialog box.

## To Open a Password-Protected Document

1. Choose File ➢ Open and select the name of the file you want to open. When you click on OK, Excel displays the Password dialog box on the screen.

2. Enter the password and click on OK.

3. If the workbook has a *modify* password, a second Password dialog box appears. Enter the password and click on OK.

4. If your passwords are correct, Excel opens the file.

## To Remove Password Protection

1. Open a password-protected file, and then choose File ➢ Save As to save it again.

2. On the Save As dialog box, click on the Options button. In the Save Options dialog box, delete the asterisks that represent the password or passwords, and then click on OK.

3. Complete the save operation. In response to the "Replace existing file?" query, click on Yes. The file can now be opened without a password.

# Patterns

You can use options on the Patterns tab of the Format Cells dialog box to apply color shades and patterns to a range of cells on a worksheet.

## To Apply Shades and Patterns

1. Select the range, choose Format ➢ Cells, and click on the Patterns tab. The dialog box contains a Color palette, a Pattern box, and a Sample display.

**2.** Click on the drop-down arrow at the right side of the Pattern box, and select a shading pattern from the top three rows of the resulting palette. Optionally, click on the drop-down arrow a second time, and select a color for the pattern.

**3.** In the Color palette, select a color for the background of the pattern.

**4.** Examine the result of your selections in the Sample box. If the pattern appears the way you want it, click on OK.

# Pivot Tables

A pivot table is a dynamic, customizable tool designed to help you rearrange, summarize, and explore information from a database or list. The PivotTable Wizard provides a simple four-step graphical approach to creating the initial version of a new pivot table; subsequently, you can use efficient drag-and-drop actions to revise and customize the table in a variety of useful ways.

## To Create a Pivot Table from a List or Database

**1.** Activate a worksheet containing a list or a database. (See the "Database" and "Lists" entries for background information.)

**2.** Choose Data ➤ PivotTable Report. The Pivot-Table Wizard Step 1 Of 4 dialog box appears on the desktop.

**3.** In the first step, keep the default selection, labeled Microsoft Excel List Or Database. (Note that you can also create a pivot table from other sources of data—a database created in a different application, a selection of similarly organized worksheet ranges, or another pivot table.) Click on the Next button.

**4.** Step 2 gives you the opportunity to define the target worksheet range. Excel automatically supplies a reference to the list or database on the active worksheet. If this is correct, click on Next again.

**5.** Step 3 is where you define the structure of the pivot table. At the right side of the dialog box you see a list of field buttons, identifying the fields of your database. In the center of the dialog box is a graphical representation of the pivot table's structure. To create a table, you drag any selection of field buttons to the four areas of the pivot table:

- Drag fields to the ROW area to create rows of summary data in the pivot table.

- Drag fields to the COLUMN area to create columns of data.

- Drag fields to the DATA area to define the numeric content of the table. Excel initially identifies each item in this area as a Sum operation, but you can select other summary functions for each field if you wish, as you'll see in the next step.

- Drag fields to the PAGE area to create drop-down lists of data categories that you can view one at a time in the pivot table.

**6.** To customize a field in the DATA area, double-click on any of the field buttons you've dragged to the area. In the resulting PivotTable Field dialog box, you can select from a list of functions (Sum, Count, Average, Max, Min, and so on) that define how your pivot table will summarize information from your database. You can also define the numeric format of a field; click on the Number button, select a format from the resulting Format Cells dialog box, and click on OK. To develop a more complex summarization formula, click on the Options button. When you have finished defining the field, click on OK on the PivotTable Field dialog box. Repeat this step for any fields that you want to customize in the DATA area.

**7.** Click on Next to move to the final step of the PivotTable Wizard (Step 4). In the resulting dialog box you can indicate where you want the pivot table to appear. To do so, enter a reference into the range box, or point to a starting cell on any worksheet while the box is active. Alternatively, select the New worksheet option and Excel will create a sheet for the pivot table, just to the left of the active worksheet.

8. Click on the Options button, and select or deselect any of the check boxes in the PivotTable Options dialog box. These options determine a variety of properties, including whether the table will contain grand totals, whether a hidden copy of the source data will be saved with the table, and whether Excel will apply an Auto-Format to the table. Click on OK.

9. Click on the Finish button to complete the process of defining your pivot table. The table appears in the location you selected on the final dialog box. By default, the PivotTable toolbar appears automatically on the desktop.

## To Change the Layout of a Pivot Table

To change a field in a pivot table, click on the field with the right mouse pointer and choose the Field command in the shortcut menu. In the PivotTable Field dialog box you can select a new option in the Orientation group (Row, Column, or Page). You can also select a summary function for the field and select a category of data to be hidden in the field.

To change the organization of the pivot table, try dragging any field button to a new row or column position in the table. This is a quick visual way to transform a page, row, column, or data field to another role in the table's layout.

For other changes in the layout of a pivot table, click on the PivotTable Wizard button on the PivotTable toolbar, or choose Data ➢ PivotTable Report. Step 3 of the PivotTable Wizard appears on the screen, and you can use this dialog box to reorganize your table in any way you wish.

## To Update a Pivot Table

1. Activate the list or database that the pivot table is based on, and make any changes that you wish to make in the source data—specifically, in the fields that are part of the data area in the pivot table.

2. Activate the worksheet that contains the pivot table.

3. Click on the Refresh Data button on the PivotTable toolbar, or click on the pivot table with the right mouse button and choose the Refresh Data command. Excel updates the information in the table.

## To Copy All the Pages of a Pivot Table

1. Point to any part of the table and click the right mouse button to view the pivot table shortcut menu. Choose the Show Pages command from the menu. The Show Pages dialog box displays a list of all the page fields on the current pivot table.

2. Select the field whose pages you want to copy, and click on OK. Excel copies each page of the pivot table to its own new sheet in the current workbook.

## To View the Source Data for a Pivot Table Item

Double-click on any item in the data area. In response, Excel creates a new sheet and copies all the source records for the item you've clicked on.

# Previewing

Before printing a worksheet, you can preview the appearance of the printout on the screen. You can also use the preview window to make adjustments in the document's format before you print.

## To Preview a Worksheet Printout

Activate the sheet that you want to preview, and choose File ➤ Print Preview (or click on the Print Preview button on the Standard toolbar). The preview window displays a full-page picture of the sheet. Across the top of the window you'll find a variety of buttons you can use to examine or modify the printed sheet.

- Click on the Next or Previous button to scroll to the next or previous page in the printout.

- Click on the Zoom button (or point to the sheet itself and click on the mouse button when you see the magnifying glass pointer) to enlarge the view of the printed document. When in Zoom mode, use the scroll bars to move up, down, or across the document. To return to the regular page preview display, click on the Zoom button again, or click on the mouse anywhere on the zoomed document.

- Click on the Print button to open the Print dialog box, or the Setup button to open the Page Setup dialog box.

- Click on the Margin button if you want to adjust margins in your document. Excel displays margin lines and handles that you can drag to adjust the top, bottom, left, or right margins. For a worksheet, Excel also displays handles to represent the current column widths; you can drag these handles to increase or decrease the width of a column. Click on the Margin button again to remove the margin handles from the window.

- The Page Break Preview button gives you a new view of the worksheet in which you can change the positions of the vertical and horizontal page breaks. Drag a page break line with the mouse to change its position. (Click on the Print Preview button on the Standard toolbar to return to the preview window.) A Normal View button will appear to return your spreadsheet to its original view.

- Click on Close to return to your document in the Excel application window.

## Printer Setup

You can change the setup properties of your printer before you begin printing a worksheet. To do so, choose File ➤ Print, and then click on the Properties button on the Print dialog box. The options displayed in the resulting Properties dialog box vary according to the characteristics and capabilities of your printer. Change any of the available settings, then click on OK to return to the Print dialog box.

## Printing Charts

You can print a chart either as an object by itself, or as part of the worksheet on which it is located. To print an entire sheet along with a chart that it contains, activate the sheet, make sure the chart is not selected, and click on the Print button on the Standard toolbar. (See the "Printing Worksheets" entry for more information.)

### To Print a Chart by Itself

1. If the chart is located on a separate chart sheet, click on the sheet's tab. If the chart is an object on a sheet, click on the sheet where the chart is located and click on the chart object with the mouse. (Selection handles appear around the perimeter of the chart.)

2. Choose File ➤ Print. If the chart is an object on a worksheet, the default Print What option is Selected Chart. Click on OK to print the chart.

Alternatively, you can simply select the chart sheet or the chart object and click on the Print button on the Standard toolbar.

## Printing Worksheets

The File ➤ Print command gives you the options of printing the active sheet or sheets, an entire workbook, or a selected range of data.

## To Print All or Part of a Workbook

1. Activate the workbook that contains the information you want to print.

2. If you want to print only part of the workbook, make one of the following selections. (The selection is unimportant if you plan to print the entire workbook.)

   - Click on the tab of the sheet that you want to print.

   - Select a group of two or more sheets.

   - Select a range of data that you want to print.

3. Choose File ➤ Print.

4. Select an option in the Print What group:

   - Click on the Selection option to print a range you have selected.

   - Click on the Selected Sheets option to print the active sheet or the group of sheets you have selected.

   - Click on Entire Workbook to print sheets or designated print areas on all the sheets of the workbook.

5. To print more than one copy, increase the value in the Number Of Copies box.

6. To print less than the entire document, click on Page(s) and enter a range of page numbers in the From and To boxes.

7. Click on OK to begin printing.

## To Set a Manual Page Break

1. Activate the sheet on which you want to define a page break.

2. Select a column for a vertical page break, a row for a horizontal page break, or a single cell for both.

3. Choose Insert ➤ Page Break.

Excel marks manual page breaks with a line of dashes. If you do not set manual page breaks, Excel calculates automatic page breaks appropriate for the page size and margin settings.

# Protecting Cells in a Worksheet

By applying cell protection to a worksheet, you can prevent any changes to the entries. You can also hide the formulas that calculate data on the sheet.

## To Protect a Range of Cells on a Worksheet

1. Select a range in which you want to change the protection options.

2. Choose Format ➤ Cells, and click on the Protection tab. The resulting dialog box has two check box options: Locked prevents changes to entries in the cells, and Hidden hides the formulas in the cells. (By default, the Locked option is checked for all cells in a worksheet.)

3. Check the combination of options that you want to apply to the current range, and click on OK.

4. To select varied protection options for different ranges on the worksheet, repeat steps 1 through 3 for each range you want to change.

5. Choose Tools ➤ Protection ➤ Protect Sheet. The Protect Sheet dialog box has three check box options: Contents, Objects, and Scenarios. (All three are checked by default; the Contents box must remain checked to activate cell protection.)

6. To use a password to enforce protection, enter a word into the Password text box. Excel displays an asterisk for each character you type. Click on OK. In the Confirm Password dialog box, enter the password again and click on OK. Cell protection is now active in the selected range.

Once you activate protection, you cannot edit locked cells. If you try to enter a new value or formula into a locked cell, a warning box appears on the desktop. Excel also dims menu commands that would result in changes to the protected worksheet. If you have selected the

Hidden option as well, no formula or other entry appears in the formula bar when you select a cell in the protected range.

## To Remove Cell Protection

1. Select the sheet where you want to remove protection.

2. Choose the Tools ➢ Protection ➢ Unprotect Sheet command.

3. If you used a password to protect the cells, you must now reenter the password to remove protection. If there is no password, Excel removes protection immediately.

# Protecting Workbooks

The Tools ➢ Protection ➢ Protect Workbook command prevents changes in the structure of a workbook and in the appearance of its window.

## To Protect a Workbook

1. Open and activate the workbook.

2. Choose Tools ➢ Protection ➢ Protect Workbook.

3. Select any combination of the two check boxes in the resulting dialog box:

   - The Structure option (checked by default) prevents changes in the sheet structure of the workbook. When this option is activated, you cannot add, remove, rename, hide, unhide, or rearrange the sheets on a workbook.

   - The Windows option (unchecked by default) prevents changes in the appearance of the workbook window. When this option is activated, you cannot move, resize, minimize, maximize or hide the window. The control-menu box is removed from the window, as are the minimize, maximize, and restore buttons.

4. Optionally, enter a password into the Password text box. Re-enter the password in the Confirm Password box.

5. Click on OK.

# Recalculation

By default, Excel automatically recalculates dependent formulas whenever you change an entry on a worksheet. You might want to switch temporarily to manual recalculation while developing a complex system of interrelated formulas; this switch can sometimes give you a clearer way to monitor the effect of new worksheet entries.

## To Switch to Manual Recalculation

1. Choose Tools ➢ Options, and click on the Calculation tab on the Options dialog box.

2. In the Calculation group, select the Manual option button, and click on OK.

To switch back to automatic recalculation, choose Tools ➢ Options, click on the Calculation tab, select the Automatic option, and click on OK. Notice that there is also a third option, labeled Automatic Except Tables. Under this option, recalculation is manual for tables produced by the Data ➢ Table command. (See the "Data Tables" entry for details.)

## To Recalculate Manually

1. Choose Tools ➢ Options and click on the Calculation tab.

2. Click on the Calc Now button to recalculate worksheets in all open workbooks, or click on Calc Sheet to calculate the active worksheet.

Alternatively, press the F9 function key to recalculate all formulas.

# References

A reference identifies a cell or a range by its position on a worksheet. In a formula, references stand for the values stored in cells and ranges. You can write a reference in any of three forms—relative, absolute, or mixed—depending on how you want the reference to appear in any copies of the formula. Excel defines two different reference styles, known as A1 and R1C1. (The A1 style is the default; the R1C1 style is seldom used.) Each style denotes relative, absolute, and mixed references in its own way.

An external reference identifies a cell or range on another workbook and creates a link between two workbooks. A 3-D reference identifies cells or ranges on two or more contiguous worksheets in a workbook. (See the "Links and 3-D References" entry for details.)

## To Change a Reference Type in the Formula Bar

Position the insertion point just after a cell reference in the active formula bar. (For a range, highlight the entire reference.) Then press F4 one or more times to cycle through the choices, from relative to absolute to mixed.

In Excel's A1 reference style, dollar signs denote absolute or mixed references. For example:

- $E$9 is an absolute reference. When you copy a formula containing $E$9 as an operand, the reference is copied unchanged and always refers to cell E9.

- E$9 is a mixed reference, in which the column reference (E) is relative and the row reference ($9) is absolute. When you copy a formula containing E$9 as an operand, the reference to row 9 remains fixed, but the reference to column E can change relative to the column of the copied formula.

- $E9 is a mixed reference, in which the column reference ($E) is absolute and the row reference (9) is relative. When you copy a formula containing $E9 as an operand, the reference to column E remains fixed, but

the reference to row 9 can change relative to the row of the copied formula.

- E9 is a relative reference, in which both the column and the row are relative. When you copy a formula containing E9 as an operand, both the column and the row can change relative to the position of the copied formula.

See "Copying Formulas" for more information.

## To Change to the R1C1 Reference Style

1. Choose Tools ➢ Options and click on the General tab on the Options dialog box.

2. Check the R1C1 reference style box button and click on OK.

When you make this change, the letter column headings are replaced with numbers on all worksheets in all workbooks. Columns are numbered from 1 to 256. For example, when viewed in the R1C1 style, the A1-style reference E9 becomes R9C5.

A relative reference in the R1C1 style is denoted with brackets around the relative portions of the reference. For example:

- R[9]C[5] is a relative reference to the cell located nine rows down and five columns to the right of the current cell. R[-9]C[-5] is a reference to the cell located nine rows up and five columns to the *left* of the current cell.

- R9C[5] is a mixed reference to the cell in row 9 located five columns to the right of the current cell.

- R[9]C5 is a mixed reference to the cell in column 5 located nine rows down from the current cell.

- R9C5 is an absolute reference to the cell at the intersection of row 9 and column 5—in other words, $E$9 in the A1 reference style.

## To Create an External Reference

1. Open the source and destination workbooks for the data and activate the target worksheets in both workbooks. For convenience, choose Window ➢ Arrange, select Tiled, and click on OK, to display the two windows side by side on the screen.

2. Select the cell in the destination workbook in which you want to create an external reference.

3. Enter an equal sign (=) to begin a formula.

4. Activate the source worksheet, and select the target cell. Excel creates an external reference in the destination workbook.

5. Press ↵ to complete the formula.

# Repeating Commands

The Edit ➢ Repeat command is available to repeat your last command or action. This command is dimmed if a repeat is not possible. The Redo button on the Standard toolbar (or the Edit ➢ Redo command) reverses the effect of an Undo operation. After you click on the Undo button, you can click on Redo if you change your mind.

# Replacing Data

The Edit ➢ Replace command replaces text or numeric data on the active sheet. You can use this command to search for and replace individual characters or digits within cell entries, or the entire contents of cells. (Alternatively, you can choose Edit ➢ Find to locate an entry first, and then click on the Replace button to replace the target data with a different entry. See "Finding Data" for information about the Edit ➢ Find command.)

## To Replace the Contents of Cells

1. Activate the sheet in which you want to replace data and choose Edit ➢ Replace. The Replace dialog box appears.

2. In the Find What box, enter the text that you want to replace.

3. In the Replace With box, enter the replacement text.

4. In the Search list, select By Rows to search your worksheet from top to bottom, or By Columns to search from left to right.

5. Check the Match Case option if you want Excel's search to be case sensitive. Otherwise, Excel performs the search without regard for alphabetic case.

6. Check Find Entire Cells Only if the text you have entered in the Find what box represents an entire cell entry; leave the option unchecked to search for the text as a portion of a cell entry.

7. To begin the search-and-replace operation, use any sequence of the following command buttons:

   • Click on Find Next to find the next occurrence of the Find What text, or hold down the Shift key and click on Find Next to find the previous occurrence.

   • Click on Replace to replace the target text in the current cell and then click on Find Next to find the next occurrence.

   • Click on Replace All to replace all the remaining occurrences of the target text and close the Replace dialog box.

   • Click on Close to close the Replace dialog box without changing any additional entries.

If Excel does not find the target text in your worksheet, an error message appears.

# Reports

The Report Manager is a convenient tool for combining different views and scenarios that you've defined for a given sheet, and printing a report from these combinations. A report may consist of multiple sections; each section shows a selected sheet, view, and scenario. (Note that if the View ➢ Report Manager command is not available, you'll need to install the Report Manager add-in before defining reports. See the "Add-Ins" entry for details.)

## To Define a Report

1. Activate the workbook from which you want to create a report.

2. Choose Tools ➤ Scenarios and develop the scenarios you want in your report. (See "Scenarios" for details.)

3. Choose View ➤ Custom Views and create the views you want to use in your report. (See "Views" for details.)

4. Choose View ➤ Report Manager. The Report Manager dialog box appears. If this is the first time you have used the Report Manager for this workbook, the list box labeled Reports is empty.

5. Click on the Add button at the right side of the dialog box to create a report. The Add Report dialog box appears.

6. In the Report Name box, enter a name to identify the report you are about to create, and then read the instructions displayed beneath the text box. A report consists of sections, where each section is defined by a sheet, a view, and/or a scenario that you select.

7. If the Sheet box does not display the sheet you want to include in the current section, pull down the Sheet list and select a name.

8. Pull down the View list and select a view for the current section of the report.

9. Pull down the Scenario list and select a scenario for the current section.

10. Click on the Add button. Excel displays a description of the section in the list labeled Sections in this Report.

11. Repeat steps 7 through 10 for each section that you want to include in your report. Click on OK when you have defined all the sections.

12. Back in the Report Manager dialog box, select the name of the report you want to print from the Reports list, and click on Print.

13. In the Print dialog box, enter the number of copies you want to print of your report, and click on OK. Excel begins printing your report.

You can define multiple reports in the Report Manager, assigning a unique name to each one. When you save your workbook, Excel also saves report definitions as well as scenarios and views. To print another defined report, choose View ➤ Report Manager, select the name of the report you want to print, and click on Print.

# Row Height

You can increase or decrease the height of selected rows to improve or clarify the appearance of data on a sheet. Choose the Format ➤ Row ➤ Height command, or use your mouse to drag the border between row headings. (If you increase the font size of a data entry, Excel automatically increases the height of the corresponding row to accommodate the new size.)

## To Change Row Heights

1. Select a cell, an entire row, or a sequence of rows.

2. Choose Format ➤ Row ➤ Height.

3. Enter a new value in the Row Height text box, and then click on OK.

Alternatively, position the mouse pointer over the line located just under a row's heading and drag the line up or down. To adjust the row height to the best fit for the current contents, double-click on the line.

## To Display a Multiple-Line Entry

1. Select a cell, and type a line of text. Then press Alt+↵ to insert a carriage return into the entry. The height of the formula bar

increases to accommodate the next line of the entry.

2. Repeat step 1 for additional lines of text in the entry.

3. Press ↵ to complete the entry. Excel wraps the text in the cell, but not necessarily in the same line arrangement as your original entry. Adjust the column width and the row height to produce the text arrangement you want.

# Saving Files

Use the File ➢ Save As command to save a workbook to disk for the first time. Use File ➢ Save to update a file after making changes in a workbook.

## To Save a New Workbook to Disk

1. Choose File ➢ Save As.

2. If necessary, use the Save In box and the folder list beneath it to select a location for the file.

3. Enter a name for the workbook in the File Name box.

4. If you want to save the file in a format other than the Excel 97 format, click on the arrow next to the Save As Type list, and select a format. (See "File Formats" for details.)

5. Click on OK to save the file.

## To Update a File

Activate the workbook and choose File ➢ Save, or click on the Save button on the Standard toolbar.

# Scenarios

Using the Scenario Manager, you can define and save sets of input data for exploring "what-if"

scenarios. The Scenario Manager is especially useful in a worksheet organized into distinct "input" and "output" areas. In this context, the input area displays the values that serve as parameters for calculations performed in the output area. When you select a scenario, Excel enters the input values into specified cells and recalculates the worksheet accordingly.

## To Define Scenarios

1. Develop a worksheet that uses a range of input values to calculate data in an output area.

2. Assign names to the cells containing the input values. (See the "Names" entry for instructions. These names are optional, but they make the Scenario Manager easier to use.) Select the range of input values.

3. Choose Tools ➢ Scenarios. If this is the first time you've created a scenario in the active sheet, a list box in the upper-left corner of the Scenario Manager dialog box displays the message "No Scenarios defined."

4. Click on the Add button. The Add Scenario dialog box appears. In the Scenario Name box, enter a name for the scenario you're about to create.

5. The Changing cells box contains the range address of the input cells you've selected. Confirm that the range is correct, or change it if necessary.

6. Optionally, revise the text displayed in the Comment box. This box is for any description you want to save along with the scenario. Then click on OK on the Add Scenario dialog box.

7. The Scenario Values dialog box appears on the screen. The text boxes contain the current data from the input cells. (If you did not assign names to the cells, the boxes will be labeled with absolute references.) Enter a new set of values for the current scenario, and then click on OK. The Scenario Manager dialog box reappears. The

Scenarios list contains the name of the scenario you've just defined.

8. Repeat steps 4 through 7 for each scenario you want to define. Each scenario you create can contain a different set of input values to be used in calculating formulas on the worksheet.

9. Click on Close to exit from the Scenario Manager. When you save the workbook, Excel saves scenario definitions with it.

## To View a Scenario

Choose Tools ➤ Scenarios, select a name from the scenarios list, and click on Show. Excel replaces the entries in the input cells with the values of the selected scenario and recalculates the worksheet accordingly.

## To Create a Scenario Summary

1. Activate the sheet on which you have defined the scenarios, and choose Tools ➤ Scenarios.

2. Click on the Summary button. The Scenario Summary dialog box appears.

3. In the Report Type group, click on the Scenario Summary option button if it is not already selected. In the Result Cells box, enter a reference to the cell or cells that you want to display as the result of each scenario.

4. Click on OK to create the scenario summary. Excel creates a new sheet in the current workbook to display the summary. The summary includes a column of input data for each scenario you have defined, along with the corresponding result cells you chose to include in the summary.

You can also create a pivot table to summarize a set of scenarios. Click on the Scenario Pivot-Table option in the Scenario Summary dialog box. (See the "Pivot Tables" entry for information about using a pivot table.)

# Series

The Edit ➤ Fill ➤ Series command is a versatile tool for entering series of numeric and date values in the rows or columns of a worksheet. (In this context, a series is a sequence of values in which the entries are calculated from a linear or exponential formula.) You can also use this command to produce trend series, for which Excel calculates the linear or exponential "best fit" and modifies the data accordingly.

## To Create a Series

1. In the first cell of a row or column range on the active worksheet, enter the initial value for the series you want to create. Then select the range for the series.

2. Choose Edit ➤ Fill ➤ Series. The Series dialog box displays three groups of option buttons: Series In, Type, and Date Unit. For the Series In option, Excel automatically selects Rows or Columns according to the range you have already selected on the worksheet.

3. In the Type group, select the type of data series you want to create. If you select the Date option, Excel activates the Date Unit group; select one of the unit options in the group.

4. Enter a number in the Step Value box to define the increment from one entry to the next in the series. The default is 1.

5. Optionally, enter a value in the Stop Value box.

6. Click on OK to create the series.

Excel's use of the step value depends on the type of series you select:

- For a linear series, the step value is added to each value to produce the next value in the series.

- For a growth series, each value is multiplied by the step value to produce the next value in the series.

- For a date series, the step value represents the number of days between one entry and the next in the series. (You can modify the steps of a date series by selecting an option in the Date Unit group.)

The end of a series is determined by either the number you supply as the Stop Value, or the end of the selected range, whichever comes first.

## To Create a Trend Series

1. In a row or column range, enter two or more tentative values for the trend series and select the entire range in which you want to create the series.

2. Choose Edit ➢ Fill ➢ Series. In the Series dialog box, check the Trend option.

3. Select either Linear or Growth in the Type group, and click on OK.

To create a trend series, Excel determines the "best fit" formula for the series—that is, the linear or exponential equation that best describes the tentative sequence of entries you have already entered into the series range. In the resulting series, Excel supplies new values in the series and also adjusts the existing values to make them fit the formula.

# Sharing Workbooks

When you save a workbook on a network, many people can read and modify the file simultaneously. You can specify in advance how Excel will handle any conflicting changes at the time the file is saved. You can also review a history of all the updates that have taken place, and make decisions about combining data from different copies of the workbook.

## Managing a Shared Workbook

1. Activate the target workbook and choose Tools ➢ Share Workbook.

2. Click on the Editing tab, and check the box labeled Allow Changes By More Than One User At The Same Time.

3. Click on the Advanced tab. Make selections in each category of options:

   - Choose between keeping a change history or not.
   - Select the frequency of updates—at the time of each save, or automatic updates after a specified time period.
   - Decide how conflicting changes will be handled. You can review conflicting changes and resolve them yourself, or you can automatically save your own changes instead of conflicting ones.

4. Click on OK. A message displays the prompt, "This action will now save the workbook. Do you want to continue?" Click on OK to save the worksheet as a shared document. On the title bar Excel displays the [Shared] notation to confirm the file's new status.

See the "Tracking Changes" entry for more information about changes in shared workbooks.

# Shortcut Menus

To view a shortcut menu for any object in Excel, position the mouse pointer over the item and click on the right mouse button. Then choose a command from the resulting menu list. Shortcut menus contain selections of the most commonly used commands for a given object.

# Solver

In a worksheet containing a system of interrelated formulas, you can use the Tools ➢ Solver command to solve a numeric problem by varying the input data. The Solver command adjusts parameters within a set of constraints, and comes to the optimal solution. (If the Tools ➢ Solver command is not available, you'll have to install the Solver add-in before using this feature. See the "Add-Ins" entry for details.)

## To Use the Solver Command

1. Set up a worksheet that includes:

   - A target formula; the Solver command will optimize the result of this formula, finding its maximum, minimum, or best value.

   - One or more data entries that can be adjusted in order to find the optimal solution.

2. Choose Tools ➤ Solver. The Solver Parameters dialog box appears on the screen. In the Set Target Cell box, enter a reference to the formula you want to optimize.

3. Click on one of the three option buttons in the Equal To group: Max to find the maximum result from the formula, Min to find the minimum result, or Value to find a specified result. If you choose Value, enter the result you want to achieve in the text box labeled Value Of.

4. Activate the By Changing Cells box. On the worksheet, select the cell or cells containing the data values that you want to adjust in order to find the optimum solution. If you want to include more than one cell reference in this box, hold down Ctrl while you make multiple selections on the worksheet.

5. Click on the Add button. The Add Constraint dialog box appears on the screen. In the Cell Reference box, enter a reference to a cell for which you want to express a constraint.

6. Click on the down-arrow next to the operation list box, and select one of the three relational operators, <=, =, >=. (Select *int* if you want the constraint cell to remain an Integer; or select *bin* for Binary.)

7. In the Constraint box, enter a value or formula that expresses the constraint you want to impose on the value in the selected cell. Then click on OK. Back in the Solver Parameters dialog box, the constraint appears in the list box labeled Subject To The Constraints.

8. Repeat steps 5, 6, and 7 for any additional constraints you want to express. (You can use the Change button to edit an existing constraint, or the Delete button to remove a constraint from the list.)

9. Click on the Solve button to attempt a solution. When Solver completes its analysis, the Solver dialog box appears on the screen. If a solution has been found, the result is now shown on your worksheet.

10. Select the Keep Solver Solution option to retain this new version of your worksheet data, or select Restore Original Values to revert to the previous version. To generate reports from the Solver analysis, select any of the report titles listed in the Reports box. (To select more than one report, hold down Ctrl while you select the titles.) Then click on OK.

When Solver completes its solution, the Solver dialog box lists the three reports that the analysis can generate:

- The Answer report shows the original data values alongside the new values produced for the Solver solution.

- The Sensitivity report indicates the sensitivity of the solution to adjustments in constraints.

- The Limit report specifies the upper- and lower-limit values of the adjustable cells and the formula result.

Excel creates a separate sheet in the current workbook for each report you select.

Finally, the Solver Results dialog box has a Save Scenario button. By clicking on this button you can supply a name for the solution and save it as a scenario. You can then choose Tools ➤ Scenarios whenever you want to review the solution.

# Sorting

The Data ➤ Sort command rearranges data in alphabetical, numeric, or chronological order.

## To Sort a List or Database

1. Activate a sheet that contains a list and select any cell within the list.

2. Choose Data ➢ Sort. The Sort dialog box appears. On the sheet, Excel selects the list range.

3. If the selected range contains a top row of field names that you do not want to include in the sort, make sure the Header row option is selected (near the bottom of the dialog box). Excel deselects the field names on the sheet.

4. Click on the down-arrow next to the Sort By box. The resulting list contains the names of all the fields in your table. (If there is no row of field names, the list identifies columns by letter.) Select the primary key to the sort, the column by which the list will be rearranged first.

5. Click on Ascending or Descending for the primary key. (For a text field, an ascending sort arranges records from A to Z; descending, from Z to A. For a date field, ascending is from the earliest date to the latest; descending, from the latest to the earliest.)

6. Optionally, select the second and third sorting keys. Repeat steps 4 and 5 to select fields in one or both of the Then By list boxes. Excel uses the second key to arrange records that contain identical entries in the first key; likewise, the third key is for sorting records that contain identical entries in the first and second keys.

7. Click on OK. Excel sorts the list.

You can return the list to its original order by choosing Edit ➢ Undo Sort immediately after the sort operation. Alternatively, press Ctrl+Z or click on the Undo button on the Standard toolbar. Notice that the toolbar also has Sort Ascending and Sort Descending buttons. To use these, select the range of data that you want to sort, and click on one of the two buttons.

## To Rearrange Columns of Data

1. Select the range of data that you want to sort.

2. Choose Data ➢ Sort and click on the Options button in the Sort dialog box.

3. In the Sort Options dialog box, click on the Sort Left To Right option.

4. Click on OK. Back in the Sort dialog box, define one or more keys for the sort, and click on OK.

## To Sort in a Custom Order

1. Select the range of data you want to sort.

2. Choose Data ➢ Sort and click on the Options button in the Sort dialog box.

3. In the Sort Options dialog box, pull down the First Key Sort Order list. The list displays predefined sort orders—including the days of the week and names of the months, along with any custom lists you've defined using the Tools ➢ Options command. (See the "AutoFill" entry for details.)

4. Select one of the entries in the list and click on OK.

5. In the Sort dialog box, define one or more keys for the sort and click on OK.

# Spelling and AutoCorrect

Like other applications in Microsoft Office, Excel has two efficient tools for checking the spelling in a document. The Tools ➢ Spelling command finds misspelled words on a sheet and suggests corrections. In addition, the AutoCorrect feature instantly corrects commonly misspelled words as you enter them into the cells of a sheet. Using the Tools ➢ AutoCorrect command, you can customize the list of words that are automatically corrected.

## To Check the Spelling on a Sheet

1. Activate a sheet and choose Tools ➤ Spelling. (Alternatively, press F7 or click on the Spelling button on the Standard toolbar.) If Excel finds a misspelled word in the sheet, the Spelling dialog box appears. The suspect word is displayed at the top of the dialog box. A suggestion for the correct spelling appears in the Change To box, with a list of additional suggestions just below. You can select any of the suggestions in the list, or you can type a new entry into the Change To box.

2. Click on one of the following buttons in the Spelling dialog box:

   - Change replaces the word with the contents of the Change To box.

   - Change All replaces all occurrences of the word in the current sheet.

   - Ignore or Ignore All leaves the word as it appears in the sheet.

   - Add inserts the word to the current dictionary file. (You can also enter the name for a new dictionary file in the Add Words To box.)

   - AutoCorrect inserts the word into the list of words that are corrected automatically.

   - Cancel stops the spelling check.

3. Repeat step 2 for each misspelled word that Excel finds.

To check the spelling on several sheets in a workbook, select the sheets before you choose Tools ➤ Spelling. Excel does not check the spelling of cells that contain formulas. Also, you can check the Ignore UPPERCASE option to omit uppercase text from the spelling check.

## To Customize the AutoCorrect Feature

1. Choose Tools ➤ AutoCorrect.

2. The first four options in the AutoCorrect dialog box pertain to capitalization errors in a sheet. They are all checked by default. You can uncheck any option that you do not want included in the AutoCorrect feature.

3. Optionally, click on the Exceptions button to open the AutoCorrect Exceptions dialog box. The First Letter tab contains a list of abbreviations that are not to be considered the end of a sentence. (The AutoCorrect feature does not capitalize the first letter after these abbreviations.) The INital CAps tab contains a list box in which you can record any irregular capitalization styles that you don't want corrected. Add entries to either of these lists. Then click on OK to return to the AutoCorrect dialog box.

4. The fifth option, labeled Replace Text As You Type, is followed by a scrollable list of commonly misspelled words and their corrections. To add a word to this list, type a misspelled word in the Replace box and its correction in the With box. Then click on the Add button.

5. Repeat step 4 for any other words you want to add to the list. Then click on OK.

To disable the AutoCorrect feature—so that Excel will no longer correct spelling errors as you enter data into cells—clear the check from the Replace Text As You Type option in the AutoCorrect dialog box. To delete an Auto-Correct item, highlight the item in the list and click on Delete.

## Statistical Functions

Excel supplies a large library of functions for specialized use in statistical analysis. You can enter these functions directly into worksheets or you can select them from the Paste Function dialog box. (The Help Topics list contains descriptions and examples for all of these functions. Choose Help ➤ Contents And Index, click on the Index tab, and enter the name of any function.) The following statistical functions are available:

- Average, median, and mode functions (AVERAGE, AVERAGEA, CONFIDENCE,

GEOMEAN, HARMEAN, MEDIAN, MODE, TRIMMEAN)

- Correlation coefficient functions (CORREL, FISHER, FISHERINV, PEARSON, RSQ)

- Counting functions (COUNT, COUNTA, COUNTBLANK, COUNTIF)

- Deviation and variance functions (AVEDEV, COVAR, DEVSQ, STDEV, STDEVA, STDEVP, STDEVPA, VAR, VARA, VARP, VARPA)

- Distribution functions (BETADIST, BETAINV, BINOMDIST, CHIDIST, CHIINV, CHITEST, CRITBINOM, EXPONDIST, FDIST, FINV, FREQUENCY, FTEST, GAMMADIST, GAMMAINV, HYPGEOMDIST, KURT, LOGINV, LOGNORMDIST, NEGBINOMDIST, NORMDIST, NORMINV, NORMSDIST, NORMSINV, POISSON, PROB, SKEW, STANDARDIZE, TDIST, TINV, TTEST, WEIBULL, ZTEST)

- Gamma function (GAMMALN)

- Linear regression functions (INTERCEPT, SLOPE, STEYX)

- Maximum and minimum functions (MAX, MAXA, MIN, MINA)

- Percentile, rank, and standing functions (LARGE, PERCENTILE, PERCENTRANK, QUARTILE, RANK, SMALL)

- Permutations (PERMUT)

- Trend functions (FORECAST, GROWTH, LINEST, LOGEST, TREND)

# Styles

A style is a combination of formatting attributes that you define for use in a particular workbook. Once you've defined a style on one workbook, you can copy it to other workbooks.

## To Create a Style by Example

1. Select a range of cells and apply any combination of formats to the range.

2. While the range is still selected, choose Format ➤ Style.

3. In the Style Name box, enter a name for the style you are creating, and click on OK.

## To Apply a Style to a Range

1. Select the range to which you want to apply a style.

2. Choose Format ➤ Style.

3. In the Style name list, select the name of the style to apply.

4. Optionally, use the check boxes in the Style Includes group to select or deselect categories of styles to include or omit from the selection. Click on OK.

## To Create a Style by Definition

1. Choose Format ➤ Style.

2. In the Style Name box, enter a name for the style you are about to define.

3. Click on the Modify button. The Format Cells dialog box appears.

4. Click on a tab representing a formatting category that you want to modify for the new style. Then select specific formatting options for the style.

5. Repeat step 3 for each formatting category that you want to change for the style you're defining. Then click on OK on the Format Cells dialog box.

6. Click on OK on the Style dialog box.

By selecting or deselecting categories in the Style Includes group, you can define the exact set of formats that the style will affect. Unchecked categories will not be changed when you apply the style to a range.

To delete a style definition, choose Format ➤ Style, select the style name, and click on the Delete button.

## To Copy Styles from One Workbook to Another

1. Open both workbooks, and activate the workbook to which you want to copy styles.

2. Choose Format ➤ Style and then click on Merge.

3. In the Merge Styles dialog box, select the name of the workbook from which you want to copy styles, and click on OK. The Style Name list for the destination document now offers all the styles from the source document.

## Subtotals

The Data ➤ Subtotals command calculates sums, averages, or other statistical values for groups of records in a list or database. For this command, the list should contain a column that effectively divides the records into groups—for example, a Region, Department, or Category field. Before choosing the Subtotals command, you begin by sorting the list by this field.

### To Use the Subtotals Command

1. Activate the sheet containing the target list. Sort the list by a field that divides the records into groups. (See the "Sorting" entry for details.)

2. Select a cell within the list range, and choose Data ➤ Subtotals. Excel selects the entire list, and the Subtotal dialog box appears.

3. In the list labeled At Each Change In, choose the field that divides the records into groups.

4. In the Use Function list, choose the calculation you want to apply to each group; the default function is Sum.

5. In the Add Subtotal To box, check each field in which you want the calculation to appear.

6. Check any combination of the three check boxes at the bottom of the Subtotal dialog box:

   • Check Replace Current Subtotals to replace any previous subtotal lines with new calculations.

   • Check the Page Break Between Groups option to insert a page break after the subtotal for each group.

   • Check the Summary Below Data option to insert a grand total line at the end of the database.

7. Click on OK. Excel inserts subtotal lines according to your instructions.

Excel creates an outline on your worksheet when subtotal rows are inserted. Click on a numbered outline level symbol to hide or view detail rows of the database. (See the "Outlines" entry for details.) You can create *nested* subtotals by choosing Data ➤ Subtotal more than one time for the same database. Each time, select a different field name in the At Each Change In list, and make sure the Replace Current Subtotals option is unchecked.

## Summation and Conditional Sum

To calculate the total of all the numeric values in a row or column, use the AutoSum button on the Standard toolbar. It automatically enters SUM formulas into selected cells and displays the resulting totals. If you want to find the sum of values from *selected* records in a list or database, use the Conditional Sum Wizard. This tool guides you through the steps of defining the criteria for selecting records and then develops the formula for computing the sum of the selected data.

### To Use the AutoSum Button

Select a blank cell at the end of a row or column of numbers, and double-click on the AutoSum button on the Standard toolbar.

Alternatively, select a range of cells at the end of several rows or columns, and click on the AutoSum button once.

You can also use the AutoSum button to calculate grand totals from several subtotals located in nonconsecutive cells of a row or column. To do so, simply select the blank cell at the end of a row or column that already contains calculated subtotals. Click on the AutoSum button and examine the resulting SUM expression in the formula bar; references to the subtotals appear as the arguments of the SUM function. Click on the AutoSum button again to accept the formula.

## To Calculate Conditional Sums

1. Select a cell inside the range of a list or database, and choose Tools ➤ Wizard ➤ Conditional Sum. The Conditional Sum Wizard dialog box appears.

2. Confirm that Excel has correctly determined the entire range of the list or database, including column headings or field names. Then click on Next.

3. In the next dialog box of the Conditional Sum Wizard, you select a target column for the summation, and then you develop conditions for selecting rows from the list or database. In the Sum box, select the name that identifies the column you want to sum.

4. In the Parameter (or Columns) box, select the column that contains data for building a condition. In the Is box, select one of six relational operators ($=$, $>$, $<$, $>=$, $<=$, $<>$). In the This Value box, select a data item to complete the conditional expression. Click on the Add Condition button to copy this expression to the condition list below.

5. Optionally, repeat step 4, above, to develop more conditions for selecting rows. (Multiple expressions in the list are "and" conditions; a record must meet every condition to be selected.) Click on Next to continue.

6. In the next dialog box, choose one of two available formats for the conditional sum output. Click on the first option if you want to enter only the conditional sum formula into a cell of your sheet. Click on the second option if you also want to enter the selection parameters for choosing rows, so that you can later modify those parameters.

7. In the next dialog boxes, select cells for the parameters and the SUM formula. Then click on Finish.

Alternatively, you can develop a conditional formula yourself, using the SUMIF function. This function takes three arguments, in the following form:

=SUMIF(Range, Criterion, SumRange)

The first argument is the range of data to which the selection criterion will be applied; the second argument is a condition; and the third argument is a range containing the numeric data you want to sum.

# Templates

A *template* is an Excel file that you design for the convenience of creating new workbooks. In a template, you can store formats and styles, along with text, numbers, formula entries, and graphic objects. When you open a new document based on a template, Excel copies all the formats and other contents of the template to the new workbook. Excel comes with a library of built-in templates for home and business use.

## To Create a Template

1. Create a workbook that contains all the formats, styles, and entries that you want to save in the template.

2. Choose File ➤ Save As. In the File Name box, enter a name for the template file.

**3.** In the Save As Type list, choose Template (\*.xlt).

**4.** Click on Save to save the template. Then choose File ➤ Close to close the template file.

### To Open a New Workbook Based on a Template

Choose File ➤ New, select a template name in the General tab, and click on OK. You can open more than one new workbook based on the same template. Excel gives each new document a temporary name. For example, suppose your template is named INVOICE.XLT. The workbooks you open from this template will be named Invoice1, Invoice2, Invoice3, and so on.

To work with a built-in spreadsheet template, choose File ➤ New and click on the Spreadsheet Solutions tab. Then select a file and click on OK.

## Template Wizard with Data Tracking

Using the Template Wizard, you create links between a workbook template and a database. Specifically, individual cells in the template are linked to fields in the database. When you create and save a workbook that is based on the template, Excel automatically copies information from the workbook to the database as a new record.

### To Use the Template Wizard

Before using the Template Wizard, create the database in which records will be stored. (One way to define the database is simply to enter a row of field names into an Excel workbook, and to save the workbook to disk.) Next, create a workbook that can serve as an input form for each new record; this workbook will be the basis for creating your template. Then continue as follows:

**1.** Open the workbook that you plan to use for creating the template.

**2.** Choose Data ➤ Template Wizard to open the Template Wizard dialog box.

**3.** The upper text box shows the name of the workbook file that the template will be based on. In the lower box enter a file name for the new template, or simply accept the suggested name. (Don't change the default Templates folder location for the new template.) Click on Next to display Step 2.

**4.** In the next dialog box, pull down the list of database types and make a selection. If your database is an Excel list, keep Microsoft Excel Workbook as the database type. Otherwise, choose the appropriate type; options include Access, dBase, FoxPro, and Paradox databases.

**5.** In the lower text box, enter the path and name of the database that will be linked to your template. If necessary, click on the Browse button to search for the database file on disk. Click on Next to move to Step 3.

**6.** In the next dialog box, the Template Wizard automatically creates a list of field names from the database you've selected. Your task is to identify the cell location on the template file that corresponds to each field in the database. (In other words, you need to designate the template cells from which field data will be copied to the database.) Enter the appropriate cell references in the Cell column. Then click on Next to go to Step 4.

**7.** If you want to copy records to the database from existing workbooks, click on the Yes option on the next dialog box. Then click on Next, and the Wizard prompts you to select the files to add. Otherwise, if no such workbooks exist yet, select No and click on Next.

**8.** Excel creates the template and links it to the database. Click on Finish to complete the process.

To add a record to the database, choose File ➢ New and create a new workbook based on the linked template. Enter data into the appropriate workbook cells and then choose File ➢ Save. A dialog box named Template File - Save To Database appears. Click on OK to save the current information as a record in the linked database.

# Text Box

A *text box* is an object that displays a block of text at a location on a sheet. Like other graphic objects, a text box can be moved and resized. (See the "Graphic Objects" entry for details.)

## To Create a Text Box

**1.** Activate the sheet where you want to add the text box. (If the Drawing toolbar is not currently available, choose View ➢ Toolbars ➢ Drawing or click on the Drawing button on the Standard toolbar.)

**2.** Click on the Text Box button on the Drawing toolbar.

**3.** Hold down the left mouse button and drag the mouse over the area where you want to display the text box. Release the mouse button to complete the box. Excel activates the box and displays a flashing insertion point at the upper-left corner.

**4.** Type the text that you want to display inside the box. Then click on elsewhere on the active document to deselect the box.

You can combine a text box with an arrow object to draw attention to a particular entry in a worksheet. (The Arrow tool appears on the Drawing toolbar.)

## To Add Text to a Chart

Activate the chart window and click on the Text Box button on the Drawing toolbar. Drag the mouse through the area of the chart in which you want to place the text, and then type the text itself. Click on elsewhere in the chart to deselect the entry. The text appears directly on the chart without a text box border.

# Text Functions and Operations

Excel has a library of text functions that you can use to perform various operations on text entries in a worksheet. (See the "Functions" entry for general information.) These are the available functions:

- Alphabetic case conversion functions (LOWER, PROPER, UPPER)
- Character code conversion functions (CHAR, CODE)
- Character removal functions (CLEAN, TRIM)
- Comparison function (EXACT)
- Concatenation (CONCATENATE)
- Length function (LEN)
- Numeric and text conversion functions (DOLLAR, FIXED, T, TEXT, VALUE)
- Repetition function (REPT)
- Replacement functions (REPLACE, SUBSTITUTE)
- Search functions (FIND, SEARCH)
- Substring functions (LEFT, MID, RIGHT)

The & operator represents concatenation. You can use this operator in place of the CONCATENATE function to join two text values in a formula.

# Time Entries

You can enter time values in any of several time formats that Excel recognizes. Excel displays the entry in a time format, but stores the time itself as a decimal fraction between 0 and 1. (This fraction represents the portion of the day that has elapsed at a given point in time.) You can perform arithmetic operations on time values, such as finding the difference between two points in time.

## To Enter a Time Value

Select the cell and enter the time in a recognizable format. Here are some examples of time entry formats that Excel recognizes:

6:00

6 AM

6:00 AM

6:00:00 AM

In response to any of these entries, Excel applies one of its built-in time formats to the cell, displaying the time as either 6:00 or 6:00 AM or 6:00:00 AM.

## To Find the Difference between Two Time Entries

Enter a formula that subtracts one time from the other. Multiply the result by 24 to find the number of hours between the two time values. (Apply a numeric format to the cell containing the formula.)

## To View the Serial Number for a Time Entry

1. Select a cell containing an entry displayed in a time format.

2. Choose Format ➤ Cells and click on the Number tab.

3. Select General in the Category box.

4. Click on OK.

# Toolbars

Excel has an assortment of built-in toolbars that you can display on the desktop. They provide dozens of different buttons designed to streamline your activities in Excel. Initially, only the Standard and Formatting toolbars appear on the screen, but the other toolbars are easily accessible. You can customize a toolbar by adding new buttons to it or removing existing buttons. You can also create new toolbars with unique sets of buttons. Menus in Excel are actually specialized forms of toolbars, and can be customized in the same ways.

## To Display a Toolbar

Point to any toolbar with the mouse, and click the right mouse button. Select the toolbar you want to display from the resulting shortcut menu. Alternatively, choose View ➤ Toolbars and choose the toolbar you want to display. Once a toolbar is displayed on the screen, you can move it to a new position or change its shape. Some of Excel's built-in toolbars appear initially as *floating* toolbars, and others are docked to specific locations at the top or bottom of the desktop.

A floating toolbar is displayed with its own title bar. To move a floating toolbar to a new place on the screen, drag its title bar with the mouse. To change its shape, position the mouse pointer over the window's border until you see a double-headed arrow; then drag the border into a new shape. To hide a floating toolbar, click on the x button at the upper-right corner of the toolbar window.

Toolbars can be docked at the top, bottom, left, and right sides of the Excel desktop. For example, the Standard and Formatting toolbars are docked by default at the top of the application window, and the Drawing toolbar is docked at the bottom. You can transform a docked toolbar to a floating one by dragging it away from the dock. Conversely, you can dock a floating toolbar by dragging it toward the top, bottom, or side of the Excel window. To hide a docked toolbar, click on any toolbar with the right mouse button, and select the name of the toolbar that you want to hide.

## To View a ToolTip

A *ToolTip* is a small text box that identifies a toolbar button. Position the mouse pointer over any button on a toolbar, and the ToolTip appears beneath the mouse pointer, showing you the button's name.

## To Add or Remove a Toolbar Button

1. Choose View ➤ Toolbars ➤ Customize.

2. Click on the Toolbars tab, and check the toolbar that you want to modify. The toolbar is displayed on the desktop.

3. Click on the Commands tab. In the Categories list, choose the category for a button you want to add to the toolbar. In the Commands list, scroll to the button you want to add. Drag a copy of the button from the Commands list to the toolbar.

4. To remove a button, simply drag it out of the toolbar.

5. Click on Close on the Customize dialog box.

## To Customize an Excel Menu

1. Choose View ➤ Toolbars ➤ Customize.

2. At the top of the desktop, pull down the menu list that you want to customize.

3. In the Customize dialog box, click on the Commands tab.

4. In the Categories list, choose the category for a command you want to add to the current menu list.

5. In the Commands list, scroll to the command that you want to add to the menu list.

6. Drag a copy of the command from the Commands list to the menu list.

7. Click on the Close button on the Customize dialog box.

## To Restore the Original Toolbar or Menu

1. Choose View ➤ Toolbars ➤ Customize.

2. Click on the Toolbars tab.

3. In the Toolbars list, highlight the name of the toolbar or menu you want to restore.

4. Click on the Reset button, and click on OK on the resulting message box.

5. Click on Close on the Customize dialog box.

## To Create a Custom Toolbar

1. Choose View ➤ Toolbars ➤ Customize.

2. Click on the Toolbars tab. Then click on the New button.

3. In the New Toolbar dialog box, enter a name for the toolbar you're about to create. Then click on OK. A new empty toolbar appears on the desktop.

4. Click on the Commands tab in the Customize dialog box.

5. In the Categories list, select a category of buttons you want to add to the new toolbar. Then drag one or more commands from the Commands list to the new toolbar.

6. Repeat step 5 until you've added all the buttons you want to see in the new toolbar.

7. Click on Close on the Customize dialog box.

To delete a custom toolbar from the set of available toolbars, choose View ➤ Toolbars ➤ Customize and click on the Toolbars tab. Select the name of the toolbar you want to delete, and click on the Delete button. Click on OK to confirm.

# Tracking Changes

In a shared workbook, Excel can keep track of changes that occur in the data. You can easily view the changes that have taken place. You can also step through all the changes and decide whether to accept them or reject them.

## To Start Tracking

1. Activate the target workbook. Then choose Tools ➤ Track Changes ➤ Highlight Changes.

2. In the Highlight Changes dialog box, check the option labeled Track Changes

While Editing. Make sure the option labeled Highlight Changes On Screen is also checked.

**3.** Click on OK. A message box informs you that the workbook will be saved. Click on OK.

The workbook is now shared, as indicated by the [Shared] notation on the Excel title bar. When any subsequent changes occur in a cell, Excel places a marker in the upper-left corner of the cell. To review the change, position the mouse pointer over the cell. A text box describes the history of changes in the cell.

## To Accept or Reject Changes

**1.** Choose Tools ➤ Track Changes ➤ Accept Or Reject Changes. A message box informs you that the workbook will be saved. Click on OK.

**2.** In the Select Changes To Accept Or Reject dialog box, specify which changes you wish to review. Click on OK.

**3.** In the Accept Or Reject Changes dialog box, review each change in turn. For each item displayed in the dialog box, click on Accept to keep the change, or Reject to revert to the original data.

# Transposing Ranges

When you transpose a data table, Excel exchanges rows for columns and columns for rows.

## To Transpose a Range of Data

**1.** Select the entire range that you want to transpose, and choose Edit ➤ Copy. Excel displays a moving border around the range.

**2.** Select the cell at the upper-left corner of the location in which you want to copy the transposed data.

**3.** Choose Edit ➤ Paste Special. In the Paste Special dialog box, check the Transpose option.

**4.** Click on OK.

# Trendlines

A *trendline* is a graphic feature you can add to an existing chart to illustrate possible trends in a selected data series. You can choose among several mathematical categories of trendlines, including linear, logarithmic, polynomial, and exponential. Trendlines are available for area, bar, column, line, and xy charts.

## To Add a Trendline to a Chart

**1.** Activate the chart sheet or the embedded chart in which you want to add the trendline.

**2.** Choose Chart ➤ Add Trendline. (If the Add Trendline command is dimmed, the feature is not available for the current chart type; switch to a different chart type and then try choosing the command again.) The Trendline dialog box contains two tabs: Type and Options.

**3.** In the Type tab, select the type of trendline that you want to create.

**4.** In the Based on series list, select a series for the trendline.

**5.** Click on the Options tab. In the Trendline name options, select Automatic to assign a default name to the trendline, or click on Custom and supply a name of your own choosing.

**6.** Optionally, in the Forecast options, specify the number of periods forward and/or backward you want to extend the trendline.

**7.** Check the Set Intercept option and enter a value if you want the trendline to cross the y-axis at a location other than the origin. Check the Display Equation On Chart option if you want to see the equation that produces the trendline. Check the Display R-Squared Value On Chart option if you want to see the R-squared value.

**8.** Click on OK to display the trendline on the chart.

# Views

Use the View Manager to define and save different views of a worksheet. A view consists of the settings that affect the information you see on the screen and the format of the sheet you send to the printer. The View Manager works along with the Scenario Manager and the Report Manager to help you control the content and appearance of reports you create from a worksheet. (See "Reports" and "Scenarios" for further information.)

## To Create Views of a Worksheet

1. Open the workbook and activate the sheet for which you want to create the views.

2. Prepare the sheet in any combination of the following ways:

   - Adjust the zoom setting to display the sheet in a new scale.

   - Adjust the size and position of the worksheet window on the screen.

   - Add panes and frozen titles if appropriate.

   - Select display settings from the View tab of the Tools ➢ Options command. For example, hide the gridlines.

   - Select print settings from the File ➢ Page Setup command.

3. Choose View ➢ Custom Views.

4. Click on the Add button. In the Add View dialog box, enter a name for the current view. Select any combination of the Include options. Then Click on OK.

5. Repeat steps 2 to 4 for any additional views you want to create for the active worksheet.

## To Show a View of a Worksheet

1. Activate a worksheet for which you have defined views, and choose View ➢ Custom Views.

2. In the Custom Views dialog box, select a name from the list of views, and click on Show.

If your view includes specific print settings, you can now print the worksheet without having to choose the File ➢ Page Setup command.

# World Wide Web

Like other applications in the Microsoft Office suite, Excel now gives you a variety of ways to use the resources of the World Wide Web:

- You can open workbooks or other documents from HTTP addresses on the Web, and view those documents as worksheets.

- Conversely, you can create an HTML Web page from the data and objects on a worksheet, and ultimately publish the page at a Web site.

- On any worksheet you can create hyperlink connections to Web sites. To jump to the destination, you simply click on the hyperlink. (See "Hyperlinks" for details.)

- The Help ➢ Microsoft on the Web menu contains a list of connections to Web addresses, resources, and support pages.

To take advantage of these features, you need a connection to the Internet—a dial-in service provider, or a direct network connection.

## To Open a Web Document

Choose File ➢ Open and enter the HTTP address in the File Name box.

## To Create a Web Page from a Worksheet

Make sure you've installed the Internet Assistant add-in. (See the "Add-Ins" entry for details.) Activate the sheet and select the data that you want to include in the page. Then choose File ➢ Save As HTML.

## To Connect to Support Pages on the Web

Choose Help ➢ Microsoft On The Web, and select one of the items on the resulting menu list. Each of these is a direct link to a Web page.

# Workbooks and Worksheets

The workbook is the basic document type in Excel. You can use a workbook to store and manage any number of interrelated sheets.

## To Create a New Workbook

Choose File ➢ New, select the Workbook icon, and click on OK, or click on the New button on the Standard toolbar. A new workbook has a default name like Book1, Book2, and so on. Initially a new workbook contains three sheets. If you want new workbooks to contain some other number of sheets, choose Tools ➢ Options, click on the General tab, and change the setting in the box labeled Sheets In New Workbook.

## To Activate a Sheet in a Workbook

Click on the sheet's tab at the bottom of the workbook window. If the tab is not visible for the sheet you want to activate, click on one of the four tab scrolling buttons at the lower-left corner of the window to move other tabs into view. Alternatively, press Ctrl+PgDn to activate the next sheet in the workbook, or Ctrl+PgUp to activate the previous sheet.

## To Insert a New Sheet into a Workbook

Choose Insert ➢ Worksheet.

## To Rename a Sheet in a Workbook

1. Activate the sheet that you want to rename.

2. Choose Format ➢ Sheet ➢ Rename. Excel highlights the current name on the sheet's tab.

3. Enter a new name for the sheet.

Alternatively, double-click on a sheet's tab, and enter a new name.

## To Move or Copy a Sheet

1. Open the workbook that contains the sheet and the workbook where you want to move or copy the sheet. Activate the target sheet.

2. Choose Edit ➢ Move or Copy Sheet.

3. In the To book list, select the name of the book where you want to move or copy the sheet.

4. In the Before sheet list, choose a position for the sheet.

5. Check the Create a copy option if this is a copy operation. Leave the option unchecked for a move operation.

6. Click on OK.

## To Hide a Sheet

Activate the sheet that you want to hide and choose Format ➢ Sheet ➢ Hide.

## To Delete a Sheet from a Workbook

Activate the sheet that you want to delete, and choose Edit ➢ Delete Sheet. Excel displays a warning box; click on OK to confirm the deletion.

# Workbook Properties

In the Properties window for a workbook, you can store information such as a title, subject, author name, group category, search keywords, and comments can be saved with a file.

## To Define Workbook Properties

1. Select the target workbook, and choose File ➢ Properties. Click on the Summary tab.

2. Complete the summary properties for such items as the workbook's title, subject, and author.

3. Click on OK, and then click on the Save button to save the properties with the file.

# Workspace

You can record a particular arrangement of open workbooks as a workspace. When you open a workspace file, Excel opens all the workbooks recorded in the workspace and displays them as they were arranged when you saved the workspace.

## To Save a Workspace

1. Open and arrange the workbooks that you want to include in the workspace.

2. Choose File ➢ Save Workspace. Excel suggests RESUME.XLW as the name of the workspace file. Accept this name or enter a name of your own choosing.

3. Click on OK to save the workspace.

## To Open a Workspace

1. Choose File ➢ Open.

2. Choose Workspaces (*.xlw) from the Files Of Type list. The File Name box lists any workspace files you've saved.

3. Select the name of the workspace file that you want to open and click on Open.

# Zooming

You can use the Zoom command either to increase or reduce the viewing scale of a window.

## To Change the Zoom Setting

1. Activate the target sheet, and choose View ➢ Zoom.

2. Click on one of the preset magnification or reduction options, or click on the Custom option and enter a value from 10 to 400 in the box.

3. Click on OK to apply the zoom scale.

Alternatively, change the setting in the Zoom box on the Standard toolbar. The Zoom setting applies only to the active sheet. Other sheets in the active workbook retain their current scale settings.

## To Find the Best Scale for a Range

1. Activate the target sheet and select the range that you want to display.

2. Choose View ➢ Zoom. In the Magnification group, click on the Fit Selection option, and then click on OK.

Alternatively, pull down the Zoom list on the Standard toolbar and choose Selection. When you select this option, Excel calculates the best scale for displaying the selection. For a small range of cells, this may mean increasing the scale. For a large range, Excel reduces the scale.

# INDEX

**Note to the Reader:** Throughout this index **boldfaced** page numbers indicate primary discussions of a topic. *Italicized* page numbers indicate illustrations.

## SYMBOLS

**Z**